Economics

Student Workbook and Reader

Pearson Education

We work with leading authors to develop the strongest educational materials in Economics, bringing cutting edge thinking and best learning practice to a global market.

Under a range of well-known imprints, including Financial Times Prentice Hall, we craft high quality print and electronic publications which help readers to understand and apply their content, whether studying or at work.

To find out about the complete range of our publishing please visit us on the World Wide Web at: www.pearsoneduc.com

Economics
Student Workbook and Reader

FOURTH EDITION

John Sloman
Mark Sutcliffe
University of the West of England

FINANCIAL TIMES
Prentice Hall

An imprint of **Pearson Education**

Harlow, England · London · New York · Reading, Massachusetts · San Francisco · Toronto · Don Mills, Ontario · Sydney
Tokyo · Singapore · Hong Kong · Seoul · Taipei · Cape Town · Madrid · Mexico City · Amsterdam · Munich · Paris · Milan

Pearson Education Limited
Edinburgh Gate
Harlow
Essex CM20 2JE
England

and Associated Companies throughout the World.

Visit us on the World Wide Web at:
www.pearsoneduc.com

First edition published 1991
Second edition published 1994
Third edition published 1997
This edition published 2000

ISBN 0–13–016605–7

British Library Cataloguing-in-Publication Data
A catalogue record for this book can be obtained from the British Library

Library of Congress Cataloging-in-Publication Data
A catalog record for this book can be obtained from the Library of Congress

10 9 8 7 6 5 4 3 2 1
05 04 03 02 01 00

Typeset by 35 in 8/12 pt Stone Serif
Printed and bound in Great Britain by Henry Ling Ltd., at the
Dorset Press, Dorchester, Dorset

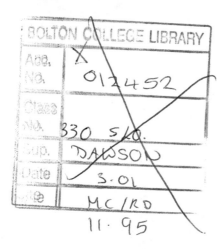

Contents

Preface

Welcome to this *Economics Workbook and Reader*. We hope that the book will help to make your study of the fascinating subject of economics both enjoyable and thought provoking and that it will improve your ability to analyse the economic problems faced by individuals and nations: problems that we hear about daily in the news or come across in our own lives.

Studying economics can be much more rewarding if it is not just seen as a body of knowledge to absorb. Applying the theories, working through problems, analysing data, examining and discussing case studies, gathering information, scouring newspapers, reports and official publications and debating with other students can all help to bring the subject alive. This *Workbook and Reader* will give you the opportunity to do all these things.

The book may be used with any introductory text, although it is specifically designed to be used with John Sloman, *Economics (4th edition)*. Each chapter in the *Workbook and Reader* corresponds to a chapter in the main text.

Each chapter is divided into five sections: (A) Review, (B) Problems, exercises and projects, (C) Discussion topics and essays, (D) Articles, (E) Answers. Between them, these sections will help you prepare for all types of examination and assessment currently used at first-year degree level and A level, and on BTEC and professional courses.

Review

This section takes you step-by-step through the material covered in the respective chapter of *Economics (4th edition)*, using a mixture of narrative and short questions.

The questions are of seven different types, six of which are signified by symbols.

≡ Multiple choice
These are set out in the standard multiple-choice format. In virtually all cases there are five alternative answers and you are required to circle the correct one. The questions are typical of those used at first-year degree level and at A level.

(?) Written answer
These require you to give one or two words or sentences. Sometimes there will be a list of points for you to give.

◗ Delete wrong word
These are sometimes *true/false* questions, sometimes *yes/no* questions, or sometimes deleting one of two or more alternative answers.

⊖ Diagram/table manipulation
These involve you completing a diagram or table, or reading things off a diagram or table.

⊗ Calculation
These involve short mathematical calculations, usually just simple arithmetic, but in some of the optional, starred questions (see below) they involve simple differentiation.

✿ Matching/ordering
These are of two types. The first involves matching a set of definitions to a set of descriptions, or a set of answers to a

set of questions. The second involves putting a set of points or events into the correct order.

The final type of question is embedded in the narrative, and involves you deleting the wrong word, phrase or sentence from two or more alternatives given.

Some questions are starred. These are on additional topics and may be omitted if desired.

Problems, exercises and projects

This section consists of longer, multi-part questions, often involving simple calculations or the manipulation of graphs. There are also questions involving the gathering and analysis of data. These 'mini-project' questions can be set by your tutor as an assigned piece of work, to be done either individually or in groups. The information gathered can then be used for in-class discussions.

Discussion topics and essays

These questions, as the name suggests, can be used for practice in writing essays or making essay plans (which will help you prepare for exams), or for discussion with fellow students. Most of the questions in this section are designed to raise issues of policy or controversy, and thus should be more stimulating than the more purely descriptive, theoretical or analytical questions sometimes used for essays. The last question in this section is usually a motion for a debate.

Articles

This section consists of newspaper, magazine or journal articles (normally three per chapter). We have written a brief introduction to each article and a set of short questions at the end of each one. These articles help to relate the economic theories you have studied to topical issues and events.

Answers

Full answers *plus*, where appropriate, full explanations are given to all section A questions. These will help you check on your understanding as you work your way through the relevant chapter of the main text. They allow section A to be used as a comprehensive revision tool.

TEACHING AND LEARNING: A NOTE TO TUTORS

In devising this Workbook and Reader, we intended that it should be both an independent study tool for the student and also a useful teaching aid for tutors. Sections A to D can all be used in a classroom context, adding variety and spice to the delivery of economic principles and policy. Outlined below are some suggestions for ways in which you might use the various sections.

Review

The main purpose of this section is to help reinforce students' learning and understanding of key principles by putting them to use in answering simple questions. The questions are built up in a sequence that mirrors that in the main text.

In addition to being used as a learning tool by students and as a useful revision and practice aid for exams, these questions could also be used in class. Students might be asked, either prior to the class meeting, or in the first part of the class, to complete a set number of questions from this section. Then, preferably in small groups, they would attempt to identify the definitive answer. Groups would be expected to explain the reasoning behind the answers they had chosen.

Alternatively, at the end of a lesson (lecture, seminar or class), a short test based on questions in this section could be set. This would be quick to administer and mark, and give you feedback on the success of your lesson in meeting its objective(s). With the answers provided to all section A questions at the end of each chapter, students could mark each other's work.

Problems, exercises and projects

As the title of this section suggests, there are three types of question to be found here.

- Multi-part problems. These longer questions provide ideal material for use in very large workshops (of up to 200 students). We have been running workshops similar to these for a number of years and find them very popular with students and a good medium for learning and applying basic economic concepts. Students can work through these multi-part questions (or a portion of them), discussing them with their neighbours as they do so, and then the lecturer can go through the answers from the front. If you leave one row free in every three in the lecture theatre, tutors can go round giving help to students if they are stuck. This is a good way of using postgraduate teaching assistants. Answers to these questions are given on the CD.

- Exercises. Many of these questions require students to look up data or other information from books or electronic media. They are best set in advance of the lesson, unless information collection is one of its main purposes. Once the information has been collected, however, students could work in small groups to devise answers to the questions. This is a very effective way of stimulating debate and discussion.

- Mini projects. These involve students gathering information, sometimes by field work, and then writing a small report or considering a question relating to the information obtained. Again, this work could be done in small groups.

These last two types of question also lend themselves well to group presentations, which help to develop useful communication skills. As part of their presentation, students could be required to consider the method(s) by which they solve problems and construct answers. Telling others how they approached such issues also helps to develop useful skills for themselves and their audience.

The questions in this section also lend themselves very well to being used as assigned pieces of work. They generally require of the student a greater depth of understanding than section A questions.

Discussion topics and essays

These questions can be set as essays, or they can be used as the basis of class discussion. Why not, mid-way through a lecture, or class, following a particular point of theory, pose one of the questions for students to discuss and to ascertain its relevance to what they have just been taught. For example, you have introduced your students to the idea of profit maximisation. You now want them to consider its relevance to real-world business decision making. Ask them the following discussion question:

Imagine you were the managing director of a fashion house producing expensive designer clothing. What achievements of you and your company would give you special satisfaction?

After a short period of time ask the supplementary question:

Are the achievements consistent with profit maximisation?

You can then proceed to discuss alternative theories of the firm and students can debate whether managerial utility maximisation might be more relevant as a goal of business rather than the maximisation of profit.

The last question in section C is usually a debate. We suggest that the debate is conducted as formally as possible, with two student proposing the motion and two opposing it. After the formal speeches we suggest that the debate is opened to question and/or contributions from the floor. Finally the proposer and opposer could give a concluding speech. By conducting the proceedings formally, you can develop an atmosphere of theatre, with students acting parts. This can make the learning environment fun.

Articles

The application of economic principles and theory to the world around us is often the most stimulating way to teach economics. Students not only come to understand economic principles better but can identify their relevance to events and issues.

The articles in this section have been carefully selected for their relevance to material covered in the chapter. Many are case studies which illustrate theory or discuss particular economic problems or policies. They are particularly suitable for using in class-based work. The articles tend to be short, and the questions at the end address both points of comprehension regarding the article, and the relevance of the article to economic concepts and theory. Small-group work is particularly successful when using such material. For example, students could be assigned to read one or more articles before the class and have some preliminary thoughts about the questions, and then, in groups of three or four, they could come up with agreed answers. The class as a whole could then debate the answers of the different groups.

ACKNOWLEDGEMENTS

The whole team at Pearson Education has been very helpful and we have really appreciated everyone's hard work. A particular thanks to Catherine Newman, the book's editor, for her encouragement and good humour, and to David Harrison for meticulously guiding the book through production. Most of all, we owe the book to the unfailing support of Alison and Sheila and the rest of our families.

John Sloman and Mark Sutcliffe
UWE Bristol, January 2000

Acknowledgements

We are grateful to the following for permission to reproduce copyright material;

Philip Allan Publishers Ltd for the article 'Why study economics?' by Alan Hamlin from *Economic Review* Vol. 14, No. 1, September 1996; BBC for the articles 'Record onion prices in India lead to state subsidies' from *BBC News Online* 9.1.98. 'Japan unveils $110bn rescue package' from *BBC News Online* 7.8.98 and 'Productivity: 'Mind the gap!' from *BBC News Online* 23.10.98; Bank of England for extracts from the article 'Monetary policy instruments: the UK experience' by Mervyn King from *Bank of England Quarterly Bulletin* August 1994 and an extract from the article 'Understanding broad money' by Ryland Thomas from *Bank of England Quarterly Bulletin* May 1996; Confederation of British Industry for the articles 'Different combinations' from *CBI News* March 1998, 'Better than feared' from *CBI News* April 1999 and 'The critical difference' from *CBI News* July/August 1999; The Director Publications Ltd for the article 'Frozen out' from *Director* August 1999 and two articles by Gail Rajgor from *Director Energy Management*, supplement of *Director* November 1998; The Economist for the articles 'Biology meets the dismal science' from *The Economist* 25.12.93, 'Investing in people' from *The Economist* 26.3.94, 'An insurer's worst nightmare' from *The Economist* 29.7.95, 'Great expectations, and rational too' from *The Economist* 14.10.95, 'Dedicated followers of fashion' from *The Economist* 23.12.95, 'What works?' from *The Economist* 6.6.96, 'Europe grows apart' from *The Economist* 7.3.98, 'Towards a new financial system' from *The Economist* 11.4.98, 'Race, sex and dismal science' from *The Economist* 6.6.98, 'The end of privatisation?' from *The Economist* 13.6.98, 'Down under' from *The Economist* 13.6.98, 'Growing old extravagantly' from *The Economist* 20.6.98, 'Turtle wars' from *The Economist* 3.10.98, and 'Making aid work' from *The Economist* 14.11.98, © The Economist, London; Financial Times for the articles 'Post-Copernican economics' from *Financial Times* 24.8.90, 'In praise of the international monetary non-system' from *Financial Times* 28.3.94, 'The heart of the new world economy' by Martin Woolf from *Financial Times* 1.10.97, 'Production lines are transformed' from *Financial Times* 11.5.98, 'Italy: Mezzogiorno tops Prodi's agenda' by James Blitz from *Financial Times* 27.5.98, 'Chile: Tiger of the south takes a tumble' by Andrea Mandel-Campbell from *Financial Times* 2.10.98, 'A yen for spending' from *Financial Times* 6.10.98, 'When the price is not right' from *Financial Times* 15.6.99, 'Voices in the air' by Samuel Brittan from *Financial Times* 2.9.99, and 'Taxation road to nowhere' by Richard Tomkins from *Financial Times* 2.9.99; The Guardian on behalf of the authors for the articles 'Free lunch as Keynes makes a comeback' by Tony Thirlwall from *The Guardian* 7.4.94, 'The growing fear of debt deters university entrants' from *The Guardian* 20.1.96, 'Stream of abuse' by Oliver Tickle from *The Guardian* 4.3.98, 'Why the poor are picking up the tab' by Larry Elliott from *The Guardian* 1.6.98, 'Why the government needs to get real on economic policy' by Tony Thirlwall from *The Guardian* 5.10.98, 'A world-tangled web' from *The Guardian* 17.10.98, 'Targeting could be hit and miss policy' by Charlotte Denny from *The Guardian* 26.10.98, 'The death of work has been greatly exaggerated' by Mauricio Rojas from *The Guardian* 28.3.99, 'Milosevic's loyal farmers join dissenters' by Jacky Rowland from *The Guardian* 10.8.99, 'The danger of growing up quickly' by Edmund Warner from *The Guardian* 4.9.99, all first published in *The Guardian*; Haymarket Publishing Services Ltd for the articles 'The ins and outs of ups and downs' from *Management Today* November 1994, 'The low-inflation challenge' from *Management Today* March 1995, 'The long, slow grind to profits' from *Management Today* October 1995, 'The balance of trade' from *Management Today* December 1995, 'The business of fast growth – the secrets of hypergrowth' from *Management Today* February 1996, 'Nirvana is not so unattainable' by David Smith from *Management Today* August 1999; Independent Newspapers (UK) Ltd for the articles 'Rising demand hides leather's limited supply' by Alison Eadie from *The Independent* 9.5.94, 'Turmoil reigns in Asia once more' by Stephen Vines from *The Independent* 11.6.98, 'Currency Bomb is still ticking' by Lea Patterson from *The Independent* 30.6.98, 'How the Post Office can be set free' by Bill Robinson from *The Independent* 26.10.98, 'The real cost of IMF rescue deals' by Gavyn Davies from *The Independent* 16.11.98, 'Successive generations of children may be "learning to be poor"' by Cherry Norton from *The Independent* 29.3.99 and 'When low prices hit the consumer' by Patrick Hosking from *Independent on Sunday* 12.9.93; Institute of Economic Affairs for the article 'The case for road pricing' by Alan Day from *IEA* Vol. 18,

No. 4, December 1998, first published by the Institute of Economic Affairs, London, 1998; Institute for Public Policy Research for extracts from the articles 'The physics of unemployment' by Rod Cross from *New Economy* Spring 1996 and the articles 'Governance and stakeholding' by Rajiv Prabhaker from *New Economy* Vol. 5, No. 2, June 1998, 'Is NAIRU worth a can of beans?' by Geoffrey Dicks and John O'Sullivan from *New Economy* August 1999 and 'Social exclusion and urban policy' by Peter Lee from *New Economy* August 1999; International Monetary Fund for the article 'The post-Communist transition: Patterns and prospects' from *Finance and Development*, September 1998; Investors Chronicle for an extract from the article 'Minding the output gap mythology' from *Investors Chronicle* 5.4.96; the author, Marc Lopatin for the article 'The crisis – A crash course in globalisation' from *Independent on Sunday* 11.10.98; The Observer for the articles 'Those whom the CAP fits only too well' by Anthony Browne from *The Observer* 1.3.98, 'The predicted death of inflation. Now, it's the death of interest rates' by Anthony Browne from *The Observer* 11.4.99 and 'Real cost of the property boom' by Will Hutton from *The Observer* 15.8.99; Organisation for Economic Co-operation and Development for the articles 'Integrating environment and economy' by Michel Potier from *OECD Observer* Vol. 198, February/March 1996, 'How agriculture benefits the environment' from *OECD Observer* April/May 1997, 'Poland: Privatisation is the key to efficiency' from *OECD Observer* August/September 1998 and 'Who pays the highest income tax? from *OECD Observer* Summer 1999, and two Figures from *Improving the Environment through Reducing Subsidies* (OECD 1998); Oxfam for 'Farmers, food and the WTO' from *Oxfam Web Site* 23.6.98; the author, Stephen Timewell for the articles 'Don't panic' by Stephen Timewell from *The Banker* March 1999 and 'How the Internet redefines banking' by Stephen Timewell and Kung Young from *The Banker* June 1999; Times News-papers Ltd for an extract from *The Times* 20.3.91 and an extract from the article 'Economic consequences of the MPC' by Roger Bootle from *The Times* 6.6.98; the author, Daniel Yergin for the article 'Bigger oil' from *Financial Times* 2.12.98.

We have been unable to trace the copyright holder in the article 'Progress and pitfalls along the path towards a "greener" method of calculating national productivity' from *Nature* October 1998 and would appreciate any information that would enable us to do so.

CHAPTER ONE

Introducing Economics

REVIEW

In this first chapter we start by looking at the subject matter of economics. What is it that economists study? How is the subject divided up? What makes a problem an *economic* one?

Although all countries face economic problems, they nevertheless tackle them in different ways. In some countries the government plays a major role in economic decision making. In others decisions are left much more to individuals. Section 1.2 examines how these different types of economy operate.

We then turn to examine types of reasoning employed by economists. Do economists proceed like natural scientists, or does being a *social* science make economics different from subjects like physics and chemistry? We also examine the extent to which economists can contribute to policy making. Can economists tell governments what they *ought* to do?

1.1 What do economists study?

(Page 2) Economists study many issues, but all of them stem from the central economic problem of *scarcity*. Scarcity occurs because there are not enough resources (labour, land and capital) to produce everything that people would like.

Q1. The problem of scarcity is *directly* relevant:
A. only to those times when rationing has been enforced.
B. only to developing countries low in resources.
C. only to those on low incomes.
D. only to those periods of history before mass production.
E. to all countries and all individuals.

Q2. The problem of scarcity will eventually disappear with the development of new technology and resulting higher levels of production. *True/False*

(Page 2) In order to tackle the problem of scarcity, societies produce goods and services for people to consume. This production involves using various resources or *factors of production*.

Q3. It is normal to group factors of production into three broad categories. These are:

1. ....

2. ....

3. ....

Q4. Which one of the following would *not* be classified as a factor of production?
A. Jim Bodget, a bricklayer for a local construction firm.
B. The cement mixer Jim uses.
C. The cement Jim puts in the mixer.
D. The building site Jim works on.
E. The wage Jim gets paid at the end of the week.

 Multiple Choice   Written answer    Delete wrong word    Diagram/table manipulation   Calculation   Matching/ordering

(Page 3) One way of understanding the problem of scarcity is in terms of *potential demand and supply*. Potential *demand* relates to the **Q5.** *wants/needs* of individuals, whereas potential *supply* is determined by **Q6.** *the level of resources available/the amount that consumers demand.*

(Pages 3–5) Because of scarcity, people are concerned that society should produce *more* goods and that the resources should be used as *fully* as possible. This is the subject of **Q7.** *microeconomics/macroeconomics*. But given that enough can never be produced to satisfy *potential demands, choices* have to be made: *what* items to produce and in what quantities, *how* to produce them and *for whom*. These choices between alternatives are the subject of **Q8.** *microeconomics/macroeconomics*.

Q9. Which of the following are macroeconomic issues and which are microeconomic ones?
(a) The level of government spending.　　*micro/macro*
(b) A grant given by the government to the UK film industry.　　*micro/macro*
(c) The level of investment in the UK by overseas firms.　　*micro/macro*
(d) The price of cotton cloth.　　*micro/macro*
(e) The rate of inflation.　　*micro/macro*
(f) The average wage rate paid to textile workers.　　*micro/macro*
(g) The total amount spent by UK consumers on clothing and footwear.　　*micro/macro*
(h) The amount saved last year by households.　　*micro/macro*

(Page 5) Choices involve sacrifices or *costs*. If as a society we consume more of one good or service then, unless there are idle resources, we will be able to consume less of other goods and services.

Q10. The cost of one good measured in terms of what we must sacrifice is called the:
A. real cost.
B. opportunity cost.
C. average cost.
D. potential cost.
E. social cost.

Q11. Economists assume that economic decisions are made *rationally*. In the case of consumers, rational decision making means:
(a) That consumers will not buy goods which increase their satisfaction by just a small amount.　　*True/False*
(b) That consumers will attempt to maximise their individual satisfaction for the income they earn.
　　True/False
(c) That consumers buy the sorts of goods that the average person buys.　　*True/False*
(d) That consumers seek to get the best value for money from the goods they buy.　　*True/False*

(e) That consumers compare (maybe very casually) the cost of an item they are purchasing with the benefit they expect to gain from it.　　*True/False*

(Pages 6–7) When we make rational choices, what we are in fact doing is weighing up the marginal benefit of each activity against its marginal (opportunity) cost. If the marginal benefit (i.e. the *extra* benefit of doing a *bit more* of the activity) exceeds its marginal cost (i.e. the extra cost of doing a bit more), it is rational to choose to do that bit more.

Even though we may not be conscious of doing so, we apply this marginal analysis on a regular basis in our day-to-day decision making.

Q12. Which one of the following statements is *not* an example of marginal analysis?
A. If I eat another chocolate bar, I might be sick.
B. If mortgage rates rise by another 1 per cent, some people will no longer be able to afford the repayments.
C. If a firm earns more from selling its products than they cost to produce, it will make a profit.
D. If J. Bloggs (Warehousing) Ltd buys a new forklift truck of the latest design it should be able to stack another 500 pallets per day.
E. Fitting flue gas desulphurisation equipment to a coal-fired power station in Britain producing *x* kilowatts will reduce the costs of acid rain pollution in Scandinavia by £*y*.

(Pages 7–12) One way in which scarcity, choice and opportunity cost can all be illustrated is via a *production possibility curve*. This depicts a simplified world in which a country produces just two goods. The curve shows all the possible combinations of the two goods that the country can produce in a given period of time.

Figure 1.1 shows the production possibility curve for a country that can produce various combinations of two goods X and Y.

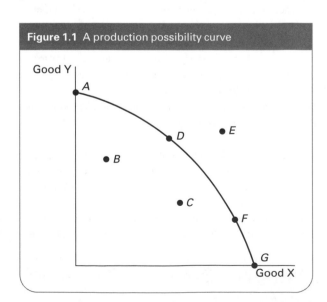

Figure 1.1 A production possibility curve

Q13. Which point or points illustrate a situation:

(a) Which is efficient? ....

(b) Which is inefficient? ....

(c) Of complete specialisation? ....

(d) Which is unobtainable? ....

Moving from one point to another round a production possibility curve illustrates the concept of opportunity cost.

Q14. Figure 1.2 shows a production possibility curve. Production is currently at point *A*. The opportunity cost of producing one more unit of good X is:

A. 10 units of X.
B. 1 unit of X.
C. 8 units of Y.
D. 6 units of Y.
E. 2 units of Y.

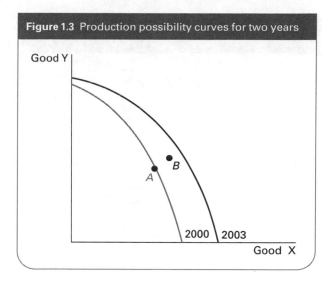

Figure 1.3 Production possibility curves for two years

A. (i), (ii) and (iii).
B. (i) and (ii), but not (iii).
C. (ii) and (iii), but not (i).
D. (ii), but not (i) or (iii).
E. It is impossible to say from the information given.

Q17. Which one of the following would directly lead to an outward shift of a country's production possibility curve?

A. An increase in the population of working age.
B. A reduction in the level of unemployment in the economy.
C. A reduction in value-added tax and duties on petrol and alcohol.
D. An increase in the general level of prices.
E. A reduction in government expenditure on education.

(Pages 11–12) A production possibility diagram can illustrate the distinction between microeconomics and macroeconomics.

Q18. Which of the following are microeconomic and which are macroeconomic issues?

(a) Whether the production possibility curve shifts outwards over time. *micro/macro*
(b) Whether the economy is operating on the production possibility curve or inside it. *micro/macro*
(c) The choice whether to produce more X and less Y, or more Y and less X (i.e. where to produce on the production possibility curve). *micro/macro*

(Pages 12–13) Another diagram that can be used to illustrate the distinction between micro- and macroeconomics and the process of satisfying consumer wants is the *circular flow of income diagram*. It shows the inter-relationships between firms and households in a money economy. A simplified circular flow diagram is illustrated in Figure 1.4.

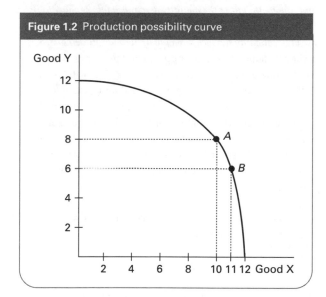

Figure 1.2 Production possibility curve

Q15. A production possibility curve is typically drawn bowed outward from the origin. This illustrates

....

Q16. Figure 1.3 shows a country's production possibility curves for two years, 2000 and 2003. The production point shifts outward from point *A* in 2000 to point *B* in 2003. The following are possible things that might have happened:

(i) Potential output has increased.
(ii) Actual output has increased.
(iii) A fuller use has been made of resources.

Which is correct?

Figure 1.4 The circular flow of incomes and of goods and services

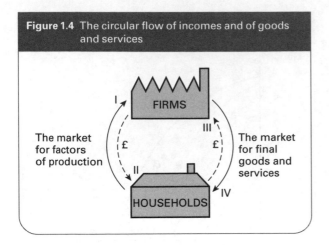

Q19. Which flow (I, II, III or IV) illustrates each of the following?

(a) Goods and services.   *I/II/III/IV*
(b) Wages, rent, profit and interest.   *I/II/III/IV*
(c) Factor services.   *I/II/III/IV*
(d) Consumer expenditure.   *I/II/III/IV*

1.2 Different economic systems

(Pages 13–14) Different countries tackle the problem of scarcity in different ways. One major way in which the economic systems of countries differ is in the extent to which they rely on the market or the government to allocate resources.

Q20. At the one extreme is the *full command economy*. Here all decisions concerning *what* should be produced, *how* it should be produced, and *for whom* are made by

....

Q21. At the other extreme is the completely free-market economy. Here all economic decisions are made by

....

(Pages 14–15) There are a number of potential advantages of a command economy.

Q22. Which one of the following is *not* a potential advantage of a command economy?

A. The planning authority can obtain an overall view of the whole economy and ensure a *balanced* expansion of its various parts.
B. Resources can be distributed according to need.
C. The system of planning can ensure that producers respond automatically to consumer wishes.

D. Resources can be diverted from consumption to investment if it is desired to increase the rate of economic growth.
E. Unemployment can be avoided.

Q23. Name two potential *disadvantages* of a pure command economy.

1. ....

2. ....

(Pages 15–18) In a totally free-market economy the questions of *what*, *how* and *for whom* to produce are determined by the decisions of individual households and firms through the interaction of demand and supply. In goods markets households are **Q24.** *suppliers/demanders/price setters*, whereas in factor markets households are **Q25.** *suppliers/demanders/ neither suppliers nor demanders* of factor services.

Demand and supply are brought into balance by the effects of changes in price. If supply exceeds demand in any market (a surplus), the price will **Q26.** *rise/fall/stay the same*. This will lead to **Q27.** *a rise in the quantity both demanded and supplied/a fall in the quantity demanded and supplied/a rise in the quantity demanded but a fall in the quantity supplied/a rise in the quantity supplied but a fall in the quantity demanded*. If, however, demand exceeds supply in any market (a shortage), the price will **Q28.** *fall/rise/stay the same*. This will lead to a **Q29.** *fall/rise* in the quantity demanded and a **Q30.** *fall/rise* in the quantity supplied. In either case the adjustment of price will ensure that demand and supply are brought into equilibrium, with any shortage or surplus being eliminated.

Goods and factor markets are linked. A change in demand or supply in one market will stimulate changes in other markets.

Q31. If the demand for houses rises, how will this affect the wages of bricklayers?

....

(Pages 18–19) Provided there are many firms competing in each market, the free-market economy can be claimed to lead to a number of advantages.

Q32. These include:
(a) A lack of bureaucracy in economic decision making.
                                               True/False
(b) Producers respond to changes in demand and consumers respond to changes in supply.   *True/False*
(c) The competition provides an incentive for producers to be efficient.   *True/False*
(d) The interaction of demand and supply ensures that resources are equally distributed.   *True/False*
(e) Firms will produce goods that are desirable for society, since only such goods can be sold profitably.
                                               True/False

(Pages 19–20) In reality no economy is a completely planned or completely free market. All economies are *mixed*. The mixture of government and the market varies, however, from one economy to another. It is thus the degree and form of government intervention that distinguishes one type of economy from another.

(?) **Q33.** List three different ways in which the government can intervene.

1. ....

2. ....

3. ....

1.3 The nature of economic reasoning

(Pages 20–1) The methodology used by economists has much in common with that used by natural scientists. Like natural scientists, economists construct *models*.

Q34. Which one of the following is *not* true of economic models?
A. They simplify reality.
B. They provide an explanation of the cause of certain economic phenomena.
C. They enable predictions of the 'if . . . then . . .' variety to be made.
B. They are constructed by conducting experiments under controlled conditions.
E. They can be tested by appealing to the facts.

Building models involves a process known as **Q35.** *deduction/induction*, whereas using a model to make a prediction involves a process known as **Q36.** *deduction/induction*.

Let us assume that an economist was attempting to establish the relationship between the rate of growth in the supply of money in the economy and the rate of inflation (i.e. the annual percentage increase in retail prices) the following year. In the process a number of steps are followed.

Q37. Rearrange the following steps in the correct order:
(a) Predict the rate of inflation next year.
(b) Collect data on the current rate of growth in the money supply.
(c) Collect data on the rate of growth in the money supply and the rate of inflation over a number of past years.
(d) If the prediction is wrong, amend the theory or abandon it.
(e) Establish a hypothesis about the relationship between the two variables.

(f) Continue collecting more evidence.
(g) Conduct observations to establish whether the prediction is correct.

Correct order: ....

(Pages 21–2) Despite using similar models to the natural sciences, economists tend to be less accurate in their predictions.

(?) **Q38.** Give two reasons for this.

1. ....

2. ....

(Page 22) Economists have an important role in helping governments to formulate and assess economic policy. In doing this it is important to separate *positive* questions about what the effects of the policies are, from *normative* ones as to what the goals of policy should be. Economists in their role as economists have no superior right to make normative judgements on the ideological/moral/political basis of the policy. They can and do, however, play a major role in assessing whether a policy meets the political objectives of government (or opposition).

Q39. Which one of the following is a normative statement?
A. The privatisation of the railways has reduced the level of traffic congestion.
B. The privatisation of the railways has led to an increase in fares.
C. Many on the political left believe that the privatisation of the railways is wrong.
D. It is fairer that rail commuters should pay the full costs of the journeys rather than having them subsidised by the government.
E. Rail privatisation has attracted private investment into the industry.

Q40. Which of the following statements are positive and which are normative?
(a) The best policy is one that will maximise the rate of economic growth for the country. *Positive/Normative*
(b) Government policies give a higher priority to curing inflation than to curing unemployment. *Positive/Normative*
(c) The government ought to higher priority to curing unemployment than to curing inflation. *Positive/Normative*
(d) If the government gave a higher priority to curing unemployment, that would be popular with the electorate. *Positive/Normative*

PROBLEMS, EXERCISES AND PROJECTS

Q41. Make a list of 5 things you did yesterday and any items you purchased. What was the opportunity cost of each? If your fellow students are doing this question, have a look at some of their lists and see if you agree with their estimates of their opportunity costs.

Q42. Imagine that country X could produce just two goods: food and clothing. Assume that over a given time period it could produce any of the following combinations:

Units of clothing	0	1	2	3	4	5	6
Units of food	24	23	21	18	14	8	0

(a) Draw the production possibility curve for country X on Figure 1.5.

(b) What is the opportunity cost of producing one more unit of clothing if the current level of production is (i) 2 units, (ii) 3 units, (iii) 4 units?

(c) Assume that technical innovation in agriculture allows a greater food output per unit of resources devoted to agriculture. What effect will this have on the opportunity cost of producing clothes?

(d) Now assume that there is a drought that halves the amount of food that can be produced per unit of resources. Draw the new production possibility curve.

Q43. Conduct a survey to establish what your fellow non-economics students believe economics to be about.

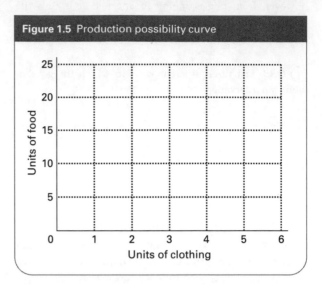

Figure 1.5 Production possibility curve

To what extent is their perception of the contents of economics the same as yours (a) was before you started your current course (b) is now?

Q44. Choose two current economics news items reported in the newspapers. Choose two newspapers of opposing political views which report this item. Give examples from these reports of *positive* statements and *normative* statements. Are there any statements that are not clearly one or the other?

DISCUSSION TOPICS AND ESSAYS

Q45. Make a list of some current problems that are the concern of economists. Are they microeconomic or macroeconomic problems, or a bit of both? How do they relate to the problem of scarcity?

Q46. Virtually every good is scarce in the sense we have defined it. There are, however, a few exceptions. Under *certain circumstances* water and air are not scarce. When and where might this be true for (a) water and (b) air? Why is it important to define water and air very carefully before deciding whether they are scarce or abundant? Under circumstances where they are *not* scarce, would it be possible to charge for them?

Q47. How can scarcity be a problem when the shops are well stocked, there are well over one million people unemployed (a *surplus* of labour), and there are butter and grain 'mountains' in many countries?

Q48. What is meant by 'economic efficiency'? Is an increase in economic efficiency the best solution to the problem of scarcity?

Q49. What are the advantages and disadvantages of (a) the pure command economy and (b) the completely free-market economy?

Q50. 'Economists can advise on economic policy and still avoid value judgements.' Explain how this could be so. Is it desirable that economists should avoid value judgements?

Q51. Debate

Each side should prepare a case in support of one of the following two statements:

1. The distinction between positive and normative economics is a very important distinction, since it clearly delineates the boundary between the legitimate areas of enquiry, analysis and pronouncements by economists and those areas where the economist has no superior right of pronouncement to the layperson.

2. The distinction between positive and normative economics is a dangerous and often bogus one. It tends to confer a legitimacy on economists' pronouncements which, while seeming to be 'positive', are in reality highly normative in their implications.

D ARTICLES

The financial situation of many students in higher education is such that increasing numbers are failing to complete their courses because of money difficulties. Of those who do complete their course, most are likely to leave with significant debt. Such prospects, as the article taken from the *Guardian* of 20 January 1996 suggests, are deterring many from pursuing higher education.

The growing fear of debt deters university entrants

Poverty and the prospect of financial hardship are driving down numbers of university applicants. A report from the Committee of Vice Chancellors and Principals, published this week, reveals that applications for third-level education have fallen for the first time in living memory, despite a steady increase in the number of school leavers.

The committee said that 54 000 first-year students had already left their courses early, 10 per cent more than last year. Almost 60 per cent of these had dropped out for non-academic reasons. Ted Nield, a spokesman for CVCP, said students from underprivileged backgrounds were more likely to leave because of money difficulties.

The report said that 11 per cent of students had not received their grants within one month of starting their course. Local education authority maintenance grants are now £2340 for students living in London and £1885 for those studying elsewhere. This year saw the second of three 10 per cent drops in the student grant.

Student loans have increased by more than 10 per cent to an average of £1695 in London and £1385 elsewhere. But loans are an unpopular option for many students. The National Union of Students has consistently hit out at the Government's steady reduction of grants. Ian Moss, NUS vice-president of welfare, says: 'Higher education is increasingly becoming the preserve of the affluent.'

Only half of all students eligible actually apply for loans. This is due in part to what are seen as unfair repayment terms. Repayments can be deferred until a graduate has a gross income of more than £15 000 with the interest rate linked to the Retail Price Index. Mr Nield says take-up figures would be higher if the repayment rates were linked to graduates' earnings. At present, the amount to be repaid depends only on the amount borrowed and the time scale of the repayment.

Many students avoid taking out loans by working to supplement their grant or relying on parental contribution. A survey from Barclays Bank found that students graduate with an average debt of £2293. The bank says that 14 per cent of the latest crop of first-year students have already taken term-time jobs, earning an average of £43.78 per week.

Louise Clarke of the National Union of Students says the figures support its opinion that the Government is doing 'absolutely nothing to help students'. She says: 'We want to encourage people to go on to further education, but high debt levels are making people reconsider enrolling for university.'

The CVCP expects that those who have just started their three-year course will owe almost £5000 when they graduate. Grant cuts and rising loans will create an even bigger burden for students on five-year courses. They will face a debt of £9517 when they complete their studies.

© The *Guardian*, 20.1.96

(a) What items would you include when measuring the opportunity cost to a student of going to university?

(b) In deciding not to attend university because the costs outweigh the benefits, the individual is assumed to be making a rational choice. Why might such a 'rational choice' for the individual not be beneficial to society and the economy as a whole?

(c) If the government wished to affect the rational decision-making of the student and encourage greater entry into higher education, what measures might it consider (other than increasing state grants)? In what ways would such measures affect the opportunity cost to the student?

Students are frequently asked to distinguish between *positive* and *normative* statements. We are told that positive statements are factual (correct or incorrect), whereas normative ones involve moral (or aesthetic) judgements. That seems a simple distinction. However, when it comes to specific examples, distinguishing between them is far from easy. In the reading below, taken from the *Economic Review*, volume 14, number 1 of September 1996. Alan Hamlin shows how positive and normative economics statements might be disentangled, and why making economic policy recommendations involves the use of both.

Why study economics?

Why do we study economics? What is economics for?

What sorts of questions can a study of economics equip us to answer?

I want to distinguish between two broad types of questions which economists address, and to emphasise that each type of question involves a rather different approach to economics.

The first type of question can be labelled 'positive' or 'scientific'. These questions are primarily concerned with explaining and understanding various economic phenomena. How do markets of a particular type work and what factors influence market prices? What would be the impact of the imposition of a tax on beer? How can we explain the wage differential between nurses and surgeons? All of these are essentially 'positive' questions.

The second type of question can be labelled 'normative' or 'moral'. These questions are primarily concerned with evaluating and judging various economic phenomena. Should we regulate a particular market to control prices? Should we raise or lower the tax on beer? Should we attempt to redistribute income? All of these are essentially 'normative' questions.

It should be clear from these examples that there are often very close links between positive and normative questions. It would surely be impossible for an economist to give a full discussion of the *normative* question of whether we should raise or lower the tax on beer without tackling the *positive* question concerning the impact of a tax on beer. But there is still an important distinction between the two types of question, and the closeness of the relationship between the positive and the normative can be dangerous since it can sometimes lead economists to think that they are engaged in positive analysis when they are actually engaged in normative analysis. This in turn can lead economists to ignore the moral dimension of economic analysis.

Positive economics

One way of thinking of the content of positive economics is illustrated in the top section of Figure 1. We begin with the simple idea of description. If we are to make any progress as economists we must be able to describe the economic

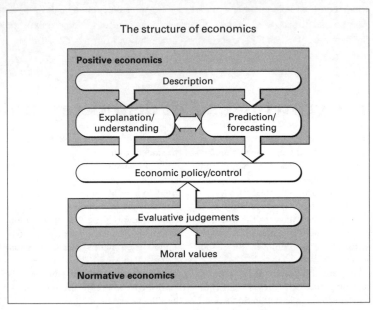

The structure of economics

Positive economics

Description

Explanation/understanding ⟷ Prediction/forecasting

Economic policy/control

Evaluative judgements

Moral values

Normative economics

world around us in a clear and recognisable way. So the first task of positive economics is to develop the terms and ideas which allow of such description.

Describing the economy is a complex task. There may be no single description which is useful for all purposes, and we need to be sensitive to the variety of functions that may be served by any part of the economic structure.

A next step is to *explain* or *understand* the workings of an economy. Explanation in positive economics emphasises the logical analysis of economic activity. The basic building blocks of positive explanation are models which attempt to capture important elements of the real world, but also to simplify it to allow a clear focus on just one or two issues. One hallmark of economic models is the assumption that individuals are rational. Indeed much economic modelling can be thought of as trying to work out the implications of rational decision-making in a variety of circumstances, thereby offering an explanation of economic phenomena as the outcomes of rational action by individuals.

Another possibility within positive economics is to shift attention from understanding some aspect of the economy to *predicting* or *forecasting* its behaviour.

So, purely positive economics can allow us to describe, explain, understand and

(sometimes) forecast aspects of the economy.

It may be interesting and intellectually exciting to understand or even forecast the economy, but unless that understanding can help us to *do* something, many people would think that economics was rather pointless. In short, most people do not simply want us to understand the economy but to make it perform better.

Normative economics

So the next step is to attempt some degree of influence or control over the economy – to think about policies that might improve economic performance in one way or another. But this is where positive economics runs out. As soon as we enter the realms of judgements about whether this or that economic arrangement is better, or whether this or that policy should be enacted, we enter the realm of normative economics.

The basic idea here is sketched in the lower panel of Figure 1. Normative or moral ideas usually begin with the identification of moral values. We might think of a range of potential moral values including human well-being, respect for human rights, equality of opportunity, and so on. There is no easy answer to the basic question of what we should value – but the question cannot be avoided. Equally, we cannot avoid the question of the extent to which these values may conflict with each other in some circumstances.

In standard economics we typically focus on two types of values as providing the normative basis for economic policy debate. On the one hand is the concern for improving each individual's own perception of his or her welfare.

On the other hand is the concern for equity or fairness across individuals. Economic policies are then defended on the grounds that they offer means of improving efficiency or improving distributional equity or fairness.

The point here is not to defend these particular values, or to offer alternatives, but simply to stress that all economics

that sets out to contribute to the policy debate – and that is virtually all economics – must be based on some specific moral stance. Economics cannot be reduced to a purely positive science and still retain policy relevance. There can be no policy conclusion without a normative input.

(a) Pick out an article in the press on some current economic issue. Identify positive and normative statements. In each case, state why they are positive or normative.

(b) How would you respond to the following argument? 'Economists should just describe, explain and predict.

Moral and evaluative judgements should be left to the politicians.'

(c) If 'all economics that sets out to contribute to a policy debate must be based on some specific moral stance', what problems does this create when we attempt to judge the findings of economists' research?

The formerly centrally planned economies of eastern Europe have moved a long way towards a free-market system. However, as the following article argues, the transition to the free market has still far to go. The article is taken from the September 1998 issue of *Finance and Development*, an International Monetary Fund (IMF) publication.

The Post-Communist Transition: Patterns and Prospects

Although the transition from a command to a market economy began in the late 1980s in some Eastern European economies, political developments following the fall of the Berlin Wall in late 1989 and the breakup of the Soviet Union two years later sharply accelerated this process. The collapse of the previous economic systems and relationships, and the ensuing large-scale reorientation and reorganization of production initially sent output and trade into a steep decline and triggered rampant inflation. Since then, however, the countries of Central and Eastern Europe and the Baltics, Russia, and other countries of the former Soviet Union have made significant progress in transition and in stabilizing output and prices.

Transition has so far comprised two distinct phases. The first, which is largely complete in most (but not all) countries, consisted of the liberalization of markets and trade, privatization of state enterprises, and withdrawal of government from many activities. In the second phase, now under way in some countries, the key challenges are to develop the public and private institutions that underpin an effective market

economy, to strengthen the state's capacity to raise revenues and provide the public services that are essential to a market economy, and to ensure that sound business practices become more firmly established. The response to these challenges will ultimately determine the extent of competition, quality of corporate governance, climate for investment, and prospects for longer-term growth. A major challenge faced by all these countries is the need to strengthen their financial sectors – the recent turmoil in East Asia provides a stark reminder of the danger of not doing so. And, for some transition economies, the process of economic reform and institutional change will be shaped by the prospect of accession to the European Union.

Progress in transition

Market liberalization. By 1994, the first year in which the European Bank for Reconstruction and Development (EBRD) compiled transition indicators (see box), most countries had made rapid progress in liberalizing markets – for example, removing price controls and restrictions on trade and access to foreign exchange. The main benefit

of liberalization was the adjustment in relative prices; prices began to reflect production costs and market demand, and were thus able to provide clear, market-based signals to producers. The liberalization of markets has been largely completed in most transition economies, with the exception of a few former Soviet Union countries and some sensitive sectors such as infrastructure and housing.

Privatization. There has been steady progress in privatizing both small and large enterprises over the past four years, and, in 1997, privatization registered the largest increase of all the EBRD indicators. Many countries quickly privatized small-scale enterprises (shops and restaurants, for example) in the early years of transition, and most small businesses in the transition countries are now privately owned international accounting standards and loan classification and provisioning requirements, it has become clear that loan-loss provisions, in particular, need to be increased.

The structure of the banking sector has begun to change in the transition countries. The typical pattern is one where a few big banks with a large share of the banking sector's total capital and assets coexist with many small, often undercapitalized banks. This pattern is likely to become even more pronounced with the closure or merger of many of the weaker banks. The entry of more foreign banks into the region has acted as a spur to competition. Further change is also inevitable in those countries negotiating to join the European Union, which will be forced to strengthen their banking sectors in order to comply with European Union banking directives, to harmonize their regulations with those of other countries, and to complete the privatization of major banks to make their banking sectors more competitive.

The development of capital markets has been slower than that of the banking sector. Although stock markets were established (or reestablished) at an early stage of transition in many countries – especially those where privatization was implemented using a voucher system, which led to initial share trading – the necessary regulatory structures and penalty enforcement mechanisms have been slower to develop. As a result, liquidity tends to be low and dealings are often not transparent, with much of the trading done off-exchange.

Private sector share of output

One indicator of the outcome of market-oriented reforms is the share of the private sector in the economy. This share has grown steadily in most transition countries; the EBRD estimates that, by mid-1997, the private sector accounted for more than 50 per cent of GDP in 19 of the 26 countries where the EBRD operates.

In some countries – Poland, for example – the response of entrepreneurs and new private business to market opportunities has been a driving force in the sharp improvement in enterprise performance and growth. The private sector's share in the economies of the Czech and Slovak Republics, Estonia, and Hungary – countries that have privatized most state enterprises – is so extensive that any further expansion of the private sector will require faster growth relative to the public sector and rapid creation of new companies. In contrast, in many of the former Soviet Union countries, a combination of unpredictable taxation, bureaucracy, and corruption have slowed the pace of private sector development. One result has been that much private sector growth has been in the informal economy, so that the share of the private sector is often understated in the official data.

Prospects for medium-term growth

In the early years of reform, output fell sharply in all of the transition economies; there is some evidence that the extent of the decline was partly related to the degree of economic distortion under the previous system. The timing and speed of the recovery in output in these economies have been linked to two factors – the successful implementation of macroeconomic stabilization programs and market liberalization – indicating a positive relationship between reform and growth.

Higher output can also be the result of increased investment, a skilled workforce, and better use of existing resources in production. Given that much past investment was misdirected and that these countries had highly educated populations before transition began, it is likely that some of the growth of the past decade reflects an improvement in the organization of production in response to market incentives. For some countries, especially those in Eastern Europe, the introduction of reforms has unleashed market forces. The results are already evident, as there has been a shift away from industrial production and toward services. With the expansion of the private sector in these countries, the breaking up of monopolies, and the growth of imports, competition has increased, leading to significant gains in productivity. In the longer term, however, it is more likely that growth will depend on increasing the rate of private investment, developing and diffusing new technologies, and acquiring the skills needed in a more advanced market economy.

(a) What economic advantages does the free market economy have over the command economy?

(b) According to the article, which areas of market reform have been successful and which ones still require improvement?

(c) What help might the western economies, and institutions such as the IMF, offer countries in eastern Europe to achieve more successful market economies? Should they help?

 ANSWERS

Q1. E. We define scarcity as the excess of human wants over the means of fulfilling those wants. Virtually everyone would like more than they have. Even very rich people would normally like a higher income, and even if money was no object at all for them, they would still have a shortage of *time* to do everything they would like to do.

Q2. *False.* Human desires are virtually boundless. For example, in 100 years people will want things that have not been invented yet.

Q3. Labour, land (and raw materials), and capital.

Q4. E. All the others contribute towards production. The wages are the *reward* for Jim's labour: they do not add to production.

Q5. *wants.* Potential demand refers to what people would *like* to have and not merely to those items that are thought of as being necessities.

Q6. *the level of resources available.* What society can produce depends on what labour, land and capital are available.

Q7. *macroeconomics.*

Q8. *microeconomics.*

Q9. *(a)* *macro.*

(b) *micro.*

(c) *macro.* (It would be micro if we were looking at overseas investment in a *specific* industry.)

(d) *micro.*

(e) *macro.*

(f) *micro.* (We are only referring to wages in a *specific* industry.)

(g) *micro.*

(h) *macro.* (We are referring to total household saving in the economy, not to the saving of specific households or to saving in specific financial institutions.)

Q10. B. The opportunity cost is the cost measured in terms of next best alternative forgone.

Q11. (b), (d), (e) *true*: (a) and (c) *false*. Rational behaviour involves weighing up the costs and benefits of any activity. For consumers this involves comparing the price of a good with the benefit the consumer expects to receive. The consumer will think (however briefly), 'Is this item worth purchasing?' The answer will vary from person to person according to their tastes (i.e. not (c)).

Q12. C. All the other statements consider the effects of a bit *more* of something (eating another chocolate bar, mortgage rates rising by another 1 per cent, purchasing another forklift truck, installing anti-pollution equipment on one more power station). In the case of C, however, we are considering the effect of *total* revenues for the firm exceeding its *total* production costs.

Q13. *(a)* A, D, F and G. All these points lie *on* the production possibility curve and thus show that the country is fully utilising its potential.

(b) B and C. These points lie *inside* the curve and thus illustrate that not as many goods are being produced as could be.

(c) A and G. Point A shows complete specialisation in good Y and point G shows complete specialisation in good X.

(d) E. Point E lies outside the production possibility curve and is thus unobtainable.

Q14. E. When production is initially at point A, producing one more unit of good X (i.e. the eleventh unit) will involve reducing production of good Y by 2 units (from 8 to 6 units).

Q15. The phenomenon of *increasing opportunity costs*. As more and more of one good is produced, increasingly larger and larger amounts of the other have to be sacrificed.

Q16. B. The outward shift of the curve illustrates an increase in potential output (i). The movement outward of the production point from A to B illustrates an increase in actual output (ii). But the fact that point A is *on* the earlier curve whereas point B is *inside* the later curve means that resources are being used less fully (or efficiently) than previously.

Q17. A. An increase in the population of working age represents an increase in (human) resources and hence an increase in production potential. Note: B represents a movement outward of the production point towards the production possibility curve; C may encourage increased *consumption* and may as a result stimulate a greater level of production (a movement outward of the production *point*) but does not directly increase *production* potential; D means that the *money* value of output potential has risen, but there is no change in *physical* output potential; E is likely to lead to an *inward* shift of the curve as the quality of the labour force declines.

Q18. (a) and (b) *macro*, (c) *micro*. In the case of (a) and (b) the whole economy is being considered: whether it is growing (a), or whether there is a full use of resources (b). In the case of (c), however, the question is one of the *composition* of production: how much of *each* good is being produced.

Q19. *(a)* IV.

(b) II.

(c) I.

(d) III.

Q20. The state or some central or local planning agency.

Q21. Individuals: households and firms.

Q22. C. In a pure command economy, firms do not have the discretion to respond to changes in consumer demand.

Q23. Costly in terms of administration; difficulty in devising incentives to ensure that the plan is carried out as the planners would like; loss of individual liberty; planners may not act in the interests of the people.

Q24. *demanders.*

Q25. *suppliers.*

Q26. *fall.*

Q27. *a rise in the quantity demanded but a fall in the quantity supplied.*

Q28. *rise.*

Q29. *fall.*

Q30. *rise.*

Q31. The rise in demand for houses will cause a shortage of houses. This will cause the price of houses to rise. This will increase the profitability of house construction. This in turn will increase the demand for bricklayers. The resulting shortage of bricklayers will lead to a rise in their wages (the 'price' of bricklayers).

Q32. *(a)* *True.*

(b) *True.*

(c) *True.* Competition will help to keep prices down and thus encourage firms to reduce their costs in order to make a satisfactory level of profit.

(d) *False.* While competition between firms may prevent very high profits in any industry and the competition between workers may prevent very high wages in any type of job, the *ownership* of

resources is not equal. Some people own a lot of property; others own none; some workers are skilled and can command high wages; others are unskilled.

(e) False. Goods that are profitable for a firm may not necessarily be socially desirable. For example, the production of certain industrial goods may damage the environment. On the other hand, some things that *are* socially desirable (such as pavements) may not be profitable for private enterprise to supply.

Q33. Examples include: state ownership of various industries (nationalisation); legislation to affect production or consumption (e.g. to control pollution); taxation (e.g. high rates on tobacco and spirits); subsidies and benefits (e.g. pensions and other benefits to help the poor); direct provision (e.g. of education and policing); price controls and controls over interest rates and exchange rates.

Q34. D. It is usually not possible to conduct controlled experiments in economics since, unlike certain of the natural sciences, it is not a *laboratory* science. It is not possible to hold other things constant. Instead, we simply have to *assume* that other things are constant (*ceteris paribus*). Note: although economic models can usually be tested by appealing to the facts (answer E), there will be a delay if a prediction of the future is being tested.

Q35. *induction.*

Q36. *deduction.*

Q37. (c), (e), (b), (a), (g), (d), (f).

Q38. Reasons include: it is impossible to conduct controlled experiments in economics; economics deals with human behaviour (it is a *social* science) and humans are not totally predictable; economic data tend to be incomplete and often inaccurate.

Q39. D. This statement is a question of *value*. Some people may regard it as fair, some may not: it depends on what they believe to be right or wrong. The other statements in principle can all be tested by an appeal to facts. They may be correct or incorrect, but they are statements about what is or is not the case. Note that statement C is positive because it is not a statement about whether privatisation is desirable or not, but about what those on the left believe.

Q40. (b) and (d) are *positive*. The person making the statements is not saying whether government policies are good or bad, or what the government ought to do. In both cases the statements can be assessed by an appeal to the facts (albeit in the case of (d) you would have to wait to see how the electorate responded). (a) and (c), on the other hand are *normative*. The person making the statements is saying what the government *ought* to do or what the *goals* of government policy *should* be. Note: in the case of (d), there *is* the implication that if the government wants to be popular with the electorate, it would be wise to give a higher priority to curing unemployment, but that does not make it a normative statement. The statement as it stands is only about means to ends, not whether those ends are desirable. Only if the person making the statement is *implying* that the government *ought* to do what is popular with the electorate does the statement have normative overtones.

CHAPTER TWO

2 Supply and Demand

A   REVIEW

In this chapter we examine the workings of the *free market*. The *market* simply refers to the coming together of buyers (demanders) and sellers (suppliers).

We look first at *demand*, then at *supply* and then put the two together to show how price is determined. We then turn to examine just how responsive demand and supply are to their various determinants and particularly to changes in price; in doing this we will examine the important concept of *elasticity*.

The response of demand, supply and price to changing market conditions is unlikely to be instantaneous. In the final section, therefore, we examine the *time dimension* of markets. We look at the process of adjustment after the elapse of different periods of time.

2.1 Demand

(Page 36) There are several determinants of consumer demand for a product. The relationship between demand and one of these determinants is expressed in the *law of demand*.

Q1. The law of demand states that:

A. quantity demanded increases as price decreases.
B. demand rises as income rises.
C. producers respond to an increase in demand by producing more.
D. an increase in demand causes an increase in price.
E. the amount purchased depends on the amount demanded.

(Page 36) The effect of a change in price on the quantity demanded can be divided into an *income* effect and a *substitution* effect.

Q2. The income effect refers to the effect on price and quantity demanded of a change in consumer income.

True/False

Q3. The substitution effect refers to the effect on the quantity demanded of a change in the price of a substitute good.

True/False

(Pages 37–8) The relationship between price and the quantity demanded can be shown graphically on a *demand* curve. A demand curve can be an individual's demand curve, or that of a group of individuals (a *section* of the market) or that of the whole market.

Q4. Consider the (imaginary) data in Table 2.1. This shows the annual demand for tennis shoes in three sections of the market.

 Multiple Choice   Written answer   Delete wrong word    Diagram/table manipulation   Calculation   Matching/ordering

(a) Fill in the column for annual market demand.

(b) Draw the annual demand curve for each of the three groups and the annual market demand on Figure 2.1.

Table 2.1 The demand for tennis shoes

Price	Tennis club members (annual) (000s)	Players but not club members (annual) (000s)	Non-tennis players (annual) (000s)	Total market (annual) (000s)
£100	6	1	0	...
£80	7	3	0	...
£60	8	6	2	...
£40	9	10	8	...
£20	10	18	20	...

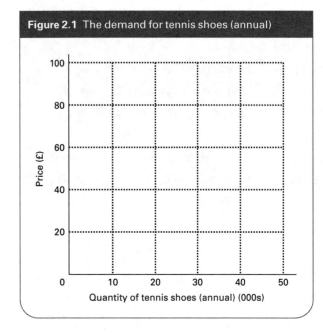

Figure 2.1 The demand for tennis shoes (annual)

(Pages 38–9) But price is not the only factor that determines how much of a good people will demand. Let us take the case of a particular product:

⚫ **Q5.** It is normal to group the various determinants of demand into categories. The categories include:

(i) The price of the good.
(ii) The price of substitute goods.
(iii) The price of complementary goods.
(iv) Tastes.
(v) Income.
(vi) Expectations of future price changes.

Into which of the above categories would you put the following determinants of the demand for tennis shoes?

(a) The price of tennis rackets.

....

(b) The amount shops charge for tennis shoes.

....

(c) The earnings of people who might possibly buy tennis shoes.

....

(d) The price of running shoes.

....

(e) The likelihood that the government will impose a tax on imported sportswear in order to protect the domestic sportswear industry.

....

(f) The amount of coverage to tennis given on the television.

....

(Page 39) When the price of a good changes, we say that this causes the **Q6.** *demand/quantity demanded* to change. This is shown by **Q7.** *a shift in the demand curve/a movement along the demand curve*. When one of the other determinants changes, however, we say that this causes the **Q8.** *demand/ quantity demanded* to change. This is shown by **Q9.** *a shift in the demand curve/a movement along the demand curve*.

◐ **Q10.** Consider the demand curve for petrol. What effect will the following have?

(a) An increase in the price of cars. *Rightward shift/leftward shift/movement up along/movement down along/need more information to say.*

(b) An increase in the proportion of the population owning cars. *Rightward shift/leftward shift/movement up along/movement down along/need more information to say.*

(c) A rise in transport costs of shipping oil. *Rightward shift/leftward shift/movement up along/movement down along/need more information to say.*

(d) A growing concern for environmental issues by the general public. *Rightward shift/leftward shift/movement up along/movement down along/need more information to say.*

(e) An increase in duty on diesel. *Rightward shift/leftward shift/movement up along/movement down along/need more information to say.*

(f) A reduction in duty on petrol. *Rightward shift/leftward shift/movement up along/movement down along/need more information to say.*

(Page 39) One of the most important determinants of demand is the level of consumer income. When considering

the effect of a change in income on demand, we distinguish between *normal* goods and *inferior* goods.

(?) Q11. We define a normal good as one

....

(?) Q12. On the other hand, we define an inferior good as one

....

2.2 Supply

(Page 42) The relationship between supply and *price* is **Q13.** *a direct/an inverse* relationship.

Q14. Which of the following are explanations of this relationship between price and market supply (there are more than one)?

(a) Costs tend to rise over time. Yes/No

(b) As price rises, producers find that it is worth incurring the higher costs per unit associated with producing more. Yes/No

(c) At higher prices it is worth using additional, less productive factors of production. Yes/No

(d) The lower the price, the more firms will switch to producing other products which are thus now relatively more profitable. Yes/No

(e) Technological improvements mean that more can be produced and this in turn will affect prices. Yes/No

(Page 42) Given that the quantity supplied is likely to rise as price rises, the supply curve is likely to be upward sloping.

(Pages 43–4) As with demand, price is not the only thing that affects supply.

(?) Q15. Other determinants of supply include:

1. ....

2. ....

3. ....

4. ....

5. ....

(Page 44) If price changes, the effect is shown by **Q16.** *a shift in/a movement along* the supply curve. We call this effect a change in **Q17.** *supply/the quantity supplied*. If any other determinant of supply changes, the effect is shown by **Q18.** *a shift in/a movement along* the supply curve. We call this effect *a change in* **Q19.** *supply/the quantity supplied*.

Q20. Consider the case of the supply curve of organically grown wheat. What effect would the following have?

(a) A reduction in the cost of organic fertilisers. *Rightward shift/leftward shift/movement up along/movement down along.*

(b) An increase in the demand for organic bread. *Rightward shift/leftward shift/movement up along/movement down along.*

(c) An increase in the price of organic oats and barley. *Rightward shift/leftward shift/movement up along/movement down along.*

(d) The belief that the price of organic wheat will rise substantially in the future. *Rightward shift/leftward shift/movement up along/movement down along.*

(e) A drought. *Rightward shift/leftward shift/movement up along/movement down along.*

(f) A government subsidy granted to farmers using organic methods. *Rightward shift/leftward shift/movement up along/movement down along.*

2.3 Price and output determination

(Pages 45–6) If the demand for a good exceeds the supply, there will be a **Q21.** *shortage/surplus*. This will lead to a **Q22.** *fall/rise* in the price of the good. If the supply of a good exceeds the demand, there will be a **Q23.** *shortage/surplus*. This will lead to a **Q24.** *fall/rise* in the price.

Price will settle at the equilibrium. The equilibrium price is the one that clears the market.

(?) Q25. This is the price where

....

(Pages 46–7) If the demand or the supply curve *shifts*, this will lead either to a shortage or to a surplus. Price will therefore either rise or fall, **Q26.** causing a *shift in/movement along* the other curve, until a new equilibrium is reached at the position where the supply and demand curves *now* intersect.

Q27. The demand and supply schedules for organically grown wheat in a free market are shown in Table 2.2.

(a) Draw the demand and supply curves on Figure 2.2.

(b) What would be the size of the shortage or surplus at a price of €180 per tonne?

Shortage/surplus of ....

(c) What would be the size of the shortage or surplus at a price of €340 per tonne?

Shortage/surplus of ....

(d) What is the equilibrium price and quantity?

P = ...; Q = ...

Table 2.2 The market for organically grown wheat (imaginary figures)

Price per tonne (€)	100	140	180	220	260	300	340	380
Tonnes supplied per week	220	260	320	400	500	640	880	1400
Tonnes demanded per week	770	680	610	550	500	460	400	320

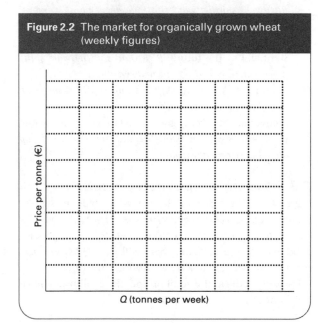

Figure 2.2 The market for organically grown wheat (weekly figures)

Q (tonnes per week)

Price per tonne (€)

(e) Now assume that the demand for organic wheat increases by 180 tonnes per week at all prices. Draw the new demand curve.

(f) What is the size of the shortage or surplus at the original equilibrium price?

   Shortage/surplus of ....

(g) What is the new equilibrium price?...............................

(h) Has the equilibrium quantity increased by more or less than the 180 tonnes per week increase in demand?
                                                        More/less
Assume that supply now changes by an equal amount at all prices.

(i) What would this change have to be to restore the original equilibrium price?

   Increase/decrease of ....

(j) What would this change have to be to restore the original equilibrium quantity?

   Increase/decrease of ....

(k) Is there any shift in the supply curve that could restore both the original equilibrium price and the original quantity?   *Yes/No*

   Explain..

   ....

Q28. If income increases, then for an inferior good, the quantity sold will decrease and the price will increase.
                                                        True/False

Q29. Figure 2.3 shows the demand for and supply of new purpose-built flats.

   The supply and demand curves are initially given by S_0 and D_0. The market is in equilibrium at point *x*. Various factors then change which have the effect of shifting the demand curve to D_1 or D_2 and/or the supply curve to S_1 or S_2. What is the new equilibrium point in each of the following cases? (Remember that in each case the market is initially in equilibrium at point *x*.)

(a) A rise in the price of building materials.
                                                     Point ....

(b) Flat living becomes more fashionable.
                                                     Point ....

(c) A fall in the price of new houses.
                                                     Point ....

(d) A rise in the price of old houses and flats.
                                                     Point ....

(e) The imposition of a new construction tax on houses (but not flats).
                                                     Point ....

(f) The belief that the price of flats will soon rise substantially.
                                                     Point ....

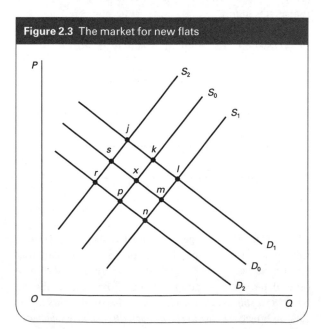

Figure 2.3 The market for new flats

(g) An increase in mortgage interest rates.

Point ....

Q30. Suppose that it is observed that the price of butter falls but that the quantity sold rises. From this we can deduce:

A. That the demand curve has shifted to the right, but we cannot deduce whether or not the supply curve has shifted.

B. That the demand curve has shifted to the left, but we cannot deduce whether or not the supply curve has shifted.

C. That the supply curve has shifted to the right, but we cannot deduce whether or not the demand curve has shifted.

D. That the supply curve has shifted to the left, but we cannot deduce whether or not the demand curve has shifted.

E. Nothing. Either curve could have shifted either way depending on which way the other shifted.

(Pages 39–41, 44–5) Demand and supply curves can be represented by equations.

Q31. The supply and demand curves for commodity X are given by the following equations:

$$Q_s = 2 + 3P$$
$$Q_d = 50 - 5P$$

(a) Without drawing a diagram or completing a table, find the equilibrium price and quantity.
(You will need to use simultaneous equations.)

....

(b) Using the two equations above, fill in the figures in Table 2.3.

(c) Draw a graph of the two curves on Figure 2.4.

(d) Assume that the demand equation now becomes: $Q_d = 66 - 5P$. Draw the new demand curve on Figure 2.4 and find the equilibrium. How is the shape of the demand curve affected?

(e) Assume that the demand equation now becomes: $Q_d = 50 - 9P$. Draw the new demand curve and find the equilibrium. How is the shape of the demand curve affected this time?

Table 2.3 $Q_s = 2 + 3P$; $Q_d = 50 - 5P$

P	0	1	2	3	4	5	6	7	8	9	10
Q_s	.	.	.	11	.	.	.	.	.	.	.
Q_d	.	.	40	.	.	.	.	.	.	.	.

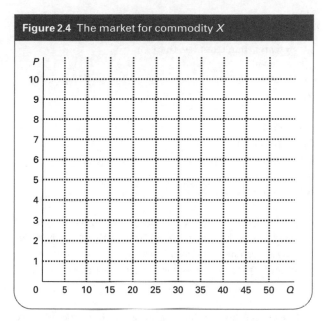

Figure 2.4 The market for commodity X

2.4 Elasticity

Elasticity (ϵ) is a measure of the responsiveness of demand (or supply) to a change in one of the determinants, and is one of the most important concepts we shall come across in the whole of economics. It is defined as the proportionate (or percentage) change in quantity demanded (or supplied) (Q) divided by the proportionate (or percentage) change in the determinant (X).

$$\epsilon = \Delta Q/Q \div \Delta X/X$$

(Pages 50–1) The *price elasticity of demand* measures the responsiveness of *Q32. the quantity demanded/price* to a change in *Q33. the quantity demanded/the quantity supplied/price*.

Q34. The formula for the price elasticity of demand ($P\epsilon_d$) is

....

If the quantity demanded changes proportionately more than the price, we say that demand is *Q35. elastic/inelastic*. If the quantity demanded changes proportionately less than the price, we say that demand is *Q36. elastic/inelastic*. Assuming that a demand curve is downward sloping, the price elasticity of demand will have *Q37. a positive value ($\epsilon > 0$)/a negative value ($\epsilon < 0$)*.

Let us now ignore the sign (positive or negative) and consider just the value for elasticity: for example $\epsilon = 1.8$ or $\epsilon = 0.43$.

Q38. Match each of the following figures for elasticity to definitions (a)–(e) below.

(i) $\epsilon = 1$

(ii) $1 > \epsilon > 0$ (This means that the figure for elasticity is greater than 0 but less than 1.)

(iii) $\epsilon = 0$

(iv) $\epsilon = \infty$

(v) $\infty > \epsilon > 1$

(*a*) Elastic.

(*b*) Unit elastic.

(*c*) Totally inelasitc.

(*d*) Inelastic.

(*e*) Totally elastic.

(*Pages 51–2*) Demand will be more elastic **Q39.** *the greater/ the less* the number and closeness of substitute goods, **Q40.** *the higher/the lower* the proportion of income spent on the good and **Q41.** *the longer/the shorter* the time period that elapses after the change in price.

⬙ **Q42.** Rank the following in ascending order of price elasticity of demand (i.e. least elastic first):

(*a*) Margarine ....

(*b*) 'Scrummy' low fat margarine ....

(*c*) Spreads for bread ....

(*d*) Low fat margarine ....

(*e*) 'Scrummy' low fat margarine with a token for the current competition

....

▤ **Q43.** The price elasticity of demand for holidays abroad (in general) is likely to be high because

A. people tend to book up a long time in advance.

B. there are plenty of different foreign holidays to choose from.

C. foreign holidays are an expensive luxury.

D. holidays at home provide no real alternative.

E. people need a holiday if they are to cope with the year ahead.

We must be careful when drawing inferences about price elasticity from demand curves.

◖ **Q44.** Referring to the two demand curves in Figure 2.5, which of the following statements are correct?

(*a*) Curve D_2 is elastic. *True/False*

(*b*) Curve D_1 has a price elasticity of –1. *True/False*

(*c*) At point *x*, curve D_1 has an elasticity of zero. *True/False*

(*d*) At point *y*, curve D_2 has an elasticity of infinity. *True/False*

(*e*) Curve D_2 is more elastic than curve D_1. *True/False*

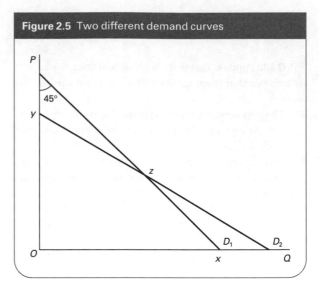

Figure 2.5 Two different demand curves

(*f*) At point *z*, the two curves have the same price elasticity. *True/False*

(*g*) Curve D_2 is more elastic than curve D_1 over any given price range. *True/False*

(*Pages 54–6*) Given that demand curves normally have different elasticities along their length, we can normally only refer to the specific value for elasticity between two points on the curve or at a single point.

? **Q45.** Elasticity measured between two points is known as

....

When applied to price elasticity of demand its formula is:

$$\frac{\Delta Q_d}{\text{average } Q_d} \div \frac{\Delta P}{\text{average } P}$$

where average Q_d is the average value of Q_d at the two points between which we are measuring elasticity. Thus if at one point $Q_d = 6$ and at the other $Q_d = 4$, then average $Q_d = 5$: i.e. average $Q_d = (Q_{d1} + Q_{d2})/2$.

? **Q46.** Similarly average $P = $ ....

✕ **Q47.** Given the following equation: $Q_d = 20 - 2P$:

(*a*) Fill in the figures for quantity demanded in Table 2.4.

(*b*) Estimate the price elasticity of demand between:

    (i) $P = 2$ and $P = 0$

    (ii) $P = 6$ and $P = 4$

    (iii) $P = 9$ and $P = 7$

    In each case state whether demand is elastic or inelastic.

(*c*) Using this arc method, how would you estimate price elasticity at a single point?

....

Table 2.4 Demand schedule: $Q_d = 20 - 2P$

P(£)	10	9	8	7	6	5	4	3	2	1	0
Q_d	.	.	.	.	8	.	.	.	.	.	.

(d) Using this method, estimate the price elasticity of demand at:
   (i) $P = 2$
   (ii) $P = 6$
   (iii) $P = 5$
   (iv) $P = 0$
   (v) $P = 10$

(Pages 52–4) One of the most important applications of price elasticity of demand concerns the relationship between the *price* of a good and the total amount of *expenditure* by consumers (and hence the *revenue* earned by firms). We define *total expenditure* as price times quantity sold: $TE = P \times Q$.

⊖ **Q48.** Fill in a new row in Table 2.4 showing the level of total expenditure at each price.

◐ **Q49.** Referring again to Table 2.4:
(a) What will be the effect on total expenditure of reducing price (and hence increasing the quantity demanded) when demand is price *elastic*?   *rise/fall*
(b) What will be the effect when demand is price inelastic?   *rise/fall*
(c) What will be the elasticity at the price where total expenditure is the maximum?

....

◐ **Q50.** When the price elasticity of demand for a good is –1.4, then a rise in the price will result in fewer goods being sold but greater consumer expenditure.   *True/False*

◐ **Q51.** When demand is price inelastic, total expenditure will vary directly with price but inversely with quantity demanded.   *True/False*

◐ **Q52.** The elasticity of a straight-line demand curve will fall as you move down the curve, from infinity at the point where it intersects the vertical axis to zero at the point where it intersects the horizontal axis.   *True/False*

(Pages 56–8) Another way of measuring elasticity is to use the point method. Remember that the arc formula for price elasticity is:

$$\frac{\Delta Q_d}{\text{average } Q_d} \div \frac{\Delta P}{\text{average } P}$$

If we want to measure elasticity at a point, then average P and Q_d simply become P and Q_d, and the 'change' (Δ)

in price and quantity becomes infinitesimally small. An infinitesimally small change is written d. The formula thus becomes:

$$dQ_d/Q_d \div dP/P$$

⑦ ***Q53.** Rearranged this formula becomes:

$dQ_d/dP \times$ ....

where dQ_d/dP is the ***Q54.** *slope/inverse of the slope* of the tangent to the demand curve at the point in question.

⊖ ***Q55.** Given the following equation for a demand curve:

$$Q_d = 50 - 20P + 2P^2$$

(a) Fill in the figures in Table 2.5.
(b) Draw the demand curve on Figure 2.6.
(c) Draw the tangent to the curve where $P = 3$, $Q = 8$. What is its slope?

....

(d) What is the price elasticity of demand where $P = 3$?

....

Table 2.5 Demand schedule: $Q_d = 50 - 20P + 2P^2$

P	5	4	3	2	1	0
Q_d						

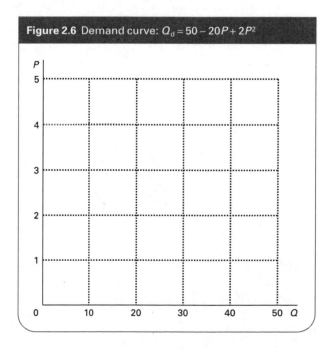

Figure 2.6 Demand curve: $Q_d = 50 - 20P + 2P^2$

(Pages 58–60) We turn now to other types of elasticity and start with *price elasticity of supply*.

◑ Q56. There are two goods A and B. Which is likely to have the more price-elastic supply in each of the following cases?

(a) It is less costly to shift from producing A to another product than it is to shift from B to another product.

A/B/cannot say

(b) The supply of A is considered over a longer period of time than B. *A/B/cannot say*

(c) The costs of producing extra units increases more rapidly in the case of A than in the case of B.

A/B/cannot say

(d) Consumers find it easier to find alternatives to A than to B. *A/B/cannot say*

(e) A is a minor by-product of B. *A/B/cannot say*

(f) A higher proportion of national income is spent on A than on B. *A/B/cannot say*

◑ Q57. Consider the three supply curves in Figure 2.7. Which of the following statements are correct?

(a) Curve S_1 has an elasticity equal to one throughout its length. *True/False*

(b) The elasticity of all three curves is the same at point x. *True/False*

(c) Curve S_2 has an elasticity greater than one throughout its length. *True/False*

(d) Curve S_3 has an elasticity equal to zero at point z. *True/False*

(e) Curve S_2 has an elasticity equal to infinity at point y. *True/False*

(f) Curve S_3 has a constant elasticity less than one throughout its length. *True/False*

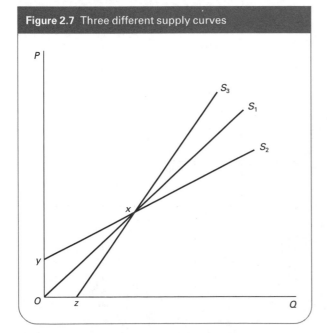

Figure 2.7 Three different supply curves

(Pages 60–1) Income elasticity of demand measures the responsiveness of demand to a change in income. For normal goods it has a **Q58.** *positive/negative* value.

⊗ Q59. Table 2.6 shows the quantity of three goods (A, B and C) purchased in two years (year 1 and year 2). The only factor affecting demand that changes between these two years is consumer incomes.

Table 2.6 Demand for goods A, B and C in years 1 and 2

	Quantity demanded Good A (000s)	Quantity demanded Good B (000s)	Quantity demanded Good C (000s)	Consumer income (Y) (£bn)
Year 1	30	52	190	45 000
Year 2	50	48	210	55 000

(a) What is the income elasticity of demand for the three goods between Y = £45 billion and £55 billion? (Use the arc method.)

Good A ....

Good B ....

Good C ....

(b) Which of the three goods has an income-*elastic* demand over the given income range? *A/B/C*

(c) Which of the goods is an inferior good over the given income range? *A/B/C*

◑ Q60. The share of income devoted to a good will increase with income if the good has an income elasticity of demand greater than one. *True/False*

(Pages 61–2) Cross-price elasticity of demand measures the responsiveness of the demand for one good to a change in the price of another and thus is a means of judging the degree of substitutability or complementarity of two goods.

◑ Q61. Match each of the following five values for cross-price elasticity (i)–(v), to the pairs of products (a)–(e).
(i) Considerably greater than zero
(ii) Slightly greater than zero
(iii) Zero
(iv) Slightly less than zero
(v) Considerably less than zero

(a) Petrol and cars ....

(b) Salt and petrol ....

(c) Cars and bicycles ....

(d) Escorts and Astras ....

(e) Petrol and cross-Channel ferry crossings ....

2.5 The time dimension

(Page 63) To get a fuller picture of how markets work we must take into account the time dimension. Given that producers and consumers take a time to respond fully to price changes, we can identify different equilibria after the elapse of different lengths of time. Generally, short-run supply and demand tend to be **Q62.** *more/less* price-elastic than long-run supply and demand. As a result, any shifts in demand or supply curves tend to have a relatively bigger effect on **Q63.** *price/quantity* in the short run and a relatively bigger effect on **Q64.** *price/quantity* in the long run.

 Q65. The short-run (retail) supply of freshly cut flowers is much less elastic than that of pot plants because

A. households generally keep pot plants much longer before throwing them away (and often never throw them away).

B. fresh flowers are more likely to be purchased for special occasions.

C. the price of freshly cut flowers fluctuates much more than that of pot plants.

D. supplies of fresh flowers fluctuate much more with the weather and the season.

E. florists cannot keep freshly cut flowers as long as pot plants.

(Pages 63–6) Realising that prices can fluctuate, buyers and sellers are likely to try to anticipate what will happen to prices if they are in a position to wait before buying or selling. In such cases, if people believe that prices are likely to

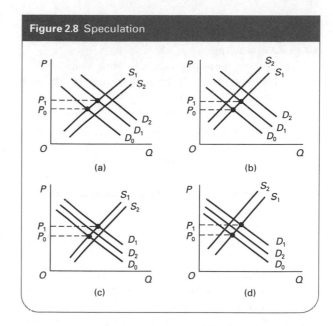

Figure 2.8 Speculation

rise, current supply will shift to the **Q66.** *left/right* and current demand will shift to the **Q67.** *left/right*. This will have the effect of causing the price to **Q68.** *rise/fall*.

This activity where buyers or sellers predict price changes and then act on these predictions, is called *speculation*. It can be of two types, *stabilising* and *destabilising*.

Q69. Figure 2.8 shows a market where demand has just increased from D_0 to D_1 with a resulting price rise from P_0 to P_1. People then make a judgement from this about future price changes. Which one of the four diagrams represents stabilising speculation and which destabilising?

Stabilising   *(a)/(b)/(c)/(d)*
Destabilising   *(a)/(b)/(c)/(d)*

B **PROBLEMS, EXERCISES AND PROJECTS**

Q70. Clearly defining the market may be crucial in explaining the effect of a price change on the quantity of a good demanded.

The market for petrol is a good example. The demand for all petrol is relatively inelastic to changes in price: there are few substitutes and it takes time for consumers to change their consumption patterns. Yet if you consider the demand for a single brand of petrol, it becomes far more elastic, as there are several substitute brands available.

Consider the two diagrams in Figure 2.9.

If the price of *all* petrol rises from 50p per litre to 70p as in diagram (a), total revenue increases from area *abc*0 to area *def*0: from (£0.50 × 50m) = £25m to (£0.70 × 45m) = £31.5m.

Alternatively, if a *particular company* raises its price *independently* of its competitors, the demand for its particular brand will fall dramatically. In diagram (b), when the

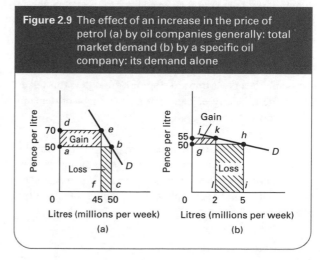

Figure 2.9 The effect of an increase in the price of petrol (a) by oil companies generally: total market demand (b) by a specific oil company: its demand alone

company raises its price to 55p its total revenue falls from area *ghi*0 to area *jkl*0: from (£0.50 × 5m) = £2.5m to (£0.55 × 2m) = £1.1m.

Generally, the more narrowly we define a market, the more substitutes there will be outside that market and therefore the more elastic the demand will be.

(a) Using the arc method of calculating elasticity, what is the price elasticity of demand between the two points on each of the two curves in Figure 2.9?

(b) Which would you expect to have the higher price elasticity: the demand for a particular brand of petrol or the demand for petrol from a particular filling station? Explain your assumptions.

Q71. Find out what has happened to house prices over the last five years.

To get details you could enquire in estate agents or building societies. The Halifax publishes quarterly leaflets on house prices; so too do newspapers. You could, for instance, try looking up the topic in *The Times Index* or *The Economist Index* (which you should find in libraries). *Economic Trends* (ONS) gives monthly data on the prices of new houses. See also web addresses B7, B8 and B11 in the websites appendix in Sloman 4th edition (page A1).

(a) Plot a time-series graph showing the movements of house prices.

(b) Identify factors over the period that have caused the demand and/or supply curves to shift. Draw diagrams to illustrate your analysis here.

(c) Forecast what will happen to house prices over the next two years, again identifying the factors that are likely to influence demand and/or supply.

Q72. Imagine that you were given a rise in grant/pay/allowance of £10 per week.

(a) Make a list of the things on which you would spend this extra income and work out your income elasticity of demand for each.

(b) Are there any items of which you would now buy less? Explain.

Now imagine you had an increase in income of £100 per week.

(c) Answer questions (a) and (b).

(d) Are your answers different this time? Explain.

Q73. Select an item that is purchased by all or most of your class or seminar group. Conduct interviews with everyone to establish the amounts they would buy at six different prices. Now divide the class into two groups (by sex or age or any other feature that you may feel relevant in determining demand).

(a) From the replies given at your interviews construct a demand curve for each group and a demand curve for the class as a whole.

(b) What is the total expenditure of each group at each price? Explain any differences between the two groups? (You will need to consider both the elasticity and the magnitude of demand.)

C   *DISCUSSION TOPICS AND ESSAYS*

Q74. Using supply and demand diagrams, illustrate the effects of a substantial fall in the world output of oil and gas on the prices of (a) oil, (b) coal, (c) cars, and on (d) bus fares.

Q75. 'An increase in demand will cause an increase in price. This increase in price will then cause a reduction in demand, until demand is reduced back to its original level.' Criticise this argument.

Q76. It is observed that over time the price and the quantity demanded of a product both rise. Does this mean that the demand curve is upward sloping? What does this tell us about the difficulty of determining the shape of demand and supply curves?

Q77. The demand for pears is more price elastic than the demand for bread and yet the price of pears fluctuates more than that of bread. Why should this be so? If pears could be stored as long and as cheaply as flour, would this affect the relative price fluctuations?

Q78. A fish and chip shop finds that on Friday early evening, Saturday lunch time and between 10.30 and 11.00 every evening it has queues out of the door, whereas at other times it is empty. Would it be a good idea to charge different prices at different times?

Q79. Imagine that a nuclear accident causes sheep flocks to be contaminated in certain areas and that before being sold for slaughter they must first be passed as radiation free by Ministry inspectors. Assume, however, that their wool is not affected. How will this affect the price of sheep meat and wool in both the short run and the long run? Make your assumptions clear and illustrate your answer with supply and demand diagrams.

Q80. When share prices move upwards on the stock market, people tend to start buying, whereas when they move downward people often sell. Does this mean that the demand curves for shares slope upwards and the supply curves slope downwards?

When extreme weather strikes, such as a hurricane or flood, it can have massive economic consequences, especially in agricultural markets. The short item below, taken from *BBC News Online* of 9 January 1998, reports on one such event in India.

Record onion prices in India lead to state subsidies

The record high price of onions in parts of India has prompted some state governments to buy up supplies and subsidise their sale to ensure this staple of Indian cooking remains affordable.

The high prices have been blamed on the early winter rains leading to crop failures in the north of the country, the region which supplies onions to most urban areas.

However, the BBC Delhi correspondent says there has been a glut of the vegetable in the western state of Gujarat, where prices have sunk below the cost of production.

(a) Show, using demand and supply curves, the effect on price of each of the following: (i) the poor onion crop in North India; (ii) the glut of vegetables in Gujarat; (iii) state governments' intervention in the onion market. How would the magnitude of these effects be influenced by the price elasticities of demand and supply?

(b) How might countries which are subject to extremes of weather better deal with the resulting economic problems? Can you see any drawbacks in the policies that you are advocating?

The collapse in house prices in the early 1990s was swift and dramatic and it was a collapse from which the market took a long time to recover, but recover it did. The late 1990s saw very rapid price increases again. But the rate of increase was not uniform across the country, or even within a particular area. Houses in more affluent areas rose much more rapidly than in poorer areas. The following article by Will Hutton, which appeared in *The Observer* of 15 August 1999, argues that this trend could have profound consequences for society.

Real cost of the property boom

Economic apartheid is being created by a massive hike in price of top-of-the-market housing

An Englishman's home may be his castle, but if he listened to the old property dealer's adage – location, location, location – it is also the source of an incredible fortune. The price of property in the country's 'hot spots' is now stunning, well beyond the pocket of any but the super-rich. A new housing apartheid is emerging, enriching those lucky enough to have bought at the right time and in the right place, but creating a social laager for the new superclass who are migrating from the rest of the country to live in the streets and districts where they know they can

find others as rich as themselves – and where their house will prove a good investment.

The simple statistics and reassuring comments by housing pundits and estate agents disguise the extraordinary condition of the housing market. The reassuring consensus is represented by the Halifax Building Society who say that on average prices have only risen some 8 per cent over the year (12 per cent in London), but that such a rise is only to be expected given that the ratio of house prices to income is in the middle of its long-run range and interest rates so low. For their part, the Council of Mortgage Lenders say that, leaving aside a few well-know exceptions, the

pace of the price rises is no more than steady. They are too complacent. The Royal and Sun Alliance Estate Agency chain are probably nearer the mark in their view that London prices have risen by more than a third over the last year; but the scale of price rises in the upper-middle class districts of London, the Thames Valley and anywhere else where the new super-class, generally backing their purchase with two incomes, is in the market – like North Cheshire or the exclusive parts of West Nottingham – easily outstrip that.

Moreover, this is building on a pattern that is now firmly entrenched; house prices in these districts fell very little even in the dog days of the early

Nineties and have been climbing steadily ever since. Today these hot spots are seeing prices rising at a pace and to a level never before witnessed in Britain. In economic terms, the open question is whether and to what degree the impact will spill over to the rest of the country with its implications for interest rates; in social terms the issue is how inequality is now transmuting into how and where the British live.

The anecdotes abound. One couple I know are on the point of selling for more than £1 million the large and cavernous house that as two poverty-stricken public-sector professionals they could easily buy 20 years ago – their peers today could not even afford the garden shed. Another couple have witnessed their open-plan, loft apartment double in value in 18 months, well beyond what they could afford either then or now. It is not average incomes driving such increases, but the incomes of those at the top – and this is what the current debate about the housing market is neglecting.

There are only a limited number of areas in which the rich want to live; we know the streets in, say, Didsbury, North Oxford or Chiswick where they want to buy, and the stock remains finite. Moreover, the old constraints about mortgage lending have long since been abandoned; banks and building societies offer mortgages that are three and sometimes four times couples' joint income – the days when the man was offered a mortgage three times his income and his partner a mortgage that was half hers have disappeared, especially in upper-income groups. The combination of financial deregulation, the explosion in top peoples' pay and a fixed stock of desirable homes has been tinder waiting to ignite; the spark has been the lowest mortgage rates for 40 years.

There is a widespread view that it is all too feverish to last, but that underestimates the capacity of markets to overshoot. Rises beget rises and, in the property market, homes in the hot spots rarely fall in price; rather they have pauses in their upward trajectory. But their performance becomes the benchmark for other prices, with a cascade effect on neighbouring districts. in London both Hackney and Newham have seen extraordinary price increases following the rises in Islington. The cascade effect will spread beyond London, helped by the affordability of houses once low interest rates are take into account.

Add on top the growing phenomenon of small investors buying houses to rent out, rather than live in, interacting with the long-term shortage of homes, and you have all the makings of two or three years of sharply rising, if not boom, conditions that will then trigger rises at the top of the market again. A sharp increase in house building, higher taxes on second and third homes, and even capital gains tax for owner-occupiers could take the heat out of the market – none of which is likely. All that remains is a hike in interest rates, but even a 1 or 2 per cent increase would do little more than weaken the pace of increase with the rich doing comfortably best of all. What is more, this is only a period of transition; prices at the top have further to rise. Britain now has an income inequality that approaches American levels, but house prices in the areas that are 'desirable', in estate agents' blurb, are nothing like those in the US. The prices that shock us today will seem cheap in five years, as Britain moves further away from the more egalitarian, regulated social structures of the post-war settlement towards American patterns of income and house-price inequality.

All this matters economically because the Bank of England will want to check the cascade effect on house prices and thus indirectly on inflation by keeping interest rates higher than they would otherwise be. But most of all it matters socially. The ever-denser clustering of the rich and poor in exclusive neighbourhoods makes any attempt at constructing socially balanced communities impossible. It undercuts the principle of comprehensive education, for example. It makes the streets more dangerous – already only some 10 per cent of children now walk to school compared with some 80 per cent 20 years ago. In short it accelerates the gallop towards the drawbridge community for the rich and the decaying housing estates locked in vicious circles of depopulation and poverty for the poor. Urban life becomes more nightmarish.

It is a high price to pay; but we are paying it because the British have always seen property as tradeable bricks and mortar rather than the physical fabric in which we live and work, and where individual profit should be secondary to wider needs and ambitions. Vast houseprice inflation for the rich; urban blight; long-term unemployment; economic decay; poorly planned cities; all are linked by an invisible thread. You might hope that a Government that believed in 'joined-upness' would recognise the fact; so far there is precious little sign.

(a) Using two supply and demand diagrams (one for houses in affluent areas and one for houses in poorer areas), show why the price gap between expensive and cheaper houses has widened.

(b) How has the fact that houses are seen as a financial investment by many people exaggerated this trend?

(c) What policies could the government pursue to reverse the widening gap in house prices? Illustrate the effects of these policies on supply and demand diagrams.

Some markets are subject to considerable price fluctuations. The magnitude of these fluctuations depends on the amount by which demand and/or supply curves shift, and the price elasticity of demand and supply. The following article, taken from *The Independent* of 9 May 1994, looks at price fluctuations in the market for sheepskin and cattle hides.

Rising demand hides leather's limited supply

For an industry in which demand for the finished product has always been steady, leather and sheepskin producers have to contend with a host of problems affecting supplies of their raw materials.

Prices of sheepskin and cattle hides have soared in recent months as suppliers have struggled to meet demand. According to the British Leather Confederation, UK abattoir prices of sheepskin are now £7 to £7.50 compared with just under £1 in autumn 1990. Oxhides (steers and heifers) fetch £40 against a low of £17 to £18 in the first quarter of 1991, although traders and tanners believe the market has now peaked, at least for the moment.

Skins and hides are an internationally traded commodity yet prices are notoriously volatile, lacking the smoothing influence of a futures market. Attempts to establish a futures market have been unsuccessful, due to inflexibility of supply and wide variations in raw material quality.

Normal laws of supply and demand do not apply as skins and hides are a by-product of the meat, wool and dairy industries. In the past 12 to 18 months, demand for leather goods has risen, yet the UK cattle kill was 9 per cent down in 1993 from the previous year and the lamb kill was 7 per cent down. Falling demand for red meat and a significant rise in the live export of UK lambs, particularly to France, are the main reasons.

UK tanners have been left short of quality raw material and prices have risen steeply. However, consumer resistance to higher prices of finished goods has prevented increases being passed on and tanners' margins have been squeezed.

There is little prospect of the by-product status of skins and hides changing. In the UK, the value of a cattle hide is only 7 to 10 per cent of the total carcass and the value of a sheepskin 10 to 15 per cent of the carcass. Farmers are more concerned about selling the meat.

Lack of a homogeneous raw material hampers the creation of an international market. Sheepskins are graded according to climate. Higher quality skins from temperate zones (less affected by parasites than skins from tropical areas) are further divided, with UK skins usually fetching a premium price over New Zealand domestics. South African Capes are considered high quality, but the supply is limited.

The quality can also fluctuate, and the way the animal has been treated makes a significant difference. Scandinavian cattle, kept indoors in winter, produce superior hides to those that remain outside. Strain from mechanised skin removal and an increase in parasitic skin damage since the lifting of compulsory sheep dipping lowered the price of UK sheepskins last year.

© Alison Eadie, *Independent*, 9/5/94

(a) Why had the supply of skins and hides fallen despite a rise in demand? Illustrate this using a demand and supply diagram.

(b) How can futures markets help to stabilise prices?

(c) According to the article, which of the following are likely to be relatively elastic and which relatively inelastic: (i) the price elasticity of supply of raw skins and hides; (ii) the price elasticity of demand for raw skins and hides; (iii) the price elasticity of demand for finished products made with skins and hides? Explain the reasoning behind your answers.

(d) Given your answer to (c), demonstrate with demand and supply curves why there had been a substantial rise in price of raw skins and hides which had nevertheless not been passed on in higher prices for finished goods made with skins and hides.

(e) Why does the lack of a homogeneous raw material exacerbate the problem of price instability?

 ANSWERS

Q1. A. There is an inverse relationship between price and quantity demanded. The higher the price the less the quantity demanded; the lower the price the greater the quantity demanded.

Q2. *False.* It refers to the effect of a change in the *price* of the good on quantity demanded as a result of the consumer becoming better or worse off as a result of the price change: in other words because of the effect of the price change on the purchasing power of the consumer's income.

Q3. *False.* It refers to the effect of a change in the price of the *good itself*, not to a change in the price of a substitute. The point is that if a good comes down in price it will now be cheaper relative to the substitute than it was before, and thus people are likely to switch to it from the substitute.

Q4. *(a)* See table below.

Price (£)	Annual market demand (000s)
100	7
80	10
60	16
40	27
20	48

(b) See Figure A2.1.

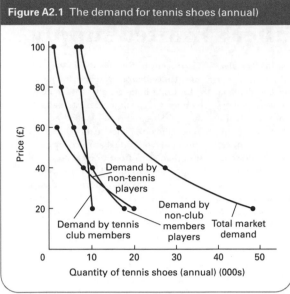

Figure A2.1 The demand for tennis shoes (annual)

Price (£) (y-axis)

Quantity of tennis shoes (annual) (000s) (x-axis)

Demand by non-tennis players

Demand by tennis club members

Demand by non-club members players

Total market demand

Q5. (a) (iii), (b) (i), (c) (v), (d) (ii), (e) (vi), (f) (iv)

Q6. *quantity demanded.*

Q7. *a movement along the demand curve.*

Q8. *demand.*

Q9. *a shift in the demand curve.*

Q10. **(a)** *Leftward shift.* There will be a reduction in the demand for cars and hence for petrol. (Petrol and cars are complements.)

(b) *Rightward shift.* With more car owners the demand for petrol will be higher.

(c) *Movement up along.* This pushes up price (a shift in the supply curve). A change in price causes a movement along the demand curve.

(d) *Need more information to say.* An increased concern for the health hazards from diesel (e.g. asthma from diesel fumes) would cause people to switch from diesel to petrol (a *rightward* shift in the demand for petrol). On the other hand, an increased concern for the problems of traffic congestion, global warming, etc. will cause people to use cars less and thus use less petrol (a *leftward* shift in the demand curve).

(e) *Rightward shift.* People will switch to petrol (a substitute for diesel).

(f) *Movement down along.* This will reduce the price of petrol.

Q11. *whose demand increases as income increases.*

Q12. *whose demand decreases as income decreases.*

Q13. *direct.*

Q14. What we are looking for is explanations of why a higher price will lead to a greater quantity being supplied (or why a lower price will lead to a smaller quantity). (b), (c), (d) are correct because they all explain this direct relationship. (a) does not provide an explanation because these cost increases are not associated with extra output. (e) is not an

explanation because changes in technology are independent of price changes. They may cause price to change, but they are not a reason why a price change affects output.

Q15. The *costs* of production; the profitability of *alternative products*; the profitability of goods in *joint supply*; *random shocks*; and *expectations* of future price changes.

Q16. *a movement along* the supply curve.

Q17. a change in *the quantity supplied.*

Q18. *a shift in* in the supply curve.

Q19. a change in *supply.*

Q20. **(a)** *Rightward shift.* A reduction in the cost of producing organic wheat.

(b) *Movement up along.* The demand for organic wheat has increased and hence also its price.

(c) *Leftward shift.* These goods are in *alternative supply.*

(d) Immediate effect: *leftward shift.* Anticipating higher prices, farmers put more organic wheat into store, hoping to sell later when the price has gone up. This reduces current supplies on the market. Subsequent effect: *rightward shift.* Farmers switch to organic methods in anticipation that they will be more profitable. Supply increases.

(e) *Leftward shift.* The supply of wheat (of all types) decreases.

(f) *Rightward shift.* (As (a) above.)

Q21. *shortage.*

Q22. *rise.*

Q23. *surplus.*

Q24. *fall.*

Q25. *Demand equals supply.*

Q26. *movement along.*

Q27. **(a)** See Figure A2.2.

(b) *Shortage of 290 tonnes per week.*

(c) *Surplus of 480 tonnes per week.*

(d) *P = €260; Q = 500 tonnes per week.*

(e) See Figure A2.2.

(f) *Shortage of 180 tonnes per week.*

(g) *P = €300.*

(h) *Less.* It has only increased by 140 tonnes per week.

(i) *Increase (rightward shift) of 180 tonnes per week.* This would mean that at the old price of €260, 680 tonnes per week would now be both demanded and supplied.

(j) *Decrease (leftward shift) of 900 tonnes per week.* This would mean that at a new equilibrium price of €380, 500 tonnes per week would once again be both demanded and supplied.

(k) *No.* Given that the demand curve slopes downwards, a rightward shift in supply is essential to restore the old equilibrium price, and a leftward shift is essential to restore the old equilibrium

Figure A2.2 The market for organically grown wheat (weekly figures)

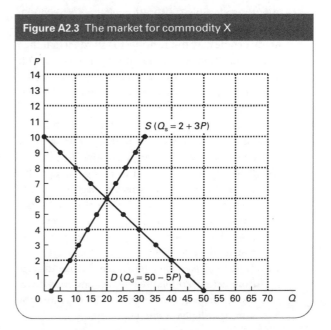

quantity. (Only a leftward shift in *demand* could restore both simultaneously.)

Q28. *False.* The demand curve will shift to the left. This will cause a decrease in the quantity sold *and also* a decrease in the price.

Q29. *(a)* *Point s.* Increased costs shift the supply curve to the left. No shift in the demand curve.

(b) *Point k.* A shift in tastes towards flats shifts the demand curve to the right. No shift in the supply curve.

(c) *Point n.* The fall in house prices reduces the demand for flats (a substitute). The demand curve shifts to the left. The fall in house prices makes their construction less profitable relative to flats (which are in alternative supply). The supply curve of new flats therefore shifts to the right.

(d) *Point k.* This will increase the demand for *new* houses and flats. The demand curve for new flats shifts to the right. No shift in the supply curve. (Builders cannot switch to building *old* houses and flats!)

(e) *Point l.* The construction tax on houses will make building flats more profitable. The supply curve will shift to the right. The higher price of houses resulting from the tax will increase the demand for flats. The demand curve shifts to the right.

(f) *Point j.* People will rush to buy flats now before prices rise. Demand shifts to the right. Builders will wait to sell their new flats until the price has risen. Supply will shift to the left.

(g) There are two possible answers here:

(i) *Point p.* If higher mortgage interest rates reduce the demand for *all* types of property,

the demand curve for flats will shift to the left.

(ii) *Point k.* If flats are seen as an inferior good (to houses) the demand may *rise* as purchasers switch from houses to flats.

Q30. C. A shift in the demand curve alone must cause price and quantity to change in the *same* direction. Thus if price and quantity change in opposite directions the *supply* curve must have shifted, causing a movement along the demand curve. In this case there must be a rightward shift in the supply curve causing a movement down along the demand curve. There may have been a less significant shift in the demand curve too, but we cannot tell.

Q31. *(a)* Set the two equations equal (given that in equilibrium supply equals demand).

$2 + 3P = 50 - 5P$

$\therefore 8P = 48$

$\therefore P = 6$

Substituting $P = 6$ in either of the two equations (since demand *equals* supply) gives:

$Q = 20$

(b) See table below.

P	0	1	2	3	4	5	6	7	8	9	10
Q_s	2	5	8	11	14	17	20	23	26	29	32
Q_d	50	45	40	35	30	25	20	15	10	5	0

(c) See Figure A2.3.

(d) *Parallel shift to the right by 16 units.* The interception point with the horizontal axis (given by the constant term) increases from $Q = 50$ to $Q = 66$. The equilibrium point now becomes $P - 8, Q = 26$.

Figure A2.3 The market for commodity X

$S (Q_s = 2 + 3P)$

$D (Q_d = 50 - 5P)$

(e) *The curve flattens.* The interception point with the horizontal axis remains at $Q = 50$, but the slope (given by the inverse of the P term) flattens from $-1/5$ to $-1/9$. The equilibrium point is now $P = 4$, $Q = 14$.

Q32. *the quantity demanded.*

Q33. *price.*

Q34. $\Delta Q_d/Q_d \div \Delta P/P.$

Q35. *elastic.*

Q36. *inelastic.*

Q37. *a negative value ($\epsilon < 0$).*

Q38. (a) (v), (b) (i), (c) (iii), (d) (ii), (e) (iv).

Q39. *the greater.* The more substitutes there are and the closer they are, the more willing consumers will be to switch from one product to the other as the price of one of them changes.

Q40. *the higher.* The higher the proportion of people's income spent on a good, the more they will be forced to cut back on its consumption as its price rises.

Q41. *the longer.* People will have more time to find alternative products and to change their consumption patterns.

Q42. (c), (a), (d), (b), (e). As we move from (c) to (e) in this order, so the number of substitutes becomes greater. Thus 'Scrummy' low fat margarine with the current competition token has many substitutes, including: 'Scrummy' low fat margarine without a token, other brands of low fat margarine, other brands of margarine, dairy low fat spreads and butter.

Q43. C. There are two reasons contained in this answer. The first is that foreign holidays are a luxury. This means that people do not regard them as vital, and will thus be prepared to substitute other items (e.g. holidays in their own country or day trips out) if the price of foreign holidays rises. What we are talking about here is a big substitution effect. The second is that, being a large item of people's expenditure, many people may not feel able to afford them if their price rises. What we are talking about here is a big income effect. Note that B would only be an answer if we were talking about a *specific* foreign holiday rather than foreign holidays in general.

Q44. (a) *False.* Except in the case of vertical and horizontal demand curves, the elasticity of straight-line demand curves will vary along their length.

(b) *False.* Again, downward-sloping straight-line demand curves have varying elasticities along their length. A curve with elasticity $= -1$ is a rectangular hyperbola (i.e. a curve bowed in toward the origin that approaches but never reaches the two axes).

(c) *True.* In *proportionate* terms any change in price from zero is an *infinite* change, and thus dividing a proportionate change in quantity by infinity will give a zero elasticity.

(d) *True.* In proportionate terms any change in quantity from zero is an *infinite* change, and thus elasticity must also be infinity.

(e) *False.* The elasticities of the two curves differ along their length (getting greater as you move down each curve). There are points high up on curve D_2 which are less elastic than points low down on curve D_1. Only if we specify that we are referring to the *same price range* in each case does the statement necessarily become true (see (g) below).

(f) *False.* At point z, curve D_2 is more elastic than curve D_1.

(g) *True.* See answer to (e) above.

Q45. *Arc elasticity.*

Q46. $(P_1 + P_2)/2.$

Q47. (a) See table below.

$P(£)$	10	9	8	7	6	5	4	3	2	1	0
Q_d	0	2	4	6	8	10	12	14	16	18	20

(b) $\Delta Q_d/(Q_{d1} + Q_{d2})/2 \div \Delta P/(P_1 + P_2)/2$
   (i) $4/18 \div -2/1 = -1/9$ *inelastic*
   (ii) $4/10 \div -2/5 = -1$ *unit elastic*
   (iii) $4/4 \div -2/8 = -4$ *elastic*

(c) Take two points an equal distance either side of the point in question, and calculate arc elasticity between these two points.

(d) (i) $4/16 \div -2/2$ $= -1/4$
   (ii) $4/8 \div -2/6$ $= -1 1/2$
   (iii) $4/10 \div -2/5$ $= -1$
   (iv) $4(?)/20 \div -2(?)/0 = 0$
   (v) $4(?)/0 \div -2(?)/20 = \infty$

Q48. See table below.

$P(£)$	10	9	8	7	6	5	4	3	2	1	0
Q_d	0	2	4	6	8	10	12	14	16	18	20
$TR(£)$	0	18	32	42	48	50	48	42	32	18	0

Q49. (a) Total expenditure will *rise* (as it does from £10 down to £5).

(b) Total expenditure will *fall* (as it does from £5 downwards).

(c) $-1.$

Q50. *False.*

Q51. *True.*

Q52. *True* (assuming that both axes start from zero).

*Q53. $P/Q.$

*Q54. *inverse of the slope.*

*Q55. (a) See table below.

P	5	4	3	2	1	0
Q_d	0	2	8	18	32	50

(b) See Figure A2.4.

(c) See Figure A2.4. The slope of the tangent is $-4/32 = -1/8.$

(d) $-8 \times 3/8 = -3.$

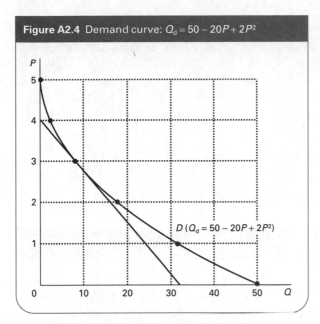

Figure A2.4 Demand curve: $Q_d = 50 - 20P + 2P^2$

$D(Q_d = 50 - 20P + 2P^2)$

Q56. **(a)** A. This means that for any given percentage fall in price, there will be a greater shift away from producing A than B.

(b) A. There is more time for supply to adjust to changing prices and hence profitability.

(c) B. For any given percentage increase in price, there will be a bigger percentage increase in resources attracted into B than into A before cost increases make it unprofitable to expand further.

(d) *Cannot say*. (A will have a more elastic *demand* than B.)

(e) B. The supply of A is unlikely to be affected much by its price if it is going to be produced anyway as a by-product.

(f) *Cannot say*. This affects elasticity of demand not elasticity of supply.

Q57. **(a)** *True*. All straight-line supply curves passing through the origin have an elasticity equal to one *irrespective of their slope*. (Try drawing some on graph paper and working out their elasticity over various sections.)

(b) *False*. See (c) and (d) below.

(c) *True*. The elasticity equals infinity at point *y* (see (e) below) and then diminishes as you move up the curve, but nevertheless stays above one. (Again, try drawing it on graph paper and working out its elasticity over various sections.)

(d) *True*. At the point where it crosses the horizontal axis the proportionate change in price is infinite, and thus the elasticity is zero (a number divided by infinity is zero).

(e) *True*. At the point where it crosses the vertical axis, the proportionate change in quantity is infinite.

(f) *False*. It has an elasticity less than one throughout its length, but this nevertheless rises towards one as you move up the curve.

(g) *False*. See (a), (c), (d) and (e).

Q58. *Positive*. A *rise* in income causes a *rise* in demand.

Q59. **(a)** Good A: $Y\epsilon_d = 20/40 \div 10\,000/50\,000 = 2.5$.
Good B: $Y\epsilon_d = -4/50 \div 10\,000/50\,000 = -0.4$.
Good C: $Y\epsilon_d = 20/200 \div 10\,000/50\,000 = 0.5$.

(b) *Good A*. ($Y\epsilon_d > 1$.)

(c) *Good B*. ($Y\epsilon_d$ negative: a rise in income leads to *less* being purchased as people switch to superior goods.)

Q60. *True*. Expenditure on the good increases by a larger proportion than does income.

Q61. **(a)** (v) (strong complements).

(b) (iii) (unrelated).

(c) (ii) (moderate substitutes).

(d) (i) (close substitutes).

(e) (iv) (mildly complementary).

Q62. *less* price elastic.

Q63. *price*.

Q64. *quantity*.

Q65. E. Once they are cut, the supply is virtually fixed. The florist cannot choose to sell a given bunch of flowers next week or next month instead of today if today's demand is low. Note: A and B refer to *demand*. C is an *effect* of supply inelasticity, not a *cause*. D refers to *shifts* in the supply curve.

Q66. *left*.

Q67. *right*.

Q68. *rise*. The speculation is thus self-fulfilling.

Q69. Stabilising: (c).
Destabilising: (b).

3 Government Intervention in the Market

Chapter 2 examined the working of the free market. In the real world, the government often intervenes in the market. This intervention can take various forms. Examples include: price fixing, taxes or subsidies on various goods and services, directly taking over production, and rules and regulations governing the supply of certain goods.

In the first section we look at the effects of controlling prices, and in particular at the effects of setting either minimum or maximum prices. In the second section we examine the 'incidence' of taxes and subsidies on goods and services: who ends up paying the tax or receiving the subsidy – the producer or the consumer? To do this we must see what happens to price and this will depend on the price elasticities of demand and supply. In the third section we look at the extreme case of where the government rejects allocation by the market and either prohibits the production of certain goods or takes over production directly. Finally, we look at agriculture as a case study of different types of government intervention.

3.1 The control of prices

(Pages 70–3) The commonest form of price control is the setting of minimum or maximum prices.

If a minimum price (a price floor) is set above the equilibrium price, a **Q1.** *shortage/surplus* will result. If a maximum price (a price ceiling) is set below the equilibrium price, a **Q2.** *shortage/surplus* will result.

Q3. Figure 3.1 shows the demand and supply for petrol. The market is initially in equilibrium with a price of 50p per litre and sales of 40 million litres per day.

(a) Assume that the government is worried about inflation and decides to set a maximum price for petrol. What will be the effect if it sets this price at:

(i) 60p?..

(ii) 40p?..

(iii) Is a black market in petrol likely to emerge in either case?

60p:	Yes/No
40p:	Yes/No

(iv) Explain your answer to (iii).

....

....

 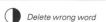

Figure 3.1 Intervention in the market for petrol

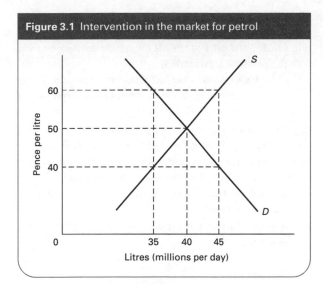

(b) Assume now that, worried about the effect of excessive fossil fuel consumption on global warming, the government passes a law forcing companies to sell petrol at 60p per litre, but agrees to buy (at 60p) any surplus and put it into store.

    (i) What will be the effect on consumer expenditure?

....

    (ii) How much will the government have to buy from the petrol companies?

....

    (iii) How much revenue will the petrol companies earn?

....

Q4. Which one of the following controls would involve setting a minimum price rather than a maximum price (where 'price' can include the price of the services of a factor of production)?

A. Controls on rents to protect tenants on low incomes.

B. Controls on wages to protect workers on low incomes.

C. Controls on basic food prices to protect consumers on low incomes.

D. Controls on transport fares to protect passengers on low incomes.

E. None of the above.

(?) Q5. Give three problems that can occur when the government imposes maximum prices.

1. ....

2. ....

3. ....

(?) Q6. Give three problems that can occur when the government imposes minimum prices.

1. ....

2. ....

3. ....

3.2 Indirect taxes

(Pages 73–4) Another form of government intervention in markets is the imposition of taxes on goods (indirect taxes). Such taxes include VAT and excise duties (on items such as cigarettes, alcohol and petrol). The taxes will have the effect of raising prices and thus could be used as a means, not only of raising revenue for the government, but also of reducing the consumption of potentially harmful products.

A tax imposed on a good will have the effect of shifting the supply curve **Q7.** *upward/downward.* A specific tax will **Q8.** *make the supply curve steeper/make the supply curve shallower/leave the slope of the supply curve unaffected.* An *ad valorem* tax will **Q9.** *make the supply curve steeper/make the supply curve shallower/leave the slope of the supply curve unaffected.*

Q10. Figure 3.2 shows the effects of imposing taxes or giving subsidies on a good.

Match each of the following to one of the four diagrams.

(a) An *ad valorem* subsidy   *(i)/(ii)/(iii)/(iv)*
(b) A specific tax   *(i)/(ii)/(iii)/(iv)*
(c) An *ad valorem* tax   *(i)/(ii)/(iii)/(iv)*
(d) A specific (per-unit) subsidy   *(i)/(ii)/(iii)/(iv)*

Figure 3.2 The effects of indirect taxes and subsidies

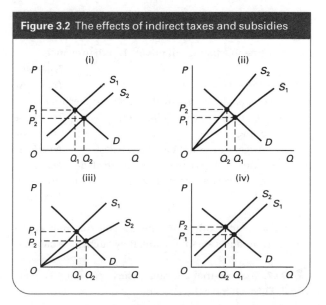

Q11. If the imposition of a tax (t) on a good has the effect of increasing the price from P_1 to P_2 and reducing the quantity sold from Q_1 to Q_2 then the consumers' share of the total tax paid is:

A. $P_2 \times Q_2$

B. $t \times (Q_1 - Q_2)$

C. $(P_2 - P_1) \times Q_2$

D. $(t - (P_2 - P_1)) \times Q_2$

E. $(P_2 - t) \times (Q_1 - Q_2)$

(Try sketching a diagram and attaching the appropriate labels.)

Q12. Referring to the information in Q11, the producers' share of the tax is:

A. B. C. D. E.

Q13. In which of the following situations would the imposition of a tax on a good involve the highest producers' share of the tax?

A. An elastic demand and an elastic supply.

B. An inelastic demand and an inelastic supply.

C. A unit-elastic demand and a unit-elastic supply.

D. An elastic demand and an inelastic supply.

E. An inelastic demand and an elastic supply.

(In each case 'elasticity' is referring to 'price elasticity'.)

3.3 Government rejection of market allocation

(Pages 75–6) With some goods and services, the government may feel that it is best to reject allocation through the market altogether. At one extreme, it may feel that certain products are so important to people that they ought to be provided free at the point of use. This is the equivalent of setting **Q14.** *a maximum price/a minimum price* of zero. The result is that there is likely to be a shortage of provision. This shortage is likely to greater, the **Q15.** *greater/lower* is the price elasticity of demand for the product.

Q16. In the case of the provision of health care, shortages result in:

(a) Some people taking out private health insurance
True/False

(b) Waiting lists
True/False

(c) Fewer people being treated than if the price were allowed to rise to the equilibrium
True/False

(d) Rationing
True/False

(e) Non-urgent cases not being treated
True/False

(f) Some non-serious cases not being treated
True/False

(g) Resources being diverted from education and social security
True/False

(Pages 76–7) At the other extreme, the government may feel that some products are so harmful, they ought to be banned.

Q17. Assume that a product (such as a drug) is made illegal. This will have the effect of:

(a) shifting the demand curve to the
left/right

(b) shifting the supply curve to the
left/right

(c) making the price in the illegal market (compared with the previous legal market)

higher/lower/either higher or lower (depending on the relative shifts in the demand and supply curves)

Q18. Assuming that making a product illegal has the effect of making the illegal market price higher than the previous legal market price, under which one of the following circumstances would the price rise be the greatest?

A. A small shift in the supply curve and a large shift in the demand curve.

B. A small shift in the supply curve and a price elastic demand.

C. A small shift in the supply curve and a price inelastic demand.

D. A large shift in the supply curve and a price elastic demand.

E. A large shift in the supply curve and a price inelastic demand.

Q19. Assume that the government wishes to reduce consumption of a certain product. To achieve the same level of reduction by using a tax as by banning the product:

(a) A bigger shift in the supply curve will be required.
True/False

(b) A smaller rise in price will be required.
True/False

3.4 Agriculture and agricultural policy

(Pages 77–9) Governments have intervened massively in agricultural markets throughout the world.

Short-term fluctuations in agricultural prices are due to problems on both the demand and supply sides.

Q20. Price fluctuations are likely to be greater,

(a) the more price elastic the supply.
True/False

(b) the greater the fluctuations in the harvest.
True/False

(c) the more price elastic the demand.
True/False

Q21. The following are possible features of the market for wheat.

(i) There is substantial technical progress leading to increased production over the years.

(ii) There is an income-inelastic demand for wheat.

(iii) There is a price-inelastic demand for wheat.

(iv) Wheat harvests fluctuate substantially with the weather.

Which of the above help to explain why incomes (i.e. revenues) of wheat farmers are likely to grow more slowly than incomes of producers of non-foodstuffs?

A. (ii) and (iii).

B. (i) and (iv).

C. (i), (iii) and (iv).

D. (i), (ii) and (iii).

E. (ii), (iii) and (iv).

(Pages 79–81) There are several different ways a government can intervene to stabilise prices and/or to support farmers' incomes.

◗ **Q22.** With each of the following schemes decide whether they will stabilise prices, support incomes or both.

(a) Buffer stocks (whose size fluctuates but is not allowed to grow bigger and bigger over the years).
Stabilise prices/Support incomes/Both

(b) Output subsidies (of a fixed amount per unit of output).
Stabilise prices/Support incomes/Both

(c) Minimum prices with the government buying any resulting surpluses.
Stabilise prices/Support incomes/Both

(d) 'Set-aside' schemes (whereby farmers are paid to let land lie fallow). *Stabilise prices/Support incomes/Both*

(e) Variable import levies (to bring imported foodstuffs up to an agreed price level).
Stabilise prices/Support incomes/Both

(f) Investment grants to farmers.
Stabilise prices/Support incomes/Both

(g) A tariff of 10 per cent on imported food.
Stabilise prices/Support incomes/Both

(h) Quotas on the numbers of cattle that farmers are allowed to keep. *Stabilise prices/Support incomes/Both*

(i) 'Lump-sum' subsidies unrelated to output.
Stabilise prices/Support incomes/Both

❖ **Q23.** Which of the schemes in Q22 will:

1. increase output of domestic producers? ....

2. decrease output of domestic producers? ....

3. either increase or decrease output of domestic producers depending on the circumstances?

   ....

4. have no effect on the output of domestic producers?

   ....

5. increase consumption? ....

6. decrease consumption? ....

7. either increase or decrease consumption depending on the circumstances?

   ....

8. have no effect on consumption? ....

(Pages 82–90) If the government wants to support farmers' incomes, rather than merely stabilise prices, then two of the most widely used policies worldwide have been output subsidies and high minimum prices.

⊖ **Q24.** Figure 3.3 shows the market for a foodstuff in which a country is self-sufficient. The market price of P_1 is regarded as too low and the government wants farmers to receive a price of P_2.

Assume first that farmers are paid a guaranteed minimum price of P_2.

(a) How much will the government have to buy from producers?

   ....

(b) How much will it cost the taxpayer? ....

Assume now that the government, instead of paying a minimum price, gives an output subsidy.

(c) What must be the size of the subsidy per unit of output to have the same effect on farmers' incomes as the minimum price of P_2?

   ....

(d) How much will it cost the taxpayer? ....

In some cases the country may be a net importer of food, in which case the diagram for such a foodstuff will look like Figure 3.4.

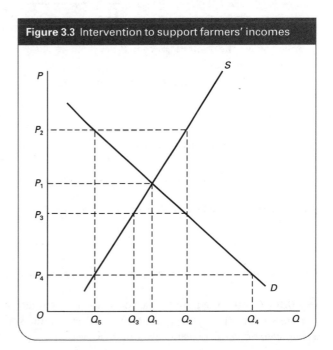

Figure 3.3 Intervention to support farmers' incomes

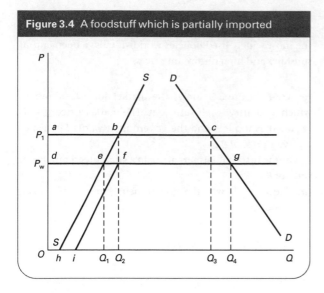

Figure 3.4 A foodstuff which is partially imported

(a) What will the supply curve be now?..............................

(b) What will be the market price?......................................

(c) What will be the level of domestic production?

....

(d) What will be the level of domestic consumption?

....

(e) What will be the level of imports?................................

Q27. Comparing the EU system of high minimum prices (and import levies) with a system of subsidies and free-market prices, the EU system
A. benefits consumers.
B. leads to less waste.
C. leads to less imports.
D. is less damaging to agriculture in developing countries.
E. leads to lower food prices.

Q25. Assume in Figure 3.4 that the world price is P_w and that initially there is no government intervention. The domestic supply and demand curves are given by *SS* and *DD* respectively.

(a) What is the total supply curve (domestic plus world)?

....

(b) What is the level of domestic production? ....

(c) What is the level of domestic consumption?

....

(d) What is the level of imports? ....

Now assume that the government imposes an import duty in order to raise the domestic price to P_1.

(e) What will the total supply curve be now?

....

(f) What will be the level of domestic production?

....

(g) What will be the level of domestic consumption?

....

(h) What will be the level of imports?................................

Q26. Continuing from the last question, now assume that instead of import duties, the government gives farmers a *subsidy* to bring their revenue per unit to a level of P_1.

Q28. Which of the following benefits could be argued to have resulted from the EU system of high minimum prices for agricultural produce?
(a) It has helped to lead to greater European self-sufficiency in food.   *Yes/No*
(b) It has led to lower food prices in the short run.
                                                                    Yes/No
(c) It has led to lower food prices in the long run.
                                                                    Yes/No
(d) It has led to increased agricultural investment.
                                                                    Yes/No
(e) It has redistributed income more equally than would a system of subsidies.   *Yes/No*
(f) It has benefited developing countries' agriculture.
                                                                    Yes/No
(g) It has led to more stable prices.   *Yes/No*
(h) It has given a roughly equal level of agricultural support (per head of the agricultural population) to all the member countries.   *Yes/No*

Q29. Give two ways in which the Common Agricultural Policy has harmed the agricultural sector in developing countries.

1.   ....

2.   ....

Compared with the free-market position, direct income support for farmers has the advantage of leading (in the short run) to **Q30.** *lower/higher/the same* prices and **Q31.** *lower/higher/the same* output.

B   PROBLEMS, EXERCISES AND PROJECTS

Table 3.1 Demand and supply of solar panels

Price (per sq. metre) (£)	Quantity demanded (sq. metres per year) (000s)	Quantity supplied (sq. metres per year) (000s)
100	5	40
90	10	30
80	15	25
70	20	20
60	25	15
50	32	9
40	40	2
30	58	0

Q32. Table 3.1 gives (imaginary) information about the market for solar panels.

(a) What is the equilibrium price?

(b) Over what price range(s) is the demand curve a straight line?

(c) What is the price elasticity of demand (using the arc method) at the equilibrium price?

(d) Assume that the government wants to promote the purchase of solar panels by householders in order to save energy. As a result it decides to impose a maximum price. What will be the effect if the maximum price is: (i) £90, (ii) £60?

(e) Will a maximum price of £50 lead to a higher or lower level of panels being sold than if the price was left free to be determined by the market?

(f) Assume that the government abandons the use of maximum prices and instead decides to grant a subsidy to producers. What size subsidy must be granted in order to reduce the price to £60?

(g) How much will this subsidy cost the taxpayer?

(h) What will be the incidence of this subsidy between consumers and producers?

Q33. Refer back to the last two Budget speeches by the Chancellor of the Exchequer. (The Budget is given in March each year.) The speech is reported in full in *The Times* and in *Hansard*. See also the Treasury website at http://www.hm-treasury.gov.uk.

Examine the Chancellor's justification for any changes in the rate of duty on alcohol, petrol, tobacco or betting. What assumptions are being made about the price and income elasticities of demand for these items? Are the arguments consistent and are there any conflicts of objectives in government policy towards taxing these items?

Q34. Do a library or web search to find articles discussing reform of the CAP and other systems of agricultural support around the world. Your search could include web addresses A_1 to A_9, E_{14}, G_3 and G_9 in the websites appendix in Sloman 4th edition. (see also the hotlinks section on the Sloman website at http://www.booksites.net/sloman)

Summarise the alternative agreements or proposals and consider their relative merits and any problems they are likely to cause.

C   DISCUSSION TOPICS AND ESSAYS

Q35. Under what circumstances are black markets likely to develop? What will determine the level of the black market price?

Q36. Consider the advantages and disadvantages of rent controls.

Q37. Give three examples of price controls. In each case identify the reasons for these controls and whether any other form of intervention could have achieved the same objectives.

Q38. Identify some measures the government could take to encourage energy conservation. Would any of these measures prevent a market equilibrium being achieved? What effects would there be in other markets from the various measures?

Q39. How do the price elasticities of demand and supply affect the incidence of an indirect tax?

Q40. Assume that the government wishes to reduce smoking. Compare the relative advantages and disadvantages of increased taxes on cigarettes with making smoking illegal as alternative means of achieving the government's objective.

Q41. Why are free-market agricultural prices and incomes subject to large fluctuations? What measures could a government adopt (a) to stabilise prices, (b) to stabilise incomes, (c) to stabilise both prices and incomes?

Q42. Compare the advantages and disadvantages of a system of subsidies and high minimum prices from the point of view of (a) the farmer, (b) the consumer and (c) the taxpayer.

Q43. Consider the relative advantages and disadvantages of alternative means of reforming the CAP.

Q44. Debate
Government price controls should never be applied in peacetime as the costs inevitably exceed any benefits.

The article below by Jacky Rowland, taken from *The Guardian* of 10 August 1999, considers the problems facing farmers in Serbia, where the government sets a maximum price for many agricultural products.

Milosevic's loyal farmers join dissenters

Milan Popov, a farmer in the northern agricultural region of Vojvodina, said the freak floods that have hit much of Serbia this summer had cost him 40 per cent of his maize crop.

But this is only part of his troubles. Maize is one of four staple crops which Serbian farmers are obliged by law to sell to the state at heavily discounted prices.

Last year, the state agreed to purchase Mr Popov's entire maize harvest for 8000 Deutschmarks (£2730).

Mr Popov said the money arrived six months late, and he was paid less than half what was due.

'The government is on the farmers' backs,' he complained. 'Everyone is on the farmers' backs.'

A few dozen farmers took part in their first demonstration in Vojvodina, demanding higher prices for crops.

'We are not satisfied with the monopolies in this country,' said Dragan Veselinov of the National Farmers' Party.

'The state alone has the right to trade wheat, corn and other agricultural products, which deprives our farmers of the chance to make profits.'

Farmers say the low price of maize, wheat and other crops has enabled the government to keep food prices down, thereby avoiding the threat of social unrest in the country.

The government is under assault from all sides, with dairy farmers adding their demands to those of other food producers. Like maize, milk has to be sold to the state at a fixed price.

Many dairy farmers say they barely break even. Nikola Hrnjak manages a 4000-head dairy farm on the outskirts of Belgrade. The farm used to be a state enterprise benefiting from subsidies, but now operates as a self-sufficient business.

Mr Hrnjak pasteurises the milk before selling it on to the state, thereby getting a better price than is paid for untreated milk. He aims to diversify into cheese, yoghurt and other more profitable dairy products.

'Milk and bread are vital to maintain people's standard of living,' said Mr Hrnjak. 'But that standard of living is being maintained at our expense. I hope we'll find a way to make up for our losses.'

Mr Popov tries to make up for his losses by cultivating crops not covered by the state compulsory purchase order. At dawn most mornings he loads his tractor trailer with potatoes, onions and garlic and sets out for Belgrade. He has been selling his produce at the same market for 30 years.

But with most shoppers feeling the pinch on their wallets, he finds his vegetables treated like luxury goods.

(a) Why might governments wish to set a maximum (low) price? What difficulties might be encountered by a government wishing to operate such a policy?

(b) Why are maximum (low) prices likely to lead to the emergence of a black market?

(c) How are the price elasticities of demand and supply relevant in determining the effects of a policy of maximum agricultural prices?

The following article, taken from the *OECD Observer* of April/May 1997, discusses what reforms are necessary if the agricultural sector is to make positive contributions to the environment.

How agriculture benefits the environment

The agricultural sectors in OECD countries are changing rapidly. Fewer people are employed on fewer farms, many of them working part-time. Farmers increasingly purchase inputs from the non-farm sector and sell under contract to the food-processing and marketing sector. Advances in technology (especially in farm chemicals, machinery and biotechnology) and better information on farm practices are available to farmers. And they are more conscious of the importance of farming sustainably – to ensure that there will be sufficient resources in the future to provide enough food, safely and in 'environmentally friendly' ways. Indeed, many farmers and farm businesses have responded to the increasing pressure from consumer and environmental groups to improve their pest-, disease- and fertiliser-management.

Farmers are also aware that the public expects them to contribute to the management of the countryside, conserve and improve the landscape, and provide spaces for recreation and tourism. The value of some of these benefits is captured by farmers through the market; some is not, such as maintaining biodiversity and wildlife habitats, or the 'positive externality' of a pleasant countryside. In many countries farmers have also to face environmental regulations and meet standards, particularly on water quality, the use of pesticides, and the disposal of animal waste – all of which can raise their production costs and depress their international competitiveness.

In agriculture, the application of the 'polluter pays' principle (which requires that polluters pay for the costs of meeting the degree of environmental protection decreed by government) often involves farmers having to meet limits for nitrates and other chemical run-off into water courses, or obey regulations on the use of pesticides. But its application to agriculture has often been poorly enforced, and can be impeded by practical problems, given the large number of farms and the difficulties in simply identifying who is doing the polluting. Moreover, it is not always easy to define property rights, which determine the environmental impacts that should be accounted for by farmers. In the event, it is often the taxpayer who ends up bearing the cost of reducing the discharge of by-products or chemical residues, through government payments to farmers to meet the costs of (for example) investments to deal with waste.

Where farming practices that maintain the quality and quantity of natural resources foster the future viability of farms, farmers have a direct incentive to adopt them. For example, by attending to the quality of the soil, farmers can reap future yields of crops at lower cost than they could otherwise. But such incentives require that farmers be aware of the environmental costs and benefits of their activities, that the market reflect these effects, which can be influenced by agricultural and environmental policies, and that farmers have the resources and the knowledge to farm in environmentally sustainable ways.

Some of these developments have been linked with high volumes of government support for farming, which on average is equivalent to around 40 per cent of the value of agricultural production, and two thirds of which is to support farm prices.

What policy framework?
Policy implications can arise where environmental effects are not captured

in markets. But one has to ensure that policy measures do improve the environment rather than make matters worse. One way to this end is to provide payments to farmers (for benefits), or levy charges on them (for harm). But that again requires the establishment of a well-defined set of property rights, embodying the entitlements and duties associated with the ownership or use of resources – for agriculture, particularly land and water.

It is generally recognised that reform of agricultural policy, by reducing production-linked support, will lower incentives that encourage farmers to use so many chemicals, will reduce intensive cropping and livestock practices, and will limit farming on environmentally fragile land. But reform may not be enough to achieve the desired degree of environmental outcomes (in part because markets are lacking or incomplete for some environmental benefits), and may have to be complemented with other measures which directly target the provision of these environmental benefits. But the policy reform of agricultural policy underway in all OECD countries could lead to some problems associated with, for example, the abandonment of land or 'traditional' agricultural practices in some regions.

An important element in reform is to target support away from production towards schemes to improve the ability of farmers to develop alternative sources of income, through for example, training and advice, start-up grants, and so on. They can, for example, provide rural amenities, which are diverse in nature, such as tourism or organic food production. A coherent approach to agricultural, environmental and rural-development policies will therefore both contribute to agricultural sustainability and give due recognition to regional diversity and local priorities. And to ensure that agriculture is economically and environmentally sustainable, the sector has to be exposed to consistent policy and market signals.

But the structure and size of farms, the population density, and the priorities attached to the environment vary considerably from one OECD country to another. Although that makes the designing of single policy solutions inappropriate, it is important that all policies take a balanced approach. If

farmers are remunerated for any environmental benefits beyond those they provide in the course of their farming activities, they should also be obliged to take account of any environmental costs they impose.

Paying farmers for the environment?
Many of the policy measures intended to address the environmental benefits of agriculture have only recently been introduced and, in general, their effects have not yet been assessed. The approaches adopted range from local and regional initiatives, voluntary schemes, through the dissemination of research results, education and training and regulation, to financial incentives and disincentives to farmers. For example, the 'accompanying measures' to the 1992 reform of the Common Agricultural Policy (CAP) in the European Union provide payments to farmers who undertake, maintain or improve their environmental performance.

The agri-environmental 'accompanying measures' of the CAP
The payments made to farmers under the Common Agricultural Policy of the EU for efforts to maintain or improve the environment can be grouped into four main types of measure.

• Land-management measures encourage low-intensity farming, lower quantities of inputs and organic farming, the main aim being to alleviate the pressure of farming on the environment. Some programmes encourage farmers to maintain genetic diversity, both of traditional crop varieties and of types of farm animals now in danger of extinction.

• Other measures seek to maintain traditional features of the landscape (stone walls, terracing and hedges, for example) and traditional craft skills – features valued not only for their aesthetic appeal but also for maintaining biodiversity – and to protect and enhance biodiversity through, for instance, the reduction of pesticides.

• The long-term set-aside of land and the maintenance of abandoned land can encourage the continuation of extensive agriculture or low-intensity grazing which may contribute to support

biodiversity and reduce risk of fire or erosion.
- The provision of information, training and demonstration can promote good farming practices and encourage public access and public leisure on land.

These measures must be made available in each EU country, although none of the measures is compulsory on any individual farmer, who may choose whether to join one or more of them. For those who decide to commit themselves, the associated obligations must be observed for at least five years; for long-term set-aside the minimum obligation is for 20 years. The design of each measure, its implementation and evaluation are the responsibility of central government, though its operation is often decentralised to the regions. In 1996, these measures accounted for over 2 billion ECU, representing about 5 per cent of the total budgetary expenditure on the CAP.

(a) Why do farmers have a tendency not to use environmentally friendly farming practices?

(b) In what manner must agricultural policy be reformed if it is to encourage more environmentally friendly farming?

(c) Why might we question the likely effectiveness of the agri-environmental measures of the CAP? What might be done to improve their effectiveness?

The reform of agricultural policy in the EU is underway as part of the Agenda 2000 programme. Central to this reform will be the reduction of financial subsidies. How will farmers cope? In the article below, taken from *The Observer* of 1 March 1998, Anthony Browne discusses the dependency of farmers on subsidies and considers the implications of cutting them.

Those whom the CAP fits only too well

The fox hunters may be dismayed, but the farmers are distraught. In the uproar from the countryside, it is the farmers who are screaming loudest, claiming their very survival is at stake.

And it's not just the beef producers. Incomes have fallen sharply in the past year on all types of farm, and the subsidies that help them stave off bankruptcy are under threat.

As if the beef ban were not enough, the strong pound has hit those meat exports that are still legal and sent international prices tumbling. In the past year, the price of broiler chickens has fallen 14 per cent; pig meat is down 30 per cent, beef 20 per cent and winter wheat 40 per cent.

Dr Michael Murphy of Cambridge University's Department of Land Economy, who is a government adviser on farm incomes, says: 'Sheep sales have collapsed because of the strong pound, the profit margin on milk has collapsed from 4p a litre to 1p; and grain that costs £100 a tonne to produce can only be sold for £72 a tonne because the world is awash with grain.'

Last year, profits earned by farms in the UK fell by 35 per cent. The average farm income is expected to fall this year to around £15 000.

The decline may seem dramatic, but it is in part a reflection of the bonanza of earlier years. When the pound collapsed after it fell out of the exchange rate mechanism in 1992, farmers cashed in on higher prices and saw their incomes double over four years.

With the pound getting stronger again, that process has simply gone into reverse.

Farmers aren't the only ones affected by the strong pound. Many exporters in all industries have suffered a catastrophic decline in profits and incomes. But farmers are unique in the support they get: the Common Agricultural Policy has turned almost the entire industry into subsidy junkies.

Last year, for the first time since 1985, the total subsidy paid to farmers exceeded the industry's profits. Without the subsidy, the farmers would be earning less than zero.

'Subsidies are 100 per cent of the profits on cereal farms, and 160 per cent on cattle and sheep farms,' says Murphy. 'Without them, huge numbers would go broke.'

The Common Agricultural Policy inflates prices by offering to buy products at a minimum price, and makes direct payment to farmers according to the amount of land cultivated. In the past four years, the amount of subsidy paid to farmers has shot up by 140 per cent, to £4.5 billion.

That is more in one year than the Government plans to spend over the entire parliament on its welfare-to-work programme – and works out as £7400 for every worker in the industry.

According to the National Consumer Council, the CAP adds £18 a week to an average family's cost of living – about half from higher food costs, the rest from higher taxes. The CAP benefits the few at the expense of the many. One commentator describes it as an extortion racket the scale and scope of which would make the Mafia proud.

The CAP was adopted in 1962, aimed at boosting food production and combating rural poverty. But now that a surfeit of food is being produced, it is a bizarre anomaly.

At certain times, so much food was produced that it had to be destroyed; farmers were paid to produce nothing; and 80 per cent of the money went to the richest 20 per cent of farmers.

Professor Allan Buckwell, of Wye College, who advises the House of Commons Agriculture Select Committee, says: 'The big farms can employ the accountants to work out how to claim all the different subsidies, whereas the small hill farmer will have no idea how to do it – and probably wouldn't get that much anyway.'

In 1994, Princess Anne's estate received £400,000 in subsidies. Her manager said: 'We are really farming the system, not the land.'

The CAP is due to be reformed in a couple of years, under the EU's Agenda 2000 programme, partly to iron out its more surreal side-effects, but largely under pressure from less subsidised producers such as those in the US. In an era of worldwide trade liberalisation and waning protectionism, the CAP could become an endangered species.

Some farmers claim to be a special case because they are subject to the vagaries of the British weather, but this is dismissed by Buckwell: 'The weather also affects small seaside hotels and small builders, who go bust by the dozen. There's no difference.'

The National Farmers Union accepts the need for and inevitability of reform, but is pressing for the subsidies to be retained for farmers as guardians of the countryside.

Many farmers are resigned to the erosion of subsidies, and are looking at ways of surviving by cutting costs. And there has been some consolidation: the size of the average farm has increased from 70 to 73 hectares over the past five years.

But, according to Murphy, farmers do face many obstacles: 'The UK has a highcost system. We don't have much land, so it is expensive; the cost of agricultural machinery is too high because the market is rigged; and fuel and labour costs are higher than in other parts of the world.'

The falling income of farmers has not yet affected land prices, which rose gradually after the recession in the early Nineties and have now steadied.

Roberts says: 'It's surprising land prices are not coming down faster. It may be because many farms' balance sheets are still relatively healthy after the good years.'

Land agents, however, are expecting farm land to fall by 20 per cent over the next year. Roberts warns: 'Farmers should be really careful about paying current prices for land.'

The large financial institutions which bought into farming in the eighties – particularly the huge grain farms of East Anglia – seem to be staying put for the moment. With the stock market so high, there are few other places for them to put their money.

(a) What evidence does the article present to illustrate the reliance of farmers on CAP subsidies to boost their incomes?

(b) What does the article suggest will be the implications of cutting such subsidies?

(c) How might farmers reduce their dependence on income from the CAP?

E ANSWERS

Q1. *surplus*. If the minimum price is set at any point above the equilibrium, supply will exceed demand.

Q2. *shortage*. If the maximum price is set at any point below the equilibrium, demand will exceed supply.

Q3. **(a)** (i) *No effect*. Maximum price is above existing price.

(ii) *Shortage of 10 million litres per day* (i.e. 45–35).

(iii)/(iv) 60p: *No*. Price remains at the equilibrium of 50p.

40p: *Possibly*. There will remain unsatisfied demand of 10 million litres, with, no doubt, some people being prepared to pay considerably more than 40p. Whether black marketeers can operate depends on whether there are any sources of supply that can avoid detection. This would clearly be difficult in the case of petrol.

(b) (i) *Increase from £20 million per day (40m × £0.50) to £21 million (35m × £0.60)*.

(ii) *10 million litres per day*.

(iii) *£27 million per day (45m × £0.60)*.

Q4. B. Wage control to help those on low incomes will involve setting a minimum wage *above* the equilibrium wage in low-paid occupations. In the other three cases, the purpose of price controls would be to keep prices *below* the equilibrium if the aim was to help those on low incomes afford the particular type of good or service. In such cases, therefore, a *maximum* price (or rent) would be appropriate.

Q5. If the maximum price is set below the equilibrium, the following problems could occur: producers' incomes will be cut and thus supplies of an already scarce product (e.g. food supplies in a drought) are likely to be reduced further (a movement down the supply curve); firms will also be discouraged from investing and thus *future* supplies are likely to be less; unless a system of rationing is in place, some consumers may be unable to obtain the product (given that there will be a shortage at the maximum price), and this clearly could be unfair; a black market may develop; queues may develop and this is time consuming.

Q6. If the minimum price is set above the equilibrium, the following problems could occur: surpluses will be produced, which is wasteful (in the case of minimum wages, levels of unemployment in such occupations could rise); the government may have to spend taxpayers' money on purchasing the surpluses; high prices may cushion inefficiency, with firms feeling less need to find more efficient methods of production and to cut costs; firms may be discouraged from producing alternative goods which they could produce more efficiently or which are in higher demand, but which nevertheless have a lower (free-market) price; firms may find ways of evading the price controls and dumping the surpluses onto the market.

Q7. *upward.*

Q8. *leave the slope of the supply curve unaffected.*

Q9. *make the supply curve steeper.*

Q10. (a) (iii), (b) (iv), (c) (ii), (d) (i).

Q11. C. $(P_2 - P_1) \times Q_2$. See Figure A3.1.

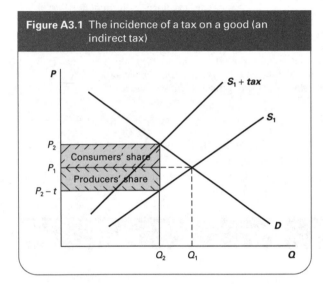

Figure A3.1 The incidence of a tax on a good (an indirect tax)

Q12. D. $(t - (P_2 - P_1)) \times Q_2$. See Figure A3.1.

Q13. D. Price will rise less, and hence the producers' share will be larger, the more elastic is demand and the less elastic is supply (see cases (2) and (3) in Figure 3.5 on page 74 of Sloman 4th edition).

Q14. *maximum price.*

Q15. *greater.*

Q16. (a) *True.*

    (b) *True.*

    (c) The answer here depends on the assumptions made. The statement would be *true* if the supply curve were upward sloping (which would occur if money earned from selling health care were ploughed back into a greater level of provision). The statement would be *false* if (i) supply were totally inelastic or (ii) the government responded to the shortage by increasing the level of provision.

    (d) *True.* Some sort of rationing will normally occur. For example, specialists may decide which patients will be given expensive treatment and which will have to go without and have a cheaper (but less effective) treatment.

(e) *False.* People would probably have to wait for non-urgent treatment, but most (if not all) serious non-urgent cases would still be treated.

(f) *True.* Some people might be refused treatment. Others may not bother with treatment (or pay for private treatment) rather than wait.

(g) *True* or *false* depending on the government's response to shortages.

Q17. (a) *left.*

    (b) *left.*

    (c) *either higher or lower* (*depending on the relative shifts in the demand and supply curves*). Normally, it would be expected that the price would rise. The reason is that the penalties for supplying illegal products are usually higher than those for buying/possessing them. Thus the supply curve would shift to the left more than the demand curve.

Q18. E.

Q19. (a) *True.* The reason is that a tax (unlike making a product illegal) will not shift the demand curve.

    (b) *False.*

Q20. (a) *False.* The more elastic the supply, the less will price fluctuate for any given (horizontal) shift in either the demand or the supply curve.

    (b) *True.* The greater the fluctuations in the harvest, the bigger the shifts in the actual supply curve, and hence the bigger the fluctuations in price.

    (c) *False.* The more elastic the demand, the less will price fluctuate for any given (horizontal) shift in either the demand or the supply curve.

Q21. D. A larger increase over time in supply (i) than demand (ii), combined with a price inelastic demand (iii) will push prices down and hence lead to a relatively small growth in revenue. Fluctuations in the harvest (iv), on the other hand, will have little effect on *long-term* supply, and may even cause revenues to grow *more* rapidly over time if the fluctuations cause uncertainty and hence a fall in investment and a resultant smaller growth in supply.

Q22. (a) *Stabilise prices.* Prices will be kept up by buying into the stocks in years of good harvest, and selling from stocks in years of poor harvest. If the stocks are not allowed to grow over the years, the average price to the farmer will be no higher, just more stable.

    (b) *Support incomes.* Output and hence prices will still fluctuate with the harvest, however.

    (c) *Both.* If the minimum price is above the market price, this will both support farmers' incomes and stabilise the price (at the minimum level).

    (d) *Support incomes.* Output will be reduced and, with a price-inelastic demand for food, farmers' revenue will thereby increase. Output will still fluctuate with the harvest, however.

(e) *Both*. If the agreed price is above the market level, this will both support farmers' incomes and stabilise the price (at the agreed level).

(f) *Support incomes*. Incomes will be supported in the short run, but in the long run, to the extent that the investment increases output, farmers' incomes will *fall*.

(g) *Support incomes*. This raises price to the farmer, but prices will still fluctuate with supply.

(h) *Support incomes (slight stabilising effect on prices)*. To the extent that supply is reduced, price will rise. Prices will still fluctuate with demand and also with milk yields, even though the number of cattle will be more stable.

(i) *Support incomes*. Output will be largely unaffected, except for those farmers who would not have survived without the subsidy, and thus prices will continue to fluctuate.

Q23. 1. (b), (c), (e), (f) and (g).

2. (d) and (h).

3. (a). In years of good harvest, the government will buy into the buffer stock to keep prices up. This will increase domestic supply above the free market level (unless supply is totally inelastic). In years of poor harvest, the government will release stocks onto the market to keep prices down. This will reduce domestic supply below the free market level (unless, again, supply is totally inelastic).

4. (i). A lump-sum subsidy, by definition, does not depend on output. The profitability of producing extra output, therefore, is not affected by the subsidy. Thus the subsidy will have no effect on supply. (The one exception is those farmers who would not have survived without the subsidy.)

5. (b) and (f).

6. (c), (d), (e), (g) and (h).

7. (a). Consumption will be kept below the free-market level in years of good harvests because the government keeps the price up by buying into the buffer stocks. Consumption will be kept above the free-market level in years of bad harvest because the government releases supplies from the stocks to keep prices down.

8. (i).

Q24. (a) $Q_2 - Q_5$.

(b) $(Q_2 - Q_5) \times OP_2$.

(c) $P_2 - P_3$. This would shift the supply curve downwards by an amount $P_2 - P_3$ and thus reduce the price to P_3. Sales would increase to Q_2. Farmers would thus earn $(P_3 + \text{subsidy}) \times OQ_2$: the same as with the high minimum price of P_2.

(d) $(P_2 - P_3) \times OQ_2$.

Q25. (a) *heg*, (b) Q_1, (c) Q_4, (d) $Q_4 - Q_1$, (e) *hebc*, (f) Q_2, (g) Q_3, (h) $Q_3 - Q_2$.

Q26. (a) *ifg*, (b) P_w, (c) Q_2, (d) Q_4, (e) $Q_4 - Q_2$.

Q27. C. For any given price to the producer, and hence given domestic supply, the EU system of high minimum prices will lead to a higher price to the consumer and thus a lower level of consumption, and hence a lower level of imports. Note that in the case of A consumers pay a *higher* price under the EU system; in the case of B there are surpluses under the EU system and no surpluses under a system of subsidies; in the case of D the EU system leads to dumped foodstuffs on world markets and involves tariffs on imports of food (including from developing countries); in the case of E the EU system is specifically designed to lead to higher prices.

Q28. *Yes:* (a), (d), (g).

No: (b), (e), (f), (h).

In the case of (c) the answer could be either *yes* or *no*. It depends on whether the additional agricultural investment resulting from the CAP (and hence a lower *free*-market price) has been sufficient to offset maintaining the price above the equilibrium.

Q29. It has been more difficult for these countries to export to the EU; cheap EU food exports into these countries have made their domestic food production less profitable.

Q30. *the same*.

Q31. *the same*. Since direct income support (as opposed to output subsidies) is unrelated to output, it should have no effect on output, and hence no effect on prices – except that, by enabling farmers to invest more and marginal farmers to survive, it could increase output (and hence reduce prices) in the *long* run.

A REVIEW

In Chapter 2 we were concerned with the *total market* demand and supply. In this chapter and the next we go behind the demand and supply curves to examine the behaviour of individuals: individual consumers and individual producers.

In this chapter we consider the behaviour of consumers. We see what determines the quantity of various goods that people will demand at various prices and incomes. By building up a picture of individuals' demand we will then be in a better position to understand total market demand.

There are two major approaches to analysing consumer demand: the marginal utility approach and the indifference approach. We examine both of them in this chapter. We also look at the problem of making rational choices when we only have limited information.

4.1 Marginal utility theory

(Pages 92–4) People generally buy goods and services because they expect to gain satisfaction from them. We call this satisfaction *utility*. An important distinction we make is between *total* and *marginal* utility.

(?) **Q1.** Total utility (*TU*) can be defined as

....

(?) **Q2.** Marginal utility (*MU*) can be defined as

....

Q3. If I gain 20 units of satisfaction from consuming 4 toffees and 23 units of satisfaction from consuming 5 toffees, then my marginal utility from the 5th toffee is
A.   43 units.
B.   23 units.

C.   20 units.
D.   3 units.
E.   −3 units.

Q4. Total utility will *fall* whenever
A.   marginal utility is falling.
B.   marginal utility is rising.
C.   marginal utility has reached a maximum.
D.   marginal utility is zero.
E.   marginal utility is negative.

A problem with the utility approach to analysing consumer demand is that utility cannot be measured.

Nevertheless in order to understand how utility relates to consumer choice it is convenient to assume that it can be measured. We thus use an imaginary unit of satisfaction called 'utils'.

Q5. Table 4.1 shows the total utility that Katie derives from visits to the cinema per week.

 Multiple Choice   *Written answer*   *Delete wrong word*   *Diagram/table manipulation*    *Calculation*   ⬛ *Matching/ordering*

Table 4.1 Katie's total and marginal utility from cinema visits

Visits	1	2	3	4	5	6	7	8
TU (utils)	12	20	25	28	30	31	31	29
MU (utils)	.	.	.	.	.	.	.	.

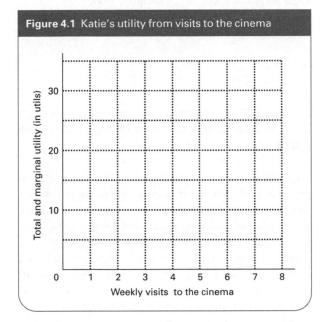

Figure 4.1 Katie's utility from visits to the cinema

(a) Fill in the figures for marginal utility. (Note that the *MU* figures are entered mid-way between the *TU* figures. This is because marginal utility is the extra utility of going from one level of consumption to the next.)

(b) Draw a graph of the figures for total and marginal utility on Figure 4.1.

(c) Assume that Katie now falls for a guy who also likes going to the cinema. As a result her marginal utility for each visit doubles. What is her total utility now for:

   (i) 3 visits?

   (ii) 6 visits?

   (iii) 7 visits?

You will notice from Figure 4.1 that the marginal utility curve slopes downwards. This is in accordance with the *principle of diminishing marginal utility*.

Q6. Which of the following are directly related to the principle of diminishing marginal utility?

(a) Rather than eating one large savoury course at dinner, I prefer to have less first course so as to leave room for a pudding. *Yes/No*

(b) I prefer to spend my time playing sport rather than watching television. *Yes/No*

(c) I like to watch a little television in the evenings. *Yes/No*

(d) I like watching comedy programmes more than documentaries. *Yes/No*

(e) I get bored easily. *Yes/No*

Q7. Diminishing marginal utility implies that total utility:

A. decreases at a decreasing rate.

B. decreases at a constant rate.

C. increases at a constant rate.

D. increases at an increasing rate.

E. increases at a decreasing rate.

(Page 94) When we draw up a utility schedule (like that in Table 4.1) we have to assume *ceteris paribus*. In other words, we assume that other factors which affect the utility gained from the product remain constant.

Q8. Make a list of 4 things that affect your marginal utility from a glass of orange juice (other than the number of glasses of orange juice you have already had). Will they increase or decrease your marginal utility?

1. .... *Increase/Decrease*

2. .... *Increase/Decrease*

3. .... *Increase/Decrease*

4. .... *Increase/Decrease*

(Pages 94–7) How much of a good will people buy? If they wish to maximise their self-interest (what is known as 'rational' behaviour), they will compare the marginal utility they expect to get from consuming the good with the price they have to pay. This will involve perceiving marginal utility in *money* terms (i.e. how much an extra unit of the good is worth to them). If the marginal utility exceeds the price, rational consumers will **Q9.** *buy more/buy less/not change their level of consumption*. If, however, price exceeds marginal utility, rational consumers will **Q10.** *buy more/buy less/not change their level of consumption*.

What we are saying is that the rational consumer will seek to maximise his or her *total consumer surplus* (*TCS*) from the good.

Q11. Table 4.2 shows the marginal utility a person gets from consuming different quantities of a good. Assume that the good sells for £10.

(a) What is the person's total utility from consuming four units?

....

(b) What is the person's total expenditure from consuming six units?

....

Table 4.2 Marginal utility for person Y from good X

Quantity consumed	0	1	2	3	4	5	6
Marginal utility (£s)		25	20	16	12	8	4

(c) What is the person's marginal consumer surplus from consuming a second unit?

....

(d) What is the person's marginal consumer surplus from consuming a fifth unit?

....

(e) What is the person's total consumer surplus from consuming two units?

....

(f) At what level of consumption is the person's total consumer surplus maxinised?

....

(g) What is the marginal consumer surplus at this level?

....

(h) What is the relationship between price and marginal utility at this level?

....

Q12. In Figure 4.2 which area(s) represent total utility at a level of consumption of Q?

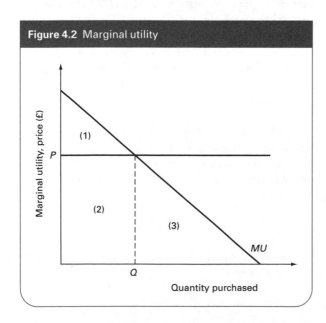

Figure 4.2 Marginal utility

A. 1
B. 2
C. 1 + 2
D. 2 + 3
E. 1 + 2 + 3

Q13. In Figure 4.2 which area(s) represent total consumer surplus at a level of consumption of Q?
A. 1
B. 2
C. 3
D. 1 + 2
E. 2 + 3

If we assume that an individual's income remains constant, his or her demand curve for a good will be directly related to **Q14.** *total utility/marginal utility.*

(Pages 97–100) Rather than focusing on how much of a *single* good people will buy, it is more satisfactory to examine how people will allocate their incomes *between* alternative goods. *Rational choice* involves comparing the marginal utility of each good relative to its price.

Take the simple case where a consumer buys just two goods, X and Y. If at the current level of consumption $MU_X/P_X > MU_Y/P_Y$, to maximise total utility the consumer should **Q15.** *buy more X relative to Y/buy more Y relative to X/ buy whichever item is the cheaper.*

(?) Q16. The consumer will continue switching until

....

Q17. Alison loves cheese. She particularly likes Dolcelatte, but also quite likes Cheddar. Her marginal utility from her last gram of Dolcelatte is double that from her last gram of Cheddar. Assuming that she consumes cheese 'rationally', and that Cheddar costs £4.00 per kilo, what is the price per kilo of Dolcelatte?
A. £1.00
B. £2.00
C. £4.00
D. £8.00
E. £16.00

Q18. Andrea spends all her income on just 3 goods X, Y and Z. If at her present level of consumption $MU_X/P_X > MU_Y/P_Y > MU_Z/P_Z$, which one of the following can we conclude?
A. She will buy more X and Y, and less Z.
B. She will buy more X, and less Y and Z.
C. She will buy more X, less Z, and the same amount of Y.
D. She will buy more X and less Z, but we cannot say whether she will buy more, less or the same amount of Y.
E. She will buy more X, but we cannot say whether she will buy more, less or the same amount of Y and Z.

4.2 Demand under conditions of risk and uncertainty

(Pages 101–4) When people buy consumer durables they may be uncertain of their benefits and any additional repair and maintenance costs. When they buy financial assets they may be uncertain of what will happen to their price in the future. Buying under these conditions of imperfect knowledge is therefore a form of gamble.

When we take such gambles, if we know the odds, then we are said to be operating under conditions of *Q19. probability/possibility/risk/uncertainty/certainty.* If we do not know the odds we are said to be operating under conditions of *Q20. probability/possibility/risk/uncertainty/ignorance.*

Q21. If you are prepared to accept odds of 10:1 on drawing an ace from a pack of cards (i.e. you win £10 for a £1 bet if you draw an ace), then how would your risk attitude be described? *Risk neutral/risk loving/risk averse*

Q22. Figure 4.3 shows the total utility that Clive, a first-year degree student, would get from different levels of annual income. Assume at the moment that his annual income (from an allowance from his parents and some part-time work in a burger bar) is £4000. Spending this rationally gives him a total utility of 500 'utils'.

Assume that he is offered the chance to gamble the whole £4000 on the toss of a coin at odds of 2:1 (i.e. if he wins, he doubles his money; if he loses, he loses the lot).

(a) If he takes the gamble, what will be his utility this year if he wins?

.... utils.

(b) If he takes the gamble, what will be his utility this year if he loses?

.... utils.

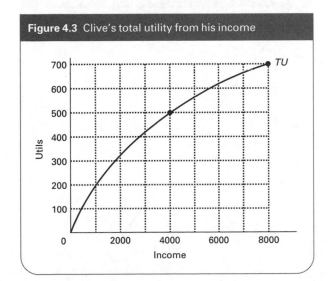

Figure 4.3 Clive's total utility from his income

(c) What would be his average expected utility from the gamble?

.... utils.

(d) Why is it likely that he will not take the gamble, and thus be risk averse?

....

Q23. People will be prepared to pay insurance premiums only if the insurance gives them 'fair odds'.

True/False

Q24. Of the following:
 (i) the law of large numbers
 (ii) the ability to spread risks
 (iii) the independence of risks
 (iv) the fact that insurance companies are technically 'risk lovers'
which help to explain why insurance companies are prepared to take on risks that individuals are not?
A. (i).
B. (i) and (ii).
C. (i), (ii) and (iii).
D. (ii), (iii) and (iv).
E. (i), (ii), (iii) and (iv).

Q25. In which of the following cases are the risks independent?
(a) Accident insurance for members of a football team travelling abroad.

Independent/Not independent

(b) Insurance against loss of income from redundancy (for people working for different companies all over the country).

Independent/Not independent

(c) Insurance against loss of income from accidents at work (for people working for different companies all over the country).

Independent/Not independent

(d) House contents insurance for houses in a particular neighbourhood.

Independent/Not independent

(e) Life assurance for people over 65.

Independent/Not independent

(f) Life assurance for soldiers.

Independent/Not independent

*4.3 Indifference analysis

(Pages 104–5) A problem with marginal utility analysis is that utility cannot be measured. An alternative approach is to use *indifference analysis.* This merely examines a consumer's preferences between different bundles of goods. It does not involve measuring utility.

Table 4.3 Sally's preferences between books and CDs (per year)

Set 1	Books	40	30	23	16	12	10	6	4	2
	CDs	3	5	8	14	19	22	30	37	46
Set 2	Books	33	22	16	13	7	4			
	CDs	7	14	20	25	37	45			
Set 3	Books	40	30	22	20	17	14	11	6	2	1
	CDs	1	2	4	5	7	10	13	20	30	37
Set 4	Books	27	20	11	5					
	CDs	6	10	20	33					
Set 5	Books	30	20	16	12	6	3	1		
	CDs	1	3	4	6	10	14	20		

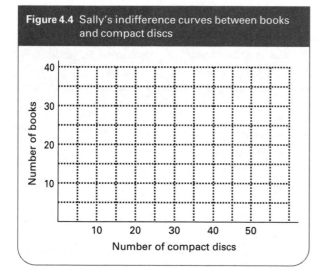

Figure 4.4 Sally's indifference curves between books and compact discs

Number of books (vertical axis: 10, 20, 30, 40)
Number of compact discs (horizontal axis: 10, 20, 30, 40, 50)

⊖ **Q26.** Sally, a first-year degree student, lives in a hall of residence and pays a fixed amount for food and accommodation. The money she has left over she spends on books and compact discs. Her preferences between various combinations of books and CDs are shown in Table 4.3. She is indifferent between the combinations in each of the five sets shown, but has preferences between sets.

(a) Plot indifference curves on Figure 4.4 corresponding to each of the sets in Table 4.3.

(b) Which set would Sally like best?

set 1/set 2/set 3/set 4/set 5

(c) Between which two sets is Sally indifferent?

set 1/set 2/set 3/set 4/set 5

(d) Which set does Sally like the least?

set 1/set 2/set 3/set 4/set 5

(e) Given the information in Table 4.3, why would Sally *not* be indifferent between the combinations in the following set: 36 books and 5 CDs, 23 books and 8 CDs, 12 books and 13 CDs, 3 books and 20 CDs?

....

(Pages 105–7) The slope of the indifference curve is given by $\Delta Y/\Delta X$, where Y is the good measured on the vertical axis and X is the good measured on the horizontal axis. The slope gives the *marginal rate of substitution (MRS)*.

(?) **Q27.** This can be defined as the amount of one good (Y) that a consumer is prepared to give up for

....

⊖ **Q28.** Referring again to Table 4.3, what is Sally's marginal rate of substitution of books for CDs in set 5 for

(a) the fourth CD? ....

(b) the sixth CD? ....

(c) the tenth CD? ....

(?) **Q29.** Why are indifference curves drawn convex (bowed in) to the origin? Explain this in terms of the marginal rate of substitution.

....

....

▤ **Q30.** The slope of an indifference curve (the *MRS*) also gives:
A. MU_X/MU_Y
B. MU_Y/MU_X
C. MU_X/P_X
D. MU_Y/P_Y
E. P_Y/P_X

(Pages 106–11)

⊖ **Q31.** Figure 4.5 shows a person's budget to spend on two goods X and Y.

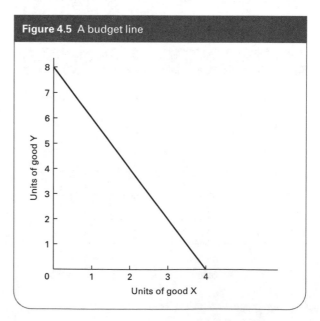

Figure 4.5 A budget line

Units of good Y (vertical axis: 1–8)
Units of good X (horizontal axis: 0–4)

(a) If the size of the budget was £20, what would be the price of X and Y?

$P_X = $ ...., $P_Y = $ ....

(b) Assume that the price of Y rises to £4 (but that the price of X and the level of money income stay the same). Draw the new budget line.

(c) If the budget line does not shift again, but the price of X is now £10, what must be the size of the total budget now?

....

(d) What will be the price of Y now? $P_Y = $ ....

(e) If the price of X and Y both double, but the consumer's money income also doubles, what will happen to the budget line?

....

Q32. Which of the following gives the slope of the budget line?
A. MU_X/MU_Y
B. MU_Y/MU_X
C. P_X/P_Y
D. P_Y/P_X
E. MRS

Q33. Referring back to Q26, assume that Sally has, £300 per year to spend on a combination of books and CDs, and assume that all the books and CDs she wants cost £10 each.
(a) Draw in her budget line on Figure 4.4.
(b) What is the optimum amount of books and CDs for her to buy with this £300?

.... books, ... CDs

(c) Assume now that the price of CDs rises to £20. Draw in her new budget line.
(d) What is the optimum amount of books and CDs per year for her to buy now?

.... books, ... CDs

Q34. Match each of the following changes in an indifference diagram to the causes (a)–(h) of those changes. (In each case assume *ceteris paribus* and that units of Y are measured on the vertical axis and units of X on the horizontal axis.)
(i) A parallel shift outwards of the budget line.
(ii) The budget line becomes steeper.
(iii) The indifference curves become flatter.
(iv) A parallel shift inwards of the budget line.

(v) A movement along the budget line to a higher indifference curve.
(vi) A pivoting inwards of the budget line round the point where the budget line crosses the X axis.
(vii) The indifference curves become steeper.
(viii) A movement along the budget line from an old tangency point to a new one.

(a) An increase in the price of Y ....

(b) A shift in tastes towards Y and away from X.

....

(c) A rise in income ....

(d) A change in the optimum level of consumption resulting from a change in tastes

....

(e) A shift in tastes towards X and away from Y.

....

(f) An increase in utility resulting from a change in consumption.
....

(g) A decrease in the relative price of Y ....

(h) A fall in income ....

(Page 111) We can use indifference analysis to show the effects of changes in price of one of the two goods on the quantity demanded of the good. This then enables us to derive an individual's demand curve for that good.

Q35. Tom has an income of £160 to spend on two goods X and Y. Assume that the price of Y is constant at £16.
(a) On Figure 4.6 plot the budget lines corresponding to $P_X = £10$, $P_X = £16$, $P_X = £20$, $P_X = £32$ and $P_X = £40$.
(b) Now show how much X will be consumed at each price. From this construct a *price–consumption curve*.
(c) Use this information to construct Tom's demand curve for good X.

The demand curve you have just derived is for the simple case where the consumer is only buying two goods (X and Y). In the real world people buy many goods.

Q36. How can we derive the demand for good X under these circumstances? The answer is to measure good X on the horizontal axis and

.... on the vertical axis.

Figure 4.6 The effect of a change in the price of good X on Tom's consumption

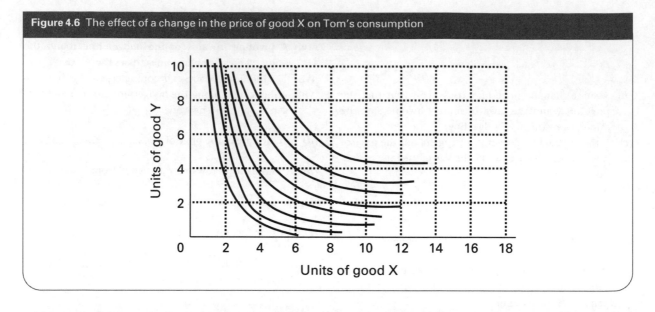

Figure 4.7 The income and substitution effects of a reduction in the price of good X

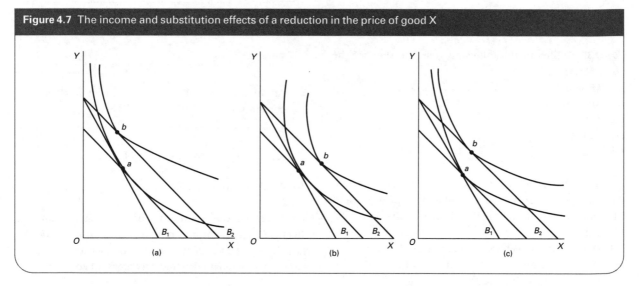

(a)   (b)   (c)

(Pages 112–16) As we saw in Chapter 2, the effect of a change in price can be divided into an income effect and a substitution effect. In examining these effects we can distinguish three types of good: a *normal good*, an *inferior (non-Giffen) good* and a *Giffen good*.

⊖ **Q37.** Figure 4.7 illustrates each of these three types of good measured on the X axis) and the effect in each case of a reduction in the price of good X and a consequent shift in the budget line from B_1 to B_2.

(a) Mark the income and substitution effects in each diagram.

(b) In which diagram is X

   (i) a normal good? ....

   (ii) an inferior, but non-Giffen good? ....

   (iii) a Giffen good? ....

Table 4.4 Income and substitution effects of a price change

Type of good	Substitution effect	Income effect	Which is the bigger effect?
Normal	positive/ negative	positive/ negative	income/substitution/ either
Inferior (non-Giffen)	positive/ negative	positive/ negative	income/substitution/ either
Giffen	positive/ negative	positive/ negative	income/substitution/ either

◑ **Q38.** Table 4.4 is used to summarise the direction and relative size of the income and substitution effects. Cross out the incorrect information.

◑ **Q39.** When the price of an inferior (but non-Giffen) good rises, people will consume more of it. *True/False*

Q40. Select three items of foodstuff that you purchase regularly (e.g. bread, eggs, potatoes).

(a) In each case estimate how much per week you would purchase at different prices.

(b) In each case work out the amount of consumer surplus you receive per week.

(c) Now ask yourself how much money you would need to be given in each case in order to persuade you not to buy any of the good at all.

(d) Are the answers to (b) and (c) similar? Should they be?

(e) Now choose one of the three goods and select a substitute good for it. How will (i) a 10 per cent rise, (ii) a 20 per cent fall and (iii) a 50 per cent rise in the price of the substitute affect the consumer surplus you gain from the original good?

(f) How will your consumer surplus for each of the three goods be affected by a change in your income?

Q41. Imagine that you have £30 to spend on three goods, A, B and C. The marginal utility you gain from each good is independent of the amount you consume of the other two goods. Your marginal utility from successive units of each of the three goods is shown in Table 4.5.

Table 4.5 Marginal utilities (in utils) from the consumption of three goods A, B and C

Units of good A	1	2	3	4	5	6	7	8	9	10
Marginal utility	45	40	25	20	16	12	9	6	4	2
Units of good B	1	2	3	4	5	6	7	8	9	10
Marginal utility	80	70	60	50	40	30	20	10	0	0
Units of good C	1	2	3	4	5	6	7	8	9	10
Marginal utility	22	20	18	16	14	12	10	8	6	4

(a) Imagine that good A costs £4, good B costs £3 and good C costs £2. How much will you consume of each?

(b) Assume now that the price of A rises to £10, that the price of B falls to £2 and the price of C remains unchanged at £2. How much of each will be consumed now, assuming the budget remains unchanged at £30?

(c) In which situation (a) or (b) is total utility higher?

*Q42. Harry gains equal satisfaction from the following combinations of annual visits to the theatre and visits to football matches:

14 theatre and 3 football
11 theatre and 4 football
8 theatre and 6 football
6 theatre and 9 football
4 theatre and 16 football

(a) Using graph paper, plot Harry's indifference curve corresponding to these figures. Plot theatre visits on the vertical axis.

(b) If Harry actually visited the theatre 5 times, how many football matches would he have to attend in order to obtain the same satisfaction as in the other 5 combinations?

(c) What is the marginal rate of substitution of theatre visits for football matches between 4 and 6 football matches?

(d) What is the marginal rate of substitution of theatre visits for football matches at the 8 theatre, 6 football point on the indifference curve?

(e) Assume that Harry decides to allocate a total of £280 per year to these two activities. Assume also that both football matches and theatre visits cost £20. How many visits to the theatre could he make if he attended 9 football matches?

(f) Draw Harry's budget line on your diagram.

(g) How many theatre performances and football matches will he attend?
Why will he not attend an equal number of each?

(h) Assume now that the price of theatre tickets increases to £40, but that Harry unfortunately cannot afford to budget for any more than the £280. Draw Harry's new budget line.

(i) Poor Harry is now going to have to economise on the number of visits to either or both types of event. So he sits down and thinks about alternative combinations that would give him equal satisfaction to each other (but less than before). He comes up with the following combinations:

12 theatre and 2 football
9 theatre and 3 football
6 theatre and 5 football
3 theatre and 8 football
2 theatre and 11 football
1 theatre and 15 football

Draw this indifference curve on the diagram.

(j) How many theatre performances and football matches will he now attend?

(k) Assume that Harry now wonders whether to try to maintain his previous level of satisfaction by allocating a bigger budget to compensate for the higher price of theatre tickets. If he did do this, what would his new budget line look like? (Draw it.)

(l) How many theatre performances and football matches would he attend under these circumstances?

(m) How much would this cost him?

(n) Had he maintained his original combination of visits, how much would this now have cost him?

(o) On second thoughts he reluctantly decides he will have to restrict himself to the original £280 and thus the answer to (j) above holds. What will be the size of the income and substitution effects of the rise in the price of theatre tickets from £20 to £40?

(p) Are theatre visits a normal or an inferior 'good' for Harry? Explain.

(q) If Harry meets Sally and she likes going to the cinema with Harry rather than to the theatre, how will this affect Harry's indifference curves between visits to the theatre and visits to football matches?

DISCUSSION TOPICS AND ESSAYS

Q43. If people buy things out of habit, does this conflict with the assumption of rational behaviour?

Q44. In the UK most domestic consumers pay for water through a system of water rates which are based on the value of the person's property. This is a flat sum and does not vary with the amount of water consumed. What would you expect a person's marginal utility for water to be? Make out a case for and against having water meters and charging for water on a per litre basis.

Q45. What are the drawbacks in attempting to measure utility in money terms?

Q46. Explain how goods with little total utility to the consumer can sell for a high price.

Q47. Explain the difference between the terms 'risk loving', 'risk neutral' and 'risk averse'. Would a risk-loving person ever be prepared to take out insurance?

Q48. How can insurance companies protect themselves against the problems of adverse selection and moral hazard?

*Q49. Could indifference curves ever intersect (i) over the same time period, (ii) over different time periods?

*Q50. Imagine that the price–consumption curve for good X was downward sloping. Are goods X and Y substitutes or complements? Explain.

*Q51. What are the limitations of indifference analysis for (a) explaining and (b) predicting consumption patterns for a given consumer?

Q52. Debate
It is wrong for the state to provide services such as health and libraries free at the point of use. With a zero price, people consume a wasteful amount. They consume to the point where marginal utility is zero.

ARTICLES

When economists build models they are required to make a series of simplifying assumptions, none more so than that concerning human behaviour. Individuals are assumed to be 'rational utility maximisers', who are motivated by self-gain. Such an assumption is, in many cases, clearly unrealistic and a major limitation on the economist attempting to explain so-called 'irrational' economic behaviour. The article below, taken from The *Economist* of 25 December 1993, shows how such a perception of human nature is being questioned and how an understanding of biology might be the key to constructing a more realistic view of human economic behaviour.

Biology meets the dismal science

In the past few years a curious flirtation has developed in the halls of academe between economists and Darwinian biologists. They talk the same language, borrow each other's techniques and come to similar conclusions. A recent issue of the *American Economic Review* contained a series of papers on altruistic behaviour. In June, at the London School of Economics, a conference explored the common ground between economics and evolution. A new discipline of evolutionary economics is being born.

To thine own self be true
The common ground between economics and evolution is a focus on the individual. In the 1960s, both economists and students of the evolution of social behaviour in animals lurched towards individualism. They became convinced that you can understand what happens to groups, populations, nations or species only by understanding what motivates individual people and animals. Societies are the sums of individuals. According to economists, individuals maximise their 'utility

functions' (roughly equivalent to consumption); according to evolutionists, they maximise their 'fitness functions' (roughly, successful offspring). But the process is much the same.

Paul Romer, an economist at the University of California at Berkeley, insists that it is not just an analogy to see fitness and utility as similar concepts. When he talks to people who study the evolution of behaviour, he finds that they, like him, are concerned with the individual organism. None of them assumes that classes and groups have distinct properties of their own. In this respect, economics is closer to biology than it is to sociology – which talks about the actions of groups.

Biologists return the compliment. Helena Cronin, an evolutionary theorist at the London School of Economics, says economists are more aware of the problems of emergent properties than other scientists – that is, of how collective effects flow from individual behaviour.

So both evolutionists and economists found themselves arguing that individuals do things for the good of the larger group only if it is also for the good of the individual. Animals rarely do selfless things for their species. And people rarely do selfless things for the good of society. (If it were otherwise, communism might have stood a better chance.)

At first, such emphasis on individualism seems to leave both disciplines committed to a ruthless and opportunistic view of human nature: man as Robinson Crusoe, alone and self-centred. Such a view of mankind is patently wrong.

Never fear. Even desiccated economists had noticed the 'voter paradox': people vote in elections, despite the fact that no individual can expect to influence the outcome. Many other examples are much more obvious. People give to charity. Executives work long hours on behalf of their firms. Travellers tip waiters they will never see again. Soldiers willingly risk their lives for their country. Trust, co-operation and altruism are all part of human life.

But guess what. They are also part of animal life. Monkeys groom each other.

Birds give alarm calls to warn each other of danger. Bees feed their queen and her daughters and defend their hives to the death. Animal altruism abounds. The question is: how do you reconcile altruism with the invisible hand and survival of the fittest?

Economists, observant folk, have always recognised that people are nicer to their children than to strangers. But they have had difficulty making sense of this in terms of their theories, because it seems to be merely an irrational whim. But as the theory of 'kin-selection' gained ground within evolutionary biology – a theory in which the survival not of the individual but of its genes (in descendants and close relatives) became the criterion of fitness – so economists have learnt to adjust their utility functions to include not just people's own consumption, but also their children's.

Any theory of how people save and spend needs to take this into account. To put it starkly, economists used to be puzzled by the way people continue saving right up to the ends of their lives. Now they recognise that 'utility' includes leaving something to your children.

A theory of preferences

Economists believe in a typical human being, whose actions they can predict based on an assumption of what motivates him or her. Evolutionary psychologists find evidence that they are right.

Utah's Alan Rogers describes economics as an elaborate theory that takes human preferences as its premise. Evolution, he says, can be construed as

a theory of those preferences. In other words, economists may assume that people generally love their children; evolutionists can explain why they love their children.

Take the issue of 'concern for fairness'. Economists have noticed that a concern for fairness seems to be a strong motive in human decisions. The desire to see fair play drives much political debate. People are not the ruthless opportunists that naive economic theory assumes.

Parallels in the business world are immediately apparent. Few businessmen would think of themselves and the others they come across as ruthless or impatient self-seekers. Instead, they see people who seek co-operation, do deals on trust, share secrets with confidants, and get ahead by building friendships and alliances. Robert Maxwells, who betray their employees and confederates, and do not care what people think of them, are the exceptions, not the rule. Lord Vinson, a successful British entrepreneur, cites as one of his ten commandments of entrepreneurship: 'Trust everyone unless you have a reason not to.'

Naive economics and naive sociobiology still teach that people are ruthlessly self-interested. But where the two disciplines have come together, a much sunnier side of mankind's nature has emerged. People are opportunistic seekers of co-operation. Nice guys, far from finishing last, may in fact attract the kind of co-operation that enables them to come out ahead.

© *The Economist*, London (25th December, 1993)

(a) Explain what is meant by the 'voter paradox'. Give some examples from your own experience of altruistic behaviour (i.e. doing things for others with no gain to yourself).

(b) If people are not always motivated by self-interest, does this make marginal utility theory redundant?

(c) Assuming that people take the interests of others into account when making economic decisions, how

would this affect the nature of demand curves? Would people still respond in the same way to price changes as under traditional assumptions of self-interested behaviour?

*(d) Would the assumptions of altruism and co-operation make indifference curve analysis irrelevant?

(e) Does the article in any way challenge the economist's definition of the central 'economic problem'?

Economists assume that individuals make rational economic decisions. They do so by weighing up the associated costs and benefits of any given purchase or decision: in other words, they estimate the total utility they might gain from such an activity. But how certain can they be about their decision? Can they guarantee that costs will not change? Once uncertainty is considered, individuals may seek ways of reducing such unpredictability: for example, by taking out insurance. The article below, taken from *The Economist* of 29 July 1995, looks at the role of insurance and the problems facing insurance companies.

An insurer's worst nightmare

Aeroplane crashes, oil spills and product failures are generally unpredictable events. But they are not totally random: their occurrence can sometimes be influenced by human actions. And although insurance can help to protect people from the financial impact of accidental misfortune, it may also inadvertently make them more accident-prone.

Insurance works on the principle of pooling risks and charging each customer a premium based only on the average risk of the pool. This approach has much appeal: as the chart shows, worldwide spending on insurance premiums continues to rise. But it also presents two problems, which economists call 'adverse selection' and 'moral hazard'.

Customers who have the greatest incentive to buy insurance are likely to be those who pose the worst risk for insurers, hence adverse selection. A person will be keener to buy health insurance, for example, if he is already ill.

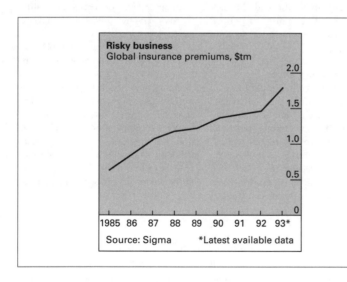

Risky business
Global insurance premiums, $tm

Source: Sigma   *Latest available data

This increases the odds that insurers will have to pay claims and so may drive up premiums for healthier people. It should not, however, increase society's total risk.

Moral hazard does. This describes the temptation for a customer, once he has bought insurance, to take greater risks than he otherwise might have done.

Moral hazard can take different forms. A customer might, for instance, increase the chances that he will incur a loss; somebody with car insurance may drive more recklessly than he would if he were uninsured. And even though an insured person may try to reduce the odds of a mishap, he may do so in a way that increases the size of the potential loss. A firm that discovers it has a defective product, for example, may withhold its finding to avoid early lawsuits it has to settle itself, while raising the risk of a huge later payout that falls on its insurance company.

Insurers have long looked for ways to cope with these problems. To counter adverse selection, they may practise a bit of their own: setting lower health-insurance rates for young people, for instance, or having their offices on the fourth floor without a lift. And to fend off moral hazard, they tend not to offer full insurance, but to pass some risk back to customers. The best technique for this depends on the kind of moral hazard an insurer faces.

When confronted with moral hazard that increases risk, insurers often resort to a 'deductible'. This requires the customer to pay in full the first portion of any claim. When someone crashes a car, for example, he often has to pay the first few hundred dollars of expenses before collecting the rest from his insurer. This not only encourages customers to drive more safely, but also cuts the insurer's administrative costs, since customers have no incentive to file small claims.

To cope with moral hazard that might increase the size of potential losses, insurers demand 'co-payments'. Rather than making customers pay the cost of a claim in full up to a certain limit, insurers require them to pay a fraction of the entire cost. Since bigger losses will mean bigger co-payments for the insured, it will remain in customers' interests to keep losses as low as possible.

Yet although insurers seem to have individual mechanisms that can cope with moral hazard, they run into trouble when they try to combine them. Many insurers, for instance, ask customers to pay an initial deductible and a small portion of all other costs above this. But this approach has a serious flaw, for deductibles can increase the moral hazard that raises the size of potential losses.

Consider, for example, a car maker that discovers a possible defect in a batch of cars that it has sold. There is a small chance that many of the cars have been built with a defective part, which would cause a string of fatal accidents. For a cost of, say, $20m, the firm can recall all of these cars and repair them. If it does nothing, it risks having to pay out several hundred million dollars if people are killed. The firm's insurer faces two kinds of moral hazard: if it insures the company against all recalls, the firm may often use them for trivial reasons; if it insures it only against large losses, the firm may avoid recalls altogether.

Mixing deductibles with small co-payments can make this worse. In some cases, the deductible will discourage a recall by more than the co-payment encourages one, even if the right decision is to recall the cars. But combining big deductibles with big co-payments might deter people from buying insurance altogether.

© *The Economist*, London (29th July, 1995)

(a) What is the function of insurance and the role of the insurance company?

(b) What is meant by the terms 'adverse selection' and 'moral hazard'?

(c) How have insurance companies attempted to overcome the problems of (i) adverse selection, and (ii) moral hazard?

E ANSWERS

Q1. The total amount of satisfaction a consumer gains by consuming a given quantity of a good or service over a given time period.

Q2. The additional satisfaction a consumer gains by consuming one more unit of a good or service within the same time period.

Q3. D. By consuming the fifth toffee, my total utility has gone up from 20 units to 23 units: a rise of 3 units.

Q4. E. If total utility is falling then the last unit must *reduce* total utility: its marginal utility must be negative.

Q5. *(a)* See table below.

Visits	1	2	3	4	5	6	7	8
TU (utils)	12	20	25	28	30	31	31	29
MU (utils)	12	8	5	3	2	1	0	-2

(b) See Figure A4.1.

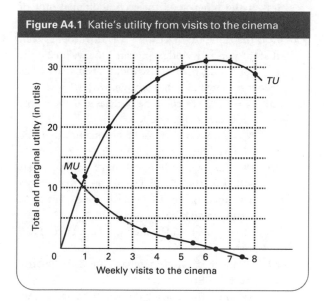

Figure A4.1 Katie's utility from visits to the cinema

(c) (i) 50; (ii) 62; (iii) 62. A doubling of marginal utility leads to a doubling of total utility.

Q6. (a), (c), (e). In each of these cases I only consume/do a certain amount and then do something else. The implication is that as the marginal utility declines, so it becomes preferable to switch to an alternative. (Note that (b) and (d) simply state a preference without saying how the preference *changes* according to the level of consumption.)

Q7. E. Marginal utility is the extra utility gained from one more unit consumed. If it falls then total utility will still rise (provided that *MU* does not become negative), but will rise *less* than for the previous unit.

Q8. The list could include increased consumption of other drinks (*MU* decreases), the weather (on a hot day the *MU* will increase), increased consumption of dry food (*MU* increases), fashion, etc.

Q9. Buy more. They are gaining more from extra consumption than it is costing them.

Q10. Buy less. The last unit being consumed is costing them more than it is benefiting them.

Q11. *(a)* £73 (= £25 + £20 + £16 + £12).
(b) £60 (6 units @ £10 each).
(c) £10 (= £20 (MU) – £10 (P)).
(d) –£2 (= £8 (MU) – £10 (P)).
(e) £25 (= £45 (TU) – £20 (TE)).
(f) 4 units (TCS = £33).
(g) (i.e. between +2 (between 3 and 4 units), and –2 (between 4 and 5 units)).
(h) P = MU = £10.

Q12. C. It is given by the area under the *MU* curve at the output (Q) in question.

Q13. A. It is given by the area between the *MU* curve and the price.

Q14. *marginal utility*. With a constant income and when the consumption of this good is too insignificant to affect the demand for other goods, the demand curve will be the marginal utility curve (where *MU* is measured in money terms).

Q15. *Buy more of X relative to Y.* If $MU_X/P_X > MU_Y/P_Y$, then people would be getting a better value (*MU*) for money (*P*) from X than from Y. They would thus consume relatively more of X and relatively less of Y. This would cause MU_X to fall (and MU_Y to rise) until $MU_X/P_X = MU_Y/P_Y$.

Q16. $MU_X/P_X = MU_Y/P_Y$.

Q17. D. If Dolcelatte gives her twice as much marginal utility as Cheddar, it must be costing her twice as much, in order for the equi-marginal principle to be satisfied.

Q18. D. We can say for certain that if she is 'rational' she will switch away from Z and towards X, but whether she alters her consumption of Y and in which direction will depend on how rapidly the marginal utilities of X and Z change.

Q19. *risk.*

Q20. *uncertainty.*

Q21. *Risk loving.* The chances of drawing an ace are 1:13. If for a £1 bet you only won £10 each time you drew an ace, then on average you would lose money. If, therefore you were prepared to accept odds of 10:1, you would be risk loving.

Q22. *(a)* *700 utils* (with a total income of £8000).
(b) *0 utils* (with a total income of £0).
(c) (700 + 0) ÷ 2 = 350 utils.
(d) because, with a diminishing marginal utility of income, by taking the gamble his average expected utility (350 utils) is less than by not taking the gamble (500 utils).

Q23. *False.* The total amount paid to insurance companies in premiums will exceed the amount received back in claims: that is how the companies make a profit. Thus the odds are inevitably unfair for the client. It is still worth-while, however, to take out insurance because people are risk averters (given the diminishing marginal utility of income).

Q24. C. A company can spread its risks over a large number of policies (ii). The more people the insurance company insures, the more predictable the total outcome (i), provided that the risks are independent (iii). Insurance companies are not risk lovers, because on average they will make a profit.

Q25. (a) *Not independent.* They may all meet with an accident in the coach or on the plane.

(b) *Not independent.* In a recession, people in many otherwise unconnected parts of the economy will be under greater threat of redundancy.

(c) *Independent.* One person having an accident will not affect the risks of others having an accident.

(d) *Not independent.* A particular neighbourhood may be more subject to burglaries. (Insurance companies charge house contents premiums based on your postcode. People living in high-risk areas pay higher premiums.)

(e) *Independent.* If a person over 65 dies, this will not affect the chances of other people over 65 dying. Under certain circumstances, however, the risks would *not* be independent. These circumstances would include an epidemic or an exceptionally severe winter.

(f) *Not independent.* In a war, soldiers' lives will generally be at greater risk.

Q26. (a) See Figure A4.2.

(b) *Set 2.* It gives an indifference curve furthest out from the origin.

(c) *Sets 1 and 4.* They lie along the same indifference curve.

(d) *Set 5.* It gives an indifference curve furthest in toward the origin.

(e) *Because a curve drawn through these combinations would cross other indifference curves, and indifference curves cannot cross.* 36 books and 5 CDs are preferable to 30 books and 5 CDs (set 1) and yet 3 books and 20 CDs are inferior to 6 books and 20 CDs (set 3) and yet set 1 is preferable to set 3! Thus, given the other sets, 36 books and 5 CDs cannot lie along the same indifference curve as 3 books and 20 CDs.

Q27. The marginal rate of substitution of Y for X is the amount of Y that a consumer is prepared to give up *for a one unit increase in the consumption of X.*

Q28. (a) $\Delta B/\Delta CD = 4/1 = 4$.

(b) $\Delta B/\Delta CD = 4/2 = 2$.

(c) $\Delta B/\Delta CD = 6/4 = 1.5$.

Q29. The *MRS* diminishes (e.g. see answer to Q28). The reason is that as more of one good is consumed relative to the other, so its marginal utility will decrease relative to that of the other. Thus the consumer would be prepared to give up less and less of the other good for each additional unit of the first good.

Q30. A. If the slope ($\Delta Y/\Delta X$) were 2/1, this would mean that the person would be prepared to give up 2 units of Y for 1 unit of X. This would mean that X has twice the marginal utility of Y, i.e. $MU_X/MU_Y = 2$.

Q31. (a) $P_X = £5$ (i.e. 4 could be purchased if the whole budget were spent on X).

$P_Y = £2.50$ (i.e. 8 could be purchased if the whole budget were spent on Y).

(b) The new budget line will join 5 on the Y axis with 4 on the X axis. The reason is that, with a new price for Y of £4, if all £20 were spent on Y, 5 units could now be purchased.

(c) £40 (i.e. 4X could be purchased at a price of £10 each).

(d) £8 (i.e. if 5Y can be purchased for £40, the price must be £8).

(e) *Nothing.* The consumer will be able to buy exactly the same quantities as before. Although money income has doubled, *real* income has not changed.

Q32. C. If the slope were 2/1, this would mean that 2 units of Y could be purchased for each 1 unit of X sacrificed. Thus X must be twice the price of Y: $P_X/P_Y = 2 =$ slope of budget line.

Q33. (a) See Figure A4.3.

(b) 16 books and 14 CDs.

(c) See Figure A4.3.

(d) 20 books and 5 CDs.

Q34. (a) (vi).

(b) (iii). (As tastes shift towards Y and away from X so MU_X/MU_Y will fall, and thus the curve will become flatter.)

(c) (i).

(d) (viii).

(e) (vii). (MU_X/MU_Y will rise.)

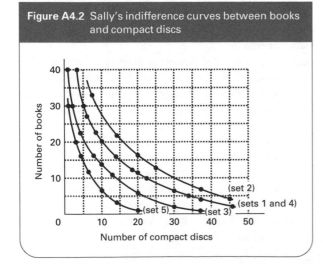

Figure A4.2 Sally's indifference curves between books and compact discs

Figure A4.3 Sally's indifference curves between books and compact discs

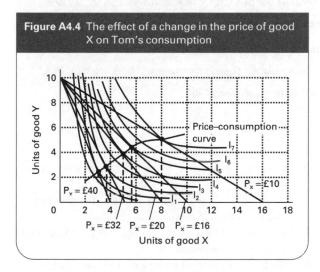

(b)

P	Q_d
10	8.0
16	5.6
20	5.0
32	3.6
40	3.0

See Figure A4.4 for the price–consumption curve.

(c) The five sets of figures (plus any others you choose to read off from the price–consumption curve) can then be plotted with *P* on the vertical axis and Q_d on the horizontal axis. The points can then be connected to give a demand curve.

***Q*36.** *expenditure on all other goods.*

***Q*37. (a)** See Figure A4.5. In each diagram the substitution effect is represented by the movement from Q_{X_1} to Q_{X_2} and the income effect by the movement from Q_{X_2} to Q_{X_3}.

(b) (i) diagram (b) (negative income (and substitution) effect), (ii) diagram (c) (positive income effect, but smaller than the negative substitution effect), (iii) diagram (a) (positive income effect which outweights the negative substitution effect).

(f) (v).

(g) (ii).

(h) (iv).

***Q*35. (a)** See Figure A4.4.

Figure A4.4 The effect of a change in the price of good X on Tom's consumption

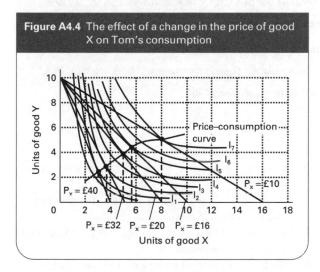

***Q*38.** See table below.

Type of good	Substitution effect	Income effect	Which is the bigger effect?
Normal	*negative*	*negative*	*either*
Inferior (non-Giffen)	*negative*	*positive*	*substitution*
Giffen	*negative*	*positive*	*income*

***Q*39.** *False.* People would only consume more if the positive income effect (because the good was inferior) outweighed the (usual) negative substitution effect. This is the case only with a Giffen good.

Figure A4.5 The income and substitution effects of a reduction in the price of good X

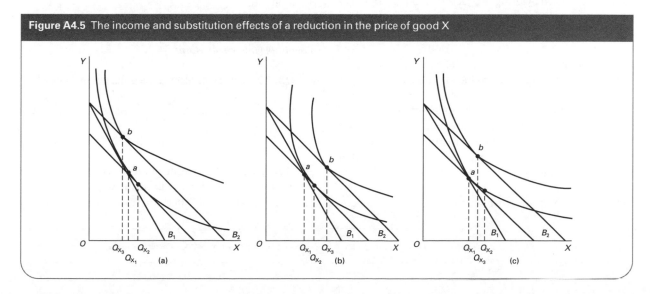

CHAPTER FIVE

5 Background to Supply

A   REVIEW

We now turn to the theory of supply. We will examine what determines the quantity that firms will produce at various prices and various costs.

In this chapter (and the next two) we will be making the traditional assumption that firms are profit maximisers: that they wish to produce the level of output that will maximise the total level of their profit ($T\Pi$). We define total profit as total revenue (TR) minus total costs (TC).

In order then to discover how a firm can maximise its profit, we must first consider what determines costs and revenue. We start by examining costs in both the short run and the long run. We then examine revenue. Finally we put the two together to examine profit.

5.1 Background to costs: the short-run theory of production

(Pages 119–22) The cost of producing any level of output will depend on the amount of inputs used. The relationship between output and inputs is shown in a *production function*.

⊗ **Q1.** In the following production function for good A, a good is produced by using two factors labour (L) and capital (K). How much will be produced if six units of labour and three units of capital are used?

$TPP = 10L + 4K$ ....
(where TPP is total physical product: i.e. total output).

Extra output involves using extra input. But increasing the amount of certain inputs may take time: it takes time, for example, to build a new factory or to install new machines. We thus make a distinction between *short-run* production and *long-run* production.

▤ **Q2.** The short run is defined as

A.   a period of time less than one year.
B.   the shortest time period in which a firm will consider producing.
C.   the period of time in which at least one factor of production is fixed in supply.
D.   the period of time it takes for raw materials to be converted into finished goods.
E.   the length of time taken for a minimum-sized production run.

In the short run, production will be subject to the *law of diminishing (marginal) returns*.

⍰ **Q3.** The law of diminishing marginal returns states that

....

....

⊖ **Q4.** Imagine that a firm produces good X with just two factors: capital which is fixed in supply, and labour which is variable. The effect on total output (*TPP*) of

---

 Multiple Choice   *Written answer*   *Delete wrong word*   *Diagram/table manipulation*   *Calculation*   *Matching/ordering*

Table 5.1 The relationship between the output (total physical product) of good X and the number of workers employed

(1) Number of workers	(2) TPP	(3)	(4)
0	0		
1	10	.	.
2	26	.	.
3	41	.	.
4	52	.	.
5	60	.	.
6	65	.	.
7	67	.	.
8	67	.	.
9	63	.	.

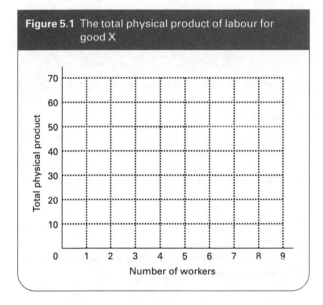

Figure 5.1 The total physical product of labour for good X

increasing the number of workers is shown in column (2) of Table 5.1. (We will fill in columns (3) and (4) later.)

(a) Draw the total physical product curve on Figure 5.1.

(b) Beyond what number of workers do diminishing returns set in?

(Pages 122–6) We can use total physical product data to derive *average* and *marginal physical product* data. We define marginal physical product (*MPP*) as **Q5.** *the number of units of the variable factor required to produce one more unit of output/the amount of extra output gained from the use of one more unit of the variable factor.*

Q6. If *L* is the quantity of labour, then of the following:

 (i) *TPP/L*

 (ii) $\Delta L / \Delta TPP$

 (iii) $\Delta TPP / \Delta L$

 (iv) $\Delta L / TPP$

(a) Which is the formula for the marginal physical product (*MPP*) of labour? *(i)/(ii)/(iii)/(iv)*

(b) Which is the formula for the average physical product (*APP*) of labour? *(i)/(ii)/(iii)/(iv)*

Q7. Referring back to Table 5.1, fill in the figures for *APP* and *MPP* in columns (3) and (4) respectively. (Note that the figures for *MPP* are entered between the lines. The reason is that the marginal physical product is the extra output gained from *moving* from one level of input to one more unit of input.)

Q8. Draw the *APP* and *MPP* curves on Figure 5.2.

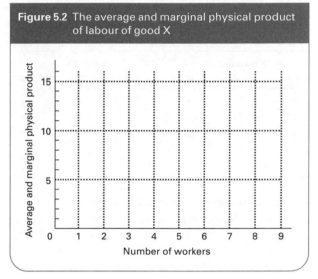

Figure 5.2 The average and marginal physical product of labour of good X

Q9. Why does the marginal product curve pass through the top of the average physical product curve?

....

....

Q10. The total physical product for any given amount of the variable factor is the sum of all the marginal physical products up to that point. *True/False*

Q11. Assume that the following two pieces of information are obtained from a production function for good X. (1) 1000 units of good X can be produced with a combination of 20 units of input A, 30 units of input B and 40 units of input C. (2) 1005 units of good X can be produced with 20 units of input A, 30 units of input B and 41 units of input C. From these two pieces of information it can be deduced that at this point on the production function:

A. the *MPP* of good X is 5 units.

B. the *MPP* of input C is 5 units.

C. the *MPP* of good X is 1005/1000 units.

D. the *MPP* of input C is 1005/40 units.

E. the *MPP* of input C is 1005/41 units.

5.2 Background to costs: the long-run theory of production

(Pages 126–9) In the long run, all factors become variable. Given time, more capital equipment can be installed, new techniques of production can be used, additional land can be acquired and another factory can be built.

If a doubling of inputs leads to a more than doubling of output, the firm is said to experience **Q12.** *decreasing returns to scale/increasing returns to the variable factor/increasing returns to scale.*

⊖ **Q13.** Assume that a firm uses just two factors of production. Table 5.2 shows what happens to output as the firm increases one or both of these inputs.

Table 5.2 The effects of increasing the amounts of both inputs

Situation (i)			Situation (ii)		
Input 1	Input 2	Output	Input 1	Input 2	Output
1	1	12	1	2	14
2	2	24	2	2	24
3	3	36	3	2	32
4	4	48	4	2	38
5	5	60	5	2	42

(a) Which situation represents the long run?   *(i)/(ii)*

(b) Does the firm experience increasing returns to scale?

Yes/No

Explain ....

(c) Are the figures consistent with the law of diminishing marginal returns?   *Yes/No*

Explain ....

If a firm experiences increasing returns to scale, it is also likely to experience *economies of scale*.

▤ **Q14.** Economies of scale can be defined as:

A. large-scale production leading to bigger profits.

B. large-scale production leading to lower costs per unit of production.

C. large-scale production leading to greater marginal productivity of factors.

D. large-scale production leading to greater output per unit of input.

E. large-scale production leading to a better organisation of the factors of production.

♟ **Q15.** The following is a list of various types of economy of scale:

(i) The firm can benefit from the specialisation and division of labour.

(ii) It can overcome the problem of indivisibilities.

(iii) It can obtain inputs at a lower price.

(iv) Large containers/machines have a greater capacity relative to their surface area.

(v) The firm may be able to obtain finance at lower cost.

(vi) It becomes economical to sell by-products.

(vii) Production can take place in integrated plants.

(viii) Risks can be spread with a larger number of products or plants.

Match each of the following examples for a particular firm to one of these types of economy of scale.

(a) Delivery vans can carry full loads to single destinations.

....

(b) It can more easily make a public issue of shares.

....

(c) It can diversify into other markets.

....

(d) Workers spend less time having to train for a wide variety of different tasks, and less time moving from task to task.

....

(e) It negotiates bulk discount with a supplier of raw materials.

....

(f) It uses large warehouses to store its raw materials and finished goods.

....

(g) A clothing manufacturer does a deal to supply a soft toy manufacturer with offcuts for stuffing toys.

....

(h) Conveyor belts transfer the product through several stages of the manufacturing process.

....

♟ **Q16.** Referring to the list (i)–(viii) of economies of scale in Q15, which arise from increasing (physical) returns to scale?

....

◖ **Q17.** Which of the following are *internal* and which are *external* economies of scale for firm A?

(a) Firm A benefits from a pool of trained labour in the area. *Internal/External*

(b) Firm A benefits from lower administration costs per unit as a result of opening a second factory. *Internal/External*

(c) Firm A is able to sell by-products to other firms. *Internal/External*

(d) Firm A benefits from research and development conducted by other firms in the industry. *Internal/External*

(e) Other firms benefit from firm A's discovery of a new technique of mass production. *Internal/External*

(Pages 129–30) Given that all factors of production are variable in the long run, a firm will want to choose the least-cost combination of inputs for any given level of output.

Q18. Assuming that a firm uses three factors A, B and C, whose prices are respectively, P_A, P_B and P_C, which of the following represents the least-cost combination of these factors?

A. $P_A = P_B = P_C$

B. $MPP_A = MPP_B = MPP_C$

C. $MPP_A \times P_A = MPP_B \times P_B = MPP_C \times P_C$

D. $MPP_A/MPP_B = MPP_B/MPP_C = MPP_C/MPP_A$

E. $MPP_A/P_A = MPP_B/P_B = MPP_C/P_C$

Q19. Table 5.3 gives details of the output of good X obtained from different combinations of the three factors A, B and C.

Table 5.3 Output of good X from various factor combinations

Quantity of input A	Quantity of input B	Quantity of input C	Output of X
100	50	30	1000
100	50	31	1005
100	51	30	1010
101	50	30	1003

Assume that the price of factor A is £6. What must the prices of factors B and C be if the least-cost factor combination to produce 1000 units of X is the one shown in the top row of Table 5.3?

Price of B ....

Price of C ....

(Pages 130–3) The least-cost combination of factors to produce various levels of output can be shown graphically by drawing isoquants and isocosts. This analysis assumes that there are just two factors.

*Q20. Table 5.4 shows the output of good X obtained from different inputs of factors A and B.

Table 5.4 Various factor combinations to produce different levels of output of good X

100 units of X	70A, 1B; 52A, 3B; 40A, 8B; 31A, 15B; 22A, 25B; 17A, 33B; 14A, 40B; 10A, 50B; 4A, 70B
200 units of X	70A, 3B; 58A, 5B; 45A, 10B; 33A, 20B; 26A, 30B; 18A, 45B; 10A, 63B; 5A, 80B
300 units of X	70A, 7B; 55A, 11B; 46A, 16B; 40A, 20B; 32A, 30B; 26A, 40B; 21A, 50B; 13A, 70B; 8A, 86B
400 units of X	70A, 11B; 58A, 15B; 50A, 19B; 39A, 28B; 32A, 38B; 26A, 50B; 20A, 63B; 12A, 83B

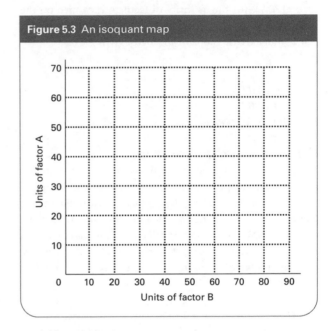

Figure 5.3 An isoquant map

(a) Draw the 100, 200, 300 and 400 unit isoquants on Figure 5.3.

(b) If factor A and factor B both cost £200 each, what is the least-cost combination of A and B to produce 300 units of good X? (You will need to draw the appropriate isocost.)

....

(c) How much will this cost the firm? ....

(d) Suppose now that the price of factor B rises to £300 but that the firm's total cost remains the same as in (b). What is the maximum output the firm can now produce for this cost?

....

(e) How many units of A and B will it now use?

....

At the point where an isocost is tangential to an isoquant, the firm is producing the highest possible output for a given cost and at the lowest possible cost for a given output.

Q21. With the quantity of factor A measured on the vertical axis and the quantity of factor B measured on the horizontal axis, the slope of an isoquant gives (for that output):
A. P_A/P_B
B. P_B/P_A
C. MPP_A/MPP_B
D. MPP_B/MPP_A
E. $MPP_A/P_A = MPP_B/P_B$

Q22. With the quantity of factor A measured on the vertical axis and the quantity of factor B measured on the horizontal axis, the slope of an isocost gives:
A. P_A/P_B
B. P_B/P_A
C. MPP_A/MPP_B
D. MPP_B/MPP_A
E. $MPP_A/P_A = MPP_B/P_B$

5.3 Costs in the short run

(Pages 134–5) We now examine how a firm's costs are related to its output. When measuring cost we should be careful to use the concept of *opportunity* cost. In the case of factors not already owned by the firm, the opportunity cost is simply **Q23.** *the implicit/explicit* cost of purchasing or hiring them. In the case of factors that *are* already owned by the firm, we have to impute an opportunity cost when they are used.

Q24. Assume that a firm already owns a machine that has a total life of 10 years. The cost of using the machine for one year to produce good X is:
A. a tenth of what the firm paid for the machine in the first place.
B. a tenth of what it would cost to replace the machine.
C. the value of one year's output of X.
D. the scrap value of the machine at the end of its life.
E. the maximum the machine could have earned for the firm in some alternative use during the year in question.

Q25. The opportunity cost of using a factor owned by the firm that has no other use and whose second-hand or scrap value is not affected by its use is zero.   *True/False*

(Page 135) In the short run, by definition, at least one factor is fixed in supply. The total cost to the firm of these factors is thus fixed with respect to **Q26.** *time/the firm's output.*

Q27. Which of the following are likely to be fixed costs and which variable costs for a chocolate factory over the course of a month?

(a) The cost of cocoa.   *Fixed/Variable*
(b) Business rates (local taxes).   *Fixed/Variable*
(c) An advertising campaign for a new chocolate bar.
                                                                          Fixed/Variable
(d) The cost of electricity (paid quarterly) for running the mixing machines.   *Fixed/Variable*
(e) Overtime pay.   *Fixed/Variable*
(f) The basic minimum wage agreed with the union (workers must be given at least one month's notice if they are to be laid off).   *Fixed/Variable*
(g) Wear and tear on wrapping machines.   *Fixed/Variable*
(h) Depreciation of machines due simply to their age.
                                                                          Fixed/Variable
(i) Interest on a mortgage for the factory: the rate of interest rises over the course of the month.   *Fixed/Variable*

(Pages 136–9) We use a number of different measures of cost: fixed and variable; and average and marginal.

Q28. Which of the measures of cost – total fixed cost (*TFC*), total variable cost (*TVC*), total cost (*TC*), average fixed cost (*AFC*), average variable cost (*AVC*), average (total) cost (*AC*), marginal cost (*MC*) – are described by each of the following?

(a) TC/Q ....

(b) $AC - AFC$ ....

(c) $\Delta TC/\Delta Q$ ....

(d) $\Delta TVC/\Delta Q$ ....

(e) $(TC - TVC) \div Q$ ....

(f) $(AFC + AVC) \times Q$ ....

(g) ΣMC ....

(h) $\Sigma MC + TFC$ ....
(Note: Σ means 'the sum of'.)

Q29. Table 5.5 gives the short-run costs for an imaginary firm.
(a) Fill in the figures for each of the columns.
(b) At what output do diminishing marginal returns set in (assuming constant factor prices)?

....

(c) Draw *TFC*, *TVC* and *TC* on Figure 5.4. Mark the point on the *TVC* curve where (i) *MC* is at a minimum, (ii) *AVC* is at a minimum.
(d) Draw *AFC*, *AVC*, *AC* and *MC* on Figure 5.5. Be careful to plot the *MC* figures mid-way between the figures for quantity (i.e. at 0.5, 1.5, 2.5, etc.).

Table 5.5 Short-run costs for firm X

Output	TFC	TVC	TC	AFC	AVC	AC	MC
0	.	.	.				
1	.	8	.	10.0	.	.	
2	.	12	.	.	.	.	4
3	10	.	25	.	.	.	.
4	.	.	27	.	.	.	.
5	.	.	.	.	4.0	.	.
6	.	.	.	.	4.0	.	.
7	.	.	.	.	.	.	5
8	.	.	.	.	.	5.75	.
9	.	48	.	.	.	6.44	.
10	.	70	.	.	.	.	.

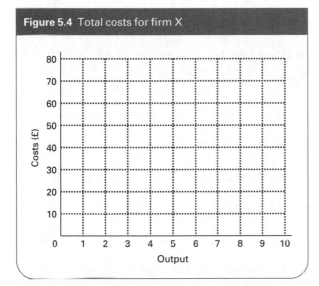

Figure 5.4 Total costs for firm X

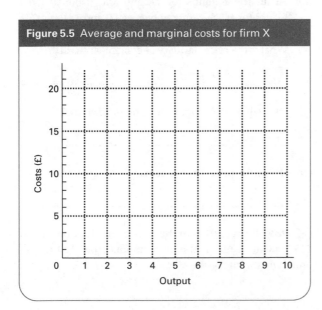

Figure 5.5 Average and marginal costs for firm X

Q30. If the marginal cost is below the average cost, then:

A. the marginal cost must be falling.

B. the marginal cost must be rising.

C. the average cost must be falling.

D. the average cost must be rising.

E. the average cost could be either rising or falling depending on whether the marginal cost is rising or falling.

5.4 Costs in the long run

(Pages 140–4)

Q31. Which of the following assumptions do we make when constructing long-run cost curves? (There may be more than one.)

(a) Factor prices are given. *Yes/No*

(b) The state of technology is given. *Yes/No*

(c) All factors are variable. *Yes/No*

(d) Firms will choose the least-cost factor combination. *Yes/No*

(e) The firm experiences economies of scale. *Yes/No*

(f) There are no fixed factors of production. *Yes/No*

(g) The MPP/P ratios for all factors are equal. *Yes/No*

Q32. Assume that a firm experiences economies of scale up to a certain level of output, then constant (average) costs, and then diseconomies of scale. Sketch its long-run average and marginal cost curves on Figure 5.6.

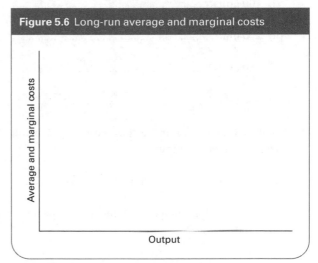

Figure 5.6 Long-run average and marginal costs

Q33. The long-run average cost curve will be tangential with the bottom points of the short-run average cost curves. *True/False*

Q34. If a firm is achieving maximum economies of scale then its $LRAC = SRAC = LRMC = SRMC$. *True/False*

*Q35. Figure 5.7 shows a (weekly) isoquant map for a firm which uses two factors of production, labour (L) and capital (K), to produce good X. The optimum factor

Figure 5.7 A firm's isoquant map for good X

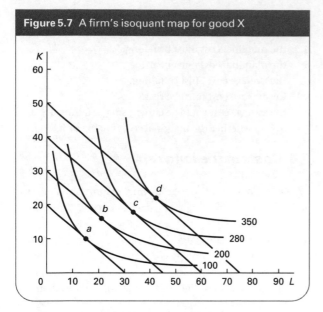

Table 5.6 The demand curve for the product of firm T

Price (Average revenue) (£)	Quantity (units)	Total revenue (£)	Marginal revenue (£)
20	0	.	
18	1	.	.
16	2	.	.
14	3	.	.
12	4	.	.
10	5	.	.
8	6	.	.
6	7	.	.

(a) What is its total revenue from selling:

   (i) 5 units?...

   (ii) 8 units?..

(b) What shape is its total revenue curve?

....

(c) What will be its marginal revenue from selling:

   (i) the fifth unit? ....

   (ii) the eighth unit? ....

(d) What shape is its marginal revenue curve?

....

Now assume that firm T faces a downward-sloping (straight-line) demand curve. This is shown in Table 5.6.

(e) Fill in the columns for *TR* and *MR*. (Note that the figures for *MR* are entered between 0 and 1, 1 and 2, 2 and 3, etc.)

(f) What is the price elasticity of demand at $P = £10$?

....

(g) Over what price range is demand price elastic?

....

(h) Over what price range is demand price inelastic?

....

combinations to produce four levels of output are shown by points *a*, *b*, *c* and *d*. These represent the following factor combinations: $a = 10K, 15L$; $b = 16K, 21L$; $c = 18K, 33L$; $d = 22K, 42L$. The cost of capital is £240 per unit per week. The cost of labour (the wage rate) is £160 per week.

(a) What is the (minimum) total cost of producing:

   (i) 100 units?...

   (ii) 200 units?..

   (iii) 280 units?...

   (iv) 350 units?...

(b) What is the (minimum) average cost of producing these four levels of output?

   (i) ...., (ii) ...., (iii) ...., (iv) ....

(c) Over what output range does the firm experience economies of scale?

....

5.5 Revenue

(Pages 145–8) Remember we said that profit equals revenue minus cost. We have looked at costs. We now turn to revenue.

Let us assume that firm S is a price taker. In other words it faces a **Q36.** *downward-sloping/horizontal* **Q37.** *demand curve/supply curve.*

⊗ **Q38.** Let us assume that it faces a market price of £2 per unit for its product.

⊗ **Q39.** If a reduction in the price of good X from £20 to £15 leads to a rise in the amount sold from 100 to 130 units, what would be the *MR*?

....

Q40. A wine merchant will supply bottles of Champagne to a wedding at £10 per bottle, but is willing to offer a 10 per cent discount on the total bill if 50 bottles or more are purchased. What would be the firm's marginal revenue for the 50th bottle?

A. £450

B. £9

C. £1

D. –£40

E. –£45

5.6 Profit maximisation

(Pages 148–9) There are two methods of showing the profit-maximising position for a firm. The first uses total revenue and total cost curves.

Q41. Figure 5.8 shows the total cost and revenue curves for a firm on the same diagram.

(a) At what output is the firm's profit maximised?

....

(b) How much profit is made at this output? ....

(c) Draw the *TΠ* curve over the range of output where positive profit is made.

(d) How much is total fixed cost? ....

(e) At what output is the price elasticity of demand equal to –1?

....

(f) At what outputs does the firm break even? ....

(Pages 149–52) The second method of showing the profit-maximising position is to use *AR*, *MR*, *AC* and *MC* curves.

Figure 5.8 A firm's total cost and total revenue

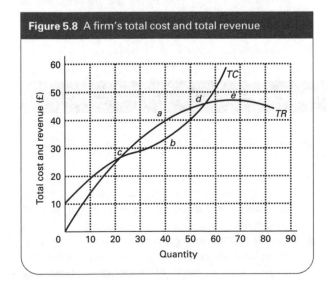

Table 5.7 Costs and revenues for the production of good X

Quantity (units)	Average costs (£)	Marginal costs (£)	Average revenue (£)	Marginal revenue (£)
100	4.80	1.40	3.20	3.20
200	3.60	0.80	3.20	3.20
300	2.90	0.85	3.20	3.20
400	2.45	1.30	3.20	3.20
500	2.30	2.30	3.20	3.20
600	2.55	4.00	3.20	3.20
700	3.05	6.30	3.20	3.20
800	3.80	(above 7.00)	3.20	3.20
900	5.10	(above 7.00)	3.20	3.20

Figure 5.9 Average and marginal costs and revenues for the production of good X

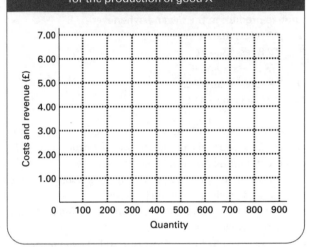

Q42. Table 5.7 gives a firm's average and marginal cost and revenue schedules for the production of good X.

(a) Draw the *AC*, *MC*, *AR* and *MR* curves on Figure 5.9.

(b) Explain the shape of the *AR* curve ....

(c) At what output is profit maximised? ....

(d) How much is average cost at this output?

....

(e) How much is average profit at this output?

....

(f) Shade in the area representing maximum total profit in Figure 5.9.

(g) How much is the maximum total profit? ....

(h) What is the lowest price the firm could receive if it were not to make a loss?

....

Q43. If at the current level of output a firm's price exceeds its marginal revenue and its marginal revenue exceeds its marginal cost, then to maximise profits it should:

A. reduce price and output.
B. raise price and output.
C. reduce price and raise output.
D. keep price the same and reduce output.
E. keep price the same and increase output.

Q44. The optimum point for a profit-maximising firm to produce will be at the bottom of the *AC* curve.   *True/False*

Q45. A firm will always maximise profits by charging a price equal to both marginal cost and marginal revenue.
                                                                True/False

Q46. A firm will choose to shut down rather than continue to produce in the *short run* whenever:

A. *AR* is less than *AC*.
B. *TR* is less than *TC*.
C. *MR* is less than *MC*.
D. *TR* is less than *TFC*.
E. *AR* is less than *AVC*.

Q47. Figure 5.10 shows a firm's cost and revenue curves. It is currently producing at an output of *OX*. In order to maximise profits it should:

A. continue to produce at *OX* in the short run and expand production in the long run.
B. continue to produce at *OX* in the short run and close down in the long run.
C. reduce output in the short run and expand output in the long run.
D. reduce output in the short run and close down in the long run.
E. close down straight away.

*Q48. A firm faces the following total cost and total revenue schedules:

$TC = 100 - 20Q + 3Q^2$
$TR = 60Q - 2Q^2$

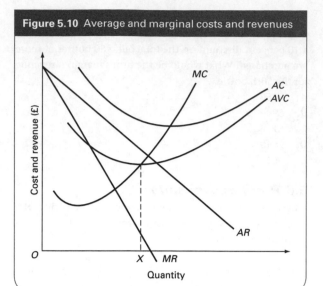

Figure 5.10 Average and marginal costs and revenues

(a) What is the equation for average cost? ....

(b) What is the equation for marginal cost? ....

(c) What is the equation for average revenue? ....

(d) What is the equation for marginal revenue? ....

(e) At what output is profit maximised? ....

(f) What is average profit at this output? ....

(g) How much is total profit at this output?......................

(h) What is the equation for total profit? ....

(i) Using this equation, find the output at which profit is maximised (thereby confirming the answer given in (e) above).

....

 PROBLEMS, EXERCISES AND PROJECTS

Q49. Table 5.8 shows the short-run total cost curves of three alternative plants producing luxury cars. The three plants are of different sizes: one small, one medium and one large.

(a) Calculate the (short-run) average cost for each level of output given in the table for each of the three plants.
(b) Plot the (short-run) *AC* curve for each of the three plants (on the same diagram).
(c) From these three short-run *AC* curves sketch the long-run *AC* curve.

(d) Are there increasing, decreasing or constant returns to scale?
(e) Assuming that a firm could choose with what size plants to operate in the long run, which of the three size plants would it choose to produce an output of 10 cars per day?
(f) Assume that a firm is producing 10 cars per day with the optimum-sized plant, and now wishes to increase output to 30 cars per day in response to a temporary

Table 5.8 Costs of car production

Output (daily)	TC small plant (£000)	TC medium plant (£000)	TC large plant (£000)
0	35	70	90
5	90	120	200
10	140	170	300
15	180	195	345
20	220	210	360
25	300	225	375
30	420	255	405
35	595	315	455
40	880	400	540
45	1260	585	675
50	1900	950	900
55	2750	1430	1265
60	3900	2400	1800

increase in demand. What will its average cost of production now be?

(g) Now assume that the rise in demand to 30 cars per day is perceived by the firm to be a permanent increase. After its long-run adjustment, what will its average cost be now?

(h) Now assume that demand increases to 45 cars per day in the long run. Would the firm alter its plant size? Would it alter its plant size if output increased to 50 cars per day? Explain.

Q50. Table 5.9 gives details of a firm's total costs and total revenue.

(a) Fill in the columns for *AR*, *MR*, *AC* and *MC* – but ignore columns for AR_1, TR_1 and MR_1 until you get to (e) below. Remember that *MC* and *MR* are the extra cost and revenue of producing *one* more unit (not ten).

(b) At what output and price is profit maximised?

(c) How much is total profit at this output?

Table 5.9 Costs and revenue for firm X

Q	AR	(AR₁)	TR	(TR₁)	MR	(MR₁)	TC	AC	MC
0	30	–	0	–			300	–	
					...	–			...
10	...	–	280	–			350	...	
					...	...			...
20	...	...	520	...			380	...	
					...	...			...
30	...	...	720	...			420	...	
					...	...			...
40	...	...	880	...			480	...	
					...	...			...
50	...	...	1000	...			600	...	
					...	...			...
60	...	...	1080	...			780	...	
					...	...			...
70	...	...	1120	...			980	...	
					...	...			...
80	...	...	1120	...			1280	...	
					...	...			...
90	...	...	1080	...			1710	...	
					...	...			...
100	...	...	1000	...			2300	...	

(d) Assume that total fixed cost rises by £200. What effect will this have on the profits maximising price and output?

(e) What effect will it have on profit?

(f) Now assume that *TFC* returns to its original level and that demand increases by 20 units at each price. Fill in the columns for AR_1, TR_1, and MR_1. (Do not fill in the spaces with a dash.)

(g) What will be the new profit-maximising price and output? (Note: It may help if you draw the *AR*, *MR*, *AC* and *MC* curves on graph paper and then show the effects of shifting the *AR* and *MR* curves.)

The remaining parts of the question continue with the assumption that demand has increased by 20 units at each price.

(h) Now let us assume that the government imposes a *lump-sum* tax of £100 on producers (i.e. a total tax that does not vary with output). What will be the profit-maximising price and output now?

(i) Now assume instead that the government imposes a *specific* tax of £12 per unit. What will be the profit-maximising price and output now? (See if you can spot the answer from the table without entering new cost columns.)

Q51. Should your educational establishment take on more students? The answer given to this question by the administrators of many universities, colleges and schools in the early 1990s was a resounding 'Yes', as they have avidly competed for students. At the same time the amount of resources they had available per student declined: and yet many of the administrators claimed that the quality of education that students received did not decline and some claimed that it even increased. The arguments they used have partly to do with the marginal cost per student being lower than the average cost and the possibility of achieving economies of scale.

Many of the academic and administrative staff, on the other hand, claimed that it was only their harder work that prevented a decline in standards and that a further reduction in moneys earned per student would lead to an inevitable erosion of the service they could provide for students.

Assess these arguments in the context of your own establishment, and in particular consider the following:

(a) What are the fixed and what are the variable costs associated with your particular course? Would the marginal cost be significantly different from the average cost? How will the answer differ in the short run and the long run?

(b) Are there any significant economies of scale associated with (i) courses with large numbers of students; (ii) large educational establishments?

(c) Should your establishment take on extra students at present?

(d) Should there be an expansion of some courses relative to others?

(e) If there were a further decline in the 'unit of resource' (i.e. the money earned per student), should your establishment take on more or fewer students?

(f) Should inefficient educational establishments close down?

Try interviewing teaching staff and administrative staff to help you answer these questions. Explain any differences in the replies they give.

DISCUSSION TOPICS AND ESSAYS

Q52. Imagine that you are a small business person employing five people, and are pleased to find that business is expanding. As a result you take on extra labour: a sixth worker this month, a seventh next month and an eighth the month after. The seventh worker discovers that when she is taken on, output increases more than when either the sixth or eighth worker was taken on. Not surprisingly, she claims that she is a more efficient worker than her colleagues. Do the facts necessarily support her case?

*Q53. Use isoquant analysis to illustrate the effect on the factor proportions used by a firm of the granting of an employment subsidy (per worker) to the firm.

Q54. Why are historical costs a poor basis for making production decisions?

Q55. A firm observes that both its short-run and its long-run average cost curves are ⌣ shaped. Explain why the reasons for this are quite different in the two cases.

Q56. A local trader complains to a disgruntled customer, 'I've had to put up my prices to cover the higher uniform business rate (local tax) I am being charged.' How might an economist advise this trader?

Q57. Would there ever be any point in a firm attempting to continue in production if it could not cover its long-run average (total) costs?

Q58. The price of pocket calculators fell significantly in the years after they were first introduced and at the same time demand for them increased substantially. Use cost and revenue diagrams to illustrate these events.

Q59. Debate

It is better to have manufacturing concentrated in just a few large plants in each industry and in just a few parts of the country. That way production will take place at minimum costs.

ARTICLES

As the general level of inflation has fallen, and consumers have become more sensitive to price rises, businesses have had to look at exerting greater control over costs in order to improve their profitability. The article below, taken from *Management Today* of October 1995, assesses the recent success of many UK companies in achieving this goal, and considers the problems they are likely to experience in attempting to squeeze costs further.

Charles Miller Smith, chief executive of ICI, recently announced plans to seek out and implement cost savings within the chemicals giant of £400 million a year. These efficiency improvements were not to be achieved through job cuts or plant closures but, said Smith, 'by improving operational performance in areas like purchasing, supply chain management and manufacturing excellence'.

Nothing unusual in this you may think; companies are constantly trying to achieve efficiency gains and, indeed, would soon fall by the wayside if they did not. But Smith was quite explicit about the reasons behind the cost-saving drive: ICI had been achieving too low a rate of return on its assets (15 per cent against a target of 20 per cent), and there was little prospect of lifting that rate through higher prices.

Indeed, the outlook for the bulk chemicals market, in the light of some softening of world industrial demand, was for weaker prices, and there was little that ICI, even as a major player, could do about it. The ICI task, therefore, has to be to approach the problem from the other side, by benchmarking itself against the best competitors in each of its businesses and achieving efficiency levels on a par with, or better than its rivals. Only thus could the rate of return be lifted to achieve the company's targets.

The chemicals business, sensitive as it is to global economic trends and unable to do much about them, might be considered a special case. But is it? Consider Merrydown, the drinks group, famous for its ciders. Although operating on a much smaller scale, its problems are identical to those of ICI. According to Richard Purdey, Merrydown's chairman, the cider price war that the company has been caught up in is a 'vicious' one which shows no sign of easing. Post-duty cider prices have retreated to their levels of 10 years ago and, in spite of cost cuts amounting to £1.5 million in the financial year which ended on 31 March, Merrydown still made a pre-tax loss of £2.7 million. And, in the absence of any indications that the pressure on prices may be easing, cost cutting seems to be the only way forward.

No business needs to be reminded that it is tough out there. But these examples from opposite ends of the industrial spectrum are symptomatic of a wider generality. We are, it seems, in an environment where it is only possible to make money by constantly pruning, cost-cutting and introducing far-reaching efficiency savings. Even then, if the competitive environment is tough enough, such measures may not be enough. The days of easy profits, often floating on a tide of rising inflation, are long gone. Making money has become a grinding process.

At the heart of it lies an old business truism – that the customer is king. And not only is the modern-day customer positively regal, but he or she is more price-sensitive than at any time in recent corporate history.

Businesses find themselves in an uncomfortable, piggy-in-the-middle situation. Powerless to exert control over their raw material costs, which themselves often reflect macroeconomic factors such as the pound's performance on the foreign exchanges, they are also unable to pass these higher costs on.

The CBI has been monitoring trends in industrial costs and prices for 40 years. Earlier this year, its reports caused mild alarm at the Treasury and the Bank of England. Industry's costs were rising, it said, and in time-honoured way these rising costs would be passed on to customers in the form of higher prices. It was a semi-official inflation alert. But then a curious thing happened. Industry's costs, both for raw materials and labour, continued to climb. In fact, in its latest quarterly survey they showed their strongest rise for four-and-a-half years. At that time inflation was in double figures. Firms, however, which had earlier been gung-ho about their ability to pass these cost increases on to customers, were now much more cautious. Price expectations eased back, as managers accepted that they would not be able to force through higher prices, and the Chancellor of the Exchequer was able to breathe a sigh of relief. Managers, of course, were left with the task of rebuilding margins in some other way, most probably by following the ICI/Merrydown cost-saving route.

'The squeeze on margins is likely to continue,' says Andrew Buxton, chairman of Barclays and head of the CBI's economic situation committee. 'Prices are rising more slowly even though cost pressures due to higher raw material prices have continued to mount. Competition is fierce in both home and overseas markets.'

Sudhir Junankar, the CBI economist whose task it is to condense the raw information from industry and turn it into the organisation's industrial trends surveys, notices several forces at work. 'In general, the closer you are to the consumer market, the more difficult it is to raise prices,' he says. 'But the pressure on margins does not begin and end with retailers. They, in turn, are putting the squeeze on their suppliers, and the effect is felt right back along the supply chain.' He also maintains that the pressure is more intense than at the comparable stage in earlier cycles, but then so too is the response of companies. 'Cost-cutting and cost-control has become a continuous process, a way of life,' he says. 'But firms have become better at it. By responding to the toughness of the pricing environment, companies have managed to improve their profitability in difficult conditions.'

But why is it so hard to force through price increases now, and is this the permanent situation facing industry? David Buck of the Chartered Institute of Purchasing and Supply (CIPS), which like the CBI has been reporting a squeeze on margins for virtually the entire period of Britain's post-1992 industrial upturn, says there is no doubt that there has been a fundamental change in behaviour. 'The '80s were different, and in many ways a lot easier,' he says. 'The '90s are all about being lean, mean and ready to rationalise. The interesting question is whether it was the 1980s that was the exceptional decade and we have merely returned to normality.'

On a practical level, Buck detects a growing awareness among buyers about what products and services should cost, and an unwillingness to accept higher prices. 'Buyers are much more knowledgeable and aware,' he says. 'They know, more than ever, what is going on in the marketplace, usually as much as the suppliers themselves, and they are highly resistant to higher prices.'

A large part of the explanation for this, of course, rests with the fact that inflation generally has been consist-ently lower than at any time in the past 30 years. Even in the 1980s, a decade in which the Thatcher Government was given credit for bringing inflation to heel, the annual increase in prices averaged 8 per cent. During this recovery, in contrast, inflation has averaged between 2 per cent and 3 per cent, a huge difference. The result is that buyers, their own incomes and budgets constrained, are unwilling to accept higher prices without challenge. The phenomenon known by economists as the 'money illusion', whereby real price changes can be achieved under the camouflage of a general rise in the price level, has been dealt a decisive blow. The Government, having set out to eradicate the mentality of the annual pay round, may also have succeeded in eliminating the annual, or twice-yearly, uprating of list prices.

'We are in a different, and difficult, environment as regards inflation,' says Doug McWilliams of the Centre for Economics and Business Research (CEBR). 'That means a lower average rate of inflation or, for many firms, no increase at all in their final prices. The result of this is a process which starts in the consumer market and is working its way right back to raw materials, and it is more obvious in Britain than elsewhere. The problem is that firms are often in no position to influence their raw material prices – there has been a shift in the terms of trade in favour of primary commodity producers. In this environment, firms either have to reduce the cost of labour or increase its productivity.'

The other side of this, suggests Buck, is that firms could be storing up problems for the future. 'Cost-saving is of course essential, but I sometimes wonder whether industry is becoming a little too anorexic,' he says. 'Companies are restructuring and rationalising so much that they are getting, or will get, skill shortages.'

This danger aside, tight control of labour costs provides part of the answer to a current conundrum. Although the pressure on margins is real, it would be highly misleading to say there has been no recovery in profitability. An analysis by Michael Saunders of Salomon Brothers shows that gross trading profits as a share of national income, having peaked at 18.4 per cent in the late 1980s, slumped to 11.5 per cent at their lowest point in the recession (in the early part of 1992). But by the beginning of this year, the share of profits in gross domestic product had made up most of the lost ground, rising to 16.3 per cent.

Tight control over labour costs, both in staff numbers and in extracting higher output from available personnel, referred to by McWilliams, is one important factor in this. The dog that has yet to bark in the current recovery is a decisive upturn in wage settlements, in spite of a falling official unemployment total. The danger for firms was that the effects of rising raw material costs would be compounded by an upturn in labour costs, a double whammy. This has not happened, allowing firms to breathe a collective sigh of relief and rebuild profitability in a tough competitive environment.

But even this would not have been possible without two other factors identified by the Bank of England in its annual assessment of company profitability and finance, published in August. Although it noted some slippage in company profits in the early months of this year, it too was struck by the general recovery in profitability, measured by the pre-tax rate of return on capital employed, since the recession's low point, against a backdrop of pressure on domestic margins.

The two factors emphasised by the Bank were, firstly, an increase in capital productivity, itself a side-effect of firms' often-criticised unwillingness to boost spending significantly on new plant and machinery. By extracting rising output from their existing capital stock – allowing capacity utilisation to rise – managers are automatically engineering an increase in the rate of return on capital. Eventually, of course, capacity ceilings are reached and the process becomes no longer tenable. However, capacity utilisation has yet to reach the levels of the late 1980s.

The second factor identified by the Bank is that, while domestic margins have been squeezed, export margins rose strongly in the wake of sterling's departure from the European exchange rate mechanism three years ago, and have continued to improve. The rise in export margins has continued this year in response to a further decline for sterling against the D-mark and other European currencies – in the first three months of the year, export prices rose by 7 per cent on the previous quarter, something that few, if any, businesses could have come close to achieving in the domestic market. And, in fact, this rise in overseas margins has been a double blessing. Without it, the pressure on domestic margins would have been sufficient to constrain severely any overall improvement in business profitability. Healthy export margins, which contrast so starkly with the tightly price-constrained domestic environment, have, in addition, persuaded companies to divert resources into export markets, with clear benefits for their profitability and the health of the economy.

This shows up in wide differences between the 'haves' and 'have-nots' when it comes to profit. Sectors with a strong export component will, according to estimates by UBS, all show healthy profit increases this year, with increases of 31 per cent for engineering, 40 per cent for vehicles and components, and 25 per cent for general manufacturing. In contrast, those reliant on the domestic market are struggling, with household goods manufacturers set for a 3 per cent profits decline, distributors down 18 per cent and general retailers 4 per cent.

Not everyone, however, can divert into export markets. And, sooner or later, the prospect of easier profits in overseas markets will end. Sterling cannot decline indefinitely, and many of the price-constraining factors that apply in Britain are present, and becoming more so, overseas.

The solution to making money in price-constrained markets, apart from tough cost controls, has to lie with product and process innovation. It is still clear that even parsimonious consumers and professional buyers are prepared to pay premium prices for new and innovative products. Even for some consumer electronic products, prices have stuck more than would have been expected from previous experience. Think of camcorders, where miniaturisation has kept prices high, or home cinema, which attracts a fat premium over conventional televisions. Even compact discs, which initially attracted huge consumer price-resistance, have in general maintained their prices. As for process innovation, this can open up a whole new range of cost reductions.

Nor is the outlook for margins necessarily bleak, even if price prospects are dull. The CEBR's McWilliams believes that the current pricing environment is here to stay, but he also thinks that industry in Britain, and in Europe generally, is on the brink of a revolution in costs that will allow a sharp increase in profitability, even if prices are constrained. 'The world is moving into a period where the trend will be towards higher profitability rather than lower profitability. Education and skills levels in the newly industrialised countries of the Far East and India are improving sharply, and labour in Britain and Europe will have to respond to survive. Labour costs will fall and what this will produce is an improvement in profitability on something like the scale that we saw in Victorian England.'

He may be right, although an enduring fall in labour costs implies a squeeze on wages that will serve to reinforce the reluctance, and for that matter the ability, of consumers to accept higher prices. One firm's redundancy programme is another's lost sales.

And there is a gloomier way of looking at the present set of circumstances. It is that, in this new era of tightly constrained prices, businesses have survived thanks to three factors: a one-off one – the devaluation of sterling; a temporary one – the tilt in the balance of the labour market in their favour; and an unsustainable one – the eking out of additional production from existing capital stock. As these diminish in importance, making money will become even harder. Nor are there any obvious hiding places; the impetus to grind down prices is as strong in, say, auditing fees and bank charges as it is in manufacturing.

The solution, then, becomes rather more drastic. Areas of business that were viable during a period of generally rising prices are no longer so. Rationalisation becomes a permanent strategy. And the apparent economic nirvana of stable prices is harder and harder to equate with vigorous business expansion.

© *Management Today*, Oct. 95

(a) Why might it be no longer possible for a business to pass its higher costs on as higher prices? Is this a good thing?

(b) What areas does the article identify where cost savings have been made?

(c) Why have companies with large export sales proved to be more profitable than companies which focus on the domestic market?

With modern technology, many manufacturing sectors are undergoing a 'new industrial revolution'. Production methods are being transformed, with the result that production costs are falling and output flexibility is being enhanced. One sector where such a revolution is taking place is the tyre industry. The following article was taken from the *Financial Times* of 11 May 1998 and examines how competition over tyre production technology is driving prices down and quality up.

Production lines are transformed

A technological revolution is gathering pace this year within the world tyre industry.

Unlike the introduction of previous major innovations such as radial or low-profile tyres, it will not be immediately evident to consumers. It is a manufacturing process revolution, and it is transforming the economics of tyre production. Its benefits to the motorist will be better and cheaper products.

For much of its history tyremaking has been a multi-stage and highly labour-intensive business, involving building up the tyre carcass in layers manually on a drum, with each layer of material often cut to length by hand before going off to be encased in its sidewall and tread compounds and then vulcanised.

Now, however, the leading tyre companies are lining up to confirm that they are bringing new technology to the industry which is cutting required labour input, increasing productivity by quantum steps and providing a degree of flexibility of which tyre plant managers would have barely dreamed a decade ago. Where commercially viable production once meant continuous output of thousands of a single size and type of tyre, it is becoming possible to turn a profit on batches as small as a few hundred.

At least as remarkable, the industry has not suddenly found collectively one breakthrough manufacturing process from which they can all benefit. Each has been making its own, closely guarded innovations, with the result that several distinctly different processes are bringing about the transformation. Even after intensive scouring

of patent offices has allowed each to gain inklings of their rivals' processes, the mainly separate development paths have continued.

The leading companies in the industry – and the top six between them control more than 70 per cent of the world tyre market – insist that their innovations will allow them to remain competitive with the strongest rival for the foreseeable future. But the developments bode ill for the dozens of smaller players who lack the financial and technical resources to make their own quantum leaps.

The developments are happening in the wake of the first leaks several years ago that the highly secretive Groupe Michelin had developed a revolutionary process called C3M.

Differing from conventional processes in all stages of production, the heavily computerised system – about which Michelin will still impart no details – requires only half the workforce and one-tenth of the usual production space, with a capital cost said to be less than $15m per 500 000 units of annual capacity. One perceived disadvantage, however, is that it does need new, dedicated facilities.

Several plants have already come on stream in France and the US. The expectation is of a gradual introduction elsewhere in order to minimise the social and employment disruptions implicit in the process.

At the time, the process appeared likely to provide Michelin with daunting competitive advantage – the ability to produce tyres considerably more cheaply than anyone else, and thus enjoy high margins if pricing up to local

market levels, or to use some of the extra available margin to increase market share.

However, Goodyear of the US, once again bent on regaining the world tyre market leadership it lost in the 1980s, has served notice that it is not in the least intimidated by the Michelin system in announcing its own manufacturing technology breakthroughs a few weeks ago.

Indeed, the company's chairman, Samir Gibara, in unveiling Goodyear's 'Impact' production system, has expressed the view – after looking at some of Michelin's patents – that Impact (Integrated Manufacturing Precision Assembly Cellular Technology) will prove superior to C3M. Not least, it can be incorporated into existing plants at lower investment costs than those of Michelin's system. 'It means we can site wherever in the world we like, close to major vehicle producers' plants or even large consumer areas for the aftermarket,' says Goodyear.

Goodyear is also reluctant to reveal in detail the technology of its systems. But key indicators of its effectiveness, says Mr Gibara, are that it improves productivity by 135 per cent, halves the number of manufacturing steps, eliminates the cutting and placing of many materials, reduces direct labour by 35 per cent, cuts materials costs by 15 per cent, halves material inventory levels and reduces energy costs. It is no wonder, perhaps, that in terms of employment such process transformation is likened by some industry analysts to a neutron bomb going off – plant and equipment being undamaged, but the human workforce devastated.

(a) What cost savings are various tyre manufacturers claiming will be realised as a result of the introduction of their new production processes?

(b) Explain the relevance of the concept of 'economies of scale' to the new production technology in tyre manufacturing. Illustrate the impact of the new technology with an appropriate diagram.

(c) What advice might you give a small tyre manufacturer which does not have access to the new technology of the big companies, such as Michelin, as to how it might stay in business, faced with the falling costs of such rivals?

For many products, style is a key component to their success. Two such products are clothing and cars. Both markets exhibit 'fashion price cycles'. However, in recent times, whereas clothing seasonal price variations have become more pronounced, the seasonal pricing variation in the market for cars has diminished. The article below, taken from *The Economist* of 23 December 1995, explores the factors affecting the price of fashion products, and in particular looks at the role of *costs*.

Dedicated followers of fashion

According to standard economic theory, Giorgio Armani, a world-famous Italian fashion designer, runs a simple business. His company combines inputs of labour (seamstresses), capital (dyeing and weaving machines) and raw material (cloth) to make clothes with the best possible trade-off between cost and quality. He then calculates what the demand is for his designs, and estimates how many units he can make without marginal costs exceeding marginal revenues. He sells these at the market-clearing price, and earns just enough profit to compensate him for his investment of time and money.

The flaw of this stylised view is that it ignores the most important thing that designers such as Mr Armani sell: fashion itself. In industries as diverse as clothing, cars and music, the key to making money is to work out (or, better still, invent) what is going to be 'in' by the time a new product comes to market.

At first glance, economists would seem to have little to say about this phenomenon. For example, they have no special means of telling which styles of clothing are fashionable (if you doubt this, take a look at what the next economist you meet is wearing), let alone what is likely to be hip in future. So when fashions wax and wane, people tend to give simplistic explanations: they say that people's tastes have changed, or that they have become more (or less) fashion-conscious.

Can economics offer more revealing insights than these? A recent study by three economists – Peter Pashigian and Eric Gould from the University of Chicago's Graduate School of Business, and Brian Bowen from the Chicago Mercantile Exchange – argues that it can. They start by looking at the pattern of prices for fashion-sensitive goods, which tends to follow well-established cycles. Prices are high at the start of the buying season, they fall gradually as the season progresses, and then they rise again as new styles are introduced for the next period.

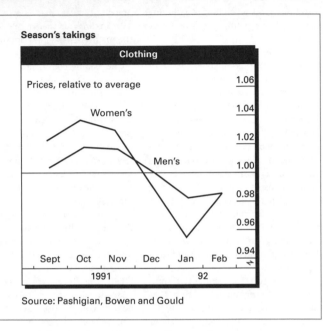

Source: Pashigian, Bowen and Gould

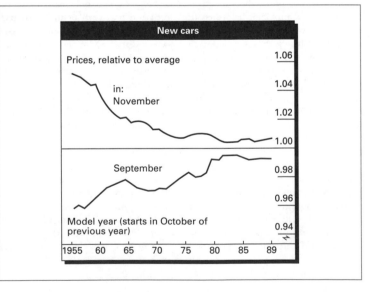

The main reason for this is uncertainty. When producers introduce a new line of, say, cars or dresses, they do not know how successful it will be. To avoid selling it for less than is necessary, they initially set a high price, then lower it for lines that do not sell well. A good way to measure the importance of fashion, therefore, is to look at the variation in seasonal prices. The first chart, for example, compares prices for men's and women's clothing during the autumn–winter season. As you would expect, fashion seems to play a more important role in women's clothing than in men's.

The strength of this pattern, however, can change over time. Over the past few decades, seasonal price variations for women's clothing have become more pronounced. However, prices in the American car market, which also tend to follow a 'fashion' cycle, have displayed the opposite trend. As the second chart shows, prices in November, at the beginning of the new model year, are higher than they are the following September. Since the mid-1950s, however, this seasonal gap has been narrowing steadily.

Explaining this is harder than it looks. It is no use, for example, simply to say that people's tastes are changing. If so, why are people caring more about fashion when buying clothing, but less when choosing cars? Or perhaps rising incomes are what matter? But these should not have opposing effects in the two markets.

Fashion cents

The three economists claim to have solved the puzzle. The answer, they say, is to focus on supply rather than demand. They argue that the different trends for cars and clothes are due less to shifts in the tastes of consumers than to changes in the technology of producers.

Advances in the textile industry, such as the development of sophisticated electronic weaving and knitting machines, have made it cheaper for designers to revamp their lines each season. But in the car industry, say the authors, it has become more costly to make radical style changes every year. Although new technology has made it easier to change the size and shape of a car's body, they show that the cost of doing so as a share of the total production costs has actually risen.

As a result, they say, most car makers have been forced to make more modest changes each year. They have focused on those that improve a car's quality, such as better engines and new gadgets, rather than its look.

© *The Economist*, London (23rd December, 1995)

(a) Why might it be very difficult to estimate the likely demand for a given fashion product? Why might Armani have fewer problems in setting price than, say, a common high-street retailer?

(b) If consumers are aware that unsuccessful lines of clothing will fall in price as the season progresses, why do they buy when prices are set high at the start of the season? What does this tell us about the shape of the demand curve for a given fashion product (i) at the start, and (ii) at the end of the season?

(c) How might we account for the differing fashion price cycles of clothing and new cars?

(d) What has happened to fixed costs as a proportion of total costs in the production of cars? How has this affected car design strategy?

 E ### ANSWERS

Q1. $(6 \times 10) + (3 \times 4) = 72$ units of output.

Q2. C. The actual length of time of the short run will vary from industry to industry depending on how long it takes to vary the amount used of all factors.

Q3. *when one or more factors are held constant, then, as the variable factor is increased, there will come a point when additional units of the variable factor will produce less extra output than previous units.*

Q4. *(a)* See Figure A5.1.

(b) Diminishing returns set in beyond point *a* (beyond 2 workers): i.e. the *TPP* curve rises less rapidly after point *a*.

Q5. *the amount of extra output gained from the use of one more unit of the variable factor.*

Q6. *(a)* (iii) Thus if an extra two workers were taken on $(\Delta L = 2)$ and between them they produced an extra 100 units of output per period of time $(\Delta TPP = 100)$, then the extra output from *one* more unit of the variable factor (i.e. labour) would be $100/2 = 50$.

(b) (i) Thus if 200 workers are employed $(L = 200)$ and between them they produce a total

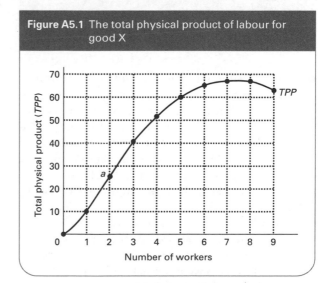

Figure A5.1 The total physical product of labour for good X

output of 30 000 units per period of time $(TPP = 30\,000)$, the average output per worker would be $30\,000/200 = 150$.

Q7. See table below.

(1) Number of workers	(2) TPP	(3) APP	(4) MPP
0	0	—	
			10
1	10	10	
			16
2	26	13	
			15
3	41	13.67	
			11
4	52	13	
			8
5	60	12	
			5
6	65	10.83	
			2
7	67	9.57	
			0
8	67	8.38	
			−4
9	63	7	

Q8. See Figure A5.2.

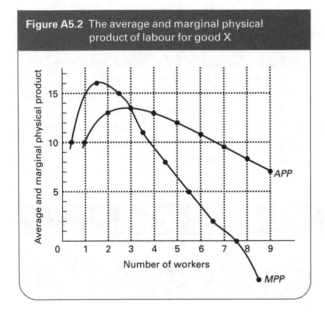

Figure A5.2 The average and marginal physical product of labour for good X

Q9. To the left of this point the *MPP* is above the *APP*. Thus extra workers are producing more than the average. They have the effect of pulling the average up. The *APP* curve must therefore be rising. To the right of this point the *MPP* is below the *APP*. Extra workers produce less than the average and thus pull the average down. The *APP* must be falling.

Q10. *True.* (Try adding the figures in the *MPP* column in Q7.)

Q11. B. $MPP = \Delta TPP/\Delta F = (1005 - 1000)/(41 - 40) = 5$.

Q12. *Increasing returns to scale.* Notice the terminology here. The 'to scale' refers to the fact that *all* the factors have increased in the same proportion: that the whole scale of the operation has increased.

Q13. *(a)* Situation *(i)*: both factors are being varied.

(b) *No.* Output increases proportionately. A doubling of inputs leads to a doubling of output. The firm is experiencing *constant returns to scale*.

(c) *Yes.* The marginal physical product of input 1 diminishes. In other words, when input 2 is held constant, each additional unit of input 1 produces less and less additional output (10, 8, 6, 4).

Q14. B. Economies of scale are defined as lower *costs* per unit of output as the scale of production increases. These lower costs will probably be in part due to increasing returns to scale (answer D), but they may also be the result of lower input prices that large firms can negotiate.

Q15. (a) (ii); (b) (v); (c) (viii); (d) (i); (e) (iii); (f) (iv); (g) (vi); (h) (vii).

Q16. (i), (ii), (iv), (vii).

Q17. External economies of scale occur when a firm experiences lower costs as a result of the *industry* being large. Thus (a) and (d) are external economies of scale for firm A, whereas (b), (c) and (e) are internal economies of scale. Note that (e) is an external economy of scale for *other* firms, but not for firm A.

Q18. E. If the *MPP/P* ratio for any factor were greater than that for another, costs would be reduced by using more of the first factor relative to the second. But as this happened, diminishing marginal returns to the first factor would cause its *MPP* to fall (and the *MPP* of the second to rise) until their *MPP/P* ratios became equal. At that point there would be no further savings possible by substituting one factor for another.

Q19. The *MPP* of A is 3 (i.e. output rises from 1000 to 1003 when one more unit of A is used); the *MPP* of B is 10; the *MPP* of C is 5. If the price of A is £6, then $MPP_A/P_A = 3/6 = 1/2$. If the least-cost combination of factors to produce 1000 units is shown in the top row of Table 5.3 then $MPP_A/P_A = MPP_B/P_B = MPP_C/P_C = 1/2$. Thus:

$$P_B = MPP_B/{}^1/_2 = 10 \div {}^1/_2 = £20$$
$$P_C = MPP_C/{}^1/_2 = 5 \div {}^1/_2 = £10$$

*Q20. *(a)* See the four curves in Figure A5.3.

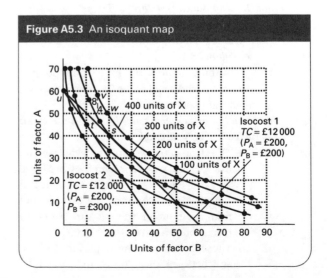

Figure A5.3 An isoquant map

(b) 40*A* and 20*B*. Production will be at point *s*, where the isocost of the slope $(-)P_B/P_A = (-)1$, is tangential to the 300 unit isoquant. This will involve using 40 units of factor A and 20 units of factor B.

(c) £12 000 (i.e. 40*A* @ £200 + 20*B* @ £200).

(d) 200 units of X. If the price of A rises to £300, the £12 000 isocost will pivot inwards on point *u*, so that its slope becomes 300/200. The maximum output that can now be produced is where the isocost touches the highest isoquant: namely at point *t* on the 200 unit isoquant.

(e) 45*A* and 10*B* (point *t*).

Q21. D. For example, if we move from point *v* to point *w* in Figure A5.3, an extra 4 units of B can replace 8 units of B and output will stay at 400 units. Thus the *MPP* of B must be twice that of A (8/4). Thus the (average) slope of the curve (8/4) must equal MPP_B/MPP_A.

Q22. B. For example, isocost 2 in Figure A5.3 has a slope of 60/40 = 3/2. But the price of B is £300 and the price of A is £200 and thus $P_B/P_A = 3/2$.

Q23. *explicit*.

Q24. E. This is what the firm is having to forgo by using the machine. The alternative forgone may be the production of some other good, or it may be the additional second-hand value from selling it at the beginning of the year rather than after producing X for a year.

Q25. *True*.

Q26. *the firm's output*.

Q27. (a) *variable*, (b) *fixed* (c) *fixed* (unless the firm deliberately chooses to spend more on advertising the more it produces), (d) *variable* (even though the bill may not be paid this month, the total cost of the electricity will nevertheless vary with the amount of chocolate produced), (e) *variable*, (f) *variable* (even though the basic wage is fixed per worker, the amount spent on basic wages will increase if extra workers are taken on to produce extra output, and will fall if workers quitting are not replaced because of falling output), (g) *variable*, (h) *fixed*, (i) *fixed* (the rise in interest rates is not the result of increased *output*: i.e. the cost is still fixed with respect to output).

Q28. *(a)* *AC*.

  (b) *AVC*.

  (c) *MC*.

  (d) *MC*. (Given that fixed costs, by definition, do not vary with output, marginal costs will consist of variable costs.)

  (e) *AFC*.

  (f) *TC*.

  (g) *TVC*.

  (h) *TC*.

Q29. *(a)* See table below.

Output	TFC	TVC	TC	AFC	AVC	AC	MC
0	10	0	10	–	–	–	
							8
1	10	8	18	10.0	8.0	18.0	
							4
2	10	12	22	5.0	6.0	11.0	
							3
3	10	15	25	3.33	5.0	8.33	
							2
4	10	17	27	2.5	4.25	6.75	
							3
5	10	20	30	2.0	4.0	6.0	
							4
6	10	24	34	1.67	4.0	5.67	
							5
7	10	29	39	1.43	4.14	5.57	
							7
8	10	36	46	1.25	4.5	5.75	
							12
9	10	48	58	1.11	5.33	6.44	
							22
10	10	70	80	1.0	7.0	8.0	

(b) 4. After this level of output *MC* begins to rise.

(c) See Figure A5.4.

(d) See Figure A5.5.

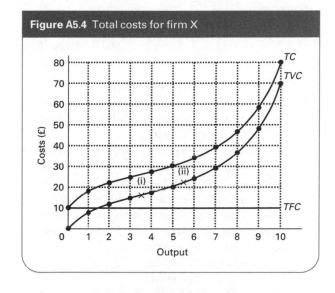

Figure A5.4 Total costs for firm X

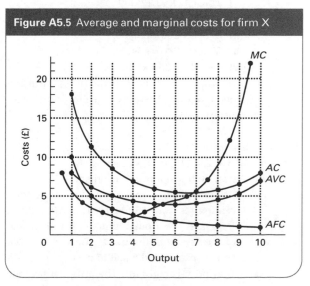

Figure A5.5 Average and marginal costs for firm X

Q30. C. If the marginal cost is below the average cost, then additional units will cost less to produce than the average and will thus pull the average down. You can see that this is the case by looking at Figure A5.5.

Q31. All except (e) are assumed. (In the case of (a) and (b), if factor prices or the state of technology change, the long-run costs curves will shift. In the case of (e) firms may or may not experience economies of scale. Note that (d) and (g) are the same.)

Q32. See Figure A5.6.

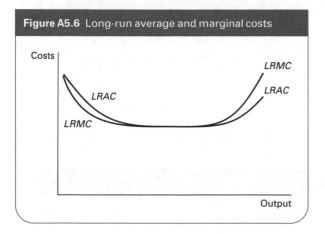

Figure A5.6 Long-run average and marginal costs

Q33. *False*. This is the so-called 'envelope curve'. It *will* be tangential with the short-run average cost curves, but only with the bottom points where the *LRAC* is horizontal. (Try drawing it.)

Q34. *True*. Maximum economies of scale will be achieved at the bottom of the *LRAC* curve. The *LRMC* must equal *LRAC* at this point – when *LRAC* is neither rising nor falling. The *LRAC* curve is tangential with the *SRAC* curves. At the *bottom* of the respective *SRAC* curve, through which point the *SRMC* curve passes.

*Q35. *(a)*   (i) $10K + 15L = £4800$.

         (ii) $16K = 21L = £7200$.

         (iii) $18K + 33L = £9600$.

         (iv) $22K + 42L = £12\,000$.

     (b)   (i) $£4800 \div 100 = £48.00$.

         (ii) $£7200 \div 200 = £36.00$.

         (iii) $£9600 \div 280 = £34.29$.

         (iv) $£12\,000 \div 350 = £34.29$.

     (c)   Economies of scale are experienced up until 280 units of output. Thereafter the firm experiences constant costs.

Q36. *horizontal*.

Q37. *demand curve*.

Q38. *(a)*   (i) $5 \times £2 = £10$; (ii) $8 \times £2 = £16$.

     (b)   A straight line out from the origin.

     (c)   (i) When sales rise from 4 units to 5 units, total revenue rises from £8 to £10. Thus $MR = 2$. (ii) When sales rise from 7 units to 8 units, total revenue rises from £14 to £16. Thus $MR = 2$. MR is thus constant and equal to price. The reason is that price is constant. The marginal revenue

from selling one more unit, therefore, is simply its price.

     (d)   A horizontal straight line and equal to the firm's demand 'curve'.

     (e)   See table below.

P(AR) (£)	Q (units)	TR (£)	MR (£)
20	0	0	
			18
18	1	18	
			14
16	2	32	
			10
14	3	42	
			6
12	4	48	
			2
10	5	50	
			-2
8	6	48	
			-6
6	7	42	

     (f)   −1. (Where $MR = 0$ and TR is at a maximum, demand is unit elastic.)

     (g)   Over £10. (A fall in price leads to a proportionately larger rise in quantity demanded and thus a rise in total revenue.)

     (h)   Under £10. (A fall in price leads to a proportionately smaller rise in quantity demanded and thus a fall in total revenue.)

Q39. $MR = \Delta TR / \Delta Q = ((15 \times 130) - (20 \times 100)) \div (130 - 100) = -50/30 = -£1.67$.

Q40. D. The total revenue for 49 bottles would be $49 \times £10 = £490$. The total revenue for 50 bottles would be $50 \times £9 = £450$. Total revenue thus falls by £40 for the 50th bottle sold.

Q41. *(a)*   40 (where the two curves are furthest apart).

     (b)   £7 (the size of the gap).

     (c)   The curve should plot the size of the gap, crossing the horizontal axis at outputs of 21 and 56 and reaching a peak of £7 at an output of 40.

     (d)   £10 (the point where the *TC* curve crosses the vertical axis).

     (e)   65 (the peak of the *TR* curve: where $MR = 0$).

     (f)   21 and 56 (where $T\Pi = 0$).

Q42. *(a)*   See Figure A5.7.

     (b)   The firm is a price taker. It has to accept the price as given by the market, a price that is not affected by the amount the firm supplies. The AR curve is thus a horizontal straight line, and the AR also equals the MR, given that each *additional* unit sold will simply earn the market price (AR) as additional revenue (MR) for the firm.

     (c)   560 units, where $MC = MR$ (point a).

     (d)   £2.40 (point b).

     (e) $£3.20 - £2.40 = £0.80$ ($a - b$).

     (f)   See Figure A5.7.

     (g) $560 \times £0.80 = £448.00$.

     (h)   £2.30 at an output of 500 (the minimum point on the AC curve).

Figure A5.7 Average and marginal costs and revenues for the production of good X

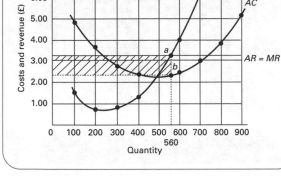

Q43. C. With $MR > MC$, the firm should increase output. With price $> MR$ the firm must face a downward sloping demand (AR) curve. In order to increase output, therefore, the firm must reduce price.

Q44. *False.* The optimum (profit-maximising) output for the firm will be where $MC = MR$. The profit-maximising firm will thus choose to produce at the bottom of the AC curve *only* if MR and MC happen to intersect at this point. (As we shall see in the next chapter, this *will* be the case in the long run under perfect competition.)

Q45. *False.* It should produce at an *output* where $MR = MC$, but unless it is a price taker whose MR thus equals price, it will sell at a price *above* MR and MC.

Q46. E. If AR is greater than AVC it will be able to cover the costs arising directly from remaining in production, and will be able to make some contribution to paying its fixed costs which, in the short run, it will have to pay anyway whether it remains in production or not. If it cannot even cover its variable costs, it will lose less by closing down.

Q47. D. In the short run it is covering its average variable cost and therefore it should continue in operation; but it will minimise its losses (i.e. maximise the contribution towards paying off its fixed costs) by producing where $MR = MC$. It should therefore reduce output. In the long run, since it is not covering its average (total) cost (AC) it should close down.

*Q48. (a) $AC = TC/Q = 100/Q - 20 + 3Q$.

(b) $MC = dTC/dQ = -20 + 6Q$.

(c) $AR = TR/Q = 60 - 2Q$.

(d) $MR = dTR/dQ = 60 - 4Q$.

(e) Profit is maximised where $MR = MC$
i.e. where $60 - 4Q = -20 + 6Q$
where $10Q = 80$
where $Q = 8$.

(f) $A\Pi = AR - AC = (60 - (2 \times 8)) - ((100/8) - 20 + (3 \times 8)) = 60 - 16 - 12.5 + 20 - 24 = 27.5$.

(g) $T\Pi = A\Pi \times Q = 27.5 \times 8 = 220$.

(h) $T\Pi = TR - TC = (60Q - 2Q^2) - (100 - 20Q + 3Q^2) = -100 + 80Q - 5Q^2$.

(i) Profit is maximised where $dT\Pi/dQ = 0$
where $80 - 10Q = 0$
where $Q = 8$.

6 Profit Maximising under Perfect Competition and Monopoly

A REVIEW

The amount firms will supply and at what price will depend on the amount of competition they face – on the market structure. In this chapter we look at the two extreme types of market structure.

At the one extreme is perfect competition. This is where there are so many firms competing that no one firm has any market power whatsoever. Firms are too small to influence market price or have any significant effect on market output. At the other extreme is monopoly, where there is only one firm in the industry which thus faces no competition at all from inside the industry (although it may well face competition from firms in related industries).

6.1 Alternative market structures

(Pages 155–6) It is usual to divide markets into four categories.

(?) Q1. In ascending order of competitiveness these are (fill in the missing two):

1. monopoly

2. ....

3. ....

4. perfect competition.

Q2. To which of the four categories do the following apply? (There can be more than one market category in each case.)

(a) Firms face a downward sloping demand curve.

....

(b) New firms can freely enter the industry.

....

(c) Firms produce a homogeneous product.

....

(d) Firms are price takers.

....

(e) These is perfect knowledge on the part of consumers of price and product quality.

....

Q3. In which of the four categories would you place each of the following? (It is possible in some cases that part of the industry could be in one category and part in another: if so name both.)

(a) A village post office ....

(b) Restaurants in a large town ....

(c) Banks ....

(d) Hi-fi manufacturers ....

(e) Growers of potatoes ....

(f) Water supply ....

(g) Local buses ....

(h) Local builders ....

(i) The market for foreign currency ....

We can get an indication of the degree of competition within an industry by observing *concentration ratios*.

Q4. A 5-firm concentration ratio shows:
A. the proportion of industries in the economy that have just five firms.
B. the share of industry profits earned by the five largest firms.
C. the sales of the five largest firms as a proportion of the total industry's sales.
D. the size of the largest firm relative to the total size of the five largest firms.
E. the output of good X produced by the five largest firms as a proportion of their total output of all types of good.

6.2 Perfect competition

(Pages 156–8) The theory of perfect competition is based on very strict assumptions.

Q5. These include the following (delete the incorrect one in each case):
(a) Firms are *price makers/price takers* and thus face a *horizontal/downward-sloping* demand curve.
(b) Firms in the industry produce a *homogeneous/differentiated* product.
(c) Producers and consumers have *complete/limited* knowledge of the market.
(d) Entry of new firms is *free/restricted*.

Q6. Before examining what price, output and profits will be, we must distinguish between the short run and the long run as they apply to perfect competition.
(a) The short run is defined as that period which

....

(b) The long run is defined as that period which

....

Q7. Which one of the following is true for the marginal firm under perfect competition?
A. It can earn only normal profits in both the short run and the long run.
B. It can earn supernormal profits in both the short and long run.
C. It can earn supernormal profits in the long run but only normal profits in the short run.
D. It can earn supernormal profits in the short run but only normal profits in the long run.
E. Whether it earns normal or supernormal profits in the short and long run will depend on the conditions in that particular industry.

(Pages 158–9) Short-run price and output under perfect competition can be found by applying the general rules for profit maximisation that we examined in the last chapter.

Q8. Under perfect competition a firm will increase output if:
A. marginal cost is less than price.
B. price exceeds marginal revenue.
C. marginal revenue equals average revenue.
D. marginal cost exceeds marginal revenue.
E. marginal cost equals marginal revenue.

Q9. Figure 6.1 shows the cost and revenue curves faced by a perfectly competitive firm.
(a) What is the maximum profit the firm can earn?

....

(b) What is the maximum output the firm can produce and still earn normal profits?

....

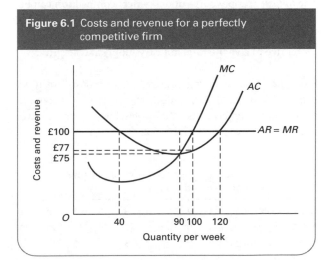

Figure 6.1 Costs and revenue for a perfectly competitive firm

(c) Assuming that there are no internal or external economies or diseconomies of scale, what will be the long-run price and output?

....

⊖ **Q10.** A perfectly competitive firm is currently earning £130 total profit per week from selling 100 units per week. Its total cost schedule is given in Table 6.1.

(a) Fill in its marginal cost schedule in Table 6.1. (Remember that marginal cost is the cost of producing *one* more unit.)

(b) What is the market price? (Clue: find its total revenue from selling 100 units.)

(c) Should the firm alter its level of production if it wishes to maximise its profit? If so, to what? If not, why not?

Table 6.1 Total and marginal costs

Output (Q)	0	20	40	60	80	100	120	140	160	180
TC (£)	100	190	270	340	420	520	640	780	940	1140
MC (£)	...	...	...	...	...	...	...	...	...	

(Pages 159–60) The profit-maximising rule tells us how much a firm will produce at any given price. From this we can derive the firm's short-run supply curve.

▤ **Q11.** A firm's supply curve under perfect competition in the short run will be equal to:

A. the upward-sloping portion of its *AC* curve.

B. the upward-sloping portion of its *MC* curve above its *AC* curve.

C. the upward-sloping portion of its *AVC* curve.

D. the upward-sloping portion of its *MC* curve.

E. the upward-sloping portion of its *MC* curve above its *AVC* curve.

The *industry* supply curve under perfect competition can be derived from the supply curves of the member firms. All we do is simply add up the amounts supplied by each firm at each price to give the total industry supply at each price.

⊖ **Q12.** A perfectly competitive industry consists of 1000 firms. Because of their location, 400 of the firms (type A firms) have higher costs. The cost schedules of the two types of firm are given in Table 6.2.

Table 6.2 Costs for two types of firm in a perfectly competitive industry

Output: weekly (Q)	1	2	3	4	5	6	7	8	9
MC: Type A firm (£)	4	3	4	5	7	10	15	23	40
MC: Type B firm (£)	3	2	3	4	5	7	10	15	23

Figure 6.2 Perfectly competitive industry's short-run supply curve

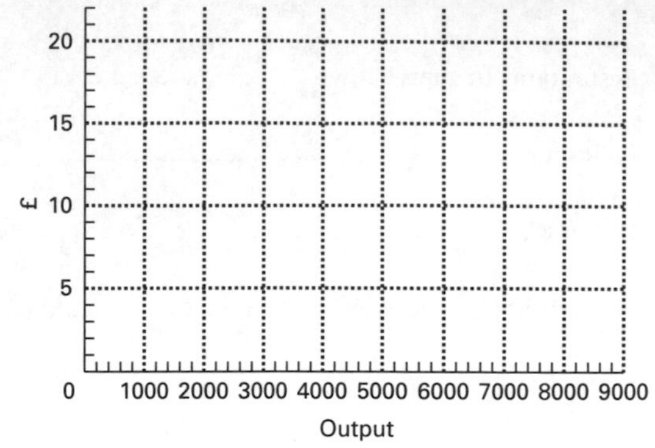

Assume that minimum *AVC* = £4.50 for type A firms and £3.50 for type B firms.

(a) What will short-run industry supply be at each of the following prices?

(i) £15 .... per week

(ii) £7 .... per week

(iii) £4 .... per week

(iv) £3 .... per week

(b) Draw the industry's short-run supply curve on Figure 6.2.

(Pages 160–1) We now turn to the long-run equilibrium under perfect competition.

◑ **Q13.** If the firm is in long-run equilibrium, the market price is equal to its:

(a)	long-run average costs.	*True/False*
(b)	long-run marginal costs.	*True/False*
(c)	short-run average costs.	*True/False*
(d)	short-run average variable costs.	*True/False*
(e)	short-run marginal costs.	*True/False*
(f)	average revenue.	*True/False*
(g)	marginal revenue.	*True/False*

▤ **Q14.** A perfectly competitive firm is producing 1000 tins of toffees per week, which it sells for £1.50 per tin. This output on 1000 tins per week incurs the following costs:

Total fixed cost	£1000
Total variable cost	£1200
Marginal cost	£1.00

What should the firm do in the short run?

A. Raise its price.

B. Decrease output.

C. Increase output.

D. Maintain output at its present level.

E. Cease production altogether.

Q15. Referring to the firm in the previous question, assuming that its long-run total cost is £1600, its long-run marginal cost is £1.50 and the price has remained unchanged, what should it do in the long run?

A. Raise its price.

B. Decrease output.

C. Increase output.

D. Maintain output at its present level.

E. Cease production altogether.

The long-run industry supply curve will reflect the changing number of firms as higher prices attract new firms into the industry and lower prices encourage firms to leave the industry.

Q16. If all firms (existing and potential entrants) face the same *LRAC* curves, then the long-run industry supply curve will:

A. necessarily be horizontal.

B. slope upwards if there are external economies of scale.

C. only be horizontal if there are constant external costs with respect to industry size.

D. slope downwards if there are external diseconomies of scale.

E. slope upwards if there are internal diseconomies of scale.

Q17. Why would it be impossible for industries which experience substantial internal economies of scale to be perfectly competitive?

....

....

....

(Page 162) Perfect competition is argued to be more in the public interest than other types of market structure.

Q18. Which of the following are claimed to be advantages of perfect competition?

(a) It leads to allocative efficiency. *Yes/No*

(b) It leads to production at minimum short-run *AC*. *Yes/No*

(c) It leads to production at minimum long-run *AC*. *Yes/No*

(d) It leads to the lowest very long-run *AC* curve. *Yes/No*

(e) It leads to high levels of investment. *Yes/No*

(f) It leads to intense non-price competition. *Yes/No*

(g) The competition acts as a spur to X efficiency. *Yes/No*

(h) It leads to firms combining their factors in the least-cost way. *Yes/No*

(i) It leads to consumer sovereignty. *Yes/No*

6.3 Monopoly

(Page 163) A monopoly may be defined as an industry which consists of one firm only. In practice it is difficult to determine whether firms are monopolies or not, because it depends on how narrowly 'the industry' is defined.

Q19. Each of the following firms could be claimed to be *either* a monopoly *or* imperfectly competitive (monopolistic competition or oligopoly) depending on how we define the market (industry) in which it is operating. In each case identify two markets in which the firm operates: (1) where it is a monopoly; (2) where it competes in imperfect competition with other suppliers. Here is an example:

British Telecom (1) Supply of telephone lines to those customers not having access to a competitor (monopoly).

(2) Sale of telephones (imperfectly competitive).

The Post Office (1) ....

(2) ....

Your refectory (1) ....

(2) ....

Car spares manufacturer (1) ....

(2) ....

Local water company (1) ....

(2) ....

Local ice skating rink (1) ....

(2) ....

An ice cream van (1) ....

(2) ....

Q20. A firm would have a 'natural' monopoly if:

A. its average revenue curve were vertical.

B. it controlled the supply of a natural resource essential to the production of the good in question.

C. there were *total* barriers to the entry of new firms.

D. it had gained significant experience of producing the good in question.

E. its long-run average cost curve were downward sloping at the profit-maximising level of output.

(Pages 163–4) In order for a firm to maintain its monopoly position there must be barriers to the entry of new firms.

Q21. Which one of the following would not be a barrier to firms entering an industry?

A. An upward sloping long-run average cost curve.
B. Patents on key processes.
C. Substantial economies of scale.
D. Large initial capital costs.
E. The threat of takeover by the existing firm(s).

(Page 165) Given its market power, a monopolist will face a downward-sloping demand curve that **Q22.** *is elastic throughout its length/is inelastic throughout its length/must be elastic for some of its length but may be inelastic for part of it.* This downward-sloping demand curve will mean that the monopolist will charge a price **Q23.** *above/below/equal to* its marginal cost of production.

Q24. Because of its market power, a monopolist can choose how much to sell and what price to sell it at.

True/False

Q25. In Figure 6.3 which letter gives the profit-maximising price: A, B, C, D or E?

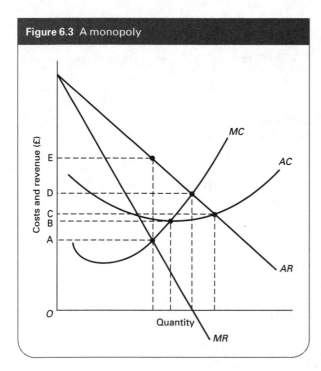

Figure 6.3 A monopoly

Q26. Table 6.3 shows the costs and revenues of a monopolist producer of specialist luxury rough terrain cars.
(a) Fill in the figures for *TR*, *MR*, *TC* and *MC*.
(b) At what daily output of cars will the monopolist maximise profits?

....

(c) How much profit will be made? ....

Table 6.3 A monopoly car producer

Quantity (cars per day)	AR (£000s)	TR (£000s)	MR (£000s)	AC (£000s)	TC (£000s)	MC (£000s)
1	100	...		110	...	
			...			...
2	95	...		90	...	
			...			...
3	90	...		80	...	
			...			...
4	85	...		75	...	
			...			...
5	80	...		74	...	
			...			...
6	75	...		76	...	
			...			...
7	70	...		81	...	

Q27. The profit-maximising monopolist will never produce where *MR* is negative. *True/False*

Q28. At the profit-maximising output, the monopolist's demand will be price inelastic. *True/False*

Q29. Referring to Table 6.3, what is the price elasticity of demand at the profit-maximising point? (Use the midpoint arc method over the price range either side of the profit-maximising price.)

....

Q30. In the long run, a perfectly competitive firm will produce at the bottom of its *AC* curve. Why will a monopolist probably not do so?

....

....

(Pages 165–9) There are several reasons why monopoly may be against the public interest, but several reasons also why the consumer may gain.

Q31. Figure 6.4 shows a perfectly competitive industry for eggs. The egg producers then get together and set up a marketing agency which becomes the monopoly seller of eggs. The agency sets the profit-maximising price and gives each producer an output quota to ensure that total output is kept to the profit-maximising level. Assuming that industry costs are not affected, the consumer will:
A. gain because price falls from P_2 to P_1.
B. gain because price falls from P_3 to P_2.
C. gain because price falls from P_3 to P_1.
D. lose because price rises from P_1 to P_2.
E. lose because price rises from P_2 to P_3.

Q32. A monopoly will always produce a lower output and at a higher price than if the industry were under perfect competition. *True/False*

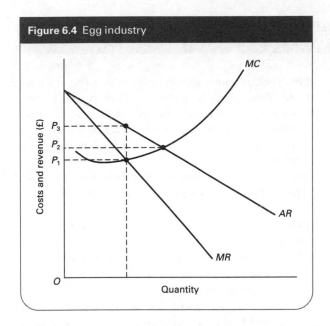

Figure 6.4 Egg industry

Referring again to Figure 6.4, assume now that the egg producers' marketing agency sets up a research laboratory into new efficient methods of egg production and as a result is able to shift the industry *MC* curve downwards. This could result in the profit-maximising industry price being lower than before the agency was set up.

⊖ **Q33.** On Figure 6.4 draw two new *MC* curves below the original curve. Draw them so that one of them results in a lower price than before the agency was set up and the other still results in a higher price.

⊗ *Q34.** A monopolist's average revenue and average cost functions are given by:

$$AR = 1200 - 4Q$$
$$AC = 400/Q + 300 - 4Q + 3Q^2$$

where *AR* and *AC* are in £s.

(a) What is the equation for the monopolist's demand curve?

....

(b) What is the equation for total revenue?

....

(c) What is the equation for marginal revenue?

....

(d) What is the equation for total costs?

....

(e) How much are total fixed costs?

....

(f) What is the equation for marginal cost?

....

(g) At what output is profit maximised?

....

(h) What is the price at this output?

....

(i) What is average cost at this output?

....

(j) How much is average profit at this output?

....

(k) How much is total profit at this output?

....

6.4 The theory of contestable markets

(Pages 169–73) Even if a firm is currently a monopoly, it may be forced to behave as if it were in a competitive market if there is potential competition: i.e. if the market is contestable. The threat of this competition will be greater **Q35.** *the higher/the lower* the entry costs to the industry and **Q36.** *the higher/the lower* the exit costs from the industry.

⑦ **Q37.** A perfectly contestable market is defined as one where

....

....

◗ **Q38.** Classify each of the following markets as highly contestable, moderately contestable, slightly contestable or non-contestable. If it depends on the circumstances, explain in what way.

(a) satellite broadcasting   *highly/moderately/slightly/non*
(b) hospital cleaning services
                                  highly/moderately/slightly/non
(c) banking on a university/college campus
                                  highly/moderately/slightly/non
(d) piped gas supply   *highly/moderately/slightly/non*
(e) parcels delivery   *highly/moderately/slightly/non*
(f) siting for the Olympic games
                                  highly/moderately/slightly/non
(g) bus service to the area where you live
                                  highly/moderately/slightly/non

B PROBLEMS, EXERCISES AND PROJECTS

Q39. A perfectly competitive industry consists of 100 equalsized firms. The firms fall into three categories according to their cost structures. Their short-run marginal costs are shown in Table 6.4.

Table 6.4 Marginal costs for firms in a perfectly competitive industry

Output per day	40 firms (type A) MC per firm (£)	30 firms (type B) MC per firm (£)	30 firms (type C) MC per firm (£)
1	20	40	20
2	25	45	30
3	30	50	40
4	35	55	50
5	40	60	60
6	45	65	70
7	50	70	80
8	60	75	90
9	70	80	100
10	80	85	110
11	90	90	120

(a) How much will a type A firm supply at a price of £40?
(b) How much will total supply of type B firms be at a price of £80?
(c) What will total industry supply be at a price of £50?
(d) Assuming that marginal cost is above average variable cost for all firms at all levels of output, construct the total industry supply schedule at £10 intervals between £20 and £90 on the following table.

P	20	30	40	50	60	70	80	90
Q_S	...	...	...	...	...	...	...	...

(e) What is the industry price elasticity of supply between £50 and £60?
(f) Assume that the demand schedule facing the industry is given by

$$Q_D = 1100 - 5P$$

Construct the industry demand schedule at £10 intervals between £20 and £90 on the following table.

P	20	30	40	50	60	70	80	90
Q_D	...	...	...	...	...	...	...	...

(g) What is the equilibrium industry price and output?
(h) If a tax of £10 per unit is levied on type A firms and a subsidy of £10 is paid to type B firms, how much will each type A and each type B firm supply at a price of £50?

Q40. Look up double glazing, builders, solicitors and taxis in the *Yellow Pages* telephone directory. Approximately how many firms are there in each category? Do any of these industries come fairly close to being perfectly competitive? Look at the advertisements appearing with the telephone numbers.

In what ways are the firms attempting to make their position less like that of firms under perfect competition?

Q41. Figure 6.5 shows cost and revenue curves for a monopolist.
(a) At what output will the firm maximise profits?
(b) What price will it charge to maximise profits?
(c) How much profit will it make?
(d) Assume that a potential rival had a minimum average cost of £3.70. How much can the monopolist sell if it does not want to attract that firm into the industry?
(e) How much profit will the monopolist now make?
(f) What would have to be the position of the monopolist's revenue curves if its maximum profit output were to be at minimum average cost?
(g) Is there any position of the revenue curves which would give a profit-maximising output at minimum average cost *and* a price equal to minimum average cost?
(h) At what price and output would this industry produce if it were a perfectly competitive industry (but with the same cost curves and demand curve)?
(i) Does this represent a long-run equilibrium position for the (perfectly competitive) industry?
(j) In the long run would *individual* perfectly competitive firms produce more or less than they did in (h)?

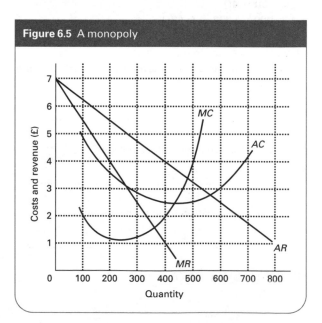

Figure 6.5 A monopoly

Q42. Look through the business sections of the 'quality' newspapers of two or three days and identify those companies that have substantial monopoly power. What are the barriers to entry in their respective industries? Is there anything in the reports that suggests that these firms act either in or against the public interest? Can this behaviour be explained by their market power?

DISCUSSION TOPICS AND ESSAYS

Q43. What is the point of studying perfect competition if it does not exist, or only very rarely exists, in the real world?

Q44. Give some example of markets where the suppliers are price takers. In each case consider whether they are operating under perfect competition.

Q45. Under perfect competition a firm's supply is entirely dependent on its cost of production. In what sense then is total industry output the result of the interaction of supply *and* demand?

Q46. Is it possible for a perfectly competitive industry to have falling long-run average costs? Explain.

Q47. Using examples, discuss the proposition that whether a firm is regarded as a monopoly or not depends on how narrowly the industry is defined.

Q48. Think of three examples of monopoly and consider what barriers there are to the entry of new firms. Are these barriers total or are they merely hurdles?

Q49. 'A monopolist's demand will always be elastic at the profit maximising output.' 'The greater a monopolist's power, the less elastic its demand curve.' 'The monopolist will try wherever possible to increase its monopoly power.' Reconcile these three statements.

Q50. Assume that an art gallery displaying a unique collection of paintings by old masters finds that all its costs (staffing, heating, lighting, rent, security, etc.) are fixed costs. What price should it charge if it wants to maximise profits?

Q51. How does the level of exit costs from an industry in which there is currently only one firm affect the level of prices the firm will charge?

Q52. Debate
Monopolies that make supernormal profits are always against the public interest because they could charge a lower price than they do.

ARTICLES

The recent case in the USA against Microsoft and its action in the market for internet browsers has highlighted a whole range of issues regarding the role of monopoly producers in high-technology markets. The article below, taken from the *Guardian* of 17 October 1998, considers the case against Microsoft and some of the issues it raises.

A world-wide tangled web

Next week history's richest man, Bill Gates, who runs the most valuable company in the world, Microsoft, will take on the United States government and 20 individual states in a seminal legal case with awesome implications.

Ron Chernow, biographer of John D. Rockefeller, said: 'This is a major case and may well define the rules of the information age just as the Standard Oil case defined the rules of the industrial age.'

The judgement will affect all who use the products of the digital age (eventually that will mean everyone)

including computers, web-based TV sets, digital phones and 'intelligent' washing machines, plus thousand of products as yet undreamed of.

Standard Oil once supplied kerosene to virtually every house in the US but was broken up by the same anti-trust authority now gunning for Microsoft. Mr Chernow told Fortune magazine that Rockefeller – who ruthlessly made then gave away a vast fortune – was 'as good and bad a man as ever lived'.

Mr Gates generates similar emotions. To his followers, and to most of his customers, he is a hugely successful

businessman who has made his fortune ($59.5 billion – £35 billion – on yesterday's count) by innovating and price cutting. To them his only crime is success. To detractors, including most of his competitors, he is a ruthless man who uses a monopoly to put competitors out of business and stifle innovation.

That he has a monopoly is not in doubt. Microsoft's MS-DOS operating system (the essential instructions for a computer) resides in over 90 per cent of the world's personal computers. Microsoft has a market share approaching that for the world's biggest-selling software packages such as Word, for word-processing, and the Excel spreadsheet.

The company has a reputation for buying up potential competitors while diversifying into areas the digital revolution is taking over, such as web-based television, cable TV, e-mail, telephony and the internet. Microsoft is also part of a consortium putting satellites into orbit to deliver instant communications, including the internet on a global basis. These are natural diversifications to the company but to critics proof of Microsoft's aim to control the world.

Microsoft is no ordinary monopoly. The typical monopolist is unpopular and uses his monopoly to keep prices up. A recent poll produced a Clinton-esque majority of two-thirds saying the government should leave Mr Gates alone. More important, instead of raising prices, he reduces them. And in the most contentious case – Microsoft's browser used for surfing the internet – he gives it away free. So what's the problem?

Giving it away free, that's the problem. Microsoft is a bit like an electricity company owning 90 per cent of global transmission giving away light bulbs to ward off the competition. That would be a clear case of abuse of monopoly power. With Microsoft it is more complicated. It argues that its browser (and other add-ons) are an essential part of its operating system and improvement programme.

The browser wars arose when a rival, Netscape, developed a commercial version of a free internet browser. It was mainly given away to build a base on which it could make profits later.

Microsoft, slow to see the potential of the internet, suddenly saw its business threatened. In retaliation it developed its own – free – browser and (a central prosecution point) it threatened some PC manufacturers that it would not supply them with Microsoft's Windows operating system unless they made its browser the one that popped up on the screen when the computer is turned on.

This is a huge competitive advantage because, while in theory users can install rival browsers, few will bother.

The government will also claim Microsoft sealed a deal with America On Line (AOL) (the world's biggest on-line provider) by pledging to give AOL a good position on its Windows computer screen in every MS-DOS computer if AOL rejected Netscape.

Microsoft contests these versions of events. Mr Gates says: 'You can't just rip the browsers out of the thing,' and the company rejects the view that it should give prominence to its competitors' products. Should McDonald's, it asks, be required to give is customers the option of buying Burger King first?

Put that way, no. But McDonald's does not control 90 per cent of the world's food outlets. As long as Microsoft is controller of the highway and a major provider of products there will be a problem. Microsoft says it cannot realistically 'unbundle' its browser. But rival Netscape can still make its browser as a stand-alone product able to be added to Microsoft's system or (distant) rivals such as Apple.

Economists backing Mr Gates say that in a fast-expanding technological market monopolies come and go, pointing to the decline of IBM. Watch out, they say, for a revived Apple, Netscape, use of Java or even Britain's Psion to oust Microsoft.

Critics say that Microsoft owes its existence to IBM's reluctance years ago to move against an incipient rival because IBM knew anti-trust officials were watching. They argue that Microsoft will stifle competition. No one wants to finance rival products because Microsoft can drop the price of its own products and snuff them out while still enjoying a huge profit from its monopoly of the new information network.

One solution is for the government to split Microsoft between its 'common carrier' obligations arising from its monopoly of PC operating systems and a second company selling software – including browsers – on an arms-length basis.

(a) In what ways does Microsoft behave like a monopolist, and in what ways is its behaviour not consistent with traditional or expected monopoly practices?

(b) If the development of an internet browser, incorporated into the Windows operating system, clearly improves the quality of the product, is not Microsoft doing what every business should, namely improving the quality of the product for its customers? If it does, should we criticise Microsoft?

(c) Why might it be difficult to introduce competition into high-technology markets? Is it necessarily desirable to have such competition?

The following article by Gail Raygor, taken from the *Director* Special Supplement on energy management of November 1998, assesses the advantages and problems of liberalising the market for energy. The article first considers the advantages consumers are likely to gain from enhanced competition, considering experiences from the United States, illustrates some of the potential problems of a privately run electricity and gas supply sector.

The power and the glory?

Competition in the electricity and gas supply markets is, at last, a reality. But what does it mean? What benefits can it bring? What opportunities does it present? And what are its drawbacks? Essentially, the opening up of both markets gives consumers the right to choose which company they buy their energy from. It should also ensure that all users – large and small businesses as well as domestic customers – get better value for money. Lower prices combined with better services; the opportunity for all businesses to lower overheads by cutting their power bills by between 10 and 20 per cent, at least – these are the promises of deregulation.

When the Labour party came to power it instigated a host of reviews, the main ones focusing on utility regulation, trading arrangements and energy sources. All have been controversial, but all should bring huge benefits for customers.

When she published the Green Paper on utility regulation, *A Fair Deal for Consumers*, earlier this year the then trade and industry secretary Margaret Beckett vowed that government proposals would 'keep the pressure on the utility companies and the utility regulators to drive prices down and standards up, and provide more choice for all'.

In the past year, there has been a crackdown on bad selling practices by suppliers, greater emphasis on providing accurate information, a drive to improve customer services, more advice on cutting energy costs by using energy more efficiently and more stress on the need for the energy industry to get prices down.

The forthcoming reform of electricity trading arrangements (which will see the market operate in line with other commodity markets) is designed to ensure lower prices while increasing flexibility in terms of trading options and the types of contracts available. According to Professor Stephen Littlechild, director general of electricity regulator Offer, the proposals will mean 'lower prices from more efficient and more competitive trading, greater choice of markets, transparency from simple bids and more flexible and effective governance'.

In essence, these reviews and reforms seek to ensure the full benefits of competition are gained by all customers.

Competition in the energy markets has long been on the agenda, but has taken years to come to full fruition. The gas market has matured most rapidly, with full competition reaching all customers in March 1998. British Gas remains the monopoly supplier at present, but there are now around 60 suppliers serving the entire market (a quarter of these serve the domestic and small-business market).

Latest figures from the gas regulator, Ofgas, suggest that in the domestic and smallbusiness sector around three million customers have switched from British Gas and a further one million plan to do so. This represents around 15 per cent of the market. All have gone with deals that claim to offer savings of around 20 per cent. Many of the one million who are waiting to switch have signed up for so-called 'dual fuel' packages – the offer of both gas and electricity at reduced rates from a single company. (They can only take advantage of these deals once the electricity market in their particular region is open.)

In the electricity market, large business customers (those with a maximum demand of more than 1 MW) have been able to choose their supplier since 1990, and in 1994 competition was extended to medium-sized businesses with a maximum demand of more than 100 kW.

Some consumers in the under-100 kW or 'franchise' market – small-business and domestic customers – were free to choose when this sector started opening to competition in mid September.

'For the first time, customers will have a choice,' Professor Littlechild says. 'Having a choice means that customers can change their supplier if they are offered lower prices or better services, or are dissatisfied with the service they are getting at the moment. Knowing that customers can switch to a competitor quickly and easily will help keep electricity suppliers on their toes.'

The traditional suppliers – RECs – face the prospect of competing not only with one another but also with a host of new entrants to the market. The move to privatisation has seen many of the UK's 14 RECs taken over by US companies, while two of the last remaining independents, Southern Electric and Scottish Hydro-Electric recently announced their merger. Meanwhile, the generator, PowerGen has snapped up East Midlands. Deregulation has also seen the birth of new energy suppliers such as Independent Energy and Union Energy.

In addition, non-energy companies have entered the market. Supermarkets, financial services companies and high-street stores have formed marketing alliances with suppliers. Barclaycard, for example, recently announced an alliance with Eastern Group. Every card holder will be offered a saving of up to 15 per cent on their energy bills when they switch to what is to be called Barclaycard Energy for both gas and electricity.

Choice extends not only to supplier but also to source, with some companies offering 'green' electricity options such as wind or solar power.

Increased competition and increased choice, however, can lead to increased confusion and complexity. Experience from deregulation of the gas market has shown that small-business customers and domestic customers can often be deterred from switching supplier due to complications in contract negotiations, confusion over tariffs and problems in getting proper advice and guidance from some companies.

This should not put users off, however. The reviews initiated by the government have sought to address the problems – in both the gas and the electricity markets – and businesses should be better off financially and receive better service.

Competition in energy markets is not just a UK phenomenon. Markets across Europe are scheduled to open fully within the next two years, as they are in Australia. And in the US some states – notably California – are already experiencing competition.

Reaction to liberalisation in America has been mixed: some customers believe that supplier companies will simply be in a position to exploit them more; others acknowledge that lower prices and better services are inevitable. Battles over state legislation continue, while the troubled Clinton administration has published its own plan to ensure that all American customers gain from the potential benefits of competition – lower prices, improved services, and, above all, the power to choose which companies they buy their energy supplies from.

Notwithstanding the fears of some consumers, the case for a shake-up appears strong. America's Mid West (around 17 states) has suffered severe power shortages and blackouts during the past two summers. The El Niño weather phenomenon has struck hard. This year, prices for electricity jumped by over 100 per cent because of pressure on demand: unexpected storms caused damage to power generating stations and a dramatic increase in temperatures saw air conditioning systems used more than ever.

To ensure that work continued and they remained competitive, companies were forced to pay astronomical fees for their electricity – in some cases 400 per cent more than normal. Others simply shut up shop.

'Price gouging is occurring and it must be stopped,' declared one US company, Steel Dynamics, calling on the Federal Energy Regulatory Commission to 'use any and all applicable legal authority to address the crisis'.

While the US regulators have launched investigations in the hope that such experiences will not be repeated, the Clinton administration has argued that the introduction of full national competition in the retail energy markets would ensure greater security of supply.

'Recent experiences in the mid west and other regions show how important it is to act to modernise this vital industry and bring competition to the electricity markets,' says Elizabeth Moler, America's acting energy secretary. 'None of the areas that have experienced supply problems has yet implemented retail electric competition. Retail competition and steps to update the institutions

that protect electric system reliability are clearly part of the solution.'

As Moler has acknowledged, however, the problem boils down to a severe lack of generating capacity. Until more investment is forthcoming in the industry, users remain vulnerable – unless they invest in back-up supply systems of their own.

(a) What advantages does the article identify from enhanced competition in the energy sector?

(b) Why has the reaction to liberalisation in America been 'mixed'?

(c) Can the theory of contestable markets be used to explain how energy suppliers might be regulated by the market rather than a regulatory authority?

E ANSWERS

Q1. Monopoly; oligopoly; monopolistic competition; perfect competition.

Q2. *(a)* All except perfect competition.
  (b) Perfect competition and monopolistic competition.
  (c) Perfect competition and certain oligopolies (e.g. sugar, regular unleaded petrol, cement).
  (d) Perfect competition only.
  (e) Perfect competition only.

Q3. *(a)* Monopoly for certain items and for certain people. Oligopoly or monopolistic competition for other items where alternative suppliers exist locally, and for people who are mobile.
  (b) Monopolistic competition.
  (c) Oligopoly.
  (d) Oligopoly.
  (e) Perfect competition (approximately), assuming no marketing agency.
  (f) Monopoly. Although there are several water companies in the UK and in some other countries, there is usually only one company able to supply each customer.
  (g) Monopoly if there is only one; oligopoly if there are more than one.
  (h) Monopolistic competition.
  (i) Perfect competition. (There are many foreign currency dealers; the product is homogeneous; dealers are virtually price takers according to demand and supply from their various customers.)

Q4. C. This measures the market share of the five largest firms in the industry. It is also common to measure the 3-firm or 4-firm concentration ratios.

Q5. *(a)* *price takers: horizontal.*
  (b) *homogeneous.*
  (c) *complete.*
  (d) *free.*

Q6. *(a)* *there is too little time for new firms to enter the industry.*
  (b) *is long enough for new firms to enter the industry.*

Q7. D. Given that in the short run there is not enough time for firms to enter the industry, supernormal profits could be earned by the firm. In the long run, however, supernormal profits would attract new firms to enter, thus driving down the market price until the marginal firm was just earning normal profits.

Q8. A. If marginal cost is less than price (= MR), the firm will make additional profits if it produces extra output. Note: price (AR) equals marginal revenue and thus B will never occur under perfect competition. C on the other hand will always occur, but thus gives no guidance as to whether a firm should expand or contract production. In the case of D the firm should reduce output. In the case of E this is the profit-maximising position and hence the firm should not change its output.

Q9. *(a)* £2300 per week. (Profits are maximised where $P = MC$, at an output of 100 units per week. Profit per unit equals £100 – £77 = £23. Total profit thus equals $100 \times £23 = £2300$.)
  (b) 120 units. (Above that $AC > P$.)
  (c) $P = £75$; $Q = 90$ (i.e. at the bottom of the AC curve: where just normal profits remain).

Q10. *(a)* $MC = \Delta TC/\Delta Q$ (in this case $\Delta Q = 20$).

Q	0	20	40	60	80	100	120	140	160	180
TC(£)	100	190	270	340	420	520	640	780	940	1140
MC(£)		4.50	4.00	3.50	4.00	5.00	6.00	7.00	8.00	10.00

(b) $P = £6.50$. (100 units are costing £520 to produce and earning £130 profit. The total revenue from these 100 units must therefore be £520 + £130 = £650. Therefore price = $TR/Q = £650/100 = £6.50$.)

(c) *Yes.* At the current output (100), $MR = £6.50$ and MC is between £5.00 and £6.00, i.e. $MR > MC$. Thus the firm should produce *more*. Profit will be maximised where $MC = MR = £6.50$. This will be at an output of approximately 120. At this output, total profit = $TR - TC = (120 × £6.50) - 640 = £140$.

Q11. E. The firm, by equating marginal cost and price, will always produce that output for each price that is given by its MC curve, but only so long as price, and hence MC, is above AVC. If price, and hence MC, were below AVC the firm would shut down.

Q12. *(a)* (i) 7600 (i.e. 400 firms producing 7 units each plus 600 firms producing 8 units each).
(ii) 5600 (i.e. 400 firms producing 5 units each plus 600 firms producing 6 units each).
(iii) 2400 (i.e. 600 firms producing 4 units each; type A firms will not produce as price is below AVC).
(iv) 0 (i.e. price is below AVC for all firms).

(b) See Figure A6.1.
Note the horizontal sections of the supply curve. These correspond to the prices where the two types of firm leave the industry in the short run because they cannot cover average variable costs.

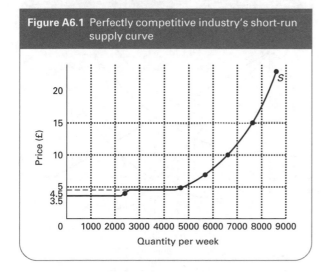

Figure A6.1 Perfectly competitive industry's short-run supply curve

Q13. All *true* except (d).

Q14. C. The firm is currently making a loss because its AC (= £2200/1000 = £2.20) is greater than the price (£1.50). It is nevertheless covering its AVC (= £1.20) and should therefore continue in production. It should increase output because MR (£1.50) is greater than MC (£1.00). This will help to reduce its loss.

Q15. E. The firm's $LRMC$ is £1.50, which is also equal to the price. The firm is thus producing at the long-run profit-maximising/loss-minimising point. But with a long-run total cost of £1600, its $LRAC$ is £1.60. It is thus making a loss and should therefore cease production.

Q16. C. If there are constant external costs firms $LRAC$ curves will not shift as the size of the industry changes. If all firms have the same $LRAC$ curves, then any increase in demand, and hence any rise in price above the bottom of firms' $LRAC$, will attract new firms. This will simply push price back down to the bottom of the $LRAC$ curve. This means that in the long run supply will increase without any increase (or decrease) in price. (Note that E is wrong because higher prices attract *new* firms which can come in at the minimum point of the $LRAC$ curve.)

Q17. Because the first firms to take advantage of large-scale production would drive the other firms out of the industry until there were too few firms left for them to remain price takers. Markets are not big enough for a large number of large firms.

Q18. (a), (c), (g), (h) and (i), *yes*.
(b), (d), (e) and (f), *no*. In the case of (b), firms can make supernormal profits or a loss in the short run. In the case of (d) and (e), firms may not be able to afford extensive research and development and investment. As a result their very long-run average costs may not be as low as if they were able to obtain long-run supernormal profits that could be ploughed back into the firm. In the case of (f), there is no non-price competition because, by definition, the firms produce homogeneous products.

Q19. The Post Office: (1) letter mail; (2) stationery.
Your refectory: (1) meals served on site; (2) food retailing.
Car spares manufacturer: (1) for particular makes of car where only one manufacturer produces them; (2) spare parts generally (i.e. general motor accessories) and spare parts for specific cars which are made by more than one manufacturer.
Water company: (1) water supply to a particular area; (2) water supply where the consumer has a choice of location (e.g. a firm setting up in business).
Ice skating rink: (1) ice skating in that area; (2) ice skating nationally; sports facilities.
Ice cream van: (1) ice cream supply at certain events or public places; (2) ice cream supply in the general area or when there is a shop or another van nearby.

Q20. E. If the long-run average cost curve is downward sloping, one firm supplying the whole market would be able to produce at a lower average cost than two firms sharing the market. The established firm would thus be able to undercut the price charged by any new entrant. (Although a downward-sloping *LRAC* curve would be a *sufficient* condition for a firm to have a natural monopoly, it is not a *necessary* condition. A firm could still have a natural monopoly if it was operating at the bottom, or even just beyond the bottom, of its *LRAC* curve, provided that two firms sharing the market would entail moving back up along the *LRAC* curve to a significantly higher level of long-run average cost.)

Q21. A. With an upward-sloping *LRAC* curve, two firms could produce at a lower *AC* than one. A new firm could thus 'steal' some of the monopoly's market by producing at a lower cost.

Q22. *must be elastic for some of its length but may be inelastic for part of it.* Although a monopolist is likely to face a less elastic demand at any given price than an imperfectly competitive firm, its demand curve *must* be elastic along part of its length. The reason is that profits are maximised where *MR* is to equal *MC*. Now *MC* will be positive and thus *MR* must also be positive. But where *MR* is positive, demand is elastic.

Q23. *above.* With a downward-sloping demand curve, price is above *MR*. Thus if *MR = MC*, price must also be above *MC*.

Q24. *False.* The monopolist can choose *either* price *or* quantity but not both. Given its demand curve, there is only one price corresponding to each level of sales and only one level of sales corresponding to each price.

Q25. E. The price given by the demand curve at the output where *MR = MC*.

Q26. *(a)* See table below.

Quantity (cars per day)	AR (£000s)	TR (£000s)	MR (£000s)	AC (£000s)	TC (£000s)	MC (£000s)
1	100	100		110	110	
			90			70
2	95	190		90	180	
			80			60
3	90	270		80	240	
			70			60
4	85	340		75	300	
			60			70
5	80	400		74	370	
			50			86
6	75	450		76	456	
			40			111
7	70	490		81	567	

(b) 4 cars per day (where *MC = MR*).

(c) £40 000 (i.e. *TR – TC*).

Q27. *True.* *MC* cannot be negative: it cannot cost less (in total) to produce more. Therefore if *MC = MR*, *MR* cannot be negative.

Q28. *False.* Demand is elastic over the output range where *MR* is positive: a rise in output causes a rise in total revenue (quantity rises proportionately more than price falls). Demand is inelastic over the output

range where *MR* is negative: a rise in output causes a fall in total revenue (quantity rises proportionately less than price falls). But since *MC* cannot be negative and thus *MR* cannot be negative where it equals *MC*, demand must be elastic at the output where the monopolist maximises profit.

Q29. $P_{\epsilon_d} = \Delta Q/\text{mid}Q \div \Delta P/\text{mid}P = 2/4 \div -10/85 = -4.25$ (which is elastic).

Q30. Given the barriers to the entry of new firms, supernormal profits will not be eliminated by competition. Price will remain above *AC*. It will only be chance if *MR* and *MC* happen to intersect at the bottom of the *AC* curve. For example, Figure 6.3 (on page 80) could represent a long-run situation as well as a short-run one. Here *MR* and *MC* intersect to the left of the minimum point of the *AC* curve.

Q31. E. Before the agency was formed the price was determined by the simple interaction of demand (given by the *AR* curve) and supply (given by the *MC* curve. Price was therefore P_2. Once the agency has been formed, it will sell that quantity where *MC = MR*, at a price of P_3.

Q32. *False.* If a monopolist operates with a significantly lower *MC* curve (e.g. because its size allows it to operate more efficiently), this could be sufficient to offset the fact that the monopolist's price will be above the *MC* whereas the perfectly competitive price will equal *MC*.

Q33. See Figure A6.2. Before the agency was set up the price was P_0, where MC_0 crosses the demand curve. If the agency reduces costs to MC_1, price will fall to P_1. If it only reduces costs to MC_2, however, price will be P_2, which is still higher than the original level.

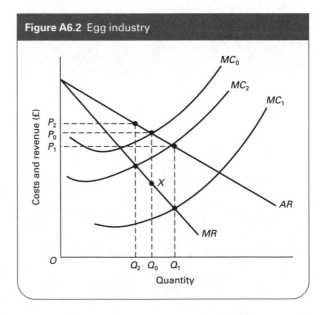

Figure A6.2 Egg industry

Q34. *(a)* $300 - P/4$.

(b) $TR = 1200Q - 4Q^2$.

(c) $MR = 1200 - 8Q$.

(d) $TC = 400 + 300Q - 4Q^2 + 3Q^3$.

(e) $TFC = 400$.

(f) $MC = 300 - 8Q + 9Q^2$.

(g) $MR = MC$

$\therefore 1200 - 8Q = 300 - 8Q + 9Q^2$

$\therefore 9Q^2 = 900$

$\therefore Q = 10$.

(h) $P = AR = 1200 - (4 \times 10) = £1160$.

(i) $AC = 400/10 + 300 - (4 \times 10) + (3 \times 10^2) = £600$.

(j) $A\Pi = £1160 - £600 = £560$.

(k) $T\Pi = £560 \times 10 = £5600$.

Q35. *lower.*

Q36. *lower.* The lower the exit costs, the less risky it will be for new firms to enter the industry: the more easily they can move to some other industry if they fail in their challenge.

Q37. *entry and exit costs are zero.*

Q38. *(a)* *slightly.*

(b) *highly* if the cleaning is put out to periodic tender.

non if the hospital employs its own cleaners or if an outside firm has a permanent contract.

(c) *moderately* if the banks are invited to tender periodically for a site licence.

non if a single bank is given a permanent site licence.

(d) *non* if the gas pipe grid is owned by a single company and if other companies are not permitted to use it or to establish a rival grid.

slightly (in densely populated areas) if companies are permitted to construct a rival grid.

moderately if rival companies are permitted to use the existing grid.

(e) *highly* unless prohibited by law or unless an existing service is heavily subsidised.

(f) *moderately* (at the bidding stage). The failure costs may be high if a city invests a lot on facilities – as several unsuccessful cities can testify (but, of course, the facilities can still be enjoyed by the inhabitants).

(g) as (e).

7 Profit Maximising under Imperfect Competition

A REVIEW

Imperfect competition is the general term we use to refer to all market structures lying between the two extremes of monopoly and perfect competition. We examine the two broad categories of imperfect competition: *monopolistic competition* and *oligopoly*. We also look at a common practice of firms under imperfect competition (and monopoly too): *price discrimination*.

In this chapter we continue with the assumption that firms want to maximise profits. In the next chapter we will drop this assumption and consider the effects of firms pursuing other goals.

7.1 Monopolistic competition

(Pages 175–7) Monopolistic competition is nearer the perfectly competitive end of the spectrum.

Q1. From the list of points below, select those which distinguish a monopolistically competitive industry from a perfectly competitive industry.

(a) There are no barriers to the entry of new firms into the market.   *Yes/No*

(b) Firms in the industry produce differentiated products.   *Yes/No*

(c) The industry is characterised by a mass of sellers, each with a small market share.   *Yes/No*

(d) A downward-sloping demand curve means the firm has some control over the product's price.   *Yes/No*

(e) In the long run only normal profits will be earned.   *Yes/No*

(f) Advertising plays a key role in bringing the product to the attention of the consumer.   *Yes/No*

Q2. At which of the following outputs would a monopolistically competitive seller maximise profits?

A. Where marginal revenue equals average cost.

B. Where price equals marginal revenue.

C. Where marginal revenue equals marginal cost.

D. Where average cost is at a minimum.

E. Where price equals average cost.

Q3. Following a rapid growth in the demand for home-delivered fast foods, Pukka Pizza is now earning substantial supernormal profits on its dial-a-pizza business. As a result of this success, a number of other local restaurants and fast-food diners are diversifying into the home-delivery market.

(a) What will be the likely effect on the position and elasticity of Pukka Pizza's demand curve from this increased competition?

....

(b) How will this depend on the type of food that the new competitors are supplying?

....

(c) At what point will firms stop entering the market?

....

 Multiple Choice   Written answer    Delete wrong word   Diagram/table manipulation   Calculation   Matching/ordering

Figure 7.1 Pukka Pizza: costs and revenue (long-run position)

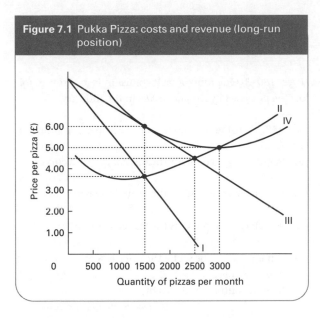

Q4. Figure 7.1 represents Pukka Pizza's long-run equilibrium position.

(a) Label the curves.

Curve I: ....

Curve II: ....

Curve III: ....

Curve IV: ....

(b) What is the long-run equilibrium price? (Tick)

£3.50 . . . £4.50 . . . £5.00 . . . £6.00 . . .

(c) What is the long-run equilibrium quantity? (Tick)

1500 . . . 2500 . . . 3000 . . .

(Pages 177–8) Firms under imperfect competition are likely to engage in advertising and other forms of non-price competition. The aim of this is to **Q5.** *shift the demand curve to the right and make it less elastic/shift the demand curve to the right and make it more elastic.*

Q6. For a profit-maximising firm, the amount it should spend on advertising should be:

A. as little as possible because advertising costs money.

B. as much as possible because advertising increases demand.

C. that where the average cost of the advertising equals the average revenue earned from it.

D. that where the average revenue from the advertising minus the average cost of it is at a maximum.

E. that where the marginal revenue from the advertising equals the marginal cost of it.

Q7. Which of the following are reasons why a monopolistically competitive firm is inefficient in the long run?

(a) It is only making normal profits.   *Yes/No*

(b) It is producing at a price above the minimum average cost.   *Yes/No*

(c) It is producing an output below that at minimum average cost.   *Yes/No*

(d) It faces a downward-sloping *AR* curve.   *Yes/No*

(e) It is producing where marginal cost is below average cost.   *Yes/No*

(f) It faces an upward-sloping *MC* curve.   *Yes/No*

Q8. The monopolistically competitive firm in the long run will produce less than a firm in perfect competition (given the same *LRAC* curve) but will charge a lower price due to the threat of rival firms.   *True/False*

Q9. A monopolistically competitive industry in the long run will experience excess capacity. To which one of the following is this due?

A. Firms will only make normal profit.

B. Firms will enter the industry if supernormal profits can be made.

C. Firms will produce along the upward-sloping portion of their marginal cost curve.

D. The tangency point of the firm's *AR* and *LRAC* curves is to the left of the minimum *LRAC*.

E. The point where *AR* equals *LRAC* is vertically above the point where *MR* equals *LRMC*.

Q10. The monopolistically competitive firm in the long run will always produce at a lower price than a monopoly because it only makes normal profits.   *True/False*

7.2 Oligopoly

(Page 179) Oligopoly is the most frequently occurring of the four market structures. Oligopolies, however, differ significantly one from another. Nevertheless they do have various features in common.

Q11. Which of the following are characteristics of oligopoly?

(a) There are just a few firms that dominate the industry.   *Yes/No*

(b) There are few if any barriers to the entry of new firms into the industry.   *Yes/No*

(c) The firms face downward-sloping demand curves.   *Yes/No*

(d) There is little point in advertising because there are so few firms.   *Yes/No*

(e) Oligopolists tend to take into account the actions and reactions of other firms.   *Yes/No*

Q12. Under oligopoly the price charged by one firm is likely to affect the price charged by other firms in the industry.   *True/False*

◖ Q13. Because oligopolists are interdependent this makes it easier to predict an oligopolist's price and output.
True/False

(Pages 179–80) Sometimes oligopolists openly compete with each other; sometimes they collude. When they collude they will attempt to act as if they were a monopoly and make monopoly profits which they then must decide how to divide between them.

When oligopolists formally collude this is known as a *cartel*. One way of dividing up the market is to assign each cartel member a quota.

(?) Q14. Assume that a member of a cartel faces the situation shown in Figure 7.2. Assuming that P_c is the price set by the cartel and Q_1 is the firm's allotted quota, why would the firm have an incentive to cheat?

....

....

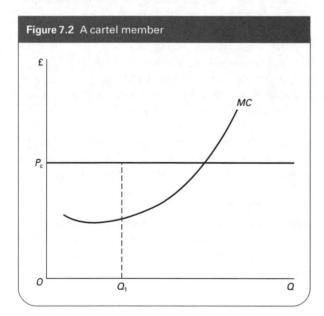

Figure 7.2 A cartel member

◖ Q15. There will be little point in non-price competition by cartel members if a strict quota system is enforced.
True/False

In most countries there are laws that restrict either the formation of cartels or their activities. When formal or open collusion is against the law, firms may collude tacitly.

◖ Q16. Which of the following are examples of tacit collusion?
(a) Price leadership by a *dominant* firm. *Yes/No*
(b) Agreements 'behind closed doors'. *Yes/No*
(c) Discounts to retailers. *Yes/No*

(d) Setting prices at a well-known benchmark. *Yes/No*
(e) Increased product differentiation within the industry.
Yes/No

(Pages 180–3) One form of tacit collusion is for firms to follow the prices set by the *price leader* in the industry.

⊗ Q17. Consider the model of price leadership shown in Figure 7.3.
(a) Which curve represents the market demand curve?
ABC/DBC/DE
(b) Which curve represents the leader's demand curve?
ABC/DBC/DE
(c) Which curve represents the leader's *MR* curve?
ABC/DBC/DE
(d) What price will be set by the price leader if it wishes to maximise profits? $P_1/P_2/P_3/P_4$
(e) Q_1 is the output produced by
the leader/all other firms together
(f) Mark total industry output on Figure 7.3.

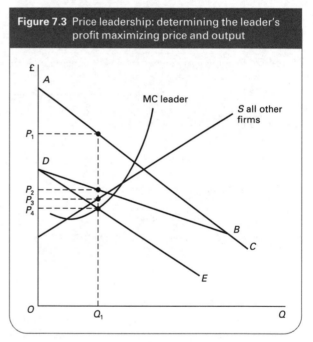

Figure 7.3 Price leadership: determining the leader's profit maximizing price and output

◖ Q18. In the *barometric price leader* model, the price leader is always the largest firm in the industry. *True/False*

An alternative form of tacit collusion is for firms to follow simple 'rules of thumb'. An example is that of *average cost pricing*.

◖ Q19. Average cost pricing involves setting price equal to average cost. *True/False*

(Pages 183–4) Sometimes, however, there will be no collusion of any sort between oligopolists, or, if there has been, it may break down.

Q20. Under which of the following circumstances is collusion likely to break down?
(a) There is a reduction in barriers to international trade. *Yes/No*
(b) The market becomes more stable. *Yes/No*
(c) One of the firms develops a new cost-saving technique. *Yes/No*
(d) One of the firms becomes dominant in the industry. *Yes/No*
(e) The number of firms in the industry decreases. *Yes/No*

(Pages 184–8) The behaviour of firms under non-collusive oligopoly depends on (a) how they think their rivals will react, and (b) their attitudes towards taking a risk. The theory of games studies the alternative strategies a firm can adopt. Two possible strategies are *maximax* and *maximin*.

Q21. Which *one* of the following is the *maximax* strategy?
A. Choosing the policy whose best outcome is better than the worst outcomes of all alternative policies.
B. Choosing the policy whose best outcome is better than the best outcome of any alternative policy.
C. Choosing the policy whose worst outcome is better than the best outcome of any alternative policy.
D. Choosing the policy whose worst outcome is better than the worst outcomes of all alternative policies.
E. Choosing the policy whose worst outcome is worse than the best outcome of any alternative policy.

Q22. Which *one* of the strategies in Q21 is the *maximin* strategy?
A. B. C. D. E.

Table 7.1

		Durashine's price	
		£5.00	£4.50
Supasheen's price	£5.00	A £6m each	B £2m for Supasheen £8m for Durashine
	£4.50	C £9m for Supasheen £3m for Durashine	D £4m each

Table 7.1 shows the annual profits of two paint manufacturers. At present they both charge £5.00 per litre for gloss paint. Their annual profits are shown in box A. The other boxes show the effects on their profits of one or the other firm or both firms reducing their price per litre to £4.50.

Q23. Which of the two prices should Durashine charge if it is pursuing
(a) a maximax strategy? *£5.00/£4.50*
(b) a maximin strategy? *£5.00/£4.50*

Q24. Which of the two prices should Supasheen charge if it is pursuing
(a) a maximax strategy? *£5.00/£4.50*
(b) a maximin strategy? *£5.00/£4.50*

(?) Q25. Why is this known as a *dominant strategy* game?

....

....

Q26. Assume now that the 'game' between Durashine and Supasheen has been played for some time with the result that they both learn a 'lesson' from it. They thus form a new agreement to fix the price at £5.00. It is now likely that:
A. both firms will cheat on the agreement.
B. both firms will stick to the agreement permanently.
C. both firms will stick to the agreement so long as costs of production remain constant.
D. Durashine alone will cheat.
E. Supasheen alone will cheat.

(Pages 188–9) One of the most famous of the non-collusive theories of oligopoly is that of the *kinked demand curve*. According to this theory, the firm under oligopoly perceives that its demand curve is steeper below the current price than it is above it: that it is kinked at the current price.

Q27. This kink is due to the firm's belief that its competitors:
A. will set a price at the kink of the demand curve.
B. will match any price increase it makes, but will not match a price reduction.
C. will not match a price increase but will match any price reduction.
D. will match all price increases and reductions.
E. will match neither price increases nor reductions.

The kinked demand curve theory suggests that a firm is likely to keep its price unchanged unless there are substantial shifts in revenue or cost curves.

Q28. Figure 7.4 shows a kinked demand curve. Which of the following represents the *MR* curve?
A. *fghi*
B. *jgkl*
C. *jghi*
D. *fgkl*
E. *jgk,hi*

(Pages 189–91) It is not possible to draw firm conclusions as to whether oligopolists act in the public interest given that there are many factors that influence their behaviour and given that circumstances differ from one oligopoly to another.

Figure 7.4 Kinked demand curve

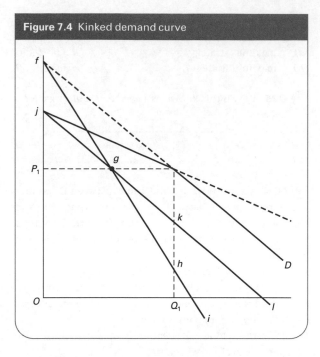

Q29. Which of the following aspects of oligopoly can be seen to be in the public interest?

(a) Prices are set collusively.	*Yes/No/Possibly*
(b) Suppliers have countervailing power.	*Yes/No/Possibly*
(c) Customers have countervailing power.	
	Yes/No/Possibly
(d) There is non-price competition in the industry.	
	Yes/No/Possibly
(e) There is substantial advertising.	*Yes/No/Possibly*
(f) The market is contestable.	*Yes/No/Possibly*
(g) The firms' products are highly differentiated from each other.	*Yes/No/Possibly*
(h) There are substantial barriers to entry.	
	Yes/No/Possibly

7.3 Price discrimination

(Pages 191–6) A firm may practise price discrimination. This is where it sells the same product (costing the same to produce) at different prices in different markets or to different customers.

In order for a firm to practise price discrimination it must be **Q30.** *a price setter/a price taker*. It must be able to distinguish between markets such that the good cannot be resold from the **Q31.** *low-/high*-priced market to the **Q32.** *low-/high*-priced market. In each market, price elasticity of demand will differ. In the low-priced market, demand will be **Q33.** *more elastic/less elastic* than in the high-priced market.

Q34. There are three types of price discrimination:
 (i) First-degree price discrimination.
 (ii) Second-degree price discrimination.
 (iii) Third-degree price discrimination.
Match each of the three types to the following definitions:

(a) When a firm charges a consumer so much for the first so many units purchased, a different price for the next so many units purchased and so on.

....

(b) When a firm divides consumers into different groups and charges a different price to consumers in different groups, but the same price to all the consumers within a group.

....

(c) When a firm charges each consumer for each unit the maximum price which that consumer is willing to pay for that unit.

....

Q35. In Figure 7.5 if the firm is able to earn the revenue shown by the shaded area, which of the following must it be practising?
A. First-degree price discrimination.
B. Second-degree price discrimination.
C. Third-degree price discrimination.
D. No price discrimination at all.
E. It is impossible to say without knowing details about its costs of production.

Figure 7.5 A firm's revenue

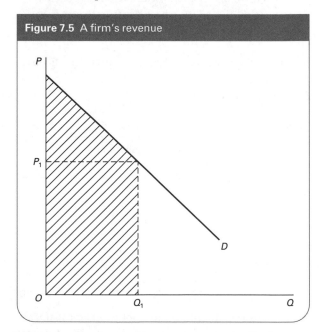

Q36. Which of the following are advantages to the firm from practising price discrimination.

(a) Higher total revenue.	*Yes/No/Possibly*
(b) Lower costs.	*Yes/No/Possibly*
(c) Less advertising.	*Yes/No/Possibly*
(d) Helps to drive competitors out of business.	
	Yes/No/Possibly
(e) Increases sales.	*Yes/No/Possibly*

B   PROBLEMS, EXERCISES AND PROJECTS

Q37. In recent years it has become fashionable for governments around the world to break up monopolies (sometimes nationalised and sometimes private but protected by licences or other regulations). The argument has been that the introduction of competition will stimulate firms to find ways of reducing costs and of providing a better service or product.

Take the case of buses and coaches. Many routes that were previously guaranteed to a single operator have now been opened up to competition. The immediate advantage is that on the routes used by a lot of passengers, the competition has often driven down the prices.

(a) Demonstrate this diagrammatically for an individual coach operator now finding itself under monopolistic competition.

On the other hand, on many routes facing cut-throat competition, coaches are running with empty seats.

(b) Does the theory of monopolistic competition predict this?

Also there is the danger that companies may cut corners (e.g. in terms of safety) in order to keep their costs as low as possible.

Then there is the problem that the less used routes may no longer be operated at all. A bus or coach company with a monopoly may be prepared to operate such routes even though it makes a loss on them. It 'cross-subsidises' them with the monopoly profits it gains on the popular routes. When the monopoly is broken up, however, the competitive firms may not be willing or able to carry on operating these routes. Thus country bus services may close down, as may also services early in the morning or late at night on the otherwise well-used routes.

(c) Is it desirable that a monopoly bus company *should* cross-subsidise loss-making routes?

(d) Would a profit-maximising monopoly bus company *choose* to cross-subsidise such routes? How may a local authority ensure that the company does so?

(e) How could a local authority ensure that loss-making routes continued to operate after the industry had become monopolistically competitive?

(f) Use the arguments contained in this case study to compare the relative benefits and costs to the consumer of monopoly and monopolistic competition.

Q38. Find out the prices of a range of foodstuffs and household items sold in two or three different supermarkets and two or three different small foodstores. Which items are sold at similar prices in all the different shops and which are sold at significantly different prices? Account for these similarities or differences.

Q39. Durashine paint company is considering what strategy it should adopt in order to maximise its profits. It is currently considering four options. The first is to introduce a 10 per cent price cut. The second is to introduce a new brand of high-gloss durable emulsion paint. The third is to launch a new marketing campaign. The fourth is to introduce no change other than increasing its prices in line with inflation.

It estimates how much profit each strategy (1–4) will bring depending on how its rivals react. It considers the effects of six possible reactions (a–f).

(a) Which of the four policies should it adopt if it is pursuing:
  (i) A maximax strategy?
  (ii) A maximum strategy?

(b) Which of the four policies might be the best compromise?

		Other firms' responses					
		a	b	c	d	e	f
Strategies	1	−25	50	−20	30	40	60
for	2	−20	20	−15	0	15	80
Durashine	3	0	15	30	0	20	30
	4	20	35	−10	40	30	70

(£000s)

Q40. A firm operating under conditions of oligopoly is currently selling 4 units per day at a price of £30. By conducting extensive market research its chief economist estimates that, if it raises its price, its rivals will not follow suit and that as a result it will face an average revenue curve given by

$$P = 40 - 5Q/2 \text{ (where } P = AR)$$

On the other hand, if it reduces its price, its rivals will be forced to reduce theirs too. Under these circumstances its average revenue curve will be given by

$$P = 50 - 5Q \text{ (where } P = AR)$$

(a) What will be the equation for the firm's *demand* curve if the firm raises its price?

(b) What will be the equation for the firm's demand curve if the firm reduces its price?

(c) How much will be demanded at the following prices?

£40 ....

£35 ....

£30 ....

£20 ....

£10 ....

(d) Plot the two demand curves on Figure 7.6, marking in bold pen the portion of each that is relevant to the firm.

(e) Plot two marginal revenue curves corresponding to each of the demand curves. (Remember that the *MR* curve lies midway between the *AR* curve and the vertical axis). Mark in bold pen the portion of each *MR* curve that is relevant to the firm.

(f) Over what range of values can marginal cost vary without affecting the profit-maximising price of £30?

....

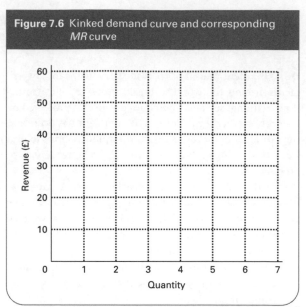

Figure 7.6 Kinked demand curve and corresponding *MR* curve

DISCUSSION TOPICS AND ESSAYS

Q41. Why does monopolistic competition lead to a less than optimal allocation of resources? Does this inevitably mean that the consumer benefits more from perfect competition than monopolistic competition?

Q42. Under what circumstances might a firm under monopolistic competition be able to earn supernormal profits in the *long* run?

Q43. Outline the main benefits and costs to society from advertising. Does advertising necessarily lead to a higher price for the product?

Q44. Imagine that a group of wall tile manufacturers decide to enter a cartel. What factors will determine whether the cartel is likely to be successful in raising prices?

Q45. Assume that an international airline cartel has been operating for a number of years. Imagine various circumstances that could lead to the breakdown of this cartel. What could the members of the cartel do to prevent its breakdown?

Q46. Describe what is meant by the *prisoners' dilemma* game. How will the outcome be affected by (a) the number of participants in the game and (b) the degree of similarity between the participants?

Q47. What are the main strengths and weaknesses of game theory as (a) a theory of oligopoly behaviour and (b) an aid to a real-world oligopolist in deciding its price and output?

Q48. The kinked demand curve theory provides an explanation of price stability under oligopoly. Does it also explain how prices are determined?

Q49. In what ways may the consumer (a) gain and (b) lose from the behaviour of oligopolists?

Q50. Debate
Advertising merely increases costs, eliminates competition and as a consequence pushes up prices.

ARTICLES

FT

The decision by Wal-Mart to purchase Asda was a significant event in food retailing. The stable, if reasonably competitive, oligopoly of the major food retailers, was suddenly faced by an international giant of retailing with a reputation for driving prices down. How were they to respond? The article below, taken from the *Financial Times* of 15 June 1999, considers the impact Wal-Mart might have on the market and what strategies existing retailers will need to adopt in order to survive.

When the price is not right

Is this the end of life as the British consumer knows it? Wal-Mart, the world's most formidable retailer, has arrived in the UK and is widely expected to transform the shopping experience for Britain's 55m inhabitants.

Almost overnight, UK retailers will find themselves facing price wars on everything from food to cosmetics and clothing to household goods. Customers should enjoy huge discounts of 10 to 15 per cent on their basic shopping needs.

That, at least, is the kneejerk reaction to news that Wal-Mart, with annual sales of $138bn a year, intends to swallow up Asda, the UK's third-largest food retailer, in an agreed £6.7bn cash deal.

But will Wal-Mart's entry into one of the most mature retail markets in Europe actually have such a dramatic effect?

True, its sheer size and efficiency allow it to sell products to US consumers at levels much lower than the cost would be to UK retailers. But there are some reasons why the anxieties might be overdone.

Wal-Mart is used to operating from significantly larger outlets than the typical Asda. On average, the UK supermarket group's stores are about 40 000 sq ft, whereas Wal-Mart's are four to five times bigger.

This may not seem important until it is combined with another simple fact. Wal-Mart's expertise lies in selling a wide range of general merchandise, while Asda's is in food. So the question might be how will Asda – physically constrained by its smaller stores – be able to widen its non-food range to benefit from Wal-Mart's buying power.

'If you are going to put fertiliser into Asda, what are you going to stop selling?' asks one analyst. 'And if you increase the toaster range, will you sell less bread?'

Moreover, Wal-Mart will be as constrained as anyone else by Britain's tight planning regime which means it cannot drive Asda forward simply by throwing up new stores or adding vast extensions.

Wal-Mart itself is keen to stress that the changes which result from its takeover of Asda will be 'evolutionary rather than revolutionary'. Jay Fitzsimmons, Wal-Mart's treasurer, says there is a lot of 'doom and gloom' spoken about the company's effect on the new markets its chooses to enter.

But it is a fact that when Wal-Mart comes to a market, the first thing it does is reduce prices, which inevitably puts pressure on other retailers.

'They cut prices on 1500 lines in Germany,' says Tony MacNeary, retail analyst at SPP Investment Management. One of the first repercussions was the decision by Interspar to sell its hypermarkets to Wal-Mart and focus on smaller stores.

In Canada, too, retailers were forced to reconsider their strategies when Wal-Mart entered in 1993. Although cutting prices and putting muscle behind the cuts with sharpened advertising hit Wal-Mart's returns for some three years, today Canada is its most profitable operation. And the Canadian food sector has begun a round of consolidation which many believe is the direct result of Wal-Mart's aggressive pricing strategy. 'No one can afford to sit back and take it easy,' says Mr MacNeary.

British retailers may have good reason to fear Wal-Mart, even though in the past the market has been relatively immune to attacks from discounters. The recent controversy over pricing in Britain could mean that the market is ripe for a big and effective discounter, say some analysts.

A recent survey by Verdict, the retail consultancy, found that more than 80 per cent of shoppers felt that prices of food and groceries were higher in the UK than elsewhere. An even greater percentage believe they pay more for certain consumer goods.

Food retailers have been the obvious focus of concern, having suffered some of the greatest adverse publicity over pricing since the government launched an enquiry into whether they are profiteering at the expense of consumers.

But Wal-Mart's takeover of Asda will almost certainly prompt closer examination of strategies employed by the three biggest rivals. They will be aware that, although Wal-Mart is relatively new to food in the US, since it began expanding rapidly it has taken a substantial share of business away from traditional supermarkets, which have fallen from 71 per cent in 1980 to 45 per cent in 1996.

And although Wal-Mart denies there will be any dramatic changes in the way Asda will be run, there is always the possibility that it could use the benefits

from improving Asda's non-food product range to lower prices significantly in food.

The struggling food retailers, such as Safeway and J Sainsbury, may well be forced to find partners to shore up their competitiveness. And it is most likely that these partners will be from abroad, since the current competition commission enquiry in to the market power of the big four would appear to rule out British mergers. 'This is the beginning of panEuropean consolidation,' says Michael Jary, of strategy consultants OC&C.

But non-food retailers could be even more vulnerable. There is a strong view among industry analysts that Wal-Mart will not use the same approach as it did in Canada or Germany. Both those businesses required substantial cultural changes and remedial action to improve their positions. That is not the case at Asda, which has largely emulated Wal-Mart's retailing approach of every day low pricing and is already on average some 5 per cent cheaper than its supermarket rivals.

The price attack will be more selective, and possibly hit the health and beauty retailers such as Boots, the high street chemist chain, hardest, say analysts and retailers. 'Health and beauty is where most food retailers make their fattest margins,' said one supermarket executive. 'They will probably go for that first.'

It is the mass-market operators which have the most to fear from Wal-Mart, says Verdict's Mike Godliman. 'Any large retailer whose customers visit them primarily because of price are exteremely vulnerable,' he says. 'You can never fight Wal-Mart on price.'

Those which focus on other aspects such as service and quality may find a way to live happily with Wal-Mart, he suggests.

Yet in the end, it is true to say that nothing will ever be the same again for UK retailers. Prices in food and non-food sectors will have to come down, making life more difficult for an already struggling sector, says one analyst, even if Wal-Mart's slowly-slowly approach to the UK market means this does not happen overnight.

'Wal-Mart will certainly not spend $11bn and write it off as some academic experiment in price versus volume.'

(a) Competition in UK food retailing has more often than not been concerned with choice and quality rather than with price. What advantages have such businesses gained from this approach?

(b) Given the size of Wal-Mart, why does it continue to focus on price competition when a case might be made that this is not the best way to maximise profits?

(c) What strategies, according to the article, should UK retailers adopt in order to survive in the market with Wal-Mart? Identify any weaknesses with these strategies.

Fancy an ice cream? What is on offer in a shop is likely to be determined by who owns the freezer. The result is that the choice open to you is likely to be limited. In the article below, taken from *Director* of August 1999, the exclusivity of freezer use, and the likely outcome of a Competition Commission investigation into the industry, are considered.

Frozen out

The holiday season is well under way. And that means work for the ice-cream industry. While the rest of us get hot under the collar, this is the time of the year when Britain's ice-cream industry watches the money roll in. The season may last barely 100 days, but the ice-cream market is nevertheless worth a total of £885m. This year, however, the 'impulse' ice-cream industry – so named because products are bought for immediate consumption – is beginning to leave a sour taste in the mouth of the Competition Commission, formerly MMC.

Next month, the Commission will report the findings of its latest investigation into the ice-cream industry. It will be the result of an inquiry launched last December, and prompted by numerous complaints to the Office of Fair Trading of anti-competitive practices. This is the third inquiry into the supply of impulse ice-cream in six years. A thorough investigation of the industry was also recommended in the MMC's July 1998 report, which found the distribution system operated by market leader Birds Eye Wall's to be uncompetitive.

The key problem, according to many ice-cream manufacturers, is freezer exclusivity. This is where the manufacturer supplies a retail outlet with a freezer on the condition that only its own products are stocked.

Many smaller ice-cream makers are effectively being 'frozen out' of shops where these 'tied' freezers are already in place. The shops themselves are usually small operations, and either don't have room for another freezer, or cannot sustain the level of turnover needed to justify more than one. So in most instances, only one manufacturer's products are available at such outlets.

Wall's, part of the Anglo-Dutch giant Unilever, has a near 70 per cent share of the wrapped impulse market and around 80 000 exclusive freezers in outlets across the UK. It holds to the belief that exclusivity makes the market grow, rather than stifles it.

Fears of exclusion

While Wall's welcomes the inquiry into the whole industry, which includes scooped and machine-dispensed ice-cream as well as wrapped, it strongly defends its position. Jill Turner, business manager at Wall's, claims the company has gained its position through investment in the market. 'From a business point of view, we want to see a return on that investment – that is why only our products can be stocked in our freezers.'

But for small ice-cream makers such as Treats, this problem is barring its growth in the sector. David Durie, marketing director, says: 'As a small company we feel extremely frustrated that we can't take some of our good ideas and do something with them.'

The Leeds-based company, which employs 50 staff, has been trying to get its products into small shops since 1991, with limited success – it currently holds a 6 per cent market share. Says Durie: 'We had a strong mobile base, and when we parted from Unilever in 1991 through a management buy-out, we decided to try and get our products into small retailers. But we came across this problem with freezers.'

Treats has between 6000 and 10 000 freezers in shops around the UK, but they're not exclusive. 'A retailer pays us between £400 and £500, but then they can stock whatever products they like,' says Durie. 'Admittedly, we give them vouchers to redeem against Treats products. But it is up to us to make sure our sales and marketing is up to scratch so they want to stock our products.'

Wall's believes the problem is that no-one else is willing to invest in freezers, which it believes is the way the market works. If Wall's didn't supply freezers, says Turner, then ice-cream in general would not be so widely available. 'The issue is that [small] retailers can't afford, or are not prepared to buy, a freezer because ice-cream sales account for only about 2 per cent of their turnover. A barrier will be created in the market if retailers have to buy their own freezer,' she says.

Durie disagrees. He believes that whatever the retailer's view, exclusivity limits the number of new players coming into the market. He believes unbranded industry freezers are the way forward. Retailers such as Fourbouys, Martins and Woolworths changed to industry freezers a couple of seasons ago and now stock Treats's products alongside other brands. 'This proves that we've got products worth selling,' says Durie.

US confectionery group Mars has been battling with Unilever over freezer exclusivity since 1991. It believes that the freezer-supply market would open up if the Competition Commission found exclusivity to be anti-competitive. According to a Mars spokesman: 'There are already many other ways for retailers to acquire good quality refrigeration, without it costing them a penny: other ice-cream suppliers and ice-cream wholesalers provide freezers without exclusivity.' Mars, which has about 13 per cent of the market for wrapped impulse ice-cream, supplies freezers to retailers on condition that about one-third of the products stocked are Mars's.

Mars believes Wall's practices of exclusivity are a key reason why the company has become so dominant over the last 20 years. 'Freezer exclusivity, outlet exclusivity and distribution exclusivity together provide Unilever with an effective shield against fair competition.'

But Turner defends Wall's position. She claims that no other company has shown that it is as willing as Wall's to invest in freezers. If no-one else is going to do it Wall's believes the market will suffer. 'Having a freezer provided by us can make the difference between someone selling ice-cream or not bothering,'

says Turner. 'Our investment in product innovation and refrigeration has led to the growth in ice-cream sales. That provides consumers with choice of whether they buy chocolate or an ice-cream. That's real choice,' she adds.

However, if exclusivity were prohibited, argues Mars's spokesman, the market would grow significantly. 'Our research shows the market would grow 30 to 40 per cent. This means overall impulse sales would go from two to three per cent, which would be a small rise, but substantial from a retailer's point of view.'

The experiences at Newspoint, a newsagent in Kingston, Surrey, support Mars's argument: since replacing its exclusive freezer, sales have rocketed.

Owner Nalin Shah, says: 'I'm loyal to the company that supplied the freezer, so about one-third of the freezer is stocked with its products. But the rest is various brands. I now stock about 36 different products, instead of the 10 I stocked before. My sales of ice-cream increased over 200 per cent last season, and I think that is down to better consumer choice.'

(a) What do you understand by the term barriers to entry? How do exclusive freezers act as a barrier to entry?

(b) How does Wall's respond to the argument that its exclusive freezers are stifling competition and consumer choice?

(c) If the Competition Commission finds against Wall's, and it is forced to remove or relax its exclusive freezer policy, what might happen to ice cream retailing?

 ANSWERS

Q1. Yes: (b), (d) and (f). The rest ((a), (c) and (e)) apply to both perfect competition *and* monopolistic competition.

Q2. C. This is the universal law for profit maximisation no matter what the type of market structure.

Q3. *(a)* The demand curve will shift to the left as the market will now be divided between a larger number of firms. The curve will probably also become more elastic as there will be a larger number of suppliers to choose from, and hence the demand for Pukka Pizzas will be more price sensitive.

(b) The more similar the product and the service provided by the competitors, the more elastic will be the demand.

(c) Firms will stop entering the market when all supernormal profits have been eroded.

Q4. *(a)* Curve I: *marginal revenue (MR).* Curve II: *marginal cost (MC).* Curve III: *average revenue (AR).* Curve IV: *average cost (AC).*

(b) £6.00. The price where $MC = MR$ and where $AC = AR$.

(c) 1500. The quantity where $MC = MR$ and where $AC = AR$.

Q5. *Shift the demand curve to the right and make it less elastic.*

Q6. E.

Q7. Yes: (b), (c), (d) and (e). The long-run equilibrium is where $AR = AC$: i.e. where the AR curve is tangential to the AC curve. But since the AR curve is downward

sloping (d), this point of tangency must be to the left of the minimum point of the AC curve (c), at a point where AC is falling and where therefore MC is below AC (e). Thus costs are not as low as they could be and therefore the price is higher (b) and output is lower than it would be (c) if production was at minimum AC.

Q8. *False.* The monopolistically competitive firm will produce less than the perfectly competitive firm if they both face the same $LRAC$ curve, *but* it will charge a *higher* price because it is not producing at the bottom of the $LRAC$ curve.

Q9. D. Normal profits will be made where the AR curve is tangential to the $LRAC$ curve. But because the AR curve is downward sloping (unlike under perfect competition), its tangency point with the $LRAC$ curve must be to the left of the minimum $LRAC$ curve. In other words the firm is producing at less than minimum average cost. It is in this sense that we say the firm and industry experience excess capacity: if industry output were to be expanded, production would take place at lower cost.

Q10. *False.* The monopoly may achieve economies of scale giving it a lower $LRAC$ curve. Also the monopoly may produce further down its $LRAC$ curve, depending on where $LRMC = LRMR$.

Q11. Yes: (a), (c) and (e). No: (b) and (d). One of the features that allows oligopolists to maintain their position of power in the market is their ability to restrict the entry of new firms. Advertising is one of the major ways in which oligopolists compete with their rivals in their attempt to gain a bigger market share and bigger profits.

Q12. *True.* As one firm changes its price this will affect the demand for its rivals' products and hence their prices.

Q13. *False.* It is very difficult to predict price and output without knowing what degree of competition or collusion there is between the rival firms.

Q14. By producing more than Q_1, it will earn more profit provided price remains at P_c. At P_c it will maximise its profits where $MR (= P_c)$ equals MC.

Q15. *True.* The firm *could* sell more at existing prices if it produced above its quota. There is thus little point in advertising or other types of non-price competition.

Q16. Yes: (a), (b) and (d).

Q17. *(a)* ABC; *(b)* DBC; *(c)* DE.
  (d) P_2: i.e. the price given by the leader's demand curve at the output (Q_1) where the leader's $MC = MR$.
  (e) Q_1 is the output produced by the leader.
  (f) Total industry output is found by reading across from P_2 to the market demand curve.

Q18. *False.* The barometric firm is simply the one whose prices the other firms are prepared to follow: the one whose price setting is taken as a barometer of market conditions.

Q19. *False.* Price is equal to average cost *plus* a mark-up for profit.

Q20. Yes: (a) and (c). (a) is likely to increase competition from imports. (c) is likely to encourage the firm with reduced costs to undercut its rivals' prices in order to gain a bigger market share.

Q21. B.

Q22. D.

Q23. *(a)* Cut price to £4.50.
  (b) Cut price to £4.50.

Q24. *(a)* Cut price to £4.50.
  (b) Cut price to £4.50.

Q25. Because both maximax and maximin strategies lead to the same decision.

Q26. C. After a period of 'tit-for-tat' price cutting, both firms will come to realise that they are both worse off for having played this 'game' (profits in box D are lower for both firms than in box A). They are thus likely to be willing to reach an agreement to fix price which *they will both stick to*. If, however, costs of production change, they may have to negotiate a new price agreement between them, or follow some rule of thumb, such as raising prices by the same percentage that costs have risen.

Q27. C. Competitors will be quite happy to see the firm raise its price and lose market share. They will feel obliged to match price reductions, however, for fear of losing market share themselves.

Q28. E. The *MR* curve corresponds to the shallower *AR* curve at levels of output lower than that at the kink and to the steeper *AR* curve at levels of output higher than that at the kink.

Q29. (a) *No*; (b) *Yes*; (c) *Yes*; (d) *Possibly*; (e) *No*; (f) *Yes*; (g) *Possibly*; (h) *No*.

Q30. a *price setter*.

Q31. *low.*

Q32. *high.*

Q33. *more elastic.*

Q34. (a) (ii); (b) (iii); (c) (i).

Q35. A. It can charge each consumer the maximum price (above P_1) that he or she is prepared to pay.

Q36. (a) *Yes*; (b) *Possibly*; (c) *No*; (d) *Yes*; (e) *Possibly*.

8 Alternative Theories of the Firm

A REVIEW

In this chapter we drop the assumption that firms are always profit maximisers. Firms may not have the information to maximise profits. But even if they did, they may choose to pursue some alternative aim.

We first examine the reasons why firms may not be able to maximise profits or may have some alternative aim. Then we look at the effects of pursuing some alternative aim: either a single aim, such as growth or sales, or several aims simultaneously.

8.1 Problems with traditional theory

(Page 198) Firms may *want* to maximise profits, but lack the information to do so.

Q1. If firms do no use *marginal* cost and marginal *revenue* concepts, they will not be able to arrive at their profit maximising output. *True/False*

Q2. If a firm uses accountants' cost concepts that are not based on opportunity cost, then it will only be by chance if it ends up maximising profits. *True/False*

Given the problems in estimating the profit-maximising price and output, the firm may resort to simple rules of thumb. One such rule is the *cost-plus* method of pricing. Under this system a firm merely adds a *mark-up* for profit to its average cost of production. Thus if its average cost were 50p and it wanted to make a 20p profit, it would set a price of

Q3. ....

By a process of trial and error, adjusting the mark-up and adjusting output, the firm can move towards the profit-maximising position.

(Pages 198–9) An even more fundamental criticism of the traditional theory of the firm is that the decision makers in the firm may not even aim to maximise profits in the first place.

Q4. On which of the following is this criticism based?
A. Many shareholders do not want to maximise profits.
B. Owners of firms are not 'rational'.
C. Shareholders are not the decision makers and have different interests from them.
D. Managers prefer to maximise profits because this is usually in their own interest.
E. Shareholders are really utility maximisers.

The divorce between the ownership and control of a firm is likely to be greater if **Q5.** *there are a few large shareholders/ there are many small shareholders*. It is also likely to be greater in **Q6.** *partnerships/private limited companies/public limited companies*.

Q7. Firms must still make enough profits to survive. But this does not make them profit maximisers.

Instead they are 'profit ....'.

◑ **Q8.** If a firm under *perfect competition* had an aim other than profit maximisation, would this make any difference to the output it would choose to produce?

(a) In the short run? *Yes/No*

(b) In the long run? *Yes/No*

The problem of managers not pursing the same goals as shareholders is an example of the *principal–agent problem*. Because of asymmetric information and different goals, agents may not always carry out the wishes of their principals. Asymmetric information, in this case, refers to the fact that **Q9.** *principals/agents* have superior knowledge and can, therefore, act against the interests of the other party.

⑦ **Q10.** In the following cases, which are the principals and which are the agents?

(a) Estate agents and house buyers:

estate agents ....; house buyers ....

(b) Shareholders and managers:

shareholders ....; managers ....

(c) House builders and architects:

house builders ....; architects ....

(d) Employers and workers:

employers ....; workers ....

(e) Shops and their customers:

shops ....; customers ....

8.2 Alternative maximising theories

(Pages 203–4) Long-run profit maximisation
The traditional theory of the firm assumes that firms are *short-run* profit maximisers. An alternative assumption is that firms seek to maximise *long-run* profits.

⑦ **Q11.** In what way might each of the following lead to smaller short-run profits but larger long-run profits?

(a) A large-scale advertising campaign ....

....

(b) Opening up a new production line ....

....

(c) Investing in research and development ....

....

(d) Launching a takeover bid for a rival company ....

....

(e) Installing expensive filter equipment to reduce atmospheric pollution from the factory's chimneys

....

A major problem with the theory of long-run profit maximisation is that it is virtually impossible to test.

⑦ **Q12.** Explain why.

....

....

◑ **Q13.** It is also virtually impossible in advance to identify a long-run profit-maximising price and output. Which of the following are reasons for this?

(a) Cost and revenue curves are likely to shift unpredictably as a result of the policy pursued. *Yes/No*

(b) Cost and revenue curves are likely to shift as a result of unpredictable external factors. *Yes/No*

(c) The firm is likely to experience economies of scale.

Yes/No

(d) Some policies may affect both demand *and* costs.

Yes/No

(e) Different managers are likely to make different judgements about the best way of achieving long-run maximum profits. *Yes/No*

(Pages 204–5) Sales revenue maximisation (short run)
The success of many managers may be judged according to the level of the firm's sales. For this reason, sales or sales revenue maximisation may be the dominant aim in a firm. Nevertheless, firms will still have to make sufficient profits to survive. Thus sales or sales revenue maximising firms will also be profit-'satisficing' firms.

⊖ **Q14.** Figure 8.1 shows a firm's short-run cost and revenue curves. (It operates under monopoly or imperfect competition.) The level of output it produces will depend on its aims. For each of the following four aims, identify the firm's output.

(a) Profit maximisation

....

(b) Sales maximisation (must earn at least normal profits)

....

(c) Sales maximisation (must cover all variable costs)

....

(d) Sales revenue maximisation (must earn at least normal profits)

....

(e) Assume now that the diagram represents a perfectly competitive industry (also in the short run). What will the equilibrium level of output be?

....

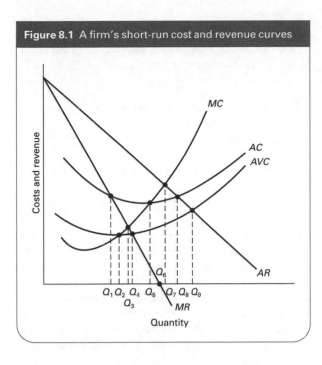

Figure 8.1 A firm's short-run cost and revenue curves

(f) Returning to the assumption that the diagram represents a firm under monopoly or imperfect competition, redraw the *AC* (and *AVC*) curves so that (b) and (d) produce the same output.

Q15. The profit-maximising output will never be greater than the (profit-satisficing) sales revenue maximising output. *True/False*

Q16. The (profit-satisficing) sales revenue maximising output will always be greater than the profit-maximising output. *True/False*

(?) Q17. If in the short run the firm could maximise sales revenue and make more than the satisfactory level of profit, this situation would be unlikely to persist in the long run even if other firms were prevented from entering the industry. Why?

....

....

(Pages 205–12) Growth maximisation
Rather than aiming to maximise *short-run* sales revenue, managers may take a longer-term perspective and aim to maximise the rate of growth of their firm. Growth can be by internal expansion or by merger.

If growth is to be by internal expansion, the firm will need to increase both its productive capacity (by investment) and the demand for its product (by advertising). Both will require finance.

(?) Q18. Name three ways in which a firm can finance such expansion.

1. ....

2. ....

3. ....

Firms may be prevented from growing too rapidly by the 'takeover constraint'.

(?) Q19. Why does a takeover become more likely when a firm expands rapidly?

....

....

A firm can grow by merging with or taking over another firm. (We will use the term 'mergers' for both mergers and takeovers.) Mergers can be of three types: horizontal, vertical and conglomerate.

Q20. Match each of the three types of merger to the following examples.
(a) A soft drinks manufacturer merges with a pharmaceutical company.

....

(b) A car manufacturer merges with a car distribution company.

....

(c) A large supermarket chain takes over a number of independent grocers.

....

(?) Q21. Various motives have been suggested for mergers other than the simple desire to grow. Name four of them.

1. ....

2. ....

3. ....

4. ....

Q22. Look at the answers to Q21. Which of the motives are consistent with the prime motive of:

(a) long-run profit maximisation? ....

....

(b) growth maximisation? ....

....

📖 **Q23.** When comparing a growth-maximising firm with a short-run profit-maximising firm, which one of the following (in the short run) is likely for the growth-maximising firm?

A. A lower level of advertising.

B. A lower equilibrium output.

C. A lower price relative to average cost.

D. A lower level of investment.

E. A higher price elasticity of demand at the price charged by the firm.

8.3 Multiple aims

(Page 212)

❓ **Q24.** Is it possible for a firm to *maximise* two objectives simultaneously?   *Yes/No*

Explain ....

....

Sometimes firms may attempt not to maximise any one objective but merely to achieve a target level of several.

📖 **Q25.** The setting of multiple targets (with no one objective to be maximised) is most likely:

A. when the firm has a complex multi-department organisation.

B. when there is a limited number of large institutional shareholders.

C. when one of the managers in the company is dominant.

D. when firms operate in highly competitive markets.

E. when firms produce a single product.

(Pages 212–15) A major development in the theory of the firm has been in *behavioural theories*. Rather than identifying various equilibrium positions for price, output, etc., behavioural theories examine how firms **Q26.** *should behave/ actually behave/could behave*.

Behavioural theories examine the conflicts that arise between different interest groups within a firm in setting and achieving targets. If targets cannot all be achieved, then a **Q27** .... procedure will be adopted to find ways of rectifying the problem. This may involve revising the targets to make them less ambitious.

To avoid constant revision of targets, managers may allow *organisational slack* to develop.

❓ **Q28.** Define organisational slack ....

....

◑ **Q29.** Which of the following will tend to lead to a higher level of organisational slack?

(a) A greater degree of uncertainty about future demand.
                                                              Yes/No

(b) A more complex organisational structure in the firm.
                                                              Yes/No

(c) The firm does better than planned (in terms of its various targets).   *Yes/No*

(d) Managers become more cautious.   *Yes/No*

(e) The number of rival firms decreases.   *Yes/No*

(f) Industrial relations deteriorate.   *Yes/No*

❓ **Q30.** A frequent complaint of junior managers is that they are often faced with new targets from above and that this makes their life difficult. If their complaint is true, does this conflict with the hypothesis that managers will try to build in slack?   *Yes/No*

Explain ....

....

....

◑ **Q31.** When firms adopt a satisficing approach with multiple targets, their production is likely to be less responsive to changing market conditions.   *True/False*

8.4 Pricing in practice

Whether firms are profit maximisers or are pursuing some alternative objective(s), many set prices, not by referring to marginal cost and marginal revenue, but by adding a profit mark-up to average cost.

◑ **Q32.** If a firm would like to maximise profits, it will be pure chance if it succeeds in doing so if it uses a mark-up system of pricing.   *True/False*

◑ **Q33.** A firm that is a profit maximiser is likely to adjust its mark-up more frequently than a firm that is a profit satisficer.   *True/False*

📖 **Q34.** For a firm which uses mark-up pricing and aims to achieve a particular level of total profit, its supply curve will be:

A. parallel to its average (total) cost curve.

B. parallel to its average variable cost curve.

C. parallel to its demand curve.

D. above its average (total) cost curve, but getting closer to it as output increases.

E. impossible to determine as long as the firm has market power.

B   PROBLEMS, EXERCISES AND PROJECTS

Table 8.1 Total costs, revenue and profit

Quantity (units)	Total revenue (£)	Total cost (£)	Total profit (£)
0	0	20	−20
1	...	...	...
2	...	...	...
3	78	...	...
4	...	52	...
5	...	...	45
6	120	...	...
7	...	...	...
8	128	116	...
9	...	137	...
10	...	...	−40

Table 8.2 Sources of capital funds of UK industrial and commercial companies

Year	Total from all sources (£ million)	Internal funds[1] (%)	Borrowing from banks etc. (%)	Shares and debentures (%)	Overseas sources (%)
1970	6 336	60.7	22.4	3.2	13.7
1980	28 913	66.1	22.3	4.9	6.7
1986	48 715	58.5	21.6	12.5	7.4
1987	79 475	49.6	21.1	25.3	4.0
1988	99 874	40.8	39.6	11.5	8.1
1989	108 025	32.7	41.7	14.9	10.7
1990	88 058	37.5	33.2	16.2	13.1
1992	53 452	68.3	−5.3	26.8	10.2
1994	82 469	72.9	−2.3	26.9	2.5
1996	114 501	53.0	20.0	19.0	8.0
1997	136 443	41.8	8.6	30.4	19.2

[1] Includes grants and tax relief.
Source: *Financial Statistics* (ONS 1998).

Q35. A firm has the following total revenue and total cost functions:

$$TR = 32Q - 2Q^2$$
$$TC = 20 + 4Q + Q^2$$

(a) Fill in the figures in Table 8.1.

(b) At what output is profit maximised? ....

(c) At what output is sales revenue maximised? ....

(d) Assume that the firm regarded £15 as the minimum satisfactory level of profit, how much would it produce now if it were concerned to maximise sales revenue?

....

Assume now that fixed costs increase by £30.

(e) What will be the profit-maximising output now? How much profit would be made at this output?

....

(f) What would be the sales revenue maximising output assuming that the minimum profit constraint of £15 still applied?

....

***Q36.** Given the *TR* and *TC* functions of Q30:
(a) What is the function for *TΠ*?
(b) At what output, to the nearest whole number, is this function maximised? (You will need to use differentiation.)
(c) At what output is the *TR* function maximised?
Check that your answers for (b) and (c) are the same as for Q35 (b) and (c).

Q37. Table 8.2 reproduces Table 8.1 from Sloman, *Economics* (4th edition).
(a) How did the proportions of investment financed from the different sources change between 1970 and 1997?
(b) Explain any major changes in these proportions over the period. To what extent have they varied with the course of the business cycle? (see Figure 13.3 on page 386 of Sloman *Economics* (4th edition)).

Q38. Look through the business pages of two or three quality newspapers for a few days to find reports of companies which are merging, attempting to take over other firms, diversifying or simply expanding fast.
(a) Try to identify the objectives of the companies and whether there are any apparent conflicts in these objectives.
(b) Assess whether the stated aims are 'final' aims or merely the means to achieving other aims (stated or not stated).
(c) In each case try to assess what type of information you would need to have in order to judge (i) whether the companies really were pursuing the objectives stated and (ii) how successful they were in achieving them.
(d) In each case assess the extent to which the company's performance and objectives are in the public interest.

DISCUSSION TOPICS AND ESSAYS

Q39. Under what circumstances is it likely that there will be a divorce between the ownership and control of a company?

Q40. Imagine you were the managing director of a fashion house producing expensive designer clothing. What achievements of you or your company would give you special satisfaction? Are these achievements consistent with profit maximisation?

Q41. Are sales revenue maximising firms likely to achieve more than normal profits in the long run (assuming that they have the market power to do so)?

Q42. Make up three seemingly outrageous business decisions and then attempt to justify each as being consistent with a policy of long-run profit maximisation.

Q43. 'Monopoly will only be against the interests of the consumer if the firm is a profit maximiser.' Discuss.

Q44. To what extent will consumers gain or lose from the three different types of merger?

Q45. Consider the proposition that satisficing is irrational since it implies that people prefer less of an objective to more.

Q46. 'Ultimately it is not the goals that a firm pursues that determine its price and output but the nature of the competition it faces.' Discuss.

Q47. 'If a firm uses a mark-up system of pricing, then it is unlikely to be aiming to maximise profits, either in the short run or the long run.' Discuss this proposition and consider what evidence you would need to have in order to establish what the aims are of a particular firm which uses cost-plus pricing.

Q48. Debate
Mergers are inevitably against the public interest as they increase monopoly power and reduce the incentive to innovate.

ARTICLES

In whose interests should business be run? Just shareholders, or all the stakeholders – customers, employees, creditors, suppliers, local residents, the wider community? In the article below, taken from *New Economy*, volume 5, number 2 of June 1998, Rajiv Prabhaker analyses the issue of corporate governance and stakeholding.

Governance and stakeholding

Corporate governance has been a key issue of controversy over recent times. This concern has been academic, political and public. Aside from public concern over issues such as executive pay, there have been a series of reports (Cadbury, Greenbury and Hampel) on corporate governance and the new Secretary of State for Trade and Industry Margaret Beckett is taking a proactive stance on the issue. The academic debate has often been polarised between supporters of stakeholding and supporters of shareholding models of the firm. The key question is whether UK corporate governance would improve if it moved from a shareholding to a stakeholding approach.

Corporate governance concerns how a firm's assets are managed. In the modern firm, the management or control of those assets has become separated

from their ownership. Hart (1995) outlines how that separation works in the shareholder model (also called the *principal–agent* model). Here the firm's owners (*principal*) are its shareholders. They seek to maximise shareholder value in the form of profits. Control is delegated to a set of managers (*agent*), however, who naturally seek to pursue their own interests. The so-called agency problem then arises: how can shareholders motivate managers to act in the shareholder's best interests?

Hart examines large UK and US public corporations. He notes the prevalence of a large number of small owners and argues that, since monitoring is costly, there is an incentive for shareholders to free-ride. Most shareholders may benefit from effective monitoring, whilst others undertake its costs. This makes it easy for managers to pursue

their own interests, up to a point, limited by the threat of takeovers and the like.

The principal–agent model rests on a number of assumptions. I focus on two core ones: firstly that all parties – employers, employees or shareholders – are rational self-interested utility maximisers; and secondly that the objective of the firm is to maximise profits.

Keasey, Thompson and Wright 1997 note that the main challenge to this paradigm arises from stakeholding theorists. They argue that 'the central proposition at the heart of the stakeholder approach is that the purpose – the objective function – of the firm should be defined more widely than the maximisation of shareholder welfare alone'. Welfare is extended to cover other persons or groups such as workers, consumers, other firms and community groups. In one sense the shareholder–stakeholder dichotomy is somewhat stylised. All models may be seen as stakeholding. The principal–agent model is simply one in which shareholders are the only stakeholders that matter.

Social institutions

An influential stakeholding model has been proposed by Kay (Gamble *et al.* 1997). Kay argues that in continental Europe and Japan corporations are viewed as social institutions, with public responsibilities responsive to a variety of stakeholder groups. Kay argues that this view of the corporation is more accurate and he puts forward a model of trusteeship. Shareholders elect a managerial team, entrusted with ensuring that the firm continues to meet various obligations. Along with shareholder value, sensitivity to other stakeholders and the history of the firm are also important. The key is managerial freedom with accountability. He argues against greater involvement of shareholders in major decisions because of the free-rider problem already mentioned. Instead,

he proposes a new Companies Act with policy instruments such as 'stakeholding statutes' for suitably defined companies (above a certain size).

Most stakeholding theorists, like Kay, have focused their attention on challenging the second core assumption that the only objective of the firm is to maximise profits but have not taken the argument much further. Often they suggest that a stakeholding approach would tend to improve the performance of firms. Kay argues that it would enable firms to gain a 'competitive edge'. But this has conventionally been taken to mean corporate profitability so is stakeholding then not so much about ends, but about mean? If stakeholding did reduce profitability would the stakeholding theorists remain wedded to it? Are there other ethical justifications for stakeholding?

I argue that the driving force behind stakeholding comes instead from challenging the first core assumption – that of rational self-interest. In an uncertain world, we have to rely on and trust others to achieve common goals. If

individuals act purely on self-interest such relationships will be hard to sustain. In fact, individuals may act according to non-instrumental reasons, for example by simply observing a social norm. Furthermore, they may not always act in a self-interested way. Both of these behaviours depart from rational self-interest, and may combine in different ways.

It might be claimed that even if this is the case, within economics the assumption of rational self-interest holds. Kay's model is essentially wedded to the conventional view of the self. It might be thought that part of the strength of his approach is that he succeeds in showing how, even on such an assumption, it is possible to favour stakeholding. However I would argue against this. The 'social capital' often seen as integral to a firm's success trades on a wider view of human motivation than used in orthodox modelling. I believe that the power behind Kay's model in fact derives from widening the view of the self. In any case, his focus on profit maximisation is different from mine.

(a) Distinguish between shareholding and stakeholding.

(b) What implications does the distinction between shareholding and stakeholding have for the aims of the firm and the strategies it is likely to adopt in their pursuit?

(c) Why is the nature of the 'principal–agent problem' in (i) the shareholder model; (ii) the stakeholder model?

(d) Is the concept of 'rational self-interested utility maximisation' the only form of self-interest? Could adherence to various social norms be a form of longer-term self-interested behaviour?

On very rare occasions there appears a company in the marketplace that grows at a phenomenal rate. What special ingredient(s) do such businesses have which enables them to perform so well? In the article below, taken from *Management Today* of February 1996, an attempt is made to identify the key ingredients and assess their importance.

The secrets of hypergrowth

Of all the beasts in the corporate jungle, the most fascinating is the one that emerges from nowhere, grows at a phenomenal rate and, before too long, is challenging some of the bigger animals. Hypergrowth companies are known in America as fast-growth tigers or threshold companies, and sometimes in Britain as baby sharks.

What are the lessons that firms with more prosaic performance records can learn from the management strategy

and techniques of the hypergrowth companies? And is it the case that there is a 'tortoise and the hare' element to the experience of hypergrowth companies *vis-à-vis* the rest? In other words, do such companies, after a period of rapid expansion, either burn themselves out, bump up against financial or market ceilings, or come to the attention of larger firms as takeover targets?

Coopers & Lybrand, in a recent study of hypergrowth companies in Britain, de-

fined them as firms which had achieved an increase in both turnover and employment of 100 per cent over the latest three years. From a sample of 501 successful medium-sized, or 'middle market' companies, 26 fell into the hypergrowth category, although there were 78 companies in all which met a less demanding 'supergrowth' definition (turnover up by 60 per cent or more over the latest three years), and 39 in all which were defined as supergrowth on the basis of a

60 per cent-plus rise in employment over three years.

The 26 hypergrowth companies tended to be young, with half under 10 years old. Most, around 70 per cent, were private, with current turnover typically ranging from £13 million to £50 million a year (although by their nature, some could be expected to expand rapidly out of this range). The vast majority served a single market, or supplied one type of product or service. In four-fifths of cases, this market was identified by the companies themselves as a niche market, either ignored by or underexploited by larger players. Although there were hypergrowth companies in manufacturing (fast-moving consumer goods, textiles and clothing, computers and electronics), they were proportionally more likely to be in service industries, notably transport, professional services and financial services.

Ann Todd and Professor Bernard Taylor of the Henley Management College, who looked at rapidly growing companies over a longer time-frame, 1980–90, found that the 'baby sharks' in their sample recorded profit and turnover growth of over 20 per cent a year, with the majority recording growth of over 40 per cent annually.

Todd and Taylor's baby sharks, like the Coopers & Lybrand companies, were often niche players, taking advantage of recently established technologies. But relatively few were in what could be described as pure high-technology markets; in other words, products or processes at the forefront of technology. Such markets often had prohibitively high entry barriers, particularly relating to the level of investment required and, in the case of untried technologies, substantial risks of failure.

They give two examples. Owners Abroad, now renamed First Choice, developed a chain of niche travel agents selling holidays on relatively high margins, by taking advantage of computer technology and proprietary software which enabled economies of scale to be achieved of a kind previously only available to the travel industry heavyweights. Indeed, it is a measure of its growth – away from its original timeshare business – that it had to change its name. Another successful niche market player was Iceland Frozen Foods, which set up a nationwide chain of low-overhead specialist food retailers.

Specialist Computer Holdings (SCH), under the chairmanship of Peter Rigby, is an example of a current hypergrowth company. Founded in 1975 by Rigby, who at the time was working for Honeywell, and based in Tyseley, Birmingham, it is a computer sales and service group involved in the integration and distribution of personal computer systems, mainframe computer bureau services and computer training. Its shift into very rapid growth has come with a move into mail order computer sales and the Byte chain of computer superstores – a network of seven such stores expanded to 17 during 1995.

SCH's turnover rose from £95 million in the 1993 financial year to £229 million in 1995. It is on target for a turnover of more than £350 million in the current financial year, ending on 31 March 1996. At the same time, group employment has risen from 500 to more than 850. Most of the company's expansion has been organic, although it has also made acquisitions, at a rate of roughly one a year. 'There is only one way to take the business – forward,' says Rigby. 'You can't stand still, or be half-hearted or complacent. You have to be forward-thinking.'

Both the Todd & Taylor and Coopers & Lybrand studies distil a number of common factors which typify the strategies followed by successful hypergrowth companies. According to Simon Greenstreet of Coopers & Lybrand, Specialist Computer Holdings is an embodiment of most of these factors. Thus, the company has improved the time to market for new products and services, vital in the rapidly-changing computer market. At the same time, it has kept tight control over stocks. SCH has reduced its risk by maintaining a close relationship and collaborating on marketing with its suppliers, which include IBM, Microsoft, Novell and the other industry giants who regard the company as an important source of information on developments in the UK market.

Thus, it has avoided confrontation with larger players, which can mean death for the hypergrowth company. SCH uses available technology effectively in its own distribution operations and benchmarks its performance against a range of yardsticks for the industry.

SCH has deliberately recruited managers with expertise outside the computer industry, notably with its expansion into the retail market. It operates an active employee incentive programme, with both share option and employee share ownership schemes. The company's borrowings are low, most of its growth having been funded by the reinvestment of profits.

But can hypergrowth ever be a realistic long-run proposition? One year on from the point at which they were identified as hypergrowth, Coopers & Lybrand's 26 companies are still going strong, and most expect to achieve performance at or near the hypergrowth level for the foreseeable future, although this could be dismissed as predictable optimism.

A study by McKinsey & Co. of fast-growth 'tiger' companies, however, found that rapid growth was sustainable. Indeed, it concluded: 'For the tigers, fast growth fuels itself. Multiple reinforcing feedback loops conspire to create a "virtuous circle", unleashing a momentum that competitors are powerless to stop.'

But research by both 3i and the Cranfield European Enterprise Centre suggests that the population of companies achieving hypergrowth is unstable between two time periods. In other words, companies are always moving in and out of the hypergrowth performance league, and relatively few are likely to sustain such performance over prolonged periods. This fits the popular image of hypergrowth companies – that their success is in exploiting a particular market niche or product advantage. Once the competition arrives, or the niche is fully exploited, the scope for continued rapid growth becomes that much more difficult. If this coincides with the typical problems of fast-growth businesses – loss of control of the finances, perhaps a falling-out between the original partners, or just a loss of impetus – the chances of sustained hypergrowth begin to look slim.

Taylor offers a middle ground between the two competing views on the sustainability of what is, on any definition, extraordinary business performance. He and Todd established a data-base of 176 high-growth, medium-sized companies, on the basis of their performance over the period 1980–85.

In the following five years, 52 per cent of the sample continued to record rapid growth in profitability and turnover, of at least 20 per cent and in most cases more than 40 per cent, annually. A further 9 per cent of the sample continued to grow, but at more modest rates, while 13 per cent experienced 'stagnation and decline' and 26 per cent were no longer in existence (as a result of poor performance, and not because their good records had led to their acquisition).

'When we started we were looking very much at the problems of growth and the strategies needed to secure rapid growth in terms of products, markets, finance and so on,' Taylor says. 'But we found that the problem of growth comes down to the people. If you're growing at 40 per cent or so every year, you are effectively creating a new business every three years. The management problems that this creates for the original entrepreneurs are enormous. Either they make their mind up to adapt to a much larger operation by taking on new management. Or, in many cases, they decide to be taken over.' This is the point, adds Taylor, when hypergrowth

is likely to come to an end. 'Large companies find it difficult to innovate, so they pick up smaller innovative companies,' he says. 'This process of concentration is going on all the time.'

The problem is that the smaller, innovative company often ceases to be innovative once part of a larger organisation. It is a familiar story. The spur that drove on the original creators of the business is often lost once they have sold out, however powerful the contracts binding them to the business. Acquisition is often more effective as a means of snuffing out a younger, aggressive and more innovative competitor than of giving the larger firm an infusion of innovative sparkle.

It is from their relationship with large companies that medium-sized hyper-

growth companies derive both their strength but also, ultimately, their vulnerability. The Coopers & Lybrand research found that hypergrowth companies tended to have a higher proportion of large company customers than their middle-market peers, and that this could be a source of problems, for example, in slow payment. At the same time, they had a proportionately bigger number of big company suppliers. The danger for hypergrowth middle-sized businesses is that they will be squeezed when they begin to become a serious threat. Either that or they get taken over by one of their bigger customers, suppliers or competitors and lose the edge that made them special in the first place.

© *Management Today*, Feb. 1996

(a) How might we define a 'hypergrowth' firm?

(b) What key characteristics do such firms have which enable them to grow so quickly?

(c) Do hypergrowth companies remain hypergrowth companies? What threats are they likely to experience?

In the following article, taken from the *Financial Times* of 2 December 1998, Daniel Yergin assesses the merger wave sweeping the oil industry and evaluates the motives for it and the possible outcomes.   **FT**

Bigger oil

'Life's just one damn thing after another,' said John Archbold to his board in 1911, as the tickertape brought word to the headquarters at 26 Broadway of the Supreme Court's order to break-up John D. Rockefeller's Standard Oil Trust. As the news sunk in, the directors sat in stunned silence. It was Archbold, Rockefeller's successor, who broke the spell. He began to whistle.

One may whistle now in amazement at the scale of the new company that will be formed from the $75.3bn takeover of Mobil by Exxon. In size, it overshadows even the recent combination of BP and Amoco and certainly yesterday's news that France's Total is taking over Petrofina of Belgium. With so much merger activity, much is being made of the reconstitution of Rockefeller's company.

In contrast to Rockefeller's days, the industry today is highly diverse and competitive. It has become even more

competitive since the oil price collapse in 1986. Many state-owned companies have been privatised – including ENI in Italy and YPF in Argentina – and have become active international participants. Smaller companies have extended their reach; and new technologies have become widely available, lowering the cost of exploration and production.

What is promoting consolidation in the contemporary oil industry is not some subconscious drive to recreate the ancient empire but an altogether different 'damn thing': hard economics.

Oil was one of the first global industries to be hit by the Asian crisis. For the past several years, the 'prize' for the world petroleum industry was Asia. Until the second half of 1997, the rapid growth in consumption in that region was increasing prices and boosting spending on exploration and production around the world. Companies complained that geologists and engineers were in such

demand, there were not enough to go around. Senior executives were being poached by other companies. The charges for drilling ships and other services were rocketing. The industry looked as though it was heading into another boom. And all this was less than a year and a half ago.

Then came the Asian debacle. The region's demand had been expected to grow by almost 1m barrels per day in 1998. Instead, it plummeted by 400 000 bdp. A warm winter and increased world output added to oversupply. Prices plummeted, falling by more than 40 per cent between 1997 and 1998.

Yesterday, crude oil futures fell to under $11 a barrel, in nominal terms the level of the oil-price bust of 1986. If inflation is taken into account, the price of a barrel of oil today is back to where it was before 1973, 25 years after the first great oil crisis.

The industry did a remarkable job of adjusting to the earlier price collapse in 1986. By restructuring and applying new technology, it brought costs down to a level that allowed oil companies to undertake exploration profitably with prices at $15–16 a barrel. A decade earlier, the break-even point for exploration in similar areas might have been nearer $30.

But with oil prices at $11 or $12, the economics of new projects become problematic. At best, projects can break even. The industry has responded by cutting budgets by 20 to 30 per cent and stretching out the timing of new projects. The risk of the business is being recalibrated.

Mergers and acquisitions are the ultimate form of cost-cutting, sometimes to be measured in the billions of dollars. Once the tumult of the merger passes, they enable companies to spread their costs over a larger base. The rapid evolution of information technology adds to the efficiencies and enables knowledge to be more widely diffused. The larger base enables companies to broaden their portfolio, manage risk, and assume more easily the multi-billion-dollar 20-year projects, such as Caspian oil or Asian natural gas, that loom in the next decade. Altogether, the savings enable the companies to work their way back to acceptable returns on capital.

But more than that, mergers are transforming the industry. Just as BP-Amoco encouraged 'merger think' and generated the idea of the 'super-major', so a combination between Exxon and Mobil is likely to foster other mergers.

By the time this period of extremely low oil prices is over, the landscape of the industry will look different. There will be further consolidations, some perhaps obvious, some likely to be surprises. And as the new combinations rationalise their operations, they will shed some holdings. That that will create opportunities in production for entrepreneurial independents, which have the same access to technology as the super-majors, to move up in scale. Parallel opportunities will be available to penny-conscious operators in refining and marketing.

The driving force for consolidation is not only lower prices but the expectation of an extended period of low prices. It is possible that the spectre of the 1930s depression might lead fearful central bankers and finance ministers to encourage global reflation over the next year. And if this were to happen, an economic recovery could lead to stronger commodity prices earlier than people might expect. But no management dare make that bet for their companies. At least, not yet.

(a) What does the article identify as the main motive for the wave of mergers in the oil industry in the late 1990s?

(b) How have they benefited oil companies?

(c) Should consumers be fearful of the mergers?

ANSWERS

Q1. *False.* Provided a firm measures cost in terms of opportunity cost, it could arrive at the profit-maximising position by a system of trial and error. It does this by sticking with policies that turn out to have increased profits and abandoning policies that turn out to have reduced profits.

Q2. *True.* If the firm does not use opportunity cost concepts, it cannot establish how much profit it is making, and whether profit is therefore at a maximum.

Q3. 70p.

Q4. C. Shareholders may well wish to maximise profits, but if they are separated from managers whose own personal interests may be better served by aiming for some other goal, such as power or prestige, profits will not be maximised. The managers may simply aim to make *enough* profits to keep shareholders quiet.

Q5. *there are many small shareholders.* If there are many of them, individual shareholders will have virtually no say in the firm's decisions.

Q6. *public limited companies.* These are companies where shares are traded publicly. Shareholders (unless they own a large percentage) are unlikely to have any influence on day-to-day decisions. They merely have a vote when broad issues of policy are put at shareholders' meetings.

Q7. *satisficers.*

Q8. *(a)* *Yes.* Provided it *could* earn supernormal profits, it may choose to sacrifice some or all of these in order to achieve some other aim (e.g. increasing output).

(b) *No.* It could only make normal profits anyway, which it must make to survive, whether it is a profit maximiser or merely a profit satisficer.

Q9. *Agents.*

Q10. *(a)* estate agents, *agents*; house buyers, *principals*.

(b) shareholders, *principals*; managers, *agents*.

(c) house builders, *principals*; architects, *agents*.

(d) employers, *principals*; workers, *agents*.

(e) shops, *agents*; customers, *principals*.

Q11. *(a)* Marginal advertising costs exceeding marginal revenue from advertising in the short run; but marginal revenue increasing in the long run as demand steadily grows with the product becoming more established.

(b) Initial high set-up costs and initial 'teething' costs, costs that would fall in the long run. Also if demand is growing and it takes time to open a

new production line, the opening of the line may lead to excess capacity in the short run, but not in the long run.

(c) Revenue from new or improved products only occurs in the future *after* the research and development has taken place. Costs occur from the outset.

(d) There may be high administrative and public relations costs associated with the bid. If successful, the acquisition of the new company is likely to lead to bigger profits (sheer size of output; economies of scale; increased monopoly power).

(e) Costs of the filter equipment with little immediate return. In the long run consumers may prefer the firm's 'greener' image and the firm may avoid government-imposed restrictions that might turn out to be more expensive in the long run.

Q12. Because a firm could always, in hindsight, use it to justify virtually *any* decisions, no matter how unprofitable they eventually turn out to be.

Q13. Yes: (a), (b) and (e). Note that (c) and (d) will not in principle make price and output impossible to predict; they are merely factors that would need to be taken into account.

Q14. *(a)* Q_3; where $MC = MR$.

(b) Q_8; the maximum level of sales consistent with AR being not less than AC.

(c) Q_9; the maximum level of sales consistent with AR being not less than AVC.

(d) Q_6; the point where $MR = 0$ and where, therefore, TR is at a maximum. (Note that in this diagram, the sales revenue maximising point more than satisfies the requirement that at least normal profits should be made. In this case supernormal profits will be made because the AR curve is above the AC curve at Q_6.)

(e) Q_7; the point where MC (the industry supply curve) equals demand (AR).

(f) The AC curve should now interest the AR curve at, or to the left of, Q_6.

Q15. *True.* At the profit-maximising point, $MC = MR$. Since MC will be positive, MR must also be positive, and thus revenue could be increased by producing *more*. The revenue-maximising firm will thus produce more than the profit-maximising firm (provided profits are above the satisfactory level and thus allow the firm to increase production).

Q16. *False.* Although the (profit-satisficing) sales revenue maximising output cannot be less than the profit-maximising output, it could be the same. This will occur when the maximum profits are no greater than the satisfactory level (e.g. under perfect competition in the long run).

Q17. Because the firm would be likely to spend the excess profits on advertising or product improvements in

order to increase sales. It would continue doing this, even when the MC from advertising exceeded MR, as long as MR was positive and as long as profits were sill above the minimum level.

Q18. 1. from borrowing.
2. from a new issue of shares.
3. from retained profits.

Q19. Because dividends are likely to fall if the firm borrows too much, retains too much profit or issues new shares. Unless shareholders are convinced that dividends and the share price will increase in the long run, they may sell their shares. The resulting fall in share prices will make the firm vulnerable to a takeover bid.

Q20. *(a)* conglomerate.
(b) vertical.
(c) horizontal.

Q21. Answers could include: to achieve economies of scale; to gain greater market power; to obtain an increased share price; to reduce uncertainty; to take advantage of an opportunity that arises; to reduce the likelihood of being taken over; to defend another firm from a hostile takeover bid; asset stripping (i.e. selling off the profitable bits of the newly acquired company); empire building; broadening the geographical base of the company.

Q22. *(a)* All could be argued to be! This is an example of the problem with the theory of long-run profit maximisation: virtually any action could be justified as potentially leading to increased profits.

(b) To achieve economies of scale; (to take advantage of an opportunity that arises); to reduce the likelihood of being taken over; empire building; broadening the geographical base of the company. These could be argued to lead directly to a faster growth in the size of the firm. Some of the others could be argued to be consistent under certain circumstances.

Q23. C. The growth-maximising firm will be prepared to sacrifice profit in order to achieve higher output and sales. Note: in the case of E, the growth-maximising firm will be operating at a lower point on its AR curve. This will correspond to a lower level of MR and hence a *lower* price elasticity of demand.

Q24. *No*: if there is any trade off between the objectives. For example, in order to sell more, a firm may have to accept lower profits. In such cases only one of the objectives can be maximised. Alternatively one of the objectives could be maximised *subject* to achieving a target level of another objective. For example, the firm could maximise sales revenue subject to achieving a *satisfactory* level of profits.

Q25. A. In a multi-department firm there may be many different potentially conflicting interests of different managers. In such cases, unless one manager is dominant, it is likely that managers will have to be prepared to be 'satisficers' rather than 'maximisers'.

Q26. *actually behave.*

Q27. *search.*

Q28. *Where managers allow spare capacity to exist in their department, thereby enabling them to respond more easily to changed circumstances.*

Q29. *All of them.* Organisational slack is likely to increase when firms face uncertain times and when they are not forced by competition to cut their slack.

Q30. *No.* The changes in targets may result from the fact the senior managers have built slack into their departments and can afford the 'luxury' of changing targets: perhaps experimentally. At the same time, the junior managers, fearing changed targets, may well be trying to increase the amount of organisational slack in their domain (but hoping not to let their bosses know for fear of being given tougher targets).

Q31. *True.* The greater the number of goals, and hence the greater the chance of conflict, the more likely firms are to build in organisational slack, and therefore the less they will need to change their level of production as market conditions change.

Q32. *False.* The choice of the level of mark-up may reflect the firm's assessment of what price the 'market will bear': what price will maximise profits. By not using marginal cost and marginal revenue, the firm may well not arrive at the profit-maximising price and output immediately (and in this sense the statement is true), but if the firm is willing to adjust its mark-up in the light of the perceived strength of demand, then it may, by an 'iterative' approach (i.e. a step-by-step approach), arrive at the profit-maximising mark-up. Note that even if a firm does try to equate marginal cost and marginal revenue, a lack of information, especially about the shape of the demand curve for its product, and hence its marginal revenue, may prevent it from arriving directly at the profit-maximising price. It may still, therefore, have to use an iterative approach.

Q33. *True.* A firm that is a profit maximiser will need to adjust its price (i.e. its mark-up) as revenue and cost curves shift. A profit satisficer, given the probability of a degree of organisational slack, will not need to be so responsive to changes in demand and costs.

Q34. D. As its output increases, it will need a smaller (average) profit mark-up on top of average cost in order to achieve a given level of *total* profit.

9 The Theory of Distribution of Income

REVIEW

In this chapter we consider what determines the incomes earned by different factors of production.

We start by having a look at the general principles governing income determination. We then turn to examine the incomes of specific factors of production. In the case of labour, this income takes the form of wages. We will look at wage determination in both perfect and imperfect markets. In doing so we will attempt to establish why wage rates can differ substantially from one occupation to another: why there can be substantial inequality in wages.

We then look at the rewards to non-human factors of production. We first look at the determination of the return to capital: at the *price of capital* that is either hired or sold and at the incomes – *profit* and *interest* – earned from the use of capital by its owners (capitalists).

Finally we look at the rewards to owners of land (landlords). This consists of the *rent* earned from hiring out land or using it to produce goods.

9.1 The market for factors of production

(Pages 220–1) In a *perfect* market the rewards to factors are determined by the interaction of demand and supply.

Figure 9.1 shows a local market for plasterers. It is assumed that it is a perfect market. This assumption means that **Q1.** *the price of plaster/the wage rate of plasterers/the profitability of employers of plasterers* cannot be affected by individual **Q2.** *employers/workers/employers or workers*. This means that **Q3.** *the supply curve of labour to/the demand curve for labour by* an individual employer is perfectly elastic, and that **Q4.** *the supply curve of labour by/the demand curve for labour from* an individual worker is perfectly elastic too.

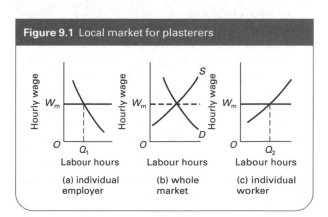

Figure 9.1 Local market for plasterers

⊖ **Q5.** In Figure 9.1(b), which of the two curves would shift and in which direction as a result of each of the following changes?

(a) A deterioration in the working conditions for plasterers.
demand/supply; left/right

(b) A decrease in the price of plaster.
demand/supply; left/right

(c) A decrease in the demand for new houses.
demand/supply; left/right

(d) An increased demand for plasterers in other parts of the country. *demand/supply; left/right*

(e) Increased wages in other parts of the building trade (as a result of union activity). *demand/supply; left/right*

(f) Increased costs associated with employing plasterers (e.g. employers having to pay higher insurance premiums for accidents to plasterers).
demand/supply; left/right

▤ **Q6.** From Q5 (c) it can be seen that the demand for a factor of production is:

A. a substitute demand.
B. a direct demand.
C. an elastic demand.
D. an inelastic demand.
E. a derived demand.

In perfect factor markets it is not just wages that are determined by the interaction of demand and supply.

◗ **Q7.** What effect would the following have on the rent on arable farmland?

(a) A rise in the demand for wheat. *rise/fall*

(b) A substantial rise in the demand for beef (but no fall in the demand for cereals). *rise/fall*

(c) A major coastal land reclamation scheme is completed.
rise/fall

(d) The ending of the EU system of setting an artificially high price for grains. *rise/fall*

(e) The introduction of a government scheme to 'set aside' 20 per cent of all farm land. Farmers would be prohibited from growing crops on such land. (What would happen to the rent on land remaining in use?)
rise/fall

(Pages 221–2) Even in a perfect market, inequality will exist between the earnings of different factors.

▤ **Q8.** Which one of the following would be a cause of inequality of wages between different occupations in the long run even if all labour markets were perfect?

A. There is short-run geographical immobility of labour.
B. Different jobs require people with different skills.
C. There is perfect knowledge of wages throughout the economy.
D. Everyone has to accept wages as given by the market.
E. Labour is homogeneous within any one particular labour market.

(Page 223) In practice, of course, factor markets are not perfect and this will provide a further reason for inequality in factor earnings.

⟨?⟩ **Q9.** Name three types of market imperfection in factor markets.

1. ....

2. ....

3. ....

9.2 Wage determination under perfect competition

We now turn to a detailed examination of the determination of wages: the price of labour services. We start by assuming perfect competition. In the next section we will drop this assumption.

The supply of labour
(Pages 223–5) We can look at the supply of labour at three levels: the supply of hours by an individual worker, the supply of workers to an individual employer and the total market supply of a given category of labour.

When an individual worker works longer hours, each extra hour worked will involve additional sacrifice.

⟨?⟩ **Q10.** This additional sacrifice is known as

....

This sacrifice consists of two elements: the sacrifice of leisure and the extra effort/unpleasantness incurred from the extra work. As people work extra hours, these two sacrifices are likely to increase. As a result the supply curve will normally be **Q11.** *upward sloping/downward sloping*.

Under certain circumstances, however, the supply curve can bend backwards at higher wages. To understand why, we must distinguish between the *income* and *substitution* effects of a wage increase.

◗ **Q12.** Which of the following is the income effect and which is the substitution effect?

(a) As wage rates rise, people will tend to work more hours since taking leisure would now involve a greater sacrifice of income and hence consumption.
income effect/substitution effect

(b) At higher wage rates people do not need to work such long hours. *income effect/substitution effect*

Thus the income effect is **Q13.** *positive/negative* and the substitution effect is **Q14.** *positive/negative*. The supply curve will thus become backward bending at high wage rates if the **Q15.** *income effect/substitution effect* becomes dominant.

Q16. The supply curve of labour to an *individual employer* in perfect competition will be perfectly elastic.

True/False

Q17. The *market* supply curve of labour will tend to be upward sloping. The position of this curve will depend on three main determinants. Of the following:
- (i) the number of qualified people,
- (ii) the wage rate,
- (iii) the productivity of labour,
- (iv) the pleasantness/unpleasantness of the job,
- (v) the wages and non-wage benefits of alternative jobs,

which three determine the position of the supply curve?
- *A.* (i), (ii) and (iii).
- *B.* (i), (iii) and (iv).
- *C.* (iii), (iv) and (v).
- *D.* (i), (iv) and (v).
- *E.* (ii), (iii) and (iv).

Elasticity of supply
(Pages 225–6) The elasticity of the market supply of labour will depend on how readily workers are willing and able to move into jobs as their wage rate increases relative to other jobs. What we are referring to here is the mobility of labour. The less the mobility (the greater the immobility), the less elastic the supply.

Q18. There are several causes of immobility. In each one of the following cases, identify whether it is a cause of geographical immobility, occupational immobility or both.
- *(a)* Social and family ties.   *geographical/occupational/both*
- *(b)* Ignorance of available jobs.

  geographical/occupational/both
- *(c)* Difficulty in acquiring new qualifications.

  geographical/occupational/both
- *(d)* Inconvenience of moving house.

  geographical/occupational/both
- *(e)* Fear of the unknown.   *geographical/occupational/both*
- *(f)* Less desirable working conditions in alternative jobs.

  geographical/occupational/both

(Pages 226–8) The elasticity of supply of labour will determine what proportion of wages consists of *transfer earnings* and what proportion consists of *economic rent*. The definition of a person's **Q19.** *transfer earnings/economic rent* is 'anything over and above what that person must be paid to prevent him or her moving to another job'.

Q20. A fashion model could earn £80 per week as a gardener, £160 per week working on a building site or £240 as a lorry driver. As a model, however, he earns £320. Assuming he likes all four jobs equally and that there are no costs associated with changing jobs, what is his economic rent from being a fashion model?

- *A.* £80
- *B.* £160
- *C.* £240
- *D.* £320
- *E.* £480

Q21. In Figure 9.2, which area represents transfer earnings?
- *A.* (i)
- *B.* (ii)
- *C.* (iii)
- *D.* (i) + (ii)
- *E.* (ii) + (iii)

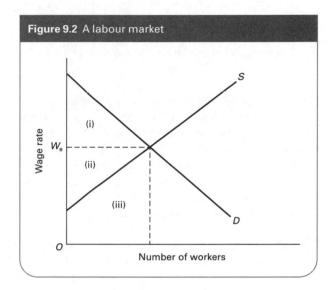

Figure 9.2 A labour market

Q22. In Figure 9.2, which area represents economic rent?
- *A.* (i)
- *B.* (ii)
- *C.* (iii)
- *D.* (i) + (ii)
- *E.* (ii) + (iii)

The demand for labour: the marginal productivity theory
(Pages 228–9) We turn now to the *demand* for labour. How many workers will a profit-maximising firm want to employ? What will be its demand for labour?

There are a number of concepts you will need to be clear about here.

Q23. Match the concepts (i)–(vii) to the definitions (a)–(g).
- (i) Marginal cost (MC)
- (ii) Marginal cost of labour (MC_L)
- (iii) Average cost of labour (AC_L)
- (iv) Marginal revenue (MR)
- (v) Average revenue (AR)
- (vi) Marginal physical product of labour (MPP_L)
- (vii) Marginal revenue product of labour (MRP_L)

(a) The extra revenue a firm earns from the employment of one more worker.

....

(b) The wage rate. ....

(c) The price of the good. ....

(d) The extra cost of producing one more unit of output.

....

(e) The extra output gained from the employment of one more worker.

....

(f) The extra revenue from producing one more unit of output.

....

(g) The extra cost of employing one more worker.

....

The most important of these concepts in understanding the demand for labour is the marginal revenue product (MRP_L). This can be derived by multiplying **Q24.** MPP_L by MR/AR by MC_L/MR by AC_L.

The rule for profit maximising can thus be stated as 'whenever MC_L exceeds MRP_L the firm should employ **Q25.** *more/fewer* workers, and whenever MRP_L exceeds MC_L the firm should employ **Q26.** *more/fewer*.

◖ **Q27.** The firm's demand curve for labour under perfect competition is given by the MRP_L curve. *True/False*

(Page 229) We can conclude that under perfect competition, there are three main determinants of the amount of labour that a firm will demand: the productivity of labour (MPP_L), the wage rate (W) and the price of the good ($P = MR$).

◖ **Q28.** Will a change in each of the following determinants lead to a shift in or a movement along the demand curve for labour?

(a) A change in the productivity of labour (MPP_L).
shift/movement along
(b) A change in the wage rate (W). *shift/movement along*
(c) A change in the price of the good ($P = MR$).
shift/movement along

(Pages 229–31) The demand curve for labour by the *whole industry* will not simply be the horizontal sum of the demand curves by individual firms.

◖ **Q29.** The (wage) elasticity of demand for labour will depend on a number of factors. Elasticity will be greater:

(a) the greater the price elasticity of demand for the good
True/False
(b) the harder it is to substitute labour for other factors and vice versa. *True/False*

(c) the greater the elasticity of supply of complementary factors. *True/False*
(d) the lower the elasticity of supply of substitute factors.
True/False
(e) the smaller the wage cost as a proportion of total costs.
True/False
(f) the longer the time period. *True/False*

◖ **Q30.** If all workers had identical abilities, if there were perfect mobility of labour, if all jobs were equally attractive, if all workers and employers had perfect knowledge, and if wage rates were determined entirely by demand and supply, then there would be complete equality of incomes.
True/False

9.3 Wage determination in imperfect markets

(Pages 231–2) In this section we shall consider the effect of economic power on wages.

♟ **Q31.** There are a number of types of economic power. These include:
(i) monopoly in goods markets
(ii) monopoly in labour markets
(iii) monopsony in goods markets
(iv) monopsony in labour markets
(v) bilateral monopoly

Match each of the following examples of economic power to the above five types.
(a) A group of local authorities get together as a purchasing consortium in order to be able to buy cheaper easy-empty dustbins from the manufacturers (dustbins that will be provided free to residents).

....

(b) A trade union operates a closed shop. ....
(c) A firm is the only domestic coal merchant supplying the area.

....

(d) The wages of postal workers are determined by a process of collective bargaining between the Post Office and the Union of Postal Workers.

....

(e) A factory is the only employer of certain types of skilled labour in the area.

....

(Page 232) Let us examine the situation where firms have power in the labour market. This is the case of *monopsony*, where a firm is the sole employer in a particular labour market (or *oligopsony*, where the firm is one of only a few employers). A monopsonist, unlike a perfectly competitive employer, will face **Q32.** *a downward-sloping/an upward-sloping/a horizontal* **Q33.** *supply curve of/demand curve for* labour.

Table 9.1 A monopsonist's supply-of-labour schedule

Wage rate (AC_L)	£50	£60	£70	£80	£90	£100	£110	£120
Number of workers	1	2	3	4	5	6	7	8
Total wage bill (TC_L)	...	...	...	...	...	...	...	...
Marginal cost of labour (MC_L)		...	...	...	...	...	...	...

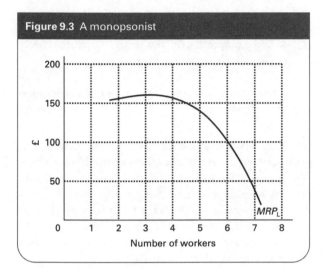

Figure 9.3 A monopsonist

Q34. Assume that a monopsonist faces the supply-of-labour schedule given in Table 9.1.

(a) Fill in the figures for TC_L and MC_L.

(b) Plot the figures for AC_L and MC_L on Figure 9.3, which also shows the firm's MRP_L curve.

(c) How many workers will the firm choose to employ in order to maximise profits?

(d) What wage rate will it pay?

(e) If Figure 9.3 were to illustrate a perfectly competitive market for labour (i.e. the sum of all firms), how many workers would now be employed and at what wage rate?

(Pages 232–6) What happens when labour also has economic power? Let us assume that a union is formed and that it has sole negotiating rights with a monopsony employer. What we have here is a case of *bilateral monopoly*. Wages are set by a process of collective bargaining, and once the wage rate has been agreed, the firm has to accept that wage. It cannot therefore then drive the wage rate down by employing fewer workers. The firm thus now faces **Q35.** *an upward-sloping/a downward-sloping/a horizontal* supply-of-labour curve which is therefore **Q36.** *below/above/equal* to the new MC_L curve.

Q37. Referring still to Figure 9.3, assume that a union now represents labour and that wage rates are set by a process of collective bargaining.

(a) Draw the AC_L and MC_L if the agreed wage rate is £100 per week.

(b) How many workers will the firm now choose to employ?

....

(c) Explain briefly why the firm is willing to take on *more* workers than before despite now having to pay a higher wage rate.

....

....

(d) What is the highest negotiated wage rate at which the firm would still wish to employ the same number of workers as before the union was formed?

£..............

(e) What is the equilibrium wage rate under bilateral monopoly?

£..............

(Pages 236–7) Let us now look at the process of collective bargaining.

The outcome of the negotiations will depend on the attitudes of both sides, their skills in negotiating, the information they possess about the other side and on the amount they are prepared to give ground. In particular, the outcome will depend on the relative power of both sides to pursue their objectives.

Q38. How will each of the following affect the *power of a union* to cause the employer to give ground at the negotiating table?

(a) New figures showing that the firm's profits for the last year were less than anticipated.

Increase/Decrease the union's power.

(b) A rise in unemployment.

Increase/Decrease the union's power.

(c) New figures showing that inflation has risen.

Increase/Decrease the union's power.

(d) A successful recruiting drive for union membership.

Increase/Decrease the union's power.

(e) Increased competition for the firm's product from imports.   *Increase/Decrease* the union's power.

(f) A rapidly growing demand for the firm's product.

Increase/Decrease the union's power.

(g) A closed shop agreement.

Increase/Decrease the union's power.

(h) The firm has substantial monopoly power in the goods market.   *Increase/Decrease* the union's power.

(Pages 237–43) Power is not the only factor that makes actual wage determination different from the perfectly competitive model. There are various other imperfections that cause labour markets to be distorted.

? **Q39.** Give three different types of labour market imperfection.

1. ....

2. ....

3. ....

⊖ **Q40.** Figure 9.4 shows the effect of imperfect information on a particular labour market. Workers looking for a job are likely to spend a period of time searching for a suitable one. Likewise firms wanting to recruit more labour are likely to spend time searching for suitably qualified workers.

The 'wage offered' (W_o) curve shows that as the period of search increases, the average worker will discover better-paid jobs (with the curve flattening off as the information becomes complete). The acceptable wage (W_a) curve shows the minimum wage the average worker would be prepared to accept.

(a) Why is the W_a curve downward sloping?

....

(b) How long will the average worker in the diagram go on searching for a job?

....

(c) Which of the two curves will shift and in which direction in each of the following cases?

  (i) Workers become more optimistic about finding a high paid job.   *W_o/W_a; up/down*

  (ii) Firms become more optimistic that there is plenty of suitably qualified labour.   *W_o/W_a; up/down*

  (iii) Unemployment benefit decreases, so that the costs to workers of searching becomes greater.
    W_o/W_a; up/down

  (iv) Demand in the goods market increases.
    W_o/W_a; up/down

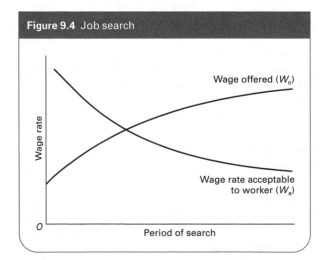

Figure 9.4 Job search

Wage offered (W_o)

Wage rate acceptable to worker (W_a)

Wage rate

O Period of search

◗ **Q41.** Which of the following could explain why the average wage of women tends to be lower than that of men?

(a) Some employers are prejudiced against women.
    Yes/No

(b) Women are less strong physically.   *Yes/No*

(c) Women tend to be less geographically mobile than men.   *Yes/No*

(d) A lower proportion of female workers are in unions than male workers.   *Yes/No*

(e) Women tend to work in more labour-intensive industries.   *Yes/No*

(f) A lower proportion of the female population seeks employment than that of the male population.
    Yes/No

(g) A lower proportion of women have higher education qualifications.   *Yes/No*

▤ **Q42.** A particular industry (which operates in a competitive labour market) discriminates against black workers. Which one of the following effects is likely? (Assume no discrimination in other industries.)

A. White workers will be paid a lower wage rate in that industry than they would have been otherwise.

B. Black workers in other industries will be paid a higher wage rate than they would otherwise.

C. White workers in other industries will be paid a lower wage rate than they would otherwise.

D. The discriminating industry will employ more black workers than it would if it did not discriminate, because it will pay black workers lower wage rates than white workers.

E. The profits of the industry that discriminates will fall.

▤ **Q43.** The marginal productivity theory states that firms will employ workers up to the point where their MRP_L is equal to their MC_L. Some labour market imperfections are consistent with this theory; some contradict it. From the following list of imperfections, which ones are consistent with the marginal productivity theory?

  (i) Firms discriminate against certain groups of workers.

  (ii) Firms have monopsony power.

  (iii) An industry has nationally negotiated wage rates.

  (iv) When reducing its labour force, a firm adopts a 'last in, first out' policy.

  (v) Firms are growth maximisers and profit satisficers.

  (vi) Wage rates (but not employment) are set by a process of collective bargaining.

A. (iv) only.

B. (iii) and (vi).

C. (ii), (iii) and (vi).

D. (i), (iv) and (v).

E. all six.

9.4 Capital and land

(Page 246) As with wages, the incomes accruing to the owners of capital and land are the outcome of the forces of demand and supply: forces affected to varying degrees by market distortions.

At the outset it is necessary to make an important distinction. This is between the money received from selling capital and land outright, and the income from the *services* of capital and land (i.e. income or interest from using or hiring out capital, and rent from land). The first is the price of the factor. The second is the price of the services of the factor.

Q44. Wage rates are the price of labour.   *True/False*

Q45. As with labour, the profit-maximising employment of land and capital *services* will be where the factor's *MRP* is equal to its *MC* (= price under perfect competition).
True/False

Capital for hire
(Pages 246–7) If firm A owns capital equipment, what determines the rate at which the firm can rent it out? The answer is that it will be determined by demand and supply.

The demand for capital services by firm B is given by the *MRP* of capital curve.

Q46. Draw the MRP_K, AC_K and MC_K curves for a firm which has monopsony power when hiring capital equipment. Mark the amount of capital equipment it will choose to hire and show what hire charge it will pay.

(Pages 247–9) The supply of capital services is determined in much the same way as the supply of goods. A firm will supply capital services up to the point where their marginal cost equals their marginal revenue. For a small firm supplying capital services (e.g. a tool hire company) the rental is given by the market and thus is the same as the **Q47.** *marginal revenue/marginal cost/average cost* from renting out equipment. The marginal cost will be the marginal *opportunity cost*.

Q48. Assume that a tool hire company already has a stock of tools. Which of the following are opportunity costs of hiring out the tools?
(a) The cost of replacing the equipment.   *Yes/No*
(b) The depreciation of the equipment due to wear and tear.   *Yes/No*
(c) The depreciation of the equipment due to ageing.   *Yes/No*
(d) Maintenance costs of the equipment.   *Yes/No*
(e) Handling costs associated with hiring out the equipment.   *Yes/No*

(Page 249) The price of capital services in a perfect market will be determined by market demand and supply.

Q49. The price of capital services will be higher:
A. the lower the marginal physical productivity of capital.
B. the lower the price of the goods produced with the capital equipment.
C. the lower the opportunity costs of supplying the capital services.
D. the lower the demand for the goods produced with the capital equipment.
E. the lower the price of complementary factors.

*Capital for purchase: investment
(Pages 249–51) The demand for capital for purchase (investment) will depend on the income it earns for the firm. To calculate the value of this income we need to use *discounted cash flow* (DCF) techniques.

These techniques allow us to reduce the future value of an investment back to a *present value* which we can then compare with the cost of the investment. If the present value exceeds the cost of the investment, the investment is worth while.

To find the present value we *discount* (i.e. reduce) the future values using an appropriate *rate of discount*.

*Q50. What is the present value of an investment in a project lasting one year that yields £110 at the end, assuming that the rate of discount is 10 per cent?

....

To work out the present value we use the following formula:

$$PV = \frac{X_1}{(1 + r)} + \frac{X_2}{(1 + r)^2} + \frac{X_3}{(1 + r)^3} \cdots + \frac{X_n}{(1 + r)^n}$$

where:
PV is the discounted present value of the investment, X_1 is the revenue from the investment earned in year 1, X_2 in year 2 and so on.

r is the rate of discount expressed as a decimal (e.g. 10% = 0.1).

*Q51. Suppose an investment costs £12 000 and yields £5000 per year for three years. At the end of the three years, the equipment has no value. Work out whether the investment will be profitable if the rate of discount is:

(a) 5% ....

....

....

(b) 10% ....

....

....

(c) 20%..

....

....

The rate of interest

(Pages 251–2) The rate of interest is the price of loanable funds. This depends on the supply of savings and the demand for finance (which includes investment demand).

Q52. Would the following changes cause the rate of interest to rise or fall?

(a) People become more thrifty.   *Rise/Fall*

(b) The productivity of investments generally increases.

     Rise/Fall

(c) The demand for goods increases.   *Rise/Fall*

(d) The cost of machinery rises.   *Rise/Fall*

Rent on land

(Pages 252–3) Rent on land, like the price of other factor services, will be determined by the interaction of demand and supply.

Q53. In what sense has the supply of land an elasticity:

(a) equal to zero? ....

(b) greater than zero? ....

Q54. The following are possible explanations of why rents are higher in city centres than in rural areas:

(i) Land in city centres is of more use to commerce.

(ii) Transport costs are lower for people living in city centres.

(iii) The supply of agricultural land is elastic.

(iv) The marginal productivity of land is higher for shop and office use than for agricultural use.

(v) City centres are more congested than out-of-town areas.

(vi) Costs of living (other than rents) are higher in towns than in the countryside.

Which are valid explanations?

A. (i), (ii) and (iv).

B. (i), (iv) and (v).

C. (iii), (iv) and (vi).

D. (i), (iii), (iv) and (vi).

E. (i), (ii), (iii), (iv), (v) and (vi).

Q55. If land is totally fixed in supply, then

A. all rent is economic rent.

B. all rent is transfer earnings.

C. the proportions of total rent that are economic rent and transfer earnings will depend entirely on demand.

D. the size of transfer earnings will depend on the *position* of the demand curve.

E. the amount of economic rent depends entirely on the position of the supply curve.

(Pages 253–5) Not all land is rented. Much of it is bought and sold outright. Nevertheless the price of land will depend on its potential annual rental value (*R*) and on the market rate of interest (*i*). The formula for working out the equilibrium price of land is *R/i*.

Q56. How much would a piece of land be worth that produces £2000 in rent each year if the market rate of interest were:

(a) 10 per cent per annum? ....

(b) 20 per cent per annum? ....

B   PROBLEMS, EXERCISES AND PROJECTS

Q57. Assume that you are offered some part-time evening work serving in a bar. You need this to supplement your meagre income/allowance. How many hours would you work if you were offered 50p per hour, £1, £2, £5, £20, £100, £1000? Is your behaviour rational? Do you have a backward-bending supply curve of labour and if so over what range? How would your behaviour differ if you were offered the job for 1 day, 1 week, 1 year, 40 years?

To what extent does your supply of labour per week depend on the number of weeks you *anticipate* being able to work at those rates? How would your behaviour differ if you were not allowed to save your wages or to invest it in shares, property, etc.?

Try discussing this question with other students. Note down their answers and tabulate the information. Does a common pattern emerge?

Q58. Table 9.2 shows how a firm's output of a good increases as it employs more workers. It is assumed that all other factors of production are fixed. The firm operates under perfect competition in both the goods and labour markets. The market price of the good is £2.

(a) Fill in the missing figures in Table 9.2.

(b) How many workers will the firm employ (to maximise profits) if the wage rate is (i) £50 per week, (ii) £110 per week, (iii) £100 per week?

Table 9.2 Total physical product of labour (weekly)

Number of workers	Total physical product (units)	Marginal physical product (units)	Marginal revenue product (£)
1	50		
		60	...
2	110		
		...	...
3	170		
		...	...
4	220		
		...	...
5	260		
		30	...
6	...		
		...	40
7	...		
		15	...
8	...		

Table 9.3 A monopsonist's labour supply and output (hourly data)

Workers (number)	Wage rate (AC_L) (£)	Total wages (TC_L) (£)	MC_L (£)	TPP_L (units)	TRP_L (£)	MRP_L (£)
10	4	...		500	...	
			...			...
20	5	...		575	...	
			...			...
30	6	...		645	...	
			...			...
40	7	...		705	...	
			...			...
50	8	...		755	...	
			...			...
60	9	...		800	...	
			...			...
70	10	...		840	...	

Q59. A profit-maximising firm has monopsony power in the labour market but its employees are not initially members of a trade union. Labour is the only variable factor and its supply schedule to the firm and the firm's total physical product of labour are shown in Table 9.3. The firm's product sells for £2.

(a) Fill in the columns for the total wage bill, MC_L, TRP_L and MRP_L. (Remember that the MC_L is the extra cost of employing *one* more worker not ten; similarly the MRP_L is the extra revenue earned from employing *one* more worker.)

(b) How many workers will the firm employ in order to maximise profits?

....

(c) What wage will the firm pay? ....

(d) Assuming that the fixed costs of production are £600 per hour, what will be the firm's hourly profit?

....

(e) If the fixed costs increase to £1200 per hour, what will be the effect on the firm's output?

....

(f) Assume now that the price of the good rises to £4. How many workers will the firm now employ to maximise profits?

....

(g) Returning to the original price of £2, assume now that the workers form a trade union and that a situation of bilateral monopoly is the result. What is the maximum wage the trade union could negotiate without causing the firm to try to reduce the size of the labour force below that in (b) above?

....

(h) How much profit will the firm make, assuming that fixed costs were at the original £600 per hour level?

....

(i) What has happened to the level of profits and the wage bill compared with (c) and (d) above?

....

(j) If the union only succeeds in pushing the wage up to £9 per hour, what will happen to the level of employment?

....

(k) If, as a result of industrial action, the union succeeds in achieving a wage rate of £12 per hour with no reduction in the workforce below the level of that in (b) above, what will the firm's level of profit be now?

....

C   DISCUSSION TOPICS AND ESSAYS

Q60. What is the relationship between the mobility of labour and the proportion of wages that consists of economic rent?

Q61. To what extent will a perfect market economy lead to equality of wage rates (a) within any given labour market and (b) between labour markets?

Q62. If, unlike a perfectly competitive employer, a monopsonist has to pay a higher wage to attract more workers, why, other things being equal, will a monopsonist pay a lower wage than a perfectly competitive employer?

Q63. Why do the most pleasant jobs often pay the highest wages?

Q64. Use the bilateral monopoly model to explain why a statutory minimum wage does not necessarily lead to a lower level of employment in a firm which would otherwise pay a lower wage rate.

Q65. Why is it impossible to identify an 'equilibrium wage' under bilateral monopoly?

Q66. Would a higher national average wage for men than women in a country be evidence of sexual discrimination in the labour market?

Q67. Consider the impact on the labour market of equal pay legislation.

*Q68. Should a profit-maximising firm always go ahead with a project that has a present value greater than the cost of the investment?

*Q69. If a project's costs occur throughout the life of the project, how will this affect the appraisal of whether the project is profitable?

Q70. How can the concept of marginal revenue product be used to explain why rents are higher in city centres than in out-of-town areas?

Q71. Mary Giles, a farmer, earns £100 000 from her farm where she owns all the land. After paying the wage bills of the two workers employed on the farm, and the bills for seeds, fertiliser, equipment, maintenance, fuel, etc. she has £20 000 left over. How should this £20 000 be classified: as her wages, her profit, her rent, or a combination of all three?

Q72. To what extent can marginal productivity theory explain inequality of income?

Q73. Debate
A society where wages are based on productivity will be an unfair and unjust society.

 D **ARTICLES**

Issues surrounding discrimination and its practice have been at the forefront of political debate for many years. How has economics contributed to this discussion? Can it add something to the debate? The article below, taken from *The Economist* of 6 June 1998, evaluates the contribution of economics and reviews some of the findings economics has made.

Race, sex and the dismal science

More than 30 years after the passage of America's landmark civil-rights legislation, discrimination is still an explosive social issue. Although it is illegal to treat female job applicants differently from males or to refuse to rent flats to Hispanic families, many Americans believe that unfair treatment persists in many parts of their economy.

There is no question that there are economic inequalities in America. Women earn less than men; Hispanics earn less than non-Hispanics; blacks are less likely to have mortgages than Caucasians. But are these inequalities due to deliberate discrimination, or are other factors at work? Economic analysis should be able to reveal the answer. But as a symposium in the *Journal of Economic Perspectives* makes clear, discrimination is devilishly difficult to pin down.

The legal definition of discrimination is disparate treatment of an individual on the basis of race, gender, age, religion or ethnic origin. The first economic attempt to understand such behaviour, developed by Gary Becker of the University of Chicago, suggested that prejudiced individuals with a 'taste for discrimination' must face additional costs if their prejudice is unfounded. A bigoted factory owner, for instance, will have to pay higher wages if he insists on hiring only white employees, and this will make his business less profitable than that of an unprejudiced competitor.

Since a price must be paid for prejudice, many economists have suggested (though Mr Becker's own model does not necessarily imply this) that in fully competitive markets discrimination should eventually disappear, because prejudiced firms will fail. Discrimination could persist only if entrepreneurs are willing to sacrifice part of their returns or if customers share – and are prepared to pay for – the employer's prejudice.

This taste-based analysis may well explain discrimination in settings where individuals interact and so tastes matter. But it is less successful at explaining prejudice in one-off or impersonal transactions. For instance, it does not clarify why blacks might find it harder than whites to get mortgage loans. In these situations, a second theory, offered by Kenneth Arrow and Edmund Phelps in the early 1970s, is more useful. Their approach, called 'statistical discrimination', suggests that people use an individual's race or sex as a proxy for individual characteristics. Thus a mortgage company might be reluctant to lend to a black client because it believes blacks, in general, have higher default rates. Using a racial 'proxy' is cheaper for the mortgage company than examining the individual's own credit history.

Unfortunately, this theory also is hard to square with persistent discrimination. The reason is that even if such a proxy is generally correct for a large group, it will not be true for all individuals within the group. Those firms able to distinguish among, say, high-risk and low-risk borrowers on an individual basis will eventually win out over those who use crude – and discriminatory – proxies.

Discrimination might be easier for economists to understand if they were able to measure it. There are two main techniques for doing this. The first is regression analysis, which seeks to measure whether an outcome, such as wage differentials between blacks and whites, is correlated with race once all other relevant factors, such as education and experience, are taken into account. Regression analysis has provided important evidence: a famous study of mortgage applications by the Federal Reserve Bank of Boston, for instance, showed that loan denial rates for blacks were eight percentage points higher

than those for whites, once a large number of factors that affected the risk of default were included.

But, as John Yinger, of Syracuse University, points out in the *JEP* symposium, regression analysis has drawbacks as a tool for measuring discrimination. In particular, it is hard to measure certain variables, such as the quality of an individual's 'human capital', which may explain employer decisions that superficially appear discriminatory. Excluding such factors overstates discrimination in the labour market; including them may understate it, since the quality of human capital may be related to discrimination in other areas, such as education.

Take a test
An alternative technique for studying discrimination involves audits. In an audit, two individuals or couples, equal in all respects save one (such as race or sex) sequentially visit an employer, banker or rental agent to look for evidence of forms of disparate treatment that would otherwise be difficult to capture statistically. A 1991 employment audit in Washington, DC, for instance, showed that white testers were almost 10 per cent more likely to be invited for job interviews than black testers.

A 1989 study involving 2000 audits of American estate agents found only 13 per cent of black testers posing as house buyers were offered assistance in mortgage financing, compared with 24 per cent of white testers.

Audits, however, have their problems as well, as James Heckman, of the University of Chicago, points out in a penetrating commentary. Audit studies assume that pairs of testers are alike in every relevant was save one. This may well not be the case. Employers may react differently to different auditors for reasons that have nothing to do with race or sex, meaning that audits may detect discriminatory behaviour when there is none. Fundamentally, audits and regressions suffer the same problem: it is hard to identify the characteristics that matter.

So how well has America dealt with discrimination against the various groups its lawmakers have sought to protect? Anecdotally, there is ample evidence that discrimination is far less rampant than it used to be, but that it is still all too common. Very few studies, however, have sought to look at changes in discrimination over time. Demonstrating incontrovertibly that it even exists is still beyond the ability of the dismal science.

(a) Why, given Gary Becker's theory of discrimination, might discrimination disappear over the longer term? Why might this seem an unlikely outcome?

(b) What problems might be encountered in attempting to measure discrimination?

The link between labour market flexibility and economic competitiveness has been at the centre of many of the economic reforms of the last 20 years, both in the UK and elsewhere in the world economy. The article below, taken from *CBI News* of March 1998, explores the various forms that labour market flexibility might take and the differing strategies adopted by countries in Europe to achieve it.

Different combinations

The debate about labour-market flexibility has never been more important or contentious, but unfortunately it is often characterised by stereotypes, misconceptions and confusion over definitions. The European labour market is typically portrayed as rigid and inflexible, whereas the US and UK are seen as possessing dynamic and flexible labour markets leading to low unem-

ployment. While there is some truth in this generalisation, we must recognise that there are strengths and weaknesses to all labour markets and that the European picture is not uniform but varied.

Dimensions
There are six different dimensions of flexibility. All are important, but in dif-

ferent ways for productivity growth and employment creation:
• Geographical mobility is clearly important to avoid regional unemployment as far as possible. Some high national levels of unemployment around Europe are essentially regional problems in each country.
• Flexible working patterns, such as part-time work and fixed-term

contracts, can be important sources of improved company performance and productivity growth and are popular with employees.

- Wage flexibility is important for maintaining competitiveness and employment, and will become more so in EMU, when countries can no longer devalue their currencies to remain competitive.
- Numerical flexibility – the ability to adjust the size of the workforce – is perhaps the most controversial dimension of flexibility. But limited numerical flexibility can distort the labour market and cause unemployment by discouraging hiring.
- The last two dimensions of flexibility – skills and functional flexibility – are the least controversial and yet, in many ways, the most important. A workforce with good and transferable skills, which can be moved easily between jobs, is essential for rapid productivity growth. Functional flexibility goes further than that and relates to the involvement of people in their work tasks, to devolving responsibility and to the willingness of both managers and employees to change their working practices – often vital to competitive success.

In order for a country to be flexible it does not need maximum flexibility in each of these areas but rather to have sufficient flexibility overall. Different countries have developed different responses and each state draws strengths from its own combination. Weaknesses in one area are often compensated for by strengths in another. Some states are strong in areas which call for active flexibility (for instance, skills and function). Others gain flexibility through a more passive use – where it is the absence of rigidity that gives the freedom to use flexibility (for instance, numerical flexibility or flexibility in working patterns). Countries need to find a combination of flexibility which delivers growth and high, sustainable levels of employment.

When examining EU states, what we find is a picture of great national variability far removed from the simplistic slogans of: UK flexible . . . Europe inflexible.

The Italian economy has seen rapid growth in productivity, accompanied by moderate wage increases. But there are large regional differences. Northern Italy has most of the manufacturing and forms part of the 'core' of Europe, sharing a similar industrial structure to France and Germany. Southern Italy has higher unemployment, a greater share of people employed in agriculture and poor skill levels. Italian unemployment is high owing to high levels of social security contributions and stringent employment protection that discourage employment creation, though the *cassa integrazione* and on-the-job training contracts provide companies with some flexibility in adjusting the size of their workforce. There is little flexibility in working patterns as the use of fixed-term contracts is restricted and part-timers cannot work overtime.

Germany's absolute productivity levels are very high and result from a skilled workforce, able to make full use of multi-skilling and teamworking. Collective bargaining is primarily conducted at the sectoral level and characterised by a high degree of informal co-ordination. As automatic indexation is forbidden and wages do not appear to be influenced by inflation expectations, pay settlements are generally sensitive to the macro-economic situation. But they do not provide for differentiation at company level. Wage dispersion is also low. This has meant the service sector is relatively underdeveloped. Numerical flexibility is limited; the General Dismissal Protection Act applies to all employees after six months' service and requires that all ordinary dismissals are qualified as socially justified. There are restrictions on the use of fixed-term contracts.

In the UK, there are few restrictions on the use of flexible patterns of work and numerical flexibility is high. Skills flexibility has been historically limited and company training has been used to remedy the lack of basic skills of the workforce. The development of functional flexibility is hindered by the weak skills base but is improving, especially in the service sector. The long-term record on wage restraint is weak, with a tendency to inflationary settlements. But a major recent shift to decentralised wage setting and improved links between company/individual performance and pay has increased flexibility.

The Netherlands has interesting lessons to offer about how labour markets can be reformed within a consensual model. Its economy is doing well, unemployment is low, and GDP growth is strong. There has been considerable reform since the 80s when both unemployment and inflation were high and growth low. Co-operation between the social partners – the government, business and unions – helped reform rigid labour market policies such as working pattern restrictions and a high minimum wage, while wage restraint has improved competitiveness. The workforce is skilled and there is significant flexibility in working patterns. However, numerical flexibility is limited; employers need authorisation before dismissing workers. Dutch labour-force participation is also low by international standards.

In France, skills flexibility is high: 77 per cent of the population are qualified to level two (five GCSEs equivalent) or above. Unit labour costs have fallen throughout most of the 90s but a high minimum wage continues to be a barrier to employment growth, especially among young people. Benefit replacement levels are also high. As in Spain, numerical flexibility is limited. Redundancies are permitted for serious and genuine failures in performance of individual employees or because of financial difficulties experienced by the firm but not to improve profitability. The number of temporary work contracts is growing rapidly as an alternative to flexibility in permanent employment. Whether this is desirable or not remains to be seen.

Spain is now among the fastest-growing countries of the European Union. It has a higher than EU average share employed in manufacturing and has made continual 'catch-up' productivity improvements, particularly helped by the devaluation of the peseta in 1992 by 20 per cent. Spain has made considerable efforts to improve its skills base over the past two decades, but gaps still remain in its education and training provision, especially with regard to vocational training and lifelong learning. Flexibility in working patterns was facilitated by a set of reforms in 1994. Functional flexibility has also improved since the abolition of the *ordenanzas laborales* – regulations that limited the responsibilities which different trades are allowed to perform. Spain has high unemployment (currently around 20 per cent), owing to deep structural problems. Wages are the most inflexible in the OECD, preventing the low skilled and young pricing themselves into the market. Numerical flexibility is severely limited. Severance payments are among the highest in the world and 30 per cent of the workforce are on temporary contracts to avoid these restrictions.

(a) Attempt a definition of a 'flexible labour market'.

(b) In what ways has the UK approach to flexibility differed from those in other European countries?

(c) Which of the countries considered in the article do you consider to have the strongest approach to flexibility? Explain your answer and identify the criteria on which you made your judgement.

Until 1999, the UK was the only major economy with no minimum wage provision. Some argued that a lack of a statutory minimum wage rate was the key to its steadily improving competitive position, whereas others argued that unscrupulous employers simply used the situation to drive wages down to poverty levels. In the article below, taken from *CBI News* of April 1999, the likely impact of the newly adopted minimum wage on business is assessed.

Better than feared

The minimum wage regulations have been hailed as a victory for common sense and CBI members recognise the wage as fair. John Cridland CBI director of HR policy comments: 'It's not bad news and it's not a sledgehammer and it's a lot better than many of our members feared.'

According to government figures, some two million workers will be up to 25 per cent better off when the minimum wage – £3.60 an hour for workers over the age of 22 – comes into force in April. The figure arrived at was the result of lengthy and detailed consultation in which the CBI reached a compromise with the government and unions who fought for a rate of above £4.

Most employers will be glad that bureaucracy has been kept at bay. There is no obligation to state the minimum wage on payslips, nor is there any obligation to keep detailed records or pay statements. The regulations recognise flexible working arrangements such as annualised contracts where hours worked vary from one month. Britain's biggest general union GMB which covers 700 000 workers in public and private sectors has few complaints having recently secured pay deals above the minimum for its public sector workers. A GMB spokesperson said: 'We're delighted to see the minimum wage come into force and security for millions of workers.' On the downside, GMB is still unhappy lower rates apply to people below the age of 22.

Industries most affected are labour-intensive, low-wage manufacturing industries like textiles and clothing and electronics and the service sector – retail, catering, leisure and fast food – where flexibility and training are an issue. Bigger companies are generally satisfied with the legislation but there are specific concerns. One is the inflationary pressure on pay differentials at the bottom end of the scale and costs will be carefully counted as some manufacturers look at their options. Max Playfer personnel director of textile group Coats-Viyella says: 'In terms of overall competitiveness it doesn't help. We are moving offshore fairly rapidly.'

In banking the issue of competiveness is being addressed by flexible working and the big change is the switch away from traditional branch network to call-centres offering out-of-hours banking. NatWest has negotiated annualised hours contracts for call-centre and branch staff, who now work to meet the changing pattern of customer demand. Steve Williamson, NetWest head of employee relations says: 'Hours can vary significantly from one month to the next and rather than asking people to work a standard seven hour day we offer flexibility.'

Training rates are an issue for many employers. Builders' merchant group Jewson currently has 80 trainees going through the modern apprentice scheme and is grateful that it does not have to bear the full costs of the minimum wage. Managing director (operations) Peter Hindle says: 'We're paying them a training wage and when they finish they'll kick into our pay structure. Hopefully these people will become our future management and supervisors.' Fast-food chain McDonalds offers a number of training places under the New Deal and pays a starting rate of £3.25 for people aged 16–18. According to the company, wage rates have been going up independently of minimum wage legislation. Personnel director Mike Love comments: 'The legislation doesn't affect us as we're already paying in excess of the national minimum rates.'

The wage will have a proportionately higher impact on small businesses. The British Retail Consortium which represents the employers of some 2.9 million shop workers believes the government is not doing enough to help small retailers. Lorraine Ford, associate director of HR policy for the British Retail Consortium, says: 'The DTI has put together a package for small businesses to pay for staff training which can increase productivity and help with retention. But in the short term that's no help at all.' The CBI's John Cridland comments: 'The reality is that most people who are going to gain from the minimum wage are going to be working for very small businesses, often part-time, often home workers and typically women.'

In the retail sector, large companies are paying above the minimum rates and are promoting flexible working through practices like part-time working, shift swapping, and holiday cover and there is little evidence of companies taking advantage of exemptions like the lower rate for workers in their first six months of a new job – often applied to women returners. Julie Mitchell-Ninnis, colleague relations manager for Asda, says: 'We have a lot of flexible working practices and paying people different rates doesn't fit with our philosophy of being a family-friendly employer.'

One of the biggest changes CBI members will feel is that the minimum wage will finally expose the cowboys and unregulated operators who have been holding down wages and undercutting employers who have adopted responsible policies on pay and conditions.

Hopes are that the minimum wage will force them to pay higher rates so levelling the playing field and giving honest companies a fair crack of the whip. Realistically, pressure may have to be brought to bear to make the cowboys comply and the new legislation will need effective policing.

(a) In any discussion of a national minimum wage, why is it crucial that we distinguish between the impact it will have on a competitive labour market and a labour market dominated by a monopsonistic employer?

(b) Why are certain industries likely to be more affected by the adoption of a minimum wage than others? How relevant might your answer above be in answering this question?

(c) Under what circumstances might the imposition of a national minimum wage lead to an *increase* in employment?

(d) What responses by business to the national minimum wage does the article identify? What might be the economic implications of such responses?

 ANSWERS

Q1. *the wage rate of plasterers.* We are referring to a perfect factor market: i.e. the market for plasterers, *not* the market for plaster or plastered walls. (These may or may not be perfect.)

Q2. *employers or workers.* Both demanders (employers) and suppliers (workers) are 'wage takers', under perfect competition.

Q3. *the supply curve of labour to.*

Q4. *the demand curve for labour from.*

Q5. *(a)* *supply; left.* Plasterers will be prepared to work fewer hours at any given wage rate.

   (b) *demand; right.* Plaster is a complementary good. Thus as its price comes down, more of it will be demanded *and* hence also more plasterers will be demanded to use it.

   (c) *demand; left.* As fewer houses are demanded so fewer plasterers will be needed.

   (d) *supply; left.* This will push up plasterers' wages in other parts of the country and hence encourage plasterers to leave this part of the country to get jobs elsewhere.

   (e) *demand; left.* This will push up the price of new buildings and hence lead to a lower quantity of them being demanded and hence a lower demand for plasterers.
   Also: *supply; left.* Plasterers will be encouraged to move into other parts of the building trade.

   (f) *demand; left.* Employers will try to economise on the number of plasterers they employ. Many small builders may do the plastering themselves instead.

Q6. E. The demand for a factor of production is derived from the demand for the good it is used to produce: the more of the good that is demanded, the more of the factor that will be demanded to produce it.

Q7. *(a)* *rise.* Being a derived demand, the *demand* for arable land would *rise* and hence the rent would *rise.*

   (b) *rise.* The rise in the demand for beef would encourage farmers to move from cereals to beef production. This would cause a shortage of cereals and hence a rise in the price of cereals. This would cause the *demand* for arable land to *rise.*

Also the switching of land to beef production would cause a *fall* in the *supply* of land for cereal production. Both effects will lead to a *rise* in rent on arable land.

   (c) *fall.* The reclamation scheme would *increase* the *supply* of land.

   (d) *fall.* The quantity of grain supplied would fall and hence the *demand* for arable land would *fall.*

   (e) *rise.* The set-aside scheme would *reduce* the *supply* of arable land.

Q8. B. The perfect labour market will cause people with the *same* skills to be paid the same in the long run, but it will not cause people with a high level of skills to be paid the same as those with a low level of skills.

Q9. Market power; barriers to entry into various markets; imperfect knowledge.

Q10. *marginal disutility* (the opportunity cost of work).

Q11. *upward sloping.* A higher wage rate will be necessary to persuade a person to work extra hours.

Q12. *(a)* *substitution effect.* People substitute income for leisure (leisure has a higher opportunity cost).

   (b) *income effect.* People can afford to take more leisure.

Q13. *negative.* Here higher wage rates will encourage people to work *less.*

Q14. *positive.* Here higher wage rates encourage people to work *more.*

Q15. *income effect.* If this becomes dominant above a certain wage, the number of hours offered by the worker will get *less* as the wage rate rises.

Q16. *True.* The firm is a 'wage taker': i.e. it has to pay the market wage, but at that wage can employ as many workers as it likes.

Q17. D. (ii) is not correct because a change in the wage rate is shown by a movement *along* the supply curve. (iii) is not correct because it determines the *demand* for labour not the supply.

Q18. *(a)* *geographical.*

   (b) *both.*

   (c) *occupational.*

   (d) *geographical.*

   (e) *both.*

   (f) *occupational.*

Q19. *economic rent.*

Q20. A. He earns £80 more than he could in the next best paid job (as a lorry driver). Thus he earns £80 more than is necessary to prevent him giving up being a model and becoming a lorry driver instead.

Q21. C. The vertical distance below the supply curve shows the wage the marginal worker must receive to persuade him or her to move to this job: it shows the marginal worker's transfer earnings. When all these transfer earnings are added together we get the total area under the supply curve.

Q22. B. The area between the supply curve and the wage rate (W_e) shows the excess of actual wages over the minimum needed to persuade workers to stay in this job.

Q23. (a) (vii); (b) (iii); (c) (v); (d) (i); (e) (vi); (f) (iv); (g) (ii).

Q24. MPP_L *by MR.*

Q25. *fewer.*

Q26. *more.*

Q27. *True.* Under perfect competition the firm will always demand that quantity of workers where $MRP_L = W$. Thus, like the demand-for-labour curve, the MRP_L curve shows for each wage the number of workers the firm will employ.

Q28. (a) *shift.*

    (b) *movement along* (given that the wage rate is measured on the vertical axis).

    (c) *shift.*

Q29. (a) *True.* A fall in W will lead to higher employment and more output. This will drive P down. If the demand for the good is elastic, this fall in P will lead to a lot more being sold and hence a lot more people being employed.

    (b) *False.* If labour can be *readily* substituted for other factors, then a reduction in W will lead to a large increase in labour used to replace these other factors.

    (c) *True.* If wage rates fall, a lot more labour will be demanded if plenty of complementary factors can be obtained at little increase in their price.

    (d) *False.* If wage rates fall and more labour is used, less substitute factors will be demanded and their price will fall. If their supply is *elastic*, a lot less will be supplied and therefore a lot more labour will be used instead.

    (e) *False.* If wages are a *large* proportion of total costs and wage rates fall, total costs will fall significantly; therefore production will increase significantly, and so, therefore, will the demand for labour.

    (f) *True.* Given sufficient time, firms can respond to a fall in wage rates by reorganising their production processes to make use of the now relatively cheap labour.

Q30. *False*: for two reasons. (1) Some people may choose to work longer hours than others (they have different leisure preferences). (2) There is unequal ownership of *non-human* factors of production (land and capital) and these also yield an income for their owners. (The statement would be *true* if it read 'there would be complete equality of *wage rates*'.)

Q31. (a) (iii); (b) (ii); (c) (i); (d) (v); (e) (iv).

Q32. *upward sloping.*

Q33. *supply curve of* labour. If the firm wants to employ extra workers, it will have to offer higher wages to attract the necessary labour into the market. Conversely, by cutting back on the number of workers it can force down the wage rate.

Q34. (a) See following table.

Wage rate (AC_L) (£)	50	60	70	80	90	100	110	120
Number of workers	1	2	3	4	5	6	7	8
Total wage bill (TC_L) (£)	50	120	210	320	450	600	770	960
Marginal cost of labour (MC_L) (£)		70	90	110	130	150	170	190

    (b) See Figure A9.1.

    (c) *5 workers* (where $MRP_L = MC_L$).

    (d) *£90* (as given by the supply curve).

    (e) *6 workers at £100* (where MRP_L = supply of labour).

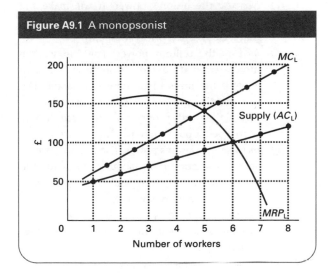

Figure A9.1 A monopsonist

Q35. *horizontal* (along to the point where it reaches the old supply curve: if it wants to employ beyond *that* point, it will have to pay *above* the negotiated rate in order to attract sufficient workers).

Q36. *equal to* (along to the point where it reaches the old supply curve: then it jumps up to the old MC_L curve).

Q37. (a) They are the same horizontal straight line at £100 up to 6 workers. Above that number of workers they are the same as the original curves.

    (b) *6 workers* (where $MC_L = MRP_L$).

    (c) Because it is no longer in the position to be able to drive down the wage rate by cutting down on the number of employees. The MC_L has now become the same as the AC_L (a horizontal straight line).

(d) £140. If this is the negotiated wage rate, it will now be the MC_L as well as the AC_L. Thus the firm will choose to employ 5 workers (the pre-union number) since this is where $MC_L = MRP_L$.

(e) There is none! The actual wage will depend on the outcome of the bargain, but that cannot be predicted with any accuracy. It depends on how successful each side is in the negotiations.

Q38. (a) *Decrease* the union's power. The union will have less scope to press its claim.

(b) *Decrease* the union's power. The firm can threaten to employ non-union labour; it can threaten redundancies (a greater threat when unemployment is high).

(c) *Increase* the union's power. The firm will be more able to pass on any wage increases in higher prices (given that it expects inflation to cause competitor firms to raise their prices).

(d) *Increase* the union's power. This will make it easier for the union to finance industrial action. It will also create more solidarity among workers and make it more difficult for the firm to recruit non-union labour.

(e) *Decrease* the union's power. It will make the firm more resolved to resist high wage claims so that it can keep its prices competitive.

(f) *Increase* the union's power. The firm will be more anxious to avoid a dispute so as not to allow other firms to capture this market. The firm may be anxious to take on extra labour. Also if the firm's profits have increased, it may be in a better position to pay higher wages.

(g) *Increase* the union's power. The firm will not be able to use non-union labour or to divide the workforce by making separate (lower) offers to less militant groups of workers.

(h) *Increase* the union's power. The firm will find it easier to pass on wage increases to the consumer in higher prices.

Q39. *Discrimination* (by race, sex, age, class, etc., i.e. not based on differences in productivity), *imperfect knowledge of labour market conditions* (by workers and/or employers), *non-maximising behaviour*.

Q40. (a) As time elapses, the costs to the worker of searching will increase. Thus the longer the typical worker is unsuccessful in getting a job, the lower the wage he or she would be prepared to settle for.

(b) The point on the horizontal axis corresponding to the intersection of the two curves.

(c) (i) W_a; *up*.

(ii) W_o; *down*.

(iii) W_a; *down*.

(iv) W_o; *up*.

Q41. Yes: all except (f).

Q42. E. If it is discriminating it is preferring to employ white workers to black even when black workers are more able. It is thus sacrificing profit. (Note that D is wrong because the lower wages are the *result* of lower demand for black workers by the employers in the industry in question.)

Q43. C. These imperfections, although they affect wages, will not affect a firm's choosing to employ people up to the point where $MRP_L = MC_L$.

Q44. *False*. Wage rates are the price of labour *services*. When a firm pays a person a week's wages, the wages are for the person's labour. The firm has not purchased the actual person.

Q45. *True*. The principle is the same.

Q46. The diagram will be similar to Figure A9.1, but with the amount of capital measured on the horizontal axis. The amount of capital equipment the firm will hire is given by the intersection of the MC_K and MRP_K curves. The hire charge is given by the AC_K curve (i.e. the supply of capital curve).

Q47. *marginal revenue*.

Q48. Yes: (b), (d) and (e). There are all opportunity costs since they vary with the amount that the equipment is hired out.

Q49. E. The lower the price of complementary factors the more of them will be demanded and hence the more capital equipment will be demanded. This will push up its market price.

Q50. £100 (i.e. £100 invested at 10 per cent will be worth £110 after one year).

Q51. Using the discounting formula gives:

(a) $PV = £5000/1.05 + £5000/1.05^2 + £5000/1.05^3$
$$= £4761.90 + £4535.15 + £4319.19$$
$$= £13\ 616.24$$
Therefore the investment is profitable at a 5 per cent discount rate.

(b) $PV = £5000/1.1 + £5000/1.1^2 + £5000/1.1^3$
$$= £4545.45 + £4132.23 + £3756.57$$
$$= £12\ 434.25$$
Therefore the investment is also profitable at a 10 per cent discount rate.

(c) $PV = £5000/1.2 + £5000/1.2^2 + £5000/1.2^3$
$$= £4166.67 + £3472.22 + £2893.52$$
$$= £10\ 532.41$$
Therefore the investment is not profitable at a 20 per cent discount rate.

Q52. (a) *Fall*. Caused by an increase in the supply of loanable funds.

(b) *Rise*. Caused by firms wanting to invest more and thus demanding more loans.

(c) *Rise*. Caused by a rise in investment demand as firms respond to the rise in consumer demand;

also by a decrease in savings as a result of the increased spending.

(d) *Rise*: if the demand for machinery is inelastic. More will now be spent on machinery and thus more funds will be required. *Fall*: if the demand for machinery is elastic and thus less funds will be demanded.

Q53. *(a)* *Land in total*: i.e. for all uses (assuming that land cannot be reclaimed from the sea or from deserts).

(b) *Land for specific uses*. The higher the rent or price of land for a specific use (e.g. building houses), the more land will be offered for sale for that purpose and thus transferred from other uses (e.g. agriculture).

Q54. A. All these cause a higher demand for land in city centres.

Q55. A. If the supply curve is totally inelastic there are no transfer earnings: all rent is economic rent. The *size* of the economic rent will depend on the position of the demand curve relative to the supply curve.

Q56. *(a)* £2000/0.1 = £20 000.

(b) £2000/0.2 = £10 000.

10 Inequality, Poverty and Policies to Redistribute Incomes

A REVIEW

In this chapter we examine the distribution of income in practice and ask why incomes are unequally distributed. We start by looking at different ways of measuring inequality and poverty, and then examine their causes.

We then turn to look at what can be done. In particular we look at the role of taxes and benefits as means of redistributing incomes.

10.1 Inequality and poverty

(Pages 258–60) There are a number of different ways of looking at the distribution of income and wealth. Each way highlights a different aspect of inequality.

 Q1. Match the following measures of inequality (i)–(x) to the examples (a)–(j).
  (i) Size distribution of income.
  (ii) Functional distribution of income: broad factor categories.
  (iii) Functional distribution of income: narrow factor categories.
  (iv) Functional distribution of income: occupational.
  (v) Distribution of income by recipient: class of person.
  (vii) Distribution of income by recipient: geographical.
  (vii) Size distribution of wealth.
  (viii) Distribution of wealth by class of holder.
  (ix) Absolute poverty.
  (x) Relative poverty.

(a) The average income of manual workers compared with non-manual.

....

(b) The percentage of people with an income below what is considered to be a minimum acceptable level.

....

(c) The average level of income in the south-east compared with that in the north-west.

....

(d) Profits as a proportion of national income.

....

(e) The proportion of total savings held by people over retirement age.

....

(f) The ratio of the income of the richest 20 per cent to that of the poorest 40 per cent.

....

▤ *Multiple Choice*   ⊘ *Written answer*   ◖ *Delete wrong word*   ⊖ *Diagram/table manipulation*   ⊗ *Calculation*   ✦ *Matching/ordering*

(g) The average income of doctors compared with that of nurses.

....

(h) The number of people without adequate food and shelter.

....

(i) The proportion of the nation's assets held by the richest 1 per cent of the population.

....

(j) The average income of one-parent families as a proportion of the national average income.

....

(Pages 260–2) The size distribution of income can be measured by the use of *Lorenz curves* and *Gini coefficients*.

⊖ **Q2.** Assume that the economy is grouped into five equal-sized groups of households according to income. The figures (imaginary) are shown in Table 10.1.

Draw two Lorenz curves corresponding to these two sets of figures on Figure 10.1.

Table 10.1 Percentage size distribution of income by quintile groups of households

	Quintile groups			
Lowest 20%	Next 20%	Middle 20%	Next 20%	Highest 20%
Income before taxes and benefits				
1.0	6.0	15.0	25.0	53.0
Income after taxes and benefits				
6.0	10.0	17.0	22.0	45.0

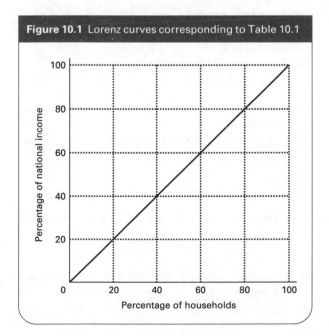

Figure 10.1 Lorenz curves corresponding to Table 10.1

? **Q3.** If the government pursues a policy of cutting taxes for the very rich but providing increased benefits for the very poor, and pays for this by increasing taxes on those with middle incomes, what will happen to the shape of the after-tax-and-benefits Lorenz curve?

....

....

The Gini coefficient is a way of measuring in a single figure the information contained in the Lorenz curve.

▤ **Q4.** In Figure 10.2 the Gini coefficient is the ratio of areas:

A. Y to Z
B. Z to $(X + Y + Z)$
C. Z to $(Y + Z)$
D. Y to $(Y + Z)$
E. Y to $(X + Y + Z)$

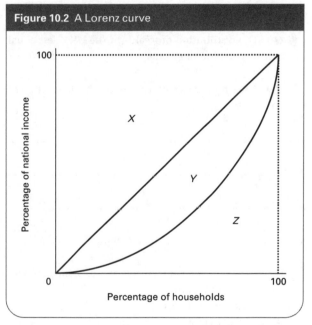

Figure 10.2 A Lorenz curve

◑ **Q5.** If the Gini coefficient rises, this means that income distribution has become more equal.   *True/False*

(Pages 262–70) A common way of representing the degree of inequality in a country is to look at the functional distribution of income by source.

⊖ **Q6.** Table 10.2 shows the sources of UK household income by quintile groups. What do the figures suggest are the major causes of inequality in incomes?

....

....

Table 10.2 Sources of UK household income as a percentage of total household income: 1997/8

Gross household weekly incomes (quintiles)	Wages and salaries (1)	Income from self-employment (2)	Income from investments (3)	Pensions and annuities (4)	Social security benefits (5)	Other (6)	Total (7)
Lowest 20%	6	1	3	5	81	3	100
Next 20%	25	4	5	13	50	3	100
Middle 20%	58	7	5	12	16	2	100
Next 20%	76	6	4	6	6	1	100
Highest 20%	78	10	5	4	2	1	100
All households	67	8	4	7	13	1	100

Source: *Family Spending* (ONS, 1998).

There is marked inequality of income between females and males. The average gross hourly earnings of full-time adult female workers is only 80 per cent of those of full-time adult male workers.

Q7. Although the average wage of women is less than that of men, the average wage of women is approximately the same as that for men *in the same occupation.*   *True/False*

Q8. The distribution of wealth in the UK is less equal than the distribution of income.   *True/False*

(?) Q9. Give four different causes of the inequality of wealth.

1. ....

2. ....

3. ....

4. ....

Q10. The following are possible causes of inequality:
 (i) Differences in wealth.
 (ii) Differences in attitudes.
 (iii) Differences in power.
 (iv) Differences in household composition.
 (v) The proportion of the population over retirement age.
 (vi) The proportion of the population below working age.

Which can help to explain inequality in wage rates?
A.   (iii) only.
B.   (ii) and (iii).
C.   (i), (ii) and (iii).
D.   (i), (ii), (iii) and (iv).
E.   (i)–(vi).

Q11. Referring to the same list of possible causes of inequality as in Q10, which can help to explain inequality between households?

A.   (iv) only.
B.   (i) and (iv).
C.   (iv), (v) and (vi).
D.   (i), (iv), (v), and (vi).
E.   (i)–(vi).

10.2 Taxes, benefits and the redistribution of income

(Pages 270–4) We turn now to the role of the government in redistributing incomes more equally. The two means of redistributing income that we shall consider are taxes and benefits. We first examine taxation.

Principles of taxation

Q12. The following is a list of requirements that people have argued should be met by a good tax system:
  (i) Equitable between recipients of benefits (the benefits principle).
  (ii) Convenient to the government.
  (iii) Horizontally equitable.
  (iv) Minimal disincentive effects.
  (v) Non-distortionary.
  (vi) Vertically equitable.
  (vii) Difficult to avoid.
  (viii) Difficult to evade.
  (ix) Convenient to the taxpayer.
  (x) Cheap to collect.

Match the following descriptions to each of the above requirements.
(a)   Taxes whose amount paid is the same for people in the same economic circumstances.

....

(b)   Taxes whose rates can be quickly and simply adjusted.

....

(c)   Taxes where the authorities can easily prevent illegal non-payment.

....

(d) Taxes with minimal administrative costs.

....

(e) Taxes where people pay in proportion to the amount of public services they use.

....

(f) Taxes which do not alter market signals in an undesirable direction.

....

(g) Taxes which people cannot escape paying by finding legal loopholes.

....

(h) Taxes which do not discourage initiative or effort.

....

(i) Taxes whose method of payment is easily understood and straightforward.

....

(j) Taxes whose rates depend on people's ability to pay.

....

(?) **Q13.** Why may there be a conflict between the principle of vertical equity and the benefits principle?

....

....

(?) **Q14.** How well do the following two taxes meet (i) the vertical equity principle and (ii) the benefits principle?

(a) Income tax:

(i) ....

....

(ii) ....

....

(b) The old community charge (poll tax):

(i) ....

....

(ii) ....

....

Taxes as a means of redistributing incomes
(Pages 274–5) The degree of redistribution will depend on the degree of progressiveness of the tax.

Taxes can be categorised as *progressive, regressive, proportional* or *lump sum* (where lump-sum taxes are an extreme form of regressive tax).

(−) **Q15.** Figure 10.3 shows how these four different categories of tax vary with income. Diagram (a) shows the total amount of tax paid. Diagram (b) shows the average tax rate. On each diagram which of the four curves correspond to which category of tax?

(a) Progressive   Curve ....

Regressive   Curve ....

Proportional   Curve ....

Lump sum   Curve ....

(b) Progressive   Curve ....

Regressive   Curve ....

Proportional   Curve ....

Lump sum   Curve ....

Figure 10.3 The variation of different taxes with income

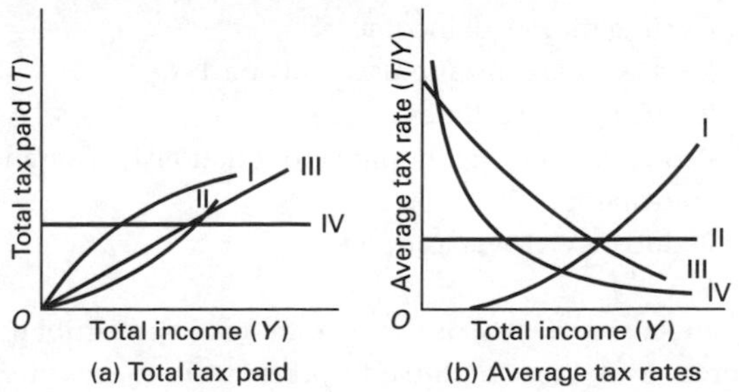

(a) Total tax paid

(b) Average tax rates

⊗ *Q16.* If Clyde's income tax goes up from £1000 to £1100 as a result of a rise in his income from £10 000 to £10 400:

(a) What was his original average rate of tax? ....

(b) What is his new average rate of tax? ....

(c) What is his marginal rate of tax? ....

◐ *Q17.* An income tax levied at a constant marginal rate with a tax-free allowance of £5000 will be a proportional tax.   *True/False*

▤ *Q18.* Indirect taxes levied at the same rate on all goods would be:
A.   progressive.
B.   regressive.
C.   proportional.
D.   lump sum.
E.   progressive at low levels of national income and regressive at high levels.

(Pages 275–9) There are various problems in using taxes to redistribute incomes. For example, there are difficulties in helping the very poor.

◐ *Q19.* Since taxes *take away* incomes, changing taxes alone cannot benefit the poor. To give additional help to the poor will require additional *benefits*.   *True/False*

▤ *Q20.* Which of the following will provide most help to the very poorest people in society? (In each case assume the total reduction in tax revenue for the government is the same.)
A.   Cutting the rate of income tax.
B.   Increasing tax thresholds on income tax.
C.   Reducing excise duties.
D.   Reducing the main rate for national insurance contributions.
E.   Reducing VAT on basic goods.

▤ *Q21.* Which of the following will provide most help to those on low incomes but who nevertheless are still liable to income tax? (As before, in each case assume the total reduction in tax revenue for the government is the same.)
A.   Cutting the rate of income tax.
B.   Increasing tax thresholds on income tax.
C.   Reducing excise duties.
D.   Reducing the main rate for national insurance contributions.
E.   Reducing VAT on basic goods.

The effectiveness of a rise in income tax in redistributing incomes away from high-paid workers will depend on the elasticity of supply of labour.

◐ *Q22.* The more elastic the supply of high-paid workers, the more effective will be an income tax in redistributing income away from this group.   *True/False*

Taxes and incentives
(Pages 279–81) Perhaps the biggest drawback of using taxes to redistribute incomes is that they create *disincentives*.

◐ *Q23.* The effects of imposing an income tax can be divided into an *income effect* and a *substitution effect*. Which of these two effects will be to:
(a) *increase* the amount people work?
                        Income effect/Substitution effect
(b) *decrease* the amount people work?
                        Income effect/Substitution effect

Whether people thus work more or less after a rise in income tax will depend on which of the two effects is the larger.

◐ *Q24.* Which of the two effects of a rise in the rates of income tax is likely to be the larger in each of the following cases?
(a) For people with large long-term commitments (e.g. mortgages).   *Income effect/Substitution effect*
(b) For second income earners in a family where the second income is not relied upon for 'essential' consumption.   *Income effect/Substitution effect*
(c) For those on very high incomes.
                        Income effect/Substitution effect
(d) For people with large families.
                        Income effect/Substitution effect
(e) For those just above the tax threshold.
                        Income effect/Substitution effect

▤ *Q25.* The Laffer curve shows that:
A.   At very high levels of income tax, the government can expect to earn very high levels of revenue.
B.   The government's tax revenue will be highest when the marginal rate of income tax is 50 per cent.
C.   A rise in income tax beyond a certain level will reduce the government's tax revenue.
D.   The government's tax revenue is at a maximum when the substitution effect begins to outweigh the income effect.
E.   Tax revenues will be at a maximum when the marginal rate of tax is equal to the average rate.

◐ *Q26.* Raising the higher rate(s) of income tax (but leaving the basic rate unchanged) will have a relatively small income effect and a relatively large substitution effect.
                        True/False

◐ *Q27.* For all those above the old tax threshold, reducing tax allowances will have no disincentive effect at all.
                        True/False

The relationship between income taxes and incentives can be examined in the context of tax *cuts* as well as that of tax increases. If income tax rates are cut, people will choose to work *more* if the income effect **Q28.** *outweighs/is outweighed by* the substitution effect. For people already above the tax threshold, this will only be likely if tax cuts come in the form of **Q29.** *cuts in the basic rate of income tax/increases in tax allowances.*

State benefits
(*Pages 281–6*) Some benefits are *means tested* and some are *universal.*

Q30. Which of the following are universal benefits and which are means-tested benefits?

(a)	State pensions	*universal/means tested*
(b)	Child benefit	*universal/means tested*
(c)	Family credit	*universal/means tested*
(d)	Working families tax credit	*universal/means tested*
(e)	Housing benefit	*universal/means tested*
(f)	Income support	*universal/means tested*

Q31. Four of the following are possible problems with means-tested benefits. Which one is *not* a problem?

A. They tend to have a lower take-up rate than universal benefits.

B. They cost the taxpayer more to provide a given amount of help to the poor than do universal benefits.

C. The application procedure may deter some potential claimants.

D. If based solely on income, they may ignore the special needs of certain people.

E. They may act as a disincentive to getting a job.

(*Pages 286–7*) When means-tested benefits are combined with a progressive tax system there can be a serious problem with disincentives. A situation known as the 'poverty trap' can arise.

Q32. What is meant by the *poverty trap*?

....

....

....

....

Q33. If the marginal tax rate is 25 per cent and if for each extra £10 of take-home pay a person loses benefits of £6, what is the marginal tax-plus-lost-benefit rate?

....

One simple combined system of taxes and benefits which avoids the poverty trap is that of the *negative income tax*.

Q34. If everyone were entitled to a tax-free benefit of £1000 per annum (a 'negative income tax') paid by the tax authorities, and if the tax rate were 20 per cent, what would your net tax liability be if your income were:

(a) zero?   ....

(b) £1000?   ....

(c) £5000?   ....

(d) £10 000?   ....

(e) What is the marginal rate of tax-plus-lost-benefit?

....

Q35. What is the major drawback of a negative income tax system?

....

....

B   PROBLEMS, EXERCISES AND PROJECTS

Q36. Refer to the latest edition of *Social Trends* (published annually by the Office for National Statistics (ONS)). This should be taken by all university, college and reference libraries. Turn to the chapter on income and wealth.

(a) Provide a summary of income distribution in the UK as described in this chapter.

(b) To what extent does the tax and benefit system redistribute incomes more equally?

(c) How has income distribution and redistribution changed between the years illustrated in the various tables? (You could also look at earlier editions of *Social Trends* for a more complete analysis, but be careful

that the methods of calculating the statistics have not changed.)

(d) Identify any measures of inequality for which you think figures ought to be given if a more comprehensive analysis is to be provided.

Two other more complete sources are (1) the *Family Expenditure Survey* which, like *Social Trends*, is published annually by the ONS; (2) the annual report on the effects of taxes and benefits on household income published in *Economic Trends* (ONS). *Economic Trends* is published monthly, but if you look in the back cover of the latest edition, it will tell you in which month's edition the last annual report appeared.

Q37. To which of the four categories in Q15 do each of the following types of tax belong?

(a) Income £10 000, tax £1000; income £20 000, tax £2000

....

(b) Income £10 000, tax £5000; income £20 000, tax £9000

....

(c) Income £10 000, tax £2000; income £20 000, tax £5000

....

(d) Income £10 000, tax £0; income £20 000, tax £400

....

(e) Income £10 000, tax £400; income £20 000, tax £400

....

(f) Income £10 000, tax £400; income £20 000, tax £4000

....

(g) Income £10 000, tax £8000; income £20 000, tax £12 000

....

Q38. Figure 10.4 shows the effect of imposing an indirect tax on a good produced under conditions of perfect competition. It can be used to illustrate the resource costs of the tax. The tax has the effect of raising the equilibrium price

from P_1 to P_2 and reducing the equilibrium quantity from Q_1 to Q_2.

(a) Which area(s) represent(s) the original level of consumer surplus?

....

(b) Which area(s) represent(s) the loss in consumer surplus after the imposition of the tax?

....

(c) Which area(s) represent(s) the original level of profits for the producers?

....

(d) Which area(s) represent(s) the loss in profits after the imposition of the tax?

....

(e) Which area(s) represent(s) the total loss to consumers and producers and producers after the imposition of the tax?

....

(f) Which area(s) represent(s) the gain in tax revenue to the government after the imposition of the tax?

....

(g) Which area(s), therefore, represent the net loss to society as a whole after the imposition of the tax?

....

(h) Name two weaknesses in using this type of analysis to criticise the imposition of taxes.

1. ....

2. ....

*Q39. Figure 10.5 uses indifference analysis to show the effect of a tax cut on a person's choice between income and leisure. Assume that the person has 14 hours per day to distribute between work and leisure.

(a) Which of the two budget lines show the person's available choices *after* the tax cut? B_1/B_2

(b) How many hours will the person work before the tax cut?

....

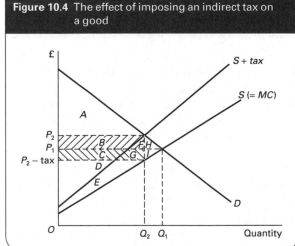

Figure 10.4 The effect of imposing an indirect tax on a good

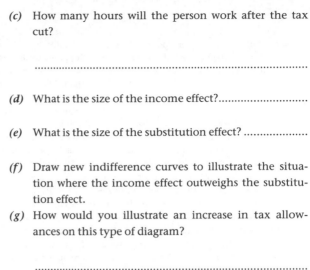

CHAPTER 10 INEQUALITY, POVERTY AND POLICIES TO REDISTRIBUTE INCOMES 137

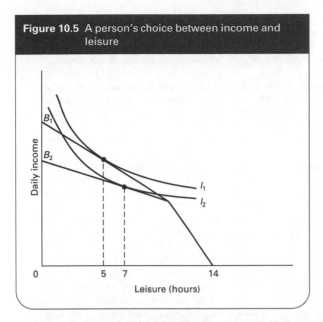

Figure 10.5 A person's choice between income and leisure

(axes: Daily income (vertical), Leisure (hours) (horizontal); markings at 0, 5, 7, 14; curves B_1, B_2, I_1, I_2)

(c) How many hours will the person work after the tax cut?

....

(d) What is the size of the income effect?............................

(e) What is the size of the substitution effect? ....

(f) Draw new indifference curves to illustrate the situation where the income effect outweighs the substitution effect.

(g) How would you illustrate an increase in tax allowances on this type of diagram?

....

....

C DISCUSSION TOPICS AND ESSAYS

Q40. What limitations are there in using Gini coefficients to compare the degree of inequality in different countries?

Q41. How well do the following taxes meet the requirements of a good tax system? (a) highly progressive income taxes; (b) VAT at a single rate on all goods and services; (c) excise duty on cigarettes.

Q42. Compare the advantages and disadvantages of a poll tax and a property tax as means of financing local authority expenditure.

Q43. 'The economic costs of an indirect tax will exceed the benefits.' Discuss with reference to its effect on producer and consumer surplus.

Q44. What effects will (a) cuts in basic rates of income tax and (b) increases in income tax allowances have on the labour supply of (i) high income earners, (ii) low income earners and (iii) those currently choosing not to work?

Q45. What are the arguments for and against universal welfare benefits?

Q46. What is meant by the *poverty trap*? Will the targeting of benefits to those in greatest need necessarily increase the problem of the poverty trap?

Q47. Debate
A local income tax is the only means of financing local authority expenditure that is both fair and efficient.

D ARTICLES

Poverty breeds poverty. That seems to be the message of two reports published by the Joseph Rowntree Foundation. What are the economic consequences of this, both for the poor themselves, and for the wider community? The following review of the report is by Cherry Norton. It appeared in *The Independent* of 29 March 1999.

Successive generations of children may be 'learning to be poor'

Children growing up in low-income families may be 'learning to be poor' from an early age as diminished expectations of what their parents can afford lead them to scale down their hopes and aspirations for the future.

The ways that children's experiences of poverty affect their future welfare are examined in two research reports published by the Joseph Rowntree Foundation. They consider how children respond to growing up in a low income family, and analyse the risks that high levels of relative poverty among today's children may carry for future generations.

Taken together, they highlight many of the pressing problems that must be tackled if the Government's 20-year goal of overcoming child poverty – set earlier this month by the Prime Minister – is to be reached.

Poor children's attitudes to money

A study based on interviews with more than 400 children shows that those who live with a lone parent or in families claiming Income Support are more likely than other children to be frequently told that things they want are unaffordable. It found that:

- Children living in households claiming Income Support (42 per cent) were five times more likely to think that their family income was inadequate than other children (8 per cent). Children in lone-parent families (39 per cent) were four times more likely to believe it than children in two-parent families (9 per cent).
- Children living in lone-parent and Income Support families were more likely to have been involved in family discussions about money and spending. Two-thirds said they were often told that their family could not afford what they wanted, compared with less than half other children.
- Asked which presents they would like if it was their birthday next week, the children in lone-parent and Income Support families listed items that were significantly less expensive on average than those identified by other children.
- Children in lone-parent and Income Support families were less likely to receive regular pocket money than others. Although children in low income families were less likely to have part-time jobs, those who did worked for longer hours and lower rates of pay than other children.

Children in lone-parent or Income Support families had much lower expectations about their future careers than their peers. They were more likely than other youngsters to want jobs that required few qualifications and little training. And they were less likely to aspire to attaining professional qualifications or occupations.

Sue Middleton of the Centre for Research in Social Policy at Loughborough University, the study's co-author, said: 'As children learn about their family's financial situation, so they form views of where they stand in relation to other families. Our research suggests that children from low income families are learning to expect and accept less from an early age and to find ways of covering up their disappointment.'

She added: 'It seems entirely possible that for some children it is early learning of this sort that reduces both their immediate expectations and their future aspirations. There is a real sense in which they are learning to be poor.'

Child poverty and its consequences

A study by researchers at the Centre for Economic Performance at the London School of Economics shows how the number of children living in homes that are relatively poor is dramatically higher than 30 years ago. As many as one in three children (over 4.3 million) were living in households with less than half average income in 1995/96 compared with one in ten in 1968.

It also finds that spending by the poorest fifth of the population on toys, children's clothing, shoes and fresh fruit was no higher in real terms in 1995/96 than it was almost 30 years earlier. This evidence suggests that increasing inequality in expenditure has had a direct impact on the well-being of children and served to exclude them from the rising living standards of the prosperous majority.

Data from large-scale national surveys enable the researchers to calculate that a fifth of the rise in child poverty is attributable to an increase in the number of children living in lone-parent families. However, they find that a more important factor has been unemployment and the increasing chances that children find themselves in 'work poor' families where no adult has a paid job.

Using results from a long-term survey that has traced the development of children born in 1958 through to adulthood, the researchers demonstrate how social disadvantage during childhood has been linked to an increased risk of low earnings, unemployment and other adversity by the age of 33. Among family-based measures, poverty has been by far the most important force linking childhood development with later social and economic problems. Growing up in a lone-parent family has only been a significant factor when associated with family poverty.

Pursuing the links between poverty affecting one generation and the next, the study also finds that 33-year old parents in the survey who were themselves, disadvantaged as children are more likely than other parents to have children who were performing poorly in school at an early age.

Stephen Machin, co-author of the report, said: 'Our study shows how the economic position of families strongly affects the present and future welfare of children. It suggests that today's high level of child poverty is likely to have continuing negative effects as the present generation of children in low income families grows up. Conversely, any measures that successfully address child poverty, especially by giving more households access to jobs, are likely to have wide-ranging, positive effects that go beyond improving the immediate welfare of children.'

(a) How does the article suggest that children 'learn to be poor', and how is this perpetuated between generations?

(b) What factors are argued to be responsible for the rise in child poverty?

(c) Given the findings of the report, what policies would you recommend to reverse the rise in child poverty?

The article below, taken from *The Economist* of 20 June 1998, investigates the growing problem that governments are facing from workers taking early retirement. It also examines the ways in which the pension and benefit systems tend to encourage early retirement.

Growing old extravagantly

In Belgium, only one man in ten is still in the labour market at the age of 65, the official retirement age. On average, men retire before their 58th birthday. Back in 1960, Belgian men typically worked until they were 63. Yet in the interim, elderly Belgians have become healthier and live longer.

Belgium is an extreme example of a trend occurring all over the rich world. The average age of retirement has been falling for both men and women in almost every OECD country, from around 66 for men in 1960 to 62 by 1995. When OECD social-security ministers meet in Paris on June 23rd, one of the main items on their agenda will be the need to reverse this trend.

Why should ministers care whether people choose, as they grow richer, to take some of their increased wealth in the form of more years of leisure? Many people doubtless love their jobs, but plenty of others would clearly prefer to grow dahlias or take up golf. The problem is that early retirement compounds the increasing imbalance between the numbers in and out of work. Moreover, unlike increases in longevity, it has a double impact: it both cuts the number of productive, tax-paying workers and raises the number of retired people. The rough rule of thumb is that, if all employees retired one year earlier, GDP would decline by about 2 per cent and the pension contributions made by those still working to pay-as-you-go schemes would increase by 7 per cent.

Several countries now see early retirement as a problem. In response, they have reversed the fall in the minimum age at which people become entitled to draw a public pension. However, two recent studies suggest that tinkering with the retirement age may have little effect. One, by Jonathan Gruber and David Wise, argues that social-security provisions in most countries place a heavy implicit tax on working beyond the age when an employee becomes eligible for early retirement. This week, the OECD published a study which reaches similar conclusions.

Both papers find that old-age pension systems powerfully discourage people from staying in work. In some countries, notes the OECD, it is illegal to combine working with drawing a pension. In others, workers can draw a

pension only if they leave their current job – which, given the difficulty older workers have in finding work, in effect condemns them to unemployment.

Not only do workers lose by staying on at work beyond the standard retirement age; they rarely gain much by working beyond the minimum age for drawing a pension. A worker who has already contributed for, say, 35 years of employment rarely earns a higher pension by contributing for additional years. In some countries, that represents a break with the past: in Belgium in the late 1960s, a 55-year-old worker could increase his eventual pension by up to a third by working another ten years.

But pensions are not the only social-security benefits which lure older workers out of the job market. For instance, one-third of Austrians aged between 55 and 64 draw disability benefits; and, in more than half of all OECD countries, workers can draw unemployment benefits from the age of 55 until they reach the formal retirement age, without being subjected to the time limits applied to younger workers or to stringent requirements that they look for work.

In many countries, the combined effect of these measures is to impose an implicit tax on those who work past the

minimum retirement age. Messrs Gruber and Wise illustrate this with the case of a 60-year-old German man, on median earnings, with a slightly younger wife. Like many older German workers, he would be eligible for disability benefits were he to leave the workforce. He could continue to work until the age of 65, but his benefit entitlement would not increase, and he would not draw the benefits to which retirement would entitle him. The effect of staying at work for an extra five years is to reduce the present value of his benefits by almost 18 per cent. Delaying retirement merely from 60 to 61 cuts the present value of benefits by 4 per cent. Measured against the income earned by staying in work, the implicit pension tax in this case comes to nearly 40 per cent.

A question of incentives

The chart, from the OECD report, illustrates the upshot. Workers tend to retire earliest where the combined effects of pensions and other benefits create the greatest incentive to do so. The relationship between different tax rates and retirement patterns is strong evidence that pensions and other benefits have not merely accommodated an existing trend in retirement ages, but have reinforced it.

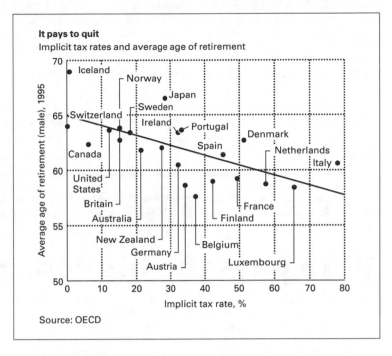

It pays to quit
Implicit tax rates and average age of retirement

Source: OECD

What should governments do about this? Clearly, they should begin by removing the disincentives to work longer. Countries that are struggling to foot a growing bill for caring for the old cannot afford the loss of productive capacity that large-scale early retirement represents. At a minimum, suggests the OECD, pension benefits should con-tinue to accrue with every extra year that is worked and contributions paid, up to and beyond the standard retire-ment age.

But ministers should not tackle pensions alone. To do so might make the problem worse, especially if higher contribution rates increased the dis-incentive to stay at work. They need also to curtail open-ended unemployment benefit and to tighten up eligibility for disability benefit. And they should act to increase the supply of jobs by deregu-lating labour markets. The main effects of the pensions problem will not be felt in most countries for at least a decade. But it will take at least that long to administer the remedies.

(a) Why is early retirement an economic problem?

(b) Explain why some workers might lose out if they delay retirement.

(c) What solutions does the article suggest are necessary, if the problems of early retirement are to be overcome? Are there any problems with these solutions?

Why is it that the highest earners in a society are not necessarily those who pay the highest rates of tax? The article below, taken from the *OECD Observer* of Summer 1999, tells you why and identifies some of the implications.

Who pays the highest income tax?

It is not always high earners who pay the highest marginal rates of taxes on income. This assertion may appear to contradict what one would expect of progressive tax systems. Yet, in most OECD countries many individuals in low- to middle-income brackets find themselves exposed to higher marginal rates – that is the rate applied to the last additional dollar, yen or franc earned – than even the very rich. The question is why? Part of the answer lies in 'bubbles', which are humps in the structure of taxes on income. Bubbles can develop in cases where income is subject to both personal income tax and social security contributions. The tax base of those contributions may be identical or sim-ilar to that used for personal income tax. But unlike for income tax, a ceiling or cap often applies; earnings above that ceiling are not subject to social security contributions. A bubble appears if the combined marginal rate of income tax and 'capped' social security contribu-tions exceeds the marginal income tax rate applicable to income earned above that contributions ceiling. For example, take a country that imposes social secu-rity contributions at a flat rate of 15 per cent on the first 50 000 units of income. Also, suppose the first 25 000 units earned are subject to 10 per cent per-sonal income tax, the second 25 000 units is taxed at 20 per cent, and all income over 50 000 is taxed at the top rate of 30 per cent. To judge by the headline rate alone, the latter rate of

30 per cent would seem like the highest of the lot. But in practice it is those with taxable income in the middle bracket who pay the highest marginal rate, since the marginal income tax and social security add up to 35 per cent of their additional earnings. But taxpayers in the highest bracket are not required to pay the 15 per cent social security contribution and so only pay 30 per cent on their highest earnings.

But bubbles do not just show up in 'all-in' rates of the combined taxes on income. Occasionally, they appear in standard personal income tax schedules as well. In the second half of the 1980s the US federal income tax had such a rate structure. At the time, income in the first bracket was taxed at 15 per cent and income in the top bracket at 28 per cent. It follows that tax relief for high-income earners, which is determined by the marginal tax rate, was almost twice the tax relief for low-income earners. To recoup the higher tax relief for well-off taxpayers, lawmakers introduced a new 33 per cent bracket which they sandwiched between the low and high brackets. The new middle rate worked like this. Suppose for the sake of illustra-tion that the personal exemption on income tax was $4000 across the board. Under the old structure before the 33 per cent band was created the tax bill of low-income earners would have been reduced by $600, since with the exemp-tion they would not have had to pay the 15 per cent tax on that $4000. The

tax bill for those in the highest taxed bracket would have been slashed by $1120, because they would have been exempt from paying 28 per cent on their highest $4000 of income. The difference of $520 in favour of higher earners was clawed back by inserting a middle bracket of $10 400 taxed at 33 per cent, that means 5 per cent more tax to pay than before, or $520. So, although the tax relief for the highest earners remained at 28 per cent, or $1120, by taxing middle earnings more, the new bracket effectively balanced the tax relief for those in the low and the top brackets at $600. The rates of the federal income tax in Switzerland show a similar 'bubble' today.

A job can make you poorer

Another rather curious situation which does not show up when studying head-line rates is that low earners can find themselves confronted with very high marginal tax rates, in some rare cases exceeding 100 per cent. The reason for this is that lower earners not only pay more tax when their income goes up, but in many cases they lose part of their means-tested tax relief, subsidies and benefits as well. The loss of this income acts as an 'implicit' tax at the margin. The rational response of workers who find themselves in this situation is to reduce the number of hours they work. Their gross wage would of course be lower if they did, but in return they would pay less tax and receive more means-tested subsidies and benefits. As a result, their net disposable income would increase despite putting in fewer hours.

This type of situation occurs to varying degrees in different OECD countries, depending on the peculiarities of various social protection programmes. Take the example of an unemployed couple with two young children. Suppose that after five years' unemployment, one of them takes up a lowly paid job. In Finland or Sweden net income in and out of work would be the same in that case, since each unit of income earned is cancelled out by a unit of benefits foregone once employment is taken up. In other words, there is an implicit tax rate of 100 per cent. In the case of Denmark and the Czech Republic, the implicit rate in a similar case would be almost 100 per cent, and in Germany and the United Kingdom it would be around 80 per cent. In France and the United States the implicit rate would be about 50 per cent, since half the increase in earnings is wiped out by a loss of benefits. In Japan, the implicit tax actually exceeds 140 per cent, meaning our one-earner couple would be worse off with the new job than without it. What's more, they may have to be wary when it comes to staying in the job itself, since small wage increases can expose low-wage earners to high implicit tax rates as their means-tested benefits get cut further.

(a) What is meant by 'the marginal tax rate'?

(b) Explain what is meant by the term 'a bubble' in the structure of taxation.

(c) How can it be that marginal tax rates can exceed 100 per cent?

(d) How are workers and non-workers likely to respond to high marginal tax rates?

FT

In 1999, the Labour government in Britain altered the system of providing support for poor families where one or more parents work. Under the old system of Family Credit, families whose income was below a certain level received a cash benefit. This benefit was progressively reduced as income rose beyond a certain level. The combination of a 20 per cent marginal tax rate, a 10 per cent national insurance rate and reduced family credit meant a marginal tax-plus-lost-benefit rate of approximately 90 per cent. Under the new Working Families' Tax Credit, which has replaced Family Credit, families where at least one parent works at least 16 hours per week are entitled to a 'tax credit'. This is effectively an income top up, paid by the Inland Revenue (the tax authority) through the employer. This too is progressively withdrawn, but less steeply. Many people, however, still pay a tax-plus-lost-benefit rate of 60 per cent or more.

The following article by Nicholas Timmins, taken from the *Financial Times* of 8 September 1999, describes reactions to the new scheme.

Work: low-paid offered cash incentive

Employers will come to love the working families' tax credit despite their marked reservations, Gordon Brown, chancellor, said yesterday at the launch of a £12m advertising campaign to persuade 1.5m families to start claiming the new credit from next month.

Smaller employers are worried about the burden of the new credit being paid through pay packets, as opposed to the Department of Social Security order books used for family credit – the benefit it replaces.

They are also worried about potential disputes with employees, and cash-flow problems if the payments are not right.

But Mr Brown said employers offering low-paid work will be able to show potential employees with children 'that the work will pay more than the wage they are offering – and that is a very powerful incentive for people to take the jobs they are offering'.

The new credit guarantees any couple or lone parent working more than 35 hours a week at least £200, against the minimum wage for the same hours of £126 – with extra help for formal child care. For people working 16 hours the minimum guaranteed is £145. On average the new benefit will pay £24 a week more than family credit.

With an estimated 1m vacancies at present, the unemployed 'should be looking at how we are making work pay,' Mr Brown said. 'It is a matter of rights and responsibilities.'

The chancellor, who was joined at the launch by Dennis the Menace, Postman Pat and a Womble, said that linking the payment to work through the pay packet meant there is 'enormous scope to increase take-up', when only 70 per cent of those eligible claim family credit.

Mr Brown refused to speculate about how many of the 1.5m eligible families will claim. However, there have been some estimates that the new incentive will add only 35 000 to 40 000 to the workforce.

He said the new credit, with a matching credit for the disabled, 'ensures for the first time in this country that work will pay more than benefits'. A similar credit for the low-paid, and possibly for housing benefit, are also being studied.

While campaigning organisations welcomed the extra generosity of the new credit, the system continued to attract criticism. David Willetts, the Conservative social security spokesman, said it was 'biased in favour of institutionalised child care'. Relatives and those who pay nannies will not be able to claim, 'penalising families who care for their own children at home', while couples where one partner does not work will get no child care allowance.

The Institute for Fiscal Studies pointed out, however, that the higher level of payment may provide incentives for one of a two-earner couple to stop work.

The Federation of Small Business reiterated its demand for an exemption for small employers. Brendan Burns, its policy chairman, said: 'It really is not on to expect small employers to act as the government's benefit agency.'

Conservative spokesmen echoed that view while Steve Webb, for the Liberal Democrats, said the potential £100m cost to business 'could be better spent boosting low pay'. He also accused ministers of a 'massive act of false accounting' by counting the expenditure as revenue foregone rather than public spending.

Mr Willetts argued that the new credit 'fails as an anti-poverty measure', because it spreads help up the income scale rather than helping the very poorest. Although the numbers paying marginal tax rates of 90 per cent fall sharply, the numbers potentially losing 60p in the pound, as the benefit is withdrawn and taxes are paid, rises by close to 500 000.

He added: 'The chancellor is creating a new poverty trap in which middle-income families who are promoted or earn a bit of overtime will be heavily penalised.'

Mr Brown insisted that higher child benefit and more help in income support meant the poorest families were also gaining.

(a) What are the advantages to (i) the government and (ii) poor families of the new scheme compared with the old?

(b) What is meant by the 'poverty trap'? How has the poverty trap been altered by changing the system of support for poor families?

(c) How would the poverty trap be affected if help was targeted at the 'very poorest' rather than 'spreading it up the income scale'?

E ANSWERS

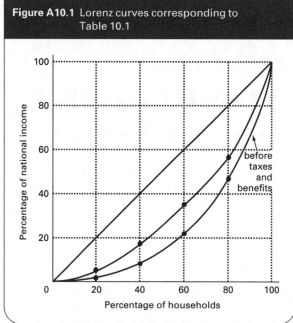

Figure A10.1 Lorenz curves corresponding to Table 10.1

Q1. (a) (iii), (b) (x), (c) (vi), (d) (ii), (e) (viii), (f) (i), (g) (iv), (h) (ix), (i) (vii), (j) (v).

Q2. See Figure A10.1.

Q3. Moving up the curve, the new curve would initially be above the original one. It would then cross the original one and thereafter be below it up to the top right-hand corner.

Q4. D.

Q5. *False.* In Figure 10.2, as income distribution becomes more equal, the Lorenz curve will move closer to the 45° line and thus area *Y* will get smaller and hence the Gini coefficient will *fall* not rise.

Q6. (i) Differences in wages and salaries between different occupations, (ii) differences between incomes from self-employment and employment and (iii) differences between incomes from employment and self-employment on the one hand and social security benefits on the other.

Q7. *False.* Women are paid less even in the same occupation. The causes include: men promoted to more senior positions; the average age of full-time female workers is lower; women do less overtime; discrimination.

Q8. *True.* The wealthiest 10 per cent owned 50 per cent of UK wealth in 1995.

Q9. 1. *Inheritance*: this allows income inequality to be perpetuated and deepened from one generation to another.

2. *Income inequality*: people with higher incomes can save more.

3. *Different propensities to save*: people who save more will build up a bigger stock of wealth.

4. *Entrepreneurial and investment talent/luck*: some people are more successful than others in investing their wealth and making it grow.

Q10. B (possibly C). Wage rates will reflect workers' and employers' attitudes and their power in the labour market. The distribution of wealth will affect wages to the extent that it affects the distribution of economic power.

Q11. E. Household income is affected by wage rates (i.e. (ii) and (iii)), by income from assets (i.e. (i)) and by household composition (i.e. (iv), (v) and (vi)).

Q12. (a) (iii), (b) (ii), (c) (viii), (d) (x), (e) (i), (f) (v), (g) (vii), (h) (iv), (i) (ix),(j) (vi).

Q13. Because those who use a service the most (e.g. the sick using the health service) may be the least able to pay.

Q14. *(a)* (i) *relatively well*, if the rate of tax increases as people's incomes increase. Note, however, that income tax in the UK is not very progressive. Most people on the basic rate of income tax pay a marginal rate of 32% (i.e. 22% income tax and 10% national insurance). People on very high incomes pay a marginal rate of 40% (i.e. 40% income tax and 0% national insurance). Thus the difference in marginal rate between the moderately poor and the very rich is only 8%. (ii) *badly*, given that poor people (who pay less income taxes) will be in receipt of larger amounts of state benefit.

   (b) (i) *very badly*, given that all except the very poor paid exactly the same amount per head within any given local authority area.
   (ii) *well*, for services which were consumed relatively equally (e.g. refuse services and street lighting), but *moderately badly* for services which were consumed unequally (e.g. education).

Q15. *(a)* Progressive – curve II; regressive – curve I; proportional – curve III; lump sum – curve IV.

   (b) Progressive – curve I; regressive – curve III; proportional – curve II; lump sum – curve IV.

Q16. *(a)* *10%* (i.e. (£1000/£10 000) × 100)

   (b) *10.58%* (i.e. (£1100/£10 400) × 100)

   (c) *25%* (i.e. $\Delta T/\Delta Y = $ (£100/£400) × 100)

Q17. *False.* It will be progressive. Although the marginal rate is constant, the average rate will rise as income rises because the tax-free allowance will account for a smaller and smaller proportion of total income.

Q18. B. The rich tend to save proportionately more than the poor and hence spend proportionately less. This means that they would pay proportionately less of this type of tax.

Q19. *False.* Provided the poor pay some taxes, *cutting* taxes for the poor *will* provide additional help. The problem comes for the very poor, who do not pay income taxes in the first place.

Q20. E. This will target the tax cuts to the poorest people, who spend a large portion of their meagre incomes on basic goods. (Note, in the case of B, that increasing tax thresholds will not help the very poor who are too poor to pay income tax in the first place.)

Q21. B. Everyone paying income tax will have the same *absolute* reduction in taxes. This will represent a larger *percentage* the lower a person's income (provided that they were paying at least as much in the first place as the size of the total tax cut).

Q22. *False.* In this case the main tax burden falls on employers: a significantly higher (pre-tax) wage will have to be offered in order to continue attacting enough workers. The employers' share of the tax is thus high.

Q23. *(a) Income effect.* Higher taxes reduce people's disposable income. They thus feel it necessary to work more or harder in order to try to recoup some of this lost income.

   (b) Substitution effect. As an hour's work now brings in less income (and hence enables less consumption), people are likely to substitute leisure for income.

Q24. *(a) Income effect.* People will feel a greater need to maintain their level of disposable income and will thus work harder.

   (b) Substitution effect. The second income earner will now be more inclined to stay at home or at least to work fewer hours.

   (c) Income effect. A rise in income tax will cause them to have a *substantial* fall in income and may thus cause them to work harder to compensate.

   (d) Income effect. These people will find it difficult to sustain a fall in income and will thus probably work harder.

   (e) Substitution effect. For these people the rise in income tax will have virtually *no* effect on disposable income. The income effect will be negligible. Each *additional* pound earned, however, will be at the higher tax rate and thus the disincentive effect will still exist. Thus the substitution effect is likely to outweigh the income effect even though the marginal utility of money is greater for poor people.

Q25. C. Note that B is wrong because that there is no reason why the curve should peak at a 50 per cent marginal (or average) tax rate. D is wrong because the point where the substitution effect begins to outweigh the income effect will be to the *left* of the peak of the curve; even when the substitution effect is bigger than the income effect and thus people work fewer hours, they could still pay more tax if the percentage reduction in hours is less than the percentage rise in tax.

Q26. *True.* The total income of higher tax payers will only be moderately affected if the basic rate is unchanged and thus the income effect is relatively small (except for extremely well-paid people). The substitution effect, however, could be quite large given that the rich tend to have a lower marginal utility of income than the poor.

Q27. *True.* The rate of tax has not changed and thus there is no substitution effect. There is an income effect, however. People will suddenly have been made poorer and are thus likely to work harder to compensate for the lost income. Thus reducing tax allowances will act as an incentive.

Q28. *is outweighed by*. The income effect (people can now afford to take more leisure) will cause people to work less. The substitution effect (the opportunity cost of leisure has now increased) will cause people to work more.

Q29. *cuts in the basic rate of income tax*. With increases in tax thresholds, there will be *no* substitution effect because the marginal rate of tax has not changed. There will only be an income effect. Thus with increases in tax allowances, people will be encouraged to work less.

Q30. (a), (b) and (d) are *universal*. (c), (e) and (f) are *means tested*.

Q31. B. *Universal* benefits cost more to provide a given amount of help to the poor. The reason is that some will go to those who are not poor. For example, child benefit is an expensive way of relieving child poverty because rich parents as well as poor are entitled to child benefit.

Q32. Where poor people are discouraged from working or getting a better job because any extra income they earn will be largely or wholly taken away in taxes and lost benefits.

Q33. *70%* (i.e. 25% + (60% × 75%)). In other words, if a person earned an extra £10, £2.50 would be taken off as taxes. Take-home pay would thus be £7.50, of which 6/10 (i.e. £4.50) would go in lost benefits, leaving a mere £3. Thus 70 per cent of the increase in pay has been lost.

Q34. (a) *–£1000*. The tax authorities would *pay you* a cash benefit (a negative tax) of £1000.

    (b) *–£800*. The tax authorities would *pay you* £1000 benefit minus £200 tax.

    (c) *zero*. You would be liable to a tax of £1000 which exactly offsets the benefit.

    (d) *+£1000*. You would be liable to a net tax of £2000 minus the £1000 benefit.

    (e) *20%*. There is *no* lost benefit. Everyone is entitled to the benefit which is offset against their tax liability. Thus the marginal tax-plus-lost-benefit rate is the same as the marginal tax rate.

Q35. If the marginal rate of tax is to be kept reasonably low (so as to avoid creating a disincentive to work), the benefit (i.e. the negative element) will have to be small, which reduces its effectiveness in providing help to the poor. If, on the contrary, the benefit were large but still only declined slowly (a low marginal rate of tax), the tax would only start to yield revenues from people with very high incomes and thus the tax would yield very little, if any, net revenue for the government!

CHAPTER ELEVEN

11 Markets, Efficiency and the Public Interest

A REVIEW

In this chapter we examine the question of *social efficiency* in the allocation of resources. It is the failure of markets to achieve social efficiency that provides much of the argument for government intervention in the economy. But likewise it is the failure of governments to achieve social efficiency in the allocation of resources that provides much of the argument for *laissez-faire*.

We start by seeing how, under certain conditions, a perfect market economy will lead to social efficiency. We then see how in the real world the market will fail to do so and we examine the causes and types of market failure. We see how a government can intervene to correct these failures and then look at *cost-benefit analysis* – a means of establishing whether a particular public project is desirable or not. We turn finally to the other side of the argument and consider the case against government intervention.

11.1 Efficiency under perfect competition

Simple analysis: MB = MC
(Pages 290–1) A socially efficient economy is defined as one that is *Pareto optimal* (named after Vilfredo Pareto (1848–1923))

Q1. A situation of Pareto optimality is one where.
A. resources are allocated in the fairest possible way.
B. people can be made better off with no one being made worse off.
C. losses to the rich will be more than offset by gains to the poor.
D. there is no X inefficiency.
E. it is not possible to make anyone better off without making at least one other person worse off.

Q2. In any economy there will be many different possible Pareto-optimal situations, some of which will involve greater equality than others. *True/False*

Q3. Bill and Ben both like apples and currently have 8 apples each in their respective fruit bowls. This is shown in Figure 11.1 as point *X*. Various other alternative quantities of apples are also shown (points *A–H*).

(a) Which points would represent a Pareto improvement compared with point *X*?

....

(b) Is point *X* a Pareto improvement on any other points? If so which?

....

(c) With the information given, can we say anything about the relative efficiency of point *B* compared with point *X*?

....

....

 Multiple Choice   Written answer    Delete wrong word    Diagram/table manipulation   Calculation   Matching/ordering

Figure 11.1 Apples for Bill and Ben

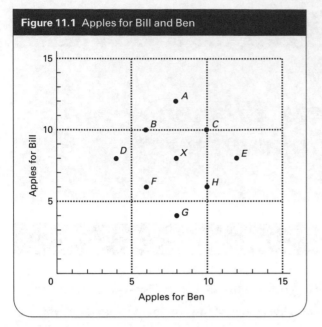

(Pages 291–3) Will a free-market economy lead to Pareto optimality, to social efficiency? The answer is that it will only do so under very strict conditions.

(?) **Q4.** What two conditions must be fulfilled for the free market to be socially efficient?

1. ....

2. ....

Under perfect competition we assume that individuals behave *rationally*. Rational behaviour involves doing more of any activity whose **Q5.** *total cost/marginal cost/average cost* is **Q6.** *greater than/less than* its **Q7.** *total benefit/marginal benefit/average benefit*. Such behaviour will lead to *private efficiency*.

(Pages 293–4) In the absence of externalities and with perfect competition in all markets, the achievement of private efficiency in each individual market will lead to a *general equilibrium* throughout the whole economy which is *socially efficient*: i.e. Pareto optimal.

(≣) **Q8.** In a perfect market, social efficiency in any activity will be maximised where the activity's:

A. marginal benefit equals marginal cost.
B. total benefit equals total cost.
C. marginal social benefit exceeds marginal social cost.
D. marginal social benefit equals marginal social cost.
E. total social benefit exceeds total social cost.

In a perfectly competitive goods market, the consumer will achieve private efficiency where **Q9.** *marginal utility/ marginal cost/marginal revenue* equals the price of the good.

The producer will achieve private efficiency where the price of the good equals the firm's **Q10.** *marginal revenue/ marginal revenue product/marginal cost.*

(?) **Q11.** Describe the process whereby social efficiency would be restored in all markets if the marginal social benefit of good X were to rise, causing initial disequilibrium. (Assume perfect competition and an absence of externalities.)

(a) Effects on the market for good X ....

....

(b) Effects on the market for factors used in producing good X.

....

....

(c) Effects on other goods markets ....

....

....

(d) Effects on other factor markets ....

....

(e) The final equilibrium state ....

....

Intermediate analysis: MB ratios equal MC ratios
(Pages 294–7)
(?) ***Q12.** If for two goods X and Y, MU_X/MU_Y (MRS) were greater than P_X/P_Y, what would a rational consumer do?

....

(?) ***Q13.** A firm produces two goods X and Y. If it finds that MC_X/MC_Y (MRT) is greater than P_X/P_Y what should it do to maximise profits?

....

(?) ***Q14.** If MU_X/MU_Y for person A exceeded MU_X/MU_Y for person B (i.e. $MRS_A > MRS_B$):
(a) How could a Pareto improvement be achieved?

....

(b) What would the Pareto optimum be?

....

⬤ *Q15.* Assuming no externalities, social efficiency will be achieved where *MRS* = *MRT* for all goods.　　*True/False*

⊖ *Q16.* Figure 11.2 shows social indifference curves (I_1 to I_4) and a social transformation curve (production possibility curve) (*TT*) between two goods X and Y. It is assumed that there are no externalities.

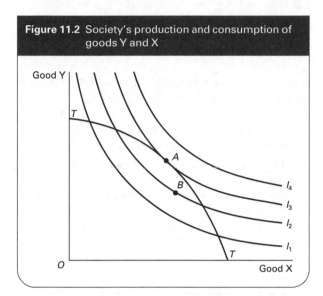

Figure 11.2 Society's production and consumption of goods Y and X

(a) What does the slope of the social indifference curves give?

....

(b) What does the slope of the production possibility curve give?

....

(c) Draw a line showing the *equilibrium* price ratio P_X/P_Y.

(d) Why are all points other than point *A* socially inefficient?

....

....

(e) If production were at point *B*, how could a Pareto improvement be achieved?

....

....

11.2 The case for government intervention

(Page 297) Real-world markets will fail to achieve social efficiency. What is more, efficiency is not the only economic objective, and real-world markets may fail to achieve these other objectives too.

(?) *Q17.* Give three other economic objectives.

1.　..

2.　..

3.　..

There are several reasons why real-world markets will fail to achieve a socially efficient allocation of resources.

⬤ *Q18.* The following are problems that cause market failings:
 (i) Externalities.
 (ii) Monopoly/oligopoly power.
 (iii) Monopsony/oligopsony power.
 (iv) Ignorance and uncertainty.
 (v) Public goods and services.
 (vi) Persistent disequilibria.
 (vii) Dependants.
 (viii) Merit goods.

Match each of the above problems to the following examples of failures of the free market. In each case assume that everything has to be provided by private enterprise: that there is no government provision or intervention whatsoever. Note that there may be more than one example of each problem. Also each case may be an example of more than one market problem.
(a) There is an inadequate provision of street lighting because it is impossible for companies to charge all people benefiting from it.

....

(b) Advertising allows firms to sell people goods that they do not really want.

....

(c) A firm tips toxic waste into a river because it can do so at no cost to itself.

....

(d) Firms pay workers less than their marginal revenue product.

....

(e) Prices take a time to adjust to changes in consumer demand.

....

(f) People may not know what is in their best interests and thus may underconsume certain goods or services (such as education).

....

(g) Firms' marginal revenue is not equal to the price of the good and thus they do not equate *MC* and price.

....

(h) Firms provide an inadequate amount of training because they are afraid that other firms will simply come along and 'poach' the labour they have trained.

....

(i) In families one person may do the shopping for everyone and may buy things that other family members do not like.

....

(j) Farmers cannot predict the weather.

....

(Pages 297–9) As we saw in the last section, externalities are spillover costs or benefits.

⊖ **Q19.** Figure 11.3 shows the production of fertiliser by a perfectly competitive profit-maximising firm. Production of the good leads to pollution of the environment, however. This pollution is an external cost to the firm.

(a) Which of the two curves, *I* or *II*, represents the marginal social cost curve? *I/II*

(b) What output will the firm produce if it takes no account of the pollution?

....

(c) What is the level of the marginal external cost at this output?

....

(d) What is the socially efficient level of output?

....

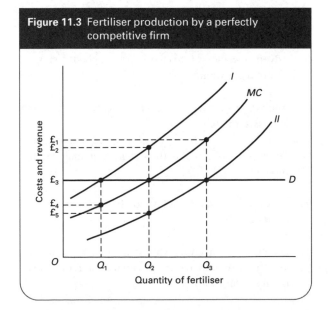

Figure 11.3 Fertiliser production by a perfectly competitive firm

? **Q20.** Give two examples of each of the following:

(a) External benefits of production ....

(b) External benefits of consumption ....

(c) External costs of consumption ....

◐ **Q21.** In the absence of externalities, a monopoly will charge a price above the level where *MSC* = *MSB* and produce an output below the level where *MSC* = *MSB*.

True/False

(Pages 299–300) A monopoly will be socially inefficient because it will result in *deadweight welfare loss*.

▤ **Q22.** Which one of the following is a definition of *deadweight welfare loss* under monopoly?

A. The loss in output compared with perfect competition.

B. The increase in price compared with perfect competition.

C. The loss of total consumer surplus compared with perfect competition.

D. The increase in total profit compared with perfect competition.

E. The loss of total consumer-plus-producer surplus compared with perfect competition.

(Pages 300–4) There is a category of goods that the free market, whether perfect or imperfect, will underproduce or fail to produce at all. These are *public goods*.

▤ **Q23.** Which two of the following features distinguish public goods from other types of goods?

(i) Large external benefits relative to private benefits.

(ii) Large external costs relative to private costs.

(iii) A price elasticity of demand only slightly greater than zero.

(iv) The impossibility of excluding free riders.

(v) Ignorance by consumers of the benefits of the good.

(vi) Goods where the government feels it knows better than consumers what people ought to consume.

A. (i) and (iv).

B. (ii) and (iii).

C. (v) and (vi).

D. (ii) and (v).

E. (iv) and (v).

◐ **Q24.** Which of the following are examples of public goods (or services)? (Note that we are not merely referring to goods or services that just happen to be provided by the public sector.)

(a) Museums *Yes/No*

(b) Roads in town *Yes/No*

(c) Motorways   *Yes/No*
(d) National defence   *Yes/No*
(e) Health care   *Yes/No*
(f) Community policing   *Yes/No*
(g) Street drains   *Yes/No*
(h) Secondary education   *Yes/No*

Q25. The equilibrium price for a pure public good is zero.   *True/False*

(?) Q26. If the provision of health care were left to the free market, there would be a number of reasons why the market would fail to provide an optimum allocation of health-care resources. Give an example from health care of each of the following categories of market failure:

(a) Externalities

....

(b) Market power

....

(c) Ignorance

....

(d) Uncertainty about the future

....

(e) Dependants

....

(f) Inequality

....

(g) Poor economic decision making by people on their own behalf

....

11.3 Forms of government intervention
(Page 305) If there were a market distortion in just one part of the economy and elsewhere there were perfect competition and an absence of externalities, then the *first-best* solution to the distortion would be possible.

(?) Q27. Define the first-best solution.

....

....

In the real world, where there are countless distortions, the first-best solution of correcting all these distortions simultaneously will be totally impossible. In this case the answer to a specific distortion is to adopt the *second-best* solution.

Q28. Which of the following represents the second-best solution to a market distortion?
A. Concentrating on making *MSB* equal *MSC* solely in the industry in question.
B. Correcting all the distortions in other parts of the economy that can be *identified*.
C. Concentrating on questions of equity and ignoring questions of efficiency.
D. Minimising the distortion relative to other distortions in the economy.
E. Tackling distortions one at a time.

(Pages 305–8) The use of taxes and subsidies
A policy instrument particularly favoured by many economists is that of taxes and subsidies.

Q29. In the first-best world, where there are no other market distortions, the problem of externalities can be corrected by imposing a tax equal to marginal social cost (at the optimum level of output) and a subsidy equal to marginal social benefit (at the optimum level of output).
True/False

⊖ Q30. Referring to Figure 11.3 (see Q19):
(a) Assume that the government imposes a 'pollution tax' on the firm at a constant rate per unit of output. What must the size of the tax per unit be in order to persuade the firm to produce the socially efficient level of output?

....

(b) Assuming that this firm is the only polluter in the industry, what effect will the tax have on the market price?

....

(?) Q31. Give two advantages and two disadvantages of using taxes and subsidies to correct market imperfections.

Advantage 1 ....

Advantage 2..

Disadvantage 1 ....

Disadvantage 2 ....

(Pages 308–9) Extending property rights
An alternative to taxes and subsidies is to extend individuals' private property rights. That way individuals may

be able to prevent others from imposing costs on them. For example, people living by a river may be granted ownership rights which allow them to decide whether a firm can dump waste into it and if so whether to charge it for so doing. Such a solution will be impractical, however, when **Q32.** *many/few* people are **Q33.** *highly/slightly* inconvenienced and when there are **Q34.** *many/few* culprits imposing the costs.

(Pages 309–10) Legal controls
Another alternative is to use laws. Laws can be used to prohibit or regulate activities that impose external costs; to prevent or control monopolies and oligopolies; and to provide consumer protection.

◗ **Q35.** From each of the following pairs of problems select the one where legal controls would be more appropriate. (Tick.)

(a) (i) preventing accidents from worn car tyres

        ....

    (ii) encouraging people to use public transport

        ....

(b) (i) preventing monopolists from charging excessive prices

        ....

    (ii) preventing manufacturers from setting the *retail* price

        ....

(c) (i) preventing false claims by tobacco companies about the 'benefits' of smoking

        ....

    (ii) preventing ignorance about the spread of infectious diseases

        ....

(Pages 310–11) Other policies
In addition to taxes and subsidies, extending property rights, and legal controls, there are other ways that a government can offset market failures. These include regulatory bodies, price controls, the provision of information, the direct provision of goods and services and public ownership.

♟ **Q36.** Match the methods of intervention (i)–(viii) to the examples (a)–(h).
  (i) Taxes and subsidies.
 (ii) Extending property rights.
 (iii) Legal controls.
 (iv) Regulatory bodies.
  (v) Price controls.
 (vi) The provision of information.
 (vii) The direct provision of goods and services.
(viii) Public ownership.

(a) Government job centres.   ....

(b) Nationalising an industry.   ....

(c) OFGEM, OFWAT, OFTEL.   ....

(d) Driving tests.   ....

(e) State education.   ....

(f) Grants for fitting loft insulation.   ....

(g) Tightening the laws on trespass.   ....
(h) Setting maximum rents that can be charged for private rented accommodation.

          ....

11.4 Cost–benefit analysis

(Pages 312–17) If the government decides to replace or modify the market, it will need a means of assessing whether particular goods or services should be produced and, if so, in what quantities. *Cost–benefit analysis (CBA)* can help a government decide whether or not to go ahead with a public project.

♟ **Q37.** All costs and benefits associated with the project should be identified. These include:
  (i) direct private monetary costs,
 (ii) external monetary costs,
 (iii) external non-monetary costs,
 (iv) direct private monetary benefits,
  (v) private non-monetary benefits,
 (vi) external monetary benefits,
 (vii) external non-monetary benefits.

Assume that a cost–benefit study is conducted to decide whether to build a road bridge across an estuary. At present the only way across is by ferry. Assume that building the bridge will drive the ferry operators out of business. Into which of the above seven categories should each of the following costs and benefits of the bridge be placed?

(a) Loss in profits to ferry operators.   ....

(b) Tolls paid by the users of the bridge.   ....
(c) Damage to local wildlife from constructing the bridge.

          ....

(d) The difference between what people would be prepared to pay in tolls and what they will actually be charged.

          ....

(e) Removal of the nuisance to local residents of people queuing for the ferry.

          ....

(f) Wages of the toll collectors. ....

(g) Increased profits from fishing in the estuary now that the ferry boats no longer disturb the fish.

....

One way of estimating both private and external non-monetary costs and benefits is to make inferences from people's behaviour.

Q38. Which of the following might be used to estimate the non-monetary benefits of a new by-pass round a village?

(a) The costs of its construction.   *Yes/No*

(b) The difference in house prices in villages with a by-pass and villages with a main road running through them.   *Yes/No*

(c) The amount that people are prepared to pay for a quicker mode of transport.   *Yes/No*

(d) The loss in profits to local traders.   *Yes/No*

(e) The savings on future road maintenance in the village.
                                                        Yes/No

Another approach is to use questionnaires: to ask people how much they will suffer or gain from a project.

(?) Q39. Give two problems with using questionnaires to assess cost and benefits.

1. ....

2. ....

Q40. Figures can be adjusted for *risk* by multiplying the value of the benefit or cost by the probability of its occurrence.   *True/False*

But what if the costs and benefits are *uncertain*? One answer to this problem is to use *sensitivity analysis*.

Q41. A project has a number of costs whose magnitudes are uncertain. Estimates for these costs range from a total of £4m to £10m. Is the project's desirability sensitive to this possible variation in costs, if the project's projected surplus of revenue over all *other* costs is:

(a) £20m?   *Yes/No*

(b) £6m?   *Yes/No*

(c) £1m?   *Yes/No*

Assume all costs and benefits are in present values.

(Pages 317–19) In a public project, the benefits and some of the costs can be expected to occur over many years. Thus to get an accurate assessment of benefits and costs, *discounting procedures* must be used.

Q42. Put the following steps in the discounting procedure in the correct sequence. (Number them.)

(a) Discount each year's net benefit to give it a present value.

....

(b) Recommend accepting the project if the net present value is greater than zero.

....

(c) Estimate the costs and benefits for each year of the life of the project.

....

(d) Add up the present values of each year's net benefit to give a total net present value of the project.

....

(e) Subtract the costs from the benefits for each year, to give a net benefit for each year.

....

It is argued that the rate of discount chosen should be a *social* rate of discount: i.e. one that reflects society's preferences for the present over the future. Just what this rate should be, however, is controversial.

(?) Q43. How may sensitivity analysis be used to ease the difficulty in choosing a social discount rate?

....

....

(Page 319) How may the *distribution* of costs and benefits be taken into account?

Q44. One alternative is to use the Hicks–Kaldor version of the Pareto criterion. This states that a project will be desirable if:

A. the gainers fully compensate the losers and still have a net gain.

B. the government fully compensates the losers and there is still a net gain.

C. if it is impossible for people to make any further gains from the project without others losing.

D. if the gainers could in principle fully compensate the losers and still have a net gain, even though in practice no compensation is paid.

E. there are no losers.

(?) Q45. What is the problem with the Hicks–Kaldor criterion?

....

11.5 *The case for* laissez-faire

(Pages 320–4)

(?) Q46. Give six possible drawbacks of government intervention: i.e. reasons why the government may fail to ensure an optimum allocation of resources.

1. ....

2. ....

3. ....

4. ....

5. ....

6. ....

 Q47. Match the following words to the blanks in the statement about the *neo-Austrian* support for free-market capitalism.

dynamic; longer-term; risk taking; monopoly; growth; oligopolies; efficiency; free-market; innovation.

The neo-Austrian school of economics argues that, rather than focusing on questions of (a)...........in the allocation of resources, we ought to judge (b)...........capitalism in its (c)...........context. The chances of (d)...........profits encourage (e)..........., (f)...........and (g)...........Thus governments ought to take a (h)...........view and not attempt excessive (or indeed *any*) regulation of monopolies and (i)...........

Q48. Even if a firm is currently a monopoly producer in the country, there are various reasons why in practice its market power may be limited. Four of these reasons are given below. One, however, is not a reason. Which one?

A. It faces a continuously falling *LRAC* curve.
B. The market may be contestable.
C. There may be competition from closely related industries.
D. The firm may face countervailing power from its customers.
E. It may face competition from imports.

B PROBLEMS, EXERCISES AND PROJECTS

Q49. Conduct an audit of your activities during the course of a day.
(a) What external costs and benefits resulted from your activities? Make sure you try to identify *all* externalities you created. You may need to think very carefully.
(b) Were you aware of the externalities at the time? If so, did the existence of them make any difference to your actions?
(c) Were there any pressures on you to avoid generating external costs? If so, were these pressures social, moral or what?
(d) How could you best be encouraged/persuaded/forced to take the externalities fully into account? Are there any costs in such methods?
(e) Present your findings in groups and discuss each other's assessments of the externalities you create. Do your findings differ substantially one to another?

Q50. Assume that a firm produces organic waste that has the effect of increasing the fertility of neighbouring farmland and thus reducing the farmers' costs. It is impractical, however, to sell the waste to the farmers. Table 11.1 shows the firm's private marginal costs and these external benefits to farmers from the firm's production.
(a) How much will the firm produce to maximise profits?

....

Table 11.1 A firm's costs and revenue (daily figures)

Output (units)	Price (£)	Marginal (private) cost (£)	Marginal external benefit (£)
1	20	16	6
2	20	15	5
3	20	15	4
4	20	16	3
5	20	17	2
6	20	18	2
7	20	20	2
8	20	22	2
9	20	24	2
10	20	27	1

(b) What is the marginal social cost of producing 3 units of output per day?

....

(c) What is the socially optimum level of output?

....

(d) What subsidy per unit would the government have to pay the firm to encourage it to produce this level of output?

....

(e) What would it cost the government?

....

(f) If new farming technology doubled the benefit of the waste to the farmer, what would be the socially optimum level of the firm's output?

....

Q51. Figure 11.4 shows an industry which was previously perfectly competitive but is now organised as a monopoly. Cost and revenue curves are assumed to be the same in both situations. (Assume that there are no fixed costs of production.)

(a) What is the perfectly competitive price and output?

....

(b) What is the monopoly price and output?.....................

(c) What areas represent consumer surplus in the perfectly competitive situation?

....

(d) What areas represent consumer surplus after the industry has become a monopoly?

....

(e) What areas represent the loss in consumer surplus after the industry has become a monopoly?

....

(f) What areas represent producer surplus in the perfectly competitive situation?

....

(g) What areas represent producer surplus after the industry has become a monopoly?

....

(h) What areas represent the gain in producer surplus after the industry has become a monopoly?

....

(i) What areas represent total deadweight welfare loss under monopoly?

....

Q52. Figure 11.5 illustrates the situation where a firm produces *two* market distortions. It creates a marginal external cost in the form of pollution, and it also has monopoly power. (Assume that it is possible for the firm to make a profit.)

(a) What is its profit-maximising price and output?

....

(b) What is the socially optimum price and output, assuming no distortions in other parts of the economy?

....

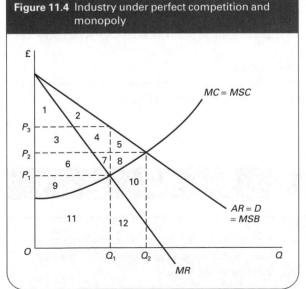

Figure 11.4 Industry under perfect competition and monopoly

Figure 11.5 A monopoly causing pollution

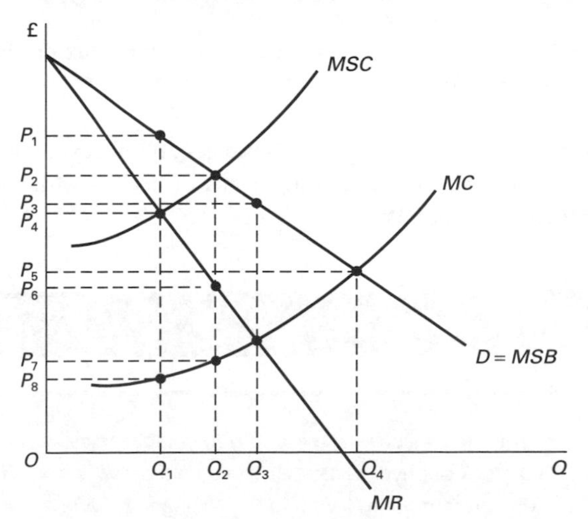

(c) If a tax were imposed equal to the marginal pollution cost, what would be the level of the tax rate?

....

(d) If there were no attempt to correct the monopoly power, what would be the new price and output resulting from the imposition of this pollution tax?

....

(e) Would this be socially efficient?   *Yes/No*

(f) If the monopoly problem were not to be corrected directly, what would be the size of the socially most efficient pollution tax?

....

(g) Would this be greater than or less than the marginal pollution cost and how much so?

greater than/less than

(h) If the marginal pollution cost were not as shown but were in fact smaller, so that *MSC* intersected with *MSB* at a higher output than Q_3, what would be the socially efficient solution if the problem of monopoly could not be tackled directly or by price controls?

....

(i) What would be the problem with this solution?

....

....

(j) How could this problem be dealt with without affecting the price and output (which with the subsidy would now be at the sociably optimal level)?

....

....

C   DISCUSSION TOPICS AND ESSAYS

Q53. Why is the Pareto test for social welfare said to be a 'weak' test?

Q54. Why will general equilibrium under perfect competition be socially efficient provided there are no externalities?

Q55. Would it be desirable for all pollution to be prevented?

Q56. Why will a free market fail to achieve an optimum allocation of resources in education? Is this an argument for the abolition of private education?

Q57. Examine the case for a 'carbon tax' (i.e. a tax on the use of fossil fuels).

Q58. Compare the relative advantages and disadvantages of taxation and regulation as means of dealing with the problem of external costs.

*Q59. How would you set about measuring the value of a human life?

Q60. Go through each of the types of failings of a free-market economy and assess whether a government is more or less likely to fail in these respects if it tries to take over from the market.

Q61. Consider the neo-Austrian argument that the possibility of large monopoly profits is of vital importance for encouraging risk taking and innovation. Does this imply that criticising a market economy for being imperfect and allocatively inefficient is to focus on the wrong issues?

Q62. Debate
Despite the weaknesses of a free market, replacing the market by the government generally makes the problem worse.

D   ARTICLES

Economic success in a modern high-technology economy is as much determined by the skills of its workforce as by its stock of physical capital. The article below is taken from *The Economist* of 26 March 1994 and considers the case for government involvement in helping to provide a greater level of training and education.

Investing in people

In recent years the term 'human capital' has become almost drearily familiar. It entered into common usage among economists 30 years ago, thanks to Gary Becker, a Nobel laureate and professor of economics and sociology at the University of Chicago; he made it the title of a seminal book on the economics of education and training.

As Mr Becker points out in the third edition of *Human Capital* (published this month by the University of Chicago Press), the term was controversial in the beginning. Many said it treated people as slaves or machines. Now, the notion that people and firms invest in skills in much the same way that they invest in plant and machinery – i.e. weighing the costs against the expected returns – seems too obvious to need stating.

Yet one of Mr Becker's most telling insights remains widely ignored. Discussion of policy towards education and training usually takes it for granted that markets fail in a particular way. Mr Becker showed otherwise.

Typically, the argument goes as follows. When a firm pays for workers to be trained, the trainees become more productive not only in their present employment, but also in any number of different jobs, with different employers. If a trained worker should be poached by another firm, the employer that paid for the training has merely subsidised a competitor. The fact that the firm cannot capture the benefits of its spending is a kind of market failure – and firms will spend less on training than they otherwise would. Hence, there is a case for public subsidy.

The argument has an impressive pedigree: as far back as 1920, A.C. Pigou, one of this century's most brilliant economic theorists, said that training was a classic case of 'externality'. But the argument is wrong.

True, employers cannot directly capture the benefits of their spending on training – but the workers who receive the training can. Once equipped with new skills, they will be paid more than untrained workers, either by their present employer or by some other. So the benefits of training do accrue chiefly to one of the parties in the transaction; they are not sprayed over the economy at large.

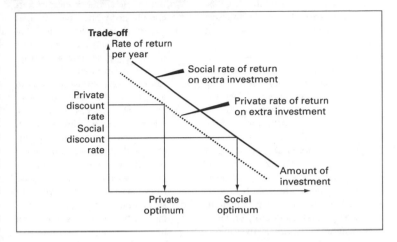

Trade-off

As far as the decision to invest is concerned, it does not matter whether this capturing of benefits is done by employers or by workers. If the benefits are captured by workers, Mr Becker showed, the market succeeds.

The market's answer is simple: workers undergoing an expensive training will be paid less, for the time being, than the value of their work to the firm. This came as a surprise to economists, but will strike trainee lawyers, accountants, architects – and anybody else receiving an education in highly marketable skills – as terribly obvious.

All such people gain skills that are not firm-specific; skills, in other words, that will be as valuable to other employers as they are to the firm that pays for the training. That being so, the market-failure argument suggests that little on-the-job training should take place. But lawyers, at least, are hardly in short supply. The reason is that workers, not employers, meet the cost – by accepting low wages during the period of training.

Less than perfect

The standard market-failure argument for subsidising investment in human capital may be wrong, but this does not mean that market forces get everything right. Markets may fail in other, subtler ways. If they do, this will just as surely upset the calculations that society makes about how much to invest in training and education.

In principle, an economy should invest in human capital (as in any other

kind of capital) up to the point where the rate of return yielded by the last bit of investment is just equal to the rate of return yielded by the best alternative use of the resources. It should invest, that is, up to the point where the marginal benefit equals the marginal cost. Please note: the idea that you can never have enough investment in human (or any other sort of) capital is nonsense. Investment is not free. You can have too much as well as too little.

To the private investor, weighing costs and benefits means investing so long as the rate of return exceeds the private discount rate (the cost of borrowing, plus an allowance for risk). For the economy as a whole, it means investing so long as the social return (which includes broader benefits to society, net of all costs) is greater than the social discount rate (which is the preference that society as a whole has for spending now rather than spending in the future). Plainly, these criteria are not the same.

The chart plots private and social rates of return against the amount of investment undertaken.* Both rates of return fall as investment increases (i.e. the two lines slope downwards). This reflects the law of diminishing returns – a truth that economists take to be

* The chart and the explanation that follows are drawn from a forthcoming study, *Britain's Training Deficit*, edited by R. Layard, K. Mayhew and G. Owen for the Centre for Economic Performance at the London School of Economics.

selfe-vident. Also, at every level of investment, the chart says that the social return is higher than the private return. There are five reasons why this might be true. In each case, the cause is indeed a sort of market failure – though not always an obvious one.

- A big **stock of skilled** labour may deliver economy-wide benefits over and above the private ones that spring from the fact that skilled labour is therefore cheaper to buy – the benefit, for instance, of greater flexibility in responding to economic change. (Michael Porter's best-selling study, *The Competitive Advantage of Nations*, made much of this point.)

- Perhaps, for lack of information, would-be trainees simply **underestimate** the return to investing in skills.

- Income taxes, especially 'progressive' ones, reduce the private (post-tax) return to training, relative to the social return. This is a good example of one form of government intervention creating a 'market failure' that another form of intervention may then be called upon to remedy.

- If unskilled workers are more likely to be **unemployed** than skilled ones (as they are), then it follows that the social return to training will exceed the private return. Here, the economics gets complicated. The idea is that society gives up less (in terms of output) to train an extra worker than the typical trainee gives up (in terms of income).

- Another argument is too tricky to go into: if firms have a degree of **monopoly power** as buyers in the market for labour (and many do), it turns out that it will be profitable for them to meet some of the cost of their workers' training – but not as much as makes sense from society's point of view. In this roundabout way, a variant of Pigou's 'poaching' argument can be valid, after all.

As well as assuming that the social return to investing in human capital exceeds the private return, the chart says that the private discount rate is higher than the social discount rate. This is plausible for two main reasons. Again, the underlying causes are varieties of market failure:

- In several ways, the **capital market** may be imperfect. For instance, borrowing to finance an investment in human capital may be difficult because would-be trainees lack collateral, or because the costs of administration and collection make such loans unattractive to private lenders. (These costs, it might be argued, would be lower if the lending were undertaken by the government, with subsequent debt-collection through the tax system.)

- Potential trainees may be unduly discouraged by the **risk** they would incur if they were to give up some of their income today in return for higher income (maybe) tomorrow. The idea is that private risks can be pooled, and thereby reduced: it follows that society as a whole should be less influenced by risk than individuals acting alone.

What is the net effect of all this? If, as in the chart, (a) the private return to investing in human capital is lower than the social return and (b) the private discount rate is higher than the social discount rate, then there will be too little investment. The investment that is actually undertaken (the 'private optimum') will be lower than makes sense for the whole economy (the 'social optimum').

© *The Economist*, London (26th March, 1994).

(a) The traditional argument states that the market will fail to provide the desirable level of education and training. What is this argument?

(b) How does Becker's argument concerning the level of education and training differ from the traditional view?

(c) Explain why the private rate of return from education and training is less than the social rate of return.

(d) If the social optimum level of education and training is greater than the private optimum, how might the government encourage greater investment in human capital? (Hint: consider what factors determine the private discount rate.)

(e) Given the arguments you have considered above, outline a case both for and against the operation of student loans in higher education.

FT

In the article below, taken from the *Financial Times* of 2 September 1999, Richard Tomkins assesses why taxation as a means of changing social habits like smoking and car use is unlikely to succeed.

Taxation road to nowhere

Cars, you could say, are like cigarettes. They pollute the air we breathe; they kill large numbers of people; and they are associated with high levels of dependency among users.

But does it follow that governments should treat drivers like smokers, portraying their habit as anti-social and trying to discourage it with punitively high taxes?

In Britain, where traffic congestion has become a troublesome political issue, the response of governments has been to try to price motorists off the roads. The country already has some of the world's highest fuel taxes, and John Prescott, the deputy prime minister, is proposing further levies, such as charging for the use of the roads on a pay-as-you-go basis.

The idea of using price to regulate people's behaviour grew in popularity in the 1980s, when – at least in the US and UK – free-market economics replaced government regulation as the favoured means of achieving social objectives.

As traffic congestion worsened, economists in the UK started arguing for a 'market' solution. Congestion imposed heavy costs on society, they said, and in a socially efficient market, motorists should meet these costs directly.

An attractive precedent appeared to have been set by attempts to control smoking, another habit with high social costs. In the 1980s, big rises in cigarette taxes had been accompanied by a gradual decline in smoking, and the government was praised by anti-smoking advocates for discouraging socially undesirable behaviour.

But, with hindsight, it seems likely that smokers who quit were motivated more by concerns about their health than by the government's price signal. In Britain, smoking also declined in the 1970s, even though the real price of cigarettes fell during the decade. And over the years, smoking prevalence has followed similar trends in the US, Canada and the UK, even though these countries have taxed tobacco at differing rates.

Moreover, in the 1990s, the long decline in smoking has ended in Britain in spite of further big tax increases. It seems that smoking has now settled at a level where those who indulge in it cannot or will not give up. Each successive tax increase simply results in higher levels of criminal activity: namely, soaring imports of contraband tobacco, now said to account for at least 10 per cent of the UK market.

The same sort of resistance to price increases is evident in people's driving behaviour. According to Britain's office for national statistics, motoring costs for the average household rose 96 per cent in the 10 years to financial year 1997–98, or 27 per cent in real terms. But the rise was not accompanied by a fall in traffic: the number of miles travelled by people in cars rose 24 per cent over the same period.

It is also interesting to note that people's ability to absorb higher motoring costs is not just a side-effect of rising incomes. Instead, it has come at the expense of spending in other areas. The percentage of household expenditure taken by motoring rose from 12.6 per cent to 14.2 per cent over the decade to 1997–98: so it seems people would rather economise on food, heat or holidays than cut down on their driving.

At this point, economists usually start talking about elasticity of demand, pointing to neat charts tracking the relationship between price and consumption.

This is fine when applied to goods for which an acceptable alternative exists, or that do not involve a high level of dependency. It is less successful at predicting outcomes when governments use taxes to stop people using things they cannot or will not go without.

In theory, economists are right: there is a point at which price will cut demand for road transport. The trouble is that such a price is by definition unacceptable. If it were not, it would fail to cut consumption.

And so, to political realities. We have seen already what happens when tobacco taxes reach the limit of acceptability: people resort to crime to avoid them, leading to social disorder.

There are signs, too, that levies on road transport are reaching the point at which the public is questioning their legitimacy. Truck drivers have taken to blockading London's streets in protest at rising taxes. Private motorists are a less cohesive community, but they are making their views known in opinion polls. And long before they stop driving, their anger will find its outlet

– if nowhere else, then at the ballot box.

So if the government cannot tax traffic growth out of existence, what is the alternative?

Some people think better public transport is a panacea. Unfortunately, it is not. Motorists like governments to spend money on public transport because they think it will encourage the idiot in the car in front to catch the train instead. But for most drivers, public transport is like the nicotine-free cigarette: it's nice to know it's there, but you would never want to use it.

Instead, the first priority should be to recognise that, contrary to popular perceptions, traffic growth is not inexorable. It will cease when everybody is driving 24 hours a day, and probably long before that. In the meantime, better traffic management will help absorb the extra traffic, and roads should be built or widened where environmental considerations permit.

But there is no magic bullet that will end traffic jams. Congestion is a part of modern life: we find it at the supermarket, the airport, the burger bar and the hospital, and the art of modern life is to learn how to deal with it.

Motorists are already doing this quite well. No new roads have been built in central London for decades, yet traffic speeds in the capital have not fallen greatly. Instead, the rush-hour has expanded to the point where it lasts all day, and is now stretching into the night.

Drivers themselves are the best judges of how to deal with congestion. They will adjust their journey times to maximise the use of the available road space, or they will change their lifestyles to minimise their travel needs.

Eventually, like smokers, they may even decide to quit. But if they do, it will be when they are ready, not when the government tells them to.

(a) Explain why taxation has been ineffective in cutting smoking beyond a certain level. Why does the article suggest that similar problems will be encountered if government attempts to price cars off the road?

(b) Why might policies to make demand for car use more price elastic fail to have much effect?

(c) What solutions to congestion does Richard Tomkins argue should be adopted (or will emerge)?

How can you price a river? Not easily is the answer. In the following article, taken from the *Guardian* of 4 March 1998, Oliver Tickell considers a recent cost–benefit analysis of the River Kennet and examines the difficulties in calculating the costs of its use by Thames Water.

Stream of abuse

How much is the river Kennet worth? The question may at first seem abstruse. But last week, following a long public inquiry in autumn 1996, the Department of the Environment put a value on the river's environmental quality. And it is now using it to uphold Thames Water's licence to pump more than 13 million litres of water from the Kennet a day, no matter how low its flow.

The move is supported by Environment Secretary John Prescott, who, speaking at last July's Water Summit, promised to 'shift the balance to help the environment', to 'give more power to the regulator' and to review abstraction licences so as to 'provide full protection for the environment'.

The Kennet, a chalk stream running west into the Thames from the Marlborough Downs, is one of England's finest trout streams. It is also of high ecological value, and has been designated a Site of Special Scientific Interest. However, low flows are contributing to the siltation of its gravel beds and the prolific growth of blanket weed.

The Environment Agency wanted to restrict Thames Water's licence to pump water from aquifers under the river to increase flows downstream of the Axford pumping station, near Marlborough, estimating that the river would be 'worth' an additional £13.6 million as a result. The sum was based on an extra 'use value' from recreation and angling of £400 000, and an extra 'non-use value' of £13.2 million.

But the head of the DETR's Water Supply and Regulation Division, Richard Vincent, determined otherwise. While accepting the EA's use-value estimate, he reduced the non-use value to £300 000, producing a total benefit worth just £700 000.

He then compared the figure with the £6.2 million cost to Thames Water of developing new infrastructure to compensate for the reduced pumping. Accordingly, he struck out the EA's attempt to reduce pumping to 3 million litres a day at times of low flow, ruling that Thames Water could continue to pump 13.1 million litres a day for the indefinite future.

But is it right to compare the value of a river with the cost of an infrastructure investment? The latter is easily calculated, but the value of the environment is not so readily tied down – as the £12.9 million gulf between the EA's and DETR's estimates in the case of the Kennet demonstrates.

The EA's non-use value was founded on the assertion that the 3 million households in Thames Water's area would be willing to pay 32p a year for the environmental benefits of reduced pumping. Taken over 30 years at the 6 per cent Treasury discount rate, that produces a capital value of £13.2 million. Vincent reduced the number of people to 100 000, each judged willing to pay 25p per year, producing a value of £300 000.

In fact, neither figure is satisfactory: both are based on arbitrary figures unsupported by credible research. And neither even begins to refloat the intrinsic value of the river, its wildlife and its landscape.

Yet the EA is stuck with the cost/benefit approach. Section 39 of the 1995 Environment Act, which brought the EA into being, requires it, in deciding whether or not to exercise a power, to 'take into account the likely costs and benefits of the exercise or non-exercise of the power or its exercise in the manner in question'.

In that it forces the EA into a cod science of dubious environmental valuation, Prescott would do well to be rid of Section 39. But the baby should not be thrown out with the bathwater. Cost–benefit analysis can usefully be deployed in comparing the relative costs and benefits of different means of achieving environmental quality targets.

At the Kennet inquiry, for example, Thames Water argued that the same benefits that would arise from reduced pumping would also result from redesigning the river channel and weirs to increase water velocity and create pools and riffles, and from reducing soil erosion and agrochemical use in the Kennet catchment – all at far lower cost.

In fact, measures such as these are promoted by the EA itself. But its powers to undertake in-channel improvements are limited, and it has no influence on farming practice. So the sensible option, that it should select the cheapest approaches to river restoration, is simply not open to it. If John Prescott wants the EA to bring about cost-efficient improvements in river quality, he needs to extend its powers.

Back to the Kennet, all is not lost Thames Water is installing phosphate-stripping at its Marlborough sewage works. And its environment manager, Dr Peter Spillett, has told the Guardian of his company's willingness to fund improvements such as those he proposed at the inquiry. The way is now open for the warring parties and others (including local farmers and the Ministry of Agriculture) to come together and agree on a catchment-wide plan for the Kennet's restoration.

(a) What is the role of cost–benefit analysis?

(b) Why is it difficult to calculate the costs of using a natural resource, such as the River Kennet, by a large user, such as Thames Water?

(c) What is meant by 'non-use value'? How do you explain the difference between the Environmental Agency's and the DETR's estimation of the non-use value of restricting pumping from the river (£13.2 billion and £300 000, respectively)?

(d) If it is so difficult to calculating costs and benefits, should we continue to use cost–benefit analysis in order to make judgements concerning use and value? Would it be better merely to set environmental targets and then find the cheapest way of achieving them?

FT

The following article, appearing in the *Financial Times* of 24 August 1990, reported on a book by Judith Marquand* which criticised the neo-classical conception of 'rational economic behaviour' and with it the arguments for a *laissez-faire* policy.

Post-Copernican economics

Many economists believe that Britain's long-term economic problems are mainly caused by microeconomic rigidities of various sorts. The Thatcher Government, they argue, has removed distortions – such as controls on credit and foreign exchange – but it has not wrought a transformation of the economy because it has failed *consistently* to follow the logic of market liberalism. Many parts of the economy, such as the labour market, remain fettered. The UK's long-term relative decline is thus likely to be reversed only when free market principles enjoy even greater sway.

Micro distortions probably do cause small inefficiencies and inequities. Other things being equal, their removal would be desirable. But the claim that a purer form of market competition alone would solve Britain's long-term problems appears wide of the mark. At bottom, this is because the assumptions on which modern or 'neoclassical' economics is based are oversimplified and misleading. Countries – such as the UK and US – which base policy unthinkingly on this model run into trouble; those – such as Japan – which adopt a less naive approach tend to prosper.

The shortcomings of neoclassical economics are ably discussed in *Autonomy and Change*, a recent book by Judith Marquand, an economist at Britain's Department of Employment. Marquand's arguments, which span several academic disciplines, including cognitive psychology, organisational theory and political science, are not easily summarised. But the core of her message is that a revolution is occurring in the social sciences which will, in time, bury the British empiricist tradition and with it the narrow neoclassical conception of 'rational economic man'.

Marquand has little sympathy for the neoclassical vision of human beings as 'individual atoms, bound together in society only as far as they calculate it to be worth their while'. She rejects both the doctrine that individuals independently seek to maximise their personal 'utility' or well-being, and the helpful fiction that tastes and preferences are simply 'given'. She also deplores its focus on static optimisation theorems. The theory, she argues, has little relevance in a rapidly changing world populated by complex organisations and individuals who lack either the brainpower or the information to adopt maximising strategies.

In place of neoclassical *homo economicus*, Marquand advances a conception of man as an 'inquiring social animal'. Rather than maximising, he seeks satisfactory solutions and his goals are heavily influenced by the opinions of others. He is not sovereign but dependent on the institutions and groups to which he belongs. But above all, he is a creature capable of learning and hence changing. Education thus lies at the heart of economic development. This new paradigm of 'learning man', she claims, will ultimately prove more helpful than the neoclassical vision of static competitive man.

Britain and the US, says Marquand, stand out for the strength of their belief in individualism. This led to an early preference for *laissez-faire*, which in turn stimulated early industrial success. But the world has since changed and such attitudes are no longer helpful. It is the quality of education, the ability of individuals to co-operate in groups and the capacity of institutions to manage change, rather than old-fashioned microeconomic efficiency, that have become the crucial determinants of economic success.

Neoclassical economics, contends Marquand, is in the condition of astronomy before Copernicus. The epicycles are multiplying but they explain less and less. The way forward is to embrace a broader vision of human nature and to accept that economic behaviour can be understood only in its wider social context. Economists may not like this message but, unless they widen their expertise in the social sciences, especially psychology, they are poorly placed to refute it.

© *Financial Times*, 24.8.90

* J. Marquand, *Autonomy and Change: The sources of economic growth* (Harvester Wheatsheaf, 1989).

(a) What implications does this article have for the role of government intervention in the market?

(b) Prepare a short reply to these arguments from the perspective of (i) a neo-classical economist, and (ii) a neo-Austrian economist.

 ANSWERS

Q1. E. This is the case when all Pareto improvements have been made. A Pareto improvement is where it is possible to make people better off *without* making anyone worse off. Note that B is not correct because if improvements can still be made the optimum cannot yet have been reached. A and C are not correct: Pareto optimality has to do with efficiency, not fairness. D is not correct because Pareto optimality is concerned with *allocative* efficiency not *X* efficiency.

Q2. *True*. The Pareto criterion is concerned with *efficiency* not with equity. A totally equal and a highly unequal distribution of income can both be Pareto optimal (i.e. efficient).

Q3. **(a)** *A*, *C* and *E*. Compared with point *X*, *C* represents a gain to both Bill and Ben. *A* and *E* represent a gain to one but no loss to the other.

   (b) *D*, *F* and *G*. Compared with point *F*, *X* represents a gain to both. Compared with points *D* and *G*, *X* represents a gain to one and no loss to the other.

   (c) No. Bill's gain is Ben's loss. The choice then is one of distribution rather than efficiency.

Q4. 1. Perfect competition in all markets.
   2. No externalities.

Q5. *marginal cost*.

Q6. *less than*.

Q7. *marginal benefit*.

Q8. D. It is merely an extension of the general proposition that the optimum level of any activity will be where $MB = MC$, only in this case it is marginal *social* costs and marginal *social* benefits that are relevant. (Note that A would be true in the absence of externalities.)

Q9. *marginal utility*.

Q10. *marginal cost*.

Q11. **(a)** People would consume more. *MU* (and *MSB*) would fall (diminishing marginal utility) and price would rise until once more $MSB = P$.

   (b) The rise in the price of the good would raise the *MRP* of factors and thus the demand for factors would rise. The resulting shortage would increase the price of factors and encourage more supply of factors until $MRP_f = P_f = MC_f$ (where MRP_f is the marginal benefit from using a factor and MC_f is the marginal cost of supplying a factor (= *MDU* in the case of labour). With no externalities this means that *MSB* of factor use equals *MSC* of factor supply.

   (c) To the extent that good X is a complement or substitute for other goods, so the changes in the price of good X will affect the *MU* of other goods. To the extent that factors used for producing good X are used for producing other goods, so the change in factor prices will affect the *MC* of other goods. The resulting disequilibria will lead to adjustments in these other goods markets until in each case $MSB = MSC$ once more.

   (d) To the extent that factors used for good X are complements or substitutes for other factors, so the demand for these other factors will change. The resulting disequilibria will lead to adjustments in these other factor markets until in each case $MSB_f = MSC_f$ once more.

   (e) These ripple effects will continue until a general equilibrium is restored where $MSB = MSC$ in all goods and factor markets.

Q12. Buy relatively more X and relatively less Y until $MU_X/MU_Y = P_X/P_Y$.

Q13. Produce relatively more Y and relatively less X until $MC_X/MC_Y = P_X/P_Y$.

Q14. **(a)** By B giving A some X in exchange for some Y. Both A and B would gain.

   (b) Where MU_X/MU_Y for person A equals MU_X/MU_Y for person B.

Q15. *True*. For any pair of goods, where $MRS = MRT$ there are no further Pareto improvements that can be made.

Q16. **(a)** (social) $MRS = MU_X/MU_Y = MSB_X/MSB_Y$.

   (b) (social) $MRT = MC_X/MC_Y = MSC_X/MSC_Y$.

   (c) The line is the tangent to point *A* since this is the point where *MRS* equals *MRT*.

   (d) Because production cannot take place beyond the production possibility curve and point *A* is the point where the production possibility curve reaches the highest social indifference curve.

   (e) (i) By moving out towards the production possibility curve. There could be a gain in production by some producers with no loss in production by others. (ii) There could be a move to a higher social indifference curve. A reallocation of consumption could lead to some consumers gaining with no one losing.

Q17. Examples include: greater equality, faster economic growth and stable prices.

Q18. (a) (v), (i); (b) (iv), (ii); (c) (i); (d) (iii), (iv); (e) (vi); (f) (viii), (iv); (g) (ii); (h) (i); (i) (vii), (ii) (but there are the benefits of economies of scale: for example, if another family member buys you the wrong flavour of yoghurt, the disappointment of this may be outweighed by the fact that you did not have to go out and buy it!); (j) (iv).

Q19. **(a)** *I*.

   (b) Q_2 (where $P = MC$).

   (c) $£_2 - £_3$.

   (d) Q_1 (where $P = MSC$).

Q20. See pages 297–9 of Sloman, *Economics* (4th edition). Two additional examples of each are:

   (a) An attractive new shopping centre built on previously ugly derelict land; the use of new cheaper, but less polluting, technology.

   (b) A person decorating the outside of their house (thus making the street more attractive); travel by bus (thus relieving congestion).

   (c) People visiting beauty spots and causing damage to wildlife; the consumption of alcohol and the effects of drunken behaviour on other people.

Q21. *True*. See Figure 11.6 on page 299 of Sloman, *Economics* (4th edition).

Q22. E. It is the loss in *total* surplus. The gain in producers' surplus (profit) will be more than offset by a loss in consumers' surplus, giving an overall net loss.

Q23. A. Large external costs relative to private costs make the goods socially desirable but privately unprofitable to produce. Once provided it is not possible to exclude people from consuming the goods or services without paying (i.e. from getting a 'free ride').

Q24. *Yes*: (b), (d), (f) and (g). In each of these cases the free market would simply not provide these services.

No: (a), (c), (e) and (h). In each of these cases the free market would provide the good or service, but probably imperfectly. There would be only a relatively small free-rider problem.

Q25. *True*. Since people cannot be excluded from consuming the good without paying, the market price would be zero (and hence it would be privately unprofitable to produce the good).

Q26. *(a)* People with infectious diseases passing them on to other people.

(b) Hospitals or doctors colluding to keep up the price of treatment.

(c) Patient ignorance about their condition. They may be persuaded to have more expensive treatment than is necessary.

(d) People taking out expensive private insurance for fear of their future health.

(e) Uncaring parents not buying adequate treatment for their children. Children not buying adequate treatment for their elderly parents.

(f) Poor people not being able to afford reasonable health. The belief that people have a moral right to health care according to need and not ability to pay.

(g) People may neglect their health. The government may regard health care as a merit good.

Q27. The solution of correcting a specific market distortion so as to restore the condition that $MSB = MSC$ in all parts of the economy.

Q28. D. Thus if prices in the rest of the economy are on average 10 per cent above marginal cost, the minimum *relative* distortion would be for prices in this industry to be set at 10 per cent above marginal cost.

Q29. *False*. The tax should be equal to marginal *external* cost. (Marginal *social* cost equals marginal external cost *plus* marginal private cost.) Likewise the subsidy should be equal to marginal *external* benefit not marginal *social* benefit.

Q30. *(a)* £$_3$ – £$_4$.

(b) *None: it will remain at £$_3$.*

Q31. Advantages: they 'internalise externalities'; rates can be adjusted according to the magnitude of the problem, thus allowing MSB to equal MSC; firms are encouraged to find ways of reducing external costs and of increasing external benefits.

Disadvantages: impractical to use when a different tax or subsidy rate is required for each case; rates would have to be frequently adjusted as external costs and benefits changed; knowledge is imperfect (for example, there is a danger of underestimating

external costs such as pollution) – it might be safer to ban certain activities.

Q32. *many* (it will be difficult to co-ordinate their actions).

Q33. *slightly* (it may not be worth the effort of pursuing the culprits).

Q34. *many* (it makes pursuing the culprits more difficult and costly).

Q35. *(a)* (i) (it is illegal to have below a minimum tread).

(b) (ii) ('resale price maintenance' is against the law).

(c) (i) (cigarette advertising is banned on television and is being phased out on hoardings and in magazines).

Q36. (a) (vi), (b) (viii), (c) (iv), (d) (iii), (e) (vii), (f) (i), (g) (ii), (h) (v).

Q37. (a) (ii), (b) (iv), (c) (iii), (d) (v), (e) (vii), (f) (i), (g) (vi).

Q38. (b) and (c). These can give an indication of the non-monetary benefits to local residents from a quieter village – (b); and to road users from the time saved – (c).

Q39. *Ignorance*: people are unlikely to know beforehand just how much they will gain or lose. *Dishonesty*: people may exaggerate the costs or benefits to them in order to influence the outcome.

Q40. *True*.

Q41. *(a)* *No*. No matter whether the uncertain costs turned out to be £4 or £10, the project would still be *profitable*.

(b) *Yes*. The project would be profitable only if the uncertain costs turned out to be less than £6m.

(c) *No*. No matter whether the uncertain costs turned out to be £4 or £10, the project would still be *unprofitable*.

Q42. 1 (c), 2 (e), 3 (a), 4 (d), 5 (b).

Q43. Two or three alternative discount rates can be tried to see if the project's desirability is sensitive to the choice of discount rate. If it is, then the project will be seen as borderline.

Q44. D. The criterion is merely that there be a *potential* Pareto improvement. The question of *actual* compensation is seen to be a question of equity and should thus be considered separately from the social efficiency of the project.

Q45. In practice compensation may not be paid. An actual Pareto improvement, therefore, may not take place.

Q46. Reasons include: shortages and surpluses, poor information, bureaucracy and government inefficiency, lack of market incentives, inconsistent government policy, unrepresentative government, unaccountable government and voters' ignorance.

Q47. (a) efficiency, (b) free-market, (c) dynamic, (d) monopoly, (e)–(g) risk taking, innovation, growth, (h) longer-term, (i) oligopolies.

Q48. A. This will *strengthen* its power: it is a barrier to the entry of new firms. Any new entrants (at less than the output of the existing firm) would find that their costs were higher than this firm's and would thus find it hard to survive.

CHAPTER TWELVE

12 Applied Microeconomics

A REVIEW

This chapter examines five topics that illustrate well the possible strengths and weaknesses of both the market and government intervention. These are: (1) the economics of the environment, (2) traffic congestion and urban transport policies, (3) monopolies and oligopolies and government policy to encourage greater competition, (4) privatisation and regulation and (5) privatisation in transition economies.

12.1 Economics of the environment

(Pages 327–9) People draw various benefits from the environment. The three main benefits are: (1) as an amenity; (2) as a source of primary products; (3) as a dump for waste. These three uses, however, tend to conflict with each other.

Q1. In what ways do the above uses come into conflict?

....

....

Q2. As population increases, so environmental degradation is likely to:

A. reduce.
B. stay constant.
C. increase at a decelerating rate.
D. increase at a constant rate.
E. increase at an accelerating rate.

Q3. Which of the following are likely to reduce pressures on the environment?

(a) An increased price of non-renewable resources.

Yes/No

(b) Growth in national income.   *Yes/No*

(c) Technological progress.   *Yes/No*

(d) An increase in living standards in developing countries.

Yes/No

(e) An increased recognition of global interdependence.

Yes/No

(Pages 329–31) What is the optimum use of the environment? The answer depends on people's attitudes towards sustainability.

Q4. The following are four different approaches to sustainability:

 (i) The free-market approach.
 (ii) The social efficiency approach.
 (iii) The conservationist approach.
 (iv) The Gaia approach.

Match each one of the following four descriptions to one of the above approaches:

(a) Downplaying the importance of material consumption and economic growth and putting greater emphasis on the maintenance of the ecosystems.

....

(b) Emphasising the importance of private property and the pressures this puts on using the environment as a

productive resource – a resource which, like other resources, should not be wasted.

....

(c) Regarding the environment as having rights of its own, with humans having an obligation to live in harmony with it.

....

(d) Taking explicit account of environmental costs and benefits in decision making.

....

⊖ **Q5.** Figure 12.1 shows the net private benefit from producing a good (curve *MB–MC*) and the marginal pollution cost to society (*MC*$_{pollution}$). Which output would be seen as optimum under each of the following approaches?

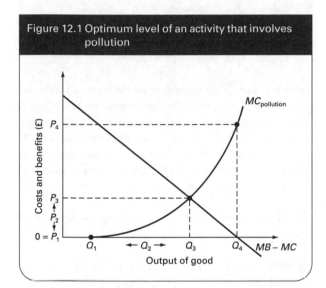

Figure 12.1 Optimum level of an activity that involves pollution

(a) The social efficiency approach $Q_1/Q_2/Q_3/Q_4$
(b) The Gaia approach $Q_1/Q_2/Q_3/Q_4$
(c) The conservationist approach $Q_1/Q_2/Q_3/Q_4$
(d) The free-market approach $Q_1/Q_2/Q_3/Q_4$

(Pages 331–4) There are various policy alternatives for dealing with environmental problems. One is to extend private property rights; another is to use green taxes. The next two questions again refer to Figure 12.1.

▤ **Q6.** According to the Coase theorem, the extension of private property rights to sufferers from pollution would allow them to levy a charge on the polluter which would (a) fully compensate the sufferers and (b) result in a profit-maximising output:

A. of Q_1.
B. between Q_1 and Q_3.
C. of Q_3.
D. between Q_3 and Q_4.
E. of Q_4.

▤ **Q7.** The socially efficient green tax would of an amount equal to:

A. zero.
B. OP_4.
C. $MB–MC$.
D. $MC_{pollution}$.
E. $OP_4–OP_3$.

(Pages 334–6) An alternative means of protecting the environment is to use command-and-control systems. Minimum environmental standards could be set. These could be any of three types: technology-based standards, ambient-based standards, social-impact standards.

⁇ **Q8.** Define these terms:

Technology-based standards ....

....

Ambient-based standards ....

....

Social-impact standards ....

....

◑ **Q9.** Command-and-control systems have the following advantages over green taxes:
(a) They are more appropriate when it is impossible to predict the precise environmental impact of pollution.
                                            True/False
(b) They have the effect of making the polluter pay for the amount of pollution generated.   *True/False*
(c) They are easier to administer than green taxes.
                                              True/False
(d) They act as a continuous incentive for polluters to reduce the amount of pollution they generate.
                                              True/False

(Pages 336–7) An alternative that has been much debated in recent years is the use of tradable permits.

⊗ **Q10.** Assume that two firms, A and B, are currently emitting 100 units of a pollutant each. Now assume that a standard is set permitting them to emit only 50 units of pollutant each. If either firm emits less than 50 units, it will be given a credit for the difference. This credit can then be sold to the other firm allowing it to go over the 50-unit limit by the amount of the credit. Assume that the marginal cost of pollution reduction for firm A is £2000 per unit and for firm B it is £1000 per unit, irrespective of the current level of emission.
(a) How many units of pollution will each firm emit after trade in credits between the two firms has taken place?

                Firm A .... Firm B ....

Table 12.1 Marginal cost of pollution reduction by firms A and B

Number of units of pollutant emitted	MC of reducing pollution by 1 unit (£000)	
	Firm A	Firm B
100	4	1
90	4	2
80	4	3
70	4	4
60	4	5
50	4	6
40	4	7
30	4	8
20	4	9
10	4	10

(b) What can we say about the price at which the credits will be traded?

....

Now assume that the marginal private cost to the firms of reducing pollution below 100 units is given in Table 12.1. (Assume for firm B that there is a straight-line *MC* curve: for example, the *MC* of reducing emissions by a 25th unit to 75 units is £4500.)

(c) How many units of pollution will each firm emit this time after trade has taken place in the permits?

Firm A .... Firm B ....

(d) What can we say about the price at which the credits will be traded?

....

(Pages 337–8) It is difficult to reach international agreements on pollution reduction.

(?) **Q11.** Give three reasons why.

1. ....

2. ....

3. ....

Q12. Assume that a country is considering whether to honour a new international agreement to cut the emission of greenhouse gases. Assume also that it is considering purely its own domestic gains from the cutting of these gases and its own domestic costs of so doing.

(a) What would be the *maximax* strategy?
Stick to agreement/Break the agreement

(b) What would be the *maximin* strategy?
Stick to agreement/Break the agreement

(c) Why could this be described as a *prisoners' dilemma game*?

....

....

12.2 Traffic congestion and urban transport policies

(Pages 339–41) The demand for road space can be seen largely as a *derived* demand.

Q13. Which one of the following demands for road space is *not* a derived demand?
A. Using a car to go to work.
B. Using a bus to go to work.
C. Using a car to go for a Sunday afternoon drive.
D. Using a car to go shopping.
E. Lorries using roads to deliver goods.

There are various determinants of the demand for road space by car users. One of the most important is the 'price' to the motorist of the journey. This is not paid directly for using a particular stretch of road, except in the case of **Q14.** *tolls/taxes/congestion/the price paid for the car*, but instead can be seen as the various **Q15.** *total/average/marginal* **Q16.** *costs/benefits* to the motorist.

Q17. This 'price' will vary according to the level of congestion. *True/False*

Q18. Which of the following motoring costs are marginal (private) costs to the motorist?
(a) Fuel consumption. *Yes/No*
(b) Fuel tax. *Yes/No*
(c) Road fund tax. *Yes/No*
(d) Congestion. *Yes/No*
(e) Car maintenance costs. *Yes/No*
(f) Depreciation due to wear and tear. *Yes/No*
(g) Depreciation due to ageing of the vehicle. *Yes/No*
(h) Time spent making a journey. *Yes/No*

One of the reasons why it is difficult to tackle the problem of a growing level of traffic has to do with elasticity of demand.

Q19. Which one of the following is likely to be elastic?
A. Price elasticity of demand for road space (with respect to the direct marginal motoring costs).
B. Income elasticity of demand for road space.
C. Cross-price elasticity of demand for road space with respect to rail fares.
D. Cross-price elasticity of demand for road space for private cars with respect to bus fares.
E. Cross-price elasticity of demand for road space with respect to the price of new cars.

(Pages 341–3) A problem is that when people use their cars they impose external costs on other people.

(?) **Q20.** Give three examples of external costs of motoring.

1. ....

2. ....

3. ....

What, then, is the optimum level of road usage?

(◗) **Q21.** The optimum level of road usage would be that at which the external costs of motoring were zero.

True/False

(⊖) **Q22.** Figure 12.2 shows the effects of increasing traffic along a particular stretch of road. At first additional cars have no effect on the speed of traffic: it flows freely. But after a point, additional cars slow down the traffic and thus impose a 'congestion cost' (an externality) on other car users. Beyond this point, therefore, the marginal social cost (*MSC*) of using the road is greater than the marginal private cost (*MC*).

(a) Assuming that there are no externalities on the demand side, so that marginal social benefit and marginal private benefit are the same, what will be the actual level of road use?

....

(b) What is the socially optimal level of road use?

....

(c) What is the marginal external cost at *OH*?

....

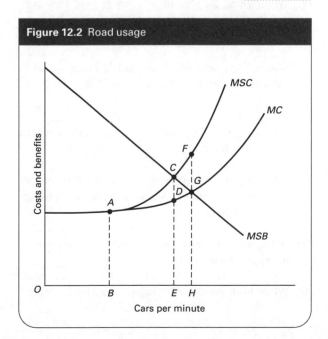

Figure 12.2 Road usage

(d) What level of 'congestion tax' (e.g. tolls) would be necessary to achieve the optimal level of road use?

....

(Pages 343–8) Various policies have been adopted for tackling the problem of traffic congestion.

(?) **Q23.** Give three problems of building more roads as the means of reducing traffic congestion.

1. ....

2. ....

3. ....

(◗) **Q24.** In order to reduce congestion, the marginal tax rate must increase as the level of congestion increases.

True/False

(▤) **Q25.** Four of the following are advantages of electronic road pricing. Which one is not?

A. The charge can be varied according to the time of day.

B. The charge can be varied according to the level of congestion.

C. The socially efficient rate to charge can easily be ascertained.

D. The revenues can be used to subsidise public transport.

E. It can be used to 'internalise' motoring externalities.

(?) **Q26.** Under what circumstances will electronic road pricing be most effective in reducing the level of traffic congestion?

....

....

....

12.3 Policies towards monopolies and oligopolies

(Pages 349–51) There are a number of possible targets of government policy concerning competition and market power.

(✪) **Q27.** The following are problems which have been the target of various government policies:

(i) An increase in industrial concentration.

(ii) The exercise of monopoly power.

(iii) Restrictive practices.

(iv) Resale price maintenance.

(v) Excessive industrial concentration.

(vi) Natural monopolies.

(vii) Cross-subsidisation.

On which of the above problems would each of the following policies be primarily targeted?

(a) A government makes it illegal for manufacturers to set the price at which their products must be sold by shops.

....

(b) A government nationalises the national electricity grid.

....

(c) A government makes collusive agreements between oligopolists illegal.

....

(d) A government sets up a body which can investigate any firm with a share of the market above a certain level.

....

(e) Firms are prohibited from using 'unfair competitive practices' whereby they use profits in one market to charge prices below cost in another, and thereby to drive competitors out of business.

....

(f) A regulatory body has the power to limit a firm's price increases where this would result in 'excessive' supernormal profits.

....

(g) A government passes legislation that enables an investigation of any mergers that will lead to the merged firms having more than a certain percentage share of the market.

....

Competition policy is concerned with three main problem areas: (i) the abuse by a firm of a dominant position in the market; (ii) oligopolistic collusion between firms; (iii) the growth of market power through mergers and acquisitions.

Q28. Which one of the above three problems is addressed by the following types of policy?
(a) Restrictive practices policy *(i)/(ii)/(iii)*
(b) Monopoly policy *(i)/(ii)/(iii)*
(c) Merger policy *(i)/(ii)/(iii)*

Q29. Monopoly policy, under both EU and UK legislation, is directed purely towards monopolies. *True/False*

Because the relative costs and benefits of monopolies and oligopolies will differ from firm to firm and industry to industry, governments in the UK, like many other governments round the world, have tended to prefer to judge each case on its merits.

Q30. What is the main criterion used under both EU and UK legislation when deciding whether action should be taken against a firm with monopoly power?

A. The firm's market share.
B. Whether its behaviour is anti-competitive.
C. Whether it is achieving economies of scale.
D. Whether it engages in excessive advertising.
E. How high its profits are.

There are various types of anti-competitive practice in which firms can engage.

Q31. The following is a list of various anti-competitive practices:
   (i) Tie-in sales.
  (ii) Collusive tendering.
 (iii) Selective distribution.
  (iv) Price rings.
   (v) Price discrimination.
  (vi) Rental-only contracts.
 (vii) Market-sharing agreements.
(viii) Vertical price squeezing.
  (ix) Predatory pricing.

Match the above practices to the following definitions.
(a) Where a firm is only prepared to supply certain selected retail outlets.

....

(b) Where a vertically integrated firm, which controls the supply of an input, charges competitors a high price for that input so that they cannot compete with it in selling the finished good.

....

(c) Where firms divide up the market between them, agreeing not to compete in each other's part of the market.

....

(d) Where firms bidding for a contract (e.g. to supply building materials for a new office development) agree beforehand all to bid high prices.

....

(e) Where a firm sells the same good at a different price (relative to costs) in different sectors of the market.

....

(f) Where a firm is only prepared to hire out equipment and not sell it outright.

....

(g) Where a firm controlling the supply of a first product insists that its customers also buy a second product from it rather than from its rivals.

....

(h) Selling a product below cost in order to drive competitors from the industry.

....

(i) Where firms get together to agree on a common price.

....

Q32. Which of the nine anti-competitive practices in Q31 are:

(a) forms of oligopolistic collusion (restrictive practices)?

....

(b) directly concerned with controlling prices?

....

(c) directly concerned with controlling supply or sales?

....

Q33. The EU and UK approaches to restrictive practices are very similar. Article 85 of the Treaty of Rome and Chapter I of the UK's 1998 Competition Act do not seek to ban all agreements between oligopolies but rather to ban various types of anti-competitive *behaviour* by oligopolists.

True/False

Q34. Which type of merger is likely to be most damaging to competition? *horizontal/vertical/conglomerate*

Q35. Give three ways in which a merger could be in the public interest.

1. ....

2. ....

3. ....

Q36. Article 86 of the Treaty of Rome is concerned with European mergers. Under this Article, what is the main criterion in judging the desirability of a merger?

....

Q37. In 1990 the EC adopted new merger control measures. Which of the following criticisms of the measures are valid, or at least have some validity?

(a) The investigations are expensive to conduct. *Yes/No*
(b) The Commission can too easily be persuaded by firms that the merger is not anti-competitive. *Yes/No*
(c) The conditions attached by the Commission to mergers that are allowed to proceed often rely too heavily on co-operation by the firms concerned.
  Yes/No
(d) The investigations are very time consuming. *Yes/No*
(e) Only a very limited number of cases meeting the minimum ECU5 billion turnover criterion are considered.
  Yes/No
(f) Not enough emphasis is placed on questions of possible cost reductions from the mergers. Instead the stress is almost exclusively on questions of competition.
  Yes/No

Q38. If, under the 1990 regulations, the European Commission decides on a full investigation of a proposed merger, it can prevent the merger if it is found to be anti-competitive. *True/False*

Q39. Under UK legislation governing mergers (covered by the 1973 Fair Trading Act):
(a) Companies must give details of any proposed merger to the Office of Fair Trading. *True/False*
(b) The Director General of Fair Trading then makes recommendations to the Secretary of State for Trade and Industry. *True/False*
(c) The Secretary of State must then refer the merger proposal to the Competition Commission (CC).
  True/False
(d) When the CC investigates merger proposals, there is no initial assumption that the merger is against the public interest. Instead the arguments for and against are weighed up. *True/False*
(e) The CC reports its findings to the Secretary of State who must then carry out the wishes of the CC and either prevent or permit the merger. *True/False*

12.4 Privatisation and regulation

(Pages 358–63) Privatisation can take various forms.

Q40. Give three forms that privatisation can take other than the complete sale of state-owned corporations by a public sale of shares.

1. ....

2. ....

3. ....

One of the major arguments used to justify privatisation was the low level of profits of nationalised industries.

Q41. Give three reasons why the level of profits may have been a poor indicator of the economic performance of nationalised industries.

1. ....

2. ....

3. ....

Q42. Imagine you are an economic consultant given the responsibility of preparing a report on the desirability of privatising the railways in a country where the railways are currently wholly stated owned. Classify the following arguments as being generally for privatisation, against privatisation or inconclusive.

(a) Many socially desirable lines are currently being run at a loss. *for/against/inconclusive*

(b) There are various ways in which competition could be injected into the industry. *for/against/inconclusive*

(c) The 'price' per mile to road users is well below the marginal social cost. *for/against/inconclusive*

(d) Studies show that the efficiency of the railways has been approximately the same as that in other countries. *for/against/inconclusive*

(e) The proceeds from the privatisation sale can be used to reduce taxes. *for/against/inconclusive*

(f) There would no longer be any government interference in setting fares. *for/against/inconclusive*

(g) The railways have had a very poor profit record. *for/against/inconclusive*

(h) A new genuinely independent body OFRAIL would be given substantial regulatory powers. *for/against/inconclusive*

Q43. Assume that a government wants to raise the maximum revenue from a privatisation sale and also wants to inject the maximum amount of competition into the industry. Why may these two objectives come into conflict?

....

....

Q44. Ownership is a less important determinant of the efficiency of an industry than the degree of competition it faces and the attitude of the government towards it. *True/False*

(Pages 363–4) If a nationalised industry is run 'in the public interest', or if the industry is privately owned but regulated so that it is required to operate in the public interest, how much should it produce and at what price? Take the case of industry X.

Q45. If all other industries were operating under perfect competition and there were no externalities, then the 'first-best' policy for industry X would be to produce where:

A. $P = AR$
B. $AR = AC$
C. $MR = MC$
D. $MC = P$
E. $MC = AC$

Q46. Consider now what price industry X should charge when the first-best situation does not apply. Assume that firms typically throughout the economy (including related industries to industry X) charge a price 15 per cent above marginal cost and that industry X's marginal cost is 5 per cent above its marginal social cost. Assume also that on average other firms' externalities are zero. The second-best price for industry X will be:

A. 10 per cent above its marginal cost.
B. 10 per cent above its average cost.
C. 20 per cent above its marginal cost.
D. 20 per cent above its average cost.
E. 15 per cent above its marginal cost.

Q47. If it is regarded as socially desirable for reasons of equity to provide loss-making rural bus services, what is the least distortionary solution to this problem?

A. Raise the fares on the urban bus services to cover the losses of the rural services so as to retain the same overall level of profit as before.
B. Keep urban fares the same and pay for the rural services from reduced bus company profits.
C. Subsidise the rural services from increased local taxes in rural areas.
D. Subsidise the rural services from increased income tax.
E. Subsidise the rural services from increased taxes on the motorist.

(Pages 364–71) In the UK, the major privatised industries have substantial market power. It was felt that the OFT and the MMC would not be sufficient to ensure that they operate in the public interest, and so the government set up independent bodies to regulate their behaviour.

Q48. Which of the following are features of UK regulation?

(a) Each regulatory body is responsible for just one industry. *Yes/No*
(b) *All* pricing decisions in the regulated industries are subject to regulation. *Yes/No*
(c) Price regulation is normally of the form: *RPI* plus *X*. *Yes/No*
(d) The *X* in the formula is designed to take account of expected increases in efficiency. *Yes/No*
(e) Price regulation takes account of cost increases beyond the control of the industries. *Yes/No*
(f) Price regulation can involve industries having to reduce their prices even when there is inflation. *Yes/No*
(g) If there is no agreement between the regulator and the industry when reviewing price-setting formulae, an appeal can be made to the Competition Commission for settlement of the dispute. *Yes/No*
(h) Once the price-setting formula has been set for a specified number of years, it cannot be changed until the end of that period. *Yes/No*
(i) Regulators are only concerned with pricing decisions. *Yes/No*
(j) The system of regulation is discretionary, with the regulator able to judge individual examples of the behaviour of the industry on their own merits. *Yes/No*

Q49. In the USA, the main form of regulation is 'rate-of-return' regulation, which involves restricting the amount of profit a firm can make. This has the major advantage that it encourages firms to find ways of reducing costs.

True/False

Q50. One of the dangers with regulation is that of 'regulatory capture'. This can be defined as a situation where:

A. the regulator is only concerned about carrying out government policy.

B. the regulator totally dominates the industry, leaving the managers no discretion to make pricing and investment decisions which might be in the *long-term* interests of the industry and the country.

C. the regulator captures an ever *increasing* amount of the decisions of the industry.

D. the managers become obsessed with doing what the regulator wants rather than what is genuinely in the interests of the industry.

E. the regulator starts seeing things from the managers' point of view rather than the consumers'.

(?) Q51. Give three advantages and three disadvantages of the UK system of regulation.

Advantages

1. ....

2. ....

3. ....

Disadvantages

1. ....

2. ....

3. ....

(?) Q52. Assume that a country has a single interconnected system of natural gas pipelines owned by a recently privatised company. Give three ways in which the government could attempt to inject competition into the supply of gas to customers.

1. ....

2. ....

3. ....

12.5 Privatisation in transition economies

(Pages 371–5) Virtually all of the previously centrally planned economies of central and eastern Europe and the former Soviet Union have been pursuing large-scale programmes of privatisation.

Q53. Which of the following problems occurred under central planning?

(a) Prices did not reflect opportunity costs. *Yes/No*

(b) Planners had insufficient information about individual workplaces. *Yes/No*

(c) Investment rates were very low. *Yes/No*

(d) It was often in managers' interests to provide planners with inaccurate information. *Yes/No*

(e) Inappropriate units were used for targets to be met by managers. *Yes/No*

(f) Bonuses were rarely awarded. *Yes/No*

(g) The prices set by the state were often above the equilibrium level. *Yes/No*

Q54. Privatisation has taken a number of forms. Which of the following forms are examples of 'insider' privatisation and which of 'outsider' privatisation?

(a) Selling an enterprise to its managers and/or workers. *Insider/Outsider*

(b) Issuing vouchers to the general public and then auctioning shares in enterprises for vouchers. *Insider/Outsider*

(c) Transferring ownership directly to the workers/managers of enterprises, with no sale of shares involved. *Insider/Outsider*

(d) Open public sale of an enterprise for cash. *Insider/Outsider*

(e) Selling an enterprise to an independent national investment trust. *Insider/Outsider*

(f) Selling an enterprise to a foreign company. *Insider/Outsider*

(Pages 375–7) There have been various problems associated with privatisation and the move to a market economy in the transition economies.

Q55. Which of the following have been problems arising from privatisation and market liberalisation?

(a) Inequality has increased. *Yes/No*

(b) Shortages have increased. *Yes/No*

(c) Inflation is higher than before. *Yes/No*

(d) Unemployment is higher than before. *Yes/No*

(e) Output fell (at least initially). *Yes/No*

(f) Relative prices are more distorted than before. *Yes/No*

(?) Q56. Name three ways in which the environment in which privatisation takes place could be made more conducive to the success of that privatisation in building a competitive market economy.

1. ....

2. ....

3. ....

B PROBLEMS, EXERCISES AND PROJECTS

Table 12.2 Time taken to travel between two points along a given road

Cars per minute	Marginal private time cost: in minutes	Total time cost: in minutes	Marginal social time cost: in minutes	Marginal external time cost: in minutes
(1)	(2)	(3)	(4)	(5)
1	4	...	...	...
2	4	...	...	...
3	5	...	...	...
4	7	...	...	...
5	10	...	...	...
6	15	...	...	...
7	25	...	...	...

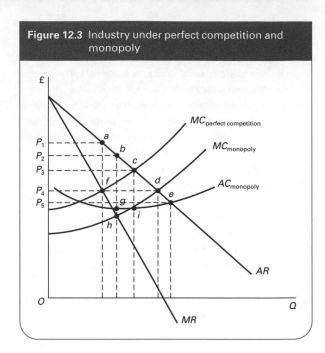

Figure 12.3 Industry under perfect competition and monopoly

Q57. Table 12.2 shows the time taken to travel between two points along a given road.

Column (1) gives the traffic density: i.e. the number of cars per minute entering that stretch of road.

Column (2) gives the journey time per car: i.e. the number of minutes taken for a car to travel along that stretch of road.

Column (3) gives the sum of the journey times: i.e. the total number of minutes for *all* the cars per minute entering the road to travel along that stretch of road.

Column (4) gives the extra total journey time as traffic density increases by one more car.

Column (5) gives the additional time costs imposed on *other* road users by one more car entering that stretch of road: i.e. column (4) minus column (2).

(a) Fill in the figures for columns (3), (4) and (5).

(b) Assume that tolls are now imposed on this road in order to reduce congestion to the socially optimal level. If time were valued at 10p per minute, what level of toll should be imposed per car when traffic density reaches:

 (i) 6 cars per minute? ....

 (ii) 7 cars per minute? ....

(c) Assume that the non-time costs of using the road are constant at 40p per car, that the marginal social benefit for the first car per minute using the road is £2.00, and that this decreases by 10p for each additional car per minute. What is the socially optimal level of road use (in cars per minute)?

....

(d) What level of toll should be imposed per car to achieve the socially optimal level of traffic on this road?

....

Q58. Figure 12.3 shows an industry that was originally perfectly competitive, but which has been taken over by a monopoly. It is assumed that this has resulted in lower costs of production. (This is illustrated by the two sets of *MC* curves.) It is also assumed that the monopoly produces no external costs or benefits. The government decides to regulate the firm's pricing behaviour.

(a) What price will the unregulated monopoly charge if it wishes to maximise profits?

....

(b) What price will the government set if it wishes the monopoly to charge the socially efficient price?

....

(c) What price will the government set if it wishes the monopoly to make only normal profits?

....

(d) What price will the government set if it wishes the price to be that which would have occurred had the industry remained under perfect competition?

....

Q59. Select an industry that has been privatised and which has a government regulatory agency (such as OFWAT) concerned with its activities. Do a library search to find articles on the industry's performance and pricing policies and on any competition it faces.

Your search could include the following sources: *The Times Index, The Financial Times Index, The Economist Index,* the *Social Science Citation Index*, the *British Humanities Index*, the *Business Periodicals Index, Keesings Record of World Events*. Your library may have information on CD ROM. You could also search for information on the world-wide web, using the references in the Website Appendix in Sloman *Economics* (4th edition).

You should use these articles to write two brief reports on the industry's performance in the private sector, and on the effectiveness of regulation and attempts to inject competition into the industry. One report should be critical of the industry's performance and one should be in support. You should then write a conclusion stating (a) where the balance of the arguments lies; (b) in what ways regulation could be made more effective; (c) in what ways additional competition could be introduced into the industry.

Q60. Do a web search to find out up-to-date reports on the progress of privatisation and progress towards a competitive market in one or more central and eastern European countries or countries of the former Soviet Union. You could use the websites referred to in the Website Appendix in Sloman *Economics* (4th edition), especially from the list in sections A, I and J. Sites G1 (European Economy Supplement C), H14 and B32 are also useful.

Write a summary of the current situation and prospects for your chosen country or countries.

C DISCUSSION TOPICS AND ESSAYS

Q61. Compare the relative merits of green taxes and command-and-control systems as means of achieving an optimum use of the environment.

Q62. For what reasons is it difficult to reach international agreements on global environmental protection?

Q63. To what extent are urban traffic problems the result of externalities?

Q64. Compare the relative merits of road pricing in cities with schemes to restrict the entry of traffic into city centres.

Q65. To what extent can the provision of public transport solve the problem of urban traffic congestion?

Q66. Should certain monopolistic and restrictive practices be banned or should firms' practices be judged on a case-by-case basis?

Q67. Is it best to define the 'public interest' in terms of the level of deadweight welfare loss, when considering whether a firm should be referred to the Competition Commission?

Q68. Compare the differences of approach to (a) monopolies and restrictive practices and (b) mergers, in UK and EU legislation.

Q69. Give two examples of industries which are in part natural monopolies and which were once nationalised and then privatised. In each case consider whether any competition has been injected into the industry by or since privatisation. Consider ways of injecting further competition and any difficulties in so doing.

Q70. 'There are no economic arguments that uniquely favour either nationalisation or privatisation.' Discuss.

Q71. How successfully does the UK system of regulating privatised utilities protect the consumer's interest?

Q72. For what reasons have privatisation and market liberalisation created so many problems for people in transition economies?

Q73. **Debate**
Regulation is always inferior to competition as a means of protecting the consumers' interests.

D ARTICLES

In the article below, taken from the *OECD Observer* of February/March 1996, an evaluation is made of current attempts to integrate environmental policy with wider economic objectives. As the article points out, economic goals and policies are frequently in conflict with ecological concerns, and sustainable development is constantly being compromised.

Integrating environment and economy

National environmental plans are a key tool for making economic, sectorial and environmental goals more consistent. A number of plans of this kind have been adopted in OECD countries, in particular in Austria, Canada, France, Japan, the Netherlands, Portugal and the United Kingdom.

These plans, which are developed by environment ministries in conjunction with other departments, set medium-term goals for environmental protection and prescribe the means necessary to achieve them. The plans vary in scope and complexity, and in the degree of co-operation that they involve. Some plans establish quantitative targets, although most set qualitative goals. The French plan debated in the National Assembly in October 1990 proposed a comprehensive approach to the environmental challenges France will face by the end of the century, and listed the goals to be achieved. Some are quantitative, such as reducing SO_2 by 25 to 30 per cent by the year 2000, stabilising CO_2 emissions at 1990 figures by 2000–2005 and increasing the rate of household wastewater purification from one-third to two-thirds by the year 2000. It said nothing about the cost of these measures, or about the contributions that individual sectors would be expected to make.

The side-effects of intervention

Governments intervene in the economy by fixing prices, imposing and monitoring standards, paying subsidies or regulating sectors such as energy, agriculture or transport. Some of this intervention can be harmful to the environment since indirectly it masks the full cost of tapping and using environmental resources in these sectors. Determining which kinds of intervention have these side-effects is by no means easy. Yet correcting harmful intervention can both improve the environment and enhance economic efficiency.

Transport

Transport is one of the most highly regulated sectors in all OECD countries. Most government intervention is aimed at controlling the overall supply of transport, changing the distribution of individual modes of transport or introducing taxes and charges paid by users. As a rule, these measures take little or no account of the environment, and their effects may in some cases be damaging. For example, road transport has been heavily subsidised through the building of highway infrastructures, resulting in oversupply and overuse of this mode of transport and, from an environmental standpoint, in increased air and noise pollution. It has been estimated that in the United States road transport pays for only 79 per cent of its total costs through taxes and tolls paid by road-users, the remaining costs being borne by the government in what amounts to a direct subsidy to road transport. Moreover, if similar subsidies granted by cities for the construction of parking facilities are included, these figures are twice as high. The lower volume of subsidy in France is no doubt explained by the fact that petrol prices and road tolls are higher than in the United States.

Some kinds of tax relief can also encourage the excessive use of cars. In Germany, it has been estimated that tax deductions for people driving to work have increased traffic and hence generated additional costs, through accidents and air pollution, in the range of a billion Deutschmarks per year. In France, the fact that the annual car-registration tax is 50 per cent lower for models over five years old has the effect of keeping older, more polluting, cars on the road. By contrast, France's policy of granting a rebate to anyone purchasing a new car provided their old one is scrapped – a measure introduced in 1994 and which the government extended last year to stimulate car sales – may perhaps be a step in the right direction.

Identifying and eliminating these contradictions should be one of the main priorities in trying to integrate environmental and transport policies more effectively.

Agriculture

For many years the agricultural sector has benefited from a vast range of subsidies that have not taken environmental concerns into account: production incentives (for wheat, for example), income support (direct payments to farmers), set-aside programmes (subsidies for withdrawing land from agricultural use in order to reduce surpluses) and crop diversification schemes (quotas).

Some countries are now reducing their total support to the agricultural sector (Canada, New Zealand), while others (Sweden, for example) are increasing support as part of a restructuring of their subsidy systems.

From an environmental standpoint, these are encouraging developments in that they will reduce incentives for farmers to plant marginal land and to practise intensive farming, which generally leads to the overuse of fertilisers and pesticides. The reduction in the subsidies and tax concessions granted for wetland draining and land clearance in Europe and the United States has had the effect of slowing down the draining of wetlands and increasing forested areas.

But reducing subsidies can also have a harmful effect on the environment if farmers compensate for the income lost from withdrawing some land from use by stepping-up intensive farming of their remaining land. In mountain areas, lowering subsidies will in many cases prove harmful to the environment, since alpine pastures will no longer be grazed. This is one reason for the increasing talk of replacing subsidies with compensation to farmers for the positive externalities generated by their activities (maintaining the countryside, preserving wild fauna and flora, and so on).

Evaluating the environmental impact of lower subsidies is a more difficult and complex task than it initially seems. Integrating environmental and agricultural policies calls for awareness of both the beneficial and the adverse effects.

The OECD has long argued in favour of the better use of market mechanisms to integrate the environment and the economy. Markets must be left free to send signals, and prices should reflect the real scarcity of natural resources and the environmental costs stemming from economic activities.

Economic instruments, such as emission taxes or charges, service charges and product taxes which influence the market through financial transfers from polluters to the community, are especially effective tools for integrating the economy and the environment. They can even lead to the emergence of new markets, as occurred with tradable emission permits. Economic instruments generally have some definite advantages over the traditional regulatory instruments, being more cost-effective, more flexible and more efficient when there is a large number of polluters, in addition to providing a continual incentive to reduce pollution and a potential source of revenue. In a sluggish economy, it is not surprising that they are being increasingly widely used.

In 1987, economic instruments were being used in approximately 150 instances in 14 OECD countries, including some 80 examples of pollution taxes and charges. Between 1987 and 1993, the number rose by 25–50 per cent, depending on the country. The largest increase was in product taxes, especially energy taxes aimed at reducing CO_2 emissions in Denmark, Finland, the Netherlands, Norway and Sweden, and sulphur taxes in France, Norway and Sweden. Deposit-refund systems in packaging also grew considerably (between 35 and 100 per cent, depending on the country), while taxes and charges on polluting emissions seemed to be developing more slowly. Programmes of tradable permits or rights were expanding in the United States, but were limited in scope elsewhere.

The introduction of these economic instruments, especially new kinds of taxes, is sometimes combined with a restructuring of the existing tax system, as was done for energy taxes in Denmark and Sweden. It can also provide an opportunity to carry out a thoroughgoing tax reform, as in Sweden in 1991, including a reduction in income and wealth taxes, offset by new environmental taxes on SO_2, CO_2 and NO_x.

To integrate the environment and the economy, it will not be enough to internalise environmental costs using tools such as economic instruments; prices must also be made to reflect the real scarcity of natural resources. Resource pricing that does not take into account the scarcity of the resource in question (water, air, land, etc.) and the costs connected with its consumption (including delivery and depletion costs) encourages overuse and will lead to the deterioration of this resource. For example, water prices that are kept artificially low can result in excess consumption, the construction of unnecessary reservoirs or a drop in groundwater levels, with serious repercussions for the aquatic system. It can also lead to overuse of water for irrigation, with further contamination of aquifers by nitrates, phosphates and pesticides, and soil deterioration through compaction and salinification.

Inappropriate pricing of water for industrial uses can also lead companies to consume excessive amounts of water to dilute effluents in order to comply with legal standards on concentration, which can then make it more difficult to eliminate these pollutants. In recent years, a number of OECD countries (such as France, Germany and the United Kingdom) have begun to raise water prices, but the user-pays principle is still a long way from becoming a reality.

Structural and institutional reform is often necessary before environmental policy and other sectorial policies can be properly integrated. It is for this reason that many countries have set up interministerial working groups or commissions of inquiry to ensure effective co-operation among all the government departments concerned.

More extensive use of analytical tools which can improve decision-making, such as cost–benefit analysis, environmental impact assessments, and environmental indicators and accounting, can also contribute to policy integration by making both private and public decision-makers more aware of the environmental consequences of their actions.

There are also macroeconomic models of the environment that can take into account the main interactions between economy and environment, and give general pointers to possible convergence or trade-offs. In the Netherlands and Norway, models of this type have encouraged increased co-operation between the finance and environment ministries. Sectorial forecasting models can also be extremely useful for evaluating the environmental impact of the expansion of a given sector such as transport or tourism.

The integration of environmental, economic and sectorial policies remains a key factor for implementing sustainable development policies. It will require a strong political commitment to develop broader and more effective co-operation among those responsible for environmental policy and other policies at all strata of government, as well as between government and the private sector, non-governmental organisations and, more generally, the public at large.

© Reprinted from the *OECD Observer*, Michel Potier, 'Integrating environment and economy', Vol. 198, Feb/March 1996.

(a) Looking at the sections in the article on agriculture and transport, identify two examples where policy in these areas works against improving the environment and may, in fact, make things worse.

(b) Why are environmental taxes superior to using various forms of environmental regulation?

(c) How may government intervention in respect to environmental policy help to make the market mechanism work more efficiently?

(d) What reasons can you suggest as to why it is likely to be very difficult to establish an integrated environmental policy?

The congested state of Britain's roads and how to relieve this problem have taxed economists and politicians alike for many years. Some economists have argued that the only way to deal with this problem is to return to the price mechanism and to ensure that road use is reflected in the cost that a motorist pays. The greater the congestion and environmental damage, the greater the cost. In the following article, taken from the *Journal of the Institute of Economic Affairs*, volume 18, number 4 (December 1998), Alan Day considers the issues involved in road pricing and some of the implications of its use.

The case for road pricing

The basic economic argument for using the price mechanism wherever possible, in order to co-ordinate the decisions and actions of millions of individuals, is that it provides a flexible and subtle information system, on the basis of which the myriad decisions are made. Moreover, the rational reactions of individuals to this information interact in order to produce a social optimum in which the efficient use of resources is maximised. Clearly, the problem of transport co-ordination is an excellent example of the more general problem of co-ordinating innumerable individual decisions, about both the present and the future. The fundamental rule of classical microeconomics is that it is rational to carry out an activity right up to (but not beyond) the point at which the marginal cost of taking the activity any further just equals the marginal benefit enjoyed from taking it further. A classical example is that a firm acting in this way will necessarily maximise profits. More generally, welfare economics has long taught that the rule for society as a whole is to push to the point where marginal social cost equals marginal social benefit. Since long before environmentalism was even heard of, economists have argued that social costs (as opposed to purely private costs which enter into the profit and loss accounts or an ordinary firm) include the adverse impact on others of pollution and other externalities. These external costs are not borne by the polluter in normal commercial practice, unlike the way it pays for costs it imposes on the rest of society for which there is a market price, such as ordinary inputs of labour and materials. Welfare economists have long concluded that external costs (and benefits) should be charged to (or credited to) the individual or firm responsible for their creation. For many decades, economists have argued that the polluter should pay.

Roads and external costs

Economists have long tended to accept that roads must be seen as public goods (except for limited-access toll roads where twentieth-century motorways in several countries have revived the eighteenth-century tradition, as a means of financing new road construction). In the late 1950s and early 1960s, a considerable number of economists came to realise that electronics was developing to the point where much more subtle charging methods than old-fashioned toll gates could be used, on any part of the road network, and that the toll charged could vary with factors such as the distance travelled, the degree of congestion, and other external costs imposed on the rest of society such as noise, pollution and accidents. Despite attempts at obfuscation by politicians, there is now no doubt about the feasibility of a variety of suitable electronic devices, of which perhaps the most attractive is the replacement of the licence disc by the purchase of a transponder whose units of electronic charge would be progressively used up as the vehicle is driven on congested roads. The economic argument is generally presented in terms of congestion costs – each additional vehicle on a road above some level of free flow will impose additional costs on every other vehicle on the road, by making their journeys slower and so less efficient than they would otherwise be. But the argument extends naturally to other external costs – for example, accident costs, where it would be logical and probably practical for insurance premiums for vehicles to be paid at least in part out of the road charge. In general, this road charge on the individual user should be related to the marginal costs imposed on the rest of society – highest in congested conditions, lower in uncongested conditions but still calculated to cover pollution, noise, accident and road repair costs.

The fundamental economic argument considers that congestion, pollution and other similar externalities should be treated in exactly the same way as other costs, such as the use of scarce resources of labour or capital. This implies several things. One is that the charges should be paid by all road users, including trucks and buses, at levels reflecting as accurately as possible the relative costs imposed by different kinds of vehicle. Thus trucks and buses, which use more road space per vehicle-mile, would pay more. Another implication is that it is right that the charges are passed on in selling prices, just like any other cost. A firm whose productive activities cause congestion to others is imposing greater costs on the rest of society than another firm using different techniques. Another implication is that these external costs should be balanced against other, equally real, costs. For example, public transport may cause less pollution than private but it uses more labour, because private transport is a perfect example of DIY. The two costs – and many others – need to enter into the balance and the outcome needs to be duly weighed. The process of weighing will commonly lead to answers which do not accord with commonly held prejudices. For example, 'everyone knows' that public transport is more economical than private. But is it, when labour costs enter the picture? Indeed, it is not even clear that the pollution costs are on average in favour of public transport. Pollution is roughly proportional to fuel consumption. An average bus carries a load of about 9 passengers and does 7–9 miles per gallon (mpg) in urban conditions – say 60–70 traveller-miles on a gallon of fuel. A small car will do up to 50 mpg in similar conditions – so with a driver alone as the only traveller in the car, it pollutes rather more than a bus to achieve a given distance of travel, but with a driver and one passenger it causes less pollution per traveller-mile. This simple example should indicate that untutored common sense and *a priori* reasoning are no substitute for careful calculation.

Another lesson from all this line of argument is that the case for road pricing is not limited to congested city centres. Undoubtedly, the appropriate price would be higher there. Public transport is far and away the most competitive with private on 'line hauls' where large numbers of people (or loads of goods for that matter) are being carried together from A to B, or in very congested areas where trains can be run underground. It seems, however, that our society is developing away from these kinds of transport demands to one of a complex pattern of criss-cross journeys – as a result of factors such as greater job mobility, the now normal situation where both husbands and wives go out to work and the choice of most people for suburban and exurban living. I have little doubt that if the traffic Origin and Destination surveys that were fashionable in the 1960s were done again today, the apparent daily tidal flow towards and from the centre of cities and conurbations would break down into much more complex cross flows with the average movement being from farther out to nearer in to the centre – simply because most people live rather further out from the centre than their work places, but with relatively few people travelling all the way from periphery to centre.

Guiding investment decisions

The last lesson of the application of basic microeconomics to road pricing is in many ways the most fundamental and the one most often ignored. In the short run, the function of the price mechanism is to allocate existing resources. But in the medium and long term, its function is also to guide decisions about adding to our productive resources (investment) or allowing existing resources to wear out (disin-

vestment). It is quite indefensible to argue, as many do, that road pricing should simply be used to ration existing road space. Road pricing should be used, both as an allocative device and as a measure of whether or not to add to (or, indeed, subtract from) the existing road space: it can and should be used as an investment criterion. All this means – but this 'all' is a great deal – is that if road users are prepared to pay a price for the use of roads that is greater than the costs of providing additional road space (including all the costs, externalities, land costs, a sensible measure of the costs of disturbing any areas with special wildlife and all the other genuine costs which can be identified) then the additional road space should be built, and as in any other economic activity, the charge for the use of the new facility should be sufficient to finance its cost.

This point – pricing as an investment criterion – is the one where

we economists start to lose some of our conventionally-minded supporters. Will not new roads lead to an indefinite demand and renewed congestion? One answer is that this only happens when the pressure of frustrated demand has built up to enormous proportions. Certainly, road traffic can be expected to grow with real incomes – but why should this growth be so wrong (as long as, one must repeat, external costs are all paid by road users) when growth in demand for and consumption of other good things is accepted as a normal part of the growth of prosperity. Indeed, it is true that transport, both private and public, is a considerable user of depletable resources – but so are very many other economic activities. The basic lesson is that all economic activities – transport or non-transport, private or public – should follow so far as is possible the rule of marginal social cost equals marginal social benefit.

(a) Why is the current system of allocating road space socially inefficient?

(b) Identify the external costs of using a car to travel to work.

(c) How could road pricing ensure that external costs would be borne by the motorist? Can you see any difficulties in administrating such a system?

(d) If road pricing were to guide investment in transport infrastructure, would it matter if this resulted in the building of many more roads?

(e) The article does not talk about equity, and whether road pricing is a fair way to allocate road space. What arguments might be made against road pricing in this respect?

One of the most difficult aspects of competition policy for the Office of Fair Trading to deal with is the area of predatory pricing. The article below, taken from the *Independent on Sunday* of 12 September 1993, assesses the practice of predatory pricing and the problems it poses for the OFT.

When low prices hit the consumer

The bus users of Southend could not believe their luck last summer when the two biggest local operators locked horns in a dramatic fares war. It seemed a godsend to the Essex town and its elderly population, many of them dependent on public transport.

Southend Transport, run at arm's length by the council, launched a welter of new services, increasing frequency on popular routes and making pioneering forays into neglected districts. It billed the move a 'New Dawn for Public Transport' and advertised in colour brochures and on local radio.

Thamesway, the rival operator, owned by the aggressive national bus group Badgerline, retaliated at once. It slashed its Dayrider ticket – allowing unlimited travel all day – from £2 to £1 in what was trumpeted as a 'Summer Fares Bonanza'.

It all seemed wonderful – competition creating better value and more services for customers. But then Southend Transport cried foul. It accused Thamesway of 'predatory pricing' – deliberately cutting fares so much that Southend Transport would be forced out of business – and dashed off a formal complaint to the Office of Fair Trading.

Allegations of predatory pricing are two a penny from companies confronted with aggressive cuts by competitors. Thousands of complaints have been made in business sectors as varied as left-luggage lockers and satellite launches.

The theory is that a company sacrifices short-term profits to force a rival out of business, or at least out of a particular market. Once the competitor is ousted, the aggressor can lift its prices back up again and reap monopoly profits. High start-up costs deter the victim from re-entering the market.

Few industries have escaped such allegations. Luton Airport accuses BAA of predatory pricing at Stansted, claiming it cross-subsidises the loss-making airport with profits from Heathrow.

Last year, several long-distance coach operators alleged that British Rail was also on the predatory track, with its cut-price SuperApex fares on InterCity routes.

Raannd Systems, based near Edinburgh, recently claimed that Mors, its French rival, unfairly undercut it in a battle to supply left-luggage lockers to railway stations. It has taken its complaint to Brussels.

No product or service is too big or too small. Russia and China have been accused of predatory pricing of their satellite-launching services for television and telephone companies, at about $60m (£39m) a throw.

Most recently, Newspaper Publishing, publisher of the *Independent* (and this newspaper), has accused Rupert Murdoch's News International of slashing the price of the loss-making *Times* in a deliberate attempt to cripple the *Independent*, which was only just breaking even before the price cut.

Complaining about predatory pricing can be a dangerous game. First, it draws more attention to the favourable price offered by a competitor. Secondly, the complainant is left open to accusations of whingeing about something that is plainly a bonus to the consumer, in the short term at least. And third, the offence is difficult to prove and even harder to correct in time.

Since the 1980 Competition Act, the Office of Fair Trading has formally investigated only seven allegations of predatory pricing. And just two of the outcomes could be considered a victory for the accuser.

Both concerned bus services. In one case, a company called Easy Rider Minicoaches withdrew from operating a route in Bognor Regis after Southdown, its main rival, slashed prices to uneconomic levels. The case was referred to the Monopolies & Mergers Commission, which found against Southdown (now operating as Sussex Coastline Buses) in June, after judging that its behaviour 'may be expected to result in higher fares and lower levels of quality and service on certain routes'.

In an earlier investigation, the MMC judged an Inverness operator, Highland Scottish Omnibuses, to be practising a predatory pricing policy that helped to propel rival company Inverness Traction into receivership in April 1989.

The only non-bus complaint investigated by the OFT concerned Becton Dickinson, a supplier of hypodermic syringes to the NHS. The OFT threw out the complaint in 1988 after judging that the company's prices were not below its short-run marginal costs – the strictest standard for establishing predatory pricing.

In the US and some other countries (see below), predatory pricing is taken more seriously, but has been just as hard to prove. In the UK, the Government has rejected proposals to upgrade the rules. Instead of introducing fines of up to 10 per cent of turnover for companies abusing market power, it opted in April for a weaker 'fine-tuning' solution.

This will give the OFT greater powers of investigation, including seizure of documents. It will also be able to restrain anti-competitive behaviour while its inquiries continue. But this is not yet law. Meanwhile, investigations take between four and 17 months to complete.

According to the OFT, the Competition Act 'is not meant to be used to protect a company whose sales are falling or static, or whose market share is being reduced simply because it is less efficient than its competitors or because, for other reasons, it is less able to meet the needs of the market'.

It does not spell out anti-competitive practices. Instead, it aims to counter policies or practices that 'prevent, exclude or restrict competition'. Critics say this catch-all phrase is so loosely worded that it catches nothing.

For a start, the scope of the Act is limited: companies with a market share of less than 25 per cent are exempt if turnover is below £5m.

Sir Bryan Carsberg, the OFT's director-general, says: 'The distinction between a vigorous response to competition, which is generally to the benefit of consumers, and a predatory response, which may offer consumers advantages in the short run but will reduce competition in the long run, can be a fine one.'

Before acting, he has to be convinced that the market is so structured that predation is a sensible and feasible business strategy for the price-cutter; that the alleged predator is incurring losses as a result of its behaviour; and that it is deliberately cutting prices to put a rival out of business.

This last factor usually means the price cutting has to be prolonged – otherwise it can be seen as a marketing ploy or special offer. And by the time the price cut is established as permanent, it can be too late for the complainant.

Newspaper Publishing, which put in a submission to the OFT on Thursday, believes it has a strong case against the *Times*, which from last Monday cut its weekday cover price from 45p to 30p.

Because about 18p of the *Times* price goes to the retailer and wholesaler, the cut is more savage than it appears. News International has reduced its sales revenue per copy from 27p to 12p – a 56 per cent cut.

But the calculation is more complicated because newspapers also receive a large proportion of their income from advertising. News International will argue that its ad revenues will be boosted by the increased circulation generated by the price cut. In the first few days, its circulation has increased by between 25 and 30 per cent.

Much may depend on how strictly the OFT interprets predatory pricing. The strictest definition is where the product price is less than marginal cost – the cost of producing one more copy of the *Times*. But the OFT, as it explained in the case of Becton Dickinson, may opt for the looser definition – where price is less than the *average* unit cost of the *Times*.

As for Southend Transport, it learnt last month that it had lost its battle. After a nine-month investigation, the OFT ruled that Thamesway's was 'a legitimate pricing strategy' and cleared it of any anti-competitive behaviour.

Graeme Torrance, director and general manager of Southend Transport, responded: 'We're disappointed, obviously, though we accept the OFT's judgment. But it took up an enormous amount of management time.'

It may also have hastened its demise as an independent company. During the course of the inquiry it was sold to a new parent, British Bus.

© Patrick Hosking, *Independent*, 12/9/93

(a) What is predatory pricing? Give examples.

(b) In what ways will the consumer gain and lose from predatory pricing?

(c) In what two ways does the article suggest that predatory pricing might be identified? Explain how they differ.

Privatisation has been, and continues to be, a contentious issue. The article below, taken from *The Economist* of 13 June 1998, shows why it is becoming increasingly difficult for those who argue against it to make a case.

The end of privatisation?

Labour's reluctance to use the p-word is oddly out of tune with its usual tendency to trumpet any successful British export. For privatisation is one British invention that continues to be emulated around the world. Flotations of privatised assets are expected to take place in more than 100 countries in 1995–2000 and to raise over £120 billion ($200 billion). The reasons for this are not hard to understand: privatisation works, as any fair reading of the British record amply illustrates.

First, the benefits to British public finances over the past two decades have been considerable. The cumulative proceeds from privatisation between 1979 and 1997 were more than £90 billion (at current prices). And the benefits go far wider than the capital account.

According to a 1997 study by National Economic Research Associates (NERA), in the first year of Mrs Thatcher's government (i.e. 1979–80) 33 state enterprises, all later to be privatised, absorbed £500m of public funds as well as more than £1 billion in loan finance. By 1987, these same companies were contributing £8 billion a year to the Treasury in share sales, tax receipts and dividends. This dramatic improvement conceals some striking individual achievements. British Steel, which ate up an annual subsidy of £600m–£1 billion on a turnover of less than £3 billion before privatisation, is now one of the lowest-cost steel producers in the world. British Airways is the world's most profitable airline, and is cited as a model by the would-be privatisers running Air France.

Customers have also benefited. A 1996 study from the National Audit Office found that service had improved significantly in telecoms and to a lesser extent in electricity, gas and water since privatisation. Since privatisation of telecoms and the introduction of digital exchanges, there has been a 50-fold reduction in faults in trunk calls and a 30-fold reduction in faults in local ones.

Most customers are also paying less for their utility bills. Since privatisation, the average telephone bill has declined in real terms by 49 per cent. But even in industries where it has taken time to introduce competition, regulation has meant that prices have fallen – the average domestic gas bill is down by 31 per cent since privatisation, and the average domestic electricity bill by 20 per cent. Real competition is just beginning in these markets, and should force prices down further. Water and sewerage are the exceptions: average domestic household bills rose by 36 per cent and 42 per cent respectively. But this is largely a result of having to meet European environmental standards, and to make up for decades of under-investment.

Water apart, the dramatic improvements in price and service give the lie to the claim that customers have been the prime victims of privatisation. Another frequently voiced fear was that privatisation would lead to a deterioration in safety. The evidence points the other way. In most privatised industries there have been 'widespread and sustained improvements in occupational safety,' according to NERA. Its 1997 study points out that the safety records at British Gas, British Steel, and in the supply of electricity and water, have also been significantly better than in the economy as a whole.

There is, of course, a valid argument that many of these post-privatisation improvements and price cuts owed as much to changes in technology and the decline in fossil-fuel prices as they did to changes in ownership. And it is also true that the performance of many of the privatised industries improved in the run-up to their sale. Yet would these improvements have taken place if the threat of privatisation had been removed? Dieter Helm, director of Oxford Economic Research Associates, is doubtful. He says the speed of change achieved could not have been matched in the public sector. Any government, whatever its ideological hue, would have been limited by public-sector borrowing constraints, as well as by the fear of industrial unrest.

Yet facts alone do not seem enough to win the argument. Poll evidence suggests that privatisation has never been wildly popular, and that it has been getting less so as time goes by. In 1983 MORI found that 43 per cent of people wanted more privatisation; by 1992 that was down to 24 per cent and last year a poll found just 19 per cent in favour of privatising the Underground.

Why is this? Many people believe that the most recent privatisations do not make sense, because it is hard to introduce competition in some industries, such as rail. But this ignores the role of regulation in mimicking competition – something that has improved the electricity and gas industries, even though the introduction of real competition is only now being completed.

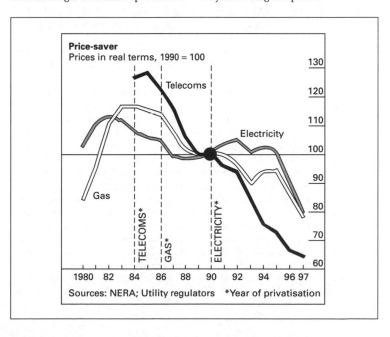

Price-saver
Prices in real terms, 1990 = 100

Sources: NERA; Utility regulators   *Year of privatisation

(a) Outline the main arguments in favour of privatisation.

(b) What evidence does the article present to support its case that privatisation has been successful?

(c) Why is regulation so important in ensuring that the benefits of privatisation continue?

One of the few remaining public-sector industries that has not been privatised is the Post Office. However, its days as a public-sector monopoly, protected from market forces, appear numbered. All that seems to be up for debate is the manner in which it should be freed to operate independently. In the article below, taken from *The Independent* of 26 October 1998, Bill Robinson considers the issues surrounding the privatisation of the Post Office and one alternative way in which the Post Office might be given market freedom.

How the Post Office can be set free

The debate about the future of the Post Office is warming up again. The market in postal services, already transformed by fax, e-mail and the private courier, faces further upheaval as collection, sorting and bulk transport of mail is opened up to pan-European competition.

There is no reason why your letter to France could not be collected and taken to France by the French PTT rather than the Royal Mail, and no reason why the two carriers should not compete directly for your business. The only natural monopoly in postal services is the local delivery network.

The post is very much a network business, rather like airlines. Other national postal carriers are already competing, as airlines compete, by forging alliances to establish the best network. The Dutch Post Office acquired TNT in 1996. The German Post Office took a 25 per cent stake in DHL earlier this year.

The UK Post Office needs to be set free to respond to these initiatives. It is a profitable organisation, and it needs to put more of those profits back into the business (it is currently required to hand over too much to the Government). It needs to be able to tap the market for funds when it sees fit. And above all it needs freedom to make acquisitions and enter into joint ventures.

So why don't we just privatise its operations? The short answer is that the Government is committed to keeping them in the public sector. And if we give it more freedom in the public sector, it will be our money that it spends. The Treasury, that zealous guardian of the taxpayer's money, has always resisted demands by nationalised industries to invest more, because such investment counts as public investment, paid for by higher taxes or higher borrowing.

However, a knee-jerk reaction against public investment is old Treasury think-

ing. In opposition, Gordon Brown repeatedly declared that Britain needed to invest more. In office he has changed the control system of public spending to relax the constraints on public investment. New Treasury thinking is the so-called 'golden rule' that government current spending must not exceed current income, but capital spending is not constrained. So under the new rules the Post Office could be allowed to invest more, even if that does drive up public borrowing.

The only good reason for stopping such investment is that it might be unproductive. Here the Treasury has a stronger argument. The Post Office borrows at the same low rate as the Government, because lenders believe the taxpayer stands behind them. The hurdle rate for its investment is thus too low. Demand for these cheap funds exceeds supply, so the Treasury rations them, both to prevent misallocation of resources (excessive investment in postal services) and to stop the Post Office gaining an unfair advantage over its competitors.

However, capital rationing is incompatible with commercial freedom. The solution is to allow the Post Office to borrow all it wants, but on commercial terms and at a commercial price. The Government must formally remove its guarantee on Post Office borrowing. This, however, requires a major rethink of the Post Office's status and of the incentives and disciplines under which its managers work.

London Economics has been doing research in this area for some years, and has long argued for the independent publicly owned company or corporation (IPOC) which would reproduce commercial discipline inside the public sector. An independent Post Office, like the independent Bank of England

or the independent BBC, would be set objectives by government and then be allowed to get on and manage. There would be no ministerial interference in pay, no Treasury control over investment, no sudden changes in the price of stamps or the Post Office's required cash contribution, just because the government of the day has problems with its own finances.

Experience from other institutions and other countries shows the benefits of creating an arm's-length relationship between the owners of an organisation, who set long-term objectives, and the managers who take all the short-term decisions. The rules of the game in an IPOC are that the managers can do what they like, but if at the end of (say) five years they have not delivered, their jobs are on the line.

This is essentially how the modern plc is run. Shareholders appoint managers to run the company and deliver a profit. They can do as they please while they are in charge, but if they fail to deliver the profits, they go.

There are important differences between the Post Office and a normal plc. Like most other organisations in the public sector it has a social objective – for example, to maintain a universal letter delivery service. These objectives could be spelt out in a charter. The task of the IPOC would be to meet these social objectives in the most cost-efficient way.

This would in practice require the imposition of three key disciplines on the IPOC, which mirror the three main commercial disciplines on the managers of a plc:

• Cost discipline in the plc comes from the objective of maximising profits. This would be reproduced in the IPOC by setting profit targets.

- Price discipline in the plc comes from competition, or failing that from regulation. The Post Office already faces stiff competition in much of its business. The monopoly part (letters under £1) would need to be regulated.

- Investment discipline in the plc comes from the requirement to make a commercial rate of return and the ultimate threat of takeover or bankruptcy if too many projects make losses. The Post Office as an IPOC must be subjected to the same disciplines of market rates of interest (no government guarantee) and the ultimate sanction of losing the business if it fails.

To impose the proper discipline on potential lenders to the Post Office, the Government must formally remove its guarantee. It must also spell out what would happen in the event that the IPOC running the Post Office fails to meet its targets. This would be a public sector version of bankruptcy, in which lenders to the IPOC would lose money (no government bailout) and those running the IPOC would lose their jobs.

People will argue that this is unrealistic – that postal services are too important to be allowed to cease. But this is to confuse the activity (postal services) with the IPOC that manages the activity. The activity must always continue,

but we must have institutional arrangements whereby it can be taken out of the hands of a failed IPOC, which is then wound up.

Wouldn't it be simpler just to privatise and regulate? Not necessarily. The key to getting public sector organisations to perform more efficiently lies not in the change in ownership *per se*, but in the accompanying changes in incentives and culture.

In the end it all comes down to human behaviour. We could get results from the Post Office operating as an IPOC under a charter as good as from a Post Office plc – and we would avoid the well-known privatisation problem of selling it off too cheaply.

(a) What is a natural monopoly? Is the Post Office a natural monopoly?

(b) Is the government's wish to keep the Post Office in the public sector based on economic arguments or merely a political judgement?

(c) What is an independent publicly owned company (IPOC)? How would it both differ from, and be similar to, a plc?

(d) 'The key to getting public-sector organisations to perform more efficiently lies not in the change in ownership *per se*, but in the accompanying changes in incentives and culture.' What are the implications of this both for the privatisation of the Post Office and privatisation as a strategy in general?

The importance of privatisation for the economies of Eastern Europe is clearly illustrated in the following article, taken from the *OECD Observer* of August/September 1998. It describes how the Polish economy will need further privatisation, if it is to maintain its impressive growth record of the past few years.

Poland: privatisation as the key to efficiency

A thriving private sector is the force behind Poland's buoyant economy, which is now in its seventh year of continuous expansion. The number of new private firms soared in the first half of the 1990s and has continued to increase rapidly since. Meanwhile, privatisation has reduced the size of the public sector, which nonetheless is still quite prominent across the economy, with a strong presence in mining, fuels, power generation, defence, heavy chemicals, telecommunications, air and rail transport, sugar, spirits and insurance.

Corporate performance in the public sector has been much weaker than in private enterprises and has acted as a brake on the economy as a whole. Profitability has improved in the private

sector since 1995 and deteriorated in the public sector, and while investment in the private sector has soared, it has stagnated in public enterprises. Yet firms in the public sector have received most of the subsidies. This difference in performance might be partly explained by the fact that privatisation began with the strongest companies, leaving the rest to struggle on under public ownership. However, some empirical studies suggest that there was no such selection bias.

Another possible reason lies in the inherited liabilities carried by some traditional heavy industries which the newly emerged private firms do not have, such as an antiquated capital stock and environmental drawbacks.

Arguably a more important cause of the discrepancy in performance is poor corporate governance in the public sector. Even unprofitable public enterprises can award relatively high wages, and spending priorities are not always geared to restructuring, as documented by Poland's Supreme Board of Inspection, which recently published a list of cases of ill-judged expenditure.

In short, financial discipline is an ingredient in short supply in Poland's public enterprises. Wages are negotiated according to a national norm established between social partners. This practice is not that unusual in Europe, but in Poland the leverage of the unions in the negotiations is particularly strong, limiting the influence of market forces on public pay deals. As a result, the national norm, which is intended to act as a ceiling to wage deals, in fact works as a floor. Also, in some firms, the remuneration of managers is set as a multiple of the workers average wage rather than as a function of corporate performance. Moreover, a number of public enterprises do not honour their tax and social security obligations, which is a *de facto* and quite perverse form of subsidy. Admittedly such arrears, and more importantly, outright evasion, are also observed in the private sector.

Although the state or the local government nominally owns those firms, in practice it fails to control them. Its inability to sanction mismanagement is in part due to political pressure from a broad range of sectoral lobbies. The fact that their demands are accommodated quite easily is helped by the lack of transparency in the handling of public money. This is a weakness which a new draft law is trying to correct. On top of that, the public administration is not equipped well enough, whether it be in logistics or skills, to be able to keep up with operations in the several thousand enterprises that are still in the public sector.

The renewed momentum

To overcome these problems the government, formed after the parliamentary elections in September 1997, has decided to accelerate privatisation. After all, private investors, be they foreign or domestic, would be in a better position than the cash-strapped state to provide the money, skills and know-how Polish firms need to boost their competitiveness. And these new stakeholders would obviously have strong incentives to impose hard budgetary constraints and would, if necessary, be freer to liquidate non-viable activities.

The menu of privatisation formulae on offer is an impressive one, but its diversity has not always helped to speed up the sales. Although the proliferation of schemes to transfer ownership reflects a multi-track approach with strong pragmatic merits, it has in some cases resulted in procrastination, slowing the process down. The new government is determined to push privatisation along quickly, since it faces strong budgetary pressures from ambitious reforms in pensions, health and education, as well as decentralisation. Moreover, the State still owes very large amounts to those whose property was illegally confiscated under communism and on account of past unpaid pension and wage hikes.

After the sale of a major bank and a large copper company last year, a whole series of important enterprises are to be privatised in the near future, particularly in banking, insurance, telecommunications, power supply and air transport. In addition, the government is considering sell-offs in sectors, such as mining, which were previously off-bounds. It is also contemplating removing some of the legal strictures which hold up privatisation, such as the approval of the Council of Ministers, which is obligatory even for some relatively small deals.

Although faster privatisation may be both feasible and desirable in Poland, it will not take place overnight. It is an inherently complex process, involving a redistribution of property and other rights on an enormous scale. It is intertwined with restructuring, deregulation and demonopolisation, each of which is a challenge on its own. Moreover, privatisation alone is not a sufficient condition of good governance; other factors include managerial skills, the existence of performance incentives, transparency and a sound legal and business environment. But can the government really afford delays? Probably not. Poland's own experience to date, as well as that of some other OECD countries, strongly suggests that the benefits of postponing the divestiture of state assets – even for prior restructuring or consolidation into larger entities – would be dwarfed by the costs. Privatising sooner, while the economy is growing strongly, rather than letting the costs build up further, would seem to be the best way forward.

(a) What forms can privatisation take in a transition economy?

(b) What weaknesses do Poland's public-sector enterprises have, and how do these weaknesses impinge upon the performance of the economy in general?

(c) What difficulties are there in achieving a faster rate of privatisation in Poland?

ANSWERS

Q1. Use of the environment for mining, farming, etc. reduces its amenity value. Use of the environment as a dump reduces its productivity for producing primary products. Use of the environment as a dump reduces its amenity value.

Q2. E.

Q3. *Yes*: (a), (c) and (e); *No*: (b) and (d). In the case of (c), technological progress has tended to be environmentally friendly (but not always so). The reasons include: greater miniaturisation, and hence a lower demand for raw materials; higher raw material prices leading to pressures to develop more resource-efficient products and processes; the pressure of public opinion; government policies (laws, taxes and subsidies promoting more environmentally friendly technology).

Q4. (a) (iii), (b) (i), (c) (iv), (d) (ii).

Q5. (a) Q_3, (b) Q_1, (c) Q_2, (d) Q_4.

Q6. C. By levying a charge that would fully compensate sufferers (i.e. a charge equal to the marginal pollution cost), the *MB–MC* line would shift downwards by the amount of the charge (i.e. by the height of the

$MC_{pollution}$ curve). Profits for the polluter would be maximised where the new MB–MC curve crosses the horizontal axis: at Q_3.

Q7. D. The socially efficient tax rate is equal to the marginal external cost of pollution: i.e. $MC_{pollution}$. At the socially efficient level of output (Q_3), this will be equal to an amount OP_3.

Q8. *Technology-based standards.* Here the focus is on restricting the amount of pollution generated, irrespective of its impact.

Ambient-based standards. Here the focus is on restricting the environmental impact of the pollution.

Social-impact standards. Here the focus is on restricting the undesirable effects on people.

Q9. (a) and (c) *True.*

(b) and (d) *False.*

Q10. *(a)* Firm A 100 units; Firm B zero. (It is more expensive for firm A to reduce the emission of the pollutant than for firm B, and so it would be profitable for both firms if firm B reduced its emission by the full 100 units and then sold its 50 units of credits to firm A, permitting firm A to continue emitting 100 units.)

(b) The price would be somewhere between £1000 per unit (the lower limit for firm B to gain) and £2000 per unit (the upper limit for firm A to gain). This is a bilateral monopoly situation (i.e. only one seller and one buyer) and thus there is no unique equilibrium price. The actual price would depend on the outcome of negotiations between A and B.

(c) Firm A 30 units (a reduction of 70 units); Firm B 70 units (a reduction of 30 units). Firm B can reduce emissions of the pollutant by up to 30 units at an MC less than £4000, and hence more cheaply than A. Beyond this level, however, it would be cheaper for A to make the necessary reductions and sell the credits to B (allowing B to continue emitting 70 units).

(d) Again, given that the firms are operating under bilateral monopoly, the price would be negotiated. If a separate price is negotiated for each credit traded, then the upper price limit for each one would be the MC to B and the lower limit would be £4000, the MC to A.

Q11. There may not be the political will, given that governments are concerned about *domestic* interests; it is difficult to measure the amount of pollution caused by each country; it is difficult to identify the global effects of individual countries reducing their pollution; it is difficult to agree on the amount that each country should reduce emissions.

Q12. *(a)* *Break the agreement.* (If it is assumed that other countries will stick to the agreement, this country would save costs by not sticking to the agreement, but would gain most of the benefits from the other countries sticking to it.)

(b) *Break the agreement.* (If it is assumed that other countries will *not* stick to the agreement, this country will save costs by not sticking to it, and would only sacrifice the small benefit it would get directly by sticking to it.)

(c) Because either strategy would lead to a breakdown of the agreement and hence all countries being worse off than without the agreement.

Q13. C. In all the other cases the demand for roads is to serve some *other* purpose than mere travelling: whether to go to work, to go shopping or to deliver goods. In the case of going for a Sunday afternoon drive, the pleasure is gained directly from the journey.

Q14. *tolls* (note that some taxes are nevertheless included in the 'price' of motoring, even though the motorist does not pay them for using a particular stretch of road).

Q15. *marginal.*

Q16. *costs.*

Q17. *True.* The higher the level of congestion, the longer will be the time taken to make a journey and the greater will be the level of frustration experienced. These are both costs to the motorists of that specific journey and are thus marginal costs.

Q18. (c) and (g) *No.* These are *fixed* costs of owning a car. There is no *additional* cost incurred under these two headings each time the motorist makes a journey. All the other costs, however, *are* variable costs with respect to car usage and therefore have a positive marginal cost. Note that (d) and (h) are not direct *monetary* costs, but nevertheless are a cost to the motorist of making the journey. In the case of (d) we are only referring to the cost the specific motorist experiences from the congestion; we are not referring to the congestion costs imposed on others by the motorist's journey.

Q19. B. As incomes grow so the demand for road use grows rapidly: more people feel they can afford private transport rather than public transport; people use cars increasingly for leisure purposes; more families can afford more than one car. The price and cross-price elasticities of demand, on the other hand, are relatively inelastic: many people feel that there is no close substitute for private motoring.

Q20. Examples include: congestion; pollution (from exhaust fumes); accidents; noise.

Q21. *False.* The optimum level would be that where the marginal social benefit is equal to the marginal social cost. This may well be at a level of road use where there are some external costs. (If environmentalists object that this involves putting too little weight on protecting the environment, an economist would reply that the answer would be simply to attach a higher value to these external costs. This value, however, would have to be very high indeed, if not infinite, if the optimum level of road use were to generate *no* environmental externalities.)

Q22. **(a)** *OH*: where marginal private cost (*MC*) equals marginal private benefit, which, in the absence of externalities on the demand side, equals marginal social benefit (*MSB*).

(b) *OE*: where *MSC* = *MSB*.

(c) *FG*.

(d) A level equal to the marginal external cost: i.e. *CD* at the optimum level of road use, *OE*.

Q23. Environmental costs.

Equity: losers are unlikely to be compensated.

Congestion may not be solved. It may encourage a faster rate of growth of traffic.

Q24. *False.* Any positive marginal congestion tax rate will *reduce* congestion. To reduce congestion to the *optimum* level, however, the congestion tax would have to equal the size of the congestion externality at the optimum level of road use.

Q25. C. It is very difficult to measure the exact size of the congestion externalities and therefore difficult to determine the socially optimal level of charge.

Q26. When there are ready alternatives for the motorist: in terms of altering the timing of journeys, or the route, or the means of transport. For example, road pricing will be more effective if there is an attractive form of public transport available.

Q27. (a) (iv), (b) (vi), (c) (iii), (d) (v), (e) (vii), (f) (ii), (g) (i).

Q28. (a) (ii), (b) (i), (c) (iii).

Q29. *False.* Any firm in a dominant market position (whether a monopolist or an oligopolist) can be investigated if it is suspected of abusing its market power.

Q30. B. The mere possession of power is not seen to be important. What is important is how the firm exercises its power: whether it abuses its power by acting to restrict competition.

Q31. (a) (iii), (b) (viii), (c) (vii), (d) (ii), (e) (v), (f) (vi), (g) (i), (h) (ix), (i) (iv).

Q32. **(a)** (ii), (iv) and (vii).

(b) (ii), (iv), (v), (viii) and (ix).

(c) (i), (iii), (vi) and (vii).

Q33. *True.*

Q34. *horizontal.* This type of merger will reduce the number of firms in the relevant segment of the market.

Q35. Ways include: economies of scale from rationalisation, greater countervailing power to drive down prices charged by suppliers to the firm, increased power to compete more effectively against an already established large firm, increased ability to afford costly research and development.

Q36. Whether the merger is likely to impede effective competition.

Q37. *Yes*: (b), (c), (f). *No*: (a), (d), (e). (See Sloman *Economics* (4th edition) page 352.)

Q38. *True.* It can decide to block the merger, permit it, or permit it subject to various conditions to safeguard competition.

Q39. *True.* (a), (b) and (d). *False* (c) (the Secretary of State can choose whether or not to refer the proposed merger to the CC), (e) (the Secretary of State can choose whether or not to accept the recommendations of the CC).

Q40. Ways include: sale of a nationalised firm directly to a private-sector firm (e.g. Rover Group to British Aerospace); sale of government's shares in otherwise private company (e.g. BP); introduction of private contractors into parts of the public sector (e.g. contract cleaners in National Health Service hospitals); introduction of private firms selling directly to the public in otherwise nationalised industries (e.g. private canteens); sale of public sector assets (e.g. council houses).

Q41. Reasons include: poor profitability may be a reflection of low demand rather than ownership; prices may be kept deliberately low by the government for social/political/macroeconomic reasons; costs may be similarly high if it were under private ownership.

Q42. Although (b), (e), (f), (g) and (h) would seem at first sight to be arguments in favour of privatisation and (a) and (c) against, most of the arguments are inconclusive (which is part of the reason why politicians will continue to argue). The extent to which any industry, private or public, operates in the public interest depends on the way in which it is run, the degree of government intervention and the amount of competition faced, and these will not necessarily depend on whether the industry is publicly or privately owned. (How would you reply to argument (e)?)

Q43. To maximise revenue from the sale, the government will want the industry to be as attractive (profitable) as possible to potential shareholders. This will be the case if the industry is sold as a monopoly with the prospect of large supernormal profits. But this will conflict with the second objective of making the industry as competitive as possible.

Q44. *True.* Monopolies can be inefficient in both the public sector and the private sector. Similarly the government can be 'tough' or take a *laissez-faire* approach with both public and private industries.

Q45. D. The socially efficient output for a firm is where *MSB* = *MSC*. In the absence of externalities and in the first-best situation this will be where *P* = *MC*.

Q46. A. The second-best pricing formula is $P = MSC + X$ (where X is the average of other industries' price above their *MSC*). Given that, on average, other firm's externalities are zero, this formula gives $P = (MC - 5\%) + 15\% = MC + 10\%$.

Q47. D. If for reasons of equity it is desired to help a particular section of the community, it is best (*ceteris paribus*) to do this from *general* taxation, otherwise it would be unfair on those who have to pay the subsidy. For example, in A, why should urban bus users have any greater obligation than others to help the rural users?

Q48. *(a)* *Yes*. There are separate regulatory bodies for each regulated industry, such as OFGEM for the fuel (gas and electricity) industry, OFTEL for the telecommunications industry and OFWAT for the water industry.

(b) *No*. Only those parts where it is felt by the government that there is inadequate competition.

(c) *No*. It is of the form *RPI* minus *X*.

(d) *Yes*.

(e) *Yes*. This enters the formula as an extra term *Y*, so that the formula becomes *RPI* − *X* + *Y*.

(f) *Yes*, if *X* − *Y* is greater than the rate of inflation.

(g) *Yes*.

(h) *No*. The price-setting formula may be changed before the end of the period if circumstances change, such as a larger value for *X* than had been anticipated.

(i) *No*. They are also concerned to prevent practices which could be anti-competitive (e.g. attempts to compete unfairly against rivals in order to prevent them getting a larger share of the market).

(j) *Yes*.

Q49. *False*. It does just the opposite: it removes the incentive to reduce costs. What is the point of reducing costs if the regulators simply reduce prices to prevent profits rising?

Q50. E. The regulator is 'captured' by the industry.

Q51. Advantages: it gives the regulator discretion to take account of the specific circumstances of the industry; it is flexible, allowing the licence and price formula to be changed as circumstances change; the price formula gives the industry an incentive to be as efficient as possible, since that way it will be able to make more profit *and keep it* (provided that this does not then lead to a higher value being given to *X*). Disadvantages: if the value of *X* is too low (which it might become if there are substantial technical advances in the industry), the firm might make excessive profits; if, on the other hand, *X* is changed to reflect reductions in costs, this then removes the incentive referred to above in the list of advantages;

a large amount of power is vested in the regulator, who is not democratically accountable; regulation has become increasingly complex, which makes it more difficult for the industries to plan; regulation can involve a time-consuming 'game' between the regulator and the industry; regulatory capture.

Q52. Dividing up the industry into a separate company owning the pipelines and other companies using the pipelines and supplying the customers; forcing the pipeline company to charge the same rates to all companies using the pipelines (including itself, if it is still allowed to supply gas); forcing the pipeline company to allow any supplier meeting safety standards to use the pipelines; breaking up the part of the industry producing gas and supplying gas to customers into several companies; allowing customers to choose from a number of different suppliers (this is possible through metering, provided that central records are kept of the gas metered into the system by each company and the gas used by each consumer allocated to that company).

Q53. *Yes*: (a), (b), (d) and (e).
No: (c), (f) and (g). In the case of (f), bonuses were nearly always awarded. The problem was that they were often awarded even though targets had not been met, or had only been met by using bogus figures. In the case of (g), the problem was that prices were often set *below* equilibrium. This resulted in shortages and queues.

Q54. (a) and (c) are examples of insider privatisation: where ownership passes to management and/or workers. The rest are examples of outsider privatisation: where the new shareholders are not employees of the company.

Q55. *Yes*: (a), (c), (d) and (e).
No: (b) and (f). Although output has fallen in many industries, shortages have been reduced or eliminated as a result of prices rising towards or to equilibrium.

Q56. Ways include: careful management of the economy to avoid inflation; creating as much competition as possible, and not merely privatising firms as monopolies; introducing a regulatory regime that will prevent the abuse of monopoly/oligopoly power; encouraging systems of corporate governance that are responsive to consumers and other outside stakeholders; improving incentives for inward investment; improving the financial, communications and transport infrastructure.

13 Macroeconomic Issues I: Economic Growth, Unemployment and Inflation

A REVIEW

Chapters 13 and 14 offer a basic overview of the principal macroeconomic variables within the economy: *growth, unemployment, inflation* and *the balance of payments*. In this chapter we focus on the first three of these variables. In Chapter 14 we will look at the open economy.

13.1 The scope of macroeconomics

(Pages 380–2)

Q1. Which of the following are macroeconomics issues?

(a) An increase in the number of job vacancies.   *Yes/No*
(b) The problems faced by a firm relocating in the south of England.   *Yes/No*
(c) Industrial action by the teaching unions.   *Yes/No*
(d) An increase in the level of taxation.   *Yes/No*
(e) A slowdown in the growth of the economy.   *Yes/No*
(f) The privatisation of the electricity industry.   *Yes/No*
(g) Unemployment in the coal industry.   *Yes/No*
(h) A rise in interest rates.   *Yes/No*

Q2. (Actual) economic growth is defined as.................

....

Q3. In which two decades between 1930 and 2000 was unemployment the lowest in most industrialised economies?

....

Q4. Inflation is defined as:
A. The difference in the price level this year compared with the same time last year.
B. The rise in costs over the previous twelve months.
C. The absolute increase in *average* prices over the previous twelve months.
D. The percentage increase in the average level of prices over the previous twelve months.
E. The percentage expansion of the economy over the previous twelve months.

13.2 Economic growth

(Pages 382–3) When discussing economic growth we need to distinguish between *actual* and *potential* economic growth.

Q5. What would be the result of each of the following events: actual growth, potential growth, both or neither? (In each case assume that other things remain constant.)

(a) The discovery of new raw materials.
Actual growth/potential growth/both/neither
(b) Firms take on more labour in response to an increase in consumer demand.
Actual growth/potential growth/both/neither
(c) A reduction in the number of vacancies in the economy.   *Actual growth/potential growth/both/neither*
(d) An increase in the level of investment.
Actual growth/potential growth/both/neither
(e) A reduction in the working week.
Actual growth/potential growth/both/neither
(f) The discovery of new more efficient techniques which could benefit industry generally.
Actual growth/potential growth/both/neither
(g) Increased expenditure on training.
Actual growth/potential growth/both/neither

 Multiple Choice   Written answer   Delete wrong word    Diagram/table manipulation   Calculation   Matching/ordering

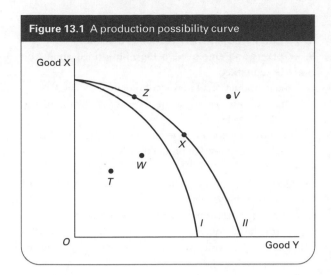

Figure 13.1 A production possibility curve

Q6. Actual growth can never be greater than potential growth. *True/False*

(Page 383) The production possibility curve can be used to illustrate the difference between actual and potential output.

Questions 7–9 refer to Figure 13.1.

Q7. A movement from *T* to *W* (but no movement in the production possibility curve) represents:
(a) An increase in potential output. *True/False*
(b) An increase in actual output. *True/False*
(c) A more efficient point of production. *True/False*

Q8. A movement from *W* to *X* and a shift of the curve from curve *I* to curve *II*, represents:
A. an increase in potential output.
B. an increase in actual output.
C. a more efficient point of production.
D. A, B and C.
E. B and C.
F. none of the above.

Q9. A movement from *X* to *Z* represents:
A. an increase in potential output.
B. an increase in actual output.
C. a more efficient point of production.
D. A, B and C.
E. B and C.
F. none of the above.

(Pages 383–7) Actual growth will tend to fluctuate over the course of the business cycle. The cycle can be broken down into four phases: the upturn, the boom, the peaking out and the slowdown or recession. In the **Q10.** *upturn/expansion/peaking out/slowdown or recession* phase the rate of growth will be at its highest, whereas in the

Q11. *upturn/expansion/peaking out/slowdown or recession* phase growth may actually cease or even become negative. Actual and potential outputs are closest during the **Q12.** *upturn/expansion/peaking out/slowdown or recession* phase of the business cycle.

Q13. Why is it unlikely that actual and potential outputs would ever be equal?

....

....

Q14. One of the major influences on the rate of actual growth within the economy is consumer spending.
True/False

(Pages 387–91) When we look at economic growth over the *longer* term, it is *potential* growth that we need to examine.

Q15. The potential output of an economy depends upon which two factors?

1. ....

2. ....

Q16. The relationship between investment as a proportion of national income (*i*) and the potential rate of economic growth (g_p) is given by the formula:
A. $g_p = i/MEC$
B. $g_p = MEC/i$
C. $g_p = MEC - i$
D. $g_p = i - MEC$
E. $g_p = i \times MEC$

where *MEC* stands for the marginal efficiency of capital: the annual extra income (ΔY) as a proportion of the investment (*i*) that yielded it.

Q17. Given that investment of £100m yields an extra £50m annual national income, and given that 25 per cent of national income is put into new investment, what will be the growth in potential output?

....

Q18. If there is an increase in the size of the population, this will cause the level of output per head to increase.
True/False

13.3 *Unemployment*
(Pages 391–6) We start by examining the meaning and measurement of unemployment.

Q19. If there are 3 million people unemployed and 24 million people employed, the rate of unemployment will be:

A. 3 per cent
B. 8 per cent
C. 9 per cent
D. 11.1 per cent
E. 12.5 per cent

Q20. There are two major measures of unemployment: the claimant count and the standardised measure used by the ILO and OECD. Why is claimant unemployment likely to be lower than standardised unemployment?

....

....

Q21. The stock of unemployment at the end of year *t* equals the stock of unemployment at the beginning of year *t* minus the outflows of people from unemployment to work or to outside the labour force, plus the inflows of people to unemployment from jobs and from outside the labour force. *True/False*

Q22. Which one of the following will increase the level of unemployment?

A. More people retire.
B. More unemployed people become disheartened and give up looking for work.
C. The school leaving age is raised.
D. The retirement age is lowered.
E. More people resign from low-paid jobs.

(Pages 396–402) We now turn to the different types of unemployment.

Q23. Which of the following defines *real-wage* unemployment?

A. Real wages being set above the equilibrium level by trade unions, or minimum wage legislation.
B. Inflation causing an erosion of real wages and hence a rise in unemployment.
C. Increased aggregate demand in the economy driving up equilibrium real wages.
D. Increased aggregate demand in the economy causing money wages to rise faster than real wages,
E. Real wages falling below the equilibrium level as a result of deficiency of demand.

Q24. Why is demand-deficient unemployment sometimes referred to as *cyclical unemployment*?

....

Q25. Frictional unemployment is the result of:

A. a shift in the pattern of consumer demand.
B. workers and employers being ill-informed about the labour market.
C. the introduction of new technology.
D. the economy entering the recessionary phase of the business cycle.
E. employers responding to the time of year and cutting back on their level of production.

Q26. Which of the following will affect the level of *structural* unemployment?

(a) The concentration of a particular industry within a particular region. *Yes/No*
(b) The speed at which structural change within the economy is taking place. *Yes/No*
(c) The immobility of labour. *Yes/No*

Q27. Given the following possible types of unemployment – *demand-deficient/real-wage/frictional/structural/technological/seasonal* – which one is likely to worsen in which of the following cases?

(a) The introduction of robots in manufacturing.

....

(b) The economy moves into recession.

....

(c) Legislation is passed guaranteeing everyone a minimum wage rate that is 60 per cent of the national average.

....

(d) The development of the single market in Europe leads to a movement of capital to the 'centre of gravity' in Europe.

....

(e) The government decides to close job centres in an attempt to save money.

....

(f) The government raises interest rates.

....

(g) More people are forced to take their annual holidays when the schools are on holiday.

....

13.4 Inflation

(Pages 403–5) The rate of inflation in the UK is normally calculated by taking the percentage increase in the retail price index (RPI).

Q28. If the RPI increased by 14 points over a 12-month period, the standard of living must have fallen.
True/False

Q29. In a period of rapid inflation which of the following would be the least desirable store of wealth?
A. Vintage wine.
B. Money.
C. Property.
D. Land.
E. Stocks and shares.

Q30. Debtors are likely to benefit from inflation.
True/False

Q31. Why is a high rate of domestic inflation likely to make the country's foreign trade balance (exports minus imports) worse?

....

....

Q32. Why might a higher rate of inflation cause economic growth to slow down?

....

....

(Pages 405–7) The level of prices in the economy is determined by the interaction of aggregate demand and aggregate supply.

Q33. As the price level in the economy rises, which of the following will occur?
(i) The quantity of 'real money' decreases.
(ii) Real aggregate demand decreases.
(iii) Total spending in *money* terms decreases.

A. (i) only.
B. (ii) only.
C. (i) and (ii)
D. (i) and (iii)
E. (i), (ii) and (iii).

The aggregate demand curve slopes downwards. This is largely because of a *substitution effect* of a rise in the price level.

Q34. Of the following, which account for the substitution effect of a rise in the price level?

(a) Higher domestic prices lead to people purchasing fewer domestic goods and more imports. *Yes/No*
(b) Exports become less competitive and thus fewer are sold. *Yes/No*
(c) People cannot afford to buy so much at higher prices. *Yes/No*
(d) As the price level rises, so the value of people's money balances will fall. They will therefore *spend* less in order to increase their money balances and go some way to protecting their real value. *Yes/No*
(e) The government is likely to raise taxes as prices rise. Higher taxes will mean that people will be able to purchase less. *Yes/No*
(f) Higher wages and prices cause a higher demand for money. With a given supply of money in the economy, this will drive up interest rates and encourage people to spend less and save more. This will have the effect of reducing real aggregate demand. *Yes/No*
(g) Higher prices will encourage the government to reduce the money supply in an attempt to reduce inflation. The reduction in money supply will reduce spending. *Yes/No*

Q35. There are various factors that can cause the aggregate demand curve to shift. What effect will the following have on the aggregate demand curve?
(a) The government increases the money supply.
Leftward shift/rightward shift/ no shift (movement along)
(b) The government increases taxes.
Leftward shift/rightward shift/ no shift (movement along)
(c) The government increases its spending.
Leftward shift/rightward shift/ no shift (movement along)
(d) People anticipate a rise in the rate of inflation.
Leftward shift/rightward shift/ no shift (movement along)
(e) Higher prices lead to higher interest rates.
Leftward shift/rightward shift/ no shift (movement along)
(f) The government reduces interest rates.
Leftward shift/rightward shift/ no shift (movement along)
(g) Higher UK prices lead to a fall in the exchange rate.
Leftward shift/rightward shift/ no shift (movement along)
(h) A reduction in prices abroad leads to a fall in the demand for UK exports.
Leftward shift/rightward shift/ no shift (movement along)

Q36. Why is the aggregate supply curve upward sloping?

....

....

(Pages 407–11) Inflation is caused by persistent **Q37.** *right-ward/leftward* shifts in the aggregate demand curve and/or persistent **Q38.** *rightward/leftward* shifts in the aggregate supply curve.

◑ **Q39.** Assume that the following factors lead to inflation. Which ones will result in demand-pull inflation and which will result in cost-push inflation? (In each case assume *ceteris paribus*.)

(a) A cut in the rate of income tax.   *demand-pull/cost-push*

(b) The expansion of public-sector works.

demand-pull/cost-push

(c) An attempt by unions to increase real wages.

demand-pull/cost-push

(d) An increase in the price of oil.   *demand-pull/cost-push*

(e) VAT is imposed on domestic fuel.

demand-pull/cost-push

(f) A company decides to increase its profits by increasing its prices.   *demand-pull/cost-push*

⑦ **Q40.** Explain the phenomenon of the wage–price spiral.

....

....

Anti-inflationary policy can focus on reducing the rate of growth in aggregate demand ('demand-side policy') or on reducing the rate of increase in costs ('supply-side policy').

◑ **Q41.** Which of the following are examples of demand-side policies and which of supply-side policies?

(a) A cut in government expenditure.

demand-side/supply-side

(b) A rise in taxation.   *demand-side/supply-side*

(c) Tougher anti-monopoly policy.

demand-side/supply-side

(d) Reducing the bargaining power of trade unions.

demand-side/supply-side

(e) Increasing the rate of interest.   *demand-side/supply-side*

(f) Offering tax incentives to encourage increased productivity.   *demand-side/supply-side*

⑦ **Q42.** How will expectations influence the rate of inflation?

....

....

....

B PROBLEMS, EXERCISES AND PROJECTS

Q43. Given the following data:

	£million
Consumers' expenditure	290 000
Government final consumption	91 000
Gross domestic fixed capital formation	80 000
Exports of goods and services	110 000
Imports of goods and services	125 000

Calculate the level of aggregate demand (*AD*)......................

Q44. Using available statistical sources, find time-series data for the last ten years for the following macroeconomic variables:

• Consumer expenditure.
• Government expenditure.
• Gross domestic fixed capital formation.
• Imports and exports.

Calculate the level of aggregate demand for each of the years found (a bar chart may be effective here) and describe the implications of your findings. Does there appear to be a regular business cycle? What is the length of time between peaks? Data may be obtained from the *Annual Abstract of Statistics* (ONS), *Economic Trends* (ONS), *UK National Accounts* (ONS) and the *National Institute Economic Review* (NIESR). See also websites B₄, B₁₂, E₂₃, E₂₄ in the Websites Appendix in Sloman *Economics* (4th edition).

Q45. Referring Table 13.1, how did the duration of un-employment change between 1979 and 1998? How did this relate to the rate of unemployment?

Q46. Table 13.2 shows the aggregate demand and supply of labour at various average wage rates.

Table 13.1 UK claimant unemployment by duration

	Up to 26 weeks	Over 26 weeks and up to 52 weeks	Over 52 weeks	Total
Oct 1979 (thousands)	771.6	194.2	337.0	1302.8
(per cent)	59.2	14.9	25.9	100.0
Oct 1981 (thousands)	1514.5	689.5	784.6	2988.6
(per cent)	50.7	23.1	26.2	100.0
Oct 1988 (thousands)	873.0	360.4	885.5	2118.9
(per cent)	41.2	17.0	41.8	100.0
Oct 1990 (thousands)	873.4	289.5	507.7	1670.6
(per cent)	52.3	17.3	30.4	100.0
Oct 1992 (thousands)	1293.1	565.7	955.6	2814.4
(per cent)	45.9	20.1	34.0	100.0
Oct 1994 (thousands)	1057.7	440.9	956.5	2455.0
(per cent)	43.1	17.9	39.0	100.0
Oct 1998 (thousands)	704.2	229.7	352.4	1286.3
(per cent)	54.7	17.9	27.4	100.0

Source: *Labour Market Trends* (ONS).

Table 13.2

Average real wage (£ per hour)	Labour demand (000s)	Labour supply (000s)	Labour force (000s)
3.00	200	100	118
3.50	170	120	136
4.00	140	140	154
4.50	110	160	172
5.00	80	180	190

(a) Plot the labour demand and labour supply curves.

(b) How might we explain the inelastic nature of the labour supply curve?

....

(c) If the wage rate were set at £4.00, what would be the level of employment and unemployment?

employment = ... *unemployment* = ...

(d) What type of *unemployment* is this? ....

(e) If the wage level were to increase to £4.50, how many workers would be classified as *disequilibrium* and how many as *equilibrium* unemployed?

disequilibrium = ... *equilibrium* = ...

Q47. From the information in Table 13.3 calculate the price index in year *X* for the basket of commodities.

....

Table 13.3

Commodity	Average price in base year	Average price in year *X*	Weight
A	£0.70	£0.75	4
B	£1.20	£1.35	1
C	£45.00	£55.00	1
D	£0.35	£0.37	2
E	£3.20	£3.55	2

DISCUSSION TOPICS AND ESSAYS

Q48. (a) What is the relationship between actual and potential output? (b) What is the relationship between actual and potential growth?

Q49. At what stage of the business cycle is the economy at the present time? Are all the macroeconomic variables behaving in the way you would expect?

Q50. How might the government set about increasing the overall level of investment in the economy? What problems is it likely to encounter in attempting to do so?

Q51. What factors have been most important in explaining the changing level of unemployment in the UK over the last 10 years?

Q52. If we were to devise a series of policies to tackle the plight of the unemployed, what factors other than the actual *number* unemployed ought we to take into account?

Q53. Solutions to the unemployment problem can be classified as interventionist or market orientated, although there is some common ground. List as many solutions to unemployment as you can, suggesting which would be supported by 'free marketeers' and which by 'interventionists'.

Q54. What are the economic consequences of inflation?

Q55. If the government insisted that everyone had wage increases to match the rate of inflation, would it matter how high the rate of inflation was?

Q56. Distinguish between demand-pull and cost-push inflation. Why in practice might it be difficult to establish the extent to which a given rate of inflation were demand-pull or cost-push?

Q57. Debate
The pursuit of economic growth is not in people's long-term interests.

ARTICLES

Business cycles are no longer purely domestic phenomena. With the progressive globalisation of trade and industry, the world economy invariably swings between boom and slump. The more a country embraces globalisation and opens its economy to trade and foreign investment, the more sensitive it will become to these global shifts in output. The article below by Marc Lopatin, taken from *The Independent* of 13 October 1998, describes the vulnerability of the UK economy to such cycles, following its willingness to embrace high levels of inward investment in the 1980s and 1990s.

The crisis – a crash course in globalisation

As factories shut, Britain's reliance on inward investment has been exposed.

'World trade and the opening of markets has been going on for centuries. Globalisation in that sense is not new. What is new is its pace and scope. It is as if someone has pressed the fast forward button on the video, and there is no sign of it stopping.' This was how Tony Blair explained the impact of globalisation to Japanese business leaders when in opposition.

Two years on, Mr Blair's words have come back to haunt him in his own Sedgefield constituency. Addressing 570 workers made redundant by the Japanese semiconductor firm Fujitsu two weeks ago, he trotted out the same rhetoric as its disconsolate casualties of globalisation listened.

UK plc has suddenly lost some of its most high-profile inward investments. In the past three months Siemens, Fujitsu, Viasystems, and National Semiconductors have all closed hi-tech plants or scaled back production, despite investing billions of pounds in state-of-the-art assembly plants.

The closures stem from a sharp cyclical downturn in the semiconductor industry caused by massive oversupply and rock-bottom prices. The bad news is one of the first manifestations of a truly globalised industry succumbing to the acute effects of a global downturn. While semiconductor makers are unlikely to be in the doldrums for long, the same cannot be said of countries left to support redundant workers each time production is switched elsewhere.

Despite Government assurances, the stream of plant closures raise serious questions about the future of inward – or foreign direct investment (FDI) – in the UK. The nation is no stranger to closing factories. But the closures of cutting edge technologies are a world away from those of shipyards and textile factories.

Government strategy has been to lure the foreign owners to use Britain as a European base of operations. But it has not yet addressed what Britain should do when these same investors cut back on their world-wide operations.

Robert Crawford, head of inward investment at accountant Ernst & Young, believes the closures are an inevitable part of globalisation. 'The semiconduc-

tor business is not a spent industry: it's a blueprint for the future of global manufacturing,' he says. 'The firms fabricate in the UK, assemble and test components in Asia, before selling chips worldwide. They must have global reach and be able to shift resources, or risk losing their foothold altogether.'

In a downturn, 'shifting risk' means deciding which plants in which countries to close. Stephen Regan, a Cranfield School of Management lecturer, says: 'When companies seek to be truly global they leave themselves nowhere to hide. So drastic action is required.'

Andrew Fraser, chief executive of the Invest in Britain Bureau (IBB), says the closures are unique to the semiconductor industry. 'Billions of pounds spent on rolling investment in new plant and products coupled with an unforeseen downturn caused the closures.'

But Mr Regan argues that other foreign investors in other cyclical industries, including commodities, oil and pharmaceuticals, may soon be copying the semiconductor business. Should this happen, Britain's impressive record in FDI might look very different. There are some 8100 foreign-owned firms in the UK generating 40 per cent of all exported manufactured goods, and 400 000 jobs in 13 years. United Nations figures show Britain has an impressive 10.66 per cent of the world's $400bn (£232bn) FDI stock, achieved with just 1 per cent of world's population and about 5 per cent of world trade.

Economists predict that, despite the crisis, global foreign direct investment will continue to grow as markets' ears are opened to the deafening mantra of free trade. Before the Asia crisis, FDI was growing at 9 per cent a year, over twice as fast as the world economy.

The IBB is bringing record levels of investment to the UK – £9.42bn for 1997/98. But with boom turning to bust the challenge is defensive: to prevent foreign companies from quitting the UK, and to persuade firms to cut production elsewhere. The IBB says the UK is still creating more FDI jobs than it is losing. But there are no loyalty cards in a global economy.

In this sense Britain could be heavily exposed. In the 1980s Britain stole a march on other Europeans by attracting massive amounts of foreign investment.

A cheap workforce and generous grant packages lured many a multi-national to the UK. But Sean Ricard, head of management economics at Cranfield School of Management, says: 'The UK has been importing industrial expertise using FDI, instead of strengthening domestic manufacturing.'

The point is not lost on Peter Mandelson, Secretary of State for Trade and Industry: 'I want to see more home-grown hi-tech industries where British know-how can be harnessed to develop and launch our own manufactured products in the UK.'

Mr Crawford says: 'For the last 20 years big assembly plants have been the order of the day. But the UK will not hold on to companies that simply assemble or manufacture products. There will always be somewhere cheaper to go. We have to provide the infrastructure and a labour force for design and development – the life blood of any manufacturer.'

The UK is now the call centre capital of Europe, but Mr Crawford says: '[They] are not connected to core product development. They are mobile assets which can be set up anywhere and will probably be gone within five years.' The IBB refutes this, but is well aware of the need to embed inward investors in the UK.

Mr Fraser, of the IBB, says: 'Fifteen years ago Nissan set up a plant factory which critics labelled a screwdriver factory. It is now the most productive car factory in Europe, exporting 80 per cent of production and sourcing 200 British suppliers. That is embeddedness.'

More recently Microsoft spent £12m setting up its first research and development facility at Cambridge Science Park where no financial inducements are on offer. The park brings together academia, training and industry to deliver an integrated long-term approach to attracting FDI.

Mr Fraser believes clustering related firms is the way forward. 'It becomes a magnet for inward investment. In the same way the City of London is a must for international finance.' Vicky Pryce, chief economist at accountant KPMG, agress: 'The growing diversity of FDI will force countries to create domestic centres of excellence.'

(a) Explain how a business cycle might be transmitted between the world's economies. For example, consider the impact on the UK of the collapse in the economies of south-east Asia in 1997/8.

(b) What strategies does the article suggest that a country, such as the UK, can adopt in order to reduce its vulnerability to a downturn in global economic activity?

(c) Should the UK restrict both inward and outward investment, and encourage more domestic investment, in order to become less vulnerable to global economic upheavals?

In the following article, taken from the *Guardian* of 28 March 1999, Mauricio Rojas attempts to dispel widely held fallacies that work, as we know it, is coming to an end. In fact, he argues that a *shortage* of labour, rather than mass unemployment, is likely to be the norm in the future.

The death of work has been greatly exaggerated

It is a remarkable epoch we are living in. Never have so many jobs been created as in the past quarter of a century. Never have so many people improved their standard of living so radically in such a short time as in the past two decades.

But instead of acclaiming this breakthrough, more and more people in the developed countries of Europe seem to be transfixed by doom-mongering about globalisation and the demise of work – often combined as one big threat. But these depressing predictions are fallacies.

Fallacy 1: work to end

Millions of old jobs are disappearing and very few new ones are created. Eventually, most of the world population will be excluded from the labour market in a world without work.

In fact, quite a number of developed countries have shown an excellent capacity for creating many new jobs. Employment in the United States, Canada, Australia and Japan grew by a startling high total of 58 million jobs between 1975 and 1995.

The assertion that work is ending will not entirely stand up, even in the case of the European Union. Some EU countries – the Netherlands, Austia and Ireland, for example – display a considerable capacity for creating new jobs. (In the UK, more people are employed now than ever.)

The end-of-work thesis becomes more remarkable still if you consider global progress over the past 20 years. We find a startling expansion of employment which, despite a rise in unemployment in the less dynamic, developing countries, has successfully absorbed the most dramatic growth ever of the employable population.

Fallacy 2: technology is taking our jobs

It is because of the information technology revolution that economic growth is not creating more jobs than are being lost. We have entered an epoch of jobless growth.

If this proposition had the slightest connection with reality, the US and Japan, which have dominated IT development since the seventies, ought to be especially hard hit. They are not.

On the contrary, tens of millions of new jobs have begun in these countries since the arrival of the computer age.

Apologists for this fallacy might, perhaps, say there are still fewer than before the IT breakthrough. But that isn't true, either. Both in Japan and the US, more jobs were created in between 1975 and 1995 than in the previous 20 years.

This is especially remarkable, given that economic growth in Japan and the US was slower between 1975 and 1995 than from 1955 to 1975. So there was a considerable increase in the job creation effect of growth.

After extensive studies, the International Labour Organisation has also concluded that growth generally is creating more jobs today than in the golden age of Fordism (mass production), the sixties.

The main reason for this is the transition from industrial to service societies. It is the highly labour-intensive services that are the backbone of the caring and educational sector which, in terms of work, have expanded most during the IT revolution.

Fallacy 3: the US creates 'trash' work

Most of the new jobs which, despite everything, are created in the developed economies are low-skilled, low-paid service work. The US typifies an economy that creates jobs through an expansive service sector consisting more and more of the 'working poor'.

The American economy, which has created tens of millions of new jobs, is frequently dismissed like this. It gives the impression that they are almost exclusively 'trash jobs' that really ought not to exist.

But this picture is profoundly misleading. Nearly half of all the new posts created in the US between 1983 and 1995 belonged to the most highly skilled occupational groups.

Nearly 12m highly qualified jobs were created in only 12 years. Seven out of 10 new jobs – just over 16.7m out of a total job growth of 24 million – came in the occupational categories of the upper income half of the American economy.

I am not condoning American poverty, of course, nor denying the existence of low-skilled jobs – only seeking to give a fair overall picture of US labour developments.

Fallacy 4: they're taking our work

Jobs are disappearing or paying less and less, owing to the pressure from new producers in poor countries. Capital and enterprise are migrating to nations where labour is cheap, using them to put developed countries out of business.

The jobs crisis is defined here as a problem of the industrialised countries, caused by the increasing mobility of capital and the ability of the transnational corporations to exploit the impoverished masses of the Third World – and Eastern Europe, too – as alternative labour.

The scene is set for a life-and-death struggle between 'us' and 'them', a struggle which we are doomed to lose because 'they' are so much cheaper.

Which is why we are becoming unemployed, poorer and more desperate.

If the fallacy had anything significant to say about real developments, the industrialised countries ought to have experienced a dramatic fall in their share of world trade over the past 15 years. However, reports of our global collapse are great exaggerations – we have slipped only very slightly. But as world exports almost doubled between 1980 and 1994, that means we made enormous gains.

What is true of trade also applies to world industrial output. In 1995 the affluent countries accounted for four-fifths of that output (80.3 per cent), roughly the same share as in 1980 (82.8 per cent), despite the enormous successes during these years by China and other Asian countries.

The relocation of certain traditional industries – textile manufacturing is a typical example – has in most cases been paralleled by the establishment of new industries. Asian successes have not been achieved at our expense.

This is not all. Even if we imported everything that was exported by South, South East and East Asia and this knocked out our own production without any compensation, it would still not impoverish us much. In 1994 the exports of this immense region equalled only 3.41 per cent of the developed world's gross domestic product.

In any case, the idea of cheap industrial products from the Third World taking away our industrial jobs conceals a fundamental fact: we export far more industrial goods to these countries than they export to us – $550 billion in 1992, while from them we imported the equivalent of $330bn.

(a) Why might technology create more jobs than it destroys?

(b) Is there *any* truth in any of the four fallacies?

(c) Given the four fallacies, what policies might governments pursue in order to ensure employment and job creation are maintained?

The article below, taken from *Management Today* of March 1995, explores the implications for management in operating within a low-inflation economy and the problems that businesses are likely to face in maintaining levels of profit.

The low-inflation challenge

For Sir James Blyth, chief executive of Boots, low inflation is not a glint in a politician's eye. It is the reality he has been living with for the past three or four years, and he expects it to continue. 'It has been with us for some time,' he says, 'and we've set out to try and plan strategies within a low-inflation environment'. The highly competitive high-street market in which Boots operates means that the company, in Blyth's words, 'under-recovers inflation'. In other words, prices rise by less than general inflation. When general inflation is low, this can mean stable or falling prices for Boots.

Initial scepticism about whether Britain's inflationary leopard had truly changed its spots is now giving way to a general acceptance that things have changed. And even those who subscribe to the cock-up theory of economic policy – which is that when governments have an opportunity to mess things up they generally do so – accept that the scope for politicians to throw away the present low-inflation advantage is limited.

The Bank of England's enhanced role in the policy process has produced a permanent anti-inflationary bias in policy. Wage bargaining behaviour has changed for the better, partly because of the labour market reforms of the 1980s. Credit growth, which reached runaway proportions during the Lawson boom, has come up against the brick wall of corporate and personal sector debt aversion. And consumers are more price-sensitive than for a generation.

But the adjustment to a low-inflation era is far from painless, even for those companies who have lived with it for some time. For Blyth of Boots, it means tough control of costs: 'We're operating on the basis of matching our wage bill to inflation and, as long as our productivity is growing by between 2 per cent and 5 per cent, our margin is very well-protected.'

Milton Friedman, the father of modern monetarist economics, drew the analogy between inflation and drug or alcohol addiction. At first, he said, the effects can appear pleasant, even benign, but very soon it gets nasty. No one doubts that they would be better off without it.

But inflation, like addiction, becomes a hard habit to kick. Right now, Britain is in the painful, cold-turkey phase of kicking a long-standing habit. Many say it would be far easier to slip back into the habit. The scepticism over Britain's ability to become a stable-price economy is being overcome, but now comes the hard part: rewriting strategies that were developed during an inflationary era.

Pressure from international forces is one factor that is forcing new thinking on companies. Increasing industrial output from newly emerging economies such as China and India will drive up the demand, and hence the price, for raw materials. At the same time, because these countries are low-cost manufacturers, their impact on world markets will be to exert downward pressure on the prices of manufactured goods. This provides Lesson One of the low-inflation era, that cost-cutting becomes a way of life. 'Most companies will find that they will have to work as hard to reduce costs during "normal" times as they ever did during the recession,' says McWilliams. 'Not surprisingly, many managers regard this as very unfair.'

Nick Morris, director of the consultancy London Economics, takes this point further: 'Many businessmen, having got used to inflation, find it hard to believe in price elasticities (the fact that demand responds to price changes). If your product isn't selling and we are in a period of no inflation, holding prices is not enough – you have to cut them.' And, because price-cutting has in the past often been regarded as a desperate throw, or as undermining a reputation for quality, it does not come easily.

Roger Bootle, chief economist at HSBC Markets (the money-market arm of the Hong Kong & Shanghai Bank) recently published a paper, *The End of the Inflationary Era*. In it he described the new psychology of low inflation among consumers, which is forcing companies to change their pricing behaviour.

'Areas which have discovered the power of price include clothing and footwear outlets, supermarkets, newspapers and insurance,' he says. 'But there are whole swathes which have yet to catch on. If they are in a line of business where demand has seemed inelastic in the past (unresponsive to price changes), they find it difficult to realise that they have become price-uncompetitive in an economy where consumers have become more sensitive to price.' Bootle believes the realisation that this is a new era will come in stages. At first, he says, many firms are reluctant to openly cut prices: 'Instead, they resort to discounts, special offers, tokens, gifts and other forms of disguised price reduction, perhaps because they regard the current "value sensitivity" in the market as temporary and wish to preserve the image of their posted price as the real price.'

The result of this, he says, is that for some time there have been two price levels in existence – the official price level, which he dubs the fictional price level because very little business is done at it. The other price level, with discounts, special deals and sales packages, is significantly lower and is one at which most business is conducted.

Over time, these two price levels will inevitably converge, Bootle predicts.

One example is in the motor trade. Traditionally, retail buyers of new cars were accustomed to regarding the manufacturers' list as a ceiling from which a discount, often a very hefty one, could be negotiated. The real price was well below the official price. In 1993, Vauxhall pioneered a shift towards more realistic list prices by cutting dealer markups. Other manufacturers followed.

Keen pricing, then, has to be the strategy in a low-inflation era. But that isn't the end of the management process. The fundamental question is how to keep prices stable, or reduce them, and still improve earnings.

Cost control, as the CEBR's McWilliams says, has to be as tough in recovery as in recession. Inevitably, one of the hardest areas in which to achieve this will be with wages. The labour market is subject to what economists call the 'money illusion', where people feel better off if they are getting a 10 per cent pay rise alongside 8 per cent inflation than if the two figures are 3 per cent and 1 per cent respectively.

Bootle points out that the cards are heavily stacked in favour of management. Widespread job insecurity has curbed labour militancy. 'The new technological revolution is labour-saving. The demand for button-pushers and lever-pullers is substantially reduced. Smaller and smaller numbers are employed in manufacturing. Even in the office, technology has made possible substantial economy in the use of clerks and typists. The structural changes stretch deep into the service sector. In transport, for instance, computerisation greatly reduces the number of people needed to run a railway system. And the potential developments are huge.'

One of the difficulties of low inflation is that it is harder to establish the differentials needed to retain key staff. In a period of moderately high inflation, the difference between a 10 per cent rise for those who could be poached by other firms and a pay freeze for others is significant. But when the total wage has to be frozen, it is hard to single out vital staff.

A low-inflation environment should also lend itself to long-term pay deals. In practice, however, both management and unions have been reluctant to commit themselves to deals stretching for more than two years. Long-term deals have not, so far, worked to the obvious benefit of companies, because in a period where both inflation and pay settlements have come in below expectations, second-year increases have tended to be higher than those that could have been freely negotiated at the time. The combination of long-term deals for basic pay coupled with a substantial profit-related element is now suggesting itself as the way forward.

Do low prices effectively take over as the main selling-point in the new era, or is there still value in brands? Boots's Blyth has no doubt that brands are a bigger advantage in a stable price era. 'They are a very large advantage,' he says. 'When you've established a reputation for very high quality, this works even more to your advantage when prices are not rising.' He cites the fact that Boots successfully saw off a pure cut-price challenge, in perfumes and other products, from Superdrug. Another example is provided by the low-price strategies of Sainsbury, Tesco and Asda, which have meant that the challenge from new discount entrants into the market, including the German retailer Aldi and the club warehouses, has been far less significant than many expected.

In the end, the challenge of low inflation has to be met by good management, which has at its heart the containment of costs and responding to the needs of increasingly price-sensitive but brand-loyal customers. This can be presented as a re-engineering task.
© *Management Today*, Mar. 95

(a) Why is low and stable inflation economically advantageous?

(b) How are businesses able to maintain high profits during periods of inflation?

(c) What new strategies have businesses been forced to adopt in order to maintain profits in a low-inflation economy?

The following article, taken from the *Investors Chronicle* of 5 April 1996, explores the problems of using the output gap of an economy as a guide to informing economic policy action.

Minding the output gap mythology

The so-called output gap – the difference between actual output and its potential level – is widely considered a key influence upon inflation. 'Roughly speaking, inflation is likely to decelerate if the output gap is negative and to accelerate if it is positive,' says Tim Congdon, one of the chancellor's panel of independent forecasters. He believes that output is currently around 3 per cent below its potential. 'On this basis, good inflation numbers are likely to be reported for the rest of 1996 and most of 1997,' he says.

However, it does not follow that interest rates should be cut further. One reason for this is that there are many problems with the idea that the output gap does determine inflation.

Not least of these is that the gap is very hard to measure. The simplest, and most popular, way of doing it is to take the peak of two economic cycles and estimate the growth rate between the two. This gives the potential growth rate. Extrapolating this rate forward gives us the current level of potential output, with which actual output can be compared.

Unfortunately, this method, and its more sophisticated counterparts, fails to give an unambiguous answer. A particular problem is that it cannot tell us whether there has been an increase in the potential growth rate since the last economic cycle. But frequently, this is precisely the point at issue between inflation optimists and pessimists, with the former claiming that structural change will enable growth to stay low, and the latter denying it.

Measures of the output gap also frequently conflict with the trade deficit. Both should show the same thing – whether supply is greater than demand. The mere existence of a trade deficit suggests that demand is greater than supply. But most measures of the output gap suggest the opposite. This could, of course, mean that there is no output gap in manufacturing, but that there is in services. And sure enough, the RPI figures, showing goods inflation rising and services inflation falling, lend credence to this claim. But this means that there is no single output gap, and no single implication for inflation.

A further problem lies in the mechanism through which the output gap influences prices. It should be simple. If output is above potential, demand exceeds supply and prices rise. If output is below potential, supply exceeds demand and prices fall. But nothing is that simple. In deciding whether to cut prices, firms consider much more than whether they have spare capacity. What will be the response of their rivals? How many more customers will they get? Will the increased demand be enough to compensate for the loss of immediate cash flow? The output gap is silent on such important questions.

But even if we reject all of these problems, and continue to hold faith in the output gap as a determinant of inflation, it does not follow that we should support lower interest rates. Indeed, Professor Congdon himself is opposed to rate cuts.

One reason for this is that it takes a long time for monetary policy to affect inflation; most estimates put the lag at around two years. In setting rates now, therefore, the government needs to know where inflation will be from April 1998 onwards. But the output gap can only tell us this if the lags between it and inflation are longer than those between monetary policy and inflation. This is improbable, not least because interest rates affect inflation through their impact on the output gap. So we need much more than the output gap to tell us where interest rates should be.

It may seem odd, therefore, that policy makers attach so much weight to the output gap. Not so. Consider the chancellor's dilemma. On the one hand, the only economic target he has is low inflation; there is no official target for growth or unemployment. On the other hand, there are political pressures to cut rates whenever the economy seems weak. How better to reconcile these conflicts than by claiming that a weak economy will eventually reduce inflation? Output gap theories may or may not be true. But they are extremely useful.

© *Investors Chronicle*, 5.4.96

(a) What is the output gap and how can it be measured?

(b) Why is it difficult to measure the rate of *potential* economic growth?

(c) Why would we expect inflation to rise when an economy nears its potential output?

(d) What would you expect to be the relationship between the output gap and the size of the trade deficit (or surplus)?

(e) What argument does Professor Congdon advance to suggest that the existence of an output gap should not automatically lead to a cut in interest rates?

(f) Given your answers to the above questions, of what use is the output gap to the policy maker?

ANSWERS

Q1. (a), (d), (e) and (h) are macroeconomic issues as they concern the whole economy rather than a segment of it.

Q2. Economic growth can be defined as the percentage increase in national output over a twelve-month period.

Q3. 1950–69.

Q4. D.

Q5. (a) *potential growth*. (Only if they are *used* will there be actual growth.)

(b) *actual growth*.

(c) *neither*. (A reduction in vacancies usually signals a reduction in output. It *could*, however, be a sign of increased labour productivity, in which case there would be *potential growth* or more vacancies being filled, in which case there would be *actual growth*.)

(d) *both*. (Increased inestment, by increasing the stock of capital, increases potential output. The purchase of new machinery and equipment stimulates growth in the industries producing the equipment.)

(e) *neither*. (Other things being equal, it will lead to a *reduction* in output.)

(f) *potential*. (It would only lead to actual growth if these techniques were used.)

(g) *both*. (It will increase labour productivity and hence lead to potential growth. The employment of instructors and other money spent on the training will stimulate demand and hence encourage an increased output in the economy.)

Q6. *False*. Provided there is some slack in the economy (i.e. production is inside the production possibility curve), actual growth can take place by using some of the idle capacity. Only when the economy is operating at full capacity will potential growth be a necessary condition for actual growth.

Q7. (a) *False*; (b) *True*; (c) *True*.

Q8. D. The movement outwards of the production point from *W* to *X*, represents an increase in potential output. Since *W* was inside curve *I*, whereas *X* is on curve *II*, *X* represents a more efficient point of production than *W*. Finally, the outward shift in the production possibility curve represents an increase in potential output.

Q9. F. In this case consumers select a new combination of X and Y. (Actual output of X has increased, but actual output of Y has *decreased*.) Potential output remains unaffected.

Q10. The *expansion* phase.

Q11. The *peaking out* and the *slowdown or recession* phases.

Q12. The *peaking out* phase. During this phase the economy will be running closest to full capacity.

Q13. In a perfect market situation it might be possible for all resources to be fully utilised. In real-world markets, however, either as a result of imperfect information, or as a consequence of other market failures, some resources will remain idle.

Q14. *True*. A major determinant of actual growth is aggregate demand, of which consumer spending is the biggest element.

Q15. Potential output depends upon the level of resources available and the state of technology.

Q16. E.

Q17. The $MEC = 50/100 = 0.5$. In order to find the potential growth rate we use the formula $g = i \times MEC$, where i is the level of investment as a percentage of national income ($i = 25\%$). Thus $g = 25\% \times 0.5 = 12.5\%$.

Q18. *False*. Whether output per head rises or not depends upon the proportion of the population as a whole that is working, and whether the marginal product of labour of new workers is above the average product of labour.

Q19. D. The formula is $U/(U + E) \times 100\%$ (where U is the number unemployed and E is the number employed): i.e. $3/(3 + 24) \times 100\% = 11.1\%$.

Q20. The claimant figures exclude those who are unemployed but are ineligible for benefit. In the UK the following categories of unemployed people are ineligible for benefit: people returning to the workforce, people over 55, people temporarily unemployed, people seeking part-time work rather than full-time work.

Q21. *True*. The level of unemployment at the end of a period is equal to that at the beginning plus the inflows and minus the outflows.

Q22. E. (Note that A will have no effect, B will have the effect of reducing unemployment, and C and D will either reduce unemployment or leave it the same depending on whether those now staying on at school and retiring were previously recorded in the statistics.)

Q23. A. The result is that the supply of labour exceeds the demand, causing disequilibrium unemployment.

Q24. Because such unemployment is closely related to the business cycle and grows in periods of recession.

Q25. B. Frictional unemployment would be reduced if workers had better knowledge of jobs available and employers had better knowledge of what workers were available. This improved knowledge would reduce the search time of workers looking for a job and firms in recruiting labour.

Q26. (a), (b) and (c). The more industrially diverse a region, the slower the rate of change, and the more flexible the workforce, the less of a problem structural unemployment will be. Those made unemployed over a period of time can more easily move to alternative employment either within the existing area or elsewhere.

Q27. (a) *technological*; (b) *demand-deficient*; (c) *real-wage*; (d) *structural*; (e) *frictional*; (f) *demand-deficient*; (g) *seasonal* (holiday areas have higher unemployment during school terms).

Q28. *False*. The RPI does not measure the standard of living as it takes no account of incomes.

Q29. B. In a period of rapid inflation the real value of money falls.

Q30. *True*. Debtors will see the value of their debt fall as prices rise. High inflation is often accompanied by low *real* rates of interest (i.e. interest rates relative to the rate of inflation). This benefits debtors.

Q31. A high rate of domestic inflation relative to those with whom we trade will cause the competitiveness of exports to fall as they become more expensive. Equally the demand for imported goods will increase since they will appear relatively cheaper than domestically produced products.

Q32. Inflation creates uncertainty for businesspeople: costs and hence profits are difficult to predict. As a consequence businesses may be reluctant to invest, thereby reducing the actual and potential levels of growth.

Q33. C. The higher prices will mean that the current stock of money will purchase fewer goods and services: i.e. the 'real' money supply has decreased (i). The movement up along the aggregate demand curve shows that fewer goods and services will be demanded: i.e. that real aggregate demand has decreased (ii). With the rise in prices and a constant nominal money supply, however, it is highly unlikely that *money* expenditure will decrease (iii).

Q34. *(a)* *Yes.* This is part of the *foreign trade substitution effect*. People substitute imports for home-produced goods and services.

(b) *Yes.* This is the other part of the foreign trade substitution effect. People abroad substitute non-UK goods for UK exports.

(c) *No.* This is the income effect. (For this to occur, prices would have to rise faster than wages.)

(d) *Yes.* This is the *real balance effect*. People substitute increased money balances for expenditure on goods and services.

(e) *No.* This will shift the curve. It is not a direct consequence of the rise in the price level: it is something the government chooses to do.

(f) *Yes.* The higher interest rates are a direct consequence of the higher price level.

(g) *No.* The reason is the same as in the case of (e).

Q35. *Leftward shift* (b), (h). (These are causes of a fall in aggregate demand other than a rise in the price level.)

Rightward shift (a), (c), (d), (f). (These are causes of a rise in aggregate demand other than a fall in the price level.) Note in the case of (d), if people believe that inflation is going to rise, they will buy more now in order to beat the price rises.

No shift (movement along) (e), (g). (These are changes in the price level that will affect aggregate demand and will thus be shown by the curve itself.)

Q36. Firms' marginal cost curves are likely to slope upwards. They would thus need to receive higher prices to encourage them to produce more. (This assumes that they believe that their cost curves will not *shift*: only that costs will rise as they move upward *along* their marginal cost curves.)

Q37. *Rightward.*

Q38. *Leftward.*

Q39. (a) and (b) are demand-pull while the rest are cost-push.

Q40. Higher wages increase firms' costs of production and thus cause them to put up their prices. These higher prices then cause unions to demand higher wages to compensate for the higher cost of living. Thus wages and prices chase each other in a spiral.

Q41. (a), (b) and (e) are demand-side policies. They have the effect of reducing the growth in aggregate demand. The others are supply-side policies. If successful, they will reduce the rate of increase in costs.

Q42. The higher the rate of inflation that employers and employees expect, the bigger will be the rate of increase in wages and prices that are set. The higher the current rate of inflation, the higher people will expect it to be in the future. (This question is examined in Chapter 21.)

14 Macroeconomic Issues II: The Open Economy

A REVIEW

A country's economy does not operate in isolation. It is affected by the state of the international economy. What is more, the macroeconomic policies it pursues will have effects on other countries, which in turn will have effects on it.

In this chapter we look at macroeconomic issues in the context of an 'open economy'. We start by examining the balance of payments and then see how it affects and is affected by the rate of exchange. These related topics of the balance of payments and exchange rates can be seen as the fourth major macroeconomic issue (economic growth, unemployment and inflation being the other three).

We then group these four issues together and see how they are related, and in particular examine the relationship between inflation and unemployment. We then look at the circular flow of income, a useful model for helping to understand the role of aggregate demand in the economy and its effects on the four issues. Finally we turn to the methods used to measure national income and its various components: again, this is done in the open-economy context.

14.1 The balance of payments account
(Page 414)

Q1. The balance of payments for country A is defined as the balance of all money transactions between the residents of country A and the residents of all other countries over a specified period of time. *True/False*

Q2. Receipts of money from abroad are counted as *credits* on the balance of payments, whereas outflows of money are regarded as *debits*. *True/False*

Q3. Which of the following are debit items and which are credit items on the UK balance of payments account?

(a) The purchase of imports. *debit/credit*

(b) Loans made to non-UK residents by UK banks. *debit/credit*

(c) Investment by UK companies abroad. *debit/credit*

(d) Dividends earned by UK shareholders on overseas investment by UK companies. *debit/credit*

(e) Investment in the UK by non-UK companies. *debit/credit*

(f) Money placed on short-term deposit in the UK by non-residents. *debit/credit*

(g) Drawing on reserves. *debit/credit*

(Pages 414–17) The balance of payments account is composed of a number of parts.

⬛ *Multiple Choice*　　❓ *Written answer*　　◐ *Delete wrong word*　　⊖ *Diagram/table manipulation*　　⊗ *Calculation*　　▦ *Matching/ordering*

Q4. A country has the following items in its balance of payments:

Exports of goods	£120m
Imports of services	£60m
Income flows and current transfers from abroad	£80m
Imports of goods	£150m
Exports of services	£50m
Income flows and current transfers going abroad	£30m

Its balance on trade in goods and services is a:

A. deficit of £40m.
B. deficit of £30m.
C. deficit of £20m.
D. deficit of £10m.
E. surplus of £10m.

Q5. Referring to the data of Q4, the country's balance of payments on current account is a:

A. deficit of £40m.
B. deficit of £30m.
C. deficit of £20m.
D. deficit of £10m.
E. surplus of £10m.

Q6. If there is a current account deficit of £1bn, then:

A. there must be a surplus of £1bn on trade in services.
B. there must be an equivalent deficit on the capital plus financial accounts.
C. there must be a net errors and omissions item of +£1bn.
D. the overall capital plus financial accounts (including net errors and omissions) must be in surplus by £1bn.
E. the financial account must be +£1bn.

Q7. The following are the various elements in the UK balance of payments account:

(i) Imports of goods (–)
(ii) Exports of goods (+)
(iii) Imports of services (–)
(iv) Exports of services (+)
(v) Incomes and current transfers to the UK from abroad (+)
(vi) Incomes and current transfers abroad from the UK (–)
(vii) Transfers of capital to the UK from abroad (+)
(viii) Transfers of capital abroad from the UK (–)
(ix) Long-term UK investment abroad (–)
(x) Long-term investment in UK from abroad (+)
(xi) Short-term financial outflows (–)
(xii) Short-term financial inflows (+)
(xiii) Adding to reserves (–)
(xiv) Drawing on reserves (+)

Into which of the above categories would you put the following items (there can be more than one item in each category)?

(a) Car imported from Germany.

....

(b) Insurance cover purchased by overseas company at Lloyds in London.

....

(c) UK pays contribution to EU Budget.

....

(d) Japanese car company builds factory in UK.

....

(e) UK resident takes a holiday in Florida.

....

(f) Interest earned by non-UK residents on assets held in UK.

....

(g) UK insurance company sets up branch in Canada.

....

(h) Running down the stock of foreign exchange in the Bank of England.

....

(i) Deposits in UK banks by foreigners.

....

(j) Scotch whisky sold in France.

....

(k) Aid given by the UK to developing countries for the construction of infrastructure.

....

Q8. Table 14.1 shows the internationally accepted way of setting out a balance of payments account.

The following are the items in country X's 2000 balance of payments:

Exports of services	£80m
Exports of goods	£74m
Income flows and current transfers from abroad to country X	£43m

Table 14.1

Credits	Debits
(1) Exports of goods	(2) Imports of goods
	1 – 2 = Balance on trade in goods
(3) Exports of services	(4) Imports of services
	(1 + 3) – (2 + 4) = Balance on trade in goods and services
(5) Incomes and current transfers from abroad	(6) Incomes and current transfers going abroad
	(1 + 3 + 5) – (2 + 4 + 6) = Current account balance
(7) Transfers of capital to UK from abroad	(8) Transfers of capital abroad from UK
	7 – 8 = Capital account balance
(9) Net direct and portfolio investment in UK from abroad	(10) Net direct and portfolio investment by UK abroad
(11) Other financial inflows (mainly short term)	(12) Other financial outflows (mainly short term)
either	*or*
(13) Drawing on reserves	(14) Building up reserves
	(9 + 11 + 13) – (10 + 12 + 14) = Financial account balance
	(15) Net errors and omissions
	Current + capital + financial account balances + net errors and omissions = 0

Net investment abroad by country X	£70m
Imports of services	£78m
Imports of goods	£82m
Net investment in country X from abroad	£56m
Short-term financial inflows to country X	£96m
Short-term financial outflows from country X	£84m
Drawing on reserves	£1m
Income flows and current transfers abroad from country X	£40m
Transfers of capital to country X from abroad	£7m
Transfers of capital abroad from country X	£5m

By referring to Table 14.1, work out the following balances in country X's balance of payments.

(a) the balance on trade in goods

....

(b) the balance on trade in goods and services

....

(c) the balance of payments on current account

....

(d) the capital account balance

....

(e) the financial account balance

....

(f) the current plus capital plus financial account balances

....

(g) net errors and omissions

....

Q9. Explain why the overall balance of payments always balances.

....

....

Q10. The current account of the balance of payments tends to fluctuate with the business cycle. The current account tends to improve during a recession and deteriorate during a boom. *True/False*

14.2 Exchange rates

(Pages 417–21) The balance of payments is closely related to the rate of exchange. The rate of exchange is the rate at which one currency exchanges for another. If the rate of exchange of a pound sterling alters from 200 to 210 Japanese yen, this means that the pound has **Q11.** *appreciated/depreciated* relative to the yen, and that the yen has **Q12.** *appreciated/depreciated* relative to the pound. This means that Japanese imports will now be **Q13.** *cheaper/more expensive* in the UK and that, therefore, they will **Q14.** *rise/fall* in volume.

Q15. Sketch a demand curve for sterling and a supply curve of sterling against the euro on Figure 14.1 and mark the equilibrium exchange rate. Make sure you label the axes correctly.

Figure 14.1 Demand for and supply of sterling

(a) Who is demanding sterling in the diagram and for what purpose?

....

(b) Who is supplying sterling in the diagram and for what purpose?

....

(c) Now illustrate what happens to the exchange rate when there is an increased demand for sterling and a decreased supply.

Q16. The demand for sterling results from the credit items in the UK balance of payments and the supply of sterling results from the debit items.   *True/False*

Q17. Only one of the following flows represents a *demand* for sterling. Which one?
A. Imports of goods and services into the UK.
B. UK investment abroad.
C. Short-term financial outflows from the UK.
D. Profit earned from UK investment abroad.
E. Overseas aid by the UK government.

Q18. Assume that there is a free-floating exchange rate. Will the following cause the exchange rate to appreciate or depreciate? In each case you should consider whether there is a shift in the demand or supply curves of sterling (or both) and which way the curve(s) shift(s).
(a) More video recorders are imported from Japan.
> Demand curve shift *left/right/no shift*
> Supply curve shift *left/right/no shift*
> Exchange rate *appreciates/depreciates*
(b) Non-UK residents increase their purchases of UK government securities.
> Demand curve shift *left/right/no shift*
> Supply curve shift *left/right/no shift*
> Exchange rate *appreciates/depreciates*
(c) UK interest rates fall relative to those abroad.
> Demand curve shift *left/right/no shift*
> Supply curve shift *left/right/no shift*
> Exchange rate *appreciates/depreciates*
(d) The UK experiences a higher rate of inflation than other countries.
> Demand curve shift *left/right/no shift*
> Supply curve shift *left/right/no shift*
> Exchange rate *appreciates/depreciates*
(e) The result of the development of the single market in the EU is for investment in the UK by the rest of the EU to increase by a greater amount than UK investment in other EU countries.
> Demand curve shift *left/right/no shift*
> Supply curve shift *left/right/no shift*
> Exchange rate *appreciates/depreciates*

(f) Speculators believe that the rate of exchange will fall.
> Demand curve shift *left/right/no shift*
> Supply curve shift *left/right/no shift*
> Exchange rate *appreciates/depreciates*

(Pages 421–2) The government may be unwilling to let the pound float freely. Instead it may attempt to fix the exchange rate, or at least attempt to reduce exchange rate fluctuations.

Q19. Which one of the following is likely to lead to persistent balance of payments deficits for country X under fixed exchange rates?
A. A lower income elasticity of demand for the country's exports than for its imports.
B. A lower rate of growth at home than abroad.
C. A higher rate of inflation abroad than in the domestic economy.
D. The long-term development of import substitutes at home.
E. A growth in the country's monopoly power in the export market.

Q20. Which one of the following would help to prevent an appreciation of sterling resulting from an excess demand for sterling?
A. An increase in interest rates.
B. Building up reserves.
C. The Bank of England purchasing sterling on the foreign exchange market.
D. A reduction in government expenditure and an increase in taxation, but with no change in interest rates.
E. A decrease in the supply of money.

Q21. Assume that, as a result of inflation, there was downward pressure on the exchange rate. List three short-term measures the government could adopt in order to prevent the exchange rate depreciating.

1. ....

2. ....

3. ....

14.3 The relationship between the four objectives

(Pages 423–7) In this section we examine the relationships between the various macroeconomic objectives, and in particular between inflation and unemployment.

Q22. Fill in the blanks in Table 14.2, which relates the state of the economy to each phase of the business cycle. You should insert one of the following words in each of the blanks: *high/low/rising/falling/surplus/deficit*.

Table 14.2

	The upturn	The expansion	The peaking out	The slow-down
Inflation	.....	.....	.....	.....
Unemployment	.....	.....	.....	.....
Balance of trade	.....	.....	.....	.....
Growth	.....	.....	.....	.....
Investment	.....	.....	.....	.....
Business confidence	.....	.....	.....	.....

Q23. What use could a Phillips curve serve for economic policy makers (assuming that it painted an accurate picture)?

A. Predicting the phase of the business cycle.
B. Showing the relationship between the level of aggregate demand and aggregate supply.
C. Showing the relationship between rates of unemployment and rates of inflation.
D. Showing the relationship between overseas trade and economic growth.
E. Showing the effects of expectations on the level of investment.

During the late 1950s and 1960s, policy makers interpreted the Phillips curve as follows: demand management policy would lead to a **Q24.** *shift in/movement along* the Phillips curve. Thus it would only be possible to reduce both inflation and unemployment together by **Q25.** *expansionary demand management policies/contractionary demand management policies/keeping the level of aggregate demand the same/ using policies to influence non-demand factors causing inflation and unemployment.*

After 1966 the Phillips curve appeared to break down, and economies began to experience both higher unemployment *and* higher inflation.

Q26. Today the evidence suggests that there is no longer any relationship between inflation and unemployment.

True/False

14.4 The circular flow of income

(Pages 428–30) An important diagram for understanding how the macroeconomy works is the *circular flow of income diagram.* It can be used to show the relationship between changes in aggregate demand and the four macroeconomic objectives.

Q27. Figure 14.2 shows a circular flow of income. Attach the correct label (*Cd, G, I, M, S, T, X, Y*) to each of the eight flows.

Q28. Which of the following are changes in injections and which are changes in withdrawals in the UK

Figure 14.2 The circular flow of income

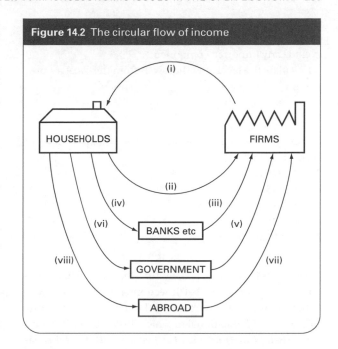

circular flow of income? In each case specify whether the change is an increase or a decrease. In each case assume *ceteris paribus.*

(a) The government raises tax allowances.
Withdrawal/Injection   Increase/Decrease
(b) The government cuts spending on roads.
Withdrawal/Injection   Increase/Decrease
(c) Firms borrow more money in order to build up their stocks in preparation for an anticipated rise in consumer demand.
Withdrawal/Injection   Increase/Decrease
(d) A depreciation in the exchange rate affects the popularity of holidays abroad.
Withdrawal/Injection   Increase/Decrease
(e) Saving is affected by a redistribution of income from the rich to the poor.
Withdrawal/Injection   Increase/Decrease
(f) Consumers demand more goods that are domestically produced (but total consumption does not change).
Withdrawal/Injection   Increase/Decrease
(g) People invest more money in building societies.
Withdrawal/Injection   Increase/Decrease

Q29. The following represent flows in the economy of a small country:

	(£m)
Saving	200
Consumption of domestic goods	1550
Income tax revenue	750
Indirect tax revenue	475
Import expenditure	600
Export expenditure	850
Government expenditure	900
Investment	575

(where government expenditure and investment include only the amount spent in the domestic economy: i.e. exclude any imported component).

Calculate the level of withdrawals from the circular flow.

....

Q30. Referring to the data in Q29, what is the level of aggregate demand?

A. £4075m
B. £3875m
C. £3275m
D. £2325m
E. £1550m

(Pages 430–1) Assume initially that injections equal withdrawals. Now assume that injections rise (or withdrawals fall), so that injections exceed withdrawals. This will cause a **Q31.** *rise/fall* in national income. This in turn will cause a **Q32.** *rise/fall* in **Q33.** *injections/withdrawals/both injections and withdrawals* until a new equilibrium level of income is reached where withdrawals once more equal injections. This change in income will tend to be **Q34.** *larger/smaller* than the initial change in injections.

Q35. What will happen to the level of national income in an economy if the following changes occur? (In each case assume other things remain unchanged.)

(a) The Chancellor of the Exchequer raises income tax.
     Rise/Fall/Impossible to tell without more information
(b) Firms are encouraged by lower interest rates to build new factories.
     Rise/Fall/Impossible to tell without more information
(c) French buyers are deterred from buying British-made goods.
     Rise/Fall/Impossible to tell without more information
(d) Both taxation and government expenditure are reduced.
     Rise/Fall/Impossible to tell without more information
(e) People decide to save a larger proportion of their income.
     Rise/Fall/Impossible to tell without more information
(f) Other countries begin to recover from recession.
     Rise/Fall/Impossible to tell without more information

Appendix: Measuring national income and output

Q36. Gross domestic product (GDP) may be defined as

....

There are three methods of calculating GDP: the product method, the income method and the expenditure method.

(Pages 432–4) The product method
In order to avoid double counting we measure the value added to a product or service as it passes through each phase of its production.

Q37. If a raw material supplier, firm A, sells some raw materials to firm B for £120, which then processes them and sells them to firm C for £160; and if firm C fashions them and sells them to firm D for £240, which uses them to produce a finished good which it sells to a wholesaler for £300, which then sells it to a retailer for £350, which then adds a £25 mark-up – what has been the total value of production? Use a value-added approach to work out the answer.

....

Q38. Which of the following would be included in the measurement of the UK's GDP?

(a) The appreciation of stock due to price increases.
                                                        Yes/No
(b) A service provided by government.   *Yes/No*
(c) A raw material that is imported.   *Yes/No*
(d) Stocks carried over from previous years.   *Yes/No*
(e) The profits from the output produced in the UK by foreign-owned firms.   *Yes/No*
(f) The benefits derived by owner occupiers from living in a property.   *Yes/No*
(g) Additions to stocks made during the year.   *Yes/No*
(h) The incomes earned by UK residents from the production of overseas companies.   *Yes/No*

(Page 434) The income approach
Q39. The factor incomes generated from the production of goods and services will be exactly equal to the sum of all values added.   *True/False*

Q40. Table 14.3 represents a simplified national income account for an economy.

(a) What is the level of gross value added?

....

(b) What is the level of gross domestic product (at market prices)?

....

Table 14.3 Items from a national income account

	(£m)
Compensation of employees	3000
Gross profit	500
Gross rent and interest	100
Mixed incomes	90
Taxes on products	150
Subsidies on products	60

(Page 434) The expenditure approach

● **Q41.** Which of the following items would be included in measuring the UK's GDP by the expenditure method?

(a) Spending on domestically produced consumer durables.
Yes/No

(b) The purchase of British cars in Europe. *Yes/No*

(c) Government spending on social security. *Yes/No*

(d) Government spending on educational services.
Yes/No

(e) The purchase of new machinery by private industry.
Yes/No

(f) Expenditure on new private housing. *Yes/No*

(g) Local government expenditure on new council housing.
Yes/No

(h) Private expenditure on old (unimproved) housing.
Yes/No

⊗ **Q42.** Table 14.4 shows GDP by category of expenditure. Calculate

(a) GDP (at market prices) ....

(b) GVA ....

Tabel 14.4 GDP by category of expenditure

	(£m)
Consumer expenditure	1050
Government final consumption	600
Gross domestic fixed capital formation	500
Exports of goods and services	850
Imports of goods and services	950
Taxes on products	500
Subsidies on products	50
Net income from abroad	60
Capital consumption (depreciation)	120

Other measures
(Pages 434–5) Three other measures which are frequently used are gross national income (GNY), net national income (NNY) and households' disposable income.

⊗ **Q43.** Using the figures in Table 14.4, calculate the following:

(a) GNY ....

(b) NNY ....

▤ **Q44.** Households' disposable income is:

A. GDP (at market prices) + taxes paid by firms – subsidies received by firms + personal taxes – benefits.

B. GDP (at market prices) – taxes paid by firms + subsidies received by firms – depreciation – undistributed profits + personal taxes – benefits.

C. GDP (at market prices) – taxes paid by firms + subsidies received by firms – depreciation – undistributed profits – personal taxes + benefits.

D. GNY (at market prices) – taxes paid by firms + subsidies received by firms – undistributed profits + personal taxes – benefits.

E. GDY (at market prices) – taxes paid by firms + subsidies received by firms – depreciation – undistributed profits – personal taxes + benefits.

Some qualifications
(Pages 435–41) When calculating real GDP we must use the *GDP deflator* for that year. This allows us to adjust figures measured in current prices for the rate of inflation, and show them in terms of a base year.

◑ **Q45.** The GDP deflator is the same as the retail price index (RPI). *True/False*

⊗ **Q46.** Assume that GDP in current prices grows from £120bn in year 1 to £160bn in year 2 and that the GDP deflator rises from 100 in year 1 to 130 in year 2, by how much has real GDP grown (as a percentage)?

....

When comparing national income statistics of different countries, they have to be converted into a common currency (e.g. dollars or euros). But the current market exchange rate may be a poor indicator of the purchasing power of a country's currency. To correct for this, *purchasing-power parity* (PPP) exchange rates can be used. PPP rates are those at which a given amount of money would buy the same in any country after exchanging it into the local currency. GDP measured at PPP exchange rates is known as *purchasing-power standard* GDP (PPS GDP).

⊗ **Q47.** If country A has a national income of $10bn and country B has a national income of $12bn at current exchange rates, and if, in PPP terms, current exchange rates overvalue the currency of B relative to A by 1.5 times, what is the ratio of the PPS GDP of country A to country B?

....

B PROBLEMS, EXERCISES AND PROJECTS

Table 14.5 Balance of payments: current account

| | Trade in goods and services | | | | | | | | |
	Exports of goods	Imports of goods	Balance of trade in goods	Exports of services	Imports of services	Services balance	Income balance	Current transfers balance	Current balance
Annual									
1986	72 997	82 614	−9 617	24 784	18 279	6 505	2 872	−2 045	−2 285
1987	79 531	91 229	−11 698	26 906	20 220	6 686	1 503	−2 074	−5 583
1988	80 711	102 264	−21 553	26 723	22 393	4 330	1 291	−1 605	−17 537
1989	92 611	117 335	−24 724	29 272	25 355	3 917	−64	−2 620	−23 491
1990	102 313	121 020	−18 707	31 188	27 178	4 010	−558	−4 258	−19 513
1991	103 939	114 162	−10 223	31 426	26 955	4 471	−1 953	−669	−8 374
1992	107 863	120 913	−13 050	35 428	29 754	5 674	2 115	−4 821	−10 082
1993	122 039	135 358	−13 319	40 039	33 416	6 623	685	−4 607	−10 618
1994	135 260	146 351	−11 091	43 507	36 979	6 528	7 770	−4 665	−1 458
1995	153 725	165 449	−11 724	48 687	39 772	8 915	5 976	−6 912	−3 745
1996	167 403	180 489	−13 086	52 900	44 003	8 897	8 111	−4 522	−600
1997	171 783	183 693	−11 910	57 259	45 417	11 842	11 124	−4 753	6 303
1998	163 704	184 302	−20 598	61 777	49 099	12 678	15 782	−6 388	1 474
Quarterly									
1994 Q1	32 096	35 250	−3 154	10 510	8 931	1 579	2 403	−1 705	−877
Q2	33 327	35 866	−2 539	10 647	9 326	1 321	1 503	−1 507	−1 222
Q3	34 228	36 688	−2 460	11 072	9 260	1 812	1 954	−1 379	−73
Q4	35 609	38 547	−2 938	11 278	9 462	1 816	1 910	−74	714
1995 Q1	37 332	38 940	−1 608	11 797	9 379	2 418	1 402	−1 519	693
Q2	37 406	40 759	−3 353	11 972	10 080	1 892	621	−1 621	−2 461
Q3	38 987	42 617	−3 630	12 189	10 160	2 029	1 799	−1 592	−1 394
Q4	40 000	43 133	−3 133	12 729	10 153	2 576	2 154	−2 180	−583
1996 Q1	41 136	44 882	−3 746	12 802	10 924	1 878	1 987	−1 656	−1 537
Q2	41 706	45 273	−3 567	13 078	10 994	2 084	2 869	−1 274	112
Q3	42 225	45 134	−2 909	13 059	10 911	2 148	1 252	−984	−493
Q4	42 336	45 200	−2 864	13 961	11 174	2 787	2 003	−608	1 318
1997 Q1	42 652	44 666	−2 014	13 687	11 069	2 618	3 101	−1 635	2 070
Q2	42 967	45 995	−3 028	14 219	11 208	3 011	2 576	−889	1 670
Q3	43 079	45 846	−2 767	14 501	11 491	3 010	3 155	−1 392	2 006
Q4	43 085	47 186	−4 101	14 852	11 649	3 203	2 292	−837	557
1998 Q1	41 412	45 665	−4 253	14 965	11 837	3 128	2 413	−1 963	−675
Q2	41 380	46 165	−4 785	15 390	12 229	3 161	1 169	−747	−1 202
Q3	41 143	46 410	−5 267	15 670	12 208	3 462	5 318	−1 116	2 397
Q4	39 769	46 062	−6 293	15 752	12 825	2 927	6 882	−2 562	954

Source: *Economic Trends* (ONS, 1999).

Q48. Table 14.5 is taken from *Economic Trends* and shows the UK balance of payments on current account.

(a) Explain the terms 'Services', 'Income balance' and 'Current transfers balance'.

(b) Which parts of the current account are subject to the greatest short-term fluctuations? What explanations can you offer for this?

(c) Which parts of the current account fluctuate with the course of the business cycle and in which direction? What explanations can you offer for this? Why do other parts appear not to fluctuate with the course of the business cycle?

Table 14.6 UK balance of payments (1997)

Item	£m
UK investment overseas	90 296
Balance of services	+11 842
Net capital transfers	+837
Net current transfers	−4 753
Net errors and omissions	+1 480
Overseas investment in the UK	52 187
Short-term capital inflows to UK	195 866
Short-term capital outflows from UK	168 757
Exports of goods	171 783
Imports of goods	183 693
Net income flows from abroad	+11 124
Changes in reserves	. . . . .

Q49. Table 14.6 shows a simplified balance of payments account for the UK in 1997.
(a) What was the UK's balance on trade in goods and services?

....

(b) Calculate the deficit/surplus on the current account.

....

(c) Calculate the deficit/surplus on the capital plus financial accounts (excluding reserves and net errors and omissions).

....

(d) Establish whether there was a loss or addition to the country's reserves and of how much. (You will first have to take net errors and omissions into account.)

....

Q50. Let us assume that there is a free-floating exchange rate: i.e. that the exchange rate is determined by free-market forces. The demand and supply schedules in Table 14.7 relate the price of sterling to the euro for a given day.

(a) What is the equilibrium rate of exchange? ....

(b) A sharp fall in UK interest rates causes the demand for sterling to fall by £8m per day at all exchange rates.

Table 14.7 Demand for and supply of sterling

Price of sterling in euros	1.10	1.20	1.30	1.40	1.50	1.60	1.70	1.80
£m demanded per day	40	36	32	28	24	20	16	12
£m supplied per day	16	20	24	28	32	36	40	44

Assuming other things remain equal, what will happen to the exchange rate for sterling in euros?

....

(c) If we relax the assumption that other things remain equal in (b) above, what might happen to the supply of sterling?

....

(d) Assume that, in addition to the fall in demand for sterling of £8m per day, the supply of sterling to purchase euros rises by £8m. What will the equilibrium exchange rate be now?

....

(e) Suppose now that the authorities decide to fix the exchange rate value between the pound and the euro. They decide on a rate £1 = €1.60. How can the reserves be used to maintain this rate of exchange?

....

(f) What will be the effect on trade between the UK and the euro-zone countries of this policy of fixing the exchange rate at £1 = €1.60?

....

(g) In order to address the problem of the over-valued pound, the authorities may be forced in the long run to reassess the fixed exchange-rate value. They might be forced to *devalue/revalue* the currency.

Q51. Table 14.8 shows UK National Income Accounts for 1998 by category of expenditure. Calculate the following:
(a) GDP.
(b) GVA.
(c) GNY.
(d) NNY.

Table 14.8 UK national income by category of expenditure

	(£m)
Consumption of households and NPISH	541 951
General government final consumption	152 361
Gross domestic fixed capital formation	145 329
Value of physical increase in stocks and work in progress	4 035
Exports of goods and services	225 481
Imports of goods and services	233 401
Statistical discrepancy	1 862
Taxes on products	100 587
Subsidies on products	4 570
Net income from abroad	12 299
Capital consumption	92 119

DISCUSSION TOPICS AND ESSAYS

Q52. In what sense is it true to say that a current account deficit will always be matched by an equal surplus elsewhere in the balance of payments?

Q53. What effect will a rise in interest rates be likely to have on the various parts of the balance of payments account?

Q54. For what reasons may the rate of exchange depreciate? What measures could the government adopt to prevent this depreciation?

Q55. What is the relationship between the balance of payments and the rate of exchange?

Q56. What problems face a government in attempting to achieve all its principal macroeconomic objectives simultaneously?

Q57. At what point of the business cycle is the country at present? Do you think that the government has managed to get the economy to the right point of the cycle in order to improve its chances of success at the next general election?

Q58. Sketch a circular flow of income diagram and describe its components. Describe the effect of (a) an increase in saving and (b) an increase in government expenditure.

Q59. Why can GDP be measured in three different ways? What adjustments have to be made to ensure that all these methods yield the same figure?

Q60. There are difficulties in making useful national income comparisons not only of different countries, but also of the same country over time. Why?

Q61. Debate
Comparing the welfare of different countries' citizens by the use of GNY statistics is so misleading that it is better not to use these statistics at all for comparative purposes.

ARTICLES

The impact of the collapse of several of the economies of south-east Asia in 1997/8, and the stagnation of Japan, was felt world wide. One country which is particularly dependent on the region is Australia. The following article, taken from *The Economist* of 13 June 1998, explores the impact the economic crisis was having on Australian trade and the Australian dollar.

Down under

The lucky country may be running out of luck. For the past decade, Australia has been one of the rich world's fastest-growing economies, thanks is part to the booming markets of East Asia on its doorstep. Now, however, its neighbours are in deep trouble, driving Australia's currency literally down under.

Worries about the country's dependence on Asia pushed the Australian dollar to a 12-year low of US$0.58 on June 10, down 25 per cent since the end of 1996. In part these worries are justified. More than 60 per cent of Australia's exports go to Asia, equivalent to almost 10 per cent of its GDP – the biggest share of any rich country (see chart). Thus the economy stands to be hit hardest by the slump in Japan and the rest of East Asia. In the four months to April exports to South-East Asia fell by 24 per cent on the same period a year ago, and exports to South Korea dropped 15 per cent.

Minerals, wool, food and live animals account for two-thirds of Australia's exports, so the economy is also being battered by weaker commodity prices. The current-account deficit is forecast to widen to between 5 per cent and 6 per cent of GDP this year. This is the main source of pressure on the Australian dollar.

Earlier this decade, in Paul Keating's days as prime minister, the government was keen to stress that Australia was part of Asia. Now, policymakers are emphasising the ways in which Australia is different from its neighbours – and therefore less likely to suffer a financial crisis. One big difference is that Australia, unlike the East Asians before their currencies plunged, has a floating exchange rate which can adjust smoothly to market pressures. In contrast, the East Asian countries' policy of pegging their exchange rates to the American dollar made their currencies susceptible to speculative attack and hence a 'currency crisis'.

The slide in the Australian dollar has revived memories of 1986, when it hit an all-time low of US$0.571 after Mr Keating, then the country's treasurer, warned that without better economic policies Australia could become a banana republic. But economic circumstances today are very different. In 1986, underlying inflation was running at almost 10 per cent, against

1.5 per cent now. Then, the budget was in deficit; this calendar year, a small surplus is expected. And the banking system is much healthier now than in the 1980s, when financial liberalisation spurred reckless lending.

Indeed, the drop in the Australian dollar today is much less alarming than the fall of the mid-1980s, when its trade-weighted index declined 40 per cent in the space of 18 months. Over the past year, in contrast, its trade-weighted value has hardly budged, because the currencies of three of Australia's most important trading partners – Japan, New Zealand and South Korea – have also tumbled against the American dollar.

How much of a dent is Asia's slump making in the Australian economy? On the surface, very little. Its GDP grew at a robust annual rate of 5.3 per cent in the first quarter of this year, the fastest growth among the main industrial economies. But look closer. Domestic demand was flat, while net exports fell. More than the whole of the increase in GDP reflected an enormous build-up of stocks. In other words, producers were caught out by a sudden drop in sales. This implies that output will slow sharply over coming months as firms slash stocks.

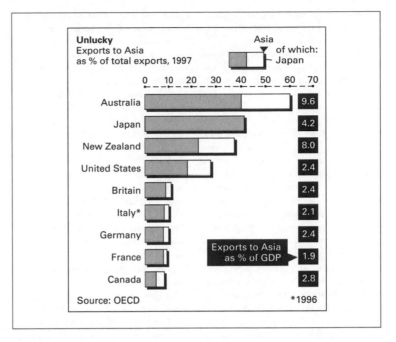

Many economists are starting to worry that the weak dollar will push up inflation, leaving the central bank no room to cut interest rates if the economy slows abruptly. It may even be forced to raise interest rates to support the dollar. For a government that is likely to call national elections later this year, slow growth, higher inflation and maybe even higher interest rates are likely to prove an awkward mix.

(a) Given the strong ties between Australia and south-east Asia – over 60 per cent of its exports go to the region – why has the Australian economy not fared far worse, given the severity of the Asian economic collapse?

(b) Why does having a free-floating exchange rate make a currency less susceptible to speculative attack than if it were pegged to the US dollar?

(c) Why might raising interest rates to support the dollar make the slump in export sales worse?

In the following article, which appeared on *The Independent* of 30 June 1998, Lea Patterson assesses the nervousness of international currency markets and how the devaluation of one currency in one part of the world is likely to lead to a ripple effect of devaluation around the global economy.

Currency bomb is still ticking

On 2 July 1997, the Thai government devalued the baht in the face of intense pressure from currency speculators. By the end of the year, the Indonesian rupiah, the Korean won, the Malaysian ringgit and the Philippine peso had all depreciated by at least 40 per cent. The world at large was forced to face facts – the once-vaunted 'tiger' economies of the East were on decidedly shaky ground.

Almost exactly a year on, currency speculators are in the news again – the

Russian rouble is faltering, the Pakistan government devalued the rupee by 4.2 per cent at the weekend, and the South African rand yesterday hit an all-time low, at 6.155 to the dollar. Are we about to see a second, perhaps more widespread, round of devaluations? And what, if anything, can the authorities do to stave off the speculators?

The amount of money traded on the world's foreign exchange markets is nothing short of phenomenal. Harry

Shutt, in his newly-published book *The Trouble with Capitalism*, estimates that the daily volume of business on the world's currency markets stood at around $1500bn in 1995, a figure which exceeds the annual gross domestic product of all but three of the world's economies.

As a result, currency speculators have immense power. When the markets become convinced that a country's currency is fundamentally overvalued, as recently has been the case in South Africa, there is little the authorities can do to avert a currency collapse.

Notwithstanding the Malaysian Prime Minister's view that the markets' attack on the ringgit was a Jewish conspiracy aimed at the Far East, most experts are now convinced that last year's Asian devaluations were inevitable, given the fundamentals. In its recently published 1997 annual report, the Asian Development Bank argues that globalisation, and the consequent rapid inflow of capital into the tiger economies, merely 'heightened the risks associated with failing to address inappropriate policies, weaknesses in financial sector institutions and problems in corporate and public governance'.

Globalisation, and the free movement of capital, may have been a spur to the heady economic growth enjoyed by the region in the early 1990s, but it also opened up the economies to an unprecedented degree of public scrutiny and evaluation. When the bubble burst in Asia, and when investor confidence began to falter, capital flowed out of the region as fast as it had flowed in just a few months before, and devaluations became inevitable.

A combination of increased globalisation – with the accompanying increase in global scrutiny – and weak economic fundamentals also lies behind the latest round of currency speculation in the emerging markets.

In Russia, the rouble yesterday steadied at around 6.22 to the dollar after the government raised interest rates on Friday to 80 per cent from 60 per cent, but analysts were gloomy about the country's long-term prospects. Paul McNamara, emerging markets economist at Julius Baer Investments, commented: 'Policy is king and neither in Asia nor Russia are we seeing any positive steps.'

In South Africa, meanwhile, the rand pulled itself off its earlier lows after the central bank raised its repo rate by almost 2 per cent but, as with Russia, experts say the outlook for the economy is negative. The central bank's use of interest rates is predicted to slow economic growth in an already fragile economy, while the fall in the exchange rate is likely to fuel inflation.

There has also been pressure on the Australian dollar, where economists are predicting that the Asian crisis will continue to hit growth. In Pakistan, meanwhile, the reasons for the currency slide are also economic in nature, albeit of a slightly different variety. Most experts have been attributing the weakness in the rupee to the economic sanctions imposed on Pakistan in the wake of its nuclear tests.

But although economic fundamentals would seem to provide the reasons for the latest bout of speculative attacks, they do not fully explain the timing. The markets have known about the weaknesses in certain of the emerging markets for some time. So why has the speculation started now? The answer here lies in the Japanese economy, and in particular in the recent bout of weakness in the Japanese yen.

David Brickman, international economist at PaineWebber, explained: 'The weakness in the yen has changed the attitude to risk in the global currency markets. There has been a flight to quality, and the markets have begun to reassess the weaker economies.' Ask the experts which of the emerging markets economies are the weakest, and the names South Africa and Russia are on almost everybody's lips.

As it is Japan that lies behind the renewed attacks by the currency speculators, so it is Japan that will determine how far the latest slump in emerging market currencies will go.

If the yen depreciates rapidly, the signs are that China will devalue the yuan. And if China devalues, this is likely to spark not only another round of devaluations in the East, but also sharp falls in global stock markets. Further emerging market gloom will also hit export demand in the developed countries, re-awakening fears of a worldwide slowdown.

It is this spectre of Chinese devaluation that prompted the US Federal Reserve to intervene in the world currency markets 10 days ago in an attempt to stem the rapid fall in the yen. The apparent success of the US intervention – the yen has not rallied but neither has it gone into free-fall – seems surprising, given the funds the currency speculators have at their disposal.

Most analysts attribute this to a mixture of nervousness in the markets, which believe that there may be no ceiling on the Fed's willingness to intervene and buy up the yen, and, perhaps more significantly, to the signals the intervention sent to the speculators. Some believe the West is now committed to rescuing the Japanese economy – and that Japan is committed to making the necessary reforms.

In sum, depreciation in the South African rand and the Russian rouble may be inevitable, given the power of the currency speculators, the renewed risk-averseness in the markets and the weak economic fundamentals.

What is less clear is whether a devaluation in the yuan is inevitable, at least in the near term. Policymakers the world over hope that co-ordinated central bank intervention combined with rapid and wide-ranging structural reforms in Japan will be sufficient to stave off the speculators. If it is not, the economic consequences may be nothing short of disastrous.

(a) What reasons does the article give to explain why currencies collapsed in south-east Asia?

(b) Why, according to the article, was Japan to blame for the uncertainty in international currency markets?

(c) 'If the yen depreciates rapidly, the signs are that China will devalue the yuan. And if China devalues, this is likely to spark not only another round of devaluations in the East, but also sharp falls in global stock markets.' Why would a round of competitive currency devaluations have very limited benefit to any country in the longer term?

Large and small companies alike, if they trade abroad, have the problem of foreign exchange risk. The article below, taken from *CBI News* of July/August 1999, considers the foreign exchange problems faced by businesses and how they might deal with them.

The critical difference

The strong pound has been wreaking havoc with British businesses for months. Furthermore, the British exporter faces two major risks: firstly from exchange rate volatility and secondly, the way in which the markets are structured. Foreign exchange is the world's largest traded market with a daily turnover of approximately £1600bn. The market is dominated by the big US and European banks led by the likes of Citibank, ABN Amro and United Bank of Switzerland. Surprisingly, 95 per cent of this enormous turnover is speculative, where trading is not based upon the sale or purchase of real goods. Therefore, even the largest exporting firms are minorities in this huge, complex flow of money around the world.

Smaller firms are even more vulnerable, and it makes no sense for hardpressed sales staff to bring in new business if already tight margins are then frittered away by ill-timed foreign exchange deals. Many firms, like clothing manufacturers Fruit of the Loom, operate the most careful hedging strategy they can, as Stephen Grisman, the company's assistant treasurer responsible for European Treasury explains. 'We are a multinational company with an American base. World-wide our sales total £1.4bn. Our European division employs about 3500 people and we have annual sales of £168m.

'I manage our integrated, centralised European cash management system and we operate a foreign exchange hedging policy. I need to be aware of where the foreign exchange markets are and I need to look ahead about 12 months. I use a mixture of spot trades, forwards and options. Historically I have worked on information from three sources, *Financial Times*, an online information system and material received from my banks.'

Stephen Grisman's problem, like that of many smaller company treasurers, is that he does not have sufficient transactions to warrant operating his own dealing room. All the time he is faced with interpreting the information he receives from his various sources, he has other tasks to perform in his working day. This means that he cannot spend long periods poring over statistics and analysing the market.

'I suppose my banks are impartial! But I am dealing with the people who want to do a trade with my money,' he adds. That, he admits, is not ideal. He is always likely to be at a disadvantage when dealing with experienced and specialist foreign exchange dealers.

'There is always a conflict of interest when banks provide foreign exchange to their clients,' says Laurence Butcher, managing director of Windsor-based Halewood International Market Strategies Ltd (HIMS). 'It is a fact that the best time for any company to sell a currency is, by the very nature of the transaction, the worst time for the bank to be buying it.'

HIMS works closely with Grisman to level up the odds. HIMS provides Fruit of the Loom's European treasury with professional expertise and analysis to assist Grisman to get the best results from the currency markets and the banks.

Nick Warburton, financial accountant at ARM Holdings Plc, the Cambridge microchip designer, faces a similar challenge. Last year the company had sales of £42m. Dual listed in London and New York's NASDAQ, ARM is mainly a sterling-based operation; however, virtually all its revenues are in dollars.

With an ongoing requirement to sell dollars for sterling, staying in tune with the market is crucial. Like Fruit of the Loom, ARM is risk averse when it comes to foreign exchange and has established clear guidelines; avoiding foreign exchange risk as far as possible. When doing a deal, Nick Warburton, for whom foreign exchange cannot be a full-time job, needs to make vital decisions.

'The main decision is when to sell US dollars. We may be in a better position to negotiate if we understand what the market is likely to do.' In other words, he needs to know more than simply the spot price. He needs to be able to understand trends in the market in order to time his sale, and protect against negative price movements. Having assessed the expected range of trade over a period of time, whether hours, days or weeks, it can make a considerable difference in protecting profits and getting the best out of the trading conditions.

Mr Warburton knows that by outsourcing advice and up-to-the-minute

information, he can assess whether the banks are giving him a fair price and making reasonable forward adjustments. 'It gives me assurance and takes the worry off my shoulders because I know that the market is being monitored all the time.'

'Simply knowing where exchange rates are is only part of the story,' explains Laurence Butcher. 'To make a decision or take action without knowing why the movement has taken place and where it is expected to move from there is pure speculation. Our clients benefit from us keeping them fully updated with realtime information where it affects their exchange rates. They know where the market is and why it is moving.

'Historically, companies have been reactive, basing their decisions on past events seen in the FT or heard on the news. Their policies tended to be based on prices quoted by their bands. Trading so blindly very often results in trades being completed at the worst price of the day, week or month in question. This bad timing is a direct result of the client being unaware of the factors and sentiment in the market at the time of the trade.

'At HIMS, we make our clients aware of the range of movement and the reasons behind the range. Then we monitor the developing trend and inform our clients when the exchange rate is at the top or bottom of expectations. This objective overview ensures that our clients never trade blind. They can make well-informed decisions on their exposure and protect against risk whenever necessary.'

Renishaw Plc is a high-technology engineering company making precision meteorology equipment with a world headquarters in Wootton-under-Edge, Gloucestershire. Sales in 1998 were £92m in dollars, deutschemarks, yen and Irish punts. The company exports about 90 per cent of its turnover.

Looking after foreign exchange is one of group financial accountant Rob Hume's jobs. 'Because we've got currencies coming in on a regular basis, and our costs are all sterling based, we have to convert the currencies to sterling. We use Halewood as an "insurance policy", they inform us of where rates are and where they are likely to move.'

Deals vary from £250 000 to £1m. Hume uses a screen-based pricing system but Halewood's information is delivered real-time with an added dimension of interaction with the analysts – something that his bankers do not supply.

'It is critical that we sell currency at the right time. HIMS inform us as to which way the currencies are moving,' says Mr Hume, 'so then we are able to optimise our dealings'.

Predicting where exchange rates may be at any given time is a pointless and exceptionally risky practice, says Laurence Butcher. 'Traditionally, the information and analysis given to UK corporates by their banks has fallen into that category. This will invariably be wrong as these guess-timates are based on variables subject to change.

'If the risk for a currency is to appreciate or depreciate, then we need to know by how much it could realistically move. From there a company can establish logical parameters of movement over any given time frame. Too many times, companies just book forward and live to regret it.'

At a time when UK companies are struggling to preserve their sales and their margins against the burden of spiralling exchange rates, good advice and specialist analysis is critical. Moreover, in the battle against the big financial institutions, who run the world's foreign exchange markets, exporters, even very large exporters, need all the help they can get.

(a) Explain how a firm's foreign trading profits might be influenced by: (i) an appreciation; (ii) a depreciation of the currency.

(b) How might a firm set about reducing its exposure to foreign exchange risk?

(c) What impact is the euro likely to have on the stability of profits for firms within the euro-zone?

Environmental economists are highly critical of conventional methods of calculating GDP. They argue that GDP should reflect the full social costs of production, which include the impact on the natural environment and its resources. In the article below, taken from *Nature* of October 1998, the issues involved, and the problems of constructing a green GDP, are considered.

Progress and pitfalls along the path towards a 'greener' method of calculating national productivity

One goal that unites most ecological economists is the desire to develop a system of national accounting that embraces environmental factors excluded from current definitions of gross domestic product (GDP).

The conventional assessment of GDP, which is around 50 years old, works by adding up all the final demands for goods and services produced annually by a nation. Although widely used by economists, journalists and politicians as the measure of the economic health of a country, GDP has been much criticized by environmentalist groups – backed by some sympathetic economists – on the grounds that it paints a potentially misleading picture of a society's health when seen in environmental terms.

'A country could exhaust its mineral resources, cut down its forests, erode its soils, pollute its aquifers, and hunt its wildlife and fisheries to extinction, but its GDP would not be affected as these assets disappeared,' says Robert Repetto, an environmental and resource economist at the World Resources Institute, an independent research organization in Washington DC.

Repetto has pioneered work on a greener GDP. His study in Indonesia in 1989 concluded that annual GDP growth corrected for depreciation in timber, petroleum and soil resources was 3 per cent lower than the conventionally calculated figure of 7.1 per cent between 1971 and 1984.

More radical ecological economists such as Herman Daly take a different view. They criticize the idea that a country's wealth can be measured just in terms of how much its citizens produce.

Daly has helped to develop what he and colleagues refer to as the index of sustainable economic welfare (ISEW). Although this takes GDP as its starting point, it adds the value of unpaid household work, and then subtracts the cost of pollution, as well as urbanization, road accidents and advertising. But, for all its intellectual attractions, the ISEW has had little success among policy-makers. It has also been criticized by more mainstream economists, mainly because of questions about the accuracy of measuring some of its components.

Despite such shortcomings, since the beginning of the decade, calls for a green GDP have been getting louder. In 1993, in response to such suggestions, the United Nations (UN) Statistical Division in New York, which is responsible for setting guidelines for national accounting systems, carried out a review of possible alternatives.

But the review concluded that there was a lack of sufficient data to be able to recommend that countries adopt a green index, or, indeed, a new welfare index.

Instead, countries were encouraged merely to publish separate indicators on the state of key environmental services, as well as their associated monetary values, in parallel with conventional measurements of GDP.

In response to such suggestions, the European Commission is already

How green is your country?

Country	GNP	Green NNP	
		($ per capita 1993)	% fall on GNP
Japan	31 449	27 374	−13.0
Norway	25 947	21 045	−18.9
United States	24 716	21 365	−11.5
Germany	23 494	20 844	−11.3
South Korea	7 681	7 041	−8.3
South Africa	3 582	2 997	−16.3
Brazil	2 936	2 579	−12.2
Indonesia	732	616	−15.8
China	490	411	−10.4
India	293	242	−17.4

Green net national product (NNP) is gross national product (GNP) minus depreciation of produced assets, depletion of forests and subsoil assets, and damage from carbon dioxide emissions.

working on 60 environmental 'pressure indices' intended to act as a measure of the health of various natural resources.

In parallel, the commission is working with the UN and the Organization for Economic Cooperation and Development (OECD) on so-called 'satellite accounts' that attempt to put monetary values on different aspects of environmental degradation.

There are several other reasons why a green GDP has not been taken up. One is the Lack of agreement on its components and on how the index would be calculated.

A second reason is that GDP was never intended to be used as an indicator of environmental health, or indeed of prosperity. And some policymakers see little point in trying to turn it into something that was not originally intended.

Third, there has been unexpected enthusiasm among governments for the human development index (HDI), a quality-of-life indicator that is based on average life expectancy at birth, literacy level, number of years at school and GDP per capita.

Another equally important reason for scepticism about a new green index is the lack of detailed knowledge of its potential components, such as an accurate measure of water pollution, or the climate change potential of greenhouse gases. The UN review team felt that the work on parallel indicators – which many countries are now carrying out – would help to address most of these issues.

'There was a feeling at the time that if we want to include environmental resources in GDP, we must have comprehensive information,' says Kirk Hamilton, a senior economist at the environment department of the World Bank. 'That means having detailed knowledge of each type of damage by each pollutant.'

Many of these gaps are now being filled. But Hamilton points out that most rich countries remain unconvinced about the desirability of a new index, partly because they derive a smaller share of their earnings from natural resources than developing countries, but also because the parallel indicators are, in themselves, an adequate guide to environmental health.

Despite the setbacks, environmental and ecological economists continue to argue the case for a single index that integrates a measure of the wealth of a country's citizens and the health of its natural environment. Progress towards this goal has been slow. But few have given up hope that it can be achieved in a generally acceptable way.

(a) In what ways do current calculations of GDP ignore environmental considerations?

(b) If GDP calculations did include some environmental estimation, what implications would this have for the level of countries' GDP? Would the gap between the GDP of rich and poor countries narrow or widen?

(c) Why has a green measure of GDP not be adopted by governments and international agencies?

 ANSWERS

Q1. *True.*

Q2. *True.*

Q3. *debits* (a), (b), (c). These all represent a monetary flow from the UK to the rest of the world.

credits (d), (e), (f), (g). These all represent a monetary flow to the UK. Note that drawing on reserves is a credit item because it credits the balance of payments (even though it represents a debit to the reserves).

Q4. A. The balance on trade in goods and services equals exports of goods and services minus imports of goods and services: i.e. (£120m + £50m) − (£150m + £60m) = −£40m.

Q5. E. It equals the balance on trade in goods and services plus net income flows and current transfers: i.e. −£40 + £80m − £30m = +£10m.

Q6. D. The three accounts, the current account, capital account and financial account (plus any net errors and omissions), must add up to zero: they must balance. Thus a deficit on the current account must be balanced by a surplus of the same amount on the sum of the other two accounts plus net errors and omissions.

Q7. (a) (i), (b) (iv), (c) (vi), (d) (x), (e) (iii), (f) (vi), (g) (ix), (h) (xiv), (i) (xii), (j) (ii), (k) (viii).

Q8. (a) £74m – £82m = –£8m.
(b) £74m – £82m + £80m – £78m = –£6m.
(c) £74m – £82m + £80m – £78m + £43m –£40m = –£3m.
(d) £7m – £5m = £2m.
(e) £56m – £70m + £96m – £84m + £1m = –£1m.
(f) –£3m + £2m – £1m = –£2m.
(g) +£2m.

Q9. After taking account of any errors and omissions, any deficit on the current account must be matched by an equal and opposite surplus on the total of the other two accounts, and vice versa.

Q10. *True.* In a boom, higher incomes lead to more imports, and higher inflation leads to both less exports and more imports. Therefore the balance of payments on current account tends to deteriorate. The reverse is true in a recession.

Q11. *appreciated.*

Q12. *depreciated.*

Q13. *cheaper.*

Q14. *rise.*

Q15. (a) Non-UK residents are buying sterling with euros in order to obtain UK exports of goods and services and to invest in the UK.
(b) UK residents are supplying sterling in order to purchase euros in order to obtain imports of goods and services from the euro-zone countries and to invest in the euro zone.
(c) The demand and supply curves in Figure A14.1 shift to D_2 and S_2 respectively. The exchange rate will appreciate to r/e_2.

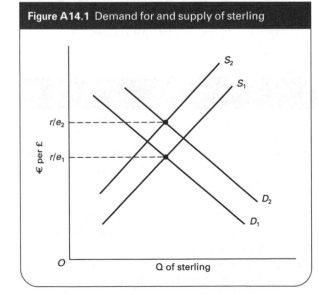

Figure A14.1 Demand for and supply of sterling

Q16. *True.*

Q17. D. It is a credit item on the balance of payments. The others are debit items. The profit earned abroad on UK investment will be in foreign currency. When this is exchanged for sterling in order to pay the dividends to UK shareholders, this will create a demand for sterling.

Q18. (a) Demand curve *no shift*; supply curve shifts to the *right*; exchange rate *depreciates*.
(b) Demand curve shifts to the *right*; supply curve *no shift*; exchange rate *appreciates*.
(c) Demand curve shifts to the *left*; supply curve shifts to the *right*; exchange rate *depreciates*.
(d) Demand curve shifts to the *left*; supply curve shifts to the *right*; exchange rate *depreciates*.
(e) Demand curve shifts to the *right*; supply curve shifts to the *right* (but less so than the demand curve); exchange rate *appreciates*.
(f) Demand curve shifts to the *left*; supply curve shifts the *right*; exchange rate *depreciates*.

Q19. A. This will mean that as world incomes grow, exports will grow less rapidly than imports. Note in the case of B that a lower rate of growth in country X will lead to a lower rate of growth in demand for imports than in other countries, and hence a lower rate of growth in demand for country X's imports than its exports.

Q20. B. Building up reserves results from the Bank of England selling sterling on the foreign exchange market. This increased supply of sterling helps to prevent an appreciation. All the other options will tend to *cause* an appreciation. In the case of option A, higher interest rates increase the demand for sterling and decrease the supply, as short-term finance flows into the country. With option C, the Bank of England is adding to the demand for sterling. With option D, there will be reduction in aggregate demand and hence a reduction in the demand for imports (and hence the supply of sterling) and, via lower prices, an increase in exports (and hence the demand for sterling).

Q21. 1. The use of reserves to buy sterling.
2. Borrowing from abroad to buy sterling.
3. Increased interest rates to attract short-term money inflows.

Q22.

	The upturn	The expansion	The peaking out	The slow-down
Inflation	*low*	*rising*	*high*	*falling*
Unemployment	*high*	*falling*	*low*	*rising*
Balance of trade	*surplus*	*deficit*	*deficit*	*surplus*
Growth	*rising*	*high*	*falling*	*low*
Investment	*rising*	*high*	*falling*	*low*
Business confidence	*rising*	*high*	*low*	*low*

Q23. C. The Phillips curve showed the apparent trade off between rates of unemployment and rates of inflation.

Q24. *movement along.* In other words, the government could trade off inflation against unemployment.

Q25. *using policies to influence non-demand factors causing inflation and unemployment.* It was believed that demand management policies could only be used to trade off inflation against unemployment: i.e. to cause a movement along the curve. Thus if the government wanted to reduce *both* inflation *and* unemployment, it would have to attempt to shift the curve inwards. This would involve policies other than demand management policies: policies to tackle cost-push inflation and equilibrium unemployment.

Q26. *False.* There is still an apparent inverse relationship between them, albeit a worse trade-off than in the 1950s and 1960s but better than in the 1980s.

Q27. (i) Y, (ii) C_d, (iii) I, (iv) S, (v) G, (vi) T, (vii) X, (viii) M.

Q28. (a) *withdrawal, decrease*; (b) *injection, decrease*; (c) *injection, increase* (building up stocks counts as investment); (d) *withdrawal, decrease*; (e) *withdrawal, decrease* (the poor save proportionally less and spend proportionally more than the rich); (f) *withdrawal (imports), decrease*; (g) *withdrawal (saving), increase* (note that whereas it is normal in everyday language to refer to depositors 'investing' in building societies, economists refer to this as 'saving'; they reserve the term 'investment' to refer to the spending by firms on capital (plant, equipment, stocks, etc.) which is an *injection*).

Q29. £2025m ($S + T$ (both) $+ M$).

Q30. B. $C_d + I + G + X$. Notice that C_d excludes imports: if the consumption figure was for *total* consumption, we would have to subtract imports: i.e. $C - M + I + G + X$.

Q31. *rise.*

Q32. *rise.*

Q33. *withdrawals.* (In the simple model, injections are not affected by the level of income.)

Q34. *larger.* The reason is that additional injections will subsequently flow round and round the circular flow of income generating additional expenditure and additional income. There is a 'multiplied' rise in income (see Chapter 16). But the process will not go on for ever, because eventually all the additional injections will leak away as additional withdrawals.

Q35. (a) *fall* (increase in withdrawals); (b) *rise* (increase in injections); (c) *fall* (fall in injections); (d) *impossible to tell without further information* (both withdrawals and injections fall); (e) *fall* ((increase in with-

drawals); (f) *rise* (increase in injections: i.e. exports to these countries rise as a result of their increased incomes).

Q36. The value of output produced within the economy over a twelve-month period.

Q37. £120 + £40 + £80 + £60 + £50 +£25 = £375 (which is the retail price).

Q38. *Yes*: (b), (e), (f) and (g). (Note that if we had been referring to gross *national income*, then (e) would not have been included but (h) would have been.)

Q39. *True.* The value added in production is simply the difference between a firm's revenue from sales and the costs of its purchases from other firms. This difference is made up of the wages, rent, interest and profit generated in the production process.

Q40. (a) £3690m: i.e. income from employment + gross profits + gross rent and interest + mixed incomes.
(b) £3780m, i.e. *GVA* + taxes on products − subsidies on products.

Q41. All except (c) and (h) would be included in the expenditure method of calculating GDP (since all except (c) and (h) involve the production of goods and/or services).

Q42. (a) £2050m (i.e. $C + G + I + X - M$).
(b) £1600m (i.e. GDP − taxes on products + subsidies on products).

Q43. (a) £2110m (i.e. GDP at market prices + net income from abroad).
(b) £1990m (i.e. GNY − depreciation).

Q44. E. It is the income available for people to spend after all deductions and additions.

Q45. *False.* The GDP deflator, unlike the RPI, includes not just the prices of consumer goods, but also the prices of investment goods, the prices of goods and services consumed by the government and the prices of exports: in other words, it includes the weighted prices of all the components of GDP.

Q46. 2.56 per cent.
This is calculated as follows:
Real *GDP* = Nominal *GDP*/*GDP* deflator × 100
Thus in year 1, real *GDP* = £120bn/100 × 100 = £120bn
and in year 2, real *GDP* = £160n/130 × 100 = £123.07bn
∴ real *GDP* has grown by (123.07 − 120)/120 × 100 = 2.56%.

Q47. The ratio of country A's GDP to country B's is 10/12 at current exchange rates. Given, however, that country B's currency is overvalued by 1.5 times in PPP terms, the ratio of country A's PPS GDP to country B's PPS GDP is 10/12 × 1.5 = 1.25.

CHAPTER FIFTEEN

Macroeconomic Ideas

A   REVIEW

'The ideas of economists and political philosophers, both when they are right and when they are wrong, are more powerful than is commonly understood. Indeed the world is ruled by little else. Practical men, who believe themselves to be quite exempt from any intellectual influences, are usually the slaves of some defunct economist.'

J.M. Keynes,

The General Theory of Employment, Interest and Money (1936)

In this chapter we examine the development of macroeconomic ideas and their influence on economic policy.

15.1 Macroeconomic controversies

(Pages 444–6) The different schools of economic thought make different assumptions about how the economy operates. The classical and new classical schools argue that prices and wages are **Q1.** *flexible/inflexible*; that aggregate supply is **Q2.** *responsive/unresponsive* to a change in aggregate demand; and that individual producers and consumers have **Q3.** *quickly adjusting/slowly adjusting* expectations concerning economic events. As a result of these assumptions, supporters of the classical position argue that the main role of government economic policy is **Q4.** *to manage the level of aggregate demand so as to maintain full employment/remove impediments to the free play of market forces/ensure that no slack is allowed to develop in the economy.* This they argue is the only way to guarantee long-term growth.

Q5. Go through questions 1–4 and summarise the key assumptions of the *Keynesian* school.

....

....

Much of the disagreement between the different schools of thought centres on the responsiveness of aggregate supply to changes in aggregate demand.

Q6. Aggregate supply may be defined as ....

....

Q7. Consider the aggregate supply curves shown in Figure 15.1.

Which of the three curves would be most likely to represent the views of:

(a) Extreme free-market economists?

....

(b) Those who argue that an expansion of demand will have no effect upon inflation?

....

≡ Multiple Choice   ? Written answer   ◑ Delete wrong word   ⊖ Diagram/table manipulation   ⊗ Calculation   ❖ Matching/ordering

Figure 15.1 Aggregate supply curves

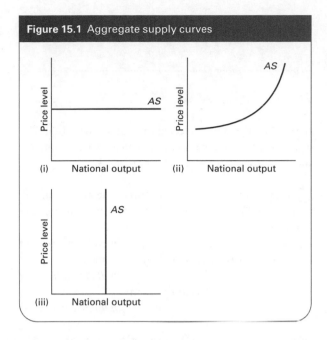

(i)   National output

(ii)   National output

(iii)   National output

(c) Those who argue that the degree of slack in the economy will determine the impact of a change in aggregate demand on aggregate supply?

....

Q8. One of the arguments used by those advocating government intervention in the economy is that people's expectations are slow to adjust to changes in the economic environment.   *True/False*

15.2 Classical macroeconomics

(Pages 446–7) The classical school of the 19th and early 20th centuries advocated minimal state intervention in the running of economic affairs, and the development of a system of free trade. Providing the government balanced its budget, in other words that it made *T* equal to **Q9.** *I/G/X/S/M/C*, achievement of full-employment macroeconomic equilibrium could be left to the free market. The free market would ensure that *S* was equal to **Q10.** *I/T/G/X/M/C*, and that *M* was equal to **Q11.** *I/T/G/X/S/C*.

Q12. What, according to the classical economists, would be the effect of a rise in saving on the level of investment?

....

....

The operation of the gold standard was supposed to ensure that the balance of payments was kept in equilibrium (*X = M*). The gold standard was a system of **Q13.** *fixed/freely flexible/partly flexible* exchange rates.

Q14. Assume that there is a balance of payments deficit (*M > X*). Trace through the steps by which the gold standard could correct this deficit.
(a) The deficit leads to an *inflow/outflow* of gold.
(b) This leads to an *increase/decrease* in interest rates.
(c) This leads to an *increase/decrease* in the price level.
(d) This leads to an *increase/decrease* in imports and an *increase/decrease* in exports.

(Pages 447–8) The classical economists argued that because the markets for loanable funds and for imports and exports would clear, then Say's law would apply.

Q15. Say's law states that, at a macroeconomic level:
A. supply will always adjust to equal demand.
B. markets are always in a state of disequilibrium.
C. demand creates its own supply.
D. supply creates its own demand.
E. price and quantity are directly related.

Q16. Say's law implied that there could be no deficiency of demand in the economy.   *True/False*

Q17. In terms of the circular flow of income diagram, Say's law would imply that *flexible prices* (as opposed to changes in national income) would ensure that withdrawals equalled injections.   *True/False*

(Pages 448–54) The classical economists also supported the *quantity theory of money*.

Q18. This states that $MV = PY$.   *True/False*

Q19. If real national income (i.e. measured in base-year prices) were £30bn, if prices had doubled since the base year, and if the velocity of circulation were 5, then the level of money supply would be:
A. £300bn
B. £75bn
C. £60bn
D. £12bn
E. £3bn

The classical economists had predicted that, provided markets were allowed to clear, there would never be a problem of **Q20.** *high inflation/mass unemployment*.

Q21. Which of the following policy decisions would have been characteristic of the classical economists' approach to the Great Depression?
(a) Encourage workers to take wage cuts.   *Yes/No*
(b) Increase the rate of interest.   *Yes/No*
(c) Expand the public sector's provision of goods and services.   *Yes/No*
(d) Reduce unemployment benefits.   *Yes/No*
(e) Increase the supply of money in circulation.   *Yes/No*

(f) The government should aim to balance its budget.

Yes/No

(g) Encourage people to save.

Yes/No

15.3 The Keynesian revolution

(Pages 454–5) J.M. Keynes rejected many of the assumptions made by the classical school, key among which was the notion that markets would clear. According to Keynes, disequilibrium was the natural state of the market and such disequilibrium would persist unless the government intervened. For example, in the labour market, if there were a fall in aggregate demand, as occurred during the Great Depression, workers would resist wage cuts and the result would be demand-deficient unemployment.

⊖ **Q22.** Show, using Figure 15.2, the effect of a fall in the aggregate demand for labour and the subsequent level of disequilibrium unemployment that would result. (Assume that the labour market is initially in equilibrium.)

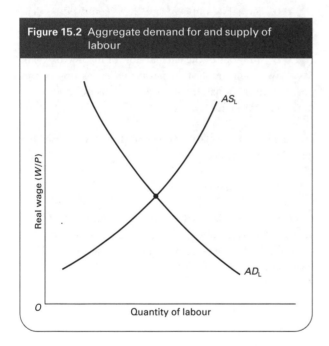

Figure 15.2 Aggregate demand for and supply of labour

But even if workers *were* willing to accept cuts in real wages, there would still be a problem of unemployment.

(?) **Q23.** Why, according to Keynes, might a successful cut in workers' wages, as advocated by the classical school, deepen the recession and not improve it?

....

....

(?) **Q24.** Disequilibrium could also persist in the market for loanable funds. Assume, for example, that there was an increase in saving. Why might the resulting fall in

interest rates fail to stimulate a rise in investment and restore equilibrium?

....

....

(Page 455) Keynes also rejected the simple quantity theory of money. Under certain circumstances, a rise in money supply may have little or no effect on prices.

◑ **Q25.** If there was an expansion of the money supply, what, according to Keynes, would happen to each of the following?

(a) V *rise/fall/stay the same*

(b) Y – if there was substantial unemployment

rise/fall/stay the same

(c) Y – if there was full employment

rise/fall/stay the same

(Pages 456–8) Keynesian theory stresses that equilibrium in the economy is brought about, not so much by changes in prices, but by changes in the level of national income.

(?) **Q26.** Describe the process whereby a new equilibrium national income will be achieved, following a rise in aggregate demand.

....

....

(Pages 458–60) Keynesian theory emphasised an active role for government in maintaining the full-employment level of national income. There are two major methods a government can use to control the level of aggregate demand. These are *fiscal policy* and *monetary policy*.

(?) **Q27.** Fiscal policy involves

....

(?) **Q28.** Monetary policy involves

....

Following the Second World War, Keynesian views became the accepted orthodoxy. If the economy was experiencing rising inflation then **Q29.** *expansionary/deflationary* fiscal and monetary policy was to be used. Alternatively, an economy suffering low rates of growth and unemployment would require **Q30.** *expansionary/deflationary* policy measures.

Because of the cyclical nature of the economy, the policies alternated between deflationary and reflationary (i.e. expansionary) measures.

(?) **Q31.** As a result the policies became known as

....

(?) **Q32.** List four criticisms of Keynesian demand management policy that were to grow over the 1960s.

1. ....

2. ....

3. ....

4. ....

15.4 The Monetarist–Keynesian debate

(Pages 460–1) The problems encountered with the Keynesian model of the economy led certain economists to return to the old classical theory of income determination. The monetarists, led by Milton Friedman, returned to the quantity theory of money. They reasserted that both V (the velocity of circulation) and Y (the level of real national income) were **Q33.** *endogenous/exogenous* variables, meaning that V and Y are determined **Q34.** *by the supply of money/independently of the supply of money*. The implication was that any change in the money supply would have a direct effect upon the level of **Q35.** *prices/national income*.

An important element of the monetarist analysis was that there was no trade-off in the long run between unemployment and inflation: that the long-run Phillips curve is **Q36.** *horizontal/vertical/upward sloping/a downward-sloping line at 45° to the axes.*

(?) **Q37.** What arguments do monetarists use to justify a long-run Phillips curve of this shape?

....

....

....

(◑) **Q38.** What effect would the following have on the natural rate of unemployment?
(a) A reduction in the level of information concerning available work. *Rise/Fall*
(b) The decline in traditional heavy industry. *Rise/Fall*
(c) An increase in the power trade unions have within the wage-negotiating process. *Rise/Fall*
(d) An expansion of job retraining schemes. *Rise/Fall*
(e) A more rapid and widespread introduction of new technology into the workplace. *Rise/Fall*
(f) An increase in unemployment benefits. *Rise/Fall*

(Pages 461–4) Not surprisingly, modern-day Keynesians reject much of the monetarist analysis.

(?) **Q39.** The modern *Keynesian* analysis of a rightward shift in the Phillips curve since 1970 focuses on a *variety* of factors, some that are argued to have influenced the rate of inflation and some the level of unemployment. List three causes of inflation and three of unemployment given by Keynesians to explain higher levels of both occurring simultaneously.
(a) Inflation

1. ....

2. ....

3. ....

(b) Unemployment

1. ....

2. ....

3. ....

One reason given by Keynesians for unemployment being higher in the 1980s and early 1990s than in the 1970s was the problem of *hysteresis*.

(◑) **Q40.** In the context of unemployment, hysteresis can be defined as the persistence of unemployment that occurred in a recession even when the economy has recovered from the recession. *True/False*

(◑) **Q41.** Keynesians offer various explanations for hysteresis. These include:
(a) A decline in capital stock during the recession.
True/False
(b) A balance of payments problem in the recession that persists in the recovery. *True/False*
(c) Having experienced a recession, firms are cautious about taking on more labour. *True/False*
(d) Insiders in firms bidding up the wage rate and making it less profitable to take on extra labour. *True/False*
(e) The unemployed have become deskilled and hence less employable. *True/False*

15.5 The current position: conflict or consensus?

(Pages 465–7) Today there is a whole range of viewpoints concerning the functioning of the macroeconomy and the most appropriate macroeconomic policies to pursue.

(⊛) **Q42.** The following are four schools of thought:
 (i) New classical
 (ii) Moderate monetarist
 (iii) Moderate Keynesian/new Keynesian
 (iv) Extreme Keynesians

Members of which school of thought hold each of the following views?

(a) A rise in aggregate demand (caused by an increase in money supply) can lead only to a temporary reduction in unemployment. As price expectations adjust upwards, so within a few months the extra demand will be translated into higher prices and unemployment will return to the natural level.   *(i)/(ii)/(iii)/(iv)*

(b) Equilibrium in the economy can persist at a very high level of unemployment and there is no automatic mechanism for bringing the economy out of recession. Indeed, recessions are likely to persist as expectations remain pessimistic. It is important, therefore, for the government to take an active role in maintaining sufficient aggregate demand. This will help to stimulate investment and lead to faster long-term growth.
     (i)/(ii)/(iii)/(iv)

(c) Markets clear virtually instantaneously. Any increase in aggregate demand by the government will be entirely reflected in higher prices.   *(i)/(ii)/(iii)/(iv)*

(d) Wage rates are sticky downwards. Unemployment can take a long time, therefore, to be eliminated by a fall in real wages. The government should take responsibility for maintaining an adequate (but not excessive) level of aggregate demand.   *(i)/(ii)/(iii)/(iv)*

Q43. New classical 'real business cycle theory' explains cyclical fluctuations in the economy in terms of *shifts in aggregate demand/shifts in aggregate supply/changes in the output of goods rather than services.*

Despite disagreements between economists, some general points of agreement have emerged in recent years.

Q44. Which of the following propositions are part of this 'mainstream consensus'?

(a) Excessive growth in the money supply will lead to inflation.   *Yes/No*

(b) Governments' ability to control their country's economy is being increasingly eroded by the process of globalisation.   *Yes/No*

(c) In the short run, changes in aggregate demand will have only a minor effect on output and employment.   *Yes/No*

(d) There is a clear long-run trade off between inflation and unemployment.   *Yes/No*

(e) Long-term growth depends primarily on changes in aggregate supply.   *Yes/No*

(f) Expectations have an important effect on the economy.   *Yes/No*

B   PROBLEMS, EXERCISES AND PROJECTS

Q45. In the version of the quantity theory of money: $MV = PY$.

(a) What are meant by the following terms?

  (i) M

  ....

  (ii) V

  ....

  (iii) P

  ....

  (iv) Y

  ....

(b) If the money supply were £20bn and money on average were spent 5 times per year on buying goods and services that make up national income, what would be the level of national income (in nominal terms)?

....

(c) Continuing with the same assumptions as in (b), what would be the price index if real national income, measured in base-year prices were £50bn?

....

(d) If money supply increases by 50 per cent and neither the price level nor the velocity of circulation changes, how much will real national income increase?   *more than 50 per cent/50 per cent/ less than 50 per cent*

(e) If money supply increases by 50 per cent and neither real income nor the velocity of circulation changes, how much will the price level rise?
     more than 50 per cent/50 per cent/ less than 50 per cent

(f) What did the classical economists assume about:

  (i) V?

  ....

  (ii) Y?

  ....

(g) What do Keynesian economists assume about:

(i) *V*?

....

(ii) *Y*?

....

Q46. The kingdom of Never Had It So Good is having it bad! Inflation has risen steadily following a series of expansionary budgets and the current account of the balance of payments has slipped into deficit. High interest rates, used to tackle the high inflation by curbing domestic demand, have led to a steady fall in household consumption. Firms have responded by cutting back on production and reducing their demand for labour, as well as postponing future investment.

Write two reports advising the chancellor of Never Had It So Good on a course of action to solve the country's economic problems. One report should emphasise the policies and beliefs of the classical school of economics, whereas the second should focus on Keynesian strategies.

DISCUSSION TOPICS AND ESSAYS

Q47. Explain the contrasting views of Keynesians and monetarists concerning the nature of the aggregate supply curve. What implications do their respective analyses have for the effect of a rise in aggregate demand on prices and output?

Q48. What are the implications of the quantity theory of money for (a) the control of inflation, and (b) the use of monetary policy to stimulate an economy in recession?

Q49. What assumptions must be made about the terms in the equation of exchange if the strict quantity theory of money is to hold? How would changes in the money supply affect the economy if you changed these assumptions?

Q50. Describe the working of the economy using classical economic theory. Clearly state your assumptions. Why did classical economists maintain that the economy would tend towards a situation of full employment?

Q51. Explain the reasoning behind Keynes' rejection of Say's law.

Q52. Keynesian demand management policies, although initially appearing to be successful, began to run into problems in the mid-1960s. What were these problems?

Q53. 'The monetarist counter-revolution is simply the restating of classical theory.' Discuss.

Q54. Describe how monetarist and Keynesian views differ regarding the Phillips curve.

Q55. What are the distinguishing features of the following schools of thought: new classical economists, moderate monetarists, moderate Keynesians, extreme Keynesians?

Q56. What is meant by 'hysteresis' (in the context of unemployment)? How do Keynesians explain this phenomenon?

Q57. Debate
Leaving the economy to private enterprise and the market system is more likely to lead to recessions and instability than to sustained economic growth.

ARTICLES

The following extracts are taken from the work of John Maynard Keynes.

We have, as a rule, only the vaguest idea of any but the most direct consequences of our acts . . . our knowledge of the future is fluctuating, vague and uncertain . . . the sense in which I am using the term (uncertain) is that in which the prospect of a European war is uncertain, or the price of copper and the rate of interest twenty years hence, or the obsol-

escence of a new invention, or the position of private wealth-owners in the social system in 1970. About these matters there is no scientific basis on which to form any calculable probability whatever. We simply do not know.[1]

1. Keynes (1937) in W. Hutton, *The Revolution That Never Was* (1986), p. 95.

Many of the greatest economic evils of our time are the fruits of uncertainty, and ignorance. It is because particular individuals, fortunate in situation or in abilities, are able to take advantage of uncertainty and ignorance, and also because for the same reason big business is often a lottery, that great inequalities of wealth come about; and these same factors are also the cause of the unemployment of labour, or the disappointment of reasonable expectations, and of the impairment of efficiency and production. Yet the cure lies outside the operation of individuals; it may even be to the interest of individuals to aggravate the disease. I believe that the cure for these things is partly to be sought in the deliberate control of the currency and of credit by a central institution, and partly in the collection and dissemination on a great scale of data relating to the business situation, including the full publicity, by law if necessary, of all business facts which it is useful to know. These measures would involve society in exercising directive intelligence through some appropriate organ of action over many of the inner intricacies of private business, yet it would leave private initiative and enterprise unhindered. Even if these measures prove insufficient, nevertheless, they will furnish us with better knowledge than we have now for taking the next step.[1]

2. Keynes in A.P. Thirlwall, Keynes and *Laissez-Faire* (1978), pp. 39–40.

Using the extracts, answer the following questions:

(a) According to Keynes, what problems did ignorance and uncertainty create?

(b) What were Keynes' remedies for ignorance and uncertainty?

(c) How would Keynes' views have differed from the classical economic orthodoxy of the day?

The conflict between monetarists and Keynesians has lasted many years. At different points in history, one view or the other has tended to dominate economic opinion. Keynesianism occupied this position throughout the 1950s and 1960s, and more recently monetarism has been the dominant theory. Between these eras of dominance we can identify a transition period in which ideas and theories are redefined. The article below, taken from the *Guardian* of 7 April 1994, assesses the relevance of Keynesian economics after 14 years of economic policy being based largely upon monetarist assumptions.

Free lunch as Keynes makes a comeback

Tony Thirlwall

Not so long ago, many economists of Keynesian persuasion, myself included, felt as if they belonged to an endangered species, with the prospect of extinction in the face of the onslaught from the doctrine of monetarism.

This argued that economies are inherently self-regulating, that governments have no role to play in the stabilisation of output and employment at the macro level, and all that matters for the control of inflation is the control of the money supply.

From the mid-1970s, this doctrine spread from the shores of America, infecting academia and policy-making in several parts of the globe. It looks now, however, that the tide is beginning to turn.

Monetarism, in its various guises, seems to be dying a slow death. Books and articles are being written on the rise and fall and rise again of Keynesian economics, and the empirical evidence of deep recession in the UK and slump in Europe is focusing again on what Keynes had to say about unemployment and how to tackle it.

The Keynesian tide should never have ebbed away in the first place, and wouldn't have done so had the 1970s not been so inflation prone and Keynesian economics been properly understood, particularly on the other side of the Atlantic.

If American monetarists had absorbed their Keynesian economics from Keynes himself and not from text book versions, how could it ever have been seriously argued (as Milton Friedman used to) that 'money doesn't matter' in Keynes, or that Keynes's central message that capitalist economies may get stuck in depression for long periods of time depends on the assumption that wages and prices are rigid, and that Keynesian economics cannot explain stagflation? None of these claims bears textual scrutiny.

The basic proposition that mainstream monetarism has always denied is that there can be such a thing as involuntary unemployment, defined as unemployed people willing to work at the going money wage (and a lower real wage if necessary) given the opportunity.

Attempts by governments to reduce unemployment by higher levels of public spending will simply raise prices and lead to money wages chasing prices in an ever-accelerating spiral of inflation with no effect on employment.

Monetarist models assume to start with what must be proved – that the labour market always clears on the basis of voluntary exchange.

But if we look back to Mrs Thatcher's 'miracle economy' in the 1980s, when unemployment peaked at nearly 3.5 million in 1986 and then fell to 1.5 million in 1990 with expansionary monetary and fiscal policy, were the two million unemployed absorbed into the system voluntarily unemployed? Clearly not.

Unemployment responded in exactly the way one would have predicted from a Keynesian model. The notion of continuous market clearing and no involuntary unemployment has been totally discredited by the bitter experience of the 1980s, and continues to be discredited today as unemployment in the UK hovers around the three million mark and unemployment in the European Community approaches 20 million.

If we want to understand what is going on in the British economy today, and the great difficulties of reconciling low unemployment with low inflation, we cannot continue to embrace the pre-Keynesian assumptions of monetarism: that all unemployment is voluntary due to a refusal of workers to accept cuts in their wages; that there are automatic mechanisms that guarantee enough private expenditure in the economy to generate sufficient demand for goods and services to ensure full employment; that all cycles in economic activity are the result of supply shocks; and that inflation is always and everywhere a

monetary phenomenon in a casual sense as if trade unions and monopolies don't exist, and money is totally exogenous to an economic system.

For the past 14 years, economic policy-making in Britain has been dominated largely by this monetarist thinking. If the primitive application of monetarism had worked in the early 1980s, it should have reduced the growth of the money supply and the rate of inflation without, in the long run, affecting the level of unemployment and the real economy.

Instead, there was an almighty slump that destroyed large sections of manufacturing industry and made thousands of workers virtually unemployable, just as a Keynesian model would have predicted. Good old-fashioned demand mismanagement then produced an

unsustainable boom in the late 1980s, and we are now in the longest, if not the deepest, recession since the 1930s. All in the name of the rejection of Keynesianism.

The fundamental Keynesian message remains that, in conditions of heavy, involuntary unemployment, there is such a thing as a free lunch; stone can be turned into bread; expenditure will generate multiplier effects; and there will be the crowding in of resources, not crowding out.

If only the Government could grasp this message, it would be a blow for monetarism but a victory for common sense.

Tony Thirlwall is Professor of Applied Economics at the University of Kent. © The *Guardian*, 7.4.94

(a) What economic assumptions does the article suggest underpin monetarist and Keynesian views?

(b) What is the difference between voluntary and involuntary unemployment? Why is this distinction seen

by the author as crucial in refuting the monetarist case?

(c) What evidence does the author cite to support his Keynesian position?

 E   ANSWERS

Q1. *flexible.*

Q2. *unresponsive.*

Q3. *quickly adjusting.*

Q4. *to remove impediments to the free play of market forces.*

Q5. The Keynesian school argues that prices and wages are relatively inflexible; that aggregate supply is relatively responsive to changes in aggregate demand; and that expectations are relatively slow to adjust. Keynesians advocate government intervention to manage aggregate demand so as to avoid recessions.

Q6. Aggregate supply may be defined as the quantity of goods and services that the nation's producers would be willing to supply at any given price.

Q7. *(a)* (iii). They argue that changes in aggregate demand will have no effect on output and therefore the aggregate supply 'curve' is vertical.

(b) (i). They argue that aggregate supply is totally elastic and that therefore output depends entirely on aggregate demand.

(c) (ii). The lower the level of output and the higher the level of unemployment, and hence the greater the degree of 'slack' in the economy, the more will output be able to increase in response to an increase in aggregate demand, and hence the shallower the curve will be. As

full employment is approached, however, the curve will get steeper, as firms find it increasingly difficult to increase output and instead respond to an increase in aggregate demand by putting up their prices.

Q8. *Ture.* Because expectations take time to adjust, interventionist policies can have a significant impact on the economy. For example, a rise in aggregate demand can lead to firms producing more if they do not expect that the rise in aggregate demand is also likely to raise inflation and hence raise their costs of production.

Q9. *G.*

Q10. *I.*

Q11. *X.*

Q12. The rise in saving would cause a surplus of loanable funds. This would drive the rate of interest down. This in turn would cause an increase in the level of investment and a reduction in the level of saving (a movement along the investment curve and the new saving curve), until equilibrium was restored where saving equalled investment.

Q13. *Fixed.* The value of each country's currency was fixed in terms of a certain amount of gold. Each country's exchange rate was therefore fixed.

Q14. (a) *outflow*; (b) *increase*; (c) *decrease*; (d) *decrease* in imports, *increase* in exports.

Q15. D. The production of goods and services will generate incomes, which in turn will generate spending, thereby creating a demand for the goods and services which have been produced. Any proportion of income that is saved will generate extra investment, and any proportion going on imports, via the gold standard, will generate extra exports. Thus, when production generates extra income, *all* of it will come back as extra spending.

Q16. *True.* Any change in aggregate supply would automatically bring about a corresponding change in aggregate demand, via the effects on aggregate demand of a change in prices and interest rates.

Q17. *True.*

Q18. *False.* The quantity theory of money states that the level of prices (P) depends on the quantity of money: if money supply increases faster than output, then prices will rise. The equation $MV = PY$ is called the 'quantity equation', not the 'quantity theory of money'.

Q19. D. The level of national income (at current prices) is equal to the real level of national income at base-year prices ($Y =$ £30bn) multiplied by the price level as a proportion of the base year price ($P = 2$): $PY =$ £60bn. Thus MV is also equal to £60bn. Given that the velocity of circulation (V) = 5, money supply must be £60bn/5 = £12bn.

Q20. *mass unemployment.*

Q21. Yes (a), (b), (d), (f) and (g). These were all advocated by classical economists during the 1920s and early 1930s.

Q22. The AD_L curve shifts to the left, but, with no resulting fall in the real wage rate, the level of aggregate labour supply now exceeds the level of aggregate labour demand, the gap between them giving the level of disequilibrium unemployment.

Q23. As workers took a wage cut their ability to consume goods and services would fall. This would deepen the recession as firms would consequently have less demand for their output.

Q24. As saving increased, consumers would consequently have less money to spend on consumption of domestic goods and services. Businesses would respond to this fall in demand by cutting back on their level of investment.

Q25. *(a)* *fall*. The average speed at which money circulates may slow down. (The reasons for this are examined in Chapter 20.)

(b) *rise*. The increased spending will stimulate extra production and extra employment.

(c) *stay the same*. Output and employment cannot be stimulated by a rise in spending as there is no slack in the economy.

Q26. The rise in injections will mean that injections exceed withdrawals. This will cause a rise in national income. This will cause withdrawals (and consuption) to rise until withdrawals equal injections. At that point income will stop rising: income will be in equilibrium.

Q27. Changing government expenditure (an injection) and/or taxes (a withdrawal).

Q28. Changing money supply or interest rates, and thereby affecting the level of spending.

Q29. *deflationary.*

Q30. *expansionary.*

Q31. *Stop/go policies*, or less provocatively, *demand management policies*.

Q32. Criticisms included: policies failed to stabilise the economy; policies were short term rather than long term; the Phillips curve relationship appeared to be breaking down; balance of payments problems meant that deflationary policies had to be pursued even when unemployment was high; it was difficult to predict the magnitude of the effects of the policy (difficult to predict size of the multiplier); there were time lags involved with the policy (see Chapter 17, review section 17.2).

Q33. *exogenous.*

Q34. *independently of the supply of money.*

Q35. *prices.*

Q36. *vertical.*

Q37. If the government expands aggregate demand in order to reduce unemployment, eventually people's expectations of inflation will increase until all the extra demand is absorbed in higher prices with no increase in output or employment. Thus in the long run the Phillips curve is vertical.

Q38. All will cause the natural rate of unemployment to rise except (d), which will cause it to fall.

Q39. *(a)* Examples include: rising costs, changes in the pattern of demand in the economy and expectations.

(b) Examples include: deficient demand, poor business expectations, structural changes in the economy, hysteresis.

Q40. *True.*

Q41. *True.* All except (b). In the case of (a), a decline in investment, and hence the capital stock, during the recession means that when the recovery comes firms reach full employment of existing capital before there is full employment of labour.

Q42. (a) (ii), (b) (iv), (c) (i), (d) (iii).

Q43. *shifts in aggregate supply.*

Q44. *Yes* (a), (b), (f) and (g).
No (c) and (d).

16.1 Background to the theory

(Page 470) In order to understand the Keynesian model, it is necessary that you are fully familiar with the circular flow of income diagram that we looked at in Chapter 14.

Q1. By way of revision, sketch the circular flow diagram and label the inner flow and all the injections and withdrawals.

The relationship between national income and the various components of the circular flow are shown in the *Keynesian 45° line diagram.*

Q2. In the model, it is assumed that consumption and withdrawals are determined by the level of national income, whereas injections are not. Which would we classify as endogenous and which as exogenous variables?

(a) Withdrawals are   *endogenous/exogenous*

(b) Injections are   *endogenous/exogenous*

(c) Consumption is   *endogenous/exogenous*

Q3. In the 45° line diagram, which of the following is given by the 45° line?

A. National expenditure.

B. Consumption of domestic goods and services.

C. Consumption of domestic goods and services plus withdrawals.

D. Consumption of domestic goods and services plus injections.

E. Withdrawals plus injections.

(Pages 471–4) The consumption function

The consumption function shows the relationship between consumption and national income.

Q4. This question is based on Table 16.1.

(a) Plot the consumption function shown in Table 16.1 on Figure 16.1 and add the 45° line.

(b) Explain why the consumption function lies above the 45° line at low levels of national income and below it at high levels.

....

....

(c) What is meant by the term *marginal propensity to consume*? Give its formula.

....

....

(d) Calculate the marginal propensity to consume between the following levels of national income:

   (i)   £50bn and £75bn ....

   (ii)   £125bn and £150bn ....

(e) The marginal propensity to consume is given by *the slope of the consumption function/the height of the consumption function above the horizontal axis*.

(f) If the marginal propensity to consume diminished as national income rose, what shape would the consumption function be?

....

....

Table 16.1

National income (£bn)	Consumption (£bn)	
50	70	...
75	90	...
100	110	...
125	130	...
150	150	...
175	170	...
200	190	...
225	210	...
250	230	...

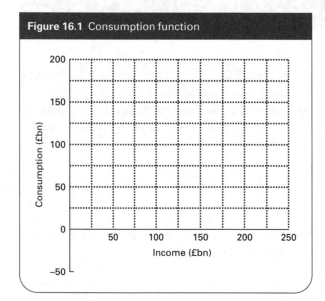

Figure 16.1 Consumption function

In the long run the marginal propensity to consume will be **Q5.** *higher/lower* than in the short run. This is the result of individuals responding relatively **Q6.** *quickly/slowly* to changes in their level of income.

(?) **Q7.** What is the difference between the marginal propensity to consume (*mpc*) and the marginal propensity to consume domestically produced goods and services (*mpc*$_d$)?

....

(Pages 474–80) Withdrawals and injections
(?) **Q8.** The major determinant of saving in the Keynesian model is

....

(—) **Q9.** Label the last column in Table 16.1 'Saving (£bn)'.
(a) Assuming that saving is the only withdrawal, fill in the figures for saving in Table 16.1.
(b) Plot the saving function on Figure 16.1.

(c) Over which range of national income is there dissaving?

....

(d) What is the marginal propensity to save between a national income of £175bn and £200bn?

....

(◑) **Q10.** What effect will the following have on saving? In each case state whether there will be a rise or fall in saving and whether there will be a shift in or a movement along the saving function.
(a) An increase in personal taxation.
                              rise/fall; shift/movement along
(b) Christmas.   *rise/fall; shift/movement along*
(c) An increase in the rate of interest.
                              rise/fall; shift/movement along
(d) Expectations of a fall in prices.
                              rise/fall; shift/movement along
(e) Moving into the recessionary phase of the business cycle.   *rise/fall; shift/movement along*

(◑) **Q11.** The marginal propensity to pay taxes (*mpt*) is the same as the marginal tax rate.   *True/False*

(?) **Q12.** The marginal propensity to import is the proportion of a rise in national income that goes on imports. If a country were predominantly an importer of luxury goods, what effect would this have on (a) the shape of the import function and (b) the marginal propensity to import?

(a) ....

(b) ....

(◑) **Q13.** Injections are assumed in the Keynesian model to be exogenously determined. This means:
(a) That injections are constant with respect to changes in national income.   *True/False*
(b) That injections are constant with respect to time.
                                              True/False
(c) That injections in the 45° line diagram are given by a horizontal straight line.   *True/False*

16.2 The determination of national income

(Pages 481–3) The injections and withdrawals approach
(—) **Q14.** Figure 16.2 shows a withdrawals and an injections function.
(a) Equilibrium national income is

....

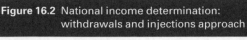

Figure 16.2 National income determination: withdrawals and injections approach

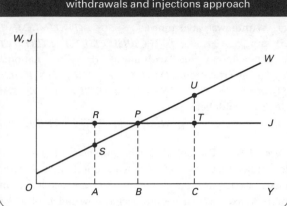

(b) Assume that the current level of national income is *OA*. Describe the process whereby equilibrium will be achieved.

....

(c) Illustrate on Figure 16.2 the effect of an increase in government spending by an amount *UT* on the level of national income.

⊘ Q15. The multiplier can be defined as

....

▤ Q16. In symbols the (injections) multiplier can be defined as:

A. $\Delta Y / \Delta J$
B. $\Delta J / \Delta Y$
C. $\Delta J / \Delta W$
D. $\Delta W / \Delta J$
E. $\Delta W \times \Delta J$

▤ Q17. Referring back to Figure 16.2, the multiplier is given by:

A. *UT/PT*
B. *PT/UT*
C. *PU/PT*
D. *PU/UT*
E. *PT/PU*

◑ Q18. The multiplier is the inverse of the *mpw*.

True/False

⊗ Q19. What are the answers to the following?
(a) $mpw + mpc_d =$

....

(b) $(1 - mpc_d) - (mps + mpm + mpt) =$

....

(where *mps*, *mpm* and *mpt* are from gross income).

⊗ Q20. What is the value of the multiplier in the following cases?
(a) $mpw = 1/3$

....

(b) $mpc_d = 0.75$

....

The full multiplier effect does not occur instantaneously. It takes time for the additional incomes to build up as they go round and round the circular flow of income. The following question demonstrates this process.

⊗ Q21. Assume that the $mpw = 1/2$ and that there is an initial injection of £200m into the economy. Fill in the missing values in Table 16.2 and calculate by how much income has increased after five periods.

Table 16.2 The multiplier

Period	ΔJ(£m)	ΔY(£m)	ΔC_d(£m)	ΔW(£m)
1	200	200	...	...
2	–	...	...	...
3	–	...	...	...
4	–	...	...	...
5	–	...	...	...
Totals				

▤ Q22. Which of the following would cause the value of the multiplier to fall?

A. A cut in the level of government spending.
B. An increase in the marginal propensity to consume.
C. A fall in the level of investment.
D. The population becomes more thrifty, and saves a larger proportion of any rise in income.
E. A balance of payments surplus.

(Page 483) The income and expenditure approach
The multiplier can also be demonstrated using the income/expenditure approach.

⊘ Q23. Consumption of domestically produced goods and services plus injections (*Cd + J*) is otherwise known as:

....

⊖ Q24. Figure 16.3 shows a Keynesian national income and expenditure diagram.
(a) Assuming that the expenditure function is given by E_1 by how much do injections exceed withdrawals at an income of *OC*?

....

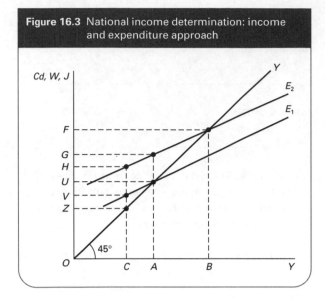

Figure 16.3 National income determination: income and expenditure approach

(b) If the expenditure line now shifts upwards from E_1 to E_2 as the result of an increase in planned consumer spending, what will be the new equilibrium level of national income?

....

(c) What is the size of the multiplier given a rise in expenditure from E_1 to E_2?

....

Q25. A rise in the marginal propensity to save is shown by a swing downwards of the expenditure function (i.e. the curve becomes less steep). *True/False*

Q26. Examine Figure 16.4.

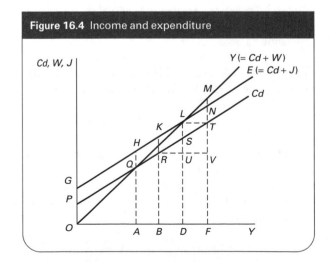

Figure 16.4 Income and expenditure

Identify the correct letters for each of the following:

(a) Equilibrium national income. *OA/OB/OD/OF*

(b) Injections at income *OA*. *AQ/AH/QH/(AQ–QH)*

(c) Withdrawals at income *OF*. *FT/TN/TM/NM/VT*

(d) mpc_d. *RU ÷ SU/SU ÷ RU/TM ÷ LT/RT ÷ VT*

(e) The amount that withdrawals rise when national income rises from *OD* to *OF*. *TN/NM/TM/LN/LM*

(f) *mpw*. *TN ÷ DF/NM ÷ DF/DF ÷ TN/DF ÷ NM*

(g) The multiplier.
 TN ÷ DF/NM ÷ DF/DF ÷ TN/DF ÷ NM

(Pages 484–5) *The formula for the multiplier is $1/(1 - mpc_d)$. Remember that mpc_d refers to consumption of *domestic* goods, from *gross* income and after the deduction of indirect taxes. When people decide how much of a rise in income to spend (their *mpc*), however, their decision is based on *disposable* income: they do not distinguish between domestic and imported goods and their spending includes the indirect taxes on the goods they purchase. How, then, do we derive the mpc_d from the *mpc* (from disposable income). We use the formula:

$$mpc_d = mpc\,(1 - t_E)(1 - t_Y) - mpm$$

where t_Y is the marginal rate of income tax, and t_E is the marginal rate of expenditure tax.

*Q27. If the *mpc* is 0.75, the *mpm* is 0.1, the rate of expenditure tax is 10 per cent and the rate of income tax is 25 per cent:

(a) What is the mpc_d?

....

(b) What is the size of the multiplier?

....

16.3 The simple Keynesian analysis of unemployment and inflation

(Pages 486–9)

Q28. When the economy is at the 'full-employment' level of national income, this means that:

A. everybody is employed.

B. there is no deficiency of demand.

C. the amount of money in the economy is at its maximum level.

D. the economy is in the expansionary phase of the business cycle.

E. the multiplier effect will generate a large number of jobs.

If the equilibrium level of national income (Y_e) is below the full-employment level (Y_f), there will be a **Q29.** *deflationary gap/inflationary gap*. Alternatively, if the level of national expenditure exceeds the full-employment level of national income, there will be a **Q30.** *deflationary gap/inflationary gap*.

Q31. Which of the following define a *deflationary* gap?
(i) The amount by which equilibrium national income exceeds the full-employment level.
(ii) The amount by which the full-employment level of national income exceeds the equilibrium level.
(iii) The amount by which injections exceed withdrawals at the full-employment level of national income.
(iv) The amount by which withdrawals exceed injections at the full-employment level of national income.
(v) The amount by which national income exceeds national expenditure at the full-employment level of national income.
(vi) The amount by which national expenditure exceeds national income at the full-employment level of national income.

A. (ii)
B. (ii) + (v)
C. (iv)
D. (iv) + (v)
E. (iii) + (vi)

Q32. Referring to the same list as in Q31, which define an *inflationary* gap?
A. (i)
B. (i) + (vi)
C. (iii)
D. (iv) + (v)
E. (iii) + (vi)

Q33. Using Figure 16.5:
(a) Mark a full-employment level of national income above Y_e. Identify the deflationary gap. Use two methods to do this.
(b) Now assume that injections rise such as to increase equilibrium national income beyond Y_f. Illustrate this and identify the resulting inflationary gap. Again use two methods to do this.

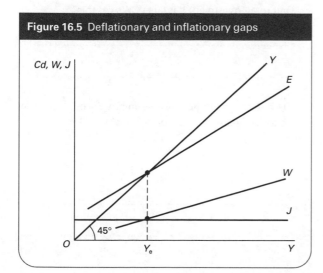

Figure 16.5 Deflationary and inflationary gaps

Table 16.3

National Income (£bn)	50	100	150	200	250	300	350	400
Withdrawals (£bn)	0	10	20	30	40	50	60	70

Q34. Table 16.3 gives country A's withdrawals schedule.
Assume that the full-employment level of national income is £250bn, and that there is an inflationary gap of £10bn.
(a) What is the size of the multiplier?

....

(b) What is the current equilibrium level of national income?

....

(c) If technological progress and increased labour productivity led to a rise of £150bn in the full-employment level of national income, and if there were no change in the equilibrium level of national income, what sort of gap would there be now and what would be its size?

....

Q35. An economy currently has a deflationary gap of £20bn and an equilibrium level of national income £60bn below the full-employment level of national income. This means that it must have an mpc_d of:
A. 3
B. 3/2
C. 2/3
D. 1/3
E. 1/6

In practice, inflation is likely to occur before the full-employment level of national income is reached. This means that the aggregate supply curve, rather than being horizontal up to the full-employment level of national income and then vertical at that point, is in fact upward sloping. How do we analyse this using a 45° line diagram?

Q36. Figure 16.6 shows an aggregate demand and supply diagram and a 45° line diagram. Assume that national income is initially in equilibrium at Y_{e_1} where $Y = E_1$ and $AS = AD_1$. Now assume that there is an increase in injections such that expenditure increases to E_2.
(a) Illustrate the effect on national income in diagram (b), assuming *no* rise in prices.
(b) Draw in the new *AD* curve on diagram (a) and again assuming no rise in the price level (i.e. a horizontal *AS* curve) mark the equilibrium level of national income.
(c) Now allowing for the fact that the *AS* curve is upward sloping, show the actual effect on income of the shift in the *AD* curve that you drew in question (b).

Figure 16.6 National income determination: upward-sloping *AS* curve

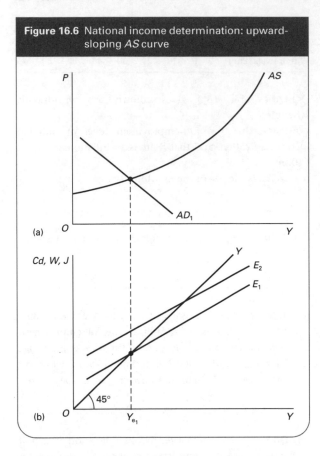

(a)

(b)

(d) Given that diagram (b) shows *real* national income and expenditure, mark the eventual (reduced) rise in the expenditure curve after allowing for the price rise.

16.4 The Keynesian analysis of the business cycle

(Pages 489–91) Keynesians seek to manage the level of aggregate demand and thereby stabilise the fluctuations in the business cycle. They argue that one of the major causes of cyclical fluctuations is the instability of investment.

Q37. The *accelerator* theory of investment states that the level of investment depends upon:
A. the rate of interest.
B. the level of saving.
C. the level of national income.
D. the size of changes in national income.
E. the degree of slack in the economy.

Q38. The marginal capital/output ratio refers to:
A. the change in investment.
B. the change in investment over a year.
C. the amount output must change in order to lead to more investment.
D. the amount of additional capital required to produce an additional unit of output.
E. the level of investment needed to achieve full employment.

The relationship between induced investment (I_i) and changes in national income (ΔY) can be expressed in the formula:

$$I_i = \alpha \Delta Y$$

where α is known as the 'accelerator coefficient'.

Q39. The accelerator coefficient is the marginal capital/output ratio. *True/False*

Q40. The accelerator gets its title because of the amount by which investment changes following a change in national income. *True/False*

Q41. Table 16.4 illustrates the accelerator effect by looking at the case of an individual firm. Assume that each of its machines produces 100 units of output and that one machine each year will need replacing.

Table 16.4 The accelerator effect

	0	1	2	3	4	5	6
Quantity demanded by consumers	500	500	1000	2000	2500	2500	2300
Number of machines required	...	...	...	...	...	...	...
Induced investment (I_i)	...	...	...	...	...	...	...
Replacement investment (I_r)	...	...	...	...	...	...	...
Total investment ($I_i + I_r$)							

Assume that the firm decides to increase the number of machines as necessary in order to supply consumer demand.
(a) Fill in the missing values.
(b) Between years 3 and 4 demand has continued to grow but total investment has fallen. Why is this?

....

....

Q42. List four difficulties we might encounter when trying to calculate the size of the real-world accelerator effect.

1. ....

2. ....

3. ....

4. ....

(Pages 491–4) The multiplier/accelerator interaction is important when analysing changes in national income. A single injection will cause a cycle of economic activity.

(?) Q43. Describe the interaction between the multiplier and accelerator following an increase in government spending.

....

....

....

 Q44. The magnitude of cyclical fluctuations resulting from any initial shock to the economy will be greater:
A. the greater the value of both the multiplier and the accelerator.
B. the smaller the value of both the multiplier and the accelerator.
C. the greater the value of the multiplier and the smaller the value of the accelerator.
D. the smaller the value of the multiplier and the greater the value of the accelerator.
E. the greater the difference in the values of the multiplier and accelerator.

Q45. If firms hold stocks, this will increase the speed with which the economy will recover from recession.
True/False

Q46. Decide in which phase of the business cycle (*upturn/expansion/peaking out/recession*) each of the following effects is most likely to appear.
(a) The accelerator leads to an increase in investment.

....

(b) Low interest rates result from only limited borrowing.

....

(c) Firms reach their full productive capacity.

....

(d) Rising stocks force firms to cut back on production.

....

(e) Firms attempt to rebuild their level of stocks.

....

(f) Replacement investment re-emerges.

....

B PROBLEMS, EXERCISES AND PROJECTS

Table 16.5

Income (*Y*)(£m)	20	40	60	80	100	120
Consumption (*Cd*)(£m)	25	40	55	70	85	100
Withdrawals (*W*) (£m)	...	...	...	...	...	...
Injections (*J*) (£m)	...	...	...	...	...	...
Expenditure (*E*) (£m)	...	...	...	...	...	...

Q47. Table 16.5 shows how national income and the consumption of domestically produced goods and services (*Cd*) are related. Government expenditure is £5 million, investment is £2 million and exports are £3 million.
(a) Fill in the missing figures in Table 16.5.
(b) Equilibrium national income is at a level of £40 million. *True/False*
(c) Using Figure 16.7 plot the line showing *Cd* + *W* against income (the 45° line).
(d) Plot the *J*, *W* and *E* functions.
(e) Identify the equilibrium level of national income from the diagram, verifying that the same result is obtained using both the injections and withdrawals approach and the income and expenditure approach.

....

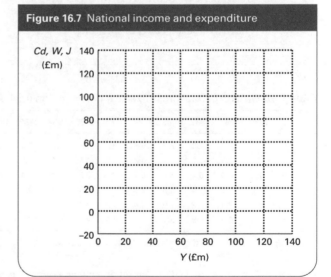

Figure 16.7 National income and expenditure

(f) Assume that withdrawals now fall by £5 million at all levels of national income. Plot the new *W* and *E* functions on Figure 16.7.
(g) What is the new equilibrium level of national income?

....

(h) What is the value of the *mpc*$_d$? ....

(i) What is the value of the *mpw*? ....

(j) What is the value of the multiplier? ....

(k) Verify that the rise in equilibrium in question (g) accords with the value of the multiplier you have just given.

....

....

Q48. At present a country has the following: exports £15bn, investment £1.5bn, government expenditure £6.5bn, *total* consumer expenditure £42bn, imports £10bn, indirect taxes £6bn. The economy is currently in equilibrium. It is estimated that the full-employment level of national income is £60bn. The *mpw* is 0.5.

(a) What is the equilibrium level of national income?

....

(b) Is there an inflationary or deflationary gap?

inflationary/deflationary

(c) What is the size of the gap?

....

(d) If the government wished to close this gap by fiscal policy but did not want to alter taxes, by how much would it have to adjust its level of spending?

....

Q49. Assume that there is an initial increase in injections to the economy of £100m. Assume that the mpc_d is 0.5 and the accelerator coefficient (α) is 1.5. Each period, therefore, C_d rises by 0.5 times the rise in income last period (i.e. $\Delta C_{dt} = 0.5\Delta Y_{t-1}$). The level of I is 1.5 times the rise in income last period (i.e. $I_t = 1.5\Delta Y_{t-1}$); this means that the *rise in I* is 1.5 times the rise in ΔY.

The effects of the initial rise in J are shown in Table 16.6 for 3 periods.

(a) Fill in the figures up to period 7.

(b) Does a cyclical effect occur?

Table 16.6 Effects of a rise in injections (£m)

Period	Initial rise in J	ΔC_d $(C_{dt} - C_{dt-1})$	ΔI $(I_t - I_{t-1})$	ΔY $(Y_t - Y_{t-1})$	Cumulative rise in income $(Y_t - Y_0)$
1	100	–	–	100	100
2	–	50	150	200	300
3	–	100	150	250	550
4	–	...	...	...	...
5	–	...	...	...	...
6	–	...	...	...	...
7	–	...	...	...	...

Q50. Table 16.7 gives data comparing the investment performance of six industrialised countries.

(a) Plot the UK's investment performance, plus that of two other countries. How does the UK compare?

(b) Using Table 16.8, assess how investment changes with output. Can you identify any time lags between changes in output and the level of investment?

(c) What are the implications for an economy of a relatively lower level of investment than that of its main rivals?

Table 16.7 Growth of total gross fixed capital formation (real percentage change over 12 months)

	1980	1981	1982	1983	1984	1985	1986	1987	1988	1989	1990	1991	1992	1993	1994	1995	1996	1997	1998	1999
USA	−8.1	0.6	−7.0	7.9	15.6	6.0	2.1	0.4	1.5	2.0	−1.4	−6.6	5.2	5.1	6.5	5.2	8.1	7.8	9.8	4.3
Japan	0.0	2.4	−0.2	−1.1	4.3	5.0	4.8	9.1	11.5	8.2	8.5	3.3	−1.5	−2.0	−0.8	1.7	9.5	−3.5	−9.0	−5.0
Germany	2.2	−5.0	−5.4	3.1	0.1	−0.5	3.3	1.8	4.4	6.3	8.5	6.0	3.5	−5.6	3.5	0.0	−1.2	0.1	1.0	1.8
France	2.6	−1.9	−1.4	−3.6	−2.6	3.2	4.5	4.8	9.6	7.9	2.8	0.0	−2.8	−6.7	1.3	2.5	−0.5	0.2	4.1	4.1
Italy	8.5	−3.1	−4.9	−1.0	3.4	0.5	2.0	4.4	6.9	4.4	3.6	0.8	−1.8	−12.8	0.5	7.1	0.4	0.6	3.5	2.9
UK	−5.4	−9.6	5.9	5.1	9.3	4.0	2.1	8.9	14.8	5.9	−2.3	−8.7	−0.7	0.8	3.6	2.9	4.9	6.1	8.0	2.7

Source: *European Economy* (Commission of the European Union).

Table 16.8 Growth of real GDP (percentage change over 12 months)

	1980	1981	1982	1983	1984	1985	1986	1987	1988	1989	1990	1991	1992	1993	1994	1995	1996	1997	1998	1999
USA	−0.5	1.8	−2.1	4.0	7.0	3.6	3.1	2.9	3.8	3.4	1.2	−0.9	2.7	2.3	3.5	2.3	3.4	4.0	3.9	2.7
Japan	3.6	3.6	3.1	2.3	3.9	4.4	2.9	4.2	6.2	4.8	5.1	3.8	1.0	0.3	0.6	1.5	3.9	0.8	−2.9	−1.3
Germany	1.0	0.1	−0.9	1.8	2.8	2.0	2.3	1.5	3.7	3.6	5.7	5.0	2.2	−1.2	2.7	1.2	1.3	2.2	2.8	1.7
France	1.6	1.2	2.5	0.7	1.3	1.9	2.5	2.3	4.5	4.3	2.5	0.8	1.2	−1.3	2.8	2.1	1.6	2.3	3.2	2.3
Italy	4.1	0.6	1.8	1.2	2.6	2.8	2.8	3.1	3.9	2.9	2.2	1.1	0.6	−1.2	2.2	2.9	0.7	1.5	1.4	1.6
UK	−2.2	−1.3	−2.9	3.7	2.4	3.8	4.2	4.4	5.2	2.1	0.6	−1.5	0.1	2.3	4.4	2.8	2.6	3.5	2.3	1.3

Source: *European Economy* (Commission of the European Union).

C DISCUSSION TOPICS AND ESSAYS

Q51. Describe the main determinants of consumption and consider whether changes in these determinants are likely to cause simply a parallel shift in the consumption function or whether they will also affect the *mpc*.

Q52. In what ways and for what reasons is a country's long-run consumption function likely to differ from its short-run consumption function?

Q53. The simple Keynesian model assumes that injections are exogenously determined. What does this mean? Are there any elements of injections that might in fact be *endogenously* determined?

Q54. Using (a) a withdrawals and injections diagram and (b) an income and expenditure diagram, illustrate and explain what you understand by the 'multiplier' effect and what determines its magnitude.

Q55. Why is it difficult to predict the size of the multiplier?

Q56. Distinguish between an inflationary gap and a deflationary gap and explain the importance of this informa-

tion for policy makers. What are the weaknesses of the analysis?

Q57. Explain the accelerator theory of investment and suggest some of the reasons why it is difficult to forecast the accelerator effect with any degree of accuracy.

Q58. Fluctuations in the level of stocks are an important feature of the business cycle. Explain how stocks are likely to change over the course of a business cycle and what effect these changes have on the cycle.

Q59. Why do booms and recessions come to an end?

Q60. Identify three key 'leading' indicators which are likely to signal the end of a recession and the recovery of the economy. Explain why they act as indicators and consider how reliable they are.

Q61. Debate
The Keynesian model presents such a simplified view of reality that it is misleading.

D ARTICLES

The central aim of UK economic policy throughout the 1950s, 1960s and 1970s was the achievement of 'full employment'. Only for short periods, however, was this goal attained. In the article below, taken from *Management Today* of August 1999, David Smith argues we are approaching full employment again, only this time it might be more long lasting.

Nirvana is not so unattainable

About 15 years ago I took part in one of those residential conferences where movers and shakers, and a few others, gather to discuss the big issues. At one point, the question came up: would we see full employment again in Britain in our lifetimes?

The movers and shakers, who included top business people, trade union general secretaries, politicians and senior civil servants, all shook their heads gravely. I, as one of the 'others', suggested tentatively that this was too gloomy a view and that when the unfavourable demographic factors unwound (baby-boomers entering the workforce), the picture might be transformed.

I say this not to boast of any forecasting triumph but merely to underline the depth of gloom into which it was all too easy to fall regarding unemployment.

For a while, it looked as if my optimism would be vindicated. Between 1986 and early 1990, unemployment virtually halved to 1.6 million and talk even turned to labour shortages in the 1990s. It was not to be. The recession of 1990–92 intervened to push the jobless total up to within a whisker of three million, and the gloomy view seemed justified once more. In the first half of the 1990s, job insecurity was again in vogue.

Now, however, it is possible to be optimistic again. Although the economy

skirted recession last winter, unemployment has continued to fall. There are 1.2 million claimant unemployed and the unemployment rate is 4.5 per cent. Since full employment is reckoned by economists to occur at an unemployment rate of 2–3 per cent (there is always some frictional – people moving between jobs – and seasonal unemployment), Britain is within sight of it. So too is the US, where the rate is a shade over 4 per cent.

Europe, by some distance, is not – average EU unemployment is still in double figures. And Japan, which until recently had full employment, is moving away from it.

There are caveats to be applied to Britain's current condition of near full employment. On the other measure of unemployment produced by the Government, based on the Labour Force Survey, the jobless rate is more than 6 per cent, and some argue that true unemployment, based on all those who say they would like a job, is between four million and five million. I take the latter with a sack of salt, and I have my doubts about the LFS measure. Just as many arguments can be used to say that even the lower claimant count overstates true unemployment – not least the fact that many unemployed people apparently melt away when faced with, for example, a New Deal interview.

A more telling argument is that the unemployment figures have been massaged down by early retirement and rising numbers on sickness and disability benefits. But the fastest-growing employment age group in the 1990s has been the over-fifties, and only partly because of rising numbers of people in this age group. Meanwhile, the labour market has had to cope in the 1990s with something as dramatic as the com-

ing of the baby-boomers in the 1980s – a sharp rise in female participation.

Compared with the golden age of the 1950s and 1960s, when the workforce was largely made up of men and pre-childbirth women, employment has reached out hugely to parts of the population for whom the norm was to stay at home.

Can this last, and what will be the consequences if it does? There is, as in the late 1980s, a sticky patch to go through before we can be said to have reached full employment nirvana. The surprise so far is that the economy's slowdown has produced no significant rise in unemployment. That doesn't mean it will not – unemployment is a lagging indicator. There is also the small matter of what happens to Britain and the rest of the global economy if, or when, the US economic bubble bursts.

If these hurdles can be overcome, and the pattern of strongly rising service-sector employment more than offsetting falling manufacturing jobs persists, would a move towards full employment bring with it an end to the present benign inflation environment? After

all, 3 per cent unemployment would be significantly below what the Bank of England, Treasury and most economists believe to be Britain's natural rate. When unemployment falls below that rate, inflation tends to rise as the wage–price spiral kicks in.

It would certainly be a test, so why am I optimistic about both unemployment and inflation? For two reasons. The first is that there are a few examples, even in Britain's chequered economic history, of a tight labour market triggering higher inflation on its own. Only in combination with other inflation-boosting factors has this happened. Second, I believe we have seen a fundamental change in inflationary psychology and, because of that, in wage behaviour.

Full employment, however, throws up new challenges, not least in raising skills levels to minimise labour shortages, and avoiding mismatches between jobs and the people capable of filling them. Like old age, however, full employment is far better than the alternative.

(a) What is meant by the term 'full employment', and why is it such an important concept in Keynesian economics?

(b) What reservations does the article suggest we should have when considering unemployment statistics and using them to identify full employment?

(c) Why does Smith argue that we are unlikely to see a wage spiral as we near full employment?

(d) If full employment is to be maintained without rising inflationary pressure, what kinds of policy will governments need to pursue?

The cyclical nature of economic activity is an accepted part of economic wisdom. As businesses experience upswings and downswings in demand for their products and services, their economic behaviour changes. In the article below, taken from *Management Today* of November 1994, the business cycle in theory and practice is assessed, and the recession of the early 1990s, which appeared to contradict accepted theory, is analysed.

The ins and outs of ups and downs

Karl Marx described the business cycle as part of 'the fundamental contradiction of capitalism'. For 30 years after the Second World War, under the influence of Lord Keynes, governments tried to smooth out the economy's fluctuations by deliberate counter-cyclical policies. Lord (Nigel) Lawson, no Keynesian, claimed, only half-jokingly, to have

eliminated the business cycle in the 1980s.

Events were to prove him wrong, with a speedy dose of reality in the form of the cyclical downturn that culminated in the 1990–92 recession. It was not the worst recession in the postwar period, but it was the longest. And, coming after the consumer and investment

boom of the late '80s, and the mood of optimism of that period, which had encouraged a widespread belief that Britain had embarked on an era of permanently faster growth, it was perhaps the most shocking.

The business cycle is taken to refer to the economy's regular pattern, whereby recovery leads to a peak in activity, followed by a downturn and a new cyclical trough. Each peak (and each trough) is, on average, four to five years apart. The short business cycle is distinct from the 10-year Juglar cycle (after the economist who identified it), which has been less easy to define in modern times. Still more controversial is the 50-year Kondratieff cycle, with 25-year upswings and downswings, named after the Russian economist who spotted it in the 1920s.

To return to the more familiar four- to five-year business cycle, its existence suggests that corporate planning should be an easy task. Recoveries last for two or three years followed by a couple of years of easier conditions where the economy turns down. There are, however, important real-world complications. The first is that the peaks and troughs are never exactly four or five years apart. This is what caught out both government ministers and many businessmen in the early 1990s, when the downturn lasted far longer than they had expected.

The second complication is that not all countries follow the same cycle. Thus, the US economy was first into the most recent recession and has now been out of it for longest. Britain, two years into the recovery phase of the cycle, followed the US out of recession, but the economies of Continental Europe did not emerge from their difficulties until around a year later. Japan was yet further down the cyclical track.

Third, each cycle will be characterised by special factors which affect the timing of upswings and downturns. In the case of Europe, Germany's post-unification boom had the effect of maintaining strong growth in the core economies of the EC (but not in Britain) for longer than would otherwise have been the case. By contrast, the response of the German Bundesbank to that boom, in the form of a prolonged period of high interest rates, meant that Europe was slow to recover.

These complications mean, according to Richard Kersley, a strategist at stock-brokers BZW, that predicting the precise cyclical performance of individual industries is 'much more of an art than a science'. He cites certain industries, such as pharma-ceuticals, and food manufacturing and retailing, which are relatively immune from the cycle. But outside these sectors, anyone who tries to base decisions on when particular

sectors are likely to kick into recovery, or suffer from a downturn, is likely to become unstuck. In the nature of these things, though, analysts are required to operate according to some cyclical model of the way the economy operates. Sushil Wadhwani of Goldman Sachs has devised a list of sectors which are particularly cyclical in nature. They are banks, building materials producers, the chemicals industry, contracting and construction firms, electricals (manufac-turers rather than the power companies and regional electricity distributors), hotels and leisure, metals, motors, property stores and textiles. Together, they account for about a quarter of quoted companies in Britain. And, so far, Wadhwani has been encouraged by the performance of the model. 'In terms of stock-market performance, these sectors have, if anything, outperformed the rest of the market by more than we would have expected,' he says.

The ground rules of business cycles are straightforward enough. Consider a situation, familiar a couple of years ago, when the economy is 'bumping along the bottom'. Companies are the first to make a move, increasing investment in response to an expected increase in demand from consumers. Thus, the first industries to experience an upturn are capital goods manufacturers. Firms also increase their demand for finance, and begin to put in place advertising and promotion programmes. Construction activity, both for commercial and resid-ential property, and for other schemes, also rises ahead of the general upturn. So, when the anticipated increase in consumer demand comes through, they are ready for it. Nor is the process an accidental one. Firms, by virtue of their actions in boosting investment, will increase income and employment among capital goods manufacturers and others, which itself will lead to an increase in consumer demand. This, in the jargon, is the Keynesian accelerator at work. Near the top of the cycle, the opposite occurs: firms cut back on their capital spending ahead of an expected slowdown in final demand. Their cut-backs here lead to the very downturn their actions were intended to anticip-ate. And so it goes on.

How do the ground rules fit the experience of the more recent cycle? At the onset of recession, the theory fitted the facts reasonably well. Manufactur-ing output effectively stopped growing

in the summer of 1989, after a parti-cularly sharp rise. Industry's growth reached a plateau at a time when retail sales were growing at more than 2 per cent a year, and a year before the sharp, mid-1990 dive into recession. Capital spending by private-sector firms reached a peak early in 1989, before embarking on its decline. There is evid-ence, then, of anticipatory behaviour by businesses, probably in direct response to the high interest rate regime of that time.

Not all sectors saw it coming. The construction industry was still growing strongly in the first half of 1990, with output growth of 3 per cent, before hit-ting the buffers in mid-year. And some industries had reason to believe that the recession would leave them relatively unscathed. Motor manufacturers saw demand dive in the home market, but this was compensated for, initially, by strong export demand. Thus, car output was still rising strongly in first-half 1991, until disappointing August regis-trations finally hit production.

In summary, the onset of recession fitted the theory of business cycles quite well. Companies anticipated a down-turn in activity by cutting back invest-ment. Many were still left holding the baby in the form of excessive debt dur-ing a period of very high interest rates, but few optimistically carried on raising output in the face of a downturn in domestic demand.

The other side of the cycle, recovery, has however been rather different. Con-sumers were the first to respond to lower interest rates. Retail sales began recovering in the spring of 1992. Until August this year, it appeared that the only segment of consumer spending not fully participating in the upturn was the housing market. But disappointing new car registrations in August, with sales to private buyers down some 4 per cent on a year earlier, suggested that a reluctance to spend on big-ticket items was more general.

If, however, the consumer was relat-ively quick to perk up, the company sector was not. There are two possible explanations for this. Industry went into recession on the back of a substan-tial investment boom, and apparently decided that capacity was adequate, at least for a time, to meet demand upturn that was expected to be rela-tively weak. In addition, firms have given a greater priority to repaying debt than boosting investment, a factor explained by high levels of corporate debt during the recession. 'We have seen a different response by industry in this recovery,' says BZW's Kersley. 'The first move has been to cut costs, followed by an attempt to get some price increases on top of those cost cuts. Only then have firms tried to generate some increases in volume.'

Slowest of all to emerge, again in contrast to the normal cyclical pattern, has been construction, which could only genuinely be said to be experiencing an upturn this year, two years after the overall economy's emergence from recession. Excess capacity is one explanation for this, but construction has also been hit by cutbacks in infrastructure spending by the Treasury, and a lacuna until new projects under the private finance initiative begin to come on stream. 'We've had to rewrite received wisdom,' says Mark Franklin, industrial economist at Oxford Economic Forecasting. 'It was always thought the construction industry was very much a leading sector of the economy. One would really have expected building to have led the rest of the economy out of recession.'

The recovery pattern, therefore, turns the theoretical model on its head. Consumers have been relatively quick on their feet, while companies have lumbered only slowly into action, with one eye firmly on the next downturn.
© *Management Today*, Nov. 94

(a) What is meant by the business cycle and, typically, how long is it?

(b) Why is predicting the cyclical behaviour of individual industries 'much more of an art than a science'?

(c) Why are some sectors of the economy more prone to cyclical movements in economic activity than others?

(d) Which are normally the leading sectors of the economy at the bottom and top of the cycle? Explain why.

(e) In what ways did the recovery from the recession of 1990–92 not follow accepted economic theory? Explain why.

E ANSWERS

Q1. See Chapter 14, Q27.

Q2. Withdrawals and consumption are endogenous in the model of national income determination: that is, they are determined (in part) by the level of national income. Injections, however, are exogenous: that is, they are determined by factors other than the level of national income.

Q3. C. Assuming that the scale of the two axes is the same, then a 45° line shows that whatever is measured on one axis *must* under all circumstances equal what is measured on the other axis. With national income measured on the horizontal axis, a 45° line shows whatever must equal national income. This is consumption of domestic goods and services plus withdrawals ($C_d + W$): income must be either spent on domestically produced goods and services or withdrawn – there is nothing else that can happen to income.

Q4. (a) See Figure A16.1.

(b) At low levels of income, people may be forced to spend more than they earn, by either borrowing or drawing on savings. By contrast, at high levels of income individuals will be able to save part of their income.

(c) The marginal propensity to consume represents the proportion of a rise in national income that goes on consumption. The formula is $\Delta C/\Delta Y$.

(d) (i) $(90 - 70) \div (75 - 50) = 0.8$

(ii) $(150 - 130) \div (150 - 125) = 0.8$

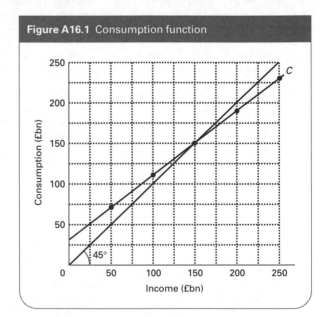

Figure A16.1 Consumption function

(e) the slope of the consumption function.

(f) It would be curved, with the slope diminishing as national income rose.

Q5. *higher*. In the long run, individuals will have time to adjust their consumption patterns.

Q6. *Slowly*.

Q7. The mpc_d includes only that part of a rise in national income that accrues to domestic firms. It thus excludes that part of a rise in consumption that goes in expenditure taxes (VAT, excise duties, etc.) and also excludes the consumption of imports. It includes, however, sales subsidies to firms.

Q8. *Income.*

Q9. *(a)* See the following table.

National income (£bn)	Saving (£bn)
50	−20
75	−15
100	−10
125	−5
150	0
175	5
200	10
225	15
250	20

(b) See Figure A16.2.

(c) At levels of national income below £150bn.

(d) $mps = \Delta S/\Delta Y = (10 - 5) \div (200 - 175) = 0.2$.

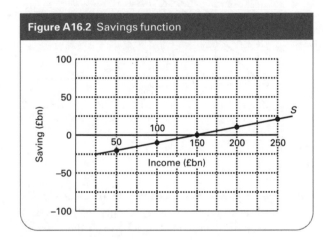

Figure A16.2 Savings function

Q10. *(a)* *fall; shift.*
   (b) *fall; shift.*
   (c) *rise; shift.*
   (d) *rise; shift.*
   (e) *fall; movement along.* (The fall in saving is due to the fall in income.)

Q11. *True.* It is the weighted average of all the marginal tax rates for each person in the country.

Q12. The import function would become progressively steeper as imports would account for a larger proportion of any rise in national income. The *mpm* would thus rise as income rose.

Q13. (a) *True* (b) *False* (c) *True.*

Q14. *(a)* *OB* (where $W = J$).
   (b) At income *OA* injections exceed withdrawals. There will be a movement towards point *P* as the additional net expenditures ($J - W$) encourage producers to increase output, which in turn lead to higher levels of national income. As income rises so will the level of withdrawals

(a movement along the *W* curve). The movement along the withdrawals curve will continue until $W = J$.
   (c) The injections curve will shift upwards by an amount *UT*. Equilibrium will now be achieved at point *U* (where the new injections curve intersects the withdrawals curve). National income will thus have risen by an amount *BC*.

Q15. The ratio of a rise in national income to the rise in injections that caused it.

Q16. A.

Q17. B.

Q18. *True.* The multiplier = $1/mpw$. The larger the *mpw*, the less of any rise in income will be spent on domestic goods and services, and thus the less will recirculate round the circular flow of income each time.

Q19. *(a)* 1.
   (b) 0.

Q20. *(a)* 3.
   (b) 4 (i.e. $1/(1 - 0.75)$).

Q21. See Table A16.1.

Table A16.1 The multiplier

Period	ΔJ(£m)	ΔY(£m)	ΔC_d(£m)	ΔW(£m)
1	200	200	100	100
2	–	100	50	50
3	–	50	25	25
4	–	25	12.5	12.5
5	–	12.5	6.25	6.25
Totals		387.5	193.75	193.75

Q22. D. An increase in the marginal propensity to save will cause the *mpw* to increase: hence the value of the multiplier will fall.

Q23. *National expenditure* (which is the same as aggregate demand).

Q24. (a) *VZ* (b) *OB* (c) *AB/UG*.

Q25. *True.* The mpc_d will fall, and thus the slope of the C_d function and hence the *E* function will fall.

Q26. *(a)* *OD* (where $Y = E$).
   (b) *QH* (i.e. $E - C_d$).
   (c) *TM* (i.e. $Y - C_d$).
   (d) $SU \div RU$ (i.e. $\Delta C_d \div \Delta Y$).
   (e) *NM* (i.e. $TM - SL$).
   (f) $NM \div DF$ (i.e. $\Delta W \div \Delta Y$).
   (g) $DF \div NM$ (i.e. $1 \div mpw$).

Q27. *(a)* $(0.75 \times 0.9 \times 0.75) - 0.1 = 0.40625$.
   (b) $1/(1 - 0.40625) = 1.68$.

Q28. B. National output is at a maximum and the level of national income is such as to ensure that all such output produced is bought, i.e. there is no deficiency in demand.

Q29. *deflationary gap.*

Q30. *inflationary gap.*

Q31. D. Note that (ii) is *not* a definition. The deflationary gap will be less than the shortfall of national income below the full-employment level. If the government adopts policies to close the deflationary gap, the multiplier will then ensure that the full shortfall is made up.

Q32. E.

Q33. *(a)* See Figure A16.3.

(b) The *J* and *E* lines will shift upward so that they now intersect with the *W* and *Y* lines respectively to the right of Y_f. The inflationary gap is now the amount by which *E* exceeds *Y* and *J* exceeds *W* at Y_f.

Figure A16.3 Deflationary gap

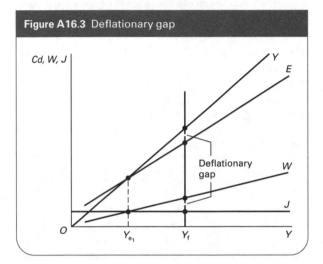

Q34. *(a)* 5. (i.e. 1/*mpw*. The *mpw* is 1/5, since for every rise in national income of £50bn, withdrawals rise by £10bn.)

(b) £300bn. (With an inflationary gap of £10bn and a multiplier of 5, the equilibrium national income must be £50bn above the full-employment level.)

(c) *Deflationary gap of £20bn.* (The full-employment level of national income has risen by £150bn to £400bn. This means that the full-employment level of national income is now £100bn above the equilibrium level of national income (of £300bn). With a multiplier of 5, the deflationary gap must be £100bn/5 = £20bn.)

Q35. C. If an increase in injections to fill a gap of £20bn leads to a rise in national income of £60bn, the multiplier must have a value of 3. Given that the multiplier = $1/(1 - mpc_d)$, the mpc_d must equal 2/3.

Q36. *(a)* In Figure A16.4(b), national income rises to Y_{e_2}.

(b) The *AD* curve shifts to AD_2, and if the price level remained at P_1 (i.e. if the *AS* curve were horizontal), income would rise to Y_{e_2}.

(c) With the upward-sloping aggregate supply curve illustrated, equilibrium will be at point *X*. National income will be Y_{e_3}.

(d) The expenditure curve will be E_3.

Figure A16.4 National income determination: upward-sloping *AS* curve

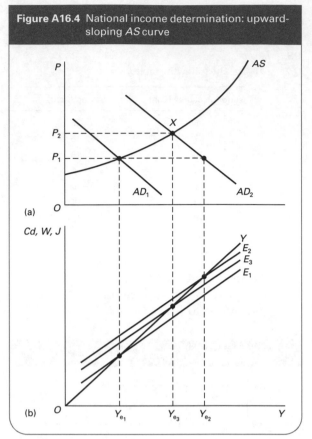

Q37. D.

Q38. D.

Q39. *True.*

Q40. *True.* Relatively small changes in national income can lead to relatively large changes in the level of investment, which in turn lead to further rises in national income.

Q41. *(a)* See Table A16.2.

(b) Even though demand has continued to grow, it has done so at a slower rate. Induced investment is determined by the rate of growth of demand.

Table A16.2 The accelerator effect

	0	1	2	3	4	5	6
Quantity demanded by consumers	500	500	1000	2000	2500	2500	2300
Number of machines required	5	5	10	20	25	25	23
Induced investment (I_i)	–	0	5	10	5	0	0
Replacement investment (I_r)	–	1	1	1	1	1	0
Total investment ($I_i + I_r$)		1	6	11	6	1	0

Q42. Firms often have spare capacity or carry stocks and thus do not need to invest more when demand rises; expectations of future demand will vary; producer goods industries may not be able to supply additional machines; replacement investment is unpredictable; firms make investment plans into the future and it may take time to change them.

Q43. Following an increase in government spending, national income will rise (multiplier effect). This rise in national income will stimulate investment (the accelerator effect). This represents a further injection into the circular flow (causing a multiplier effect). Whether the subsequent effect on national income is greater than the previous change in national income will determine whether investment continues to increase. If the change in national income is bigger, investment will rise and there will be a resulting multiplied rise in income. If it is smaller, investment will fall and there will be a resulting multiplied fall in income. The interactions continue indefinitely.

Q44. A.

Q45. *False.* It will slow down the recovery. The firm, rather than employing more labour to increase output, may simply draw on its stocks to meet the additional rise in demand.

Q46. (a) *expansion*; (b) *recession or early part of upturn*; (c) *peaking out*; (d) *recession*; (e) *expansion*; (f) *upturn*.

A REVIEW

In the 1950s and 1960s, fiscal policy was seen as the major means of either achieving full employment or avoiding inflation. Although in the late 1970s and the 1980s fiscal policy was relegated by many governments around the world to the relatively minor role of supporting monetary policy, many economists today once again regard it as an important weapon in the government's economic armoury.

17.1 The nature of fiscal policy

(Pages 497–500) Fiscal policy involves altering the size of the *budget deficit* or *budget surplus*.

Q1. If the government runs a budget deficit, this will necessarily cause an increase in national income.

True/False

The size of the budget deficit or surplus is linked to the size of the *public-sector borrowing requirement* (PSBR) or *public-sector debt repayment* (PSDR).

Q2. A public-sector borrowing requirement (or 'public-sector net cash requirement') is defined as:
A. the amount central government has to borrow in a given year.
B. the national debt.
C. the increase in government securities in a given year.
D. the excess of public-sector spending over public-sector receipts in a given year.
E. the budget deficit in a given year.

Q3. Explain why the size of the public-sector deficit or surplus will be influenced by the level of national income.

....

....

Q4. Fiscal stance refers to:
A. the total level of government spending.
B. whether the government supports the use of fiscal policies to manage the economy.
C. the effect of the budget deficit or surplus on the level of aggregate demand.
D. the existence of inflationary or deflationary gaps in the economy.
E. the size of the government's budget surplus or deficit.

Q5. Those taxes and government expenditures that increase and decrease respectively as national income rises are called.

....

The more that taxes increase and government expenditure decreases as national income rises, the **Q6.** *larger/smaller* will be the multiplier. What is more, if taxes are progressive, then *ceteris paribus*, a rise in national income will cause the multiplier to **Q7.** *rise/fall*.

(Pages 500–2) *Discretionary* fiscal policy refers to the specific adjustment of government expenditure and/or taxation with the aim of influencing the level of aggregate demand.

⬤ Q8. Which of the following fiscal policy measures would have an expansionary and which a contractionary impact upon the level of economic activity?

(a) A cut in direct taxation.

expansionary/contractionary

(b) A rise in personal allowances.

expansionary/contractionary

(c) An increase in the PSBR.

expansionary/contractionary

(d) A reduction in social security benefits.

expansionary/contractionary

(e) A move from a budget deficit to a budget surplus.

expansionary/contractionary

The multiplier effect of increasing government expenditure by £xm is different from that of reducing taxes by £xm. The tax multiplier is given by $\Delta Y/\Delta T$.

⬤ Q9. The tax multiplier is smaller than the government expenditure multiplier. *True/False*

▤ Q10. If the mpc_d is 0.75, the tax multiplier is:
A. 4
B. −4
C. 3
D. −3
E. −1⅓

▤ Q11. If investment exceeds saving by £10m and there is a balance of payments surplus of £30m, then for the economy to be in equilibrium there must be a:
A. budget deficit of £40m.
B. budget surplus of £40m.
C. budget deficit of £20m.
D. budget surplus of £20m.
E. budget balance.

17.2 The effectiveness of fiscal policy

(Pages 503–10) One problem with fiscal policy is that it can lead to 'crowding out'.

▤ Q12. Crowding out is defined as:

A. increased public expenditure replacing private-sector expenditure.
B. increased taxes pushing up interest rates.
C. when there are insufficient tax revenues to finance increased government expenditure.
D. the difficulty some people find in paying their taxes.
E. that part of public expenditure financed from borrowing.

(?) Q13. Give three reasons why it is difficult to forecast the magnitude of the impact of fiscal policy on the economy.

1. ....

2. ....

3. ....

▦ Q14. Fiscal policy suffers from a number of timing problems. Match the following problems to the various time lags between a problem occurring and the full final effect of fiscal policy measures taken to correct the problem.
 (i) The time taken for the multiplier process to work.
 (ii) The long-run consumption function is different from the short-run one.
 (iii) The business cycle is irregular.
 (iv) Administrative delays.
 (v) The Budget occurs only once a year.

(a) Time lag to recognition ....
(b) Time lag between recognition and changes being announced.

....
(c) Time lag between changes being announced and changes coming into force.

....
(d) Time lag between changes in taxes and government expenditure and the resulting changes in national income.

....
(e) Time lag before people's spending patterns fully adjust to changes in incomes.

....

⬤ B   PROBLEMS, EXERCISES AND PROJECTS

Q15. Table 17.1 shows the consumption schedule for a closed economy (i.e. one that does not trade with other countries). Investment is currently £40bn.

(a) Assuming that the government is currently spending £20bn, what is the equilibrium level of national income?

....

Table 17.1 National income and consumption for country A (£bn)

National income	30	60	90	120	150	180	210	240	270	300
Consumption	20	40	60	80	100	120	140	160	180	200

(b) Assuming that at this equilibrium level of national income the government is running a budget deficit of £5bn, what must be the level of saving in the economy?

....

(c) What is the government expenditure multiplier?

....

(d) What is the tax multiplier?

....

Q16. Referring to Q15, assume that full employment is achieved at a national income of £240bn.
(a) What is the size of the deflationary gap?

....

(b) How much would government expenditure have to be raised (assuming no change in tax rates) in order to close this gap?

....

(c) Alternatively, how much would taxes have to be changed (assuming no change in government expenditure) in order to close the gap?

....

(d) Alternatively, assume now that the government decides that it wants to close the gap and *also* to balance its budget (i.e. to raise taxes £5bn more than it raises government expenditure). How much must it raise government expenditure and how much must it raise taxes?

....

....

Q17. The Budget is when the Chancellor of the Exchequer announces changes in taxation and government expenditure for the coming financial year commencing 5 April. Using references that you have available, find out the main fiscal measures in the most recent Budget. Assess how these measures related to the state of the economy at the time of the Budget, and how the economy was forecast to change in the future. This may require your referring to government statistics. These can be found in *Economic Trends* (ONS), *Financial Statistics* (ONS) and the *Annual Abstract of Statistics* (ONS). Forecasts of economic performance can be found in the *Treasury 'Red Book'* (published at the time of the Budget). Independent forecasts and assessments can be found in the quality press. There is usually a wealth of information in the press concerning the Budget and the state of the economy at the end of November (when the Budget is usually held). Information on the Budget can also be found at the following two web addresses:
http://www.hm-treasury.gov.uk/
http://www.ft.com/

C DISCUSSION TOPICS AND ESSAYS

Q18. 'The existence of a budget deficit or a budget surplus tells us very little about the stance of fiscal policy.' Explain and discuss.

Q19. What factors might prevent the government from effectively fine tuning the economy?

Q20. Adam Smith remarked in *The Wealth of Nations* concerning the balancing of budgets, 'What is prudence in the conduct of every private family can scarce be folly in that of a great kingdom.' What problems might there be if the government decided to follow a balanced budget approach to its spending?

Q21. Aaron Wildavsky refers to the Treasury's forecasting as 'a compound of knowledge, hunch and intuition'. What difficulties are there in forecasting the effects of changes in

fiscal policy? What are the future policy implications if past and present policies are based on inaccurate forecasts? Give some hypothetical examples.

Q22. What are the advantages and disadvantages of the government sticking to a fiscal rule? (An example of such a rule is the UK Labour government's 'golden rule', where by the government pledges that, over the economic cycle, it will borrow only to invest and not to fund current spending.)

Q23. Debate
The problems of magnitude and the problems of timing conspire to make fiscal policy unpredictable. As such, intervention of this sort should be avoided and the government should aim to balance its budget.

With the stagnation of the Japanese economy well into its second year, the reflationary economic measures adopted by the Japanese government were proving to be totally ineffective. In the article below, taken from *BBC Online News* of 7 August 1998, the latest attempt by the Japanese government to get the economy moving was revealed.

Japan unveils $110bn rescue package

Japan's new Prime Minister, Keizo Obuchi, has unveiled a package of measures aimed at restoring consumer confidence and boosting the ailing economy.

The measures include tax cuts worth more than $40bn and plans to boost government spending by nearly $70bn dollars.

Jobs on the line

To cheers from members of his Liberal Democrat Party Mr Obuchi said he was confident the measures will lead to a recovery within two years and was prepared to sacrifice his own Cabinet in order to put the economy back on track.

'By staking the future of the Cabinet, I am determined to spare no effort to bring the Japanese economy back on track in one or two years,' Mr Obuchi said in his inaugural policy speech to Japan's parliament. In an address keenly awaited by the international financial community, Mr Obuchi also pledged to clean up the bad debt situation in the finance sector. He said he would implement a plan to prevent bank failures as a matter of priority.

Cautious response

Mr Obuchi speech struck a confident and determined tone that was designed to reassure financial markets that Japan was acting decisively to clear up its financial problems.

But the package of reforms will not come into effect until next year and received a lukewarm reception from Japanese investors. Japanese shares slipped after the announcement, with dealers concerned that Mr Obuchi failed to reveal any fresh measures to stimulate the economy. The Nikkei index fell 47.05 points to close at 15 829.17. The Japanese yen also lost ground on Friday, falling to more than ¥145 against the dollar.

Yasuhisa Morikuni, assistant vice president at Bank of America, said: 'Obuchi's speech was not surprising at all. His remarks were generally in line with his comments made when he formed the new cabinet.' 'I feel that Obuchi still lacks clear vision and there are still questions about how he can carry out these plans effectively and quickly,' he added.

Tax cuts

Mr Obuchi has pledged to cut taxes by far more than the 6 trillion yen ($41bn) that he originally proposed. Under the plan the highest rate of tax is set to be reduced to 50 per cent from 65 per cent. The corporate tax rate will also be lowered from 46 per cent to 40 per cent.

The Japanese government plans to issue new bonds to finance the tax cuts and its spending spree.

Under pressure

Mr Obuchi has been under pressure to produce a more decisive economic policy than his predecessor, Ryutaro Hashimoto, who stepped down after the ruling Liberal Democrats performed poorly in elections for the Japanese Upper House.

It is hoped that the tax cuts will stimulate consumer spending and help bring some companies back from the brink of bankruptcy by restoring sales and profits.

Fiscal policy is one of the last economic tools the Japanese government can resort to. The country's interest rates are among the world's lowest. Cutting taxes, however, will add to Tokyo's headaches, as it will increase an already high public deficit.

Japan's recently appointed Finance Minister Kiichi Miyazawa earlier said the government would finance the tax cuts by issuing new bonds. He said future taxpayers would face serious financial burdens as a result. He indicated, however, that his main priority was the economic recovery.

International concerns

Governments, economists and investors around the would have been closely watching what Mr Obuchi has to offer.

Japan is the lynchpin of Asia's economy, and worries about the country's economic future were the reason for this week's dramatic losses on stock markets in Europe and the USA.

The US Government has repeatedly called on Japan to push through economic reforms as quickly as possible, including a radical shake-up of the country's troubled banking sector which is struggling under a $600m mountain of bad debts.

(a) Using a relevant diagram, explain how the fiscal measures announced by the Japanese government would hopefully stimulate the Japanese economy.

(b) In order to raise the $70bn extra spending, and finance the $40bn of tax cuts, the Japanese government planned to issue new bonds. What were the implications of this course of action?

(c) The article refers to the large debts of Japanese banks. What were the implications of these debts for the Japanese government's attempts to stimulate the economy?

In 1974, Mr Healey, the then Chancellor of the Exchequer, expressed some serious reservations about the accuracy and usefulness of economic forecasts. In the November Statement 1974, quoted in P. Browning, *The Treasury and Economic Policy, 1964–1985*, p. 64 (Longman, 1986), he was to remark:

Like long-term weather forecasts, they are better than nothing. But no one who has held office in the Treasury, or who has had the job of following Treasury activity from outside, will deny that they are subject to wide margins of error.

The numbers contained in the forecasts – specific to 0.5 per cent in every case – give a spurious impression of certainty. But their origin lies in the extrapolation from a partially known past, through an unknown present, to an unknowable future, according to theories about causal relationships between certain economic variables which are hotly disputed by academic economists, and may well in fact change from country to country or from decade to decade. The current state of our economic knowledge allows of nothing better . . .

Errors in forecasting the level of the PSBR in *1974/5* made it virtually impossible for the Labour government of the day to achieve its policy objectives, which were set in accordance with the *Social Contract*, an agreement drawn up between the government and unions, whereby social policies (involving significant amounts of government spending) were introduced in return for union agreements on wage restraint.

Today, forecasting remains crucial in dictating government policy. Below is an extract from *The Times* of 20 March 1991, the day following that **year's** Budget.

The Treasury forecasts are likely to attract headline attention because they at last recognise a severe recession, with a fall of 2 per cent in real GDP expected this year, after a rise of only half a per cent in 1990. But the forecasters are only recognising what has already happened. They are predicting a moderate recovery in output from now on, with output rising at an annual rate of 1¼ per cent in the second half of 1991 and by 2¾ per cent in the first half of 1992. The last figure is very near to the Treasury's estimated trend rate of growth for non-North Sea output.

But there is a more interesting approach. Output growth started to slow down to below trend rates in the second half of 1989. By the first half of 1991, it should have fallen to 7 per cent below trend. Rough Treasury calculations suggest that there is now slightly more slack than is required to establish a stable rate of inflation. In other words, downward pressure should continue to be exerted from excess slack in the economy, as well as from favourable price expectations, for some time to come.

Even so, the official forecast of a fall in RPI inflation from 10 per cent at the end of 1990 to 3¾ per cent in early 1992 much exaggerates what is in prospect even on the Treasury's own expectations. A more realistic idea of disinflation is given by the forecast of producer price increases, which is expected to decelerate from 6¼ per cent at the end of 1990 to 4 per cent in early 1992. Adding back something for non-traded goods and services, this would amount to an underlying rate of inflation of around 5½ per cent. There would be still some way to go before German-type rates are reached.

And I nearly forgot the balance of payments. The deficit, on statisticians' guesses, is expected to fall from just below £13bn in 1990 to £6bn in 1991, before rising to an annual rate of £8bn with economic recovery in the first half of 1992, by which time it will represent 1 to 1½ per cent GDP. But if sterling and inflation come right without a worsening depression, we will be able to relegate these figures to those who like works of fiction and guessing games in general.
© *The Times*, 20.3.91

(a) What problems are there in forecasting correctly?

(b) Can forecasting ever be avoided if the government insists on intervening in economic affairs?

(c) Is forecasting simply a guessing game?

 ANSWERS

Q1. *False*. A budget deficit will only cause national income to rise if it results in *total* injections exceeding *total* withdrawals. Note, however, that an increase in the size of the budget deficit will, *ceteris paribus*, be expansionary.

Q2. D. The answer is not A, C or E, because the PSBR refers to the borrowing of the *whole* public sector: central government, local government and public corporations. The answer is not B, because the national debt refers to the accumulated debt over the years, not just to this year's borrowing.

Q3. As national income rises, so tax revenue will rise. Conversely, if national income rises fast enough for unemployment to fall, government expenditure on transfer payments such as unemployment benefit will fall. The net effect is that the budget deficit will fall (or the surplus rise). The opposite will happen if national income falls.

Q4. C. Fiscal stance refers to the effect of the government's fiscal policy on total aggregate demand: will the effect be reflationary or deflationary, and how much so. The answer is not E because the mere size of the deficit or surplus alone is not enough to determine whether aggregate demand will increase or decrease and by how much. It is also necessary to know what is happening to the other two injections and the other two withdrawals.

Q5. *automatic fiscal stabilisers.*

Q6. *smaller*. The more that taxes increase, the higher the *mpt* and hence the higher the *mpw* and the smaller the multiplier. The smaller the multiplier, the more stable will the economy be.

Q7. *fall*. The *mpt* will rise.

Q8. (a), (b) and (c) are expansionary. (d) and (e) are contractionary.

Q9. *True*.

Q10. D. The full multiplier is 4, but only ³/₄ of the cut in taxes is spent on domestic goods and services. Thus the rise in income is only ³/₄ as much as with the full multiplier. In fact, you can easily demonstrate that the tax multiplier is always 1 less than the full multiplier. (Note that the tax multiplier is negative: this is because a *fall* in taxes leads to a *rise* in income and vice versa.)

Q11. B. In equilibrium $I + X + G = S + M + T$. Thus if I exceeds S by £10m, and X exceeds M by £30m, $I + X$ must exceed $S + M$ by £10m + £30m = £40m. Thus for the economy to be in equilibrium T must exceed G by £40m: i.e. there must be a budget surplus of £40m.

Q12. A. Increased public expenditure can lead to a shortage of resources available for the private sector (resource crowding out) or a shortage of finance for private sector borrowing (financial crowding out).

Q13. Reasons include: the amount of crowding out is difficult to predict; the impact of tax cuts (or benefit increases) will depend on how consumers decide to allocate additional incomes (which in turn depends on expectations of future price and income changes); the size of the accelerator is difficult to predict and subsequent multiplier/accelerator interactions are virtually impossible to predict; random shocks.

Q14. (a) (iii), (b) (v), (c) (iv), (d) (i), (e) (ii).

18 Money and Interest Rates

The financial sector has changed a great deal in recent years, primarily as a result of the introduction of new technology and of the policy of deregulation.

This chapter and the next will review the monetary sector of the economy, examining how it operates and how it is controlled. We will also consider the relationship between money and interest rates, and examine the importance of money and interest rates in determining the level of activity in the economy.

18.1 The role of money in the economy

(Pages 513–17)

Q1. The supply of money in the economy is a flow concept since money circulates by being passed from hand to hand.   *True/False*

Q2. Money has four main functions. These are

1. ....

2. ....

3. ....

4. ....

Q3. Which of the following items would be included in:

(i)   both narrow and broad definitions of money?

(ii) broad definitions alone?

(iii) neither narrow nor broad definitions?

(a) Current accounts in banks.   ....

(b) Share certificates.   ....

(c) Cash in banks' tills.   ....

(d) Cash in a person's pocket.   ....

(e) Deposits in savings accounts in banks and building societies.

          ....

(f) A debit card.   ....

(g) Wholesale deposits in financial institutions.

          ....

The amount of money in the economy influences the level of economic activity. It does this by affecting aggregate demand.

Q4. Are the following responses to an increase in the money supply examples of the *direct* or *indirect* transmission mechanisms between changes in money supply and changes in aggregate demand?

(a) Lower interest rates, and hence an increase in investment.   *Direct/Indirect*

(b) Depreciation of the pound, and hence higher exports and lower imports.   *Direct/Indirect*

 Multiple Choice   *Written answer*   *Delete wrong word*   *Diagram/table manipulation*   *Calculation*   *Matching/ordering*

(c) An increase in money holdings, and hence an increase in the demand for goods and services. *Direct/Indirect*

(d) Lower interest rates, and hence an increase in consumption financed by consumer credit.

Direct/Indirect

Before we can examine just how money supply affects aggregate demand, we must see what determines money supply itself. We begin by looking at the various financial institutions involved.

18.2 The financial system in the UK

(Pages 517–20) Financial intermediaries provide a number of important services, two of which are in providing expert advice to their customers, and channelling funds to those areas that will yield the greatest return. They also lend long and borrow short. This is known as **Q5.** *risk transformation/maturity transformation/credit creation.* Also by lending to a large number of individuals they reduce the impact of loan defaults by any one borrower. This is known as **Q6.** *risk transformation/maturity transformation/ credit creation.*

There are several different types of institution in the financial sector.

♟ **Q7.** Match the following financial institution with the role in which they tend to specialise.
 (i) Finance houses
 (ii) Wholesale banks
 (iii) Retail banks
 (iv) Building societies

(a) They provide branch banking facilities, current accounts and overdraft facilities.

....

(b) They receive large deposits from and make large loans to industry. They also provide assistance to firms when raising new capital through an issue of shares.

....

(c) They specialise in granting loans for house purchase.

....

(d) They specialise in providing hire-purchase finance for consumer durables.

....

(Pages 520–4) The deposits made in banks and building societies are **Q8.** *liabilities/losses/costs/assets/profits* of these institutions. Whereas the loans they make to their customers are **Q9.** *liabilities/losses/costs/assets/profits* of these institutions.

An important distinction is between wholesale and retail loans and deposits.

◖ **Q10.** Which of the following are wholesale and which are retail?

(a) Large-scale deposits made by firms at negotiated rates of interest. *retail/wholesale*

(b) Loans made by high street banks at published rates of interest. *retail/wholesale*

(c) Deposits in savings accounts in high street banks. *retail/wholesale*

(d) Deposits in savings accounts in building societies. *retail/wholesale*

(e) Large-scale loans to industry syndicated through several banks. *retail/wholesale*

Financial institutions keep a range of liabilities and assets. The balance of items is dictated by considerations of *profitability* and *liquidity*.

♟ **Q11.** Rank the following assets of a commercial bank in order of decreasing liquidity.
(a) Money at call with money market institutions.
(b) Government bonds.
(c) Bills of exchange.
(d) Operational balances with the Bank of England.
(e) Cash.
(f) Personal loans.

High liquidity

 (i) ....

 (ii) ....

(iii) ....

(iv) ....

 (v) ....

(vi) ....

Low liquidity

⦸ **Q12.** Profitability is the major aim of most financial institutions. Why does the motive of profitability tend to conflict with the need for liquidity?

....

....

....

▤ **Q13.** The liquidity ratio of a bank refers to:
A. the ratio of Treasury bills to government bonds that it holds.
B. the ratio of liquid to illiquid assets.
C. the ratio of cash to advances.
D. the ratio of liquid assets to total liabilities.
E. the ratio of total assets to total liabilities.

(?) **Q14.** What adverse consequence for a bank might follow if it maintained a liquidity ratio that was:

(a) too low? ....

....

(b) higher than necessary? ....

....

(Pages 524–6) The *money market* plays a central role in the financial system. The money market is **Q15.** *the market for short-term loans and deposits/the Issue Department of the Bank of England/the institutions dealing specifically in cash transactions*.

(?) **Q16.** There are two parts of the London money market:

(a) the..., and

(b) the..

(?) **Q17.** Bills of exchange are one major type of monetary instrument. Bills pay no interest. Why, then, is it profitable for banks to buy bills (thereby providing liquidity to the issuers of the bills – the government in the case of Treasury bills and firms in the case of commercial bills)?

....

(◑) **Q18.** The process of purchasing bills from the banks and discount houses by the Bank of England is known as 'rediscounting'.   *True/False*

(▤) **Q19.** Another major type of monetary instrument is a sale and repurchase agreement (repo). Which of the following describes a repo?

A. Where a bank agrees to buy certain assets from an institution for cash in return for being able to borrow from that institution in the future.

B. Where a bank sells some assets (e.g. bonds) and agrees to buy them back at a particular price after a set period of time.

C. Where bank A lends to bank B provided that bank B is prepared to lend to bank A in the future.

D. Where a bank sells assets to person or institution A in return for buying assets from person or institution B.

E. All of the above.

(?) **Q20.** Give three reasons why the parallel money market has grown in importance in recent years.

1. ....

2. ....

3. ....

Behind the scenes, acting as overseer to the monetary and financial system, is the Bank of England.

(◑) **Q21.** Which of the following statements about the Bank of England are true?

(a) The Bank of England is the sole issuer of banknotes in the UK.   *True/False*

(b) The Bank of England acts as banker to the banks.
                                                      True/False

(c) No matter whether the government runs a budget surplus or a budget deficit, the Bank of England still has to manage the national debt.   *True/False*

(d) The Bank of England is lender of last resort to the banking system.   *True/False*

(e) The Bank of England not only operates domestic monetary policy but it also manages the country's exchange rate policy.   *True/False*

18.3 The supply of money

(Pages 527–9) If the money supply is to be monitored and controlled then it must be measured.

(▦) **Q22.** Match the following UK money supply measures:
 (i) M0
 (ii) M2
 (iii) M3H
 (iv) M4
 (v) Divisia money

with the descriptions below.

(a) Notes and coin in circulation + private-sector retail and wholesale sterling bank and building society deposits and certificates of deposit

....

(b) Notes and coin in circulation + public- and private-sector retail and wholesale sterling and foreign currency bank and building society deposits and certificates of deposit

....

(c) Notes and coin in circulation + that portion of private-sector retail and wholesale sterling bank and building society deposits used for transactions purposes

....

(d) Notes and coin in circulation + banks' till money + banks' operational balances in the Bank of England

....

(e) Notes and coin in circulation + private-sector retail sterling bank and building society deposits

....

(Pages 529–34) The process by which banks increase the money supply is known as **Q23.** *maturity transformation/ credit creation/profit generation/liquidity preference*. The amount by which the money supply can increase depends on their liquidity ratio.

⊗ **Q24.** If banks operate with a liquidity ratio of 20 per cent, by how much would they eventually increase their advances if they received an additional £175m from a government investment project?

....

(?) **Q25.** If the banks decide to hold a lower liquidity ratio, what effect will this have on the bank multiplier?

Increase it/Reduce it

Explain ....

....

◐ **Q26.** Which of the following will cause the UK money supply to rise; which will cause it to fall; and which will cause no direct change?

(a) A fixed exchange rate where the demand for sterling is greater than the supply. *Rise/Fall/No change*
(b) The government finances its PSBR by selling securities to the Bank of England. *Rise/Fall/No change*
(c) The government decides to increase the proportion of the national debt financed by bonds rather than by bills. *Rise/Fall/No change*
(d) The government finances its PSBR by selling bonds and bills to the general public and non-bank private sector. *Rise/Fall/No change*
(e) The government imposes a statutory liquidity ratio on banks higher than their current ratio. *Rise/Fall/No change*

(Pages 534–5) The various effects on money supply can be shown in a *flow-of-funds equation*.

◐ **Q27.** Decide whether each of the following elements should be added (+) or subtracted (–) to arrive at the total change in money supply.
(a) The PSBR. +/–
(b) Sales of public-sector debt to the non-bank private sector. +/–
(c) Bank lending to the private sector. +/–
(d) A total currency flow deficit (on the balance of payments). +/–

(Page 535) The relationship between the money supply and the rate of interest is one of debate.

(?) **Q28.** What does it mean in simple monetary theory when it is assumed that the money supply is *exogenously* determined?

....

....

(?) **Q29.** Give two reasons why Keynesian models assume that the money supply is *endogenous*.

1. ....

2. ....

18.4 The demand for money
(Pages 536–9)
▤ **Q30.** What do we mean by the term the 'demand for money'? Is it:
A. the demand by individuals for greater wealth?
B. the demand to hold financial assets in money form?
C. a means of controlling the money supply?
D. a sign of individuals wishing to change from sight to time deposits?
E. a term used by the Bank of England to refer to the demands placed upon it by the banking sector?

It is common to distinguish three motives for holding money: the transactions motive, the precautionary motive and the speculative motive. The principal determinant of the size of transactions balances is **Q31.** *national income/ interest rates/the exchange rate/tastes*, and the principal determinant of the size of speculative balances is **Q32.** *national income/interest rates/the exchange rate/tastes*.

(Pages 539–40) Keynesians and monetarists disagree over the shape and stability of the liquidity preference curve (the demand-for-money curve).

◐ **Q33.** Distinguish which of the four propositions below reflect Keynesian views and which monetarist views.
(a) 'Money and financial assets are relatively close substitutes for each other. Thus, as interest rates rise, so will the demand for financial assets. Consequently the demand for money will fall significantly. The liquidity preference curve therefore is relatively elastic.'
Keynesian/monetarist
(b) 'Expectations concerning changes in the exchange rate, in interest rates and in inflation have important effects upon the holding of speculative balances.'
Keynesian/monetarist
(c) 'Money is not a close substitute for financial assets. Hence changes in the rate of interest will have little effect upon money demand. The liquidity preference curve is thus relatively inelastic.' *Keynesian/monetarist*
(d) 'The liquidity preference curve is stable and relatively inelastic, as speculative balances are relatively insignificant.' *Keynesian/monetarist*

Figure 18.1 The effect of a change in money supply: the interest rate mechanism

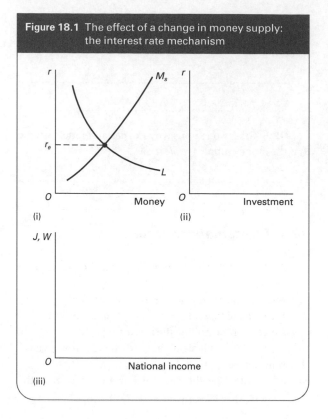

18.5 Equilibrium

(Pages 540–3)

 Q34. Figure 18.1(i) shows equilibrium in the money market. In each of the following situations, which curve shifts and what will the effect be on the equilibrium rate of interest?

(a) The government funds the PSBR by borrowing from the Bank of England.

....

(b) A rise in national income ....

(c) Speculation that sterling will appreciate ....

 Q35. We shall now use Figure 18.1 to show the relationship between changes in the money supply and the level of national income.

(a) On diagram (ii) draw a curve relating investment to the rate of interest. On diagram (iii) draw an injections 'curve' and a withdrawals curve.

(b) On diagram (i) illustrate the effect of a decrease in the money supply. Trace through the effects on to diagrams (ii) and (iii).

(c) What would the curves look like if a Keynesian had drawn the diagram?

....

....

(d) What would the effect have been on diagram (iii)?

....

(e) What would the curves look like if a monetarist had drawn the diagram?

....

....

(f) What would the effect have been this time on diagram (iii)?

....

Q36. Consider the items in Table 18.1 selected from Bank A's balance sheet.

(a) Using these items compile a balance sheet for the bank. When doing so make sure you order the sterling assets in descending order of liquidity.

(b) What are the bank's total sterling assets (and liabilities)?

(c) What is the liquidity ratio?

Q37. Assuming that banks choose to maintain a liquidity ratio of 25 per cent, that new cash deposits of £100m are made in the banking system and that all loans made are redeposited in the banking system:

Table 18.1 A range of sterling assets and liabilities of Bank A

	£bn
Notes and coin	3.5
Sight deposits by UK private sector	100.0
Time deposits by UK private sector	120.0
Investments in the public sector	16.0
Certificates of deposit in Bank A	50.0
Advances to UK private sector	200.0
Bills of exchange	14.0
Debit items in suspense and transmission	9.0
Time deposits by overseas customers	57.0
Operational balances with Bank of England	0.5
Market loans	102.0

(a) Complete Table 18.2.

Table 18.2 The creation of money

	£m		£m
Banks receive	100	Hold	25
		Lend	75
Second round deposits rise by	...	Hold	...
		Lend	...
Third round deposits rise by	...	Hold	...
		Lend	...
Fourth round deposits rise by	...	Hold	...
		Lend	...
Fifth round deposits rise by	...	Hold	...
		Lend	...
Total deposits after five rounds	...		

(b) To what level will total deposits eventually increase (after an infinite number of rounds!)?

....

(c) How much credit will have been created?

....

(d) What is the size of the bank multiplier?

....

Q38. Look up the liabilities and assets of the banking sector for the most recent month available and for 10 and 20 years ago. You will find the information in *Financial Statistics* (ONS) and the *Bank of England Monetary and Financial Statistics*. How has the balance of items changed over the years? How have the cash and liquidity ratios changed? What explanations can you offer for these changes?

DISCUSSION TOPICS AND ESSAYS

Q39. Describe the main functions of money. What attributes should money have if it is to fulfil these functions?

Q40. 'The aims of profitability and liquidity tend to conflict.' Explain this statement in respect of the banking sector.

Q41. Define the term 'liquidity ratio'. How will changes in the liquidity ratio affect the process of credit creation? Why might a bank's liquidity ratio vary over time?

Q42. How is the objective of injecting competition into the banking sector likely to conflict with the government's objectives of maintaining stability and security in the banking sector and of carrying out effective control of the money supply?

Q43. What factors might cause the money supply to rise and why? To what extent are these factors within the government's (or central bank's) control?

Q44. Describe the main motives for holding money and the main determinants of each of these money balances.

Q45. How do monetarists and Keynesians differ in their analysis of the elasticity and stability of the money demand curve? What implications do their respective analyses have for the effect of monetary variables on the level of aggregate demand?

Q46. Debate
Total deregulation of banks is in the interests of their customers as it is the best way of ensuring maximum competition between banks.

ARTICLES

The internet is set to revolutionise all aspects of economic life. One sector that is currently witnessing a flurry of internet activity is banking and financial services, as providers attempt to establish a presence in this new marketplace. The article below, by Stephen Timewell and Kung Young, taken from *The Banker* of June 1999, considers some of the implications for those banks who are shifting services on to the internet.

How the internet redefines banking

The internet is not particularly new but, for the financial sector, the last few months have witnessed not only a massive surge of interest from banks around the globe but also an explosive growth in online activities.

As the technology focus of banks shifts away from preoccupation with projects on the euro and year 2000, institutions are beginning to realise the full potential of the internet. Some online enthusiasts predict that the internet will reshape the global economy over the next five years but while this may be over-optimistic, it would be dangerous for financial institutions to underestimate the impact of Internet technology and e-commerce.

Internet commerce is already changing companies' approach to business: take, for example, the shift in buying books from the bookstore to online supplier amazon.com. And this is only the beginning.

Tim Jones, the retail head of Nat-West Bank, says: 'We expect that the two fundamental impacts of these technologies will be a massive reduction in transaction costs and the dramatically lessening importance of geography. At present, many people's horizons are governed by their capital cities since this is where they are governed from and often where their money is managed.

'In future, people's horizons may diverge, getting larger and smaller simultaneously. They may use some extremely large pan-national financial services companies but also perhaps some very local, personalised financial services.'

So, what is happening now at banks and in banking as competition increases, the 'end of geography' is at hand and non-traditional players enter the fray? Banks have been somewhat slow to realise the full potential of the internet and have been distracted by preparations for the euro but recent months have seen a quantum shift in both attitudes towards activities on the internet.

While the actual number of online customers is still relatively small (the bank with the largest number of online customers at the end of March was BankAmerica with 1.2 million), the rate of growth in online customer accounts in the first quarter of 1999 amongst the largest banks in the US shows that, across the board, online accounts will more than double this year.

The median growth is put at 118 per cent for the year with banks such as First Union and US Bancorp showing large annualised growth rates of 253 per cent and 400 per cent respectively.

For retail banking leaders, such as Wells Fargo, the accelerating customer growth implies a year end total of 1.5 million accounts compared with 700 000 at the end of 1998.

The growth surge is not just in the US. According to Sandra Alzetta, senior vice president for electronic commerce at Visa International, internet sales on Visa worldwide doubled in 1998 to $15 billion and are forecast to reach $100 billion by 2002.

Visa believes that although e-commerce accounts for only 1 per cent of total sales volume now, it will reach 10–15 per cent in the next five years.

And many countries are well advanced in their online usage, especially countries in northern Europe. Recent reports on Nua Internet Surveys showed that the percentage of the population connected online was (at the end of March, 1999): Iceland (45 per cent), Sweden (38 per cent), Finland (28 per cent), Denmark (22 per cent) – compared with the UK (18 per cent).

Nua noted in May that of the 3.6 million people online in Sweden, 3.1 million use the internet once a month and 950 000 have made an online purchase. Another May 1999 report showed that 64.2 million US adults, representing 42.2 per cent of the adult population in the US, were regular internet users, a 20 per cent increase on the previous year.

The acceptance of the internet reflects a need in the market that is redefining the relationship between the institution and the customer and in turn redefining the banking industry.

According to Robert Baldock, a partner in Andersen Consulting's financial services practice, banks up until now had driven the process, deciding what products customers would have and what prices they would be at. Now, with the internet and e-commerce, the customer will be able to drive the process: 'In the 21st century the customer is going to be the dictator, not the banks.'

With customers becoming more intelligent and sophisticated, their behaviour suggests that they will demand many more product offerings than the simple savings account. The internet allows for much more transparency in assessing products, where customers can now peruse their screens for the best products, services and prices for their banking needs.

This new-found ability for customers to choose rather than have products chosen for them represents a critical shift in the customer relationship and will be vital to an institution's future survival. The crucial issue is that if a product or service is not offered or priced competitively online, then customers will go elsewhere at the click of a mouse button.

The ability to win or lose customers at the click of a mouse poses critical challenges for banks. Customers will demand even more control over their personal finances. They will value 'anytime, anyplace, anywhere' customised access to financial services and those institutions that can satisfy this demand will be rewarded, they hope, by the benefits of profitable customer loyalty. But what mix of products, channels of distribution and technology will be rewarding for banks?

BankAmerica, for example, provides the following products and services online: bill payment, credit cards, discount brokerage, and mutual funds. This is contrasted by Wells Fargo's larger online offerings, which include: bill payment, bill presentment, credit cards, home equity, mortgages, other loans, discount brokerage and mutual funds.

According to management at Wells Fargo, online banking customers are on average more profitable – they generate 50 per cent more revenue than the bank average, hold 20 per cent higher balances and use 50 per cent more products; at the same time, their attrition is 50 per cent of the bank rate and their servicing costs are, on average, 14 per cent lower once online.

But banks will have to offer more products and services on the internet because customers are likely to be loyal to more than one bank. There may be a direct correlation between the number of products/services offered online and customer loyalty but this may not necessarily apply.

A new institution may focus on a narrow product range and with good marketing and brand recognition carve out market share at the expense of traditional suppliers. In the UK, the Prudential's new direct banking arm, called Egg, has accumulated a massive £5 billion ($8 billion) in deposits and 500 000 customers since its launch last October; the fact that it appears to have also accumulated enormous losses in the process may not necessarily be important in the long run if it can maintain customer satisfaction.

The convenience factor of the internet, coupled with customer demand, is changing how banks do business. Instead of being productcentric, they are becoming more customer-centric.

Customer satisfaction is key and banks are looking at different mediums, including the internet, to consolidate information to customise products and services suited to the customer's specific needs. This is consistent, with the idea of 'convergence', where ideally, different electronic mediums such as web TV, call centres, mobile phone and other internet-related networks begin to converge to form a common 'customer destination point' or 'portal'.

The idea is to provide customers with a single contact point to alert them about new product offerings. The scope of internet technologies has no boundaries.

(a) The authors argue that the internet will have two major impacts on banking; (i) reduced transaction costs, and (ii) the decline in the importance of geography. Explain what they mean by these changes and how they will change the face of banking.

(b) Why is it suggested that banking with the internet will become a more consumer-driven, rather than bank-driven process?

(c) How is the expansion of internet banking services likely to affect the amount of credit created?

FT

The problems facing the Japanese economy have had a long history. It is argued that they began in 1985, and that a series of policy errors since then have caused a protracted recession. The Japanese government have been driven to taking desperate measures to get the economy moving again. In the article below, taken from the *Financial Times* of 6 October 1998, the use of gift vouchers to stimulate consumption is considered.

A yen for spending

In most places handing out wads of crisp new notes is a fine way to get things moving. But not in Japan. The government there is so desperate to revive the economy that it is looking for a way to force people to spend the cash as well. Its latest idea is to give ¥30 000 ($223) gift vouchers to all Japanese inhabitants, with an expiry date by which they must be spent. The plan sounds bizarre, but does have a certain logic.

None of the Japanese government's measures for fiscal reflation is working. Its plans for a massive infrastructure boost are being thwarted by an unenthusiastic response from local governments, which are already over-indebted. And in a country where infrastructure is already well-developed, any new spending that does happen may boost demand, but will do little to improve the economy's long-term growth potential.

The tax cuts being introduced, meanwhile, will probably end up in people's bank accounts (or, more likely, under their mattresses), rather than being spent. The reasons are not hard to understand. Prices in Japan are stable or falling, so that little is lost by deferring consumption. Job insecurity is growing. And individuals approaching retirement are increasingly concerned about the shaky state of the life assurance industry.

Faced with these constraints, handing out money which people are forced to spend straight away could be the only way to achieve a quick fiscal boost.

The policy may prove administratively impossible. But even if it could be done, it would fall well short of a panacea. The main effect would probably be to change the timing of consumption, as people brought forward their spending plans. After the vouchers were used up, spending could quickly fall back.

And the scheme is too small to counteract the deflationary forces in the Japanese economy. It might produce a boost of 0.7 per cent of gross domestic product. But the International Monetary Fund estimates that the Japanese economy is now running at about 8 per cent of GDP below full capacity. The painful process of bank restructuring, if it ever gets going, can only make matters worse in the short term.

The voucher idea is not crazy, and could help procide a much-needed short-term stimulus to a rapidly deteriorating economy. But it needs to be part of a much more substantial macroeconomic policy, including large-scale monetary expansion by the Bank of Japan. And for the economy to return to a reasonable long-term growth path, there is no alternative but for Japan's politicians to tackle the structural reforms that the country needs.

(a) Demonstrate, using money supply and money demand curves, how an increase in money supply could stimulate the economy. Why might the demand curve for money be highly elastic, and what would be the consequences of this for the effectiveness of the policy?

(b) Why, with interest rates barely above zero, are people so willing to save and so unwilling to spend?

(c) Why is the voucher system likely to have only a short-run impact on the economy?

(d) From the article, what do you think is necessary to get the Japanese economy back on a path of long-term economic recovery?

Broad money is a key element in determining the level of economic activity. But just what is meant by 'broad money', and what determines changes in the amount of it that is held? The following extract considers these issues. It is taken from an article by Ryland Thomas appearing in the May 1996 edition of the *Bank of England Quarterly Bulletin*.

Understanding broad money

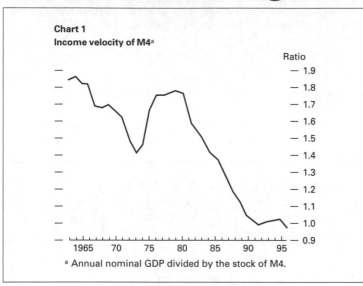

Chart 1
Income velocity of M4[a]

Ratio

a Annual nominal GDP divided by the stock of M4.

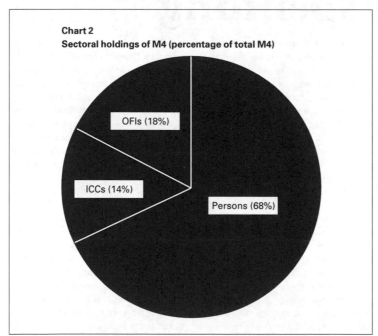

Chart 2
Sectoral holdings of M4 (percentage of total M4)

OFIs (18%)

ICCs (14%)

Persons (68%)

almost 30 times the size of the stock of sterling notes and coin in circulation.

The relationship between the growth of M4 and the growth of nominal activity has been quite variable over the past 30 years. The income velocity of M4, which measures the ratio of nominal GDP to the stock of M4, has shown several distinct phases (see Chart 1). In the period before 1980, velocity did not exhibit any consistent trend. But it declined steadily during the 1980s when – in response to financial deregulation and liberalisation – banks' and building societies' balance sheets expanded more rapidly than nominal income. Between 1991 and 1994, M4 velocity was fairly stable. But during 1995, velocity started to decline once more, raising the issue of whether this indicates incipient inflationary pressures or is simply a reflection of further changes in the structure of the financial sector.

Within M4, there have also been some interesting patterns in *sectoral* money holdings. Chart 2 shows a breakdown of M4 holdings by sector. At the end of 1995, the personal sector was the dominant holder of M4 assets, accounting for roughly two-thirds of the stock of M4. Of the remainder, 14 per cent was held by industrial and commercial companies (ICCs), and 18 per cent by other financial institutions (OFIs).

The pattern of growth for each of these three sectors has been quite different over the past 20 years (see Chart 3). Personal sector M4 growth has been much less volatile than the growth of corporate sector holdings (both ICCs and OFIs). In particular, OFIs' M4 holdings have grown at a considerably faster and more erratic rate than those of either ICCs or persons. Thus, although personal sector holdings are important in determining trend movements in M4, shorter-term fluctuations in M4 are typically dominated by changes in corporate sector money holdings. That was again true in 1995.

Another way of decomposing M4 holdings is to look at its 'counterparts' on the bank and building society sector

Broad money and its sectoral components and counterparts

The measure of broad money used by the UK authorities, M4, consists of holdings by the 'M4 private sector'[1] of

1. All UK residents except the public sector, banks and building societies.

sterling notes and coin, and of sterling deposits (including certificates of deposit and similar bank and building society deposits) held at banks and building societies in the United Kingdom. At the end of December 1995, the stock of M4 totalled £623 billion, roughly equal to one year's nominal GDP and

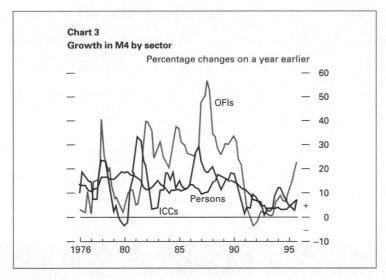

Chart 3
Growth in M4 by sector
Percentage changes on a year earlier

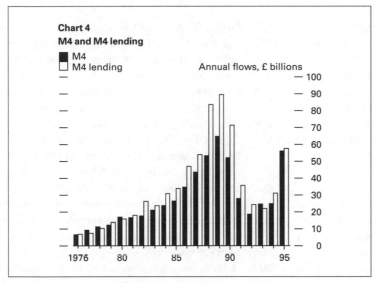

Chart 4
M4 and M4 lending
■ M4
□ M4 lending
Annual flows, £ billions

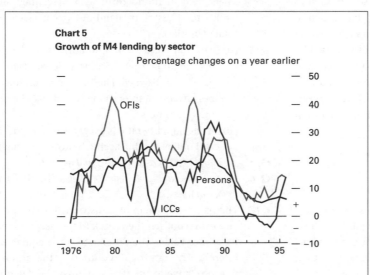

Chart 5
Growth of M4 lending by sector
Percentage changes on a year earlier

balance sheet. As Chart 4 shows, the most important counterpart to M4 growth has been sterling lending to the M4 private sector – 'M4 lending'. This too has exhibited interesting sectoral patterns over the recent past. Chart 5 shows that corporate sector (ICCs and OFIs) borrowing, like corporate sector M4 deposits, has historically been more volatile than personal sector borrowing; it has also been the most important factor driving recent fluctuations in M4 lending. In particular, there has been a rapid turnaround in the position of ICCs from being net repayers of debt for much of 1992–94 to substantial net borrowers during 1995. The growth of personal sector borrowing, by contrast, has remained subdued for much of the 1990s.

Money, credit and the transmission mechanism

In general, movements in M4 will depend on both the *demand* for broad money and on its *supply*. The second of these can be linked to developments in the credit market, given the way in which banks and building societies typically manage their balance sheets.

Looking first at the *demand* side, broad money balances are held for two main reasons. First, they serve as a medium of exchange, since banks' and building societies' deposit liabilities are generally accepted as a final means of settlement, in much the same way as cash. Second, bank and building society deposits can serve as a store of value. A large proportion of M4 is interest bearing, so agents will hold broad money as part of a diversified wealth portfolio alongside other financial (such as equities) and real (such as houses) assets. Taken together, these two roles suggest that the aggregate demand for broad money is likely to be determined by real spending, prices, wealth and the opportunity cost of holding money (the difference between the return on money and the return on non-monetary assets, real and financial).

The *supply* of broad money depends on the behaviour of banks and building societies. A useful approach in this context is to think of the banking system as managing its liabilities. The banking system undertakes profitable lending opportunities at the prevailing level of interest rates and this, in turn, determines the extent to which it needs to bid for deposits from the rest of the private sector. This implies that conditions in the credit market determine the supply of broad money. The demand for credit – borrowing from banks and building societies – is likely to depend on the current and expected future level of activity in the economy, (real) borrowing rates, and the difference between the cost of credit from banks and building societies and other forms of finance, such as retained earnings or capital market issues. For certain types of borrowers, most notably small businesses and consumers, substitution possibilities between borrowing from banks and building societies and other forms of finance are likely to be limited. The amount of lending will then also depend on the willingness of banks and building societies to provide credit. Ultimately, it is the interaction of these demand and supply – or money and credit – factors which determine holdings of broad money at any one time.

© Bank of England Publications Group, *Bank of England Quarterly Bulletin (Ryland Thomas), May 1996*

(a) What is the definition of M4?

(b) How has the proportion of total M4 held by different sectors of the economy changed over time?

(c) What is meant by 'counterparts' to M4?

(d) What are the main determinants of the demand and supply of broad money?

 ANSWERS

Q1. *False.* The amount of money in supply is a stock concept. At any one point in time there is a given amount of money in circulation.

Q2. The four main functions of money are: as a medium of exchange, a store of wealth, a means of valuing different types of goods and services, and a means of establishing future claims and payments, e.g. the setting of wages or an estimate from a builder tendering for a future contract.

Q3. *(a)* (i).

(b) (iii).

(c) (iii). Cash in banks is not included as a separate item because it has *already* been included under the heading of accounts. To count it again would be a case of 'double counting'.

(d) (i).

(e) (i). Under old definitions deposits in savings accounts were only included in broad definitions of money. Now, however, since savings accounts can normally be accessed rapidly (albeit with some loss of interest) they are also included in the narrow definition of money, M2. (M2 includes all *retail* deposits: i.e. deposits in branches of banks and building societies at published interest rates.)

(f) (iii).

(g) (ii).

Q4. *Direct* (c).
Indirect (a), (b), (d).

Q5. *maturity transformation.* This process is possible because not all depositors wish to withdraw their deposits at the same time. If they did, the financial intermediary would be unable to return their money!

Q6. *risk transformation.* This is where the risks of lending are spread over a large number of borrowers.

Q7. (a) (iii), (b) (ii), (c) (iv), (d) (i).

Q8. *liabilities.* Institutions that take depositors' money are liable to the claims that the individuals may make on their money.

Q9. *assets.* These are claims that the financial institution has on others, e.g. personal loans to customers.

Q10. (a) *wholesale*, (b) *retail*, (c) *retail*, (d) *retail*, (e) *wholesale*.

Q11. (i) (e) Cash, (ii) (d) Operational balances with the Bank of England, (iii) (a) Money at call, (iv) (c) Bills of exchange, (v) (b) Bonds, (vi) (f) Personal loans.

Q12. The more liquid an asset, the less profitable it is (the less interest it will earn). However, banks and other financial institutions must keep part of their assets liquid, e.g. to act as till money and cover day-to-day transactions.

Q13. D. The liquidity ratio refers to the bank's total assets held in liquid form as a percentage of the bank's total assets or liabilities (total assets equal total liabilities).

Q14. *(a)* The consequence of a liquidity ratio that is too low might be that customers' demands for cash cannot all be met. The bank may be forced to borrow, or in an extreme case it may be driven out of business.

(b) If the liquidity ratio is excessively high, the bank will not be making as much profit as it might.

Q15. *the market for short-term loans and deposits.*

Q16. (a) the *discount and repo markets*, (b) the *parallel money markets*.

Q17. The banks buy them at a discount (i.e. below their face value) but sell them back to the issuer on maturity at face value. The difference is the equivalent to interest. The rate of discount (i.e. the annualised return relative to the face value) will be determined by demand and supply and will reflect market rates of interest.

Q18. *True.* Rediscounting refers to the buying of bills by the Bank of England before they reach maturity. Banks and discount houses will only sell to the Bank of England in this way if they are short of liquidity as the rediscount rate will be a penal one (i.e. the Bank of England will pay a low price for these bills).

Q19. B. As with bills, the difference between the sale and repurchase price is the equivalent of interest. Repo rates may be determined by demand and supply. Alternatively, the central bank can set the repo rates at which it deals with the banks, and thereby seek to influence interest rates generally. Here we are talking about government bond (or 'gilt') repos between banks and the central bank (the Bank of England in the case of the UK). This is a means whereby the central bank, by temporarily buying back government bonds from the banks, provides them with a short-term source of liquidity.

Q20. The parallel money market has grown due to: the abolition of exchange controls and the expansion of international dealing, the deregulation of the money market, and the volatility of interest rates and exchange rates making it more desirable to have a stock of funds that can be quickly converted from one asset to another and from one currency to another.

Q21. *(a)* *False.* The Bank of England is the sole issuer of banknotes in England and Wales. In Scotland and Northern Ireland the clearing banks can also issue notes.

(b) *True.* The banks keep operational balances with the Bank of England for clearing purposes.

(c) *True.* When the government runs a budget deficit, the Bank of England arranges the necessary borrowing. But even when the government runs a budget surplus, the Bank of England will still need to manage the national debt and the issuing of new bonds if the budget surplus is insufficient to repay all maturing bonds.

(d) *True.* The Bank of England thereby ensures there is always sufficient liquidity within the banking system.

(e) *True.* The Bank of England manages the nation's stock of foreign currency and its gold reserves.

Q22. (a) M4, (b) M3H, (c) Divisia money, (d) M0, (e) M2.

Q23. *Credit creation* is the process whereby bank deposits expand by more than the cash base.

Q24. £700m. The *total* increase in bank deposits will equal $1/L \times \Delta R$ (where R = the change in the reserve base). $1/0.2 \times £175m = £875m$. The additional advances are found by deducting the initial increase in the reserve base (£175m).

Q25. If the bank decides to hold a lower liquidity ratio, the bank multiplier will increase. More will be lent to customers, thereby creating more money when it is redeposited back in the banking system.

Q26. *(a)* *Rise.* If the exchange rate is to be maintained at this value, additional pounds will need to be supplied to the market. These additional pounds will then find their way back to banks as deposits by those that trade overseas.

(b) *Rise.* If the government finances its PSBR in this way, this will lead to the creation of new money. When the government spends the money, banks' accounts in the Bank of England will be credited, thereby increasing their liquid assets and allowing credit to be created.

(c) *Fall.* Changing the way the national debt is funded by substituting bonds for bills will cause the asset base of banks to become more illiquid. As a result, advances to customers will be reduced.

(d) *No change.* Funding the PSBR in this manner will simply lead to a reshuffling of money between individuals and government. No new money is created.

(e) *Fall.* Statutory reserve requirements effectively mean that banks cannot lend as much as they would like to. Thus the initial imposition of such a ratio will cause the money supply to fall.

Q27. (a) *added*, (b) *subtracted* (given that this is the part of the PSBR that does *not* lead to an increase in the money supply), (c) *added* (this is credit creation), (d) *subtracted* (a balance of payments deficit will mean that the Bank of England has to *purchase* the excess pounds on the foreign exchange market, thereby 'retiring' them from circulation).

Q28. That the level of the money supply is determined by government rather than by the demand for money.

Q29. Reasons include: higher demand for credit will force up interest rates, encouraging banks to supply more credit and causing the money supply to expand as a consequence; higher interest rates may encourage depositors to switch deposits from sight to time accounts, but since such money is less likely to be withdrawn quickly from time accounts, banks may be encouraged to lower their liquidity ratio and create more credit as a result; higher interest rates will attract deposits from overseas.

Q30. B. The term demand for money reflects the desire by individuals to hold their assets in money form as opposed to any other (such as stocks and shares or property).

Q31. *national income.*

Q32. *interest rates.*

Q33. (a) and (b) are the Keynesian views. The demand-for-money curve is elastic and unstable. By contrast the monetarists see the demand-for-money curve as inelastic and stable. (The reasons for this an be found in Sloman, *Economics* (4th edn), pp. 539–40.)

Q34. *(a)* The M_s curve will shift to the right as the money supply grows. This will cause the rate of interest to fall.

(b) As income rises, the *L* curve will shift to the right (as a result of increased transactions and precautionary demands). The rate of interest will rise.

(c) Again the *L* curve will shift to be right (as people hold higher speculative balances in anticipation of the increased foreign exchange value of these balances). The rate of interest will rise.

Q35. *(a)* and *(b)*. See Figure A18.1.

(c) Diagram (i): the Keynesian view of the money demand curve is that it is elastic, and even relatively large changes in the money supply curve will have little effect upon the rate of interest. Diagram (ii): the investment curve is relatively inelastic since Keynesians argue that interest rates are a relatively minor determinant of the level of investment.

(d) The subsequent effect on national income in diagram (iii) of a change in money supply will be relatively small.

(e) Monetarists assume that the money demand curve is relatively inelastic and that the level of investment is highly responsive to changes in the rate of interest.

(f) The effect on aggregate demand, therefore, will be substantial (albeit with the long-run effects being felt in changed *prices* rather than changed *output*).

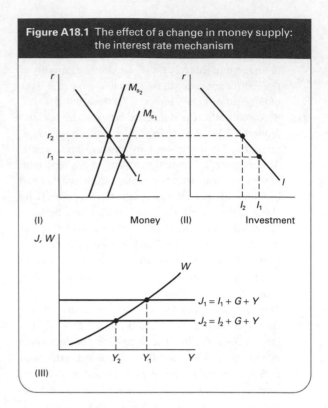

Figure A18.1 The effect of a change in money supply: the interest rate mechanism

19 Monetary Policy

A REVIEW

In the previous chapter we considered the role of money and interest rates in the economy. In this chapter we see how money and interest rates can be controlled and examine the relative effectiveness of different techniques of monetary policy.

19.1 Attitudes towards monetary policy

(Pages 546–7)

Q1. Which of the following would be classified as monetary policy? The attempt to:

(a) reduce the level of taxation. *Yes/No*

(b) control the supply of money by various means. *Yes/No*

(c) regulate wages by the use of formal agreements with unions. *Yes/No*

(d) ration credit. *Yes/No*

(e) manipulate aggregate demand via the use of interest rates. *Yes/No*

(f) regulate aggregate demand through changes in government spending. *Yes/No*

Q2. Keynesians argue that the relationship between money supply and aggregate demand is strong and predictable. *True/False*

Q3. Monetarists argue that discretionary policy, whether fiscal or monetary, can have a destabilising effect on the economy. Long-run price stability can only be achieved through adhering to monetary targets. *True/False*

19.2 Varieties of monetary policy

(Pages 547–9) Controlling the growth of the money supply over the longer term

Q4. Which one of the following would not be a cause of growth in the money supply?

A. The banks decide to hold a lower liquidity ratio.

B. There is a total currency flow surplus on the balance of payments.

C. The PSBR is financed by selling Treasury bills to the banking sector.

D. The government imposes a statutory reserve ratio on banks that is higher than their current reserve ratio.

E. National income rises and money supply is endogenous.

If over the longer term the government wishes to control the growth of the money supply, it will have to tackle the underlying causes.

Q5. Give the two major sources of a long-term growth in the money supply.

1. ....

2. ....

One way of restricting the growth in private-sector borrowing would be to impose statutory reserve requirements on banks.

 Multiple Choice   Written answer   Delete wrong word   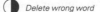 Diagram/table manipulation   Calculation   Matching/ordering

(?) **Q6.** Why do monetarists oppose statutory reserve requirements?

....

....

(≣) **Q7.** Goodhart's law states that 'to control an indicator is to distort its accuracy as an indicator'. An example of this law when applied to monetary policy is that:

A. all forms of intervention in financial markets will have little impact on the money supply.

B. regulation in one part of the financial system will divert business to other areas of the financial system.

C. government borrowing will lead to financial crowding out.

D. control of the money supply will not be possible without control of the PSBR.

E. private-sector borrowing is a more important determinant of monetary growth than is public-sector borrowing.

If there is a substantial PSBR, it is nevertheless possible to avoid an increase in the money supply by financing the PSBR by government borrowing from **Q8.** *the banking sector/the non-bank private sector.* If the government does this, however, there is likely to be a problem of financial crowding out. This will involve **Q9.** *higher/lower* interest rates and **Q10.** *more/less* private-sector borrowing.

This financial crowding out will be reduced, however, (but there will be less reduction in the growth of aggregate demand) if the velocity of circulation of circulation **Q11.** *increases/decreases.* This change in the velocity of circulation will be greater the **Q12.** *more/less* elastic the liquidity preference curve that we looked at in the last chapter.

(Pages 549–53) Short-term methods of monetary control
There are three approaches to short-term monetary control: controlling the *supply* of money; controlling the *demand* for money by controlling interest rates; rationing credit.

Controlling the supply of money will involve manipulating the liquid assets of the banking sector.

(⚽) **Q13.** The following are methods of controlling banks' liquidity base:

(i) open-market operations

(ii) the central bank changing the amount it lends to banks

(iii) funding

(iv) changing minimum reserve ratios

Match each of the following actions of a central bank to the above methods of control, and in each case state whether money supply will *increase* or *decrease.* (In each case, assume that the actions are not in response to changes in the PSBR.)

(a) It sells more government bonds and the equivalent amount fewer Treasury bills.

(i)/(ii)/(iii)/(iv); increase/decrease

(b) It sells more government bonds (but the same amount of Treasury bills). *(i)/(ii)/(iii)/(iv); increase/decrease*

(c) It buys back bonds from banks under a repo agreement.

(i)/(ii)/(iii)/(iv); increase/decrease

(d) It requires banks to hold a larger proportion of liquid assets. *(i)/(ii)/(iii)/(iv); increase/decrease*

(e) It sells fewer bonds and bills.

(i)/(ii)/(iii)/(iv); increase/decrease

(f) It replaces £1m of gilts that are maturing with £1m extra Treasury bills. *(i)/(ii)/(iii)/(iv); increase/decrease*

(g) It keeps its interest rate to the banks below market rates, but then reduces the amount it allows banks to borrow at that rate. *(i)/(ii)/(iii)/(iv); increase/decrease*

(✕) **Q14.** If banks operate a rigid 10 per cent liquidity ratio and the Bank of England repurchases £10m of government bonds on the open market, what will be the eventual size of the change in the level of bank advances?

....

(Pages 554–6) The prime form of monetary policy in the UK has been to control *interest rates.*

(◗) **Q15.** Interest rates are controlled by the Bank of England through its operations in the discount and repo markets. *True/False*

(◗) **Q16.** Assume that the Bank of England decides that it wants a rise in the rate of interest and conducts open-market operations in the discount market to achieve this. What should it do if:

(a) banks have excess liquidity?

Buy/Sell   more/fewer bills.

(b) banks are currently having to borrow from the Bank of England? *Buy/Sell   more/fewer* bills.

19.3 Problems of monetary policy

(Page 557) It is difficult to control the growth of the money supply over the longer term without controlling the size of the PSBR. This can be difficult, however.

(◗) **Q17.** Which of the following make the control of PSBR difficult?

(a) The political desirability of cutting taxes. *Yes/No*

(b) The political desirability of increasing government expenditure. *Yes/No*

(c) Automatic fiscal stabilisers in times of a boom. *Yes/No*

(d) Automatic fiscal stabilisers in times of stagflation (recession plus inflation). *Yes/No (e)* Pressure on the government to increase expenditure on education, R&D and transport infrastructure as a means of improving productivity and long-term growth. *Yes/No*

(f) An ageing population. *Yes/No*

(Pages 557–60) Controlling the money supply is difficult whether the authorities use monetary base control or attempt to control broad liquidity.

(?) Q18. What is meant by 'monetary base control'?

....

....

Q19. Four of the following are problems associated with monetary base control. One is not. Which one?

A. Banks could currently have a cash ratio above their prudent (or statutory) level.

B. Goodhart's law.

C. Disintermediation.

D. There may be a high demand for liquidity in the financial system.

E. The Bank of England will always lend money to banks if demanded.

(?) Q20. Give two problems for the authorities in attempting to control broad liquidity.

1. ....

2. ....

Q21. If the government is successful in keeping the money supply stable, it will have succeeded in keeping interest rates stable too. *True/False*

(Pages 560–1) Credit rationing may seem to be the solution to the problems of monetary control. Governments around the world, however, are increasingly opposed to it.

Q22. Which of the following statements about credit rationing are correct?

(a) It reduces competition and thus creates inefficiency. *True/False*

(b) It leads to interest rates being higher than they would be otherwise. *True/False*

(c) It will have an uneven impact upon different sectors of the economy. *True/False*

(d) Goodhart's law is likely to apply. *True/False*

(e) It only affects lending indirectly. *True/False*

(?) Q23. In the short run the supply of money is to a large extent demand determined. Why?

....

....

(Pages 561–4) Because the supply of money is demand determined in the short run, monetary policy has tended to concentrate on controlling the demand for loans via the control of interest rates. This, however, may require the authorities setting very high interest rates. This is because the demand for loans is relatively interest **Q24.** *elastic/inelastic.*

Q25. A tight monetary policy involving high interest rates can lead to a number of related problems. Identify which of the following might be a consequence of such a policy.

(a) Reduced investment. *Yes/No*

(b) A deteriorating competitive position overseas. *Yes/No*

(c) Increased costs of production. *Yes/No*

(d) Slow growth in potential output. *Yes/No*

(e) Expensive for the government to maintain. *Yes/No*

(f) Increased cost-push pressures. *Yes/No*

B PROBLEMS, EXERCISES AND PROJECTS

Q26. Using relevant statistical sources, such as *Financial Statistics* (ONS), the *Annual Abstract of Statistics* (ONS) and the *Bank of England Quarterly Bulletin*, investigate recent movements in the various monetary aggregates. How do such movements compare with those in earlier years? Does this tell you anything about the current tightness of monetary policy and the economic position of the UK economy?

Q27. Assume that the banking sector's assets and liabilities consist of the following items: cash £10m; advances £60m; time deposits £50m; bonds £15m; market loans £10m; bills £5m; sight deposits £40m; certificates of deposit in the banking system £10m. Assume that there are no other items.

(a) Compile a balance sheet for the banking sector.

(b) What is its current cash ratio?

(c) What is its current liquidity ratio?

Assume in each of the following that banks want to maintain the *cash* ratio in (b) above. What will be the effect of each of the following?

(d) An open-market purchase by the central bank of £1m of bonds.

(e) An open-market sale by the central bank of £5m of bonds.

(f) An open-market sale by the central bank of £2m of bills, where these bills are purchased by the banking sector.

(g) An open-market sale by the central bank of £2m of *bills*, where these bills are purchased by the non-banking sector.

Assume in each of the following that banks want to maintain the *liquidity* ratio in (c) above. What will be the effect of each of the following?

(h) An open-market purchase by the central bank of £1m of bonds.

(i) An open-market sale by the central bank of £5m of bonds.

(j) An open-market sale by the central bank of £2m of bills, where these bills are purchased by the banking sector.

(k) An open-market sale by the central bank of £2m of bills, where these bills are purchased by the non-banking sector.

Q28. Using the Bank of England and Treasury web sites, http://www.bankofengland.co.uk/ and http://www.hm-treasury.gov.uk/, and the Bank of England's *Inflation Report*, trace the decisions of the Bank of England's Monetary Policy Committee on interest rates over the last two years. Why were the changes made? In retrospect, were they the correct decisions?

Alternatively you could answer this question in terms of the interest rate decisions of another central bank, such as the European Central Bank (see http://www.ecb.int/) or the US Federal Reserve Bank (see http://www.federalreserve.gov/).

DISCUSSION TOPICS AND ESSAYS

Q29. What is the relationship between the money supply and the public-sector borrowing requirement?

Q30. What difficulties is the government likely to face in preventing an excessive expansion of the money supply over the longer term?

Q31. When the Bank of England's Monetary Policy Committee announces that it is putting up interest rates, how will it achieve this, given that interest rates are determined by supply and demand?

Q32. How might the targeting of a foreign exchange rate value be a means of controlling inflation?

Q33. 'The precise monetary policy tactics to be employed by the authorities depend upon the particular monetary aggregate to be controlled.' Explain this statement.

Q34. 'It is impossible to target both the money supply and the rate of interest. If you control one, you have to let the other be as it will.' Discuss.

Q35. Are targeting the rate of inflation and targeting the rate of growth in the money supply compatible policies?

Q36. Debate
If you want to control aggregate demand then monetary policy is not the answer.

ARTICLES

The Bank of England uses interest rate changes as its instrument of monetary policy. This has not always been so, however. The following extract, taken from an article entitled 'Monetary policy instruments: the UK experience', by Mervyn King which appeared in the *Bank of England Quarterly* of August 1994, looks at the history of monetary control.

Monetary instruments and monetary targets

Let me for a moment examine instruments other than interest rates. When considering these, UK history is very revealing. And by this I mean not just the history of how monetary policy in practice was conducted, but also the history of policy objectives, both final and intermediate. In the 1950s and 1960s, Keynesian demand management was the macroeconomic orthodoxy. The key policy objective was full employment, subject to maintaining external balance. Interest rates were held down, partly because demand was thought to be restrained by fiscal policy backed up by direct controls on credit, and partly because low rates helped to restrain the budget deficit. Monetary policy was tightened almost only when the external constraint was threatened – although this occurred frequently.

During the 1950s, direct controls on hire-purchase terms, qualitative calls for restraint on bank lending and controls on capital issues were widespread. Cash ratios (of 8 per cent of deposit liabilities) and liquidity ratios (of 30 per cent) were already in place and for most banks were binding constraints on balance-sheet growth. Bank rate adjustments, while important as a signal of restraint, were believed to be slow and ineffective in controlling aggregate demand. The use of quantitative controls reflected the widespread use of planning during the war, and the belief that if planning had won the war, then it could equally 'win the peace'.

But there was clearly an efficiency cost to doing this. The Radcliffe Committee, set up in 1957, alerted the wider public to the significance of these distortions. Their report, published in 1959, concluded that the authorities must 'regard the structure of interest rates rather than the supply of money as the centrepiece of the monetary mechanism'. Direct controls should, in the main, only be used in extreme conditions.

The move to more market-oriented instruments was, however, delayed. In the 1960s, direct controls became, if anything, more specific in their application. Lending ceilings were imposed on all banks and finance houses, with guidance on lending giving priority to export finance; hire-purchase controls were progressively tightened; and a special deposits scheme was introduced, obliging banks to hold a proportion of their liabilities at the Bank of England, remunerated at Treasury bill rates but not counting a part of the banks' liquidity ratios, thus placing further pressure on banks' liquidity positions.

The 1970s marked something of a watershed. Two factors were responsible for this. First, a change in the intellectual climate led to a preference for market solutions. Second, there emerged a growing dissatisfaction with the deadweight efficiency losses resulting from a directly controlled financial system. Disintermediation had already begun to eat into the effectiveness of direct controls, as the UK financial system grew in size and sophistication during the 1960s. In 1971, a series of reforms was introduced, known as Competition and Credit Control (CCC). CCC served notice of the freer hand that was to be given to interest rates in monetary policy. Quantitative controls were dismantled, together with the clearing banks' interest rate cartel. Cash and liquidity ratios were retained, but at much lower levels – 1½ per cent and 12½ per cent respectively – with the latter retitled 'reserve asset ratios'. The ability to call special deposits was retained, but with the intention that the option be exercised only infrequently to reinforce upward movements in interest rates. The key element of CCC was the emphasis placed on the level – and structure – of interest rates as the primary instrument for influencing the growth of money and credit.

Rapid bank balance-sheet growth followed the ending of direct controls. With the authorities reluctant to increase interest rates far or rapidly enough to limit inflationary pressures, direct controls were reintroduced sporadically throughout the 1970s. Hire-purchase controls, calls for special deposits and restrictions on the scale and direction of bank lending were old favourites. But they were buttressed by a new control – the Supplementary Special Deposit scheme or 'corset'. This was a penalty (in the form of non-interest-bearing deposits at the Bank) on the rate of growth of banks' interest-bearing eligible liabilities rather than on the size of the balance sheet as such.

Although these controls were in principle temporary, they persisted through much of the 1970s. Their downfall – this time for good – was inevitable as a consequence of a different liberalisation measure: the abolition of exchange controls in 1979. With banks' customers now free to borrow offshore funds to meet financing needs, domestic controls on banks' balance-sheet growth were rendered obsolete. By the end of 1980, all quantitative restrictions had been withdrawn (with the exception of a residual form of lending guidance which remained notionally in force until December 1986).

Among other reforms, the *corset* was scrapped. And while the option to call special deposits was retained, it has never been exercised subsequently, although it remains available. The cash ratio was also retained, but at a much reduced level of ½ per cent and with a new name, *cash ratio deposits*. This requirement has since been progressively reduced and currently stands at just 0.35 per cent of banks' eligible liabilities. Moreover, the function of cash ratio deposits today is strictly non-operational: they serve the sole purpose of providing income for the Bank. The fulcrum for money-market management is provided by the requirement that the banks avoid overdrafts on their operational accounts. The reserve asset ratio requirement was also abolished as a monetary control device, although liquidity requirements were retained for supervisory purposes as a purely prudential measure, and therefore play a part in affecting banks' behaviour and thus the context in which the authorities conduct their monetary operations.

The effect of the 1980–81 reforms was, at long last, to focus the spotlight firmly upon interest rate management – a decade after CCC had first proposed this. The prime mover in this shift was unquestionably financial liberalisation – whose invisible hand was in turn steered by a new economic orthodoxy.

In this intellectual climate, monetary targets had risen to prominence as an intermediate monetary objective. The United Kingdom had been obliged by the IMF to introduce targets for domestic credit expansion in 1968. But the Bank made voluntary use of unpublished targets for broad money growth (at the time, M3) from 1973 onwards. Annual target ranges were first announced in 1976, following their introduction in Germany and the United States. And this gradual progression reached its zenith with the publication of medium-term broad money targets by the incoming Conservative government in 1980. These were intended to influence inflation expectations over a medium-term horizon.

But there was to be a twist in the tail. Financial liberalisation and increasing competition among newly-liberated financial institutions caused banks' balance sheets to swell rapidly. Broad money targets came under threat. The authorities' reaction was to draw more heavily upon yet another instrument: debt management. The intention was to withdraw liquidity from the private sector by the sale of government debt – even at times in excess of that required to meet the government's borrowing requirement, so that it became known as *overfunding* – in order to hit the broad money target. In that way, broad money growth could be reduced. Overfunding operated between 1981 and 1985, until broad money targets themselves fell out of favour. Even overfunding was rarely sufficient to bring broad money growth back within its target range, and as a by-product it placed strains on the Bank of England's money-market operations by draining large amounts of liquidity from the money market.

Since the mid-1980s, interest rates have been pretty much the sole and exclusive monetary control tool of the UK authorities. Foreign exchange intervention has, on occasion, played a supporting role – when sterling shadowed the Deutsche Mark in 1987–88 and, of course, during the period of sterling's membership of the ERM. But outside these episodes, the use of intervention has been sparing. Its effectiveness is in any case short-lived without supporting monetary policy action.

The United Kingdom's new monetary framework, introduced following sterling's departure from the ERM in the autumn of 1992, is based on the use of interest rates to achieve an inflation target of 1–4 per cent, with the intention of bringing inflation down below 2½ per cent by the end of the present parliament. This is a simple and transparent framework. Equally simple and transparent instruments will help us to achieve our objective.

© Bank of England Publications Group, *Bank of England Quarterly Bulletin* (Mervyn King), Aug. 1994

(a) What is the efficiency cost of using quantitative controls?

(b) Why did the abolition of exchange controls make the downfall of quantitative controls inevitable?

(c) Why was overfunding necessary in the mid-1980s and what effect did it have?

(d) If interest rates operate on the demand for money, how can they be used to affect its *supply*?

Every since the Bank of England was given independence, interest rates have been set by the Monetary Policy Committee (MPC). In the article below taken, from *The Times* of 6 June 1998, Roger Bootle considers some of the factors the MPC need to take into account prior to their monthly meeting to set interest rates.

Economic consequences of the MPC

If you can keep your head when all about you are losing theirs, then you don't really understand what is going on. Or perhaps you should be setting interest rates? This week's meeting of the Monetary Policy Committee (MPC) is going to be a nail-biter. The new monetary policy regime was supposed to induce boredom but in fact it has done exactly the reverse. Last month hardly any economists expected the MPC to raise interest rates. They were wrong (yours truly included). Since then, many economists' forecasts (or are they postcasts) have become more bearish. The markets are nervous that the MPC is going to raise rates again this Thursday.

After last month's performance, I would forgive you if you concluded that you would do better to consult Mystic Meg, but in my view the MPC should not raise rates and, although this is very far from being the same thing, I also think that they will not.

Why did they raise rates last month? The prime influence was the surge in average earnings, with private sector pay growing by 5.75 per cent and the overall total held back only by continued restraint in the public sector. This was backed up by a sharp fall in the pound.

Since then there has been a further rise in average earnings and the latest inflation figures appeared to be disastrous, with the headline figure hitting 4.2 per cent and the underlying rate, for which the official target is 2.5 per cent, hitting 3.2 per cent. Moreover, the growth of retail sales surged back up to 4.6 per cent, prompting renewed talk of a consumer boom.

These apparent warning signs of emerging inflationary pressure, however, have coincided with a good deal of evidence to the contrary. The pain in manufacturing is intense and, now that the pound has bounced back, this may well prompt a bout of job-shedding. True, much of the service sector looks to be robust, but here, too, cracks are starting to appear.

In particular, if you muttered the words 'consumer boom' to the average high-street retailer you would get a very rum response. Several retailing companies have issued profit warnings. Consumers remain canny about prices, so that the volume figures do not tell the whole story. Moreover, it seems that June was an absolutely dire month in the high street, despite the booming business in 'sou'westers'. Meanwhile, the Asian crisis has deepened. It is not difficult to imagine that a sharp slowdown in UK growth is already under way.

Yet what about those average earnings numbers? Several members of the MPC are scarred by the experience of the late 1980s boom and determined that the same mistakes should not be made again. But they would do well to pay heed to the behaviour of average earnings during that episode. They reached their peak growth of 11 per cent in August 1990. At that point, having been slowing for two years, the growth of GDP turned negative.

To put it simply, wages are a lagging indicator of the economy. If interest rate policy is tied to the behaviour of average earnings, then there is a real risk of plunging the economy into recession. Of course, you could argue that even this outcome could be justified because otherwise the inflation target will be grossly overshot. After all, inflation already stands at 3.2 per cent. But measurement distortions greatly exaggerate the seriousness of Britain's inflation problem. The recent rise in the underlying rate is primarily because there have been two Budgets in the past year, while about half of last month's surprising high increase was because of a huge rise in potato prices caused by the adverse weather. (Perhaps the Government should target the ex-spuds RPI?).

The still unjustly neglected European harmonised inflation measure (HICP) puts UK inflation at 2 per cent, admittedly somewhat higher than the European average of 1.6 per cent, but hardly grossly so. This gives a much more accurate picture of the rate at which British businesses, on average, can raise their prices.

Of course, this average covers many different situations. Service sector inflation is much higher, but that also looks to have stabilised. Manufacturing businesses, though, are on the brink of deflation. Accordingly, overall inflation on the target measure is going to fall later on this year, whatever happens to average earnings.

(a) In assessing whether or not to raise or lower interest rates, what factors does the MPC need to take into account?

(b) The article suggests that different sectors of the economy were experiencing different inflationary pressures. What problems does this present to the MPC and its interest rate setting decision?

(c) What is meant by 'wages are a lagging indicator of the economy'? What dangers are there in using wage inflation as a guide for setting interest rates?

One of the biggest challenges facing the European Central Bank (ECB) is attempting to find a monetary policy that suits all 11 countries in the euro-zone. In the article below, taken from *The Economist* of 7 March 1998, the problems of determining a common interest rate are considered.

Europe grows apart

Europe's finance ministers have a spring in their step again. After several years of meagre growth and fiscal austerity, they suddenly have plenty to cheer about. Europe's economies are on the up: Germany and France are starting to grow strongly, and Spain and Ireland are positively booming. Meanwhile, the painful slog to qualify for the single currency is nearly over. Eleven countries, having slimmed their budget deficits enough to meet the requirements for joining Europe's new single currency, the euro, plan to hand responsibility for monetary policy to the European Central Bank (ECB) in less than ten months' time.

But although Europe's economies are growing, they are still not growing in unison. That poses a difficult challenge for the ECB. The central bank's main task will be to create a single monetary policy for all 11 states in euro-land. But on present evidence, it will be hard pressed to find a single policy that is right for Finland as well as France, that will stop an inflationary boom in Spain without pushing Germany back into recession.

The ECB will set interest rates according to economic conditions across the euro-zone. In general, these conditions are favourable, aside from stubbornly high unemployment. The economy of the 11 euro countries grew by 2.5 per cent in 1997 and is likely to do better this year. Inflation was only 1.4 per cent in the year to January and shows few signs of picking up soon. With such a benign outlook, the ECB will probably set short-term interest rates at about 4 per cent, not far from the current European average.

What is good for euro-land as a whole, however, may not be right for its constituent parts. Although the euro-11 had broadly similar inflation rates, long-term interest rates and budget deficits last year, they achieved those figures by pursuing markedly different monetary and fiscal policies. GDP growth, short-term interest rates and unemployment vary significantly from country to country (see chart on next page). Broadly speaking, there are at least two different European economies with conflicting needs: a core which includes Germany, Austria, France, Luxembourg and Belgium, and a periphery which includes Spain, Portugal, Italy and Ireland.

The core is finally recovering from several years of sluggish growth. Germany grew by 2.2 per cent last year, while France achieved 2.4 per cent. The economies in the core countries have plenty of slack, as prices are barely rising. Yet last year these countries maintained tight monetary and fiscal policies. Short-term interest rates rose by about a quarter of a point, while budgets were squeezed by around 1 per cent of GDP. As it feeds through to the economy this year, that tightening will restrict growth. Now, if anything, the core needs lower interest rates to make sure its recovery does not falter.

The periphery, in contrast, is growing so fast it is in danger of overheating. Spain's GDP increased by 3.4 per cent last year and Ireland's by 7.5 per cent. Italy's growth is accelerating rapidly: although its GDP rose only 1.5 per cent in 1997, year on year, it was up 2.8 per cent in the year to the fourth quarter. Growth in these countries seems likely to accelerate this year. The periphery needs higher interest rates soon to avoid an inflationary boom.

With a common monetary policy, both the core and the periphery are about to get the opposite of what they need. If the ECB sets the euro short-term interest rate at 4 per cent, that will mean higher rates for short-term borrowers in Germany and France, where three-month borrowing now costs about 3.5 per cent. As neither country plans to loosen its fiscal stance – if anything, Germany plans to crunch its budget deficit even more this year – a single monetary policy is thus likely to give their economies an untimely knock.

For the periphery, a euro rate of 4 per cent implies sharply lower interest rates. These countries have traditionally had much higher interest rates than Germany. While their rates have dropped substantially over the past year and are now much closer to Germany's, the differences are still large. Three-month rates are currently about 4.5 per cent in Spain, 5.5 per cent in Italy and 6 per cent in Ireland.

Lowering them is bound to stoke inflation. For Spain and Italy, those rate cuts would come on top of a marked loosening of monetary policy in the past year-and-a-half, the full impact of which has still not been felt. And whereas last year the monetary easing was offset by a huge fiscal tightening – Spain cut its budget deficit by 1.8 per cent of GDP and Italy by 4 per cent – this year both countries plan to loosen their budgetary belts. Moreover, inflation in Spain and Italy still tends to be about a percentage point higher than in Germany and France at equivalent points in the business cycle, according to Robert Prior-Wandesforde, an economist at HSBC James Capel, a British investment bank. If that is correct, the two countries will require higher interest rates than France and Germany to achieve similar inflation rates.

And what of the two other countries in the euro-zone? The single monetary policy will probably not fit there, either. Output in the Netherlands grew by

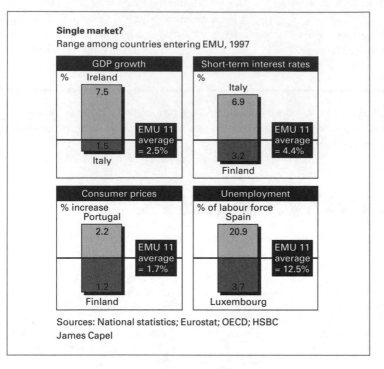

Single market?
Range among countries entering EMU, 1997

Sources: National statistics; Eurostat; OECD; HSBC
James Capel

3.3 per cent last year, and Finland grew by 4.6 per cent. Neither is experiencing runaway growth but, without higher interest rates, both will soon face inflationary pressures. Setting interest rates at about 4 per cent, the ECB's likely target, will probably not be enough to keep these in check.

This leads to an unpleasant scenario all around. Because Europe's governments have signed away national control of interest rates, fiscal policy is the only tool to hand if the single monetary policy leaves their economies growing more slowly than they might, or faster than they can sustain without pressure on wages and property prices. But many countries have only limited options. Germany and France, which already have budget deficits of roughly 3 per cent of GDP, are not well placed to cut taxes or boost government spending should the ECB's policies hold their economies back. At the other extreme, Ireland, which ran a large budget surplus last year, might be forced to run an even bigger one if the single monetary policy is not tight enough to suit its needs.

In the longer run, such problems will recede. The euro's effect – indeed, one of its purposes – will be to bring the performance of Europe's economies more closely into line. But the process of bringing that convergence about may prove unpleasant. The politicians who wax enthusiastic about Europe's fledgling central bank today are likely to be far less enamoured when that reality hits home.

(a) Why might setting interest rates at the euro-zone average of 4 per cent fail to benefit either growing or stagnant economies?

(b) The author states that the problems faced by the ECB will 'in the longer run recede'. Why?

(c) Recent studies into the effects of interest rate changes on economies in Europe have shown that they respond differently. For example, it has been found that the deflationary impact of a rise in short-term interest rates is much stronger in Italy than in Germany and France, and stronger again than in Spain. What are some of the implications of this for the ECB's monetary policy?

Monetary authorities around the world have less control over their economies than in the past. Increasingly, as governments and central banks struggle to tame the business cycle, they are having to rely not simply on changing current interest rates, but on talking about possible *future* interest rate changes that might be necessary if people fail to respond sufficiently to current changes. In the following article, taken from the *Guardian* of 4 September 1999, Edmund Warner (chief executive of Albert E. Sharp Securities) argues that attempting to control people's expectations in this way is virtually impossible to do with any precision.

The danger of growing up quickly

Like a gangly teenager, the global economy is experiencing its share of growing pains. All the signs are that the world is in the middle of a growth spurt.

Although this brings immediate benefits it also carries the threat of dislocation. Much hinges on the skills of the policy masseurs.

Although impossible to measure it seems as if each major statistical release in the US is awaited with yet greater trepidation. This is a sure sign that investors appreciate how much they have riding on a continuation of the 'new paradigm' – strong growth and low inflation. It is as if markets have begun to expect an acceleration in the rate of inflation while continuing to pray for the opposite.

Inflation is a notoriously difficult variable to model. Sure, it is too much money chasing too few goods, but what makes the money *want* to do the chasing? What, in the modern economy, determines the total quantum of money available to join the chase? The explosion in sources of credit and electronic commerce have transformed money creation. The monetary authorities have less direct control over economies than ever before.

Economic management increasingly involves the manipulation of inflation expectations. Interest rate rises of 25 basis points (¼ per cent) are unlikely, in themselves, to effect a significant change in the behaviour of an economy's participants. It is the accompanying rhetoric that magnifies the import of rate changes. Employers, employees and consumers are encouraged to display restraint by threats of future action from policymakers.

This fine-tuning approach is fraught with difficulties, not least because any individual within an economy might assume the masses will exercise restraint – leaving him or her to borrow, spend and issue extravagant wage demands at will.

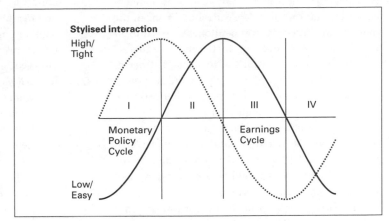

It is not just in America that monetary authorities are responding to stronger economic growth with dark hints of higher rates. Wim Duisenberg, president of the European central bank, has responded to the recovery by signalling the need for policy tightening at some point in the future. One of the Bank of England's deputy governors, Mervyn King, is fulfiling the same role of inflation hard man in Britain.

This policy shadow-boxing is typical of the present stage of the global economic cycle. The chart shows the stylised interaction of the cycles of monetary policy and corporate earnings. The world is now in stage I, a period of rising profits and easy but tightening monetary policy. This stage normally witnesses equities outperforming cash, and both cash and equities outperforming bonds.

This has indeed been the experience this year.

The challenge for investors is to assess whether inflation can be averted without tighter policy crushing corporate profitability in the process. If this is possible then the cycles can be stretched and their amplitude compressed.

History suggests this is a difficult stunt to pull off – although that is just what America's Federal Reserve has managed in recent years.

If the authorities fail to avert inflation and hence are forced to raise rates dramatically to reassert control, corporate profits are likely to pop.

In this stage of the global cycle – stage II in the chart – falling corporate earnings and tightening monetary policy typically push equities to the bottom of the performance pile and cash to the top.

(a) Why is the relationship between money supply and inflation very difficult to model?

(b) Why is the fine-tuning approach to managing the business cycle 'fraught with difficulties'?

(c) Explain the relationship between the two cycles in the chart.

E   ANSWERS

Q1. (b), (d) and (e) are all examples of monetary policy. (a) and (f) are examples of fiscal policy, and (c) incomes policy.

Q2. *False.* Keynesians argue the opposite of this, suggesting that monetary policy is unpredictable and ineffective in controlling the level of aggregate demand.

Q3. *True.* Monetarists do not favour discretionary policy, either fiscal *or* monetary, arguing that time lags tend to make discretionary changes in policy destabilising.

Instead they prefer to set money supply or inflation targets and stick to them.

Q4. D. This will reduce the credit multiplier. For the current reserve base, banks will now have to reduce the amount of non-reserve assets (i.e. loans, etc.).

Q5. The two major sources are: increased government borrowing (a PSBR) and increased private-sector borrowing (from banks being prepared to operate with a lower liquidity ratio).

Q6. Their main argument against statutory reserve requirements and other forms of direct monetary control is that they interfere with the working of the market and prevent competition. Such controls could become sources of inefficiency. Regulated institutions would be unable to expand, whereas non-regulated ones (and probably less efficient ones) would take business from them. Another reason is Goodhart's law (see next question).

Q7. B. Goodhart's law states that regulation of one part of the financial system would cause unregulated parts to expand. Thus the amount of lending by the regulated institutions would be a poor indicator of total lending: 'to control is to distort'.

Q8. *the non-bank private sector*. If the borrowing is not from the banks, there will be no expansion of the money base and no resulting credit creation.

Q9. *higher*. The excess government spending will increase the demand for money, and so, with no increase in the supply of money, there will be a rise in interest rates.

Q10. *less*. Higher interest rates will reduce private-sector borrowing, including private-sector investment. This 'crowding-out' of investment is seen by monetarists to be a serious problem of attempting to restrain the growth of the money supply *without* also reducing the PSBR.

Q11. *increases*. If existing money circulates faster, there will be less upward pressure on interest rates.

Q12. *more*. The more elastic the liquidity preference curve, the more will idle balances fall as the rate of interest rises, and hence the faster will money circulate.

Q13. (a) (iii): *decrease*, (b) (i): *decrease*, (c) (i): *increase*, (d) (iv): *decrease*, (e) (i): *increase*, (f) (iii): *increase*, (g) (ii): *decrease*.

Open-market operations will involve altering the total amount of government borrowing on the open market (as opposed to from the central bank). If the central bank deliberately keeps banks short of liquidity and then manipulates the amount that it lends to them, this will directly affect banks' liquid base. Funding involves altering the *type* of government borrowing (e.g. switching from bills to bonds). In some countries (but not the UK), the central bank requires banks to maintain a minimum ratio of reserve assets to total assets – a ratio which is above the ratio banks would choose. By raising this ratio it can force banks to contract credit.

Those actions that increase the liquidity base of the banking sector will increase the credit creation. Those that decrease the liquidity base will decrease credit creation.

Q14. £90m. The liquidity base will expand by £10m, on which banks can create £90m credit, making a total increase in the money supply of £100m (a bank multiplier of 10).

Q15. *True*. When banks run short of liquidity they will borrow from the Bank of England through gilt repos or offer bills of exchange for rediscounting. The Bank of England can dictate the repo and discount rates. This then has a knock-on effect on interest rates generally throughout the financial system.

Q16. (a) *Sell more*. If banks have surplus liquidity, they will be buying bills. If the Bank of England sells them more, this will force down the price of bills and hence force up the rate of discount and hence the rate of interest.

(b) *Buy fewer*. If banks are short of liquidity, they will be 'in the Bank' (selling bills to the Bank of England). If the Bank of England is prepared to buy fewer at any given price, this will force down the bill price and hence force up the rate of rediscount and hence the rate of interest.

Q17. (a) *Yes*. If the government cuts taxes, then other things being equal this will increase the PSBR.

(b) *Yes*. Similarly, if the government wants to increase government expenditure, this will increase the PSBR.

(c) *No*. A booming economy will automatically lead to higher tax revenues and reduced government expenditure (e.g. on unemployment benefits).

(d) *Yes*. In a recession, however, the PSBR will increase as tax revenues fall and government expenditure automatically rises.

(e) *Yes* (short term). The extra government expenditure will raise the PSBR.
No (long term). A faster growth in output will lead to a faster growth in tax revenues.

(f) *Yes*. This will reduce the tax base and increase government expenditure on health care, pensions and other benefits.

Q18. This is where the authorities seek to control cash and banks' balances with the central bank.

Q19. D. In this case, any reduction in the cash base is likely to 'bite' more effectively. In the case of A, banks could suffer a loss of liquidity without reducing loans; in the case of B and C, there is a diversion of business between institutions, which will limit the size of the total reduction in loans; in the case of E, the Bank of England is supplying liquidity on demand (albeit at a price).

Q20. Banks may reduce their liquidity ratios; they may initially have surplus liquidity; disintermediation may occur (possibly abroad).

Q21. *False*. If the supply of money is stable, but the *demand* for money is unstable, then the rate of interest will fluctuate as the level of demand fluctuates.

Q22. (a) *True*. Competition is stifled if only one part of the financial system is under regulation, whereas the rest is not. Uncontrolled (and possibly inefficient) institutions will be given an unfair advantage, which may allow them to charge monopolistic interest rates.

(b) *False*. Credit rationing will allow interest rates to be *below* the free-market equilibrium.

(c) *True*. Credit rationing will hit hardest those industries that depend upon consumer hire purchase to buy their goods. The car and other consumer durable industries are likely to be particularly hard hit by credit controls.

(d) *True*. Banks as well as other financial institutions will attempt to find ways around credit restrictions.

(e) *False*. Unlike interest rates, it directly affects the amount of bank lending.

Q23. If people wish to borrow (demand), then the financial institutions will attempt to lend (supply), even if controls are in place restricting institutions from doing so.

Q24. *inelastic*.

Q25. All are possible consequences of a policy of high interest rates. Note that in case of (b), higher interest rates will lead to an appreciation of the exchange rate, which will make exports and home-produced import substitutes less competitive. In the case of (d), higher interest rates will discourage investment, which will reduce the rate of growth of capital and of technical progress.

20 Macroeconomic Controversies I: The Control of Aggregate Demand

This chapter looks at the debates over the relative effectiveness of fiscal and monetary policy for controlling aggregate demand.

20.1 Monetary policy and aggregate demand

(Pages 567–8) The quantity theory of money

The debate between Keynesians and monetarists over the effects of monetary policy on aggregate demand can be shown by considering the *quantity theory of money*. This states that **Q1.** *money supply/the average level of prices* is a function of **Q2.** *money supply/the average level of prices/the velocity of circulation*.

Q3. The relationship between money supply and prices can be expressed in the *quantity equation*. One version is as follows:

A. $M/V = PQ$
B. $M/V = Q/P$
C. $MQ = VP$
D. $MV = PQ$
E. $MP = VQ$

Q4. If the money supply as measured by M4 = £150bn and GDP = £300bn:

(a) What will be the (GDP) velocity of circulation (of M4)?

....

(b) If the money supply were cut by 50 per cent, what must happen to the velocity of circulation if there were no change in the value of final goods and services sold?

....

Q5. Monetarists and Keynesians disagree over the nature of V and Q. Who argues the following cases?

(a) Changes in V are small and predictable, hence any increase in the money supply M will have a significant effect upon total spending.

Keynesian view/monetarist view

(b) M and V vary inversely.

Keynesian view/monetarist view

(c) V is determined by people's desire to hold speculative balances, which in turn is determined by expectations.

Keynesian view/monetarist view

(d) V is exogenously determined.

Keynesian view/monetarist view

(e) If MV falls as a result of a tight monetary policy, then Q will fall as well as P. *Keynesian view/monetarist view*

(f) In the long run, Q is determined independently of the level of aggregate demand, such that any rise in MV will ultimately simply lead to a rise in prices.

Keynesian view/monetarist view

(Pages 568–70) The interest rate transmission mechanism (the traditional Keynesian mechanism)

According to the interest rate transmission mechanism, a rise in money supply will lead to a **Q6.** *rise/fall* in interest rates, which, in turn, will lead to a **Q7.** *rise/fall* in investment and hence a **Q8.** a *rise/fall* in aggregate demand. These effects of monetary policy on aggregate demand depend upon the elasticity of the money demand curve and the responsiveness of investment to a change in interest rates.

 Multiple Choice   Written answer   Delete wrong word   Diagram/table manipulation   Calculation Matching/ordering

Figure 20.1 The interest rate monetary transmission mechanism: Keynesian and monetarist views

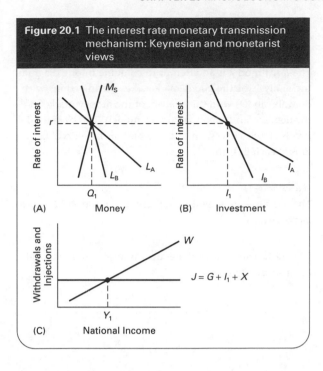

(a) A rise in demand for exports and a fall in demand for imports.

(b) A fall in interest rates leading to an outflow of finance overseas.

(c) A rise in the money supply.

(d) A multiplied rise in national income.

(e) A depreciation of the exchange rate.

Order: (c) ....

(?) Q12. What effect would a fixed exchange rate have on the exchange rate transmission mechanism?

....

....

(Pages 571–4) The monetarist transmission mechanism

(▤) Q13. The monetarist analysis is based on the theory of portfolio balance. This states that:

A. in times of recession individuals will use up their savings rather than cutting down on excess spending.

B. people hold their wealth in a number of different forms, the balance depending on their relative profitability and liquidity.

C. individuals will keep an equal balance between financial assets and money in their portfolios, irrespective of the rate of interest.

D. individuals with stocks and shares spread their risks by having a broadly balanced portfolio of equities.

E. high inflation will cause people to sell their low-earning financial assets and substitute them for cash, which, by definition, is totally liquid.

(?) Q14. How does the theory of portfolio balances help to explain the direct transmission mechanism between money supply and aggregate demand?

....

....

....

(▤) Q15. Monetarists claim that the velocity of circulation (V) is relatively stable over the longer run. Of the following, which are used by monetarists in support of this claim?

(i) Sufficient time has elapsed for the direct mechanism to have worked fully through.

(ii) The demand for money is relatively elastic in the long run.

(iii) Increased money supply would lead to inflation and hence a higher nominal rate of interest, thus offsetting any fall in the real rate of interest (and any initial fall in V).

(⊖) Q9. Figure 20.1 illustrates the interest rate transmission mechanism.

(a) Of the four curves, L_A, L_B, I_A and I_B in Figure 20.1, which two are based on monetarist assumptions?

....

(The other two are based on Keynesian assumptions.)

(b) Using Figure 20.1, show the effect of an increase in the money supply on the level of national income using both monetarist and Keynesian curves.

(c) Under which assumption does a change in money supply have the greater impact? *monetarist/Keynesian*

(d) The money supply curve in diagram (a) has been drawn as upward sloping (albeit steeply) rather than vertical. The assumption here is that money supply in the model is: *endogenous/exogenous*

(e) If the money supply curve had been drawn under strict monetarist assumptions, would there have been a bigger or smaller effect on national income from an increase in money supply? *bigger/smaller*

(?) Q10. Keynesians argue not only that changes in money supply will have a relatively small effect on investment, but also that the relationship between money supply and investment is an *unstable* one. Why?

....

....

(Pages 570–1) The Keynesian analysis of the open economy transmission mechanism

(♦) Q11. Order the following points in a logical sequence, assuming that there is a free-floating exchange rate.

(iv) Increased money supply would lead to inflation and hence people holding smaller money balances, thus offsetting any initial tendency for V to rise.

A. (i) and (ii).
B. (i) and (iii).
C. (ii) and (iii).
D. (ii) and (iv).
E. (iii) and (iv).

20.2 Fiscal policy and aggregate demand
(Pages 575–9)

? **Q16.** Assume that the government runs a budget deficit. Describe what will happen to:

(a) The supply of money ....

....

(b) The demand for money ....

....

(c) Interest rates   *rise/fall/either/neither*

Explain ....

....

Assume that, despite an increase in government expenditure and a resulting budget deficit, the government does not allow the money supply to increase. Interest rates will **Q17.** *rise/fall*. This in turn will cause the level of investment to **Q18.** *rise/fall*. As a consequence **Q19.** *crowding in/crowding out/additional investment/pump priming* will occur. The level of injections into the circular flow will **Q20.** *increase further/fall back again* causing the level of national income to **Q21.** *increase further/fall back again*.

If the government operates an expansionary fiscal policy but does not allow money supply to increase at all, this is known as *pure* fiscal policy.

◐ Q22. Which of the following analyses of the crowding-out effects of pure fiscal policy are Keynesian and which are monetarist?

(a) The increased demand for money will cause a relatively large rise in interest rates.   *Keynesian/monetarist*
(b) The increased demand for money will cause a relatively small rise in interest rates.   *Keynesian/monetarist*
(c) The increased interest rates will cause a relatively large fall in investment.   *Keynesian/monetarist*
(d) The increased interest rates will cause a relatively small fall in investment.   *Keynesian/monetarist*
(e) Crowding out is thus substantial and possibly total.   *Keynesian/monetarist*
(f) Crowding out is thus relatively minor and may be even non-existent.   *Keynesian/monetarist*

*20.3 ISLM analysis: the integration of the goods and money-market models

The *ISLM* model is an attempt to combine in one diagram the analysis of the goods market (i.e. the injections/withdrawals model) with the analysis of the money market (i.e. the demand and supply of money model). The *ISLM* model involves two curves: an *IS* curve and an *LM* curve. Let us look at each in turn.

(Pages 580–1) The IS *curve*
The *IS* curve represents equilibrium in the **Q23.** *goods market/money market*.

? **Q24.** The *IS* curve slopes downwards from left to right because, as interest rates fall,

....

....

The elasticity of the *IS* curve is determined by the responsiveness of investment (and saving) to changes in the rate of interest and by the size of the multiplier. The more responsive are investment and saving to changes in interest rates, the more **Q25.** *elastic/inelastic* will the *IS* curve be. The smaller the value of the multiplier, the more **Q26.** *elastic/inelastic* will the *IS* curve be.

Keynesians argue that the *IS* curve is relatively **Q27.** *elastic/inelastic*. Monetarists by contrast argue that the *IS* curve is relatively **Q28.** *elastic/inelastic*.

? **Q29.** Why do Keynesians and monetarists disagree over the slope of the *IS* curve?

....

....

....

◐ Q30. What effect will the following have on the *IS* curve?
(a) Business expectations of the future improve.
    Shift left/Shift right
(b) Minimum deposits are required before mortgages are given.   *Shift left/Shift right*
(c) Consumer durables fall in price as VAT is cut.
    Shift left/Shift right
(d) The economy experiences a consumer boom.
    Shift left/Shift right
(e) Firms anticipate an oncoming recession.
    Shift left/Shift right

(Pages 581–3) The LM *curve*

◐ **Q31.** The *LM* curve represents those points where the demand for money is equal to the equilibrium rate of interest. *True/False*

? **Q32.** The *LM* curve slopes upwards from left to right because, as national income rises,

....

....

The elasticity of the *LM* curve is determined by (i) the responsiveness of the demand for money to changes in national income and (ii) the responsiveness of the demand for money to changes in the rate of interest.

In the case of (i), the greater the marginal propensity to consume, the more the money demand curve (*L*) will shift to the **Q33.** *left/right* with a given increase in national income. Hence the more will the equilibrium rate of interest rise and the **Q34.** *steeper/shallower* will the *LM* curve become.

In the case of (ii), the more elastic the money demand curve, the **Q35.** *more/less* will the equilibrium interest rate change from a given shift in the money demand curve caused by an increase in national income. Hence the **Q36.** *steeper/shallower* will the *LM* curve be.

The Keynesians argue that the *LM* curve is relatively **Q37.** *steep/shallow*, whereas the monetarists argue that it is relatively **Q38.** *steep/shallow*.

? **Q39.** Why do Keynesians and monetarists disagree over the slope of the *LM* curve?

....

....

....

◐ **Q40.** What effect will the following have on the *LM* curve?

(a) Banks decide to hold a higher liquidity ratio.
Shift upwards/Shift downwards

(b) Speculation that the price of securities is about to fall.
Shift upwards/Shift downwards

(c) The government funds the PSBR by selling bonds to overseas purchasers. *Shift upwards/Shift downwards*

(d) People are paid on a less frequent basis.
Shift upwards/Shift downwards

(e) It is expected that the foreign exchange value of the domestic currency will fall.
Shift upwards/Shift downwards

(Page 583) Equilibrium in the ISLM *model*

⊖ **Q41.** Figure 20.2 shows an *IS* and an *LM* curve, showing equilibrium in the goods and money markets respectively.

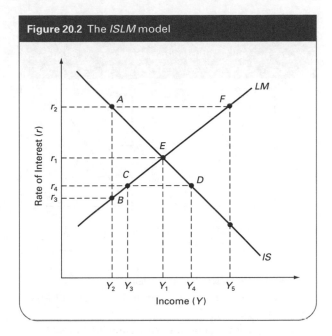

Figure 20.2 The *ISLM* model

(a) Equilibrium in both markets simultaneously is identified by which point?

....

(b) Describe the position of the economy at point *A* referring to both the goods and the money markets.

....

....

(c) By what process would the economy return to an equilibrium position?

....

(d) Describe the position of the economy at point *C*, again referring to both the goods and the money markets.

....

....

(e) By what process would the economy return to an equilibrium position this time?

....

....

(f) Using Figure 20.2, demonstrate the effects of the following:
   (i) An inflow of funds coming from abroad as the result of a balance of payments surplus.
   (ii) An increase in business confidence.

Figure 20.3 (a) Increased government expenditure and increased money supply
(b) Deteriorating business expectations and increased money supply

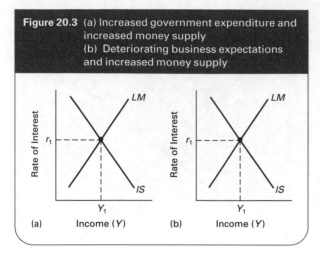

(a) Income (*Y*)

(b) Income (*Y*)

(Pages 584–6) Fiscal and monetary policy

⊖ **Q42.** Using the two diagrams in Figure 20.3, illustrate the following situations.

(a) Government expenditure grows and is financed by an expansion in the money supply. Avoid any crowding out in your model.

(b) Business expectations deteriorate and in response the government expands the money supply in order to maintain the level of aggregate demand.

⊖ **Q43.** Using Figure 20.4 sketch the following effects of government policy. On diagrams (a) and (b) sketch *ISLM* curves to represent a contractionary fiscal and contractionary monetary policy from a Keynesian perspective. On

Figure 20.4 Keynesian and monetarist views on fiscal and monetary policy

(a) Contractionary fiscal policy

(b) Contractionary monetary policy

KEYNESIAN VIEW

(c) Contractionary fiscal policy

(d) Contractionary monetary policy

MONETARIST VIEW

(c) and (d) sketch *ISLM* curves to represent contractionary fiscal and contractionary monetary policy from a monetarist perspective.

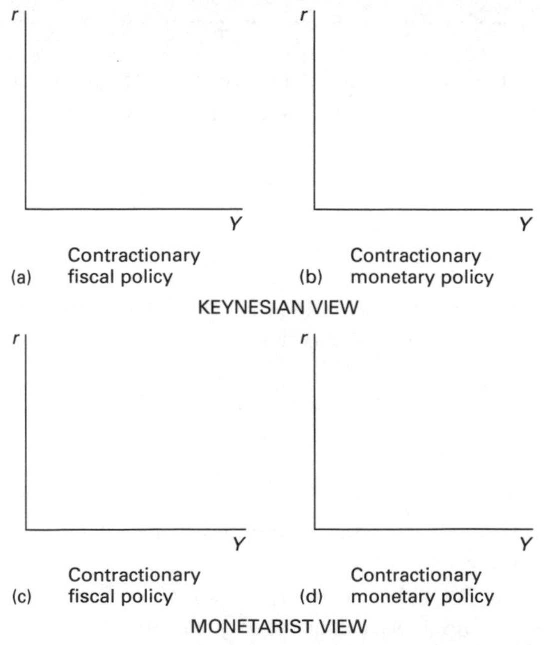

20.4 The control of aggregate demand in the UK

(Pages 587–96)

◗ **Q44.** Which of the following arguments would a Keynesian use concerning government macroeconomic intervention in the economy?

(a) The management of aggregate demand by the government can reduce the degree of instability in the economy.   *Yes/No*

(b) Control over the money supply is the best way to regulate aggregate demand in the short run.   *Yes/No*

(c) Control over the money supply is the best way to regulate aggregate demand in long run.   *Yes/No*

(d) The 'natural' state of the market system is one of disequilibrium.   *Yes/No*

(e) 'Intervention' should focus on removing government barriers to the free operation of the market.   *Yes/No*

(f) The business cycle is damaging to economic performance.   *Yes/No*

(g) Fine tuning can reduce cyclical fluctuations.   *Yes/No*

▦ **Q45.** What was the dominant constraint on demand-led growth policies in the 1950s and 1960s?

A. The level of unemployment.

B. Time lags.

C. Money supply targets.

D. The balance of payments.

E. The size of the budget deficit.

(?) **Q46.** List five possible causes of the stagflation experienced by the UK economy in the 1970s.

1. ....

2. ....

3. ....

4. ....

5. ....

◗ **Q47.** Which of the following policies were pursued by the Thatcher government in the early 1980s?

(a) The setting of targets for the growth in the money supply.   *Yes/No*

(b) Attempts to cut the PSBR.   *Yes/No*

(c) The implementation of statutory requirements. *Yes/No*

(d) Reductions in the rate of income tax.   *Yes/No*

(e) The use of incomes policy to regulate the growth of wages.   *Yes/No*

(f) The tendering of public-sector services to the private sector.   *Yes/No*

(?) **Q48.** List three problems that were encountered.

1. ....

2. ....

3. ....

(?) **Q49.** Were any economic indicators targeted in the late 1980s, and if so, what?

....

(◗) **Q50.** UK entry into the ERM (the exchange rate mechanism of the European Monetary System) meant that government had less discretion in monetary policy than before. *True/False*

(▤) **Q51.** Which one of the following was a direct consequence of UK membership of the ERM?
A. The rate of inflation was driven up to the European average.
B. Fiscal policy was dominated by European budgetary issues.
C. The money supply grew more rapidly.
D. Aggregate demand was caused to expand faster than the government had wished.
E. Interest rates had to be set at whatever level was necessary to maintain the exchange rate.

(◗) **Q52.** Since 1992, the main focus of UK demand-side policy has been the control of inflation. *True/False*

(◗) **Q53.** If the UK rate of inflation is forecast to be below 2¹/₂ per cent, the Monetary Policy Committee of the Bank of England is obliged to reduce the rate of interest. *True/False*

(◗) **Q54.** If the rate of inflation for the euro-zone countries is forecast to be below 2 per cent, the ECB is obliged to reduce the rate of interest. *True/False*

20.5 Rules versus discretion
(Pages 596–9)

(?) **Q55.** Outline the monetarist case in favour of rules.

....

....

....

(?) **Q56.** Outline the Keynesian case in favour of discretion.

....

....

....

B PROBLEMS, EXERCISES AND PROJECTS

Q57. Using diagrams (such as those in Figure 20.8 of Sloman, *Economics*, 4th edn), illustrate the effect on aggregate demand, via the exchange rate transmission mechanism, of a contraction in the money supply, making (a) Keynesian assumptions; (b) monetarist assumptions.

Q58. Using data for the money supply (M4) and GDP (where $GDP = PQ$), calculate values for the velocity of circulation for each of the last 15 years. How has the value of V changed over the period? What explanations can you offer for these changes?

How does the velocity of circulation alter when different measures of the money supply are used in its calculation? Use M0 as an alternative to M4. What are the consequences of your findings for the quantity theory of money?

Figures for GDP and the various money supply measures can be found in *Economic Trends* (ONS), the *Annual Abstract of Statistics* (ONS) and *Financial Statistics* (ONS). See also the Bank of England web site, http://www.bankofengland.co.uk/mfsd/

*****Q59.** In Figure 20.5, simultaneous goods and money-market equilibria are achieved at point E (r_1, Y_1). Two alternative *LM* curves are shown, one representing the monetarist position, the other the Keynesian position.
(a) Which *LM* curve represents the monetarist position? *LM_I/LM_{II}*
(b) Which *LM* curve represents the Keynesian position? *LM_I/LM_{II}*
(c) Draw on Figure 20.5 the new *IS* curve following an expansionary fiscal policy. Clearly identify the new rates of interest and levels of national income for each *LM* curve.
(d) Extend the line from r_1 to the new *IS* curve. What would be the full multiplied rise in national income from the shift in *IS*, assuming that money supply expanded sufficiently to keep the rate of interest at r_1?

....

(e) Dropping the assumption of a constant rate of interest, identify the crowding out that occurs from the shift in the *IS* curve if the *LM* curve is:

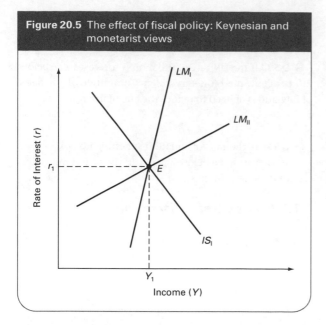

Figure 20.5 The effect of fiscal policy: Keynesian and monetarist views

(i) LM_I ....

(ii) LM_{II} ....

(f) What would the *LM* curve look like if there were no crowding out?

....

(g) What would the *LM* curve look like if crowding out were total?

....

C DISCUSSION TOPICS AND ESSAYS

Q60. 'The dismantling of controls on international financial flows and the integration of international financial markets have made the transmission mechanism from exchange rates to the money supply to prices far more important.' Discuss and consider the implications for the conduct of monetary policy.

Q61. 'The quantity equation $MV = PQ$ is true by definition.' Explain why this is so. Does it imply that a rise in money supply will necessarily lead to a rise in the price level? Discuss how monetarists and Keynesians disagree over the nature of V and Q. What are the implications of their disagreement for the effectiveness of monetary policy in controlling inflation?

Q62. 'The effectiveness of discretionary fiscal policy is reduced by the phenomenon of crowding out.' Explain what is meant by 'crowding out'. What determines its magnitude?

*Q63. Use *ISLM* analysis to explain the difference in monetarist and Keynesian views on the efficacy of fiscal and monetary policies.

Q64. What is stagflation? What reasons have been advanced to explain the stagflation experienced by the British economy during the 1970s? What problems did stagflation create for the management of economic affairs during this period?

Q65. Outline and assess the success or otherwise of the monetarist experiment in the 1980s.

Q66. 'Discretionary demand management policy in the early 1990s, like that in the early 1980s, was made virtually impossible by the adherence to a policy rule. The rule was a different one, but the effects were similar.' Do you agree?

Q67. To what extent has macroeconomic policy in the 1990s been geared to achieving a target rate of inflation?

Q68. Debate
The only way of achieving a stable macroeconomic environment is to set clear macroeconomic targets and then stick to them.

D ARTICLES

The article below by Anthony Browne, taken from the *Observer* of 11 April 1999, considers the likelihood that we have entered a period of prolonged low interest rates, and if so why.

They predicted the death of inflation. Now, it's the death of interest rates

The cut in interest rates to 5.25 per cent last week brought them to levels not seen since 1994, and to within a whisker of historic lows.

The tumbling rates of the last six months have come down to within a mere 0.25 per cent of the lowest rate enjoyed for more than 20 years – the 5 per cent reached in the Queen's silver jubilee year of 1977.

If the Bank of England cuts a further 0.5 per cent, as many economists predict, UK rates will be the lowest since 1963, the year President John Kennedy was assassinated.

There's been much talk about the death of inflation. Now we seem to be witnessing the death of interest. In the US, rates are already at their lowest since the sixties. Last week, rates in Europe were cut to 2.5 per cent. In Japan, interest is effectively dead: rates are less than 0.5 per cent.

Low UK rates are already giving welcome relief to mortgage holders and debt-laden businesses – but causing misery for pensioners living off the interest on savings. But will rates stay low – or, as so often before, simply bounce back up?

Those with good memories see little room for optimism. Rates might have been 5 per cent in 1977, but by 1979 they had jumped to 17 per cent. They might have fallen back to 7.5 per cent by 1988, but by 1989 they had doubled to 15 per cent – pushing many home-buyers into arrears. The victims warn that history has a habit of repeating itself.

But an increasing number of economists think it might not. There are strong reasons to believe Britain and other countries around the world are entering a prolonged period of low interest rates.

John Llewellyn, global chief economist at Lehman Brothers, was among the first to foresee that the US was heading for the sort of rates it last had in the fifties and sixties, and thinks the same is set to happen in the UK. What's more, he believes things are likely to stay that way: 'We have a sporting chance that we're in a sustained period of low rates. The only danger is that governments muck it up by going on a spending spree.'

Roger Bootle, the managing director of the consultancy Capital Economics who found fame with his book, *Death of Inflation*, also reckons we're entering a long, low-rate era. 'I think they'll settle in the normal range of 3 to 5 per cent, so that a rate of 6 per cent will be seen as abnormally high. We could even have rates as low as Japan's 0.5 per cent if we entered deflation.'

The interest optimists claim recent history is no guide to the future. Rates may have been bouncing up and down, but they have been on a clear downward path since reaching this century's high of 17 per cent in 1979, only a few years after the 1973 oil crisis sent shockwaves around the world economy. Since then, each peak and each trough in the cycle has been lower than the last. The most recent peak – 7.5 per cent in 1998 – was in fact no higher than the eighties' lowest point.

If history is to be a guide, it would be better to look at what things were like before that oil crisis. In 1932, rates were set at 2 per cent. They stayed there until 1951, except for a few months in 1939. For 20 years, they basically never changed. Between 1955 and 1972, rates stayed between 4 and 8 per cent.

It is to this sort of world that the optimists believe we are returning, after the aberration of the seventies and eighties.

There are many good arguments for this. The main one is the evidence for the death of inflation. In every major economy, and most minor ones, serious inflation has been cast into the dustbin of history. In Britain, inflation has fallen to 2.4 per cent (below the Government's target), while in the US and Europe it is around half that. In Japan and a few other countries, prices are actually falling. Low inflation – the product of increased global competition and cheap commodities – allows governments to cut interest rates with impunity.

Rates have also been tumbling because governments have been slashing their borrowing – and in the US and Canada turning in budget surpluses, reducing the competition for savers' money that pushes rates up.

Llewellyn believes the demise of budget deficits has knocked as much as 2 per cent off interest rates.

Whatever the arguments, low UK interest rates are pretty much guaranteed if this country joins the euro, giving us the same interest rates as other member nations. European rates have been lower than the UK's for decades, and they're now less than half of ours.

We may have entered the age of permanently low rates, but most people and businesses have yet to be convinced. If – or when – they are, their behaviour is likely to change.

With low rates come low returns on savings. 'It will push people out of bank and building society accounts and into things like equities, government bonds, and very long term saving plans,' said Bootle. Yet people are likely to save more. With declining state provision, workers are likely to put away larger lump sums to guarantee a decent retirement income.

Low rates mean cheaper mortgages, but this does not necessarily mean an eighties-style house price boom.

Martin Ellis, economist at the Halifax, said: 'You're not going to get the rapid wage inflation which in the seventies meant you could get a huge mortgage knowing that pay rises would rapidly make it more affordable. Now you have to be certain you can afford it right away. There won't be a boom, but more muted price rises.'

(a) What are the economic advantages of low and stable interest rates?

(b) What factors does the article identify as being responsible for the falling level of interest rates?

(c) What impacts are low interest rates likely to have on savers and the housing market?

The following extract is from an article entitled 'Monetary policy instruments: the UK experience', appearing in the *Bank of England Quarterly* of August 1994. The author, Mervyn King, argues that whereas the transmission mechanism between money and aggregate demand and prices is itself relatively uncontroversial, the size and timing of the effects are far from certain, depending as they do on expectations.

Money, aggregate demand and prices

If money were neutral – in the sense that a change in the money supply produced an immediate equiproportionate change in the price level – then the uncertainties of the transmission mechanism would be reduced to the link between the discretionary actions of the authorities and the behaviour of money. In practice, of course, the link between money and activity and inflation is far from clear.

The traditional view of the transmission mechanism of monetary policy is, at least *qualitatively*, relatively uncontroversial. A decrease in the monetary base or, equivalently, higher short-term official interest rates, will feed through to interest rates at all maturities and alter asset prices. Given some inertia in the setting of nominal wages and prices, the higher level of nominal interest rates will, in the short run, imply a higher level of real interest rates. Higher nominal interest rates will reduce the demand for money, and higher real rates will reduce the demand for credit. Real asset prices will fall, and there will be a process of substitution among various real and financial assets, >and between assets and spending. With fewer profitable lending opportunities, the banks will wish to attract fewer deposits, and the broad money supply will fall.

The fall in money has as its counterpart a fall in nominal incomes, as households and companies adjust their portfolios and spending plans to the new levels of real money balances and interest rates. How does this come about? The rise in real interest rates and fall in asset prices will reduce real aggregate demand in three ways.

First, the higher real rate of interest will lead to a switch of spending from the present to the future, as saving becomes more attractive. Second, higher real interest rates will lower asset prices and hence wealth. Both effects will reduce consumer spending and private investment. Third, the rise in real

short-term interest rates is also likely to lead to an appreciation of the exchange rate to a level from which it will be expected to revert slowly to its original real level. In turn, this will lead to lower prices for imports in terms of domestic currency and also a depressing effect on the economy through a reduction in the net trade balance. Eventually, the contraction of the real economy will affect prices and wages, and real demand and output can, in the long run, return to their original levels.

As I mentioned, there is nothing particularly controversial here. Turning this qualitative story into a *quantitative* account of how monetary policy affects the economy is, however, a different story. And both recent research and experience have made us aware of the importance of expectations about future inflation in determining how long and how variable are the lags between changes in interest rates and their effect on inflation.

One of the most contentious issues in assessing the role of money is the direction of causation between money and demand. Textbooks assume that money is exogenous. It is sometimes dropped by helicopters, as in Friedman's analysis of a 'pure' monetary expansion, or its supply is altered by open-market operations. In the United Kingdom, money is endogenous – the Bank supplies base money on demand at its prevailing interest rate, and broad money is created by the banking system. The endogeneity of money has caused great confusion and led some critics to argue that money is unimportant. This is a serious mistake. In his latest (April 1994) forecast, Tim Congdon[1] – who could never be accused of understanding the role of money – argues that 'the upturn in monetary growth has done its usual work in bolstering balance sheets and encouraging more spending

on big-ticket capital items'. Some of his critics might reverse the causation and say 'the upturn in spending on big-ticket capital items and the bolstering of balance sheets had done its usual work in raising monetary growth'. In other words, spending and activity determine money, not the other way round.[2] I would prefer to say that interest rates have been kept at a level such that monetary growth has turned up, balance sheets have improved and there has been an increase in spending on big-ticket capital items.

Monetary policy does affect nominal growth in the economy, but the point is that money and interest rates are twins – two sides of the same coin. Many of those who find it difficult to accept that money plays a key role find it quite natural to assign great importance to the role of interest rates in determining expenditure and output. And equally, some of those for whom money is the key driving variable in the economy sometimes overlook the crucial role of interest rates in the transmission mechanism.

Of course, there may be times when the relevant interest rates are unobservable, either because of lack of data on rates charged to certain types of borrower or because of credit rationing – in which case the observed monetary flows will contain unique information. This was especially true in the circumstances of the credit crunch in the early 1990s, which affected particularly the banking systems of Japan, the United States and the Nordic countries. But this issue concerns the question of which variables we should be monitoring, rather than the underlying transmission mechanism.

© Bank of England Publications Group, *Bank of England Quarterly Bulletin* (Mervyn King), August 1994

1. Professor Congdon is the Managing Director of Lombard Street Research.

2. Kaldor, N. (1982) *The Scourge of Monetarism*, Oxford University Press.

(a) What is the connection between changes in money supply and changes in aggregate demand?

(b) Does the direction of causation between money supply and aggregate demand matter as far as the operation of monetary policy is concerned?

(c) Does the endogeneity of money mean that monetary policy is not important?

The use of inflation targeting, and monetary policy targeting in general, has radically changed attitudes towards economic policy and the management of aggregate demand. The following article by Charlotte Denny, taken from the *Guardian* of 26 October 1998, considers what targeting involves and examines its recent history.

Targeting could be hit and miss policy

What is inflation targeting?

It's the latest fashion for running monetary policy. Policymakers announce a target level for inflation and then set interest rates to meet their goal. If their forecasts suggest inflation is going to rise above the target, they raise rates to slow the economy. In the UK, the Government sets the target and the central bank manipulates interest rates to get inflation to the goal. But in some countries the central bank gets to decide both what the target should be and the level of interest rates needed to achieve it.

Who came up with the idea?

New Zealand introduced an inflation target in 1990 and since then nearly a dozen countries have followed suit. Britain adopted the present 2.5 per cent target under the Conservative government in October 1992, after the pound was pushed out of the exchange rate mechanism.

What's the point?

Most western governments, whether left- or right-wing, accept the economic orthodoxy which holds that economies have speed limits – in other words, it is not possible to let output grow at full tilt without sparking price rises.

Maintaining low and stable inflation has been the Holy Grail of policymakers since the early 1980s.

Does that mean economic growth is not important any more?

No, but policymakers think they cannot influence growth except in the short term. In the longer term, higher growth can be bought only at the expense of higher inflation. So that they are not tempted to inject inflationary demand into the economy, their hands are bound by policymakers who announce some kind of nominal anchor for setting the policy levers. Inflation targets are the latest such anchor to be tried in the UK.

What else has been tried?

When inflation was first declared economic enemy number one by the last Conservative government, ministers decided the best way of combating it would be to announce limits to the growth of the money supply. The monetarist economists advising them believed there was a direct relationship between inflation and monetary growth. It was the attempt to meet a rigid target for the money supply which caused the 1980–81 recession.

Did they give up after that?

No, they tried to find alternative money-supply targets which might behave more like the textbooks said they should. When those proved equally unreliable, the Government started targeting the exchange rate instead. At first, the pound shadowed the German mark and then, in October 1990, the Government made the fateful decision to join the ERM. When that policy collapsed on Black Wednesday, the Government adopted the 2.5 per cent target.

Has it worked?

Inflation has come down steeply since 1991, when it was running above 5 per cent. However, cynics note that inflation has come down in many countries with and without inflation targets since then, and that the UK has benefited from a worldwide fall in commodity prices. The real question is what price will be paid for reaching the target. The Bank of England is expecting growth to slow and unemployment to rise by around 200 000 next year. But, if it turns out that it has stomped on the economy too hard in order to meet its forecasts for inflation, the new policy-making rules may come under fire.

(a) Compare the relative advantages and disadvantages of adhering to macroeconomic policy rules with those of taking a more discretionary approach to policy.

(b) In the UK's recent history, targets have been adopted for various measures of the money supply, and at other times for the exchange rate. These policies proved to be largely unsuccessful. Currently, the government has set a target for the rate of inflation which the Bank of England must pursue in setting interest rates. Why has this policy proved to be more successful (so far)?

In 1997, the incoming Labour government made the Bank of England independent, giving its Monetary Policy Committee responsibility for setting interest rates. But, as Tony Thirlwall argues in the following article, taken from the *Guardian* of 5 October 1998, this leaves the government with both too little and too much power in determining macroeconomic policy.

Why the Government needs to get real on economic policy

It was a mistake to make the Bank of England independent, giving the Monetary Policy Committee (MPC) the sole task of achieving a target rate of inflation as low as 2.5 per cent per annum. I say this for two reasons.

First, the prime task of economic policy-making should be to maximise the growth of real living standards (i.e. the growth of real output per head) not to minimise the rate of inflation. There is no economic theory, or convincing empirical evidence, that a rate of inflation of 2.5 per cent is in any sense 'optimal' from the point of view of generating the maximum use of the country's resources.

Secondly, monetary and fiscal policy need to be co-ordinated if the macroeconomic goals of stable growth, low unemployment and low inflation are to be achieved simultaneously; now much more difficult with the Bank of England responsible for monetary policy and the Government in charge of fiscal policy, with apparently no effective dialogue between the two.

It would make more sense to depoliticise both monetary and fiscal policy and put economic policy-making into the hands of a group of technocrats which could be called the Real Economy Policy Committee. Such a group would be charged with the task of achieving a stable growth of GDP per head in line with the country's rate of growth of productive capacity, subject to a much more flexible target for inflation. The Real Economy Policy Committee would replace the MPC and take decisions on monetary policy consistent with decisions of fiscal policy and the overall state of the real economy.

The MPC was given a fruitless and too easy a task: fruitless because control of inflation is only one of many goals of economic policy; too easy because to control inflation through the use of interest rates, without regard to the real economy, requires no particular skills. (This is no criticism of the members of the MPC.)

The really difficult task is to control inflation while preserving growth, full employment and a healthy, tradeable goods sector. But these other objectives are outside the remit of the MPC. In the early days of independence, the MPC had an easy ride because growth was buoyant, unemployment was falling, and decisions to raise interest rates appeared benign. The situation is now very different, but the committee is powerless to change its stance.

How much more sensible it would be to have a Real Economy Policy Committee with a much wider brief.

Recent studies of the relation between inflation and economic growth within countries and across the world show that 2.5 per cent inflation is far below the rate at which inflation may damage the real economy. Studies by the IMF and World Bank* show a positive or neutral effect of inflation on growth up to about 8 per cent inflation. There are good economic reasons why this should be so. First, a mild demand inflation encourages investment by keeping entrepreneurs' expectations buoyant and real interest rates low. Second, inflation is to be expected in the process of growth and structural change.

Controlling inflation by monetary policy alone implicitly assumes that all

* M Bruno and W Easterly, Inflation Crises and Long-run Growth, *Journal of Monetary Economics*, 1998; M Sarel, Non-Linear Effects of Inflation on Economic Growth, *IMF Staff Papers*, 1996.

inflation is monetary in origin, which clearly it is not.

It is also a grave mistake for economic policy-making to be indifferent to the exchange rate. If tight monetary policy raises the exchange rate to levels which damage the tradeable goods sector, this calls for other instruments to be used to achieve the inflation target: proper co-ordination of monetary and fiscal policy is needed.

It is ostrich-like to ignore the fortunes of the manufacturing sector on the grounds that it constitutes only 20 per cent or so of total output and employment. More than 50 per cent of foreign exchange earnings still come from manufactured exports.

The current approach to economic policy-making which sets only a monetary target and no real targets, and which divorces monetary and fiscal policy, is doing great damage to the UK economy, as many economists predicted. There would appear to be three alternatives. The first would be to abolish the MPC and for the Government to once again co-ordinate monetary and fiscal policy itself. The second would be for both monetary and fiscal policy to be 'depoliticised' and for decision-making to be put in the hands of a Real Economy Policy Committee with the objective of achieving a high and stable rate of economic growth. The Government is unlikely, however, to relinquish control of fiscal, as well as monetary, policy, so a third (compromise) option would be a UK equivalent of the US Council of Economic Advisers with strong advisory powers, with the Government obliged to give reasons if the advice preferred is not taken. Macroeconomic policy as currently practised, effectively based on one target and one instrument, has no merit or logic.

(a) What are the disadvantages of having a low rate of inflation as the central goal of monetary policy?

(b) Why, according to Tony Thirlwall, is the current approach to economic policy-making doing 'great damage to the UK economy'?

(c) Critically evaluate the case made out in the article for a 'Real Economic Policy Committee'.

E ANSWERS

Q1. *the average level of prices.*

Q2. *the money supply.*

Q3. D. The quantity theory of money is $MV = PQ$. PQ, the money value of national output, is equal to MV, the total spending on national output.

Q4. *(a)* If we rearrange the quantity theory of money equation, then $V = PQ/M$. Thus if $PQ = GDP = £300bn$ and $M = M4 = £150$, $V = 300/150 = 2$. Hence money (M4) is spent, on average, twice a year on final goods and services.

   (b) If the money supply were to be cut by 50 per cent, then the velocity of circulation would have to *double* in order for total spending to remain the same and hence there to be no change in the value of final goods and services sold.

Q5. (a), (d) and (f) are all monetarist arguments, (b), (c) and (e) are Keynesian. (For a full explanation of the Keynesian and monetarist views, see Sloman, *Economics*, 4th edn, pp. 568–75.)

Q6. *fall.*

Q7. *rise.*

Q8. *rise.*

Q9. *(a)* The monetarist curves are L_B and I_A. The Keynesian curves are L_A and I_B.

   (b) See Figure A20.1. A rise in money supply to M_{S_2} leads to a fall in the rate of interest to r_{2_K} (Keynesian assumptions about L) or r_{2_M} (monetarist assumptions about L). This fall in the rate of interest leads to a rise in investment to I_{2_K} (Keynesian assumptions about I) or I_{2_M}

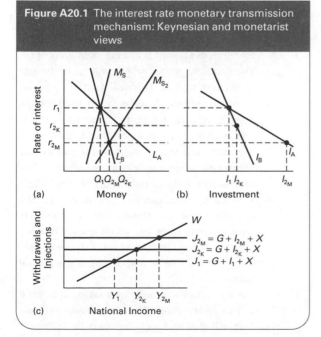

Figure A20.1 The interest rate monetary transmission mechanism: Keynesian and monetarist views

(monetarist assumptions about I). This rise in investment leads to a rise in injections to J_{2_K} (Keynesian assumptions about I) or J_{2_M} (monetarist assumptions about I) and a resulting rise in national income to Y_{2_K} (Keynesian assumptions) or Y_{2_M} (monetarist assumptions).

   (c) *monetarist.* (National income rises to Y_{2_M} in Figure A20.1(c).)

   (d) *endogenous.* With an upward-sloping M_S curve, the level of money supply depends on the rate of interest, which in turn depends on the demand for money.

   (e) *bigger.* If the money supply were exogenous (the strict monetarist assumption), the M_S curve would be vertical. A given rightward shift would lead to a bigger reduction in the rate of interest and hence a bigger increase in aggregate demand.

Q10. Because the other determinants of investment, and especially business confidence, are themselves subject to considerable fluctuations.

Q11. The points should be ordered in the following sequence; (c), (b), (e), (a) and (d). They show the effect of an increase in money supply on national income via the exchange rate transmission mechanism.

Q12. The more rigidly fixed the exchange rate, the less its value will appreciate or depreciate. Hence the less effect changes in money supply will have via this mechanism. In fact, any attempt to alter the money supply will be largely frustrated. For example, a rise in the money supply would cause the balance of payments to go into deficit. This would then cause the money supply to fall again as reserves were used to buy in excess sterling and as interest rates had to rise again to protect the overvalued exchange rate (see Sloman, *Economics*, 4th edn, Chapter 24, Section 24.2).

Q13. B. The theory of portfolio balances argues that individuals hold their assets in various forms – money, financial assets and physical assets such as housing.

Q14. Assume that the money supply expands. As it does so, people find that their portfolios change as well: they become more liquid. The additional money may be used to purchase more securities (driving up their price and forcing down the rate of interest), or more goods and services. This readjusting of individuals' portfolios will continue until balance has been restored. In the process, spending will have increased.

Q15. B. In the case of (ii), monetarists argue that the demand for money is relatively *inelastic*. In the case of (iv), the initial tendency would be for V to *fall* as increased money supply drove down the rate of interest and encouraged people to hold *larger* money balances.

Q16. **(a)** The increased PSBR will lead to an increase in the money supply if it is financed by borrowing from the Bank of England or by selling bills to the banking sector.

(b) The increased aggregate demand will lead to an increased transactions demand for money.

(c) *either.* The effect of (b) will be to increase interest rates. The effect of (a) will be to offset this. Whether interest rates do rise, and whether as a result some crowding out will occur, will depend on just how much the money supply increases.

Q17. *rise.*

Q18. *fall.*

Q19. *crowding out.*

Q20. *fall back again.*

Q21. *fall back again.*

Q22. (a), (c) and (e) are monetarist. (b), (d) and (f) are Keynesian.

Q23. *goods market.*

Q24. As interest rates fall, investment will expand and the level of saving will decrease. Both will cause a multiplied rise in national income.

Q25. *elastic.*

Q26. *inelastic.*

Q27. *inelastic.*

Q28. *elastic.*

Q29. They disagree over the responsiveness of investment and saving to changes in the rate of interest. Keynesians argue that investment and saving are relatively unresponsive, whereas the monetarists argue that they are relatively responsive.

Q30. (a), (c) and (d) will all lead to shifts to the right. They will all lead to a higher level of national income for any given rate of interest.

Q31. *False.* The *LM* curve shows all the various combinations of interest rates and national income at which the demand for money equals the supply ($L = M$).

Q32. As national income rises, transactions and precautionary demands for money increase, shifting the liquidity preference curve to the right. Assuming the money supply is fixed, this will lead to a rise in the rate of interest.

Q33. *right.*

Q34. *steeper.*

Q35. *less.*

Q36. *shallower.*

Q37. *shallow.*

Q38. *steep.*

Q39. The disagreement between the two groups centres on the speculative demand for money and its

responsiveness to changes in the rate of interest. Keynesians argue that the speculative demand is significant and responsive to interest rate changes, and that the *LM* curve is therefore correspondingly shallow. Monetarists argue that the demand for money is relatively inelastic, and that therefore the *LM* curve is relatively steep.

Q40. **(a)** *Shift upwards.* A higher liquidity ratio will cause the supply of money to fall. This, in turn, will cause the rate of interest to rise. Thus for any given level of national income the rate of interest will be higher.

(b) *Shift upwards.* As speculation mounts, there will be an increase in the demand for money. This will cause the money demand curve to shift to the right. The rate of interest will rise at the current level of national income.

(c) *Shift downwards.* If the PSBR is funded in this manner, the money supply will increase. The rate of interest will fall at the current level of national income.

(d) *Shift upwards.* The transactions demand for money will rise. Thus the same reasoning as in (b) applies.

(e) *Shift downwards.* If domestic currency is expected to fall in value, the demand for it will fall. The liquidity preference curve will shift left, causing the rate of interest to fall at the current level of national income.

Q41. **(a)** *E.*

(b) At point A, given national income of Y_2 and a rate of interest of r_2, the economy is in goods-market equilibrium and money-market disequilibrium. The rate of interest r_2 would lead to a national income of Y_2. But at this level of income the demand for money is less than the supply (point A is above the *LM* curve). At this level of income, the money market would be in equilibrium at point B, at a rate of interest of r_3.

(c) The excess supply of money will cause the rate of interest to fall. This will lead to a movement along the *IS* curve as saving declines and investment picks up. National income will rise. The higher national income will lead to an increased transactions demand for money and hence a movement up along the *LM* curve. The process will continue until point E is reached.

(d) At point C, given national income of Y_3 and a rate of interest of r_4, the economy is in money-market equilibrium and goods-market disequilibrium. At this low rate of interest, the desired level of investment and saving are equal at point D.

(e) The excess of investment over saving at point C will cause the level of national income to rise. This will lead to a movement up along the *LM* curve and a rise in the rate of interest. As the rate of interest rises, the desired level of investment will fall and saving increase. This will cause a movement back along the IS curve until equilibrium is reached at point E.

(f) (i) This will cause the LM curve to shift downwards (towards a point such as D) as the money supply expands. The equilibrium rate of interest will fall and the level of national income will rise. The new equilibrium in both markets will be where the new LM curve intersects with the IS curve. (Thus in the case of point D, the equilibrium rate of interest would be r_4 and the equilibrium level of national income would be Y_4.)

(ii) This will cause the IS curve to shift right, towards a point such as F. This pushes interest rates and national income upwards. The new equilibrium is where the new IS curve intersects with the LM curve. In the case of point F, this would give a national income of Y_5 and a rate of interest of r_2.

Q42. *(a)* In Figure A20.2(a), the increase in government expenditure causes an increase in aggregate demand and a rightward shift in the IS curve to IS_2. If it is financed by an increase in the money supply, the LM curve will shift to LM_2. The rate of interest remains at r_1. Hence there is no crowding out and there is a full multiplier rise in income to Y_2.

(b) In Figure A20.2(b), the deterioration in business expectations causes a leftward shift in the IS curve to IS_2. If the government increases the money supply, this will shift the LM curve downwards. If income is to be maintained at Y_1, the LM curve must shift downwards to LM_2 and the rate of interest fall to r_3.

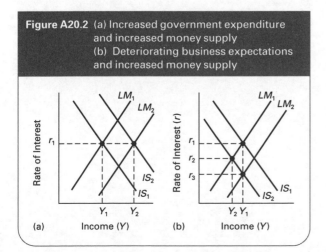

Figure A20.2 (a) Increased government expenditure and increased money supply
(b) Deteriorating business expectations and increased money supply

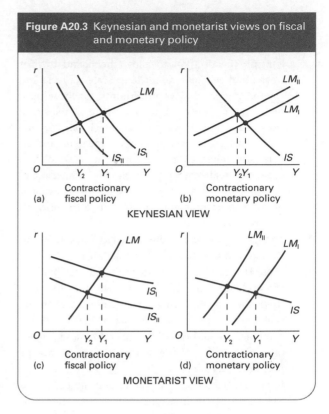

Figure A20.3 Keynesian and monetarist views on fiscal and monetary policy

Q43. See Figure A20.3. Given their assumptions about the shapes of the curves. Keynesians conclude that fiscal policy has a relatively large effect on aggregate demand, whereas monetary policy has a relatively small effect. Monetarists conclude the opposite.

Q44. (a), (d), (f) and (g) are all justifications used by the Keynesians for government intervention in the economy.

Q45. D. As the balance of payments moved into deficit, a deflationary policy was adopted in order to stop people buying imports and to improve the competitive position of UK exports by reducing the rate of inflation. As the economy slowed down and inflation fell, the balance payments would move into surplus. This was the cue for government to reflate the economy, and the start of a new cycle.

Q46. There are many arguments put forward to explain the stagflation of the 1970s. These include: a relaxation of monetary controls; a massive increase in the money supply in 1972/3; the move to floating exchange rates; the rise in oil prices; rising costs in the domestic economy; the decline in the UK's competitive position overseas; the effects of technology on jobs; poor expectations of future economic performance. (For a more comprehensive consideration of these points, see Sloman, *Economics*, 4th edn, pp. 589–91.)

Q47. (a), (b), (d) and (f) are all policies that characterised the approach to economic management in the early 1980s.

***Q*48.** A range of problems were encountered: the PSBR was very difficult to reduce; money supply measures moved in different directions and proved difficult to control; the decision to allow the pound to float freely, and the subsequent large-scale appreciation, created a great deal of uncertainty for those businesses trading overseas; the removing of credit controls contributed to the credit boom of the mid-1980s that proved to be too large to be sustainable; the reliance on high interest rates to curb spending created great difficulties for businesses and consumers. (For a more comprehensive assessment of these policy problems, see Sloman, *Economics*, 4th edn, pp. 591–2.)

***Q*49.** The D-Mark exchange rate was effectively targeted in the late 1980s (before entry to the ERM).

***Q*50.** *True*. The ERM imposed an exchange rate band. If the exchange rate moved to the limits of its band, then the government had to adopt appropriate policies to maintain the exchange rate value. For example, it could have been forced to raise interest rates if the value of the pound moved towards the bottom of its band.

***Q*51.** E. With a fixed exchange rate, monetary policy has to be geared to maintaining that exchange rate. This substantially reduces flexibility in the use of monetary policy. In the case of A, the UK inflation rate was *higher* than the European average. In the case of B,

fiscal policy was largely dominated by the domestic issue of reducing the growing PSBR. In the case of C and D, maintaining the exchange rate meant maintaining high rates of interest, and this tended to reduce the growth of the money supply and the growth of aggregate demand.

***Q*52.** *True*.

***Q*53.** *True*. The Monetary Policy Committee (MPC) is charged with targeting a rate of inflation of $2^1/_2$ per cent. It has to reduce interest rates if it believes that otherwise inflation would be below $2^1/_2$ per cent, and raise interest rates if it believes that otherwise inflation would be above $2^1/_2$ per cent.

***Q*54.** *False*. The ECB has set itself a target of maintaining inflation at no more than 2 per cent, but the rate can go *below* 2 per cent. Also, it has more discretion than the MPC in carrying out this policy.

***Q*55.** Monetarists favour rules because, they argue, they will reduce inflationary expectations and create a stable environment for investment and growth. Discretionary policy, by contrast, owing to time lags and uncertainty, will at best be ineffective, and at worst actually destabilise rather than stabilise the economy.

***Q*56.** Keynesians favour discretion because the economic environment is always changing; hence government must change its policy in response. Better forecasting and speedier action will help to increase the effectiveness of discretionary policy.

21 Macroeconomic Controversies II: Aggregate Supply, Unemployment and Inflation

A REVIEW

To what extent will aggregate supply respond to changes in aggregate demand? Will the effects be solely on prices? Or will they be solely on output and employment? Or will the effects be partly on prices and partly on output and employment, and if so, in what combination? As you will discover, the different schools of economics give different answers to these questions.

The nature of aggregate supply and its responsiveness to changes in aggregate demand will also determine the shape of the *Phillips curve*. It is the shape of the Phillips curve that has been at the centre of the *expectations revolution* in economics. Later in the chapter we will look at the theories of expectations and their implications for policies to tackle inflation and unemployment.

21.1 Aggregate supply

(Page 601) The effect that a change in aggregate demand has on the economy is determined by the nature and shape of the aggregate supply curve.

 Figure 21.1 illustrates two extreme aggregate supply curves. Aggregate supply curve I represents the extreme **Q1.** *Keynesian/monetarist* position, whereas aggregate supply curve II represents the extreme **Q2.** *Keynesian/monetarist* position.

Q3. Consider Figure 21.1. To which of the aggregate supply curves will the following statements apply?

(a) Up to the full-employment level of national income, an expansion in aggregate demand will progressively close a deflationary gap. AS_I/AS_{II}

(b) A rise in aggregate demand will have no effect on output and employment. AS_I/AS_{II}

(c) The only way to achieve higher levels of national income in the long run is through the use of supply-side policies. AS_I/AS_{II}

Figure 21.1 Different shaped aggregate supply curves

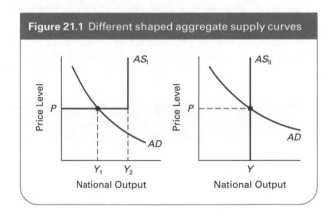

(d) Fiscal and monetary policy used to regulate aggregate demand will have a significant effect upon economic activity. AS_I/AS_{II}

When looking at aggregate supply we must distinguish between short-run and long-run *AS* curves.

(Pages 601–2) Short-run aggregate supply

To understand the short-run aggregate supply curve we need to look at its *microeconomic* foundations.

 Multiple Choice   Written answer   ◐ Delete wrong word   ⊖ Diagram/table manipulation   ⊗ Calculation   ▣ Matching/ordering

In the short run we assume that individual firms respond to a rise in demand for their product **Q4.** *by considering/ without considering* the effects of a general rise in demand on their suppliers and on the economy as a whole.

⊖ **Q5.** Figure 21.2 shows the profit-maximising price and output of a firm facing a downward-sloping demand curve. Look back to Chapters 5 and 6 (review sections 5.6 and 6.3) if you are uncertain of this material.

(a) Using Figure 21.2, show the effect of a rise in demand on price and output.

(b) Add a further *MC* curve that is flatter than the one already shown in the diagram (but still passes through point *x*). How does this influence the effect upon price and output of a rise in demand?

....

....

(c) Near full capacity, is the *MC* curve likely to become steeper or flatter?　　　　　　　　*steeper/flatter*

(d) Explain your answer to (c).

....

....

....

If there is now a *general* rise in demand in the economy, but firms assume that their cost curves are given (i.e. that the rise in demand for their products is not accompanied by a shift in their cost curves), then the aggregate supply curve

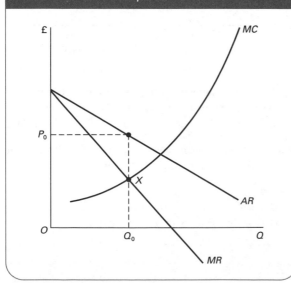

Figure 21.2 Profit-maximising price and output for a firm in an imperfect market

will be **Q6.** *horizontal/similar in shape to the MC curve illustrated in Figure 21.2/horizontal then vertical/vertical.*

(Pages 602–3) Long-run aggregate supply

In the long run (which might not be very long at all), we cannot assume that firms' cost curves are unaffected by a change in aggregate demand. Three factors will have an important influence on the aggregate supply curve in the long run: the *interdependence* of firms, *investment* and *expectations*.

⊖ **Q7.** Figure 21.3 illustrates two situations (diagrams (a) and (b)) in which the slope of the long-run aggregate supply curve is different from that of the short-run *AS* curve. In each diagram there is an initial increase in aggregate demand. In each situation we assume that in the long run firms' cost curves are affected by the change in aggregate demand. One situation is the result of firms being interdependent; the other, the result of investment by firms in response to the change in aggregate demand.

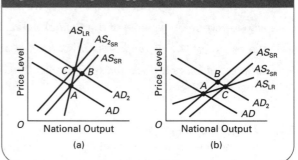

Figure 21.3 Long-run aggregate supply curves

(a) In which diagram is the interdependence of firms the dominant effect on the long-run *AS* curve?

　　　　　　　　　　　　Diagram(a)/Diagram(b)

(b) Explain the reason for your answer.

....

....

(c) Explain why the diagram you did not select in (a) represents the impact of new investment on aggregate supply.

....

....

....

◗ **Q8.** Expectations can make the long-run *AS* curve either steeper or shallower than the short-run *AS* curve.

Which of the following effects of a rise in aggregate demand will make the long-run *AS* curve steeper, and which will make it shallower?

(a) People expect that the rise in aggregate demand will lead to a general rise in prices. *steeper/shallower*

(b) People expect that the rise in aggregate demand will lead to firms increasing the level of investment. *steeper/shallower*

(c) People expect that the rise in aggregate demand will cause unemployment to fall. *steeper/shallower*

(d) People expect that the rise in aggregate demand will cause a general rise in wages throughout the economy. *steeper/shallower*

(e) People expect that the rise in aggregate demand will lead to increased economic growth. *steeper/shallower*

(f) People expect that the rise in aggregate demand will strengthen the bargaining position of trade unions. *steeper/shallower*

(Pages 603–5) Aggregate supply, the labour market and unemployment

What is the relationship between aggregate supply and unemployment?

⊖ **Q9.** Figure 21.4 shows short-run aggregate demand and supply of labour curves. The total labour force is shown by curve N; the effective supply of labour (those working plus others willing and able to work) is shown by curve AS_L. Aggregate demand for labour is initially given by AD_{L_1} and the wage rate by W_1.

(a) How much is equilibrium unemployment?

....

(b) How much is disequilibrium unemployment?

....

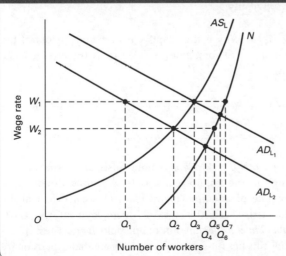

Figure 21.4 Short-run response to a fall in aggregate demand in the labour market

Now assume that aggregate demand falls to AD_{L_2} and that wages are *flexible* downwards.

(c) How much is total unemployment now?

....

(d) How much is disequilibrium unemployment?

....

(e) How much is equilibrium unemployment?

....

Now assume that aggregate demand has again fallen from AD_{L_1} to AD_{L_2}, but that this time wages are fixed at W_1.

(f) How much is total unemployment this time?

....

(g) How much is disequilibrium unemployment?

....

(h) How much is equilibrium unemployment?

....

▤ **Q10.** Keynesian models of long-run aggregate supply make one or more of four assumptions. Which of the following is *not* one of these four?

A. The existence of money illusion.

B. Firms will take on more labour only if there is a fall in the real wage rate.

C. Downward stickiness of wages.

D. Expectations by firms that changes in aggregate demand will affect sales.

E. Hysteresis.

(Pages 605–7) Aggregate demand and supply, and inflation

So far we have used aggregate supply and demand analysis to illustrate the effect of a single increase in aggregate demand and a single increase in the price level. Aggregate demand and aggregate supply analysis can also be used to illustrate the causes of *inflation* (the rate of *increase* in prices). It can be used to distinguish between demand-pull and cost-push pressures on inflation.

⊖ **Q11.** This question is based on Figure 21.5 and illustrates an inflationary sequence that starts with *demand-pull* pressures. The economy is initially at point X on curves AD_1 and AS_1. Each of the following events will shift either the *AD* or the *AS* curve. Assuming they occur in a sequence, to which point on the diagram will the economy move after each event?

(a) The government undertakes an extensive new programme of public works.

point ....

(b) Subsequently the government decides to fund the programme by selling bonds to the banking sector in an attempt to prevent crowding out.

point ....

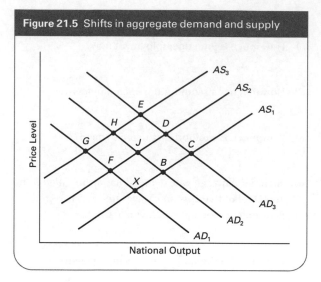

Figure 21.5 Shifts in aggregate demand and supply

(c) Higher production costs have a knock-on effect throughout industry.

point ....

(d) Workers demand higher wages to cover rising costs of living.

point ....

⊖ **Q12.** This question is also based on Figure 21.5 but this time illustrates an inflationary sequence that starts with *cost-push* pressures. To which point on the diagram will the economy move after each of the following events, which, as before, shift either the *AD* or the *AS* curve? Again assume that point *X* is the starting point and that each event follows the previous one.

(a) Firms expect their suppliers' prices to rise following the collapse of an agreement between government and unions over pay restraint.

point ....

(b) Trade unions demand and get higher wages.

point ....

(c) Falling national output and rising unemployment persuade the government to increase public expenditure.

point ....

(d) The government, believing that its fiscal policy is inadequate, decides to cut interest rates.

point ....

21.2 Inflation and unemployment: the moderate monetarist position

(Pages 607–9) The Phillips curve had an important influence upon economic thinking and analysis during the 1960s and 1970s.

▤ **Q13.** The original Phillips curve showed:

A. the influence of fiscal policy on the level of inflation and unemployment.

B. the direct relationship between price inflation and unemployment.

C. the relationship between aggregate labour demand and aggregate labour supply in the long run.

D. the inverse relationship between wage inflation and unemployment.

E. the effect of expectations about changes in economic activity on the level of unemployment.

The main contribution of the monetarists to the study of the Phillips curve was to introduce the effects of expectations. The moderate monetarists have a theory based upon adaptive expectations.

▤ **Q14.** Adaptive expectations state that:

A. people never make the same mistake twice.

B. people adapt their expectations according to the policies the government is currently pursuing.

C. expectations are formed on the basis of information from the past.

D. expectations are based upon forecasts made about the future performance of the economy.

E. government economic policy will always be predicted and hence people will adapt to it before it takes effect.

▤ **Q15.** Which of the following equations are consistent with the adaptive expectations theory?

(i) $\dot{P}^e_t = a\dot{P}_t$

(ii) $\dot{P}^e_t = a\dot{P}_{t-1}$

(iii) $\dot{P}_t = b + c(1/U) + d\dot{P}^e_t$

(iv) $\dot{P}_t = b + c(1/U) + d\dot{P}^e_{t-1}$

where $\dot{P}$ is the percentage annual rate of inflation, $\dot{P}^e$ is the expected rate of inflation, t is the time period and U is the percentage rate of unemployment.

A. (i) and (iii).

B. (ii) and (iii).

C. (i) and (iv).

D. (ii) and (iv).

E. (iv) only.

⑦ **Q16.** Why is the adaptive expectations theory of the Phillips curve sometimes referred to as the *accelerationist theory*?

....

....

(Pages 609–12) Moderate monetarists argue that in the long run the Phillips curve is **Q17.** *horizontal/vertical*. At this rate of unemployment, real *AD* is equal to real *AS*. Monetarists call this rate of unemployment the **Q18.** *natural rate/accelerating rate* of unemployment. The implications this has for government policy are that expansionary monetary (and fiscal) policy will only have the effect of

reducing unemployment in **Q19.** *the long run/the short run.* In the **Q20.** *long run/short run,* the effect of expansionary policy will be purely inflationary.

⊖ **Q21.** Figure 21.6 shows an economy moving clockwise over time from points *A* to *J* and back to *A* again.

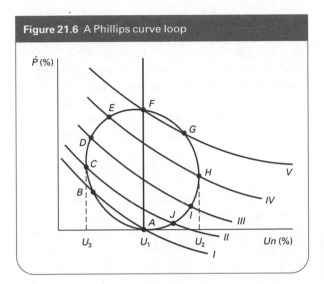

Figure 21.6 A Phillips curve loop

(a) What is the natural rate of unemployment? $U_1/U_2/U_3$
(b) What is the non-accelerating inflation rate of unemployment (NAIRU)? $U_1/U_2/U_3$
(c) Between what points will the economy experience positive demand-pull pressures on inflation?

....

(d) Between what points will the economy experience stagflation?

....

(e) How could the economy move from point *F* back to point *A* more rapidly?

....

◗ **Q22.** A fall in the rate of frictional unemployment will cause the Phillips curve to shift to the right. *True/False*

21.3 Inflation and unemployment: the new classical position

(Pages 613–17) The *new* classical economists take an extreme view of the Phillips curve and the aggregate supply curve. They argue that both curves are vertical in **Q23.** *the short run alone/the long run alone/both the short run and the long run/neither the short run nor the long run.* Therefore the effect of any expansionary monetary policy will be simply to **Q24.** *raise prices/increase output and employment.*

The new classical school assumes that markets clear **Q25.** *very slowly/virtually instantaneously.* Therefore all unemployment is **Q26.** *voluntary/involuntary.*

The new classical economists reject adaptive expectations theory. Instead they base their analysis on *rational expectations.*

◗ **Q27.** Rational expectations theory states that:
(a) Expectations are formed using currently available information. *True/False*
(b) Errors in prediction are made at random and therefore do not result in systematic divergences between the actual and expected rate of inflation. *True/False*
(c) The current economic situation will have only limited impact on expectations. *True/False*
(d) Expectations are based on imperfect information. *True/False*

⊖ **Q28.** Figure 21.7 shows the effects upon price and output of a rise in the level of aggregate demand under rational expectations. Aggregate demand rises from AD_1 to AD_2.

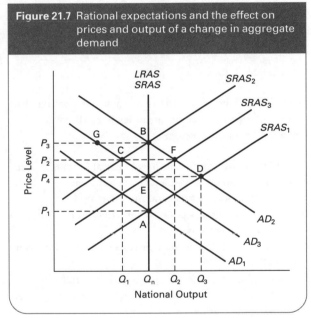

Figure 21.7 Rational expectations and the effect on prices and output of a change in aggregate demand

(a) Assuming the long-run *AS* curve is vertical, then given rational expectations theory, to which point on Figure 21.7 will the economy move in the *short run*, assuming that people correctly predict that the *AD* curve will shift to AD_2?

....

(b) If expectations prove to be incorrect, and people anticipate that aggregate demand will rise only to AD_3 and that the price level will rise only to P_4, to what point will the economy move in the short run?

....

(c) Returning to point *A*, assume now that aggregate demand in reality only increases to AD_3, but that people *over*predict the rate of inflation and believe in effect that aggregate demand will rise to AD_2 and that

prices will rise to P_3. To what point will the economy move in the short run?

....

(?) **Q29.** What happens to the Phillips curve if inflation is (a) underpredicted and (b) overpredicted?

(a) ....

....

(b) ....

....

(Pages 617–18) One of the major criticisms made of the new classical approach concerns the assumption of perfect wage and price flexibility.

(?) **Q30.** Why is total price and wage flexibility unrealistic?

....

....

....

Even with this criticism, the new classical school has had an important influence on attitudes towards government management of the economy.

(≣) **Q31.** According to the new classical school, governments should, in order to manage the economy:
A. use discretionary fiscal and monetary policy.
B. use only monetary policy when attempting to increase output and employment.
C. leave everything to market forces and not intervene at all.
D. announce monetary rules to control inflation and attempt to reduce voluntary unemployment by liberalising the market.
E. announce monetary rules to control inflation and otherwise do not interfere with the market.

If new classical economists argue that unemployment deviates from its natural rate only very temporarily and by chance, how do they explain cyclical fluctuations in unemployment and output? They have developed 'real business cycle theory' to explain this.

(≣) **Q32.** Real business cycle theory explains cyclical fluctuations in terms of:
A. fluctuations in real aggregate demand (i.e. after correcting for inflation).
B. fluctuations in the money supply, caused by banks expanding credit in anticipation of real increases in output and hence demand.

C. the effects of changes in rational expectations on real output.
D. fluctuations in aggregate supply, caused by technological or structural changes in the economy that take place over a number of months.
E. fluctuations in real output causing changes in expectations.

21.4 Inflation and unemployment: the modern Keynesian position
(Pages 619–23)

(◗) **Q33.** Which of the following are given as reasons by Keynesians for the problem of both higher inflation and higher unemployment in the 1980s and 1990s (or at least a worse trade-off) than in the 1950s and 1960s?
(a) An increase in equilibrium unemployment (at least up to the early 1990s). *Yes/No*
(b) Expectations of higher inflation and/or higher unemployment. *Yes/No*
(c) High unemployment persisting after the end of a recession (hysteresis). *Yes/No*
(d) Unions targeting real wage increases. *Yes/No*
(e) A growth in monopoly power. *Yes/No*
(f) The absence of a trade-off, even in the short run, between inflation and unemployment. *Yes/No*

(?) **Q34.** Why are 'insider workers' in firms able to secure higher wage rates, if there are 'outsiders' willing to work at lower wage rates?

....

....

(◗) **Q35.** According to Keynesians, which of the following are suitable policies to tackle the problem of hysteresis?
(a) An increase in aggregate demand. *Yes/No*
(b) Retraining programmes. *Yes/No*
(c) Grants to firms to take on the long-term unemployed. *Yes/No*
(d) A tight monetary policy. *Yes/No*

(◗) **Q36.** Modern Keynesians argue that structural changes experienced by the economy over recent years have resulted in higher levels of technological, structural and frictional unemployment. They argue that freer markets would solve this problem. *True/False*

(?) **Q37.** Give two reasons why modern Keynesians reject the notion of a natural rate of unemployment.

1. ....

2. ....

(◗) **Q38.** Modern Keynesians are critical of free-market thinking, arguing that government policy should involve the maintenance of a steady expansion of demand.
True/False

PROBLEMS, EXERCISES AND PROJECTS

Table 21.1 An expectations-augmented inflation function: $\dot{P}_t = (40/U - 4) + \dot{P}_t^e$

Year	U	40/U − 4	+	$\dot{P}^e$	=	$\dot{P}$
0	...	...	+	...	=	...
1	...	...	+	...	=	...
2	...	...	+	...	=	...
3	...	...	+	...	=	...
4	...	...	+	...	=	...
5	...	...	+	...	=	...
6	...	...	+	...	=	...
7	...	...	+	...	=	...

Q39. Assume that inflation depends on two things: the level of aggregate demand, indicated by the inverse of the rate of unemployment ($1/U$), and the expected rate of inflation ($\dot{P}_t^e$). Assume that the rate of inflation ($\dot{P}_t$) is given by the equation:

$$\dot{P}_t = 40/U - 4 + \dot{P}_t^e$$

Assume initially (year 0) that the actual and expected rate of inflation is zero.

(a) What is the current (natural) rate of unemployment?

....

(b) Now assume in year 1 that the government wishes to reduce unemployment to 5 per cent and continues to expand aggregate demand by as much as is necessary to achieve this. Fill in the rows for years 0 to 4 of Table 21.1. It is assumed for simplicity that the expected rate of inflation in a given year ($\dot{P}_t^e$) is equal to the actual rate of inflation in the previous year ($\dot{P}_{t-1}$).

(c) Now assume in year 5 that the government, worried about rising inflation, reduces aggregate demand sufficiently to reduce inflation by 2 per cent in that year. What must the rate of unemployment be raised to in that year?

....

(d) Assuming that unemployment stays at this high level, continue Table 21.1 for years 5 to 7.

Q40. In Tables 21.2 and 21.3, you are provided with unemployment and consumer price data for three countries.

Table 21.2 Unemployment rates (percentage)

	1970	1971	1972	1973	1974	1975	1976	1977	1978	1979	1980	1981	1982	1983	1984
USA	5.0	6.0	5.6	4.9	5.6	8.3	7.7	7.0	6.1	5.8	7.2	7.6	9.7	9.6	7.1
Japan	1.2	1.2	1.4	1.3	1.4	1.9	2.0	2.0	2.2	2.1	2.0	2.2	2.3	2.7	2.6
France	2.5	2.7	2.8	2.7	3.0	4.3	4.5	5.0	5.4	6.0	6.4	7.6	8.2	8.4	10.2

	1985	1986	1987	1988	1989	1990	1991	1992	1993	1994	1995	1996	1997	1998	1999
	7.1	7.0	6.2	5.4	5.2	5.4	6.6	7.3	6.7	6.0	5.6	5.5	4.9	4.4	5.0
	2.6	2.8	2.8	2.5	2.3	2.1	2.1	2.2	2.5	2.9	3.2	3.4	3.4	4.6	4.6
	10.2	10.4	10.5	10.0	9.4	8.9	9.4	10.3	11.7	12.3	11.6	12.4	12.4	11.5	11.2

Source: OECD. © OECD Publications.

Table 21.3 Consumer prices (annual percentage increase)

	1970	1971	1972	1973	1974	1975	1976	1977	1978	1979	1980	1981	1982	1983	1984
USA	5.8	4.3	3.3	6.2	11.1	9.1	5.7	6.5	7.6	11.2	13.5	10.3	6.1	3.2	4.3
Japan	7.7	6.1	4.5	11.7	24.5	11.8	9.3	8.1	3.8	3.6	8.0	4.9	2.7	1.9	2.2
France	5.2	5.5	6.2	7.3	13.7	11.8	9.6	9.4	9.1	10.8	13.6	13.4	11.8	9.6	7.4

	1985	1986	1987	1988	1989	1990	1991	1992	1993	1994	1995	1996	1997	1998	1999
	3.5	1.9	3.6	4.1	4.8	5.5	4.2	3.0	3.0	2.5	2.9	2.9	2.3	1.6	2.0
	2.1	0.4	−0.2	0.5	2.3	3.1	3.3	1.6	1.3	0.7	−0.1	0.0	1.7	−0.1	−0.6
	5.8	2.7	3.1	2.6	3.7	3.4	3.2	2.4	2.1	1.7	1.8	2.0	1.2	0.2	0.6

Source: OECD. © OECD Publications.

(*a*) Using the data, plot inflation against unemployment for each country, clearly marking the year of each point.

(*b*) Can you identify any Phillips curve loops?

(*c*) Does the evidence suggest that the Phillips curves have shifted to the right over time?

(*d*) Do you think that the Phillips curve relationship is of any value to economic policy makers?

Q41. Figure 21.8 gives a monetarist perspective of the relationship between real GDP, unemployment and inflation over the course of the business cycle.

(*a*) Explain the relationship between actual and real GDP, unemployment and inflation at each of the points 1–7 in the top part of the diagram. Why does the top of the curve in the top diagram (point 6) not correspond to the bottom and top respectively of the curves in the other two parts of the diagram (point 5)?

(*b*) If the magnitude of the cycle in the top part of the diagram became greater, would there be a similar change in magnitude in the fluctuations in unemployment and inflation?

(*c*) To what extent would (i) a Keynesian and (ii) a new classicist agree with the relationships portrayed in the diagram?

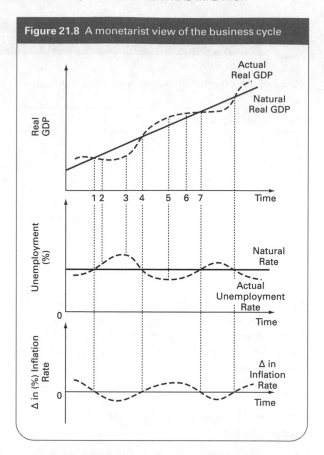

Figure 21.8 A monetarist view of the business cycle

DISCUSSION TOPICS AND ESSAYS

Q42. How does the shape of the aggregate supply curve affect the relationship between inflation and unemployment?

Q43. Why will the long-run aggregate supply curve have a different slope from the short-run aggregate supply curve? What determines the relationship between the two?

Q44. What is meant by the 'natural' rate of unemployment? Is it possible to reduce unemployment below the natural rate in (a) the short run and (b) the long run?

Q45. Distinguish between adaptive and rational expectations and describe how they are formed. What effect will each type of expectation have on the relationship between inflation and unemployment?

Q46. Outline the main assumptions made by the new classical school and describe the implications these assumptions have for macroeconomic policy.

Q47. If real wages are 'sticky' downwards, what implications does this have for the shape of the Phillips curve and for government macroeconomic policy?

Q48. How do new Keynesians explain the persistence of unemployment in the recoveries of the mid-1980s and mid-1990s?

Q49. Debate
Governments invariably resort to demand-side policies for short-term political gain. But such policies are useless in the long run as a means of increasing aggregate supply.

ARTICLES

One of the true strengths of a theory or idea is how it changes people's views and understanding of the world around them. Rational expectations is one such influential theory. The article below, taken from *The Economist* of 14 October 1995, assesses the work of Robert Lucas in developing rational expectations theory.

Great expectations, and rational too

Robert Lucas, a professor at the University of Chicago, is the most influential macroeconomist of his generation. Mr Lucas developed the idea known as 'rational expectations'. His work transformed both macroeconomic theory and the way that economists think about the effects of economic policies.

Expectations are fundamental to economic behaviour. A trade union negotiating with employers, say, will base its wage demands in part on its forecast of inflation. And the final deal will affect the actual inflation rate once it feeds through to prices. By definition, you might think, expectations are forward-looking. But until the 1970s, economists modelled expectations as if they were based on the past: next year's expected inflation rate might be a weighted average of current and past rates. That was not daft: it is impossible to observe expectations directly; and it is reasonable to suppose that they will be based largely on experience.

Yet it was wrong, because it supposed that people might go on believing what they knew to be false. Mr Lucas was not the first to see this. In the early 1960s, John Muth, another economist, argued that it would be better to assume that people have 'rational expectations'. These are forward-looking, in that they are based on all data to hand; expectations that are persistently wrong will be discarded.

Mr Lucas showed just how important this simple idea is. Governments' models of the economy are, of necessity, based on the past behaviour of consumers and firms. But unless they incorporate rational expectations, said Mr Lucas, they are useless for assessing changes in economic policy. This is because economic behaviour in the past will have depended on the economic policies of the time. When governments change their policies, expectations will change too; so the economy's response to a new policy may be different from what governments expect.

Although this principle is quite general, the best-known examples concern monetary policy. Until the 1970s, governments thought they could buy lower unemployment with a bit more inflation. That conceit had already been shredded by Milton Friedman, another Nobel prizewinner from Chicago, and Edmund Phelps, another American economist. But they had used backward-looking expectations. By applying rational expectations, Mr Lucas nailed the illusion for good.

In the short run, an inflationary monetary policy will boost jobs – but only because firms are fooled into thinking that a rise in the price they can charge signals stronger demand for their goods; in fact, it merely reflects a rise in prices in general. In the long run, under rational expectations, there can be no trade-off between inflation and unemployment, because people cannot be fooled for ever. Once they see that inflation has risen, unemployment will return to its old level.

Many forecasting models now include at least some element of rational expectations. For instance, predictions about the inflation rate that people will come to expect are typically made consistent with the model's own predictions of inflation. The one used by America's Federal Reserve is being revised to make its characterisation of the bond market more forward-looking; in the labour market, where adjustment to news is slower, expectations based on history will also still be used.

Warning governments against bad policy based on unreliable models is all very well. But how do rational expectations help them to choose a policy? To some economists and politicians in the early 1980s, one answer looked obvious. To reduce inflation, governments had to do little more than announce a strict monetary target. In the face of such a tough policy, workers, consumers and firms would expect lower inflation. They would moderate their wage demands and prices, and – hey presto – inflation would tumble at little cost in output and jobs.

How to be believed

That idea turned out to be wrong, but not because of any flaw in the notion of rational expectations. One reason was that markets do not always 'clear' quickly – i.e., supply and demand may be out of balance for a while – so unemployment may rise when monetary policy is tightened. 'New Keynesian' economists, such as Mr Mankiw, say that wages and prices take time to adjust, so that markets often clear only slowly. However, such theories often assume that expectations are rational.

The principle also explains why neither an announcement of tight money nor even a brief period of monetary stringency will lead quickly to low inflation: governments may not be believed. If people do not think that the government is in earnest, they will go on expecting high inflation. So financial markets will continue to demand high bond yields; workers will not curb their pay demands, nor will firms hold down prices.

Thus, again thanks to Mr Lucas, economists are now obsessed with the issues of credibility and sustainability. Can governments keep their promises, and for how long? Post-Lucasian economics recognises that governments are perpetually in temptation: although tough policies eventually bring the benefits of low inflation, politicians can earn popularity through an unexpected burst of inflation, which temporarily boosts incomes and employment; but if they succumb, their credibility is lost.

© *The Economist*, London (14th October, 1995)

(a) What makes rational expectations 'rational'?

(b) How did the theory of rational expectations, developed by Lucas, differ from the accepted way in which expectations were seen to be formed?

(c) How has the theory of rational expectations influenced the process of policy making?

The following are extracts from an article by Rod Cross which appeared in the *New Economy* of Spring 1996. Cross argues that the concept of a 'natural rate of unemployment' is based on the notion of a self-adjusting equilibrium – a concept lying at the heart of most mainstream economics and one borrowed from century physics. He argues that a more appropriate notion (or 'metaphor') would be that of hysteresis.

The physics of unemployment

Obsession with equilibrium stems from an old physics metaphor

What do the following propositions have in common?

- The drop in output and rise in unemployment that result from macroeconomic policy measures to reduce inflation – as used in 1979–81 and 1990–92 – are only temporary phenomena.

- Policies to stimulate demand would have only short-term beneficial effects for output and employment.

- The upward ratchets in unemployment since the mid-1960s can be explained only by increases in labour market rigidities and supply-side inflexibilities – such as over-generous unemployment benefits, minimum wages and trade union power – which have raised the natural, or equilibrium, rates of unemployment.

- A return to a lower, full-employment equilibrium can be achieved only by supply-side strategies.

The most obvious link is that these cornerstones of policy debates since the 1970s are part of the 'natural rate of unemployment' doctrine regarding what causes, and what can be done about, unemployment. If the propositions followed from self-evident or highly plausible accounts of economic systems that were well supported by empirical evidence, there would be little point in pursuing the matter further. But as many commentators have pointed out, this is not the case: the coarseness of the analysis, and the weakness of the empirical results, suggest there is some other reason why intelligent and well-intentioned economists might adhere to such propositions.

As Keynes remarked, the influence of ideas, for good or evil, is more powerful than is commonly understood. Keynes himself railed against the idea that economic systems are self-adjusting, with temporary disturbances having no effect on equilibrium levels of output and unemployment.

It turns out that this notion of a self-adjusting equilibrium, which has remained at the centre of mainstream economic analysis, was not invented by economists but borrowed from 19th century physics during the neoclassical economics 'revolution' of the 1870s. This metaphorical borrowing involved the assumption that economic systems behave, in important respects, like the physical systems described in Newtonian mechanics, or conservative fields of force. The metaphor was retained when neoclassical economics was re-specified using formal mathematical axioms in the 1950s (as in the Arrow–Debreu 'general equilibrium' model). Present-day economists who adhere to the propositions cited at the beginning of this article are thus, albeit indirectly, deriving their language from Newtonian mechanics or conservative fields of physical force. In doing so, they beg the question of whether such metaphors are appropriate to economic systems.

Alternative metaphors

. . . Metaphors have played an important role in the articulation of alternative theories of economic systems: theories of economic systems: theories of evolution in biology, and notions of self-organisation and self-reinforcement in physical systems, have provided fertile sources. The policy implications of applying alternative metaphors to economic systems can be illustrated by replacing the neoclassical metaphor of a conservative field of force with that of hysteresis.

Hysteresis

Shortly after the field of force vision of physical reality emerged, physicists in Germany, France and Britain observed that electromagnetic fields in ferric metals did not behave in accord with Maxwell's equations. Instead, they displayed the property of hysteresis. This term was coined by the physicist James Ewing in 1881 to describe the process whereby the application and removal of a temporary magnetising force is not followed by a return to the initial magnetic field characteristics, but instead leads to a change in the field, at least some of the groups of atoms affected remaining magnetised. A general

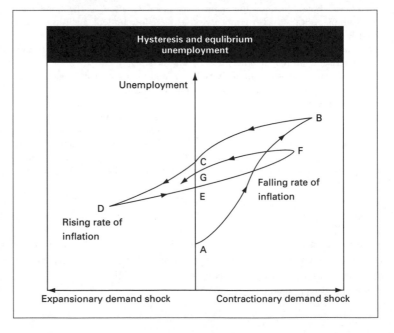

Hysteresis and equlibrium unemployment

definition is that hysteresis effects are those that remain after the initial causes giving rise to the effects are removed.

Hysteresis and unemployment

The implications of this metaphor for unemployment are illustrated in the chart. The axes, which show how unemployment responds to temporary demand shocks, could just as well show how electromagnetic fields in ferric metals respond to a magnetising force. The contraction in demand of 1979–81 sees unemployment increase along the trajectory AB. At B the rate of inflation falls and, as the level of real demand recovers, unemployment falls to a new equilibrium at C. This is higher than the initial level at A because not all the effects of a recession are reversible: workers experiencing long spells of unemployment are tainted by the experience, and firms made bankrupt do not reappear in production by some magic of reversibility. The equilibrium rate of unemployment thus displays hysteresis in the form of higher unemployment in the new steady inflation equilibrium of 1984–87.

The expansionary shock of 1988–89 reduces unemployment along the trajectory CD; but at D the rate of inflation is increasing, the level of real demand starts to fall, and unemployment rises back towards a new equilibrium at E along the trajectory DE. In 1990–92, this equilibrium is disturbed by the contractionary demand effects of moving to, and maintaining, an Exchange Rate Mechanism parity of DM2.95, leading to an increase in unemployment along the trajectory EF. At F the rate of inflation falls and, as the level of real demand recovers, further stimulated by the departure from the ERM in 1992, unemployment falls back along the trajectory FG towards a steady inflation equilibrium at G.

How hysteresis happens

. . . The implications of the non-linear, heterogeneous responses to shocks which characterise systems with hysteresis are 'remanence' and 'selective memory'. 'Remanence' means that an increase in demand followed by a decrease of the same amount will lead to a higher equilibrium level of output rather than the previous state, whereas a decrease in demand followed by an increase of the same amount will leave lower equilibrium output in its wake. The 'selective memory' property is that the equilibrium level of output at any point in time does not depend on all the past shocks experienced, but only on the extreme values which have not been superseded. Thus, the equilibrium level of output in the United Kingdom at present would still bear the marks of the slumps of 1979–81 and 1990–92, and of the 1988–89 boom.

The bad news for policy

The bad news is that the recessions in output and employment engendered by anti-inflation squeezes on demand, as in the UK in 1979–81 and 1990–92, are not temporary, as the natural rate orthodoxy would suggest. They remain even after economic recovery occurs. This is the implication of remanence: workers made unemployed and firms becoming bankrupt or closing down plants during recessions are not all converted back into jobs or production by a reversible arrow of time. Instead, there is a choice to be made between the benefits of a lower, steady rate of inflation, and the cost of the lower output and higher unemployment in the new equilibrium. The benefits and costs in this trade-off depend on how the initial equilibrium for the economy was shaped by previous recessions and booms.

The good news for policy

The other side of the coin is that higher output and lower unemployment will remain in a new steady inflation equilibrium reached after a temporary expansion of demand. Thus, the hysteresis framework provides a means of restat- ing the case that government demand stimuli can yield sustainable increases in output and unemployment. There will be some costs in terms of having a higher rate of inflation in the new equilibrium, but the actual increase in the inflation rate may be quite small.

Further, the selective memory property implies that demand stimuli, especially when coordinated between nations, could wipe out many of the legacies of past recessions so evident in the UK and international economies at present.

Two blades

The natural rate orthodoxy continues to hold sway over much of the contemporary discussion about unemployment. Hence the preoccupation with seeking out supply-side rigidities to explain rising unemployment, and hence the infatuation with supply-side cures for unemployment.

The problem is that natural rate models have been singularly unsuccessful in explaining the upward ratchets in unemployment since the 1970s, and that the supply-side measures taken since the 1980s to reduce unemployment have been accompanied by higher, not lower, unemployment. Perceptions about the world are heavily coloured by the models or metaphors employed. It could well be that the standard metaphor of equilibrium underlying the natural rate orthodoxy is the culprit.

Changing the metaphor might help. Viewing equilibria for output and unemployment by way of the hysteresis metaphor produces a different view of what explains and what can be done about unemployment. Supply-side measures, as one blade of the pair of scissors, still have an important role, but the other blade – demand – is restored to working order in the hysteresis framework. This not only provides a more coherent explanation of unemployment, but also presents a less dispiriting view of what can be done to cure unemployment.

© *New Economy*, 1996

(a) Why would the rate of unemployment in an economy recovering from a recession not fall back to previous levels?

(b) What are the implications of hysteresis for demand management policy?

(c) Are hysteresis models consistent with clockwise Phillips loops?

(d) What would be an appropriate mix of demand-side and supply-side policies to achieve substantial reductions in unemployment?

In the article below, taken from *New Economy* of August 1999, Geoffrey Dicks and John O'Sullivan consider the value of NAIRU as a guide for policy, and how theory, reality and policy action do not always seem to correspond.

Is NAIRU worth a can of beans?

In the first half of 1998, unemployment was falling slowly and from August it was virtually stable at a rate of 4.6 per cent according to the claimant count, or 6.2 per cent on the ILO survey definition. Private-sector earnings growth peaked at 6.3 per cent in May 1998 and, on the headline measure, fell throughout the rest of the year. To anyone schooled in the NAIRU analytical framework, the implications are self-evident: since earnings were decelerating, unemployment must have been above the NAIRU.

The analysis could be refined by examining what was happening to real wages – falling, against the yardstick of underlying inflation which was stable at 2.5 to 2.6 per cent in the second half of the year – or to settlements which were edging lower. But without a more complex theory that brings in inflation expectations or lagged adjustment, the basic premise is inescapable. Unemployment at the start of 1999 had not fallen far enough to generate higher wage inflation – it must have been above the NAIRU.

In the first half of 1998 it all seemed very different. Interest rates reached a peak of 7.5 per cent in June 1998. The immediate cause of the final rate hike was the strength of earnings, particularly in the private sector, which confirmed the growing conviction of the Monetary Policy Committee (MPC) that output had risen significantly above trend and that unemployment had fallen below the level consistent with the inflation target.

Evidence has emerged over the last month that the cumulative tightening of the labour market has resulted in a rate of private sector earnings growth that jeopardises achievement of the inflation target over the medium term. (MPC statement accompanying the hike in interest rates to 7.5 per cent, 4 June 1998)

The next three months saw newspaper columnists and leader writers compete with City economists to produce the most hair-shirt estimate of how far unemployment would have to rise

simply to stabilise inflation at the 2.5 per cent target.

How can the data from the second half of 1998 be interpreted? What seemed clear cut in June 1998 – that unemployment had fallen below the NAIRU and earnings were accelerating – was turned on its head as unemployment continued to fall and employment to rise. Yet all the froth went out of earnings. In the MPC's analysis, the labour market was at a 'turning point', begging the question as to whether a turning point was all that was necessary. In fact, is the whole analytical concept of the NAIRU worth a can of beans?

Nice concept . . .

Successive generations of MBA students at the London Business School in the 1980s were schooled in the NAIRU/output gap framework (by Alan Budd before us): that there is no trade-off between output and inflation in the long term; that there comes a point at which excess demand in the labour market results in accelerating wages, and that attempts to hold unemployment below the rate consistent with stable wage growth are ultimately self-defeating (since they produce rising inflation), all make intuitive sense. There seems to be no difficulty with the concept as such.

It came as no surprise therefore to read in the minutes of the MPC's December 1997 meeting (the first that Alan Budd attended as a member) that the focus of the discussion was shifting away from rates of growth of demand and output towards levels of output and unemployment. The following passage from the minutes sets out definitively how the MPC was looking at the economy in the first half of 1998.

The Committee began by discussing the importance to its assessment of the inflation outlook of levels of economic variables as well as their growth rates . . . Above-trend growth rates of output and employment need not entail short-run inflationary pressures when there was plenty of spare capacity, as was typically the case when the economy was coming out of a prolonged recession.

But as spare capacity was used up, underlying inflationary pressures would increase.

Once the level of economic activity was above trend and/or the level of unemployment below the natural rate, increasing inflation would generally result. If the levels of output and employment then remained above trend, inflationary pressures would be exacerbated, requiring a more severe or prolonged slowdown to bring them back to trend levels.

From concept to application

The message is clear. A recovery that began in 1992 had, by early 1998, exhausted the spare capacity built up in the recession of the early 1990s. The MPC probably endorsed Treasury estimates which suggested that output was about on trend in the first half of 1997 and that by the turn of the year there was a (positive) output gap of around one per cent of GDP. Similarly, for the labour market. Unemployment had been falling steadily since early 1993 and, while the initial effect on wages was negligible, average earnings had, since early 1995, been on a rising trend. Put the two together and it was clear to the MPC that above-trend output and unsustainable low unemployment posed a major threat to the 2.5 per cent inflation target.

The MPC has been consistently cautious in its assessment. Even when it was spooked by a sudden jump in earnings growth last spring and raised rates to 7.5 per cent, its language was still that of central bankers: 'the earnings data *suggested* that it was *more likely* that unemployment was below the rate compatible with stable inflation. In that case, it was *probable* that unemployment would have to rise to hit the inflation target on a sustainable basis.' (MPC Minutes, June, 1998).

Where the MPC was cautious, others were more dogmatic, believing that the trend in average earnings growth, upwards since early 1995, said it all. The leader writers on the *Financial Times* typified the attitude: 'pay inflation has been rising since unemployment fell much below eight per cent [claimant count]. The labour market reforms of the past two decades seem to have left the structural rate of unemployment at between seven per cent and eight per cent, two to three percentage points greater than today.' (*Financial Times* 17 July)

Not content with that, they went on the offensive again two months later: '. . . unemployment must now be allowed to rise – perhaps by 500 000 – to bring the economy back to a non-inflationary path.' (*Financial Times* 11 September 1998) prompting our reply: 'by arguing for a 500 000 rise in unemployment you are implicitly saying that unemployment has been below the natural rate for two and a half years. If the strict theory of the NAIRU has any validity, by now inflation should surely be on an increasing (accelerating?) trend. Is it? Quite the reverse. Does this not imply that there is something wrong with the theory?' (*Financial Times* 15 September, 1998).

. . . shame about the application

Even if the concept of the NAIRU is acceptable or the output gap is a useful analytical tool, it is possible to take exception to the attempts by FT leader writers, who were typical of a whole strand of thinking, to translate this into an explicit policy prescription (or perhaps it was the prescription itself that we objected to). How can these two positions be reconciled?

The NAIRU is lower than has previously been estimated

It is very easy to obtain a spurious estimate for the NAIRU from an inappropriate regression specification. For

Estimates of the natural rate of unemployment in Britain in the mid-1990s (as a percentage of the labour force (claimant count))

	%
Patrick Minford	3.5
Andrew Sentance	4–6
Tim Congdon	6–7
David Currie	6.5–7.5
Andrew Brittan	7–8
Gavyn Davies	7–8

example, by regressing inflation against lagged inflation and unemployment and solving out for the NAIRU. This may have been the approach of some of the Chancellor's 'Wise Men' in 1995 (see table). These estimates were made more than three years ago and it is possible that they (or some of them) were accurate at the time, but that the NAIRU has subsequently fallen. The MPC itself believes that there has been a reduction in the NAIRU: '. . . in each year of this recovery, the percentage increase in real unit labour costs has been lower than would have been expected based on the average relationship since 1980. The most likely reason for the shift in this trade-off is that the equilibrium, or natural rate, of unemployment is lower now than it was in the 1980s.' (*Inflation Report* February 1998).

There are many reasons why the NAIRU might have shifted down between the 1980s and the 1990s (changes in the benefits regime, lower rates of unionisation, the reduction in job protection legislation and so on). It is hard to argue, however, that the NAIRU has

shifted in the last year to the extent that unemployment has fallen, yet at the same time moved from below to above the NAIRU. It is possible that unemployment is above the NAIRU, and has been throughout the recent experience, but the puzzle then becomes why earnings growth was on an upward trend from 1995 to 1998.

The answer is that earnings growth has not been rising *in real terms*. The wage bargain starts with the headline rate of inflation (rather than the underlying rate that the MPC is targeting) and, mainly as a result of interest rate increases, this was on a generally rising trend from about mid-1996 onwards. If real earnings are defined as the difference between the current rate of growth of nominal earnings and retail prices, real earnings growth has been approximately stable for the last two years at one to two per cent – less than trend productivity.

It makes sense to look at real wage costs, since unemployment is a real variable and should in theory be related to real, rather than nominal, wages. And if real wages are rising at less than trend productivity, they do not in themselves pose a threat to inflation. That is not to say that the six per cent-plus peak in private sector earnings growth seen in 1998 was consistent with the 2.5 per cent inflation target, but neither can it automatically be concluded that unemployment fell below the NAIRU. The distinction between nominal earnings growing too rapidly for the inflation target (which they were) and real earnings being pushed higher by levels of unemployment falling too low (which they were not), was lost on some commentators.

(a) What is NAIRU and how should it inform the economic policy of government?

(b) Why might the NAIRU have fallen in recent years?

(c) Why do the authors maintain that the true value of the NAIRU is lower than is generally accepted?

(d) Why might *real* wage increases be a better guide than simple price inflation as to whether unemployment is below the NAIRU?

FT

In article below, taken from the *Financial Times* of 2 September 1999, Samuel Brittan takes a look at the current state of the Keynesian–monetarist debate. He suggests that the two sides tend to caricature each other's position in order to make their own position seem more reasonable and their opponent's position more extreme. Most *practising economic advisers*, however, take elements from both sides of the debate: indeed there has emerged a large measure of consensus about the need for government intervention on the one hand, and the adherence to inflation targets on the other.

Voices in the air

During the 1970s and 1980s there developed a counter-revolution against, not necessarily the core doctrines of Keynes, but against the 'Keynesianism' which governed official policy in so many countries, especially in the US and UK. It could better be described as a reaction against overambitious economic management.

The counter-revolutionary ideas were partially put into effect by the Reagan and Thatcher governments – which for some people was enough to condemn them. In fact the UK and US counter-revolutions started in the closing years of the Callaghan and Carter administrations – Callaghan's famous 1976 denial that governments could spend their way into full employment was a landmark.

The counter-revolution has indeed been carried forward by the present Labour government and has no keener exponent than the chancellor, Gordon Brown. Evidence is provided by his grant of operational independence to the Bank of England, his remit to the Bank to follow a strict inflation target, his devotion to a medium term financial framework limiting government borrowing, and his insistence on 'supply-side' cures for unemployment.

None of this prevents many leftwing economic intellectuals from disliking this counter-revolution intensely – a dislike which is shared by some on the right who are still attached to the postwar consensus. Hence the series of claims that Keynes is back and that free market and monetarist economists are discredited. How are these claims reconciled with the fact that in so many of the world economies there are independent central banks pursuing targets for inflation rather than for real growth?

Much of the battle reflects a 'Kulturkampf' among the economic chattering classes, which is a good deal fiercer than the ordinary party political battle. The most important rule of this game is to draw the dividing line between the Keynesian and the counter-revolutionary school in a way favourable to your own side.

If you want to exclaim that Keynes is alive and kicking you attribute to the counter-revolutionaries the most extreme doctrines possible: for instance that the economy automatically balances at full employment and is self-

stabilising. They are also supposed to believe that the only instrument of economic policy is money supply rules, which have to be followed rigidly. As soon as it is clear that the money supply can neither be defined nor controlled so easily, and that in any case it cannot be the sole guide to policy, the other side exclaims with glee: 'Keynes is alive: classical economists fall down dead.' If, on the other hand, you want to pull down the Keynesian flag you pretend that any concern with inflation, other than by pay and price controls, is antipathetic to the Great Man's memory.

Those who want to claim victory for the anti-Keynesian side can point to the widespread agreement on what is called a 'nominal framework'. This means that even authorities such as the US Federal Reserve, which openly admit to a concern with the level of demand, think of it as demand in money terms. Those of us who would like the European Central Bank or the Bank of England to adopt similar objectives are really saying that at very low rates of inflation central banks should not be afraid of promoting output and employment; but this must be subject to an overriding concern with preventing an inflationary take-off.

A closer inspection shows that much of the argument is shadow boxing. The counter-revolutionaries have demonstrated that there is no long-run trade-off between unemployment and inflation and that there may even be a trade-off the other way at high and fluctuating inflation rates. That is their Big Idea. There is an underlying or structural rate of unemployment which cannot easily be treated by monetary, fiscal or exchange rate policy. This is sometimes called the natural rate, or more politely the NAIRU – non-accelerating inflation rate of unemployment.

Yet on reflection there is no incompatibility between the 'natural rate' and at least one reasonable interpretation of Keynes's doctrines in his 1936 *General Theory of Employment, Interest and Money*. The inclusion of 'employment' in the title was no accident. Before then economists believed that increases in savings could be nothing but beneficial. Interest rates would fall, investment rise and the growth rate increase. The heresy of Keynes was to demonstrate that these

moralising tales might not always be true.

The traditional analysis, by focusing only on interest rates, overlooked other variables that could respond: namely output and employment. An attempted increase in savings might reduce national income and raise unemployment. This could happen because interest rates fail to fall enough or because investment is not sufficiently sensitive to them. It is this oversavings doctrine that was Keynes's Big Idea, for which he would have deserved a Nobel prize – had it existed in his lifetime for economics – several times over. In contemporary terms this means that you might not get unemployment even as low as the 'natural rate' if attempted savings are too high and demand is therefore inadequate.

There can be honest disagreement about how fast to try to restore price stability or squeeze inflation out of the system once it has taken hold. Similarly, when there is some depressive force, there can be disagreement on how aggressively governments should try to restore demand. But the interesting thing is that these arguments do not centre around any of the slogans used by the flagwavers of the two sides. Those economists who still call themselves monetarists, including Milton Friedman himself, are often in the forefront of saying what Japan or the emerging countries should have done to restore activity.

There are almost no practising economic advisers who believe that the economy can be left on its own to approach an underlying equilibrium. It can be knocked off course by events ranging from oil price explosions to German reunification, not to speak of capital flights away from emerging countries or into western economies whose exchange rates then overshoot.

On the other side many practising Keynesians are now 'reconstructed'. This means that they do not believe that governments can promote full employment regardless of what is happening to inflation: and in practice they support the inflation targets now in force.

There is also a good deal of acceptance of the primary role of monetary policy in fighting both inflation and depression, although in some cases this is based on perceived political possibilities rather than genuine conviction. There are plenty of disagreements left on what remains for fiscal policy to do.

The most famous quotation from Keynes runs: 'The ideas of economists and political philosophers, both when they are right and when they are wrong are more powerful than is commonly understood. Indeed the world is ruled by little else. Practical men, who believe themselves to be quite exempt from any intellectual influences are usually the slaves of some defunct economist. Madmen in authority, who hear voices in the air, are distilling their frenzy from some academic scribbler from a few years back.' This remains true.

(a) Outline the arguments used by (i) Keynesians to criticise the monetarist counter-revolution; (ii) monetarists to criticise Keynesianism.

(b) Where do the counter-revolutionaries and Keynesians share common ground concerning how the economy operates and the role of government policy?

(c) Is the concept of the NAIRU consistent with the theory that aggregate demand might be inadequate if there is a high level of saving?

 E **ANSWERS**

Q1. *Keynesian.*

Q2. *monetarist.*

Q3. (a) and (d) relate to the Keynesian aggregate supply curve, AS_1. Changes in aggregate demand will have no effect on prices until the full-employment level of income (Y_2) is reached. (b) and (c) relate to the monetarist aggregate supply curve. Changes in aggregate demand will have no effect on output, but instead will be reflected solely in changes in the price level.

Q4. *without considering.* We assume that firms assume that a rise in demand is confined to their product.

Q5. *(a)* See Figure A21.1. The average and marginal curves shift to AR_2 and MR_2 respectively, giving

Figure A21.1 Profit-maximising price and output for a firm in an imperfect market following a rise in demand

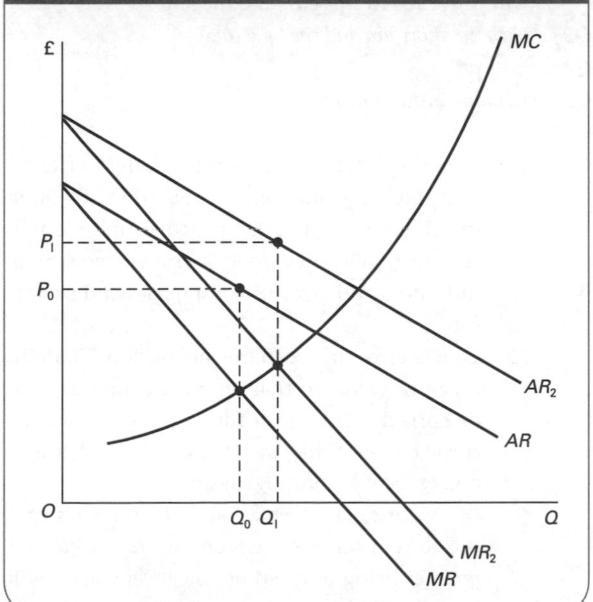

a new profit-maximising price and output of P_2 and Q_2.

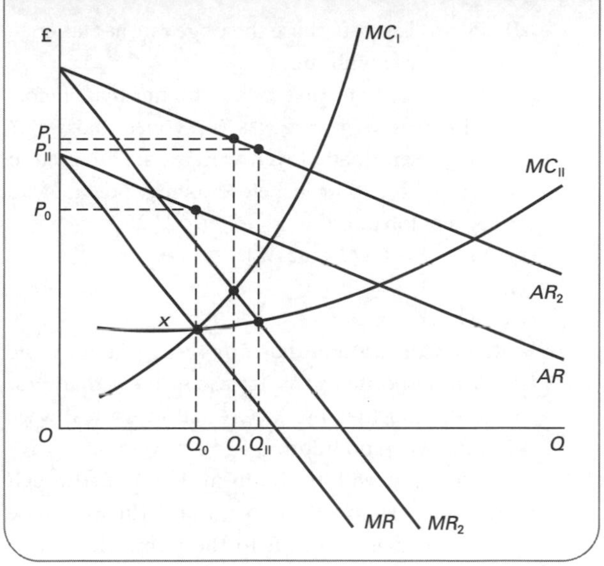

(b) See Figure A21.2. The flatter the MC curve, the more will a rise in demand affect output rather than price.

(c) *steeper.*

(d) The nearer a firm gets to full capacity, the more costs per unit will rise for each extra unit produced. This is in accordance with the principle of diminishing marginal returns.

Q6. *similar in shape to the MC curve illustrated in Figure 21.2.*

Q7. *(a) Diagram (a).*

(b) As AD rises, prices throughout the economy also rise. Because firms are interdependent, the

Figure A21.2 Profit-maximising price and output for a firm with alternative cost curves

price rise by one firm will be passed on as additional costs of production to another firm. This will cause the short-run *AS* curve to shift upwards.

(c) As demand rises, firms will be encouraged to invest. As a result they will be able to increase output without significantly increasing prices.

Q8. (a), (d) and (f) will tend to make the *AS* curve *steeper*. All of these will tend to stimulate inflation and lead firms to believe that they can raise their prices without losing market share. The effect will therefore be to shift the short-run *AS* curve upwards and hence make the long-run *AS* curve steeper.

(b), (c) and (e) will tend to make the *AS* curve shallower. They will all encourage firms to invest, in the belief that their market is expanding. The effect will therefore be to shift the short-run *AS* curve to the right and hence make the long-run *AS* curve shallower.

Q9. *(a)* $Q_7 - Q_3$ (the gap between AS_L and N at W_1).

(b) There is no disequilibrium unemployment. The wage rate is at the equilibrium.

(c) $Q_5 - Q_2$.

(d) It is still zero, because the wage rate has fallen to the new equilibrium.

(e) $Q_5 - Q_2$. Note that this is higher than before when the wage rate was W_1. Given that wages are lower, unemployed workers are inclined to search for longer before being prepared to accept job offers.

(f) $Q_7 - Q_1$ ($N - AD_{L_2}$ at W_1).

(g) $Q_3 - Q_1$.

(h) $Q_7 - Q_3$.

Q10. B. Keynesians assume that firms will take on more labour in response to an increase in the demand for the goods that they produce. A fall in the real wage rate is not a precondition.

Q11. The economy will move from point X through points B, C, D and E. Both (a) and (b) will cause aggregate demand to shift to the right, whereas (c) and (d) will cause aggregate supply to shift upwards.

Q12. The economy will move from point X through points F, G, H and E. Both (a) and (b) will cause aggregate supply to shift upwards. If, in response to falling output and rising unemployment, the government then stimulates economic activity, as in (c) and (d), aggregate demand will shift to the right.

Q13. D. The Phillips curve showed the inverse relationship between wage inflation and unemployment. Wage inflation was replaced in later modifications by price inflation.

Q14. C. Adaptive expectations are based upon past events. It is assumed that people learn from experience. Hence, if the rate of inflation is under-predicted one year, the following year expectations will be adapted and revised upwards.

Q15. B. (ii) states that the expected rate of inflation ($\dot{P}^e$) depends on the actual rate of inflation in the last time period ($\dot{P}_{t-1}$): i.e. expectations adapt to what was actually the case previously.

(iii) states that actual inflation ($\dot{P}_t$) depends on some constant amount (b), on the inverse of unemployment ($1/U$) and on the expected rate of inflation in the current time period ($\dot{P}_t^e$).

Q16. It is sometimes called the accelerationist theory because, in order to keep unemployment below the equilibrium rate, price increases must accelerate: i.e. inflation must rise. As long as unemployment is kept below the equilibrium rate, each year expectations will underpredict the rate of inflation and hence adapt and rise the following year. Thus the trade-off is not between unemployment and inflation but between unemployment and the rate of *increase* in inflation.

Q17. *vertical.*

Q18. *natural rate.*

Q19. *short run.*

Q20. *long run.*

Q21. *(a)* U_1. This is where real aggregate demand equals real aggregate supply.

(b) U_1. In this model, the NAIRU is the same as the natural rate. It is the rate of unemployment consistent with a stable rate of inflation.

(c) Between points A and F. Unemployment is reduced (temporarily) below the natural rate, but inflation rises.

(d) Between points C and F. Between these points both inflation and unemployment rise.

(e) By a more drastic contraction of aggregate demand. Unemployment would rise above U_2, but inflation would fall more rapidly.

Q22. *False.* A fall in the rate of frictional unemployment will shift the Phillips curve to the left.

Q23. *both the short run and the long run.*

Q24. *raise prices.*

Q25. *virtually instantaneously.*

Q26. *voluntary.*

Q27. *(a)* *True.* Expectations are formed using currently available information. People do not look merely at what has happened to inflation in the past, but they look at *current* economic indicators and government policies and project forward.

(b) *True.* If errors in prediction are made at random, it can be assumed that on *average* forecasts will be correct. (The mean forecasted value will be correct over time, but there will be random divergences around the mean.)

(c) *False.* Rational expectations theory argues that the current state of the economy, or the current policies being pursued by the government, will have a crucial impact upon expectations.

(d) *True.* Expectations are based on the information available. Such information might well be incomplete or even wrong.

Q28. *(a)* The economy will move to point *B*. Here the effect of rising demand is correctly anticipated and simply causes aggregate supply to shift upwards to $SRAS_2$ as aggregate demand expands to AD_2. The price level rises to P_3.

(b) *F.* Believing that aggregate demand will only rise to AD_3 and the price level to P_4 the aggregate supply curve will only shift up to $SRAS_3$. The excess demand at P_4 of $D - E$ will push up the level of prices. Believing that this represents a *real* rise in prices, firms increase output (they move up along $SRAS_3$.) Short-run equilibrium is achieved at point *F* with a higher price and output of P_2 and Q_2. Eventually, when people realise their mistake, long-run equilibrium will be achieved at point *B*.

(c) *C.* The converse of (b) occurs. The *AS* curve shifts up to $SRAS_2$. Firms believe that there is a fall in real demand (they perceive a demand deficiency of $B - G$). They thus reduce prices and output. Short-run equilibrium is achieved at point *C* with a price and output of P_2 and Q_1. Eventually, when people realise their mistake, long-run equilibrium will be achieved at point *E*.

Q29. The Phillips curve will always be vertical in the long run as errors in prediction are made at random. However, underprediction will shift the short-run Phillips curve to the left: unemployment temporarily falls below the natural rate. Overprediction will shift the short-run Phillips curve to the right: unemployment will be temporarily above its natural rate.

Q30. There are a number of reasons why the assumption of price and wage flexibility is unrealistic. For example, wage contracts are negotiated on a yearly basis (hardly flexible); trade unions and monopoly producers of goods fix wages and prices; administrative costs in changing prices on a frequent basis would be very high, and may outweigh the advantage of adjusting prices.

Q31. D. The new classical school advocates the setting of clear monetary rules and the adoption of libertarian supply-side measures to reduce the natural rate of unemployment (e.g. reducing the power of trade unions).

Q32. D. The new classical school explains the business cycle in terms of fluctuations in aggregate supply, rather than fluctuations in aggregate demand. These changes in aggregate supply may be the result of changes in technology or other supply-side factors. The effects do not take place instantaneously, but over a period of time. These 'build-up' effects cause periods of expansion (or contraction) in the economy.

Q33. *Yes.* All except (f).

Q34. Because there would be additional costs to employers from employing outsiders, including training costs and the costs of demotivating the insiders. Also insiders may be members of unions who might be able to push their wage rates above market rates. Alternatively, insiders may simply have power and influence within the firm, as a result of having become established members of staff. For these reasons, firms may be willing to pay insiders more, rather than attempting to bring in outsiders.

Q35. (a) *No*; (b) *Yes*; (c) *Yes*; (d) *No*. Supply-side policies are needed to tackle the supply-side problems that have been caused by previous recessions.

Q36. *False.* Keynesians tend to argue that free markets will not offer sufficient incentives to cure this problem. They will fail to encourage sufficient people to retrain or move to where employment might be found.

Q37. Two reasons are: rising demand makes firms more confident about their future sales and encourages them to invest and consider expanding their labour force; if existing rates of unemployment include a high level of long-term unemployed or those unemployed due to structural change, the inflationary impact of their employment and retraining may be offset in the long run by higher levels of productivity.

Q38. *True.* Leaving things to the market is seen by modern Keynesians as a slow and highly ineffective way to deal with economic problems such as unemployment.

22 Long-term Economic Growth and Supply-side Policies

A   REVIEW

If an economy is to achieve sustained economic growth over the longer term, there must be a sustained increase in potential output. This means that there has to be a continuous rightward shift in the aggregate supply curve. But what causes such shifts and what policies can be adopted to encourage such shifts. This chapter examines these issues.

22.1 Economic growth in the long run

Although industrialised countries experienced recessions in the mid 1970s, the early 1980s and early 1990s, OECD countries have averaged rates of economic growth of **Q1.** *between 0 and 2 per cent/2 and 4 per cent/over 4 per cent* per annum over the last 30 years.

Q2. Which of the following are major explanations of this sustained economic growth?

(a) A closing of the gap between actual and potential output.   *Yes/No*
(b) Increases in labour productivity.   *Yes/No*
(c) Technological progress.   *Yes/No*
(d) Sustained increases in the capital stock.   *Yes/No*
(e) Reductions in unemployment.   *Yes/No*
(f) Increases in human capital.   *Yes/No*

Q3. Figure 22.1 shows a simple model of economic growth. Assume that the economy currently has a capital stock of K_0.

(a) What is the level of total investment? ....

(b) What is the level of net investment? ....

(c) What is the current level of national income? ....

(d) Explain the process whereby national income increases.

....

....

(e) Will national income go on rising for ever? Explain.

....

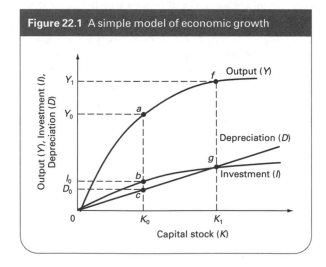

Figure 22.1 A simple model of economic growth

(f) Now assume that there is an increase in the rate of saving and hence investment. Illustrate the effect on Figure 22.1.

(g) Why will national income not go on rising for ever as a result of this higher rate of investment?

....

(h) Illustrate the effect of technological progress on Figure 22.1.

Q4. Given that an increase in saving means a reduction in current consumption, and has a declining effect in terms of extra long-term output, economists have developed the concept of a 'golden-rule saving rate'. This can be defined as the rate of saving that leads to:

A. the maximum level of output.
B. the maximum rate of growth.
C. the maximum level of consumption.
D. the minimum rate of depreciation.
E. the maximum level of investment.

Q5. An increase in technological progress is the main condition for achieving a faster rate of economic growth.

True/False

Q6. According to endogenous growth theory:

A. increases in aggregate supply depend on increases in aggregate demand.
B. the rate of technological progress depends on purely on developments in science and engineering which, in turn, depend on random inventions and discoveries.
C. economic growth can only be a temporary phenomenon caused by 'one-off' discoveries.
D. the rate of technological progress and diffusion can be increased by appropriate incentives and government policies.
E. a faster rate of economic growth is likely to lead to a lower rate of technological progress.

22.2 Supply-side policies

(Pages 632–5) It is important to distinguish clearly between demand-side and supply-side solutions to economic problems.

Q7. Which of the following measures to cure unemployment would we call supply-side and which demand-side solutions, and which have elements of both?

(a) The encouragement of pay restraint to keep costs down by preventing excessive wage increases.

Supply-side/Demand-side/Both

(b) The launch of a new government training programme for school leavers.

Supply-side/Demand-side/Both

(c) A new computer network is set up to provide more detailed national information at job centres on vacancies.

Supply-side/Demand-side/Both

(d) A government investment programme targeted on key growth industries.

Supply-side/Demand-side/Both

(e) Income tax is cut by 2p in the pound.

Supply-side/Demand-side/Both

(f) Lower interest rates to prevent the exchange rate appreciating.

Supply-side/Demand-side/Both

Q8. What effect will successful supply-side measures have on the following curves?

(a) The production possibility curve.

Outward shift/Inward shift/Movement along

(b) The aggregate supply curve.

Rightward shift/Leftward shift/Movement up along/Movement down along

(c) The aggregate demand curve.

Rightward shift/Leftward shift/Movement up along/Movement down along

(d) The Phillips curve.

Rightward shift/Leftward shift/ Movement up along/Movement down along

(e) The withdrawals curve in the Keynesian 45° line diagram.

Upward shift/Downward shift/No shift in

(f) The injections 'curve' in the Keynesian 45° line diagram.

Upward shift/Downward shift/No shift in

(g) The full-employment level of income in the Keynesian 45° line diagram.

Rightward shift/Leftward shift/No shift in

Q9. List three supply-side policies which might be used to achieve the effect on the production possibility curve in Q8 (a) above.

1. ....

2. ....

3. ....

Q10. Monetarists argue that there is a clear distinction between demand-side and supply-side policy. Which of the following would be maintained by monetarists?

(a) In the long run, demand-side policy is suitable only for tackling inflation. *True/False*

(b) In the long run, only supply-side policy will reduce unemployment and increase output. *True/False*

(c) Supply-side policies will help to shift the Phillips curve to the right by reducing the natural rate of unemployment. *True/False*

(d) Supply-side policies should aim to make markets freer.

True/False

Keynesian arguments concerning the nature and role of demand-side and supply-side policies differ considerably from those of the monetarists. Keynesians argue that demand-side policies **Q11.** *can/cannot* cause increase in output and employment. They also argue that, on their own, supply-side policies **Q12.** *can/cannot* lead to increases in output and employment *and* a reduction in inflation.

Q13. Keynesians maintain that supply-side policies can reduce the need for deflationary demand-side policies.
True/False

Q14. 'Third way' supply-side policies aim to help people to help themselves. Such policies involve a mixture of government support and market incentives. *True/False*

22.3 Market-orientated supply-side policies

(*Page 635*) The main emphasis of the supply-side policies of the UK, the USA and many other countries in the 1980s was on the liberation of market forces.

Q15. Which one of the following supply-side policies was not used in the UK in the 1980s?
A. Controls on both public- and private-sector prices and incomes to prevent inflation.
B. Deregulation and privatisation of British industry.
C. Attempts to reduce the PSBR.
D. Regional grants to encourage industrial relocation.
E. Limiting the automatic entitlement to certain welfare benefits.

(*Pages 635–7*) *Reducing government expenditure*
(?) Q16. List four supply-side measures adopted by the UK government during the 1980s designed to reduce public expenditure.

1. ....

2. ....

3. ....

4. ....

Q17. Reducing the level of government expenditure, while at the same time adopting a tight monetary policy to reduce inflation, proved to be difficult. Which one of the following help to explain why this was so?
A. The government also wanted to cut taxes.
B. Reducing the PSBR was itself inflationary.
C. Reducing the PSBR increased the money supply.
D. Statutory reserve ratios for banks had been abolished.
E. The deflationary monetary policy triggered automatic fiscal stabilisers.

(*Pages 637–8*) *Tax cuts*
Q18. Cuts in the marginal rate of income tax are claimed to have various beneficial supply-side effects. These are:

(a) People work longer hours because the substitution effect from cutting the marginal rate of income tax is less than the income effect. *True/False*
(b) More people wish to work. *True/False*
(c) People work more enthusiastically. *True/False*
(d) Both equilibrium and disequilibrium unemployment fall even when wage rates are inflexible downwards.
True/False
(e) Employment rises. *True/False*

(*Pages 638–9*) *Reducing the power of labour*
Q19. If the government succeeds in reducing the power of labour, equilibrium unemployment may well rise.
True/False

Q20. Figure 22.2 shows an aggregate labour market. N is the total labour force; AS_L is the effective demand for labour; AD_L is the aggregate demand for labour. Assume that wages are fixed above the equilibrium at a rate of W_1.

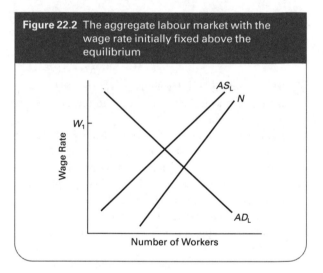

Figure 22.2 The aggregate labour market with the wage rate initially fixed above the equilibrium

(a) Mark on the diagram the levels of equilibrium and disequilibrium unemployment.
(b) Now assume that the government reduces union power, so that wages are freely set by forces of demand and supply. Mark the new wage rate and the resulting levels of equilibrium and disequilibrium unemployment.
(c) Now assume that the effect of reducing wages is to reduce the level of consumer expenditure. Illustrate the effect of this on aggregate demand.
(d) Illustrate the effect of this on employment (both equilibrium and disequilibrium), assuming that the wage rate is no longer flexible downwards below that in (b) above.
(e) Returning to (c) above, illustrate the effect of this on unemployment (both equilibrium and disequilibrium), assuming that the wage rate continues to be flexible downwards.

◐ **Q21.** The disequilibrium unemployment in Q13(d) above is of which type?

....

(Page 639) Reducing welfare

Monetarists argue that a **Q22.** *small/large* difference between wages and welfare benefits will cause a high level of **Q23.** *frictional/structural* unemployment. The extra income that an individual would receive from taking employment would be small. We would say these individuals are caught in a **Q24.** *poverty/unemployment* trap. If the level of benefits were cut, the effective labour supply curve (AS_L) would shift to the **Q25.** *left/right*.

(Pages 639–41) Encouraging competition

⁇ **Q26.** List three policies favoured by the Thatcher and Major governments as means of encouraging competition.

1. ....

2. ....

3. ....

22.4 Interventionist supply-side policy

(Pages 642–50) The UK has for decades had a **Q27.** *lower/ higher* level of investment relative to national income than other industrialised countries.

▓ **Q28.** The following series of points reflect the consequences of low investment. Order these points into a logical sequence of events. Number them from 1 to 6. (Number 1 is already shown.)

(a) Low investment.   1

(b) A widening balance of trade deficit.   ....

(c) Low productivity growth.   ....

(d) Low investment.   ....

(e) Falling international competitiveness.   ....

(f) The adoption of deflationary fiscal and monetary policy measures.

....

▤ **Q29.** Deindustrialisation refers to:
A. the modernisation of manufacturing industry.
B. the growth in science parks where only high-technology industries are located.
C. the growth in the service sector.
D. the decline in the country's manufacturing base.
E. the movement back to an agriculturally based economy.

⁇ **Q30.** Give four arguments why the free market might lead to a sub-optimal level of investment.

1. ....

2. ....

3. ....

4. ....

◐ **Q31.** Which of the following could be classified as *interventionist* supply-side policy?
(a) Government provision of infrastructure.   *Yes/No*
(b) Privatisation.   *Yes/No*
(c) Investment grants for private firms.   *Yes/No*
(d) A reduction in corporation tax.   *Yes/No*
(e) Government-funded workplace training schemes.
                                                                          Yes/No

The most extreme form of interventionist supply-side policy is national economic planning.

▤ **Q32.** Which of the following describes *indicative* planning?
A. A type of planning undertaken by a group of countries acting together.
B. Commands issued to different sectors of the economy to produce targeted amounts of output.
C. Consultation between government, business and unions in order to co-ordinate their policies and plans.
D. Government intervention in the operation of markets for short periods of time.
E. The nationalisation of large sections of the economy.

◐ **Q33.** Although governments in most industrialised countries do not engage in national economic planning, virtually all intervene selectively in order to bring supply-side improvements.   *True/False*

⁇ **Q34.** Give three arguments against interventionist industrial policy.

1. ....

2. ....

3. ....

22.5 Regional and urban policy

(Pages 650–7) There are significant regional and local disparities in the UK economy, many of which grew over the 1980s and early 1990s.

◐ **Q35.** If market prices were perfectly flexible, and there were perfect factor mobility:

(a) There would be no specifically regional or local unemployment problem. *True/False*

(b) There would be no problem of regional or local inequality of wage rates for given occupations. *True/False*

 Q36. If market prices were perfectly flexible, but there was significant factor immobility:

(a) There would be no specifically regional or local unemployment problem. *True/False*

(b) There would be no problem of regional or local inequality. *True/False*

 Q37. Which of the following regional or urban policies would be advocated by the radical right and which by interventionists?

(a) The offering of local facilities and improvement of local infrastructure for potential new business. *Radical right/Interventionist*

(b) The migration of labour should be encouraged by the reduction of benefit levels. *Radical right/Interventionist*

(c) High-spending local authorities, which impose excessive local taxation, should be capped. High taxation is a disincentive to firms locating in particular areas. *Radical right/Interventionist*

(d) Government should prevent the location of firms in already prosperous parts of the country. *Radical right/Interventionist*

(e) Nationally negotiated wage agreements should be replaced by locally negotiated ones. *Radical right/Interventionist*

(f) The provision of a range of local subsidies and grants to firms. *Radical right/Interventionist*

(g) The setting of a uniform business rate (local business tax) across the whole country. *Radical right/Interventionist*

 Q38. Which of the following have been part of successive UK governments' approach to regional policy?

(a) Increasing government expenditure on regional assistance in *real* terms and targeting it more carefully. *Yes/No*

(b) Increasing government expenditure on regional assistance in *money* terms and targeting it more carefully. *Yes/No*

(c) Making regional assistance more cost-effective. *Yes/No*

(d) Abolishing Regional Development Grants (which were *automatically* available to firms in development areas.) *Yes/No*

(e) Abolishing Regional Selective Assistance (which was granted at the *discretion* of the government). *Yes/No*

(f) Increasing the reliance placed on grants from the European Regional Development Fund. *Yes/No*

(g) The introduction of a system of grants to small businesses in assisted areas. *Yes/No*

(?) Q39. Give three factors that have limited the effectiveness of UK urban policy in regenerating deprived inner-city areas.

1. ....

2. ....

3. ....

B ## PROBLEMS, EXERCISES AND PROJECTS

Q40. Figure 22.3 illustrates the effect of a tax cut on the level of employment. N is the total labour force; AS_L is the effective aggregate supply of labour; AD_L is the aggregate demand for labour.

(a) Assume that Q_1 represents an equilibrium in the labour market, and that labour supply depends on the after-tax wage rate (W), whereas the demand for labour depends on unit labour costs: the pre-tax wage rate (Lc). What is the average level of income tax per worker?

....

(b) With employment at Q_1, what is the level of *equilibrium unemployment*?

....

(c) Assume now that income tax falls to $b - c$. What is the new unit labour cost to firms (pre-tax wage), assuming that wage rates are flexible?

....

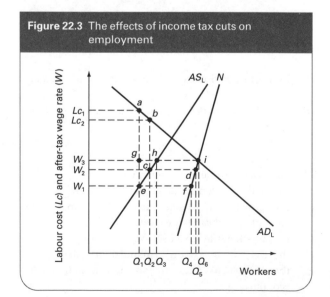

Figure 22.3 The effects of income tax cuts on employment

(d) How many workers will now be employed?

(e) Has equilibrium unemployment risen or fallen?

Risen/Fallen

Q41. Referring still to Figure 22.3, assume now that (pre-tax) wage rates are inflexible downwards.

(a) Still assuming a cut in income tax to $b - c$: if the pre-tax wage rate did not fall, but instead the after-tax wage rate rose to W_3 (i.e. $a - g = b - c$), how many workers would be willing to work at this wage now?

....

(b) What would be the level of disequilibrium unemployment?

....

(c) What would be the level of equilibrium unemployment?

....

(d) Has total unemployment risen or fallen as a result of the tax cut, given that the pre-tax wage rate is not flexible downwards? *Risen/Fallen*

Q42. Using various statistical sources, in particular *Regional Trends* (ONS), *Economic Trends* (ONS) and *Social Trends* (ONS), write a report on the significance of regional and local inequalities. Identify a range of economic and social inequalities and comment upon their growing (or declining) significance. Your report should include some assessment of whether these inequalities are likely to widen or narrow in the future. It should also review the main policies that might be adopted in order to remove or narrow such imbalances.

C   DISCUSSION TOPICS AND ESSAYS

Q43. Under what circumstances will an increase in the rate of saving in an economy lead to a faster rate of *long-term* economic growth?

Q44. What do you understand by 'endogenous growth theory'? What implications does the theory have for government supply-side policy?

Q45. Describe how Keynesian and monetarist approaches to supply-side policy differ. Illustrate this difference with reference to policies concerned with reducing unemployment and inflation.

Q46. Has there been a supply-side 'miracle' in the UK?

Q47. Outline the main supply-side policies introduced by the Thatcher and Major governments. Does the evidence suggest that they achieved what they set out to do?

Q48. In what ways do the supply-side policies of the Blair government differ from those of the previous Conservative governments? Provide a comparative critique of the two sets of policies.

Q49. What normative objections and justifications can be put forward to criticise and support market-orientated supply-side policies?

Q50. What do you understand by the term 'deindustrialisation'? What arguments have been advanced to explain the UK's experience of this phenomenon? Consider the relative merits of alternative policies for reversing the process.

Q51. Given large regional and local variations in economic prosperity and economic performance, what problems might occur in using a free-market policy to rectify such imbalances?

Q52. To what extent is it possible for a government to make a significant impact on urban deprivation without spending considerable sums of money?

Q53. Debate
We should not tolerate the uncertainty of markets when indicative planning will guarantee a degree of reliability and predictability in industrial decision making. The reason for rejecting indicative planning is purely political with little if any economic rationale.

D   ARTICLES

With the increasingly global nature of many businesses and their ability to shift production locations between countries, economies must be able to offer the most productive, and hence competitive, resources they can. The article below, taken from *BBC Online News* of 23 October 1998, considers the productivity gap that exists between Britain and some of its rivals, and explains why the gap exists and how it might be closed.

Mind the gap!

The workforce of Rover Motor Cars has been told to improve its productivity or face job cuts. Their German colleagues at BMW assembly lines for example, are 30 per cent more productive.

But what is productivity – and why does Britain lag behind?

Productivity refers to how efficiently a company makes its products. It is usually measured as output per worker. In the long run, the growth of productivity is the most important factor in raising living standards and driving economic growth.

By this measure Britain is well behind its continental rivals. According to government figures, British workers in the manufacturing sector produced on average around £30 000 of output, as compared with over £40 000 per worker in France, Germany and Italy.

But one of the problems faced by Britain is the big variation in efficiency between different companies in the same industry.

In car production, for example, Britain has both the most efficient plant in Europe – Nissan, Sunderland – and one of the least efficient – Rover's Longbridge plant.

It is this 'long tail' of underperforming companies that has been particularly concerning the government. It has been urging firms to copy the best practice in their industry, and to spur them on it has been publishing comparisons.

Investment the key

But it is difficult for companies to improve productivity in the short term.

One of the main factors that affects productivity is the level of capital investment in new plants and equipment.

Britain's Japanese-owned car plants, built on greenfield sites, have the latest technology and have agreed flexible working practices with their employees.

The situation at Rover is very different, despite the substantial new investment made by BMW during the last four years.

In the short run, productivity can only increase if there is new investment and increased sales. But with a vast over-capacity in the European auto industry, sales growth will be difficult.

So more job cuts may be necessary if the company is to achieve its productivity targets.

The British problem

Over the last decades British industry has invested less in capital equipment than rival companies in the US and Germany – leading to a gap which will take years to close.

And it is also thought that the structure of British industry – dominated by a few large firms in many sectors – has inhibited competition and investment.

Long-term prospects

Productivity is good for you: more productive firms are more profitable and pay their workers more.

At the start of the industrial revolution Britain led the world in manufacturing productivity.

But Britain lost its advantage in manufacturing industry nearly 100 years ago, as more efficient US and German firms came to dominate.

They made better use of technology, spending more on research and development. They employed a more educated workforce, and they used more modern management techniques. And their higher sales and profits allowed them to increase investment even more.

The UK is still trying to catch up on these long-run supply side weaknesses. The government is committed to boosting spending on education and research and has given tax breaks to encourage investment.

In recent years the productivity gap between the UK and Germany has begun to narrow. But it will take a long time before Britain can change the institutions and mentality which have contributed to its slow-growth economy.

Britain has both the most and least productive plants

Who is most productive?

Cars per worker per year

Bar chart showing cars per worker per year (y-axis 0 to 100):
- NISSAN SUNDERLAND: ~99
- GM GERMANY: ~77
- VW SPAIN: ~70
- TOYOTA EURNASTON: ~58
- ROVER LONGBRIDGE: ~33

Source: Economist Intelligence Unit, August 1998, 1997 figures by plant

(a) How might productivity be measured?

(b) What factors would improve the productivity of an economy?

(c) If the government is keen to improve productivity, what policy measures should it adopt?

The article below, taken from *The Economist* of 6 April 1996, assesses the value of state-run training programmes and considers whether training provision might be enhanced via alternative strategies.

What works?

When politicians who normally disagree about everything start agreeing on one particular thing, a degree of scepticism is in order. These days, they all agree that there should be more and better training.

On the face of it, the case for generous public support for training is strong. Unskilled people are much more likely to be out of work than skilled ones; if only their qualifications could be improved, they might find jobs more readily. Not only would they benefit, but so would the economy as a whole. A better-trained workforce would be a more productive one; so more training ought to mean not just lower unemployment, but also faster growth and higher living standards. Unions like training programmes because they can use them to push up wages. Academics like them because they increase demand for education. Parents like them because they give out-of-work, out-of-school youths something to do. Prophets of a post-modern society praise them as part of an ethic of life-long learning. And employers don't mind them because the public pays the bill.

As if all that were not enough, there is even a neat 'market failure' argument to explain why privately provided training is bound to be inadequate. Why should firms pay to equip employees with improved skills when those workers can be poached at a moment's notice by competitors? The state must pay, or nobody will. Here, apparently, is a case where government intervention can do some good.

All in all, then, the case for publicly supported schemes seems solid. There is just one problem. In practice, they rarely work.

The evidence

In a growing body of research, economists have compared groups of unemployed people who enter government training schemes with similar groups who do not. In almost every case, these studies have found that the schemes have failed to improve either the earnings or the employment prospects of their clients. After surveying the results of various broadly-based training programmes for unemployed adults, the training-friendly OECD was forced to

conclude in 1994 that there is 'remarkably meagre support for the hypothesis that such programmes are effective'.

Youth Training, Britain's flagship programme for 16- and 17-year-olds, enrols about 200 000 youngsters a year. A government evaluation in 1994 found that almost half of those who joined dropped out before the schemes ended. Unemployment rates of those who did finish, at 27 per cent, were higher than for the age group as a whole.

Now Britain is shifting the emphasis toward apprenticeships. These account for perhaps 20 000 places, and are based in the workplace. But these places are selective and therefore tend to serve the 'ones who would have been okay anyway', according to Ianthe Maclagan of a British charity, Youthaid. For occupations such as engineering, which have traditionally hired apprentices, the government is subsidising something that would have happened anyway – albeit not to the same extent. For non-traditional apprenticeships, such as in child care and information technology, start-up problems are still being sorted out.

Britain's other big training vehicles, Training and Enterprise Councils, are private companies that contract with the government to deliver training. This year, these will cost £1.6 billion ($2.4 billion). But an evaluation in February by the House of Commons Select Committee on Employment found that only 27 per cent of adults in TECs courses had work; even the best courses reported a success rate of less than half. The committee concluded that the TECs may have made a 'modest contribution' to the economy, but that 'their performance in placing people in work and gaining qualifications appears to reflect economic conditions, and not to overcome them'.

What about the biggest single scheme of all, Germany's highly regarded 'dual-education system'? Under this system, most German 16-year-olds sign an apprenticeship contract with a local firm to work part-time, for below entry-level wages, in return for training at the firm. The rest of the time they go to a vocational school (e.g., one for insurance, another for chemists) run by the local government. When the apprentice-

pupils finish, most get – or used to get – jobs either with their employer, or at least in their field. There are a lot of good things in the German model, but this is not a government training scheme in the ordinary sense.

Rather, it is a company apprenticeship scheme inextricably tied to the education system. Apprenticeships take place in a workplace, not at a training centre. Part of the cost is borne by the apprentices themselves, in the form of reduced wages and forgone opportunities. The largest chunk comes from businesses: of the total of DM312 billion ($211 billion) spent on all education in Germany in 1993, DM67 billion was spent by companies on vocational training. The teachers who train the apprentices at work are paid by the firms themselves; examinations under the system are set up by local Chambers of Commerce.

The system is certainly better than most. It provides firms with a supply of qualified workers. Through their influence over the curriculum, employers (who know what sorts of jobs will be needed in future) can ensure that school-leavers have the skills needed to do new jobs – in theory anyway. For their part, apprentices get a skill that should be marketable and gain experience of how companies really work.

Such a scheme, which has its roots in Germany's consensus system of rule linking companies, unions and government, would be extremely hard for others to copy. But even if they could, it is doubtful whether they should. The system is not a solution to unemployment, something particularly apparent now that German unemployment has hit a postwar high of over 4m (11.1 per cent). Almost half of Germany's unemployed are graduates of work-based apprenticeships; the problem is that once they have to be paid adult wages, many are too expensive to keep on. In this sense, one of the main benefits of the 'dual-education system' is nothing to do with skills: it merely provides cheap labour – but only for a short time.

Employers remain supportive but increasingly critical: they complain that it can take years – even decades – to change the curriculum, leaving training toiling in the wake of technological change. Worse, the system churns out lots of skilled blue-collar workers suitable for the super-engineering businesses that made German industry great (luxury cars, machine tools). But it churns out relatively few lesser-skilled but flexible workers able to switch easily from one task to another, which is what is needed now by businesses using intelligent computer-controlled machinery. Worse still, it churns out even fewer low-skilled (and therefore cheap) workers that German businesses need to cut labour costs.

Does this mean that government-backed training schemes are doomed to fail? No. Some do work. They tend to be small, expensive and with strong links to local employers. In-house

training benefits companies as well as workers. That is why firms do it. Intel, for example, an American chip-maker, has a more or less continuous retraining programme, enabling the firm to adapt to the volatility of the chip business. Mass-training schemes administered by civil servants cannot meet such needs. This is a reason employers prefer to take raw recruits and train them the company way, rather than take on training-scheme graduates.

The conclusion seems to be that the supposed market failure of training is greatly exaggerated: firms will train workers, despite the risk of poaching, provided that workers are willing to meet some of the cost through lower

wages, and/or that the skills concerned are firm-specific (i.e., not easily sold to another employer). For most workers in most firms, these conditions are met: that is why in-company training is alive and well without benefit of public subsidy.

Where government-supported training programmes have succeeded, they have been either small and focused, concentrating on helping people search for work, or else they have equipped people with basic skills. Arguably, the closer training is to general education (as in Germany), the more likely it is to succeed.

© *The Economist*, London (6th April, 1996)

(a) Outline the case in favour of government-funded training schemes.

(b) What evidence does the article present for the success, or lack of success, of training programmes in the UK?

Why has the German system of training proved more successful?

(c) How might the government support training programmes without providing such training itself?

UK urban policy has received fresh impetus in recent years as the problem of social inequality has moved up the political agenda. In the following article, taken from *New Economy* of August 1999, Peter Lee examines the way in which urban deprivation is measured and how these measures are used as the basis for identifying target areas for urban policy. As he argues, 'a consistent measure is needed, which can regularly be updated to gauge changes in levels of deprivation and the success of regeneration initiatives.'

Social exclusion and urban policy

Since June 1998, three important policy changes have occurred within the context of debates on targeting deprivation and social exclusion:

- there has been a marked shift in language away from 'worst estates' to a discourse on 'poorest neighbourhoods', reflected in the Social Exclusion Unit's (SEU) Autumn 1998 report
- the launch of the New Deal for Communities has refocused and re-emphasised the competitive element of regeneration policy and resulted inadvertently in a competition *between* 'poorest neighbourhoods'
- changes in the measurement of deprivation have lead to a shift in the location of the 'poorest neigh-

bourhoods' away from London towards the North and Midlands.

A national strategy for neighbourhood renewal

In its report, the SEU set out an agenda on how to '. . . develop integrated and sustainable approaches to the problems of the worst housing estates, including crime, drugs, unemployment, community breakdown, and bad schools . . .'. Reference to the 'worst estates' is made only once, the language shifting away from tenure specific references towards the preferred 'poorest neighbourhoods' – a phrase which appears 13 times in the report. Identifying how many 'poorest neighbourhoods' there are in Britain depends on the thresholds and indicators used to identify them. The SEU

report refers to three separate studies that estimate the size of the problem:

- 1370 'worst estates' in England (Department of the Environment, 1997)
- 3000 run-down neighbourhoods (English House Condition Survey)
- 1600 to 4000 neighbourhoods classified by socio-economic group (SEU, 1998).

The Index of Local Deprivation

The Index of Local Deprivation (ILD), released in the summer of 1998 as the official measure of deprivation (DETR, 1998), superseded the Index of Local Conditions (ILC). Like its predecessor, the ILD remains a multi-level index capturing deprivation at three spatial scales: local authority district, ward and

Table 1 The 70 most deprived authorities on the ILD: movers up and down

Movers up the Index				Movers down the Index			
Local authority	ILC	ILD	Change in rank	Local authority	ILC	ILD	Change in rank
Liverpool	6	1	5	Newham	1	2	−1
Manchester	13	3	10	Hackney	3	4	−1
Tower Hamlets	7	6	1	Southwark	2	8	−6
Sandwell	9	7	2	Islington	4	10	−6
Knowsley	12	9	3	Lambeth	8	12	−4
Greenwich	14	11	3	Haringey	10	13	−3
Barking and Dagenham	18	15	3	Lewisham	11	14	−3
Nottingham	25	16	9	Camden	15	17	−2
Brent	29	20	9	Hammersmith and Fulham	16	18	−2
Sunderland	34	21	13	Newcastle upon Tyne	17	19	−2
Salford	28	23	5	Waltham Forest	20	22	−2
Sheffield	36	25	11	Bradford	23	28	−5
Kingston Upon Hull	31	26	5	Wandsworth	21	30	−9
Rochdale	50	29	21	Gateshead	33	35	−2
Walsall	44	31	13	Hartlepool	35	37	−2
Leicester	37	32	5	South Tyneside	22	38	−16
Oldham	39	33	6	Blackburn	32	41	−9
Halton	51	34	17	Blackpool	30	51	−21
Ealing	38	36	2	City of Westminster	26	57	−31
Doncaster	41	39	2	Brighton and Hove	40	60	−20
Coventry	46	40	6	North Tyneside	52	62	−10
Barnsley	54	42	12	Kensington and Chelsea	19	63	−44
Wirral	61	44	17	Burnley	57	65	−8
St. Helens	55	45	10	Norwich	59	66	−7
Lincoln	48	46	2	Preston	47	68	−21
Bolton	49	47	2	Bristol	43	69	−26
Stoke-on-Trent	64	48	16				
Stockton-on-Tees	69	49	20				
Rotherham	60	50	10				
Easington	58	52	6				
Tameside	65	53	12				
Sefton	73	54	19				
Barrow-in-Furness	93	55	38				
Leeds	56	56	0				
Wansbeck	63	58	5				
Hounslow	99	59	40				
Wear Valley	75	61	14				
Thanet	81	64	17				
Mansfield	84	67	17				
Enfield	96	70	26				

Birmingham (ranked 5), Middlesborough (24) and Wolverhampton (27) had no change in ranking; Redcar and Cleveland, ranked 43rd on the ILD, had no ranking on the ILC.

enumeration district (ED). The main changes were made to the local authority district level of the index with data being added and updated. Changes at the local level (ward and ED) involved the dropping of one variable (children in unsuitable accommodation, which referred mainly to children living in flats) following considerable criticism of the indicator.

Table 1 shows the 70 local authorities that make up the most deprived local authority districts according to the ILD. The overall trend, comparing the ILD with the ILC, shows some London

Table 2 Regional comparisons of the percentage share of EDs comparing the ILC and ILD

Region (% share of all EDs)	ILC		ILD	
	Most deprived 10%	Most deprived 5%	Most deprived 10%	Most deprived 5%
London (15)	47	59	31	34
North West (11)	8	6	13	12
Merseyside (3)	6	5	8	9
Yorkshire & Humberside (10)	8	6	12	13
North East (5)	4	3	8	7
West Midlands (11)	10	8	12	12
South West (11)	4	3	3	3
Eastern (11)	3	2	2	2
South East (15)	7	6	5	4
East Midlands (8)	3	2	5	4

ILC figures reproduced from Harvey, J et al (1997) Mapping Local Authority Estates Using the Index of Local Conditions, DoE: London.

boroughs moving down the index and appearing less deprived, while authorities in the North and Midlands have generally moved up. Among these:

- 13 London boroughs have moved down the index compared with seven moving up
- 13 north western local authorities have moved up compared with three moving down
- 4 West Midlands authorities have moved up the ILD, with none moving down
- 8 authorities in Yorkshire and Humberside have moved up and one down.

Changes in the rankings at local authority level appear to show real changes in levels of deprivation. New data were added at the local authority level updating the index in some cases to 1997.

Analysis of the ILC at small area level showed that while London contained 15 per cent of England's EDs, it contained almost half (47 per cent) of EDs ranked in the top 10 per cent on the ILC (see Table 2). London's share of deprived EDs at the 10 per cent threshold on the ILD had dropped to just below a third. At the 5 per cent threshold, the differences in the spatial distribution of EDs, when comparing the ILC and ILD, changed more markedly. Almost 60 per cent of EDs, at the ILC 5 per cent threshold, were located in London, whereas less than 35 per cent were identified as such using the

ILD. The North West, Yorkshire and Humberside, the North East and East Midlands regions all doubled their share of deprived EDs at the 5 per cent threshold. The evidence on deprivation, therefore, shows a shift from London and the South to the Midlands and the North using both the updated local authority level index and the adjusted small area index.

New Deal for Communities

These changes in the rankings at both local authority and small area level are important as the ILD is used as the basis for identifying targets for regeneration policies. The 70 most deprived local authorities in Table 1 were used as the basis for selecting 'Pathfinder' authorities to take part in the New Deal for Communities (NDC) by the DETR.

The NDC was launched in the same month as the SEU report and will give £800 million to the most deprived neighbourhoods over the 1999 to 2001 period. To ensure a 'geographical spread of Pathfinder districts across England,' the DETR identified at least one local authority area in each region of England from the list in Table 1. Regions with disproportionate shares of deprivation were awarded additional Pathfinder authorities.

A more divisive strategy?

The NDC represents just one arm of regeneration policy. The most significant arm, the Single Regeneration

Budget, introduced a competitive bidding process to determine the allocation of resources. Previous policies, such as City Challenge, were based largely on levels of urban deprivation, with funding limited to the most deprived local authorities.

Writing about the competition for resources in inner-city policy, with particular reference to the SRB, Edwards (1997) argues that there are '. . . moral grounds on which the use of competition in social policy gives rise to disquiet. They concern rights and justice and derive from the precepts that if people have rights to things, then they should not have to compete for them or be subject to random selection or arbitrary power to get them . . .'.

Competition continues to be at the heart of government policy and in this respect it is difficult to side step the argument that the NDC has created a more divisive regeneration strategy than the SRB, by intensifying competition for resources between deprived communities. In the case of the NDC the stakes have been raised and the level of disappointment sharpened as a few communities scrap for the top prize.

The most deprived communities may lose out in this process because NDC Pathfinders have been chosen on the basis of previous regeneration spending, with a clear preference for 'spreading resources around'. Judgement on the ability of 'competitors' to succeed – their capacity to form partnerships in addition to having the most exploitable mix of economic and demographic factors – could also rule out the 'worst' areas.

'Form over substance'

Urban policy has increasingly emphasised the use of partnerships involving local authorities, the private sector and voluntary agencies whilst a consensus has emerged which has championed the role that community involvement and sustainability plays in regeneration. Edwards claims this is a victory of form over substance, where urban policy has lost sight of the principle objectives of regeneration: the reduction of poverty and deprivation.

Some local authorities used the ILD to determine which areas should be considered, whilst others used a combination of the ILD and previous spending on regeneration. However, where local authorities have attempted to be objective in their choice of NDC areas, how confident can we be that the areas chosen are the *most* deprived? The ILD identifies growing problems of deprivation in the northern regions and the Midlands, while the small area index identifies proportionally more deprived areas in these areas than does its predecessor, the ILC. The latter had been used as the basis for identifying the 'worst estates' and much press attention focused on the fact that 60 per cent of the worst areas were in London.

Clearly, a consistent measure is needed, which can regularly be updated to gauge changes in levels of deprivation and the success of regeneration initiatives. Additionally, a contract between government and *all* deprived areas should be established, to avoid leaving desperate communities to fight over scraps.

(a) What is the aim of urban policy?

(b) If you were constructing an index by which to measure social exclusion and urban deprivation, what variables would you include in your index?

(c) What reservations does the author have about the system whereby areas have to bid for money from the SRB?

FT

The article below by James Blitz, taken from the *Financial Times* of 27 May 1998, considers the economic difficulties faced by the south of Italy and how the Italian government hopes to improve the region's economic status.

Italy: Mezzogiorno tops Prodi's agenda

Amid the heroic effort of budget deficit-cutting that has enabled Italy to join the European monetary union, one problem with roots deep in history has been largely ignored: the 'Mezzogiorno', or the underdeveloped south.

Northern Italy is home to one of Europe's most powerful economies, with almost the highest per capita gross domestic product on the continent. But the south is the mirror image, among the least competitive regions in the new euro-zone and with almost the lowest level of per capita GDP.

Unemployment in much of the south stands at 25 per cent. Its black economy employs between one-third and one-half of the population. The recent mudslide disaster near Naples which killed 150 people confirmed the lamentable level of infrastructure and development.

With entry into the euro-zone achieved, Romano Prodi's government is turning its attention to the south more and more. The prime minister says his administration is entering a period in which the problems of unemployment will be tackled directly.

A new department has been set up in the treasury – Development Italy – aimed at co-ordinating public and private sector investment for the region. Carlo Azeglio Ciampi, the treasury minister, said this week the south had become the 'new frontier of Italian enterprise'.

Political pressure is increasing. Unemployed workers held large demonstrations last weekend in Naples. There are growing tensions within Mr Prodi's centre-left alliance. 'I want to see the same effort being made for the south as was made to get us into the euro,' said Antonio Bassolino, the powerful Naples mayor and a coalition supporter.

But even if money were available, Mr Prodi would be cautious about using it. Mammoth public sector transfers to the south over the last 25 years – providing the Mezzogiorno in the late 1980s with 75 per cent of its annual income – almost crippled the region. The transfers turned southerners into managers of state cash, not entrepreneurs.

Gianfranco Viesti, the government's adviser on the Mezzogiorno, believes the crucial question is whether the government can encourage Italian and European companies to invest in the region.

'The government says overall private sector investment should rise over the next three years as the economy grows,' he said. 'What local politicians want to see is a far higher proportion of this extra investment going to the south than has happened in the past.'

Some signs suggest that investment is picking up. The UK's BAA recently took a 70 per cent stake in Naples Capodicchino airport. Gioia Tauro, on the toecap of Italy, has become the premier container port for the Mediterranean. Exports from southern companies have nearly doubled in the last four years.

But debate is still raging over whether other factors may hold back the south's growth in future years.

One is organised crime. Although the best-known mafia leaders have been toppled, Mr Ciampi admits that the problem of security remains 'real'. Organised crime remains rooted in the cultural attitudes of many parts of the south and in the poor public administration.

Then there is the cost of labour. Giampaolo Galli, an economist at Confindustria, says trade unions still insist on inflexible, all-Italian wage levels for the public and private sectors, despite significantly lower productivity in the south. 'This is a huge disincentive to investors.'

However, some politicians believe that, in many parts of the south, nationally agreed settlements are no longer respected and that Confindustria is refusing to admit this. Mr Prodi insists that unit labour costs in the south are the lowest in Europe outside Spain.

The third factor is the burden of non-wage costs on new investment. Italy's expensive pay-as-you go pension system can be funded only by putting a tax burden on employers that ranks among the highest in Europe. This deters international companies from investing in the south.

Moreover, the region's fledgling enterprises, rather than pay tax, slide into the black economy where they often breed the culture of crime that investors fear.

Given this mixture of constraints, the government aims to boost about 40 defined areas of the Mezzogiorno, by means of tax subsidies and a commitment from unions to lower wage costs.

'It is a bottom-up policy of economic development, in which some areas of the south will grow faster than others,' Mr Viesti said.

In his view, this policy must start to produce real improvement in investment and job creation within three

years. If it succeeds, the stronger southern economy will transform Italy's overall economic performance. If it does not, many politicians believe the crisis of the south will overwhelm the government that took Italy into EMU.

(a) What problems does the Mezzogiorno face?

(b) Why is foreign investment not attracted to this area?

(c) The Italian government has adopted a largely interventionist approach to supporting the region. Identify the main ways in which it is seeking to improve the region's economic performance.

E ANSWERS

Q1. *between 2 and 4 per cent* per annum. The average growth rate of the OECD countries between 1970 and 1999 was 2.94 per cent.

Q2. *Yes* (b), (c), (d) and (f). These all help to explain the rightward shifts in the aggregate supply curve. In the case of (a), closing the gap between actual and potential output has not taken place, and even if it had, would be insignificant over the long run compared with increases in potential output. In the case of (e), reductions in unemployment have not occurred, except in the last few years, and do not help to explain long-term growth.

Q3. *(a)* I_0 (point *b*).

(b) $I_0 - D_0$ (points *b* – *c*). D_0 has to be subtracted for capital depreciation.

(c) Y_0.

(d) The net investment of $I_0 - D_0$ leads to an expansion of the capital stock and hence a rise in national income. As national income rises, however, diminishing returns to capital take place (the *Y* and *I* curves get less and less steep). Eventually all the new investment is taken up with replacing worn out capital (it all goes on depreciation) and national income stops rising. A steady state has been reached at Y_1 and K_1.

(e) No (see answer to (d)).

(f) The *I* line will shift upwards and a new equilibrium will be reached where it crosses the *D* line.

(g) Because all the extra investment will be eventually absorbed by depreciation (see answer to (d)).

(h) The *Y* line will shift upwards and there will be a corresponding upward shift in the *I* line. If it is a 'one-off' technological advance, rather than progress that goes on building over several years, there will be a single upward shift in the *Y*

and *I* curves and a 'one-off' increase in national income. The new equilibrium national income will correspond to the level of capital stock where the new *I* line crosses the *D* line.

Q4. C (see Figure 22.4 on page 629 in Sloman, *Economics*, 4th edn).

Q5. *True.*

Q6. D. It is important for the government to create the right climate (through appropriate supply-side policies) to encourage more research and development and a correspondingly faster rate of technological progress and hence economic growth.

Q7. (a), (b) and (c) are supply-side solutions. (f) is a demand-side solution. (d) and (e) can have an effect upon both the demand side and the supply side. In the case of (d), investment will stimulate aggregate demand, but it will also increase potential output and/or reduce costs by increasing the capital stock, especially if investment is targeted on key growth industries or to bottleneck sectors. In the case of (e), tax cuts, as well as stimulating aggregate demand, will also offer an incentive for workers to work (assuming the substitution effect outweighs the income effect). In the case of (f), lower interest rates will increase demand generally, and a lower exchange rate will increase the demand for exports at existing *sterling* prices. A lower exchange rate, however, will *not* reduce costs.

Q8. *(a)* *Outward shift.*

(b) *Rightward shift.*

(c) *Movement down along* (caused by the rightward shift in the aggregate supply curve).

(d) *Leftward shift* and/or *Movement down along*. The leftward shift would result from a lower equilibrium level of unemployment. The movement down along would result from increased output from a given quantity of labour, and thus less

employment for any given level of real aggregate demand.

   (e) *No shift in* (except as a side-effect: e.g. tax cuts to provide greater incentives would, *ceteris paribus*, shift the withdrawals curve downwards).

   (f) *No shift in* (except as a side-effect: e.g. incentives for firms to conduct research and development or training may lead to an increase in net investment and hence a vertical shift upwards in the injections line).

   (g) *Rightward shift.*

Q9. Three supply-side policies that could be used to push the production possibility curve outward are: incentives to encourage investment; the expansion of labour training programmes; the use of taxation policy to encourage more people to work or the same people to work harder.

Q10. *(a)* *True.* Demand-side policy for the monetarist is monetary policy which should be directed to the control of inflation. Given a long-run vertical Phillips curve, demand-side policy cannot be used to control long-run output and unemployment.

   (b) *True.* In the long run only by shifting the natural rate of unemployment to the left will unemployment fall, or by shifting the production possibility curve outward will output rise.

   (c) *False.* If supply-side policy causes the natural rate of unemployment to fall, the Phillips curve will shift to the *left.*

   (d) *True.* Free-market philosophy dominates the monetarist view of supply-side policy.

Q11. *can.*

Q12. *can.* With an upward-sloping aggregate supply curve, a rightward shift in the curve will both reduce prices and increase output. With a downward-sloping Phillips curve, a leftward shift in the curve can lead to lower unemployment and lower inflation too.

Q13. *True.* If supply-side policies can reduce inflation, there is less need for deflationary policies and the attendant problems of higher unemployment.

Q14. *True.* An example is the use of mixture of tax incentives and the provision of training to encourage unemployed people to take up unemployment.

Q15. A. Prices and incomes policy was not used during the 1980s. Note in the case of D, that regional grants were substantially reduced: see section 22.5 of Sloman (4th edition).

Q16. Examples included: cash limits on government departments; reductions in grants and subsidies to private industry; reductions in central government grants to local authorities as a proportion of local authority revenue; reductions in public-sector capital project; cuts in the size of the civil service; tough stance on public-sector pay; reductions in the

amount of government support given to nationalised industries; rate capping of local authorities; privatisation.

Q17. E. As the deflationary monetary policy led to increased unemployment, so the expenditure on unemployment and other social security benefits increased. (In the case of A, the desire to cut taxes would further stimulate the need to cut government expenditure; in the case of B and C, reducing the PSBR tends to lead to *reductions* in the money supply; in the case of D, this had no direct effect on government expenditure.)

Q18. *(a)* *False.* The supposed beneficial effect is that the tax cut will act as an incentive for workers to work more. This will occur only if the substitution effect (substituting work for leisure) is *larger* than the income effect (being able to afford to work less).

   (b) *True.* Lower tax rates are seen as a work incentive to those who are not the main income earners: for example, parents looking after children.

   (c) *Unsure.* This is very difficult to prove or disprove. The argument is that people will be prepared to put more effort into their work if they can keep more of their pay.

   (d) *False.* If tax rates are cut, take-home pay will increase, and thus it becomes more worthwhile for unemployed people to accept job offers. The level of *equilibrium* unemployment will fall. However, if (pre-tax) wage rates are sticky downwards, firms will not be willing to take on the extra supply of labour. Thus *disequilibrium* unemployment will *rise.*

   (e) *True.* Provided the increased supply of labour has some downward effect on *pre-tax* wages, firms will take on extra labour.

Q19. *True.* As union power is reduced, wages will fall, leading to a fall in the incentive to find employment. (Note, however, that disequilibrium unemployment will fall.)

Q20. The following answers refer to Figure A22.1:

   (a) Equilibrium unemployment equals $c - b$. Disequilibrium unemployment equals $b - a$.

   (b) Wage equals W_2. Equilibrium unemployment equals $e - d$. There is no disequilibrium unemployment.

   (c) The aggregate demand for labour shifts to the left (e.g. to AD_{L_2}).

   (d) Equilibrium unemployment equals $e - d$. Disequilibrium unemployment equals $d - f$.

   (e) Assuming no further fall in AD_L, the wage rate will fall to W_3.

   There will be no disequilibrium unemployment, but equilibrium unemployment will now be $h - g$. (In practice, there may be a further fall

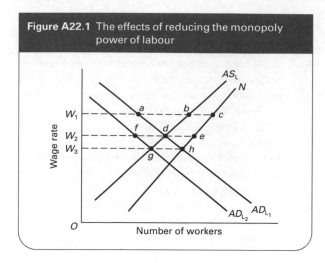

Figure A22.1 The effects of reducing the monopoly power of labour

---

in consumer demand – given a further redistribution away from wages to profits – and thus there will be a further leftward movement in AD_L. If there is any sluggishness downwards in wages, further disequilibrium unemployment will occur.)

Q21. Demand deficient.

Q22. *small.*

Q23. *frictional.*

Q24. *poverty.*

Q25. *right.* (More people would feel forced to look for a job.)

Q26. Examples include: privatisation; deregulation (e.g. financial markets and the bus industry); introducing market relationships into parts of the public sector, such as health and eduction; removing barriers to trade and international capital movements.

Q27. *lower.*

Q28. 1 (a); 2 (c); 3 (e); 4 (b); 5 (f); 6 (d).

Q29. D.

Q30. Reasons include: many markets are monopolistic (this removes some of the incentive for investment); firms may only be interested in short-term profits; investment might appear too risky, especially if the free market is subject to cyclical fluctuations; investment decisions by private firms may not take into account the social rate of return (for example, the full benefits from the training of labour); financial institutions may be unwilling to finance long-term investment.

Q31. (a), (c) and (e).

Q32. C. The key feature of indicative planning is one of consultation. Targets and goals are agreed upon between government, firms and possibly unions, and become the basis of a national plan.

Q33. *True.* Examples include: government financed training schemes, financing research and development, providing assistance to small firms, increasing

expenditure on infrastructure projects as a means of increasing national productivity.

Q34. Arguments include: firms have no incentive to be efficient if they know they can rely on government subsidies; the provision of grants and subsidies distorts economic signals; the government may finance extravagant projects that would otherwise not be economically viable.

Q35. **(a)** *True(?).* Prices and wages would simply adjust to equate demand and supply. There would be no disequilibrium unemployment. There would merely be a residual frictional unemployment, which nevertheless could vary from one locality to another.

(b) *True(?).* Workers would migrate to where wages were highest and businesses would locate where labour was cheapest. Any disparity in wages would be largely eliminated in this manner (unless there were significant non-monetary benefits from staying in the areas of reduced demand).

Q36. **(a)** *True(?).* Prices and wages would simply adjust to equate demand and supply. There would be no disequilibrium unemployment. To the extent, however, that wages differed from one region to another, the lower-wage regions might have a slightly higher frictional unemployment (but expectations of a normal wage would also be lower in these regions, which might make people more willing to accept lower-paid jobs).

(b) *False.* Considerable regional disparities in wages might continue to exist if some regions were more productive/more rapidly growing than others.

Q37. (a), (d) and (f) are all interventionist strategies. They have in common the fact that they all interfere with the free working of the market. The remainder are radical-right proposals as they all attempt to limit state or local authority intervention and/or to free-up the market. Note that (g) was designed in part to prevent 'high-spending' local authorities in areas of high unemployment charging higher than average business rates and thereby discouraging the inflow of capital to those regions.

Q38. **(a)** and **(b)** No. There was a decline in government expenditure, not only in real terms, but in money terms also. Part of the reason for this has been an increase in expenditure on urban policy.

(c) and **(d)** *Yes.* The intention has been not only to save money, but also to target the money more carefully to investments that will be effective in promoting jobs.

(e) *No.*

(f) *Yes.*

(g) *Yes.*

Q39. Factors include the following: government restrictions on local authority expenditure have reduced the support that the local authorities can give to deprived areas; the total amount of government spending on urban policy has been relatively low compared with other areas of government expenditure; many of the jobs 'created' may have been merely diverted from marginally less deprived areas nearby which did not receive support; some of the new jobs may have been filled not by local residents, but by people commuting into the area.

23 International Trade

A REVIEW

In this chapter we will look at the advantages and disadvantages of international trade. We start by examining the arguments in favour of trade and then ask, if trade is potentially beneficial to all participating countries, why do countries frequently seek to restrict trade? We then turn to examine the case for establishing trading blocs between countries where the members give each other preferential treatment. The final topic is the European Union, probably the most famous of all preferential trading arrangements.

23.1 The advantages of trade

(Pages 659–64) The theory of comparative advantage
Countries can gain from trade if they specialise in producing those goods in which they have a comparative advantage.

Q1. A country has a comparative advantage in good X compared with good Y if:
A. it can produce more X than Y in total.
B. it can produce more X than Y for a given amount of resources.
C. it can produce more X than other countries.
D. it can produce more X relative to Y than other countries.
E. it can produce X with less resources than other countries.

Q2. Consider the following five situations for a world with just two countries. Each one shows alternative amounts of goods X and Y that the two countries F and G can produce for a given amount of resources. Assume constant costs. In each case give the (pre-trade) opportunity cost of X in terms of Y.

(i) Country F: 10 units of X or 20 units of Y.
$$1X = \ldots\ldots\ldots Y$$
Country G: 10 units of X or 10 units of Y.
$$1X = \ldots\ldots\ldots Y$$

(ii) Country F: 12 units of X or 12 units of Y.
$$1X = \ldots\ldots\ldots Y$$
Country G: 6 units of X or 8 units of Y.
$$1X = \ldots\ldots\ldots Y$$

(iii) Country F: 8 units of X or 8 units of Y.
$$1X = \ldots\ldots\ldots Y$$
Country G: 10 units of X or 10 units of Y.
$$1X = \ldots\ldots\ldots Y$$

(iv) Country F: 20 units of X or 5 units of Y.
$$1X = \ldots\ldots\ldots Y$$
Country G: 18 units of X or 2 units of Y.
$$1X = \ldots\ldots\ldots Y$$

(v) Country F: 10 units of X or 8 units of Y.
$$1X = \ldots\ldots\ldots Y$$
Country G: 6 units of X or 6 units of Y.
$$1X = \ldots\ldots\ldots Y$$

Q3. Referring to the six different situations given in Q2, and assuming no transport costs:

 Multiple Choice   Written answer   Delete wrong word   ⊖ Diagram/table manipulation   ⊗ Calculation   ⬗ Matching/ordering *(a)* In which situations will country F export good X and import good Y?

....

(b) In which situations will country F export good Y and import good X?

....

(c) In which situations will country F either import or export both goods?

....

(d) In which situations will no trade take place?

....

⊗ **Q4.** In situation (i) in Q2, assume that before trade the price ratios of the two goods were equal to their opportunity cost ratios.

(a) What would the pre-trade price ratio (P_X/P_Y) be in country F?

....

(b) What would the pre-trade price ratio (P_X/P_Y) be in country G?

....

(c) Now assume that trade is opened up and that 1 unit of X exchanges for 1.5 of Y. Demonstrate how both countries have gained.

....

....

In what type of goods will countries have a comparative advantage? Which goods will they be able to produce at a low opportunity cost?

♟ **Q5.** The following are four items that are traded internationally:

  (i) Wheat
 (ii) Computers
(iii) Textiles
 (iv) Insurance

In which one of the four is each of the following most likely to have a comparative advantage?

(a) India   ....

(b) UK   ....

(c) Canada   ....

(d) Japan   ....

These four countries have a comparative advantage in these four products because they are intensive in the respective country's **Q6.** *scarce/abundant/intermediate* factor.

Specialising in these goods and exporting them will have the effect of **Q7.** *reducing/increasing/maintaining existing* factor price inequalities.

In practice there will be a limit to specialisation and trade. This will result in part from **Q8.** *increasing/decreasing/constant* opportunity costs. In other words the country will face a **Q9.** *bowed in/bowed out/straight line* production possibility curve. As a country specialises and has to use resources that are less and less suited to producing its exports, so its comparative advantage will **Q10.** *increase/remain constant/disappear*.

(?) **Q11.** There are other factors also which will have the effect of limiting specialisation and trade. Name two.

1. ....

2. ....

(Pages 664–6) The terms of trade
What will be the relative price of exports and imports? This is given by the *terms of trade*.

◑ **Q12.** In a simple world of just one export (X) and one import (M) the terms of trade are defined as P_M/P_X.

True/False

⊗ **Q13.** If 2 units of exports exchange for 3 units of imports, what are the terms of trade?

....

In the real world where countries have many imports and exports, the terms of trade are given by a weighted average price of exports divided by a weighted average price of imports, expressed as indices.

⊗ **Q14.** If in year 1 (the base year) the terms of trade index is 100, what will it be in year 5 if, over the period, the weighted average price of exports doubled while the weighted average price of imports went up by 50 per cent?

....

How will the trade price of each individual import and export be determined? Let us again assume for simplicity that there are just two countries.

⊖ **Q15.** Figure 23.1 shows the demand and supply of good Z in the two countries F and G.

(a) Which country will export the good?

....

(b) What will be the equilibrium trade price?

....

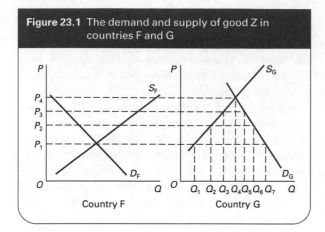

Figure 23.1 The demand and supply of good Z in countries F and G

(c) How much of good Z will be consumed in country G?

....

(d) How much will be traded? ....

The relative price of imports and exports, and hence the terms of trade, will also depend on the rate of exchange. For example, if the rate of exchange changes from £1 = €1.50 to £1 = €1.30, then, other things being equal, the UK terms of trade will have **Q16.** *improved/deteriorated.*

(Pages 666–7) Other reasons for trade
Current comparative cost differences are not the only basis for trade.

Q17. The following is a list of other factors that can make trade beneficial:
  (i) Decreasing costs.
 (ii) Differences in demand.
(iii) Increased competition.
(iv) Trade is an engine of growth.
 (v) Non-economic factors.

Into which one of these five categories do the following examples fit?
(a) When the rest-of-the-world economy expands, this will increase the demand for a country's exports and also improve its terms of trade.

....

(b) By specialising in certain exports, the country may become increasingly skilled in their production.

....

(c) Free trade between countries may encourage closer political co-operation.

....

(d) Allowing imports freely into a country may stimulate domestic producers to be more efficient.

....

(e) The marginal utility ratios for products differ between different countries.

....

23.2 Arguments for restricting trade

(Pages 667–71) Many arguments are used by governments to justify restricting imports or giving specific help to domestic industries. These arguments can be put into four categories: (i) those arguments with some general validity in a world context, (ii) those arguments with validity for specific countries, but where there is nevertheless a net world loss, (iii) non-economic arguments, (iv) fallacious arguments.

Q18. Into which of the above four categories do the following arguments belong?
(a) Putting tariffs on certain imports is desirable if it can thereby drive down the price-less-tariff.

....

(b) Industries that are subject to external economies of scale should be protected or promoted if that will result in their gaining a comparative advantage.

....

(c) Trade sanctions are desirable against countries which abuse human rights.

....

(d) The international community should permit countries to retaliate with equivalent-sized tariffs against countries that subsidise their exports.

....

(e) If imported goods undercut the price of home-produced goods, it is desirable to put tariffs on them to bring them up to the price of home-produced goods.

....

(f) A domestic computer firm should be protected from a giant competitor abroad if there is the danger that the domestic one will not survive the competition.

....

Q19. Figure 23.2 shows a large country which as a whole has monopsony power in the purchase of a given import. Assume, however, that *individual* consumers in the country are price takers. What would be the size of the optimum tariff (assuming no externalities) to allow the country best to exploit its power?
A. *HJ*
B. *OJ – FH*
C. *GH*
D. *FH*
E. *GJ – FH*

Figure 23.2 Country with monopsony power in the purchase of an import

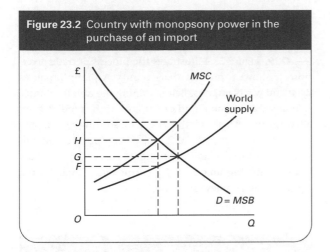

(*Pages 671–6*) Even if there are valid arguments for government intervention, protection through trade restrictions will rarely be the optimum solution. The point is that trade restrictions impose costs. Take the case of a tariff.

⊖ **Q20.** Figure 23.3 shows a country's domestic demand and supply curves (D_{dom} and S_{dom}) for a product. Part of demand is satisfied by imports. The country is a price taker and the world price for the product is given by P_{w} with the world supply curve given by S_{w}. A tariff is then imposed on the product whose amount is shown by the vertical difference between S_{w} and $S_{\text{w+t}}$.

Figure 23.3 A country's demand for and supply of an importable good

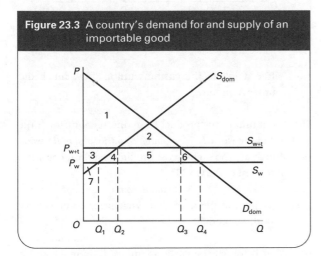

(a) How much is imported before the tariff is imposed?

....

(b) How much is imported after the tariff is imposed?

....

(c) What area(s) represent(s) total consumer surplus before the tariff is imposed?

....

(d) What area(s) represent(s) total consumer surplus after the tariff is imposed?

....

(e) What area(s) represent(s) the loss in consumer surplus from the imposition of the tariff?

....

(f) What area(s) represent(s) the producer surplus before the tariff is imposed?

....

(g) What area(s) represent(s) the producer surplus after the tariff is imposed?

....

(h) What area(s) represent(s) the gain in producer surplus from the imposition of the tariff?

....

(i) How much revenue does the government gain from the imposition of the tariff?

....

(j) What area(s) represent(s) the total net loss from the tariff?

....

Part of these 'costs' may be warranted. For example, if there were negative externalities in consumption (e.g. from cars), then it might be desirable to reduce consumption to Q_3 in Figure 23.3. But it is not *also* desirable to increase domestic production from Q_1 to Q_2. This, after all, involves diverting production from **Q21.** *high-cost producers to low-cost producers/low-cost producers to high-cost producers*. Thus protection in this case would be **Q22.** *first best/definitely second best/at most second best*.

▣ **Q23.** Referring to Figure 23.3, if there were external benefits of domestic production equal to $P_{\text{w+t}} - P_{\text{w}}$, but no externalities in domestic consumption such that $D_{\text{dom}} = MSB$, what would be the optimum form of government intervention?

A. A consumption tax so as to reduce consumption to Q_3 but leave production unchanged.

B. A tariff on imports, equal to $P_{\text{w+t}} - P_{\text{w}}$.

C. A production subsidy, equal to $P_{\text{w+t}} - P_{\text{w}}$.

D. A tax on the product, equal to $P_{\text{w+t}} - P_{\text{w}}$.

E. A complete ban on all imports of this product.

(?) **Q24.** What would be the 'first-best' solution to negative externalities in consumption (as in Q21 and Q22)?

....

(?) **Q25.** Name three other possible drawbacks from protectionism.

1. ....

2. ....

3. ....

23.3 *Preferential trading*

(Page 677) Countries may make a partial move towards free trade by removing trade restriction with selected other countries. These *preferential trading arrangements* may take different forms, but there are four broad types.

Q26. The four types of arrangement are as follows.
 (i) Free trade areas.
 (ii) Customs unions.
 (iii) Common markets.
 (iv) Economic and monetary unions.

Match each of the above to the following definitions:

(a) Where countries have no tariffs or quotas between themselves and have common external tariffs and quotas with non-members.

....

(b) Where countries have no trade barriers whatsoever between themselves, whether in terms of tariffs, quotas, differences in regulations governing the activities of firms, restrictions on factor movements or differences in indirect taxation.

....

(c) Where countries have no tariffs or quotas between themselves and are free to impose whatever restrictions they each individually choose on non-members.

....

(d) Where countries have no trade or other economic restrictions between themselves, have a fixed exchange rate or even a common currency, and pursue common economic policies: fiscal, monetary, labour and industrial.

....

(Pages 678–80) When a country joins a preferential trading system its trading patterns will change. The result can be either *trade creation* or *trade diversion*.

Q27. Trade creation is defined as a situation where production shifts from a higher-cost to a lower-cost source.

True/False

Q28. Which of the following defines a situation of trade diversion resulting from the formation of a customs union?

A. Production is diverted from a higher-cost producer outside the union to a lower-cost producer within the union.

B. Production is diverted from a lower-cost producer outside the union to a higher-cost producer within the union.

C. Production is diverted away from trade within the union to trade with non-union members.

D. Production is diverted away from tradable goods to those which are not traded.

E. Trade between non-union members is diverted to trade with union members.

Q29. Figure 23.4 illustrates the process of trade diversion. It shows a product that country A partly produces itself and partly imports. Before joining the union, country A imposed a common tariff on imports of the product from all countries. This had the effect of shifting the supply curve of imports from S_w to $S_{w+tariff}$. After joining the union, the country faced a (tariff-free) supply curve of the product from within the union of S_{union} (this curve includes the country's own domestic supply).

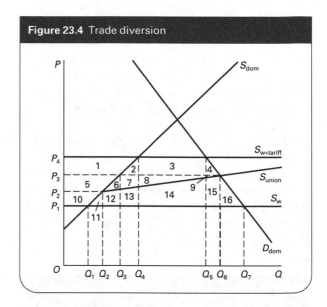

Figure 23.4 Trade diversion

(a) Before it joined the customs union, how much did country A import?

....

(b) Did it import the product from union countries or the rest of the world? *union countries/rest of the world*

(c) Which are the higher-cost producers: union countries or the rest of the world?

union countries/rest of the world

(d) After joining the union, at what price could it now import the product?

....

(e) After it joined the customs union, how much did it import?

....

(f) Did production move to a higher- or a lower-cost producer? *higher-cost producer/lower-cost producer*

(g) What area(s) represent the gain/loss in consumers' surplus from joining the union?

gain/loss of area(s) ....

(h) What area(s) represent the gain/loss in domestic producers' surplus from joining the union?

gain/loss of area(s) ....

(i) What area(s) represent the loss in tariff revenue for the government?

area(s) ....

(j) What area(s) represent the net gain or loss from the trade diversion?

area(s) ....

◗ **Q30.** A customs union is more likely to lead to trade diversion rather than trade creation when

(a) the union's external tariff is very high. *True/False*

(b) there is a substantial cost difference between goods produced within and outside the union. *True/False*

23.4 The European Union

(Pages 680–7)

▤ **Q31.** Which of the following best describes the European Community as it was in the 1980s?

A. A customs union.

B. A common market.

C. A free trade area.

D. An economic and monetary union.

E. A monetary system.

In 1993 the European Community (EC) was renamed the European Union (EU).

▤ **Q32.** Referring to the list in Q31, which one best describes the European Union today as envisaged in the Single European Act of 1986?

A/B/C/D/E

Despite the elimination of tariffs between member states, there were significant *non-tariff* barriers before the completion of the single European market after 1992.

◉ **Q33.** The following are various types of non-tariff barrier:

(i) Market-distorting barriers.

(ii) Quotas imposed by individual members on imports from outside the EU.

(iii) Tax barriers.

(iv) Labour market barriers.

(v) Regulations and norms.

(vi) State procurement bias.

(vii) Licensing.

(viii) Financial barriers.

(ix) Customs formalities.

Match each of the following examples from the pre-single market EU to the above types of barrier. There is one example of each type.

(a) A requirement by an EU country that all new buildings must be constructed using a certain type of girder made only in that country.

....

(b) The delays experienced by checking paperwork when goods cross from one EU country to another.

....

(c) Higher rates of excise duty on alcoholic drinks not produced in the country in question but produced elsewhere in the EU.

....

(d) A restriction on the quantity of shoes that one EU country allows to be imported from Poland, thereby encouraging Polish shoes to be diverted to other EU countries, making it harder for their domestic shoe industries to compete.

....

(e) Subsidies granted to domestic sheep farmers to enable them to compete unfairly in the EU lamb and wool markets.

....

(f) Professions that only recognise their own national qualifications.

....

(g) Governments or local authorities permitting only national firms to operate domestic coach and bus services.

....

(h) Governments preferring to buy military equipment from domestic armaments manufacturers.

....

(i) Credit controls that favour domestic firms.

....

⑦ **Q34.** Give three advantages of the completion of the single market in the EU.

1. ....

2. ....

3. ....

A complete common market also entails problems.

◗ **Q35.** In which of the following cases are there most likely to be adverse regional multiplier effects from the development of the single market?

(a) Capital and labour move towards the geographical centre of the Union. *Yes/No*

(b) Firms gain substantial plant economies by centralising production. *Yes/No*

(c) Rents and land prices are flexible. *Yes/No*

(d) A larger proportion of the EU budget is spent on regional policy. *Yes/No*

(e) The impossibility of euro-zone countries altering exchange rates between themselves. *Yes/No*

(f) The development of information technology reduces communication costs. *Yes/No*

(g) Infrastructure expenditure is financed locally. *Yes/No*

Although the development of the single market encourages trade creation, it can also encourage trade diversion.

 Q36. Which of the following cases would make trade diversion more likely?

(a) Substantial initial internal barriers to trade are now completely abolished. *Yes/No*

(b) External barriers remain high. *Yes/No*

(c) European industries have a wide range of available technologies and skills. *Yes/No*

(d) Many European industries experience decreasing costs at the level of individual national markets. *Yes/No*

B PROBLEMS, EXERCISES AND PROJECTS

Table 23.1 Pre-trade production possibilities for goods X and Y in countries F and G (per period of time)

Country F		Country G	
Good X (units)	Good Y (units)	Good X (units)	Good Y (units)
180	0	200	0
135	90	150	50
90	180	100	100
45	270	50	150
0	360	0	200

Q37. Table 23.1 shows the pre-trade production possibilities of countries F and G per period of time.

(a) Which country has a comparative advantage in good Y? *Country F/Country G*

(b) Assuming that $P = MC$, what would be the pre-trade price ratio (P_X/P_Y) in country F?

....

(c) Draw the production possibility curves for the two countries on Figure 23.5.

(d) Assuming that the exchange ratio after trade which balances the supply and demand for both imports and exports is $2X = 3Y$, draw a new line on each diagram showing the post-trade consumption possibilities if each country specialises completely in the good in which it has a comparative advantage.

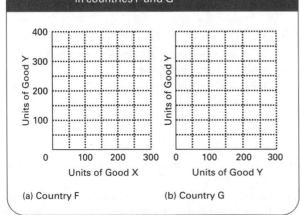

Figure 23.5 Production possibilities for goods X and Y in countries F and G

(a) Country F

(b) Country G

(e) What will be the level of production and consumption in each country after trade has commenced, assuming tha country F consumes 240 units of good Y?

Country F produces .... *units of X and* .... *units of Y.*
Country F consumes .... *units of X and 240 units of Y.*
Country G produces .... *units of X and* .... *units of Y.*
Country G consumes .... *units of X and* .... *units of Y.*

.... *units of X are exported by country* ....

.... *units of Y are exported by country* ....

(f) Mark the level of imports and exports of each country on diagrams (a) and (b) of Figure 23.5.

Q38. A country's domestic supply and demand schedules for good X are as follows:

$$Qs_{dom} = -10 + 10P$$
$$Qd_{dom} = 130 - 10P$$

(a) Using these two equations, fill in the figures in Table 23.2.

Table 23.2 Demand and supply of good X

Price (£)	0	1	2	3	4	5	6	7	8
Qs_{dom}	...	...	...	...	30	...	...	...	...
Qd_{dom}	...	...	110	...	...	...	...	...	...

(b) What is the equilibrium price and quantity?

$P =$ .... $Q =$ ....

(c) Plot the curves on Figure 23.6.

Now assume that the country starts to trade and faces an infinitely elastic world supply curve at a price of £3 per unit.

Figure 23.6 Demand and supply of good X

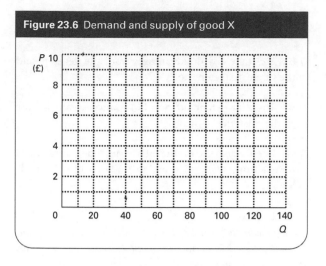

(d) How much will the country now consume?

.... units

(e) How much will the country now produce?

.... units

(f) How much will the country now import?

.... units

(g) How much extra consumer surplus will consumers now gain?

....

(Clue: look at Figure 23.6 and work out the extra area gained.)

(h) How much producer surplus do domestic producers lose?

....

(i) What is the net welfare gain?

....

Q39. Given the information in Q38, now assume that a tariff of £2 per unit is imposed on the good.

(a) What will be the new market price?

....

(b) What will be the new level of imports?

.... units

(c) What is the reduction in consumer surplus?

....

(d) What is the increase in producer surplus?

....

(e) What is the tariff revenue for the government?

....

(f) What is the net welfare loss from the imposition of the tariff?

....

Now assume that the country joins a customs union, which has an infinitely elastic supply of good X at a price of £4.

(g) What is the new market price?

....

(h) What will be the new level of imports?

.... units

(i) Has there been trade creation or trade diversion?

trade creation/trade diversion

(j) What is the increase in consumer surplus?

....

(k) What is the reduction in producer surplus?

....

(l) What is the reduction in tariff revenue?

....

(m) What is the net gain or loss in terms of good X from joining the customs union?

....

Q40. Find out how the composition of UK imports and exports has changed over the last 25 years. The best sources are *United Kingdom Balance of Payments (the 'Pink Book')* (ONS) and *Annual Abstract of Statistics* (ONS).

(a) How has the *area* composition changed? (What proportions of imports and exports come from which areas of the world?) Attempt an explanation for these changes.

(b) How has the *commodity* composition changed in primary products, semi-manufactures, manufactures and services? Have such changes reflected changes in comparative costs?

Q41. Find out what has happened to the UK's terms of trade over the last 15 years. Details are given in *Economic Trends Annual Supplement* (ONS).

(a) Have these changes reflected changes in the exchange rate index (also given in *Economic Trends Annual Supplement*)?

(b) What else determines the terms of trade? Are the figures consistent with your answer here?

 DISCUSSION TOPICS AND ESSAYS

Q42. Can different endowments of factors of production fully explain countries' differences in comparative costs?

Q43. Make out a case for restricting trade between the USA and the UK. Are there any arguments here that could not equally apply to a case for restricting trade between Scotland and England or between Liverpool and Manchester?

Q44. 'Far from leading to specialisation by country, free trade simply leads to a proliferation of products within any one country. The result is the relatively minor gain of an increased number of brands to choose from.' Discuss.

Q45. Are any of the arguments for restricting trade based on the criticism that free trade *prevents* countries from fully exploiting their comparative advantage?

Q46. Are import restriction ever a first-best policy for aiding declining industries?

Q47. Are tariffs ever superior to subsidies as a means of correcting market distortions?

Q48. 'Administrative barriers are a much more damaging form of protection than tariffs.' Discuss.

Q49. Are there any disadvantages from the development of the single market in the EU?

Q50. To what extent do non-EU countries gain or lose from the existence of the EU?

Q51. Is enlargement of the EU to include countries of Eastern Europe likely to result in trade creation or trade diversion?

Q52. Debate
All arguments for restricting trade boil down to special pleading for particular interest groups. Ultimately there will be a net social cost from any trade restrictions.

ARTICLES

The division of the world trading system into clearly defined regional trading blocs is not a new phenomenon, but it is a process that has intensified in recent years. The following article, taken from *Management Today* of December 1995, examines this trend and the implications for world trade and the WTO.

The balance of trade

The World Trade Organisation (WTO) is 'alive and functioning' says Dr Vincent Cable, director of International Economics at Chatham House. Yet, in the past two years, there have been a series of dramatic new initiatives to try and create regional free trade areas (FTAs) in North America and the Asia-Pacific region. Do these initiatives herald the demise of an open world trading system and the transition to a more conflictual, tripolar system of trading blocs? Or can British companies have some faith in the durability of the multilateral principles embodied in the new World Trade Organisation (WTO)?

While the WTO digests the Uruguay Round, what scope is there for an increase in trading ties between countries in the same geographical region? Contrary to the WTO's multilateral approach, the perceived advantage of FTAs is that they permit countries to choose their closest trading companions. Ideally, members of an FTA should be economically homogenous either in trade patterns or in levels of economic development. Countries can then reap the benefits of an expanded market base,

while minimising the problems that tend to flow from the desire of one nation's manufacturers to relocate to the markets of other FTA members with lower labour costs.

The FTAs have the advantage of being flexible. Member states need not lose the right to use ADDs or safeguards against other FTA members in case of a sudden surge of imports. FTAs are also accompanied by detailed negotiations on the 'rules of origin' for products that will be eligible for preferential treatment within the FTA. This means that national border controls can still prevent third countries from using neighbouring FTA members as launching pads for preferentially priced imports. Instead, those countries which are part of an FTA find their membership acts as a magnet to attract direct investment from foreign companies seeking to gain a foothold within the FTA.

Despite these advantages, there will still be winners and losers in an FTA. Successful FTAs, therefore, must rely upon a certain level of shared political cohesion in order to smooth over the disputes which are bound to surface

periodically as economic interpenetration accelerates.

European Union
The European Union offers the clearest example of a regional agreement that blends economic and political self-interest. EU member states operate from the principle that their national economies cannot compete effectively either in domestic or in global markets unless they give their companies a wider regional base from which to operate.

The European Union is a customs union rather than an FTA. This means that member states have dismantled most national trade barriers and replaced them with a Common External Tariff (CET). EC member states also pooled control over their national trade policies into a Common Commercial Policy in which the European Commission acts as the single representative of the collective wishes of EC governments in international trade negotiations. As part of the drive for 'ever closer union', EC governments also extended freedom of movement to three other areas: services, capital and labour.

NAFTA

Regional integration in other parts of the Western hemisphere does not yet face the complex dilemmas which currently trouble the EU. The North American Free Trade Area (NAFTA) between Canada, Mexico and the United States was signed as recently as January 1994. It is a free trade area and not a customs union, and hence aims at a lower level of economic interpenetration at this stage. Nevertheless, reflecting the importance of foreign direct investment for all signatories, NAFTA's parameters go well beyond the mere liberalisation of tariffs. The agreement provides a detailed framework to remove barriers to direct investment, the free flow of services (including financial services) and the free movement of transportation. It also tackles the issues of environmental and labour standards, and has established an effective dispute settlement mechanism.

NAFTA has much in its favour. The US cannot afford to see Mexico's political and economic reform programmes descend into chaos, and has clear political and economic reasons to want NAFTA to succeed.

First, Mexico offers US multinationals a low-labour cost, contiguous market from which to import components for final assembly in the US. Second, the potential for trade-led growth in the Americas is enormous. NAFTA makes good economic sense for any other Latin American countries. Participation in NAFTA will help them to sidestep the worst excesses of future US unilateral trade actions. More fundamentally, most Latin American governments want to use a deepening of regional trade to encourage imports and to attract foreign direct investment.

However, NAFTA faces a number of challenges. The disparity in incomes between Mexico and its northern American partners, although part of the reason for integration, may also become a source of friction (in 1994, US GDP per capita stood at $25 000 and Canada's at $21 000, while Mexico's was $5000). In the short term, it seems unlikely that NAFTA can meet the wealth-creating expectations placed on it by Mexican politicians. Unlike the EU, NAFTA lacks any formal financial redistributive mechanisms to assist Mexico adapt to the rigours of a market economy.

East Asia

Regional trade arrangements in East Asia are far less developed than either in Europe or the Americas. The Association of South East Asian Nations (ASEAN) pledged in January 1992 to trim intra-regional tariffs to a mere 5 per cent by 2003 and to create a free trade area for manufactured goods by 2007. Subsequently, the Prime Minister of Malaysia, Dr Mohamad Mahathir, proposed the creation of an East Asian Economic Caucus (EAEC) to include ASEAN members and also Japan. However, strong US opposition to this 'Caucus without Caucasians' has kept the initiative on the backburner. Instead, the US has given its backing to a broader regional initiative entitled Asia-Pacific Economic Co-operation (APEC) which is designed to link the economies of ASEAN, NAFTA, Japan, China, some other East Asian states, Australia and New Zealand.

At their summit in November 1994, leaders of APEC committed themselves to create a free trade area across the Pacific by the year 2010 for industrialised members, and by 2020 for the rest. From the American perspective, APEC would prevent the emergence of an exclusionary regional agreement that might be detrimental not only to US business interests, but also to its regional political influence.

The primary logic for Asian regionalism, however, is market-driven. It is based, in particular, on increasing levels of foreign direct investment by the most advanced East Asian states, such as Japan and Singapore. Some 61 per cent of FDI flows into East Asian economies in 1986–90 were from within the region and such trade within East Asia has increased at a faster rate than in the other two blocs, averaging 20 per cent a year to reach 50 pe rcent of total Asian trade in 1993. A large part of this growth in FDI and in trade generally simply reflects the rapid growth of the economies in the region. It is nevertheless striking that when North America is included, trade within the entire Asia-Pacific region accounts for 65 per cent of world trade, making it comfortably the largest trading 'zone' in the world.

It would be wrong, however, to deduce from these figures that either the Asia-Pacific region or East Asia itself is developing into some form of institutionalised trade bloc. First, the region is riven by unresolved disputes and

political fault-lines. Second, Asian nations are extremely cautious about US intentions. Singapore, Malaysia and China, in particular, suspect the US of plotting to force through Western standards of democratic accountability on the back of APEC trade initiatives.

Low levels of economic institutionalisation in East Asia also reflect the differing levels of development that exist there. In ASEAN alone, annual GNP per capita ranges from $22 250 in Singapore, $2315 in Thailand, to $220 in Vietnam.

Regionalism and the WTO

Looking in detail at the dynamics behind the EU, NAFTA, APEC and ASEAN, it is easy to agree with the view of Dr Vincent Cable that the concept of three neat 'trade blocs' is flawed. 'Vast differences exist between the EU, NAFTA and East Asia,' he argues, 'both in terms of the depth of economic integration and the political underpinnings of economic regionalism'.

Statistically speaking, however, a 'tripolarisation' of the world economy is taking place around the EU, NAFTA and the Asia-Pacific region. At the corporate level, multinationals have lobbied for regional integration, seeing regionalism as an integral part of the changing structure of international trade. This new structure is based partly upon the growing dependence of companies on international trade. It is also based upon the growing importance to companies of being able to invest in as many countries as possible. Between 1985–1993, foreign direct investment (FDI) by firms grew twice as fast as their direct exports.

Assisted by rapid technological modernisation, FDI serves many purposes, among them to allow firms to produce goods for local, regional or global markets in the most competitive manner; to produce or co-produce intermadiate products in the most efficient locations, then move them across borders for final assembly; and to provide services on an international basis. The importance of the interaction between international trade and FDI is illustrated by the fact that one-third of world exports in 1993 consisted of trade within multinationals.

From the corporate viewpoint, anything which facilitates international trade and investment is to be welcomed – whether on a regional or global basis.
© *Management Today*, Dec. 1995

(a) Outline the economic benefits that countries might gain from joining together in a free trade area (FTA).

(b) How might the objectives of FTAs conflict with those of the WTO?

(c) Compare and contrast the three major trading blocs, the EU, NAFTA and East Asia. What factors are likely to determine their success?

Is free trade always desirable? Environmentalists would argue not. In fact, many environmentalists argue that the encouragement of free trade by the World Trade Organisation (WTO) makes the situation far worse. In the article below, taken from *The Economist* of 3 October 1998, the issue of the WTO and the environment is considered.

Turtle wars

Cesar Luna leafs through photographs of a 'border reality trip' to Tijuana. Corroding drums of chemicals litter an industrial site open to the elements. There is nothing to keep children out, says Mr Luna, a campaigner with the Environmental Health Coalition in San Diego. Water runs down an escarpment towards people's homes below. He talks about heavy metals and acids contaminating the environment and damaging people's health: 'We're not talking about skin rashes and cold sores, but serious long-term health problems.'

Mr Luna explains that he is not against a 'just' free-trade agreement between America and Mexico, but that in Tijuana some companies are getting away with far too much. The side accords to the North American Free-Trade Agreement, which oblige NAFTA countries to uphold their own labour and environmental laws, have no teeth.

Environmental campaigners such as Mr Luna are becoming more vocal in arguing that world trade is already too free for the planet's good. And if they are cross about NAFTA, they are hopping mad about the WTO.

They have two main complaints. First, a string of national laws aimed at protecting the environment or human health have fallen foul of the WTO's dispute-settlement panels, beginning in 1995 with the very first case to be heard by one of these tribunals. The way in which America administered its cleanpetrol laws was held to discriminate against imports from Venezuela.

Since then, say the greens, things have got worse, citing two cases decided earlier this year. In the first, the WTO upheld a complaint by India, Malaysia, Pakistan and Thailand against an American law banning the sale in the United States of shrimps caught in nets that do not allow sea turtles to escape. Shrimp nets are the biggest killers of sea turtles, says Peter Fugazzotto of Earth Island Institute, a marine-conservation group in San Francisco. It was Earth Island that prodded the American government into taking up the turtle case. The second decision was that a longstanding EU ban on beef treated with growth hormones – i.e. most American meat – was incompatible with WTO rules.

The environmentalists also fret that WTO rules may undermine some international agreements to protect the global environment (known as multilateral environmental agreements, or MEAs). Of the total of around 200 such MEAs, about 20 either ban trade in certain pollutants or in goods made using them, or permit the use of trade sanctions as tools of enforcement. For example, the Montreal Protocol bans trade in chlorofluorocarbons (CFCs), which deplete the ozone layer. This trade ban, says Duncan Brack of the Royal Institute of International Affairs in London, played a big part in persuading countries to sign the protocol and end CFC production.

Luckily, so far no government has challenged the trade provisions of any MEA, but that luck may run out. For instance, a country that has not signed the Basle Convention on hazardous wastes (which bans trade in some waste chemicals and metals) might want to import blacklisted goods in order to recycle them or use them in some manufacturing process. Its goods might be barred by a signatory to the convention. The non-signatory could take the reluctant importer to the WTO, and stand a good chance of winning.

All this might worry environmentalists less if the WTO's dispute-settlement system were as limp as the old GATT's, but in fact it is remarkably effective. If one government believes that another is blocking its imports in breach of WTO rules, it can ask for talks. If these fail to resolve the dispute, the complaining government can ask for a panel of trade officials to adjudicate. If the panel finds the rules have been broken, the 'guilty' party is supposed to amend its laws or practice to conform with WTO rules. Appeals are possible, but once a final decision is reached, it can be blocked only by a consensus of WTO members. This is a big change from the old GATT system, under which every member (including guilty parties) had the right of veto. So far, no one has ignored a panel decision, because no one wants to jeopardise the credibility of the system of rule-based trade. But if someone did, the offended party could eventually retaliate with trade sanctions of its own.

The WTO's rules do in fact allow countries to impose trade restrictions for environmental and health reasons. Article XX of the GATT permits trade measures 'necessary to protect human, animal or plant life or health . . . [or] relating to the conservation of exhaustible natural resources if such measures are made effective in conjunction with restrictions on domestic production or consumption.'

However, some supposedly 'green' rules are not necessary to protect health or the environment at all, but are protectionist in either intent or effect. America's ban on Venezuelan petrol is one example. The EU's refusal to accept beef treated with hormones is another. There is little scientific evidence to suggest that such meat is any more dangerous than hormone-free beef.

Some greens insist that the WTO has no business sitting in judgment on laws passed by sovereign governments. Yet judging the compatibility of national laws with trade accords is precisely what the WTO's dispute-settlement process – set up with the agreement of all its member states – is there for. Both the disputed cases are examples of governments doing more than they should. Americans can surely make up their own minds on which shrimp to eat, helped if necessary by clear labelling. And if Europeans are happy to eat hormone-treated beef, and science judges it safe, why shouldn't they? John Jackson of Georgetown University Law School, an authority on WTO law, says the hormone case is particularly interesting because: 'It's the first to grapple heavily with the question of what scientific evidence a government has to present and the degree of risk [to consumers] it is obliged to negotiate.' WTO rules suggest that governments can decide how much risk they will accept in imported food. In effect, says Mr Jackson, the EU decided to run no risk at all. But if governments have so much leeway, they could get away with any import ban, however flimsy its scientific foundations.

A shrimp's a shrimp for a' that

A more important reason why the WTO and the greens are at loggerheads is another GATT rule requiring 'like products' to be treated identically. This means that with very few exceptions – e.g. goods made by prisoners – countries cannot ban imports because they do not like the way they have been produced: if they could, it would give rise to all sorts of protectionist jiggery-pokery. So WTO panels, like GATT panels before them, have regarded production methods as irrelevant: a shrimp is a shrimp, whether or not the net in which it was caught has a turtle-excluder.

Many environmentalists object. If the WTO rules out all trade sanctions that discriminate between more and less conservationist methods of production, then what chance is there of cleaning up? There should be exceptions to allow countries to favour goods made in less polluting ways.

According to Mr Brack, in some circumstances they may be right. Where pollution spans or crosses borders, the threat of trade sanctions can be an efficient way of achieving an environmental goal. The Montreal Protocol is a case in point. Other MEAs might be more effective if their trade clauses were immune from challenge by non-signatories at the WTO.

But this is far from straightforward. Suppose that the signatories to an MEA – to reduce emissions of certain gases, say – were mainly rich countries and

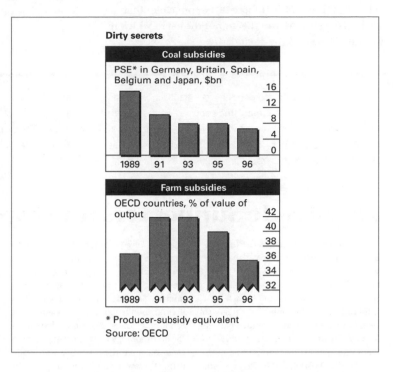

Dirty secrets

Coal subsidies
PSE* in Germany, Britain, Spain, Belgium and Japan, $bn

16
12
8
4
0

1989 91 93 95 96

Farm subsidies
OECD countries, % of value of output

42
40
38
36
34
32

1989 91 93 95 96

* Producer-subsidy equivalent
Source: OECD

the non-signatories were mainly developing ones. The developing countries might be less concerned about reducing pollution, or they might think they were being asked to bear too much of the burden. Would the rich be justified in banning imports from the poor? Clearly any exceptions to Article XX for MEAs would have to be chosen with care.

In any event, where pollution is confined to a single country, the argument for using trade sanctions against it is hard to stand up. Different parts of the world, Mr Brack points out, can tolerate different levels of pollution, depending on climate, the preferences of local people and governments, and existing pollution levels. Imposing the same environmental rules on every country, backed by trade sanctions, would destroy the comparative advantage of many countries, especially developing ones. It would be easy for protectionists to use greenery as an excuse for import restrictions.

Coming out of the shell

The WTO is looking around for ways of accommodating the greens' complaints. For example, it plans to open up its procedures by allowing non-governmental organisations to provide briefs to dispute-settlement panels and to attend hearings. It is already taking more advice from experts: in

the shrimp-turtle case, for example, it assembled a clutch of marine biologists. That should help to deflect the environmentalists' charge that the WTO is secretive and lacks know-how.

Changing the WTO's rules, however, is a taller order. In theory, says Mr Jackson, it would be easy to add a paragraph to Article XX to the effect that nothing in the WTO's rules prevents the application of certain MEAs. But he adds: 'Politically, I can't see it going through.' Such an amendment would have to be approved by three-quarters of all WTO members, and opposition from non-signatories to those MEAs would be robust.

But there are things governments can do that would make trade freer and the planet cleaner at the same time. According to a recent OECD study*, governments continue to support agriculture, energy and transport in ways that damage the environment (see chart). Minimum farm prices, for example, encourage farmers to produce too much, using more energy and more chemicals than they should. Coal subsidies encourage power companies to use dirty methods of electricity generation. Such subsidies are already in decline. Speeding their demise would please both free-traders and environmentalists.

* 'Improving the Environment through Reducing Subsidies', 1998.

(a) How does the WTO damage the environment?

(b) Why has the WTO adopted the principle that a 'shrimp is a shrimp, whether or not the net in which it was caught has a turtle-excluder'?

(c) How is the WTO looking to deal with the environmental issues of free trade?

Many people criticise the policy of free trade as one that benefits the strong (large countries and powerful multinationals) and penalises the weak (small poor countries and firms with little or no economic power, such as small farmers). In the following article, taken from *The Independent* of 13 September 1999, Diane Coyle challenges these arguments and maintains that it is often the poorest who have most to gain from the law of comparative advantage and from the activities of the World Trade Organisation.

Free-trade Supporters must speak frankly

The idea of free trade is under attack as never before in the post-war era

One of the many fresh starts in the next century will be the launch of a millennium trade round, a three-year negotiation intended to reduce barriers to trade in more areas, particularly services and agriculture. The annual meeting of the World Trade Organisation in early December is meant to agree the scope and terms of the negotiations, and it is no exaggeration to say its success will determine whether the 21st century will see extended to developing countries the improvements in welfare and prosperity enjoyed by the populations of developed countries these past hundred years.

Trade growth that gives them access to the world's big markets is one of the main ways that poorer countries can capture some of the benefits of globalisation. For very many countries, exports have been the engine of long-term growth. As the chart shows, for developing countries as a whole trade has been the motor for the past two decades, growing faster than national income, and its share rising most rapidly during the years of fastest growth.

Yet the idea of free trade is under attack as never before in the post-war era. The WTO's meeting in Seattle is likely to turn into a zoo of protest, as a coalition of campaigners, including aid charities and environmental groups, converge to proclaim their view that the world trading system is organised to benefit the rich and powerful through exploiting the poor. This could not be more wrong.

Yet the campaigners' false and malicious view of the WTO, and the continuing process of liberalisation, is in danger of becoming conventional wisdom. Few commentators bother to engage with it, or to correct it. Some even exploit it irresponsibly. For example, a recent discussion paper by economists Francisco Rodriguez and Dani Rodrik, published by the Centre for Economic Policy Research, challenged the methodology used in earlier research claiming countries with lower trade barriers grow faster. This rather technical paper was gleefully and wrongly acclaimed in some quarters as proving the stronger counter-claim that trade does not help boost growth.

The time has come for the supporters of free trade and globalisation to speak out. The global trading system has in fact been weighted very much more in favour of the developing countries by the establishment of the WTO. The reason is that it is a rule-based system, which does create a formally level playing field for all those who sign up to it. Systems based on rules, rather than negotiating weight, work to the advantage of the weak. In practice, of course, it is not quite so fair. For example, as the forthcoming World Development Report from the World Bank will point out, developing countries have very many fewer officials at the WTO than the industrial countries. Most are not in such a good position to exploit the opportunities.

Even so, the poorest country has, formally, the same market access as the richest. Poorer countries will be aided further by the fact that trade liberalisation is being extended to sectors in which they should have a comparative advantage, notably agriculture. If trade barriers and government subsidies can be reduced in farming, the whole world will benefit. Consumers everywhere will get cheaper food. Farmers in the rich countries, the lame-duck industry of

the turn of the century, will no longer be diverted into unprofitable lines of business by daft subsidies. Taxpayers will save billions. And farmers in the developing countries will enjoy a much bigger market for their produce.

Unfortunately, the politics of trade are notoriously complicated even if the economic analysis is straightforward. There are always potential losers as well as winners, with the losers often an identifiable and powerful group able to lobby government effectively. And not only is there protest against trade liberalisation from campaigning organisations, the radical fringe of modern politics, there are currently serious tensions between the EU and US that could derail the new round of talks.

The banana case was an example. The American producer Chiquita was backed by the US government in a complaint that the EU had not fulfilled pledges to allow imports of its Latin American bananas. After a 10-year transition period the EU rules were still weighted in favour of former colonial producers in the West Indies and Africa. Portrayed as a big, bad US multinational throwing its weight around, the WTO nevertheless ruled in favour of the US. On this one the EU was in the wrong.

Potential future rows could make the bananas look like peanuts. Disputes over hormone-treated meat, genetically modified foods and aircraft are all in the pipeline. On the one hand is the EU's usual suspicion of free trade, reinforced now by the fact that the strongest liberal voice in Europe, the UK, is in the second division of decision making thanks to its decision not to join the euro in the first wave. On the other is a US administration with basically liberal instincts and a good record but a yawning trade deficit and an impending

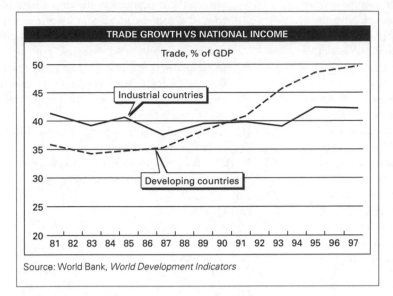

TRADE GROWTH VS NATIONAL INCOME

Trade, % of GDP

Source: World Bank, *World Development Indicators*

oped countries and the developing. The latter see the labour standards link as backdoor protectionism, especially as its most fervent advocates have been unions in industries in the rich countries most at risk from cheap imports.

After all, low wages are the core comparative advantage of developing nations. While it might be possible enough to identify, say, the use of prisoners paid no wages in export industries as unacceptable, other aspects are not so clear-cut. What if children's incomes are essential to families in a country where all children over a certain age do work? It would be considered abhorrent in the industrialised countries, but these countries are rich enough for households to have several dependents. Poor countries have to be allowed the opportunity to enjoy enough economic growth to reach that state of wealth themselves. That growth will come through exports of cheap goods.

The auguries for trade in the new millennium are not all that good. In the end, however, trade liberalisation is so important that policy makers will almost certainly hesitate to throw away its benefits. But they must not be diverted by the ill-informed and damaging circus of anti-trade campaigners descending on the negotiations. *d.coyle@independent.co.uk*

presidential election campaign. Between candidate Pat Buchanan's rhetoric and the need for union contributions to the campaign, there will be little scope for the American negotiators to make a strong push for further trade liberalisation in the early stages of the millennium round.

Even worse, one area on which the EU and US have reached agreement is the need to incorporate minimum labour standards in the trading rules. This means outlawing the use of child or slave labour, for example. Awful as these practices are, linking their abolition to access to world markets is potentially catastrophic, according to experienced and senior trade experts. They warn that it is a disaster, that the decision will open up a chasm between the devel-

---

(a) How can free trade help to reduce income inequality?

(b) In what ways has protectionism been weighted in favour of the richer and more powerful countries or groups?

(c) What are the arguments for and against outlawing child labour in developing countries?

 ANSWERS

Q1. D. A country will have a comparative advantage over another in the production of a good if it can produce it at a lower opportunity cost. This will apply to case D: the opportunity cost of X in terms of Y is lower. Note that B does not apply because other countries could possibly produce even more X relative to Y. Also E does not apply because the country could produce Y with even less resources than other countries.

Q2. (i) Country F: $1X = 2Y$.
Country G: $1X = 1Y$.
(ii) Country F: $1X = 1Y$.
Country G: $1X = 1.33Y$.
(iii) Country F: $1X = 1Y$.
Country G: $1X = 1Y$.

(iv) Country F: $1X = 0.25Y$.
Country G: $1X = 0.11Y$.
(v) Country F: $1X = 0.8Y$.
Country G: $1X = 1Y$.

Q3. *(a)* (ii) and (v). In these cases the opportunity cost of X in terms of Y is lower in country F than country G. Thus F specialises in good X and G in good Y.

(b) (i) and (iv). In these cases the opportunity cost of X in terms of Y is lower in country G than country F. Thus G specialises in good X and F in good Y.

(c) None. If there are only two goods and two countries, trade must involve one good being exported in return for the other being imported.

(d) (iii). In this case the opportunity cost of X in terms of Y is the same in both countries. Thus although country G has an *absolute* advantage in both cases, no trade will take place.

Q4. *(a)* $P_X/P_Y = 2$. Since 1 unit of X exchanges for 2 of Y, X must be twice the price of Y.

(b) $P_X/P_Y = 1$.

(c) Country F has gained because, before trade, to obtain 1 unit of X it had to sacrifice 2 units of Y (the opportunity cost of *X* was 2*Y*); whereas with trade, it can import 1 unit of X by exporting only 1.5 units of Y (the opportunity cost of *X* is now only 1.5*Y*).

Country G has gained because, before trade, to obtain 1 unit of Y, it had to sacrifice 1 unit of X (the opportunity cost of *Y* was 1*X*); whereas with trade, it can import 1 unit of Y by exporting only 2/3 of a unit of X (the opportunity cost of *Y* is now only 0.67*Y*).

Q5. (a) (iii), (b) (iv), (c) (i), (d) (ii).

Q6. *abundant.* Abundant factors will tend to have a relatively low price as will goods that are intensive in them.

Q7. *reducing.* The effect of countries specialising in goods that are abundant in their relatively cheap factor will be to increase the demand for this factor and push up its price, thereby reducing factor price differentials.

Q8. *increasing.*

Q9. *bowed out.*

Q10. *disappear.*

Q11. Factors include: transport costs; factors of production moving rather than goods (e.g. labour migration); government restrictions.

Q12. *False.* The terms of trade are defined as P_X/P_M.

Q13. If 2*X* exchange for 3*M*, then P_X/P_M must be 3/2.

Q14. Terms of trade equal $P_{\text{index of exports}} \div P_{\text{index of imports}} = 200/150 \times 100 = 133.3$.

Q15. *(a)* Country F.

(b) P_2 (where the exports from country F ($S_F - D_F$) equal the imports to country G ($D_G - S_G$).

(c) Q_6.

(d) $Q_6 - Q_2$.

Q16. *deteriorated.* If the exchange rate depreciates, then less imports can be purchased for a given quantity of exports: P_X/P_M has fallen. This is known as deterioration in the terms of trade.

Q17. (a) (iv), (b) (i), (c) (v), (d) (iii), (e) (ii).

Q18. *(a)* (ii) This is where the country is able to exercise its monopsony power.

(b) (i) This is the infant industry argument. It is justifying short-term protection (or better promotion) in order to be able to experience long-term comparative advantage.

(c) (iii) This is a political/moral argument.

(d) (i) This will prevent the move *away* from comparative advantage that dumping tends to create.

Note, however, that the losers from dumping are *not* the consumers in the importing countries: they get the goods at a lower price! The losers are the firms in the importing country and the taxpayers in the dumping country.

(e) (iv) If followed, this policy would lead to a huge decline in trade, with no imports (however much more efficiently produced) being able to gain a price advantage.

(f) (i) This will help to prevent the establishment of a monopoly situation.

Q19. D. This is the amount of the tariff necessary to bring consumption to the point where *MSC* = *MSB*.

Q20. *(a)* $Q_4 - Q_1$.

(b) $Q_3 - Q_2$.

(c) $1 + 2 + 3 + 4 + 5 + 6$.

(d) $1 + 2$.

(e) $3 + 4 + 5 + 6$.

(f) 7.

(g) $3 + 7$.

(h) 3.

(i) 5.

(j) $4 + 6$ (i.e. the gain in producer surplus (3), plus revenue to the government from the tariff (5), minus the loss in consumer surplus $(3 + 4 + 5 + 6)$).

Q21. *low-cost* (foreign) *producers to high-cost* (domestic) *producers*.

Q22. *at most second best.* Some other policy (if such existed) which only increased production part of the way to Q_2 would be second best.

Q23. C. The production externalities but no consumption externalities imply that consumption should remain at Q_4 (where $P = MSB$), but that domestic production should be increased to Q_2. Both a production subsidy and a tariff (alternative B) will achieve the required increase in production, but a tariff, by raising the price to P_{w+t}, will also reduce consumption – side-effect distortion. A production subsidy, however, will not raise the price of imports. The product will continue to be sold at the world price of P_w.

Q24. A tax on consumption. This will have the desired effect on consumption, but by leaving the *producer* price unchanged, domestic production will remain unchanged and the reduced consumption will simply mean reduced imports. In terms of Figure 23.3, D_{dom} will shift downward by the amount of the tax, but domestic production will remain at Q_1.

Q25. Examples include: deflationary effects on the world economy may reduce demand for the country's exports; other countries may retaliate; protection may reduce competition and encourage firms to remain inefficient; protection may involve high administrative costs; it may encourage corruption as firms bribe officials to waive restrictions.

Q26. (a) (ii), (b) (iii), (c) (i), (d) (iv).

Q27. *True.* Trade creation is where the removal of trade barriers allows greater specialisation according to comparative advantage.

Q28. B. The reduction in tariffs within the union may mean that members now buy imports from each other rather than from outside the union, even if the non-union members were more efficient producers of the product.

Q29. *(a)* $Q_5 - Q_4$ at a price of P_4.
(b) *rest of the world.* (S_{union} is at a higher price for each output than S_w. If there were equal tariffs, therefore, on both union and non-union imports, the country would import from non-union countries.)
(c) *union countries.*
(d) P_3.
(e) $Q_6 - Q_3$.
(f) *higher-cost producer.* Trade is diverted from non-union suppliers who without tariffs would have supplied at the lower price of P_1.
(g) *gain* of areas $1 + 2 + 3 + 4$.
(h) *loss* of area 1.
(i) $3 + 8 + 14$. (Since nothing is now imported from outside the union, the government loses the whole of the tariff revenue it had previously earned.)
(j) $(1 + 2 + 3 + 4) - 1 - (3 + 8 + 14) = 2 + 4 - 8 - 14$.

Q30. *(a)* *True.* The abolition of such a tariff between union members will lead to a large reduction in the price of goods imported from other union members.
(b) *False.* If there is a substantial cost difference, the abolition of tariffs between union members is less likely to divert trade away from the (very) low-cost non-union producers.

Q31. A. There was an absence of tariffs and quotas within the EC and common tariffs with the outside world.

Q32. B. The Act envisaged the complete abandonment of all barriers to inter-EC trade and factor movements.

Q33. (a) (v), (b) (ix), (c) (iii), (d) (ii), (e) (i), (f) (iv), (g) (vii), (h) (vi), (i) (viii).

Q34. Advantages include: trade creation; reduction in the direct costs associated with barriers (such as administrative costs and delays); economies of scale, with firms better able to operate on an EU-wide scale; greater competition.

Q35. *(a)* *Yes.* If firms now see their market as the EU as a whole rather than mainly just their own country, they are likely to want to locate nearer the geographical centre of the EU.
(b) *Yes.* This will attract firms to merge and again to locate towards the geographical centre of the EU.
(c) *No.* A fall in rents and land prices will attract capital to the regions.
(d) *No.* This will help to offset regional problems.
(e) *Yes.* Individual euro-zone countries with severe regional problems are unable to devalue in order to gain competitiveness.
(f) *No.* This will reduce the need for centralising office functions.
(g) *Yes.* Depressed regions may be unable to afford the improvements to their infrastructure necessary to attract enough capital to halt their decline.

Q36. *(a)* *Yes.* This is likely to lead to a bigger switch in consumption from non-EU goods to EU goods, irrespective of whether many of them may be produced at higher cost. (On the other hand, the substantial increase in inter-EU competition may, over time, significantly reduce EU costs.)
(b) *Yes.* This will prevent low-cost non-EU products competing with higher-cost EU products.
(c) *No.* This is likely to lead to trade creation as consumers are now able to purchase from lower-cost producers.
(d) *No.* The economies of scale from serving an EU-wide market will reduce costs of production and hence encourage trade creation.

CHAPTER TWENTY-FOUR

24 The Balance of Payments and Exchange Rates

 A **REVIEW**

In this chapter we will look at ways of dealing with problems of the balance of payments and exchange rates. We begin with an overview of the range of alternative types of exchange rate 'regime' and how the balance of payments is corrected under each. We then look in detail first at fixed exchange rates and then at free-floating exchange rates. There are then some optional questions on the extension of the *ISLM* model (see Chapter 20) to take account of balance of payments issues.

We then look at the various intermediate exchange rate regimes that have been tried since 1945. We start with the adjustable peg – a semi-fixed exchange rate system that was used round the world from 1945 to 1971. Finally we consider the system of 'dirty' floating that has been used since 1971.

24.1 Alternative exchange rate regimes

(Pages 692–6) Correction under fixed exchange rates
In order to maintain the exchange rate at a fixed level, the central bank will have to intervene in the foreign exchange market whenever there is a **Q1.** *current account/capital account/currency flow* deficit or surplus. If the UK has a currency flow deficit, the Bank of England will have to **Q2.** *buy/sell* sterling.

Central bank intervention to maintain a fixed exchange rate will tend to affect the money supply.

Q3. Other things being equal, central bank intervention in the foreign exchange market to prevent a deficit leading to a depreciation in the exchange rate will increase the money supply. *True/False*

The effects on money supply can be offset by a process of *sterilisation*.

Q4. Assume that there is a currency flow surplus and that the Bank of England intervenes in the foreign exchange market to prevent the pound appreciating. Which of the following additional actions by the Bank of England would sterilise (i.e. offset) the consequent effects on money supply?
A. A reduction in interest rates.
B. Buying government securities on the open market.
C. Selling government securities on the open market.
D. Buying pounds on the foreign exchange market.
E. Selling pounds on the foreign exchange market.

If a currency flow deficit persists and if the government is to maintain the fixed exchange rate, it will have to tackle the underlying deficit. One approach is to try to improve the current account balance. It can use **Q5.** *deflationary/reflationary* fiscal or monetary policy for this purpose. This will lead to both 'expenditure changing' and 'expenditure switching' (an income effect and a substitution effect respectively).

 Multiple Choice   **(?)** Written answer   **◖** Delete wrong word   **⊖** Diagram/table manipulation   **⊗** Calculation   **✦** Matching/ordering

Q6. Which of the following are examples of expenditure changing and which are examples of expenditure switching?

(a) Relatively lower export prices lead to an increase in exports. *expenditure changing/expenditure switching*

(b) Lower aggregate demand leads to less imports. *expenditure changing/expenditure switching*

(c) The resulting slow down in economic activity leads to less demand for imports of raw materials and capital equipment from abroad. *expenditure changing/expenditure switching*

(d) A fall in the rate of inflation makes home-produced goods more competitive relative to imports. *expenditure changing/expenditure switching*

Q7. Unlike expenditure changing, expenditure switching from deflationary policy will not have an adverse effect on unemployment. *True/False*

(Pages 696–8) Correction under free-floating exchange rates
Free-floating exchange rates automatically correct any balance of payments deficit or surplus by depreciation or appreciation respectively. As with a regime of fixed exchange rates, expenditure changing and expenditure switching will occur.

Q8. Unlike with a fixed exchange rate, only expenditure changing will help to correct the disequilibrium: expenditure switching will make the problem worse. *True/False*

Whenever there is a shift in the demand and/or supply of sterling, there will be a depreciation or appreciation of the exchange rate until a new equilibrium is reached. A depreciation will correct a current account deficit only if the Marshall–Lerner condition is fulfilled. If the condition is not fulfilled, there will not be a stable equilibrium exchange rate (unless though financial account movements).

Q9. Which of the following is the Marshall–Lerner condition?

A. The price elasticity of demand for imports is greater than that for exports.

B. The price elasticity of demand for exports is greater than that for imports.

C. The sum of the price elasticities of demand for imports and exports is greater than one.

D. The sum of the price elasticities of demand for imports and exports is less than one.

E. The sum of the price elasticities of demand for imports and exports is greater than two.

Q10. The greater the price elasticities of demand for imports and exports, the greater will be the level of expenditure switching from a depreciation and the smaller will

be the amount of depreciation necessary to restore equilibrium. *True/False*

(Pages 698–9) Intermediate exchange rate regimes
There are a number of alternative exchange rate regimes between the extremes of a completely fixed and a completely free-floating exchange rate.

Q11. The following is a list of exchange rate regimes:
(i) Crawling peg.
(ii) Free floating.
(iii) Adjustable peg.
(iv) Totally fixed.
(v) Dirty floating.
(vi) Exchange rate band.
(vii) Joint float.

Match the above to each of the following descriptions.

(a) Where a currency is allowed to float between an upper and lower exchange rate but is not allowed to move outside these limits.
....

(b) Where countries peg their exchange rate permanently to gold or to another currency.
....

(c) Where exchange rates are fixed for a period of time, but may be devalued (or valued) if a deficit (or surplus) becomes substantial.
....

(d) Where a group of currencies are pegged to each other but collectively are free to fluctuate against other currencies.
....

(e) Where governments do not intervene at all in foreign exchange markets.
....

(f) Where the government allows a gradual adjustment of the exchange rate by small amounts.
....

(g) Where the government intervenes in the foreign exchange market to prevent excessive exchange rate fluctuations.
....

24.2 Fixed exchange rates
(Pages 700–2) The effects of internal and external shocks under fixed exchange rates are analysed differently by new classical and Keynesian economists.

Q12. Assume that there is an *internal* shock under fixed exchange rates. According to new classical economists, if the government does not intervene, which of the following will occur?
(i) Internal balance will be restored.
(ii) Current account balance will be restored.
(iii) Overall external balance will be restored.

A. None.
B. (i) only.
C. (i) and (iii).
D. (ii) and (iii).
E. (i), (ii) and (iii).

Q13. What answer would Keynesian economists give to Q12? *A/B/C/D/E*

Now consider the effect of an *external* shock under fixed exchange rates. Assume that there is a rise in demand for UK exports. According to new classical economists, the current account will to into **Q14.** *surplus/deficit*. The **Q15.** *higher/lower* aggregate demand will **Q16.** *reduce/increase* wages and prices. This will therefore tend to **Q17.** *increase/reduce/eliminate* the current account imbalance.

The rise in demand for exports will have a **Q18.** *small/large* effect on the financial account depending on whether there is any net pressure on interest rates. The current account surplus will tend to **Q19.** *increase/reduce* the money supply, putting **Q20.** *upward/downward* pressure on interest rates. A rise in prices, however, will increase the transactions demand for money, putting **Q21.** *upward/downward* pressure on interest rates. Thus the restoration of overall external balance is **Q22.** *assured/possible* and the restoration of current account balance is **Q23.** *assured/possible*.

Q24. Keynesian economists argue that an external shock will, via the multiplier, destroy internal balance and may lead to a persistent current account imbalance given the inflexibility of prices. *True/False*

Balance of payments problems do not simply arise from 'one-off' shocks. There are other factors that can lead to *persistent* balance of payments problems under fixed exchange rates.

Q25. Which one of the following is likely to lead to persistent current account deficits under fixed exchange rates?
A. A lower income elasticity of demand for the country's exports than for its imports.
B. A lower rate of growth at home than abroad.
C. A higher rate of inflation abroad than in the domestic economy.
D. The long-term development of import substitutes at home.
E. A growth in the country's monopoly power in the export market.

(*Pages 702–4*) Under fixed exchange rates the government will probably have to use fiscal and/or monetary policy to control the level of demand for imports and the level of inflation.

Q26. Assume that there is a balance of payments deficit caused by a high rate of domestic inflation.
(a) What effect will a deflationary *monetary* policy (a reduction in money supply) have on interest rates?
Raise/Lower them.
(b) What effect will this have on the financial account?
Cause an *inflow/outflow* of finance.
(c) What effect will this have on the money supply?
Increase it again/Reduce it further.
(d) What effect will this have on inflation?
Help to reduce it/Increase it.
(e) What effect will a deflationary *fiscal* policy have on interest rates? *Raise/Lower* them.
(f) What effect will this have on the financial account?
Cause an *inflow/outflow* of finance.
(g) What effect will this have on money supply?
Increase/Reduce it.
(h) What effect will this have on inflation?
Help to reduce it/increase it.
(i) Which will be more effective under fixed exchange rates: fiscal or monetary policy? *fiscal/monetary*

Q27. Give three advantages of fixed exchange rates.

1. ....

2. ....

3. ....

Q28. Give three disadvantages of fixed exchange rates from a new classical perspective.

1. ....

2. ....

3. ....

Q29. Give three disadvantages of fixed exchange rates from a Keynesian perspective.

1. ....

2. ....

3. ....

24.3 Free-floating exchange rates

(*Pages 705–9*) Under a free-floating exchange rate, the balance of payments will automatically be kept in balance by movements in the exchange rate.

If there are any internal shocks, then, provided that monetary policy maintains interest rates at international levels, the purchasing-power parity theory will hold.

Q30. The purchasing-power parity theory states that
A. inflation will adjust to the level of that abroad.
B. exchange rates will adjust so that the same quantity of internationally traded goods can be bought in all countries with a given amount of one currency.
C. interest rates will adjust so that the inflation rate is equalised in all countries so as to maintain the relative value of real incomes.
D. the exchange rate between currency A and B and between B and C and between C and A will be such that all three rates are consistent.
E. the exchange rate between any two currencies at any one time will be the same in all foreign exchange dealing centres in any part of the world.

Q31. Assume initially that the exchange rate is £1 = $1.50. Assume also that UK inflation is 50 per cent, but that US inflation (and also that in other countries) is zero. According to the purchasing-power parity theory, what will be the exchange rate after one year?

....

If we drop the assumption that interest rates are maintained at the same level at home as abroad, the purchasing-power parity theory will break down.

Q32. Assume that UK inflation is 10 per cent more than the (trade-weighted) average of that in other countries and that there is an expansion of domestic money supply that forces interest rates below the level of those abroad.
(a) What will happen to the current account balance (assuming it was initially in balance)?
Move into *deficit/surplus*.
(b) What will happen to the capital account balance (assuming it was initially in balance)?
Move into *deficit/surplus*.
(c) By how much will sterling depreciate?
more than 10 per cent/10 per cent/less than 10 per cent

(Pages 709–11) Let us consider how effective monetary and fiscal policies will be under free-floating exchange rates.

Q33. Exchange rate movements will reinforce monetary policy but will dampen fiscal policy. *True/False*

Q34. Assume that the government wishes to pursue a deflationary policy.
(a) What will happen to the exchange rate if it uses deflationary *monetary* policy? *Appreciate/Depreciate*
(b) What effect will this exchange rate movement have on aggregate demand? *Increase it/Decrease it*
(c) What will happen to the exchange rate if it uses deflationary *fiscal* policy? *Appreciate/Depreciate*
(d) What effect will this exchange rate movement have on aggregate demand? *Increase it/Decrease it*

Q35. Give three advantages of free-floating exchange rates.

1. ....

2. ....

3. ....

Q36. Under which of the following conditions are fluctuations in exchange rates likely to be severe?
(a) The Marshall–Lerner condition is satisfied only in the long run. *Yes/No*
(b) Speculators believe that fluctuations in exchange rates are likely to be considerable. *Yes/No*
(c) Governments pursue a policy of setting interest rates in accordance with international interest rates. *Yes/No*
(d) Large amounts of the country's currency are held abroad. *Yes/No*
(e) There are many substitutes abroad for the country's exports. *Yes/No*

The uncertainty for importers and exporters associated with fluctuating exchange rates can be lessened in the **Q37.** *short term/long term* by firms dealing in the **Q38.** *spot/forward* exchange market. This allows traders to plan future purchases of imports and sales of exports at a known **Q39.** *price/exchange rate/interest rate/inflation rate*.

*24.4 The open economy and ISLM analysis

(Pages 711–14) ISLM analysis (see Chapter 20) can be extended to incorporate the balance of payments. This is done by introducing an additional curve to the IS and LM curves: this third curve is the BP curve.

Q40. Figure 24.1 illustrates a BP curve (we will look at the other two curves in the next question).
(a) What does the BP curve show?

....

(b) What will happen to the balance of payments if the rate of interest increases?
Current account/Financial account moves into deficit/surplus.
(c) What will happen to the balance of payments if the level of national income increases?
Current account/Financial account moves into deficit/surplus.
(d) Why does the BP curve slope upwards?

....

....

(e) What combinations of interest rate and national income would cause a surplus on the balance of payments?

Combinations in area of diagram
above/below BP curve

(f) What will happen to the slope of the *BP* curve if the marginal propensity to import increases?

It will get *steeper/shallower*.

(g) What will happen to the slope of the curve if the elasticity of supply of international finance decreases?

It will get *steeper/shallower*.

(h) What will happen to the curve if there is an autonomous increase in exports?

It will shift *upwards/downwards*.

(i) What will happen to the cruve if there is an appreciation of the exchange rate?

It will shift *upwards/downwards*.

⊖ **Q41.** Figure 24.1 shows an economy which initially has an interest rate of r_1 and a level of income of Y_1 (point *a*). This is an equilibrium position because it is where *IS* = *LM*. Let us assume that the balance of payments is also in equilibrium (the *BP* curve passes through point *a* too). Assume a system of fixed exchange rates.

(a) What curve would initially shift and in which direction if the government pursued a deflationary fiscal policy? (It may help you answer the following questions if you draw the effects on Figure 24.1.)

The *IS/LM* curve would shift to the *left/right*.

(b) What effect would this have on the rate of interest?

rise/fall

(c) What effect would this have on national income?

rise/fall

(d) What effect would this have on the current account of the balance of payments? *improve/deteriorate*

(e) What effect would this have on the financial account of the balance of payments? *improve/deteriorate*

(f) The way the diagram is drawn, what would be the overall effect on the balance of payments?

move into *deficit/surplus*.

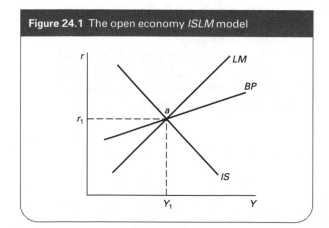

Figure 24.1 The open economy *ISLM* model

(g) If there were to be the opposite effect on the balance of payments, how would the diagram have to have been drawn?

....

(h) What effect will the balance of payments position in (f) above have on the money supply?

increase/decrease

(i) What effect will this have on the *LM* curve?

Shift it to the *left/right*.

(j) Where will equilibrium finally be achieved?

....

(k) Will the secondary monetary effects of a fixed exchange rate (i.e. the shift in the *LM* curve) have strengthened or weakened the deflationary effects of the fiscal policy? *strengthened/weakened*

▤ **Q42.** Monetary policy under fixed exchange rates will be ineffective because:

A. any initial shift in the *LM* curve will simply be reversed because of the monetary effects of the change in the balance of payments.

B. the *BP* curve will shift so as to eliminate the effect of any shift in the *LM* curve.

C. the *IS* curve will shift so as to eliminate the effect of any shift in the *LM* curve.

D. the *BP* curve is steeper than the *LM* curve.

E. the *BP* curve is shallower than the *LM* curve.

⊖ **Q43.** Illustrate on a diagram like Figure 24.1 the effects of a deflationary fiscal policy under a system of free-floating exchange rates. Assume initially that the economy is in equilibrium at a national income of Y_1 with a rate of interest of r_1.

24.5 Exchange rate systems in practice

(Pages 715–17) After the Second World War, the world adopted an adjustable peg system where currencies were pegged to the US dollar. This was the Bretton Woods System (named after the town in the USA where the system was devised).

✪ **Q44.** The following are various measures that can be taken under an adjustable peg system:
(i) Drawing on reserves.
(ii) Building up reserves.
(iii) Deflation.
(iv) Reflation.
(v) Devaluation.
(vi) Revaluation.

Which of the above measures is suitable for each of the following balance of payments problems?

(a) A severe and fundamental deficit.

....

(b) A temporary balance of payments surplus.

....

(c) A moderate surplus arising from the economy operating with a low level of aggregate demand.

....

(d) A mild deficit that is expected to disappear as the world economy recovers from recession.

....

(e) A large and persistent surplus because of the country's much lower underlying rate of inflation.

....

(f) A moderate deficit associated with a too rapid recovery from recession.

....

There were serious problems with the system.

(?) **Q45.** Governments were sometimes reluctant to devalue, even when a deficit was fundamental. Why?

....

....

(≣) **Q46.** One problem of devaluation was the so-called 'J-curve effect'. This effect arose because:

A. governments tended to back up devaluation with deflationary fiscal and monetary policies.

B. after several months speculators came to believe that the balance of payments would begin to move into deficit again.

C. devaluation tended to make inflation worse in the long run.

D. the IMF only provided support for the exchange rate on a temporary basis.

E. the Marshall–Lerner condition was only satisfied in the long run.

(?) **Q47.** Why was there a problem of excess liquidity in the late 1960s and early 1970s?

....

(Pages 717–22) Since 1972 the world has been largely on a dirty floating exchange rate system (although groups of countries, such as those in the former European Monetary System, may peg their rates to each other).

(?) **Q48.** What are the two major ways in which countries seek to prevent short-term fluctuations in their exchange rate?

1. ....

2. ....

(◑) **Q49.** Floating exchange rates after 1972, by reducing the need for international liquid assets, reduced the inflationary pressures that were building up in the international economy. *True/False*

(≣) **Q50.** One of the problems experienced in the 1970s and 1980s was the growth in 'hot money'. Hot money may be defined as:

A. illegal exchange rate transactions designed to circumvent exchange controls.

B. currency deposits earning very high interest rates.

C. dollars that are used for international trade rather than transactions in the USA.

D. currency used for buying property and other assets abroad.

E. money put on short-term deposit in the country paying the most favourable interest rates relative to expected movements in the exchange rate.

The use of interest rates as the main weapon for stabilising the exchange rate has often led to conflicts with internal policy objectives.

(◑) **Q51.** In which of the following cases is there a clear conflict between internal and external policy objectives if interest rate changes are the only weapon available to the government?

(a) The government wants to prevent an appreciation of the exchange rate and to reduce demand-deficient unemployment. *Yes/No*

(b) The government wants to help UK exporters and to reduce the rate of inflation. *Yes/No*

(c) The government wants to reduce the price of imports and to curb the rate of growth in the money supply. *Yes/No*

(d) The government wants to prevent a depreciation of the exchange rate and to stimulate investment. *Yes/No*

(e) The government wants to halt a rise in the exchange rate and to reduce the rate of growth of the money supply. *Yes/No*

(f) The government wants to reverse a recent fall in the exchange rate and to reduce its unpopularity with home owners. *Yes/No*

(◑) **Q52.** Which of the following are likely to contribute to the volatility of exchange rates between the major currencies?

(a) A growth in the size of short-term financial flows relative to current account flows. *Yes/No*

(b) The abolition of exchange controls. *Yes/No*

(c) A harmonisation of international macroeconomic policies. *Yes/No*

(d) The adoption of money supply targets by individual countries. *Yes/No*

(e) The adoption of exchange rate targets by individual countries.   *Yes/No*

(f) The adoption of inflation targets by individual countries.   *Yes/No*

(g) A growing belief that speculation against exchange rate movements is likely to be stabilising.   *Yes/No*

(h) A growing belief that speculation against exchange rates movements is likely to be destabilising.   *Yes/No*

(i) A growing ease of international transfers of funds.   *Yes/No*

(j) Countries' business cycles become more synchronised with each other.   *Yes/No*

B   PROBLEMS, EXERCISES AND PROJECTS

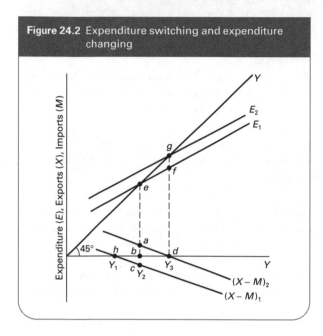

Figure 24.2 Expenditure switching and expenditure changing

(e) Why will the *E* line shift upwards as a result of the expenditure switching?

....

(f) Why does the *E* line shift upwards to E_2, but no further?

....

(g) What is the size of the multiplier?   ....

(h) What is the size of the substitution effect (expenditure switching) on the balance of payments from the depreciation?

positive/negative effect of ....

(i) What is the size of the income effect (expenditure changing) on the balance of payments from the depreciation?

positive/negative effect of ....

(j) What is the total effect on the balance of payments of the depreciation?

positive/negative effect of ....

Q53. Expenditure switching and expenditure changing are shown diagrammatically in Figure 24.2.

Assume initially that the total expenditure function is given by E_1. The balance of payments is given by the line $(X - M)_1$. This shows that the higher the level of national income, the higher the level of imports relative to exports.

(a) What is the initial equilibrium level of national income?

....

(b) What is the balance of payments surplus or deficit at this initial equilibrium level of income?

surplus/deficit of ....

(c) Beyond what level of national income will there be a balance of payments deficit?

....

Now assume that there is depreciation of the exchange rate. This will alter the relative price of imports and exports and cause expenditure switching.

(d) How is this expenditure switching illustrated in the diagram?

....

Q54. Free-floating exchange rates are likely to give rise to speculation. The two diagrams of Figure 24.3 both show an original demand and supply curve for sterling and an exchange rate of r_1. Assume that the UK experiences a lower rate of inflation than other countries.

(a) Show on each diagram the effect on the demand and supply curves and the exchange rate.

(b) Now assume that, as a result of the change in the exchange rate, people expect the government to cut interest rates and reflate the economy. On Figure 24.3(a) illustrate the effect on the demand and supply curves of these expectations.

(c) Alternatively assume that people expect inflation to continue falling and that as a result the exchange rate will continue to move in the same direction as in question (a). Use Figure 24.3(b) to illustrate the effect of these expectations.

(d) Which of the two diagrams represents destabilising speculation?   *Figure 24.3(a)/Figure 24.3(b)*

(e) In which of the two diagrams is speculation self-fulfilling?   *Figure 24.3(a)/Figure 24.3(b)/both/neither*

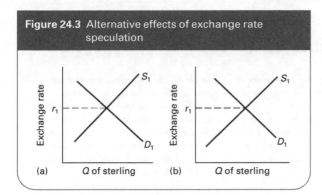

Figure 24.3 Alternative effects of exchange rate speculation

Q55. Construct a table showing the following figures for the UK economy since 1975: the exchange rate index, interest rates, the current account on the balance of payments, the rate of economic growth, the rate of growth in money supply (M4), the rate of inflation. Plot the figures on a graph (or two or three graphs if it is easier). The graph(s) should show time on the horizontal axis and the other variables on the vertical axis (you can use different scales up the *same* axis for the different variables).

(a) Comment on the movement of these variables over time and whether there are any apparent relationships between them.

(b) Are these relationships as you would expect? Explain.

(c) What other factors would influence the movement of these variables and explain any apparent unexpected movements of one variable relative to others?

Sources: *Economic Trends Annual Supplement* (ONS); *Financial Statistics (Monthly)* (ONS); *National Institute Economic Review (Quarterly)* (NIESR).

Q56. Compare movements in the volume of exports, the volume of imports, consumer prices, average earnings and the effective exchange rate over the last ten years for Germany, Japan, the UK and the USA. Plot these relationships on a separate graph for each country. (See Q55.) Explain the relative performance of the three countries.

Sources: *OECD Economic Outlook* (OECD); *European Economy Annual Report* (Commission of the European Union); *National Institute Economic Review (Quarterly)* (NIESR).

 DISCUSSION TOPICS AND ESSAYS

Q57. Why may an expansion of aggregate demand lead to a balance of payments surplus under a fixed exchange rate system?

Q58. To what extent can dealing in forward exchange markets remove the problems of a free-floating exchange rate?

Q59. 'If a country moves from a system of floating exchange rates to fixed or pegged exchange rates, it should switch its emphasis from monetary policy to fiscal policy when attempting to manage the level of aggregate demand.' Discuss.

Q60. How do elasticities of demand and supply for imports and exports influence the effectiveness of (a) depreciation and (b) deflation as means of correcting a balance of payments disequilibrium?

*Q61. Using *ISLMBP* analysis, compare the relative effectiveness of fiscal and monetary policy as means of controlling aggregate demand (a) under a system of fixed exchange rates and (b) under a system of free-floating exchange rates.

Q62. Was a system of managed flexibility (dirty floating) the best compromise between fixed and free-floating exchange rates in the 1970s? Is it the best compromise today?

Q63. What are the causes of exchange rate volatility? Have these problems become worse in the last ten years?

Q64. Debate
A movement towards fixed exchange rates is to be wholly regretted. It is a denial of political and economic sovereignty and can force countries to adopt quite inappropriate domestic macroeconomic policies.

 ARTICLES

FT

The following article, taken from the *Financial Times* of 28 March 1994, assesses the general debate concerning the advantages and disadvantages of alternative exchange rate regimes. In particular, it focuses upon the performance of floating exchange rates since 1971, following the demise of the Bretton Woods system.

In praise of the international monetary non-system

The floating exchange rate non-system comes of age this month. It was 21 years ago, in March 1973, that the attempt to sustain the postwar system of fixed but adjustable exchange rates was abandoned. But that is not the only anniversary. It was also 50 years ago, in July 1944, that the conference at Bretton Woods, New Hampshire, designed the system that expired in 1973.

It is timely, therefore, to ask whether the global system of dirty floating either will, or should, endure for the next 21 years, or more. The answer is that it both will and should.

Floating exchange rates have had relatively few friends and many enemies. Yet nothing successful has been put in their place. Small countries are able to make credible commitments to fixed exchange rates, be it through currency boards (in the case of Hong Kong, for example), the ERM (in the case of the Netherlands) or just a unilateral target (in the case of Austria). Large countries find it far more difficult. Even France, most devoted to the cause of fixed exchange rates of the members of the group of seven leading industrial countries, had to concede 15 per cent fluctuation bands within the ERM last summer.

It looks as though the world must learn to stop worrying and love floating exchange rates. Would that be so bad?

The chart shows what has happened to exchange rates of the three major currencies – the dollar, the yen and the D-Mark – since 1971, the year when President Nixon's administration devalued the dollar, a decision that led ultimately to generalised floating. Five points emerge:

- there is a considerable amount of short-term 'noise' in the movement of nominal exchange rates;
- there was one huge swing in nominal exchange rates, which began in 1980 and ended in 1987;
- that swing went into reverse in early 1985, well before the celebrated meeting of the G7 finance ministers at the Plaza Hotel in New York;
- there has been a fairly close correlation between swings in nominal and real exchange rates, although this has been less true for the D-Mark than for the other two, because Germany is shielded by the ERM;

- there have now been some seven years of reasonable exchange rate stability.

This last fact explains why schemes to reform the international monetary system – common in the mid-1980s – have ceased to attract much attention today. But it also helps put the earlier dollar 'bubble' in proper perspective.

Neither credible exchange rate commitments nor intervention explain the long period of relative stability, at least after 1987. This underlines the point made by Professor Max Corden of the Johns Hopkins University School of Advanced International Studies in Washington DC, in a book to be published later this year that 'managed floating is not incompatible with considerable exchange rate stability'.*

The conditions for this are low and stable inflation in all participants and the absence of major shocks. Destabilising shocks do have to be major ones. Even the fall of the Berlin Wall resulted in only a modest appreciation of the D-Mark against the dollar, though it did lead to a melt-down in the more rigid ERM.

In the mid-1980s, the non-system looked far more erratic. Now it is

---

* W. Max Corden, *Economic Policy, Exchange Rates and the International System* (Oxford: Oxford University Press, forthcoming).

possible to recognise that the ultimate cause of the rise of the dollar was an exceptionally large shock in the world's biggest economy: the tightening of monetary policy under Paul Volcker, chairman of the Federal Reserve, combined with the loosening of fiscal policy under President Ronald Reagan.

It is also unlikely that any other exchange rate system could have coped better with such a shock. Professor Corden's book, which shows just how economic analysis ought to be used to clarify important questions for an educated general public, indicates why.

Suppose that it is accepted that the dollar had begun to overshoot seriously by 1983 and 1984, what would have been the consequences of using monetary policy to stop the trend? The likely answer, as we know from British experience with a similar bubble in 1987 and 1988, is that US inflation would have risen instead. It is possible that the total real exchange rate appreciation would then have been smaller. What is much more important is that the loss of competitiveness would have been more difficult to reverse under greater exchange rate stability. It would have required falling prices or at the least rapidly falling inflation, rather than the depreciation of the nominal exchange rate that occurred.

Not only has the present non-system been functioning quite well for some years, it is also difficult to conceive of

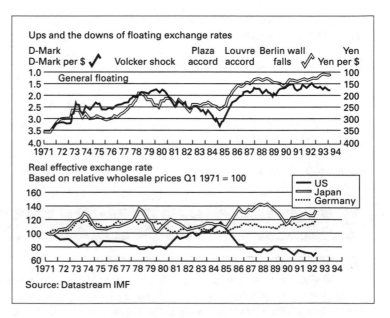

Ups and the downs of floating exchange rates

D-Mark / D-Mark per $ — Volcker shock — Plaza accord — Louvre accord — Berlin wall falls — Yen / Yen per $

Real effective exchange rate
Based on relative wholesale prices Q1 1971 = 100

— US
— Japan
······ Germany

Source: Datastream IMF

any workable alternatives. The fate of the ERM has demonstrated the vulnerability of any fixed exchange rate system with imperfect credibility and free capital movement. One alternative would be a credibly fixed exchange rate system, such as a currency board or, for large countries, a currency union. The only other would be a float, but the more explicitly the exchange rate is managed within the float, the greater its vulnerability to speculation.

As Professor Corden puts it, 'the current laissez-faire international monetary system is simply a market system, which co-ordinates the decentralised decisions reached by private and public actors, and is likely to be as efficient at this as the market system within the domestic economy'. In other words, floating exchange rates among major currencies offer the worst possible system, except for all the others.

© *Financial Times*, 28.3.94

(a) Using the two graphs presented in the article, explain what has happened to the exchange rate value of the D-Mark, dollar and yen since 1971.

(b) Does the evidence support the view that 'managed floating is not incompatible with considerable exchange rate stability'? What other conditions might be necessary for such a claim to be made?

(c) Do the events within the ERM in recent years confirm that semi-fixed or fixed exchange rate systems are doomed to failure?

The volatility of currency markets in south-east Asia continues, and speculative movements of currency send regular tremors throughout the region. The article below by Stephen Vines, taken from *The Independent* of 11 June 1998, considers one such tremor and illustrates the uncertainty stalking the markets within the region.

Turmoil reigns in Asia once more

An awesome combination of fear and hope about Asia's two regional superpowers sent Asian market-makers into a bearish trading frenzy yesterday.

The hope is that the Japanese government's economic stimulus plans will work and the Chinese government will resist the temptation to devalue the yuan ren minbi. The fear is that precisely opposite will happen.

Although the Chinese government still denies that it has any intention to devalue, and the Japanese government insists that it is finally grasping the nettle of fiscal reform and is prepared to stump up enough public money to reflate the economy, big investors are resolutely sceptical.

This scepticism sent Hong Kong's blue-chip Hang Seng Index tumbling 4.9 per cent yesterday to its lowest point in more than three years. Closing at 7979 points, the index has lost more than half its value since last summer's high.

In Taiwan, the country in the region whose economy has been hit least badly by the Asian financial crisis, the stock market fell more than 3 per cent to a seven-year low and the New Taiwan dollar tumbled to its lowest level since March 1987.

The Thai stockmarket, no slouch when it comes to testing new lows, plunged more than 5 per cent to hit a 10-year low. Piling on the agony the credit-rating agency Standard and Poors issued a warning that some 35 per cent of all Thai bank loans were problematic.

Elsewhere in the region, stocks and currencies marched in step in a downwards direction as the Japanese yen proved that Tuesday's modest recovery was no more than a aberration when it headed back towards an exchange rate of 141 yen to the US dollar.

It is hard to be sure what spurred the carnage. The most common explanation is that this bout of contagion spread from Hong Kong, where there was alarm about a statement by Dai Xianglong, China's central bank governor. He is reported to have told a private meeting that 'the depreciation of the Japanese yen is having a very negative impact on Chinese imports and exports and the utilisation of foreign capital'.

Combined with figures showing exports slowing to a level of 12 per cent growth in the first four months of the year from 21 per cent last year, and others showing output expanding only 7.9 per cent in the first five months of the year, well below the 10.5 per cent target, this led investors to conclude that the Chinese leadership was ready to break its pledge to maintain the value of its currency.

This, in turn, focused attention on the possibility of a break in the Hong Kong dollar peg with the US dollar, which would be hard to sustain in the face of a Chinese devaluation. It only needed a hint of this kind to send Hong Kong interest rates soaring. Overnight, interbank rates reached up to 8 per cent compared with Tuesday's close at 6 per cent.

The stock market has no hope of staying firm in the face of interest-rate movements of this order, although they were far less alarming than the treble-digit overnight rates seen at the end of last year when the Hong Kong dollar was under speculative attack.

China, meanwhile, is attempting a strategy of reflating the domestic economy to avoid devaluation. Interest rates have been lowered and banks' borrowing ratios relaxed.

But with rising levels of unemployment, the financial sector in a shambolic state and the government unable to come to grips with reform of the lumbering state-owned industries, domestic demand-led reflation is hardly an easy option.

The suspicion is that it simply will not work. Nevertheless, yesterday both Hong Kong and Chinese leaders rushed to deny rumours that a weak yen will prompt China to devalue.

Some analysts accept these denials. 'The cheaper yen will not take away the market from Chinese exporters,' said Chi Lo, from the Hongkong Bank China Service.

But this is not a majority view. As Alex Tang, research director at Core Pacific-Yamaichi Iternational in Hong Kong put it: 'Fund managers are not buying the story.'

Nor are they buying the story of an impending Japanese economic recovery. A finance ministry survey released in Tokyo yesterday showed that in the first quarter of the year corporate profits were down 25 per cent while investment had declined 5.8 per cent and sales were off 6.8 per cent.

'It seems that fiscal 1997/98 was the worst for companies and that they could expect some pick up in 1998/99,' said Mamoru Yamazaki, a senior economist at Paribas Capital Markets in Tokyo. 'But it's questionable whether this will happen.'

Speaking in Taipei yesterday, Premier Vincent Siew said that he thought the worst was over for most South-East Asian countries. But he added: 'The situation in Japan is unclear. I fear it will take one or two years to improve.'

Mr Siew was being quite restrained. Some analysts believe that the yen is heading down to as low as 180 yen to the US dollar and that the major stumbling block of weak domestic consumption cannot be shifted by current government policies.

This means that Japan, traditionally the main engine of Asian economic growth, is incapable of reviving other troubled Asian economies.

The most optimistic assessment yesterday came from Marcel Souza, of INVESCO Asset Management in Hong Kong, who said: 'If policy measures being taken in Japan at the moment deliver economic growth 12 months down the road, we would be looking at a recovery in Asia.' But this is hardly an affirmation of confidence, more like a timid prediction of things being not quite as black as they are painted.

The underlying fear in East Asia is that things will keep getting worse, not only because China and Japan can do little to help their neighbours, and may even damage them, but because the Asian economies are all awash with seriously devalued assets. And with falling credibility, many Asian governments are hardly in a position to lead their countries out of the crisis. Big-league investors are in no mood to help them out.

(a) Explain how speculation in the foreign exchange market can destabilise the market, making things far worse.

(b) What does the article identify as being the main cause of the uncertainty at that time in the market?

(c) Would greater government intervention in foreign exchange markets in south-east Asia improve things or potentially make things worse?

With the nervousness in international foreign exchange markets following the problems in south-east Asia, even relatively successful economies like Brazil were not free from speculative attack. The article below by Stephen Timewell, taken from *The Banker* of March 1999, assesses the end of Brazil's Real Plan and the economy's future prospects.

Don't panic

At the start of the year, Brazil was subject to some not very pretty sights. On 6 January, the former president Itamar Franco, now running the third richest state, Minas Cerais, and seeing himself as a presidential candidate in 2002, announced a 90-day moratorium on his state's R$18 billion debt to the federal government.

With President Cardoso's failure in December to steer his fiscal adjustment programme through Congress, and capital outflows apparently unstoppable, Franco's fit of pique was enough to tip Brazil into crisis and bring not only the collapse of the crawling peg but force Brazil to allow the real to float.

And float it has done. While the São Paulo stock exchange soared 33.4 per cent on the news of the collapse, the real kept falling against the dollar during January, ending the month at R$2.05 to the dollar, a more than 40 per cent devaluation since the 13 January float. February, however, has seen a halt in the real's slide and, while it has firmed to around R$1.8 to the dollar at one point, it has tended to hover around R$1.9.

So where is Brazil heading? A pessimist would suggest that the four years of Cardoso's Real Plan are unravelling fast, and the shift from 50 per cent inflation a month in mid-1994 to below 2 per cent for the whole of 1998 is now part of history.

There is no doubt that Brazil faces crucial problems, and the effect of the devaluation on inflation will prove critical in the coming months. But the damage wrought by the devaluation needs to be seen in perspective.

Brazil has a lot of positives, including the strength and preparedness of its financial sector, and it needs to be viewed very differently than a Russia or a wounded Asian tiger.

Stephen Rose of UBB Capital Markets says: 'The crucial problem is the level of total net public debt, which has been estimated to have risen to 48 per cent of GDP from 35.1 per cent at the end of October as a result of the devaluation of the real. Twenty per cent of Brazil's domestic debt is dollar indexed while as much as 75 per cent is indexed to the Selic [overnight] rate, now a crippling 35.5 per cent [at end January].

'The problems that the government might have in rolling it over during 1999 may have been evidenced by the sale of only one-third of R$500 million Three Year National Treasury Notes which the Central Bank offered to the market [at end January] at 21.9 per cent plus exchange variation.'

As Rose concludes: 'The size of the debt is serious, the rate of growth worrying and the servicing cost horrendous. This is the crunch point in all the government's plans.'

But despite its problems, the devaluation has spurred progress on other fronts. The crisis has awakened Congress to Brazil's stark choices. While 70 per cent of Cardoso's fiscal adjustment programme had been approved before the International Monetary Fund agreement late last year, key legislation had not been approved and the failure of a pension reform bill on 2 December had been a bitter blow to the government.

The devaluation, however, changed the atmosphere and forced Congress to acknowledge the necessity of Cardoso's fiscal programme. By the end of January, all the pending legislation, covering social security reform, CPMF legislation, the pension reform bill had been effectively passed and hence Congress has virtually completed all the important fiscal adjustment programme.

Whether the legislation would have cleared anyway is arguable but the devaluation certainly forced many in Congress to reconsider their opposition to certain fiscal reforms and come around to the Cardoso/IMF programme.

According to Marcos Caramuru at the Ministry of Finance in Brasilia, the passing of the legislation will enable significant restructuring to take place and, in a joint statement with the IMF on 4 February, the Brazilians agreed to reduce the ratio of the public debt to GDP by the end of 2001 to below the 46.5 per cent of GDP projected in the original $41.5 billion IMF package.

Fernao Carlos Bracher, president of Banco BBA Creditanstalt and a former central bank president, noted: 'Brazil is in a much better position [at the end of January] than at the beginning of the year. The fiscal programme now has support, the budget deficit will be turned into a surplus and the current account deficit will be reduced since there will be a trade surplus of $6–8 billion.'

Bracher and others believe the 'overshooting' of the real in the immediate aftermath of the devaluation will be short-lived and, by the end of February,

a certain equilibrium will be found with the rate settling against the dollar at a range of 1.5–1.7.

Fernando Sotelino, president of the wholesale banking group of Unibanco, thinks that it will not be until March that people can see more clearly ahead and take a better position on the initial 'overshooting'.

But while Brazil's currency market waits to calm down and interest rates in mid-February remain excessively high, certain aspects of the economy, especially the financial sector, are in stronger shape than not only many comparable emerging economies but also Brazil itself going back to the early 1990s and certainly the 1980s debt crisis.

After all, the core problems of the current crisis have been the fiscal and current account deficits, and they have now been addressed.

Given the fiscal reforms have been enacted, it is now up to the international community to demonstrate its confidence in Brazil. In the first 11 months of 1998, foreign direct investment reached $23.4 billion; an important indicator in 1999 is whether the pace of FDI will continue.

(a) Brazil operated a crawling peg exchange rate system prior to being forced to abandon it. What is a crawling peg and how does it work?

(b) What kinds of problems are a 40 per cent currency depreciation in less than a month likely to produce in a country like Brazil?

(c) Commentators suggest that the fall in the exchange rate of the real was subject to 'overshooting'. What is meant by this term?

(d) Why are the longer-term prospects of the Brazilian economy reasonably sound even given the problems faced by its currency in 1999?

E ANSWERS

Q1. *currency flow*. Note that if a deficit on current account is offset by a surplus on the capital plus financial accounts (excluding reserves) or vice versa, there will be no need for intervention.

Q2. *buy* sterling (with currencies in the reserves).

Q3. *False*. Purchases of domestic currency by the central bank to support the exchange rate will reduce the money supply.

Q4. C. To prevent the pound rising on the foreign exchange market the Bank of England will sell pounds. This will increase the money supply; so to offset this – sterilise it – the Bank of England must reduce the money supply by selling government securities.

Q5. *deflationary*.

Q6. (a) and (d) are examples of *expenditure switching*.
(b) and (c) are examples of *expenditure changing*

Q7. *True*. Lower domestic prices will lead to an *increase* in demand for domestically produced goods.

Q8. *False*. It is the other way round. Expenditure changing from increased export demand and reduced import demand will, via the multiplier, cause an increase in national income and an *increase* in the demand for imports.

Q9. C. A depreciation will improve the balance of payments on the export side if the price elasticity of demand for exports is greater than zero and on the import side if the price elasticity of demand for imports is greater than one. Thus provided the sum of the two is greater than one, the balance of payments will improve.

Q10. *True*.

Q11. (a) (vi), (b) (iv), (c) (iii), (d) (vii), (e) (ii), (f) (i), (g) (v).

Q12. C. Flexible wages and prices will restore internal balance. Any current account deficit (surplus) will put upward (downward) pressure on interest rates which will lead to a financial (plus capital) account surplus (deficit) which will offset the current account imbalance and restore overall external balance.

Q13. A. Wage and price rigidity will prevent internal balance being restored: a recession could persist. An endogenous money supply will remove the pressure on interest rates which would otherwise cause changes in the financial account to offset a current account imbalance.

Q14. *surplus.*

Q15. *higher.*

Q16. *increase.*

Q17. *reduce.*

Q18. *small.*

Q19. *increase.*

Q20. *downward.*

Q21. *upward.*

Q22. *assured.*

Q23. *possible.*

Q24. *True.*

Q25. A. As the world economy grows so the growth in the country's exports will be less than the growth in its imports if the income elasticity of demand for exports is lower than that for imports.

Q26. *(a)* *Raise* them.
(b) Cause an *inflow* of finance.
(c) *Increase it again.*
(d) *Increase it.*
(e) *Lower* them.
(f) Cause an *outflow* of finance.
(g) *Reduce* it.
(h) *Help to reduce it.*
(i) *fiscal.*

Q27. Advantages include: certainty for the business community; little or no speculation (provided people believe that the rate will remain fixed); automatic correction of monetary errors; prevention of the government pursuing 'irresponsible' macroeconomic policies.

Q28. Disadvantages from the new classical perspective include: they make monetary policy totally ineffective; an imbalance between current and financial accounts may persist; they contradict the objective of having free markets.

Q29. Disadvantages from the Keynesian perspective include: deficits can lead to a recession, or if severe, to a depression; there may be problems of international liquidity to finance deficits; inability to adjust to shocks given sticky wages and prices; speculation if people believe that the fixed rate cannot be maintained.

Q30. B. The theory implies that the exchange rate will adjust so as to offset the effects of different inflation rates in different countries.

Q31. $1.00. To keep the purchasing power of the pound the same abroad as at home, the 50 per cent reduction in the purchasing power of the pound at home as a result of the 50 per cent inflation must be matched by a 50 per cent depreciation in the exchange rate (i.e. whereas originally £1 exchanged for $1.50, now £1.50 must exchange for $1.00).

Q32. *(a)* Move into *deficit.*
(b) Move into *deficit.*
(c) *more than 10 per cent.* The deficit on the capital account will cause the exchange rate to depreciate by more than that necessary to restore purchasing power parity.

Q33. *True.*

Q34. *(a)* *Appreciate.* A deflationary monetary policy will lead to higher interest rates, which will cause an inflow of finance and thus extra demand for (and reduced supply of) the domestic currency on the foreign exchange market.
(b) *Decrease it.* The higher exchange rate will discourage exports (an injection) and encourage imports (a withdrawal).
(c) *Depreciate.* A deflationary fiscal policy will lead to a lower transactions demand for money and hence a lower interest rate. This will encourage an outflow of finance and thus an increased supply of (and reduced demand for) the domestic currency on the foreign exchange market.
(d) *Increase it.* The lower exchange rate will lead to increased exports and reduced imports.

Q35. Advantages include: automatic correction of external disequilibria; elimination of the need for reserves; governments have a greater independence to pursue their chosen domestic policy.

Q36. *(a)* *Yes*: if the Marshall–Lerner condition is not satisfied in the short run, the inelasticities of currency demand and supply will cause severe fluctuations. There will be no stable short-run equilibrium.
(b) *Yes*: speculation tends to be self-fulfilling.
(c) *No*: this will tend to prevent large-scale financial movements and thus avoid large-scale exchange rate fluctuations.
(d) *Yes*: this can cause large-scale financial movements.
(e) *No*: this will make the demand for the currency more elastic and thus the exchange rate more stable.

Q37. *short term*: long-term movements in exchange rates over a number of years *cannot* be offset by forward currency dealing. Forward exchange deals are only for a few weeks or months hence.

Q38. *forward.*

Q39. *exchange rate.*

Q40. *(a)* All those combinations of national income (Y) and the rate of interest (r) where the balance of payments is in equilibrium.

(b) *Financial account* moves into *surplus* (as finance is attracted into the country).

(c) *Current account* moves into *deficit* (as higher incomes cause an increase in imports).

(d) Because an increase in national income causes the current account to move into deficit and therefore if the balance of payments is to stay in balance there must be a rise in the rate of interest to cause a counterbalancing surplus on the financial account.

(e) Combinations in area of diagram *above* the *BP* curve. This area shows higher interest rates or lower levels of national income than are necessary to achieve a balance. Higher interest rates will improve the financial account. Lower national income will improve the current account.

(f) It will get *steeper*. A rise in national income will cause a bigger rise in imports and thus there will have to be a bigger rise in interest rates to cause the necessary counterbalancing inflow of finance.

(g) It will get *steeper*. A bigger rise in interest rates will be needed to attract the necessary inflow of finance to offset any deterioration on the current account from an increase in income.

(h) It will shift *downwards*. The current account will improve at any level of national income and thus a lower interest rate will be necessary to achieve the counterbalancing level on the financial account.

(i) It will shift *upwards*. If there is currently a balance of payments surplus (the economy is in the part of the diagram above the *BP* curve) the exchange rate will appreciate. The resulting increased imports and reduced exports will cause the balance of payments surplus to disappear. The *BP* curve will shift upwards.

Q41. *(a)* The *IS* curve would shift to the *left*.

(b) It would *fall*.

(c) It would *fall*.

(d) It would *improve*. A lower income would mean that less imports were purchased.

(e) It would *deteriorate*. A lower rate of interest will encourage an outflow of finance.

(f) It would move into *deficit*. The intersection of the new *IS* curve with *LM* is below the *BP* curve. The financial account effect is stronger than the current account effect (this is likely in the short run, given the massive financial flows that take place on the foreign exchanges).

(g) The *BP* curve would have to be steeper than the *LM* curve.

(h) *Decrease* as finance flows out of the country.

(i) Shift it to the *left*.

(j) Where the *LM* curve has shifted far enough to the left so that it intersects with the new *IS* curve *along* the *BP* curve. Only then will the balance of payments deficit be eliminated and thus money supply stop falling.

(k) *Strengthened*. The leftward shift of the *LM* curve will cause a further fall in equilibrium national income.

Q42. A. A rise in money supply (a rightward shift in the *LM* curve) will reduce interest rates. This will encourage an outflow of finance, which will reduce money supply again (a leftward shift in the *LM* curve).

Q43. See Figure A24.1. The deflationary fiscal policy shifts the *IS* curve to the left (say to IS_2). The resulting lower interest rate causes a balance of payments deficit (point *b* is below the *BP* curve). This causes the exchange rate to depreciate and thus the *BP* curve to shift downwards. But the depreciation will encourage more exports (an injection) and discourage imports (a withdrawal) and thus cause a rise in aggregate demand. The *IS* curve will shift back towards the right, reducing the original deflationary effect. Eventual equilibrium is reached at point such as *c*, where all three curve intersect.

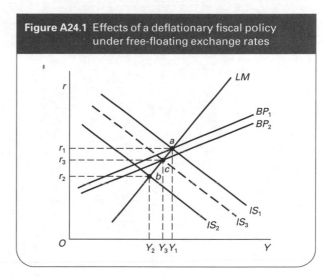

Figure A24.1 Effects of a deflationary fiscal policy under free-floating exchange rates

Q44. (a) (v), (b) (ii), (c) (iv), (d) (i), (e) (vi), (f) (iii).

Q45. It could be very disruptive to firms and might be seen as a sign of weakness of the economy and of the government's political failure. If so, it could possibly lead to speculation about a further devaluation. Also it would be inflationary.

Q46. E. In the short run, the demand for both imports and exports may be relatively inelastic, given that consumers and producers take time to adjust to price changes (arising from the devaluation). Thus the current account may deteriorate directly after the devaluation and only improve after a number of months (the J-curve).

Q47. Because the USA ran persistent balance of payments deficits.

Q48. Using reserves to intervene on the foreign exchange market; changes in interest rates.

***Q*49.** *False.* By reducing the need to deflate if a country was experiencing a deficit, the system encouraged the expansion of countries' money supply.

***Q*50.** E. It is 'hot' because it can easily be switched from one country to another as interest rates or expected exchange rates change.

***Q*51.** *(a)* No: external and internal $r \downarrow$.

(b) Yes: external $r \downarrow$; internal $r \uparrow$.

(c) No: external and internal $r \uparrow$.

(d) Yes: external $r \uparrow$; internal $r \downarrow$.

(e) Yes: external $r \downarrow$; internal $r \uparrow$.

(f) Yes: external $r \uparrow$; internal $r \downarrow$.

***Q*52.** Yes: (a), (b), (d), (h) and (i).

No: (c), (e), (f), (g) and (j).

Note in the case of (d) that the adoption of money supply targets is likely to involve the government having to adjust interest rates to keep money supply within the target range and that this could lead to large inflows or outflows of short-term finance with a resulting effect on the exchange rate. In the case of (f) the adoption of inflation targets by countries (assuming that the targets are similar) will lead to greater harmonisation. In the short run, it could lead to greater exchange rate volatily if countries had different underlying inflation rates, but in the long run, it should lead to greater exchange rate stability as harmonisation increases. In the case of (j), if business cycles become more synchronised, country's consumption, interest rates and inflation rates are likely to be more synchronised.

CHAPTER TWENTY-FIVE

25

Global and Regional Interdependence

A   REVIEW

A rapid growth in international trade and financial flows has made countries much more inter-dependent. The result has been that countries' domestic economies are increasingly being governed by the world economy and by world international financial movements. We start by seeing just how countries are inter-related. We then look at what can be done to create a greater co-ordination of international economic policies. The extreme solution to currency instability is for countries to adopt a common currency. We then turn to look at the euro and how economic and monetary union (EMU) operates. Finally we look at some alternative suggestions for reducing currency fluctuations.

25.1 Globalisation and the problem of instability

(Pages 725–8) There are two main ways in which countries are economically interdependent: through trade and through international financial markets.

When the US economy expands, assuming no change in US interest rates, this will lead to **Q1.** *an expansion of output in other countries/a contraction in other countries approximately equal to the expansion in the USA*. This is the international trade multiplier effect.

 Q2. Which one of the following defines the inter-national trade multiplier?

A. The amount by which international trade expands for each $1 expansion in exports of country A.

B. The amount that country A's income expands for each $1 increase in its exports.

C. The amount that country A's income declines for each $1 increase in its imports.

D. The amount that country B's imports grow for each $1 increase in country A's national income.

E. The amount that country B's national income rises (via an increase in exports to A) for each $1 rise in country A's national income.

The effects of the international trade multiplier may be amplified by, or more than offset by, international financial flows.

Q3. Assume that the US economy expands. Assume also that the US Federal Reserve Bank (the central bank of the USA), worried by rising inflation, raises interest rates. What will be the consequences?

(a) There will be an outflow of finance from the USA.
True/False/Uncertain

(b) The US dollar will appreciate.   *True/False/Uncertain*

(c) This will lead to a fall in US exports.
True/False/Uncertain

(d) As a result of the action of the Federal Reserve Bank, US national income will fall below what it would otherwise have been.   *True/False/Uncertain*

(e) There will also be a fall in US imports.
True/False/Uncertain

 Multiple Choice   Written answer   Delete wrong word   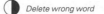 Diagram/table manipulation   Calculation   Matching/ordering

(f) The current account of the USA's trading partners will improve. *True/False/Uncertain*

(g) Interest rates in other countries will fall. *True/False/Uncertain*

(h) Investment in other countries will rise. *True/False/Uncertain*

(i) Other countries' national incomes rise. *True/False/Uncertain*

From the example given in Q3, it can be seen that a change in US monetary policy will probably have a **Q4.** *similar/opposite* effect on *other* countries' national incomes to that on US national income. This is the result of **Q5.** *the international trade multiplier effect/international financial flows.* The larger the level of international financial flows, the **Q6.** *more/less* will interest rate changes in one country affect the economies of other countries.

Q7. Consider the following policy changes in the USA:

 (i) an expansionary fiscal policy, combined with lower interest rates.

 (ii) an expansionary fiscal policy, combined with higher interest rates.

(iii) a contractionary fiscal policy, combined with lower interest rates.

(iv) a contractionary fiscal policy, combined with higher interest rates.

In which case(s) will international financial flows amplify the foreign trade multiplier effect on other countries?

A. (i) and (ii)
B. (iii) and (iv)
C. (i) and (iv)
D. (ii) and (iii)
E. (i) and (iii)

(Pages 728–9) Given the growing economic interdependence of nations of the world, it is important for countries to adopt complementary economic policies and not to engage in 'beggar-my-neighbour' tactics.

Q8. Assume that the world is suffering from a recession. Which of the following policies adopted by country A would benefit other countries and which would hinder them in attempting to pull out of recession?

(a) An expansionary fiscal and monetary policy. *benefit/hinder* other countries

(b) A devaluation of the currency. *benefit/hinder* other countries

(c) Raising interest rates in an attempt to reduce inflation and make exports more competitive. *benefit/hinder* other countries

(d) Using protectionism to help domestic industry. *benefit/hinder* other countries

(e) Giving investment grants to industry. *benefit/hinder* other countries

25.2 Concerted international action to stabilise exchange rates

(Pages 729–30) Currency fluctuations can be lessened if countries' economies were harmonised: in other words, if they were at a similar stage in the business cycle and if they did not experience excessive exchange rate fluctuations. In order to achieve these objectives, the Group of 7 major industrialised countries (Canada, France, Germany, Italy, Japan, the UK and the USA) meet periodically to discuss joint economic policies.

Q9. For which of the following reasons is it likely to be difficult for the G7 countries to achieve harmonisation of their economies?

(a) The G7 countries are usually more concerned about their own national interests than international ones. *Yes/No*

(b) Countries today have little power, given the huge scale of international financial flows. *Yes/No*

(c) Monetary policy is generally determined by central banks. *Yes/No*

(d) Achieving similar rates of economic growth may involve considerable differences between the countries with respect to other macroeconomic indicators. *Yes/No*

(e) General harmonisation of policies is only possible if there is convergence of the G7 countries, and that has not been achieved. *Yes/No*

Q10. For each of the following pairs of objectives, explain why it may be difficult to achieve harmonisation of *both* simultaneously.

(a) Interest rates and inflation rates

....

(b) Budget deficits and economic growth

....

(c) Inflation rates and exchange rate stability

....

Q11. If countries attempt to achieve similar rates of economic growth through demand management policy, for which of the following reasons may the equilibrium rate of exchange change over the longer term?

 (i) The marginal propensity to import differs from one country to another.

 (ii) The relative income elasticities of demand for imports and exports differ from one country to another.

(iii) The rate of growth of productivity differs from one country to another.

A. (i) and (ii).
B. (i) and (iii).
C. (ii) and (iii).
D. (ii) alone.
E. (i), (ii) and (iii).

(Pages 730–4) One example of an attempt to achieve greater exchange rate stability was the exchange rate mechanism (the ERM) of the European Monetary System (EMS).

Q12. Which one of the following describes the ERM?
A. A fixed exchange rate system between member countries and a joint float with the rest of the world.
B. A dirty floating system between member countries and a clean float with the rest of the world.
C. A pegged exchange rate system at a single point between member countries and a joint float with the rest of the world.
D. A pegged exchange rate system within bands between member countries and a joint float with the rest of the world.
E. A fixed exchange rate system within bands between member countries and a crawling peg with a basket of rest-of-the-world currencies.

Q13. Under an exchange rate mechanism, which of the following could be used to reduce inflation if there is upward pressure on the exchange rate and if it is already near the top of its band?
  (i) Raising interest rates.
 (ii) Reducing aggregate demand through fiscal policy.
(iii) A prices and incomes policy.

A. (i) only.
B. (i) and (ii).
C. (i) and (iii).
D. (ii) and (iii).
E. (i), (ii) and (iii).

Q14. Which of the following were reasons for the crisis in the ERM in September 1992 which led to the withdrawal of Italy and the UK from the system?
  (i) Speculators perceived that Italy and the UK were not committed to maintaining their exchange rates within their bands.
 (ii) The Bundesbank felt obliged to maintain high rates of interest in order to dampen the inflationary effects of German reunification.
(iii) US interest rates were cut in order to halt the slide into recession.
(iv) There were worries that the Maastricht Treaty would not be ratified.

A. (i) and (ii).
B. (i), (ii) and (iv).
C. (ii) and (iii).
D. (ii), (iii) and (iv).
E. (i) and (iv).

Q15. The main reason behind the crises in the ERM in September 1992 and July/August 1993 was the lack of convergence of the economies of the ERM members.
True/False

Q16. As 1999 approached, so convergence between the economies of the ERM countries grew and exchange rate fluctuations diminished. *True/False*

25.3 European monetary union (EMU)
(Pages 735–8)
Q17. The Maastricht Treaty set out three stages in the process of achieving full economic and monetary union. According to the treaty, which of the following would apply to those countries adopting full EMU in Stage 3?
(a) A fixed exchange rate between their currencies.
Yes/No
(b) A pegged exchange rate between their currencies.
Yes/No
(c) A single central bank for all the countries.   *Yes/No*
(d) A single currency for all the countries.   *Yes/No*
(e) Identical tax rates.   *Yes/No*
(f) Free trade between the countries.   *Yes/No*
(g) Free financial movements between the countries.
Yes/No
(h) Common external tariffs.   *Yes/No*
(i) The abolition of all special EU help for different regions of the various countries.   *Yes/No*
(j) A common monetary policy.   *Yes/No*

Q18. Give two advantages of monetary union.

1. ....

2. ....

Q19. Give two disadvantages of monetary union.

1. ....

2. ....

The success or otherwise of the euro will depend on how close the euro-zone is to an 'optimal currency area'.

Q20. An optimal currency area can be defined as one which:
A. maximises the growth rates of the member countries.
B. minimises the degree of economic fluctuations between member countries.
C. maximises the amount of trade between the member countries.
D. minimises the average inflation rate between member countries.
E. would involve a decrease in net benefits from having a single currency if the size of the area were either to grow or diminish.

25.4 *Achieving greater currency stability*

(Pages 738–9) If there is a consensus in markets that a currency will depreciate, there is very little in the short term that governments can do to stop it.

⊗ **Q21.** If there were a 50 per cent chance that by this time next week a currency will have depreciated by 20 per cent, then selling the currency now will give an expected return of approximately 10 per cent for the week. *True/False*

⊗ **Q22.** The weekly interest in Q21 is equivalent to approximately 520 per cent per annum. *True/False*

◐ **Q23.** If neither changes in interest rates nor central bank intervention from the reserves can halt a depreciation/appreciation of a currency that is perceived to be not at its equilibrium exchange rate, then which of the following exchange rate regimes are viable over the longer term?
(a) Free-floating exchange rate. *Yes/No*
(b) Adjustable peg system (with just occasional adjustments). *Yes/No*
(c) Fixed with an independent monetary policy. *Yes/No*
(d) Adopting the dollar or the euro or some other international currency as the domestic currency. *Yes/No*

(Pages 739–40) What then can be done to reduce the scale of speculative flows and create greater currency stability? One approach is reduce the *mobility* of international finance by introducing controls over financial flows. Such controls pose problems of their own.

? **Q24.** Identify two problems of using controls over financial flows (sometimes known as 'capital controls').

1. ....

2. ....

◐ **Q25.** One type of control is known as a 'Tobin tax' (named after James Tobin). This is a small tax on foreign exchange transactions. *True/False*

? **Q26.** Controls are likely to dampen speculation, not eliminate it. Why might this be seen to be a desirable outcome?

....

....

◐ **Q27.** An alternative to controlling financial flows would be to use a system of exchange rate target zones. This system would have the following features:
(a) Currencies would be allowed to fluctuate within bands. *True/False*
(b) These bands would be very narrow, say ±1 per cent. *True/False*
(c) Central parity would be set so as to maintain it at the 'fundamental equilibrium exchange rate'. *True/False*
(d) The central parity would be adjusted very infrequently. *True/False*
(e) There would be 'soft buffers', with exchange rates occasionally allowed to move outside their bands. *True/False*

? **Q28.** Give two problems of the system of exchange rate target zones.

1. ....

2. ....

B   PROBLEMS, EXERCISES AND PROJECTS

Q29. Construct a table and four graphs showing the movements of the following rates of exchange over the last three years: $/€, ¥/$, €/£, $/£. Plot the exchange rates at monthly intervals. Now plot interest rates for the four countries/areas over the same period. How closely have the exchange rate movements reflected interest rate movements? Identify any rapid changes in exchange rates and do a search through newspapers to find articles explaining such changes.

Sources: *International Financial Statistics* (IMF); *Datastream*; *The Economist*; newspapers; various web sites, including the *Financial Times* (http://www.ft.com), The Bank of England (http://www.bankofengland.co.uk), Euro-

pean Central Bank (http://www.ecb.int), Bank of Japan (http://www.boj.or.jp/en/index.htm), US Federal Reserve Bank (http://www.federalreserve.gov), International Monetary Fund (http://www.imf.org), US Administration (http://www.whitehouse.gov/WH/html/briefroom.html).

Q30. Do a web search to find articles considering whether or not the UK should adopt the euro. Prepare two reports, one putting the case for the UK adopting the euro and one putting the case against.

Sources: various newspapers (see web addresses in section A of Appendix A in Sloman, *Economics* (4th edition)); see also http://euro-emu.co.uk.

DISCUSSION TOPICS AND ESSAYS

Q31. Under what circumstances will the effect of international financial flows reinforce the international trade multiplier effect? Under what circumstances will the effect of such flows offset the international trade multiplier effect?

Q32. Why is it important for countries' economic policies to be harmonised?

Q33. What are the economic (as opposed to political) difficulties in achieving an international harmonisation of economic policies?

Q34. To what extent were the benefits and costs of membership of the exchange rate mechanism of the European Monetary System similar to those experienced under the old Bretton Woods system?

Q35. Why did the ERM with narrow bands collapse in 1993? Could this have been avoided?

Q36. Would economic and monetary union between a group of countries reduce any individual country's economic problems to those of a region *within* a country?

Q37. What are the arguments for and against a common currency for (a) the whole of the existing EU; (b) a considerably enlarged EU; (c) the whole world?

Q38. What difficulties are there for the euro-zone countries in achieving continued convergence of their economies?

Q39. Consider the arguments for and against imposing controls over international financial flows.

Q40. Debate
A world of just three currencies (the dollar, euro and yen) would be one which was much more stable economically, where international economic policies could be much more easily harmonised and where international economic growth could be higher.

ARTICLES

The article below by Martin Woolf, taken from the *Financial Times* of 1 October 1997, examines how and why the world economy has become more integrated and open. In particular he focuses on the role of the multinational corporation in this process.

FT

The heart of the new world economy

Globalisation is a word that now leaps readily to every tongue. Like the idea or loathe it, few deny its existence or understate its significance. But how far has it progressed? And what role do companies play?

Behind the growing integration of the world economy lies the decline in the costs of transport and communication. Between 1930 and 1990 average revenue per mile in air transport fell from 68 US cents to 11 cents, in 1990 dollars. The cost of a three-minute telephone call between New York and London fell from $244.65 to $3.32. Between 1960 and 1990, the cost of a unit of computing power fell 99 per cent.

Technological change makes globalisation feasible. Liberalisation allows it to happen. Under the agreement reached at the end of the Uruguay round of multilateral trade negotiations, average advanced country tariffs on imports of manufactures will be reduced to under 4 per cent. Tariffs of developing countries are set to fall from 34 per cent between 1984 and 1987 to 14 per cent. Between 1970 and 1997, the number of countries that eliminated exchange controls affecting imports of goods and services jumped from 35 to 137.

Restrictions on investment have been reduced virtually everywhere. Around the world, there have been some 570 liberalising changes in regulations governing foreign direct investment since 1991. Some 1330 bilateral investment treaties involving 162 countries are now in effect, a threefold increase in half a decade.

Technology and deregulation work together. The unit cost of sea freight, for example, fell 70 per cent in real terms between the beginning of the 1980s and 1996. Behind this sharp decline lay not just technical innovations, but increased competition generated by bigger, more liberal markets.

The extent of globalisation must not be exaggerated. At its pre-1914 peak, the UK's net capital outflow was 9 per cent of gross domestic product, twice as big a share of GDP a outflows from Germany and Japan in the 1980s. In the same period the number of workers moving across frontiers was greater than now.

Nevertheless, international economic integration has, on balance, probably gone further than ever before. According to Angus Maddison, an economic historian, ratios of exports to global output were 9 per cent in 1913, 7 per cent in 1950, 11 per cent in 1973 and 14 per cent in the early 1990s. Financial markets are ever more closely linked; and governments are increasingly bound by a web of multilateral agreements and institutions.

Such constraints are one difference between today and a century ago. More fundamental still is the role of companies. Where once integration tended

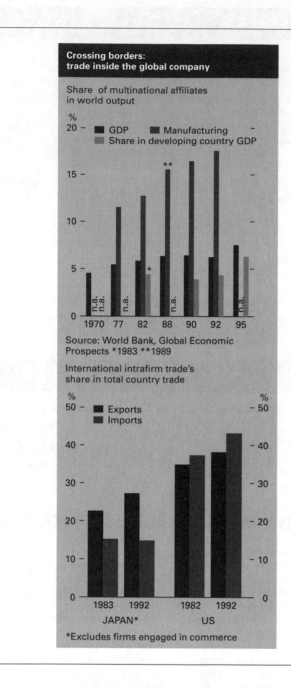

**Crossing borders:
trade inside the global company**

Share of multinational affiliates
in world output

Source: World Bank, Global Economic
Prospects *1983 **1989

International intrafirm trade's
share in total country trade

*Excludes firms engaged in commerce

the US, intra-firm imports were more than 40 per cent of total imports by the early 1990s. Similarly, an estimated 70 per cent of global payments of royalties and fees are transactions between parent firms and their foreign affiliates.

Large companies have long dominated industries characterised by economies of scale and scope, by firm-specific skills in innovation, production or sales or by valuable trademarks or brands. Companies usually find it more profitable to exploit such assets in-house than sell or license them to other companies or engage in joint ventures.

As sophisticated and more differentiated goods and services become more important in demand, output and trade, so do companies with the capacity to supply these competitively. Inevitably, it is the most successful companies of the most advanced economies that do best beyond the borders of their country of origin.

The largest 100 multi-nationals, ranked on the basis of their foreign assets, own $1700bn in their foreign affiliates, one-fifth of global foreign assets. All but two of the companies are from advanced countries, 30 from the US alone. The top 25 US multinationals are responsible for half of the country's stock of foreign capital – a share that has remained almost unchanged over four decades.

The big change in recent years, however, is a shift in the reasons why companies move production overseas. Historically, companies have located production abroad in order to overcome natural or artificial barriers to trade. If production efficiency were the only criterion, it would have made sense for many companies to locate all their production at a single base, to maximise economies of scale. In practice, however, governments in consuming countries have pushed them to spread production more widely.

For example, much of the Japanese investment in the US and the European Union was a response to protection against its exports. The same is true of investment in many developing countries – in car and truck production, for example.

Other barriers to centralised production were inherent in the nature of the business. The provision of many services used to require face-to-face contact. Expansion of service firms therefore required the creation of elaborate overseas networks. Similarly, fear of fluctuations in real exchange rates encouraged

to take the form of trade and capital movements at arm's length, it now occurs increasingly within companies.

In 1996, the global stock of foreign direct investment (FDI) was valued at $3200bn. Its rate of growth over the previous decade was more than twice that of gross fixed capital formation. FDI flows grew at 12 per cent a year between 1991 and 1996, while global exports grew at 7 per cent. FDI is also widely spread: last year, 37 per cent of total FDI went to developing countries.

Investment leads to production. By 1995, 280 000 foreign affiliates generated $7000bn in global sales, which exceeded global exports of goods and services by 20 per cent. According to the World Bank, the share in world output of multi-national affiliates jumped from 4.5 per cent in 1970 to 7.5 per cent in 1995. Their share in manufacturing output was 18 per cent in 1992, up from 12 per cent in 1977.

Multinational production generates further international transactions. In

the spread of production capacity across frontiers.

Many of these trends are now changing. Trade liberalisation makes traditional protection-jumping production unnecessary. Improvements in communications are eliminating natural barriers to long-distance commerce; services can now be produced in one country and exported to another, just like manufactured goods. And in Europe, at least, economic and monetary union will eliminate exchange rate fluctuations.

So, creating overseas production sites merely in order to meet local consumption looks an increasingly fragile base for foreign investment. A much better one is the ability to make the best use of a company's competitive advantage by locating production wherever it is most efficient. Today's multi-nationals create widely spread networks of research, component production, assembly and distribution.

Evidence of this trend can be seen in the growing role of exports in multi-national production. Between 1966 and 1993, exports from US-majority owned foreign affiliates rose from about 20 per cent of sales to 40 per cent. For affiliates in developing countries, exports rose from 10 per cent to close to 40 per cent.

This sort of internationalisation reflects – and augments – the economic liberalisation and technical change binding the world's economies closer together. To the extent that reflects such forces, globalisation of companies is here to stay.

(a) What do you understand by the term globalisation?

(b) How far is technology responsible for this globalising tendency?

(c) Why does Woolf see multinational corporations as central to the process of globalisation?

(d) Woolf argues that the reasons why businesses go multinational are changing. What are these changes and what are their implications?

It is hardly surprising that, in the wake of the south-east Asian crisis, economists and politicians have been debating the possible regulation of global capital markets. Is more regulation desirable or even possible? In the article below, taken from *The Economist* of 11 April 1998, some of the issues involved in this discussion are analysed.

Towards a new financial system: the perils of global capital

Robert Rubin, America's Treasury secretary, wants to 'modernise the architecture of the international financial markets'. Eisuke Sakakibara, Japan's top international finance official, is thinking of a 'Bretton Woods II'. Alan Greenspan, chairman of the Federal Reserve, wants to review the 'patchwork of arrangements' governing international finance. After East Asia's crisis, activism is in the air.

It is easy to see why. After East Asia's spectacular crisis, policymakers worry that today's financial architecture, designed at Bretton Woods in 1944 for a world of limited capital mobility, may not be capable of dealing with an ever more global capital market. For international finance has been revolutionised. Formerly closed economies have cast off controls and embraced foreign funds. Better technology and financial innovation have made it easy to move money instantaneously.

The benefits are obvious: the expansion of private flows to developing countries, from $34 billion a decade ago to $256 billion in 1997, has brought much-needed capital to emerging economies, and healthy returns to rich-country savers. But vast inflows can quickly become huge outflows. And financial crises can spread overnight between apparently unconnected markets. The five worst-affected Asian economies (South Korea, Indonesia, Thailand, Malaysia and the Philippines) received $93 billion of private capital flows in 1996. In 1997 they saw an outflow of $12 billion. This shift of $105 billion in one year was the equivalent of 11 per cent of their combined GDP.

Yet bouts of activism have occurred before. After the demise of the fixed exchange-rate system in the early 1970s, a group of finance ministers and central bank governors, 'the Committee of 20', set out to design a wholly new architecture. As the oil shock hit, Henry Kissinger had big ideas for the International Energy Agency. During the 1980s debt crisis, a score of new bureaucracies, such as an International Debt Discount Corporation, were mooted.

But actual innovation was modest and incremental. After the fixed exchange-rate system collapsed, today's non-system of floating rates emerged from the wreckage. After the oil shocks, the IMF created new credit lines to help countries cope with sudden shifts in commodity prices. The debt crisis was finally resolved with the introduction of Brady bonds. Since Mexico's most recent crash in 1995, the G7 has led more tinkering, including a new credit line to lend the IMF money in an emergency.

Cumulatively, such changes have allowed the post-war blueprint to evolve. At issue is whether it has evolved enough.

First identify the problem
Much depends on what caused East Asia's crash. Explanations abound, but – with some simplification – they divide into two broad categories. One emphasises that the crisis was homegrown, the product of crony 'Asian capitalism'. The other emphasises panic. It points out that no one foresaw the crisis; that by conventional indicators of economic

health (budget deficits and so forth) the Asian economies were in good shape; and that no economic change occurred in 1997 to justify such a massive loss of confidence.

There is probably some truth to both interpretations, and most observers believe the crisis was a combination of the two. Where analysts differ is the relative weight they assign to each. American triumphalists and some academics, such as Paul Krugman, emphasise crony capitalism. Others, notably Jeffrey Sachs of Harvard University and Joseph Stiglitz, chief economist at the World Bank, believe panic was more important.

Crucially, these two interpretations imply different conclusions about how best to prevent and deal with future crises. If you regard Asia's crash essentially as a crisis of Asian capitalism – especially its opacity, poor regulation and cronyism – then systemic reforms should be geared towards reinforcing transparency, improving supervision and limiting moral hazard. But if the crisis was primarily one of panic, then the goal should be to control unstable markets while providing more public money or creating new, reassuring rules.

The market-reinforcing view starts by calling for greater transparency. Thailand's secret sales of foreign-exchange reserves in the forward markets made a mockery of its official reserve levels. No one had any idea how enormous South Korea's short-term debt burden was. This opacity worsened the crisis, suggesting global markets would work better if there were more information, of better quality, on a broader range of economic items.

Since Mexico's crash in 1994–95 there have been efforts to improve the information available to investors. But too many emerging economies are still too secretive. Only 39 countries post their economic statistics on the IMF's new electronic bulletin-board. Few countries (rich or poor) publish details of their forward foreign-exchange operations. Worse, much important information is simply not collected, or collected too late. Aggregated information on firms' foreign indebtedness, for instance, simply does not exist. Sorting out these statistical shortcomings is an obvious priority.

Policing the banks
A second reform to reinforce capital markets is better regulation. Banks are uniquely vulnerable institutions, capable of wreaking havoc if inadequately supervised. Countless banking crises – in rich and poor countries alike – have shown that the combination of free capital flows and badly regulated banks is disastrous. To improve supervision, the Basle Committee of international bank supervisors issued '25 core principles' of sound banking last year.

For many observers, however, East Asia's crisis shows that more needs to be done. Perhaps the standards of financial safety themselves need updating. The key internationally agreed rules for banks are the Basle capital-adequacy standards set up by the industrialised countries in 1988. A decade on, they look inadequate and arbitrary. The minimal capital necessary for safety in a developed banking system may be insufficient in volatile emerging markets. And it seems odd that lending short term to banks, particularly emerging-market ones, is considered always less risky than making long-term loans to companies such as Microsoft.

Others go much further, arguing that a global capital market needs global financial regulation, not a hotch-potch of national supervisors of varying quality. Henry Kaufman, an American markets-watcher, has put forward the most ambitious proposal. He wants to create a new international institution that would supervise participants in global capital markets. It would establish uniform trading, reporting and disclosure requirements, set minimum capital requirements and eventually rate the credit quality of institutions under its jurisdiction. Some of these ideas have found resonance in official circles. Stanley Fischer, deputy managing director of the IMF, is wary of creating a new institution but keen on more systematic supervision of existing regulators.

Cut moral hazard
A third market-reinforcing reform is to reduce moral hazard. Bail-outs, on this view, breed more crises. For many conservatives, particularly in America's Congress, the answer is to curb, or even eliminate, the IMF. It is the prospect of bail-outs, they argue, that encourages governments to profligacy and investors to recklessness.

The most libertarian want nothing in the IMF's place. They argue that governments can protect themselves privately against sudden flights of capital. In 1995, Argentina faced a liquidity crisis, as capital fled in the aftermath of Mexico's crash. To avoid a repeat, the Argentines entered into $6.7 billion worth of 'reverse repo' arrangements with 14 international banks. For promising to provide liquidity should capital suddenly flee, the banks charge Argentina a fee and demand Argentine bonds as collateral. Many reformers think this approach is the best way to avoid liquidity crises. They may be right, but it is untested.

Some argue that public money can bolster such private liquidity lines. The Argentines, for instance, have suggested that international institutions could give guarantees in place of the collateral banks now demand. Ricardo Hausmann, chief economist at the Inter-American Development Bank, wants international institutions to promote this market by offering countries such liquidity lines jointly with commercial banks. This way, public money helps boost liquidity without worsening moral hazard, and private creditors cannot simply flee when panic hits.

If credit lines could pre-empt crises of illiquidity, that still leaves the problem of insolvency. Or, put another way, the question of how Asia's mess should have been dealt with. Again, the most orthodox free-market types would say that South Korean, Thai and Indonesian banks and firms should simply have defaulted, making foreign bankers and other investors lose money.

International default, however, is thought to come at a heavy price. Countries that reneged on their bonds in the 1930s did not regain access to capital markets for decades. This history has spawned a deep-seated fear of formal default (though many poor countries have had *de facto* defaults as their debts have been rescheduled). Formal cross-border default seems frightening, for it takes place in a legal and institutional vacuum. Hence a further market-reinforcing reform aims to fill this void: to find a way in which creditors can take a hit without the chaos of uncontrolled default.

Unfortunately no one has worked out how to do it. Jeffrey Sachs is the most ambitious. He would like a fully fledged international bankruptcy framework, modelled on chapter 11 of the American bankruptcy law. His proposals* would not only ensure that creditors took a hit, but would also provide debtors with a framework within which they could

---

* S Radelet and J Sachs, 'The East Asian Financial Crisis: Diagnosis, Remedies and Prospects', *Brookings Papers on Economic Activity*, forthcoming.

gain access to new credit. He claims that South Korea's 'voluntary' rescheduling of its short-term debts was the right approach. It should simply be formalised. Many 'pro-market' reformers abhor the idea of debt work-outs. They argue that a generous international bankruptcy procedure would worsen the problems of moral hazard, as default became an easy option.

Or channel the flows

For those who see East Asia's crisis primarily as one of panic, these market-reinforcing reforms mostly miss the point. Far more urgent is the need to control the capital flows themselves.

Ironically, the most ambitious of such proposals is touted by George Soros, a man who made his fortune and reputation in financial markets. He now believes the private sector is ill suited to allocating international credit and thinks bureaucrats would do a better job. He wants to create an International Credit Insurance Corporation. This bureaucracy would, for a modest fee, guarantee all international loans to a country up to a debt level it deemed appropriate. Any further lending would be uninsured.

This proposal has so many weaknesses it is hard to believe anyone takes it seriously. Consider only two. Blanket insurance up to a cut-off point would precipitate a rush to lend up to a country's limit (with commensurately bad investment decisions). And there is no evidence that bureaucrats are any better at determining optimal debt levels than the market. Think only of the marvellous job they did in the former Soviet Union.

While most policymakers consider Mr Soros's ideas crazy, a far broader consensus surrounds the usefulness of capital controls. For those who are uneasy with the speed with which funds flow around the globe, the perennial idea of a tax on currency transactions has surfaced again. Even more popular is the idea of 'prudential' capital controls on short-term inflows. The World Bank's Mr Stiglitz is a big fan. He likes to compare global capital markets to a wild and choppy sea: small economies, like small boats, can easily sink. Chile is often cited as an example of a country that has flourished using such controls. It discourages hot money by demanding that 30 per cent of all inflows be deposited without interest at the central bank for one year. For short-term inflows this implies a hefty tax.

Judging by Chile's performance, such controls may work. But they come at a price. Chile's real interest rates are higher than they need be, and its financial markets are segmented: big firms borrow abroad; small ones face high rates at home. And, most importantly, sophisticated financiers eventually find ways around them.

While less hot money might reduce the risks of a market panic, it would not eliminate it entirely. Hence a further reform option is to create a true global lender of last resort. The IMF partially fulfills the role but compared with a central bank (the domestic lender of last resort), it is severely constrained: it cannot print money and so cannot lend freely. Its resources are paltry compared with today's cross-border flows. It does not lend at penal interest rates (though it attaches exacting conditions to its money) and does not demand collateral.

In serious crises, the IMF has not been the main lender of last resort. In 1982, when Mexico teetered on the edge of default, it was the United States that stepped in, pre-paying for $2 billion of Mexican oil. When Mexico hit trouble in 1995, it was again the Americans that provided most of the instant money. And, for all the talk of 'huge IMF bail-outs' in East Asia, only modest sums have been lent. So far, the Fund has disbursed less than $20 billion.

Recent reforms have made the IMF more like a lender of last resort. A new credit facility allows countries in trouble to borrow more money, quickly, at penal interest rates (but still with economic conditions attached). Its capital base is being expanded. But even with a capital increase, the IMF will have only another $90 billion in its kitty. To be a credible lender of last resort would demand much more.

With such an array of possible reforms, it is hardly surprising that international officials are confused and uncertain. Their political masters demand quick action, to show they have 'dealt with' Asia's crisis. But the issues are complicated, and many proposals inconsistent.

(a) What are the advantages and problems with global capital markets as they currently operate?

(b) The south-east Asian crisis has prompted proposals for reform of international capital markets. The nature of the proposals depends on the analysis of the problem. Identify the reform proposals (i) based on the assumption that the crisis was essentially one of Asian capitalism and (ii) based on the assumption that the problem was largely one of panic.

(c) In what ways do these two sets of proposals conflict?

The article below by Gavyn Davies, taken from *The Independent* of 16 November 1998, explores the role of the IMF and the manner in which it attempts to deal with problems in international capital markets.

The real cost of IMF rescue deals

The role of the International Monetary Fund (IMF) in the world economy has never been more crucial than now – or more vulnerable to attack. In the past few weeks the IMF has been central in stitching together a package of international financial assistance for Brazil – an effort which culminated with the $41bn (£25bn) loan announced on Friday. By avoiding a disorderly series of devaluations in Latin America (for a while at least), this breakthrough reduces the recession risks facing the world economy in 1999.

But at the very same moment that the IMF has been critical to the health of the world system in this regard, a powerful political and intellectual assault on the institution is being mounted, especially in the United States. This raises huge question marks about the future role of the organisation, and indeed whether it has any real future at all.

The present structure of the IMF is a relic of the reconstruction of the world financial system which immediately followed the Second World War. Learning the lessons of the 1930s, the great Western powers decided that free trade should be made central to the new world economic order and, because of the risk of competitive devaluations, they decided that this would not be compatible with an era of floating exchange rates. Under the Bretton Woods system, the major exchange rates were therefore fixed, both against gold and against each other, subject only to infrequent adjustments when 'fundamentals' changed irrevocably.

The key role of the IMF in this system was to provide a multilateral source of temporary liquidity for countries which ran into balance of payments difficulties. By providing such liquidity, the IMF could give troubled countries more time in which to adjust their domestic economic policies in response to international trade problems, thus maintaining political support for the free trade/fixed exchange-rate system.

With the break-up of the fixed exchange-rate system in the early 1970s, the Fund increasingly focused its attention on the emerging world. Initially, the bulk of this work related to traditional balance of payment financing for countries which hit problems on their trade balances. But, by the 1990s, the massive increase in the scale of private sector capital flows into the emerging world meant that the IMF inevitably became enmeshed in problems on the capital account of the balance of payments, rather than on the trade account.

This soon entailed a wide range of new dangers and pitfalls. In the 1994/95 Mexico crisis, and in the 1997/98 Asian and Latin American crises, IMF lending to troubled economies has had little to do with the traditional task of smoothing the process of trade adjustment, but instead has been intended to prevent widespread defaults in the financial system. The provision of liquidity to help countries with trade problems had been transformed into a form of bridge lending for countries with insolvent financial systems.

In the rare instance that the IMF has bungled in this new role – notably, Russia 1998 – the consequences for the world's financial system have been extremely disturbing. However, according to many economists, the deeper long-term consequences of the IMF packages themselves, even where successful, have been equally disturbing. For example, it is clear in retrospect that the allocation of IMF funds to Korea last year had the effect – whether intended or not – of bailing out the Western banking system. International money sent to Korea was immediately used to pay down foreign bank debt which would otherwise have been subject to a high risk of default.

Up to a point, this result was to be highly welcomed. The Russian example shows that the alternative to IMF action – major defaults on bank debt, leading to a much greater risk of recession in the world economy – would have been much worse in the short term. But the IMF programmes inevitably involve major disadvantages, and it is disingenuous to deny this.

First, the money has to come from somewhere – in point of fact, either from taxpayers in Western economies or from the central banks which they ultimately own. Typically, though, these taxpayers have no idea that their money is being spent in this manner.

Admittedly, the vast majority of IMF lending is repaid in full, and at attractive rates of interest for the lending country. But sometimes (for example, in the recent case of Russia), these loans are not repaid, disappearing instead into Swiss bank accounts. And, in all cases, IMF programmes imply that taxpayers are assuming risks that the private sector is not willing to assume. This means that there is an implicit transfer of wealth away from the taxpayers of the lending countries.

Who are the beneficiaries of this implicit transfer? Obviously, the most direct beneficiaries are the shareholders of Western banks, who would otherwise suffer much larger write-offs on their emerging market loan books. This transfer from the general taxpayer to the bank shareholder almost certainly implies gains by the rich at the expense of the poor. It is not difficult to imagine what would happen if a political party openly proposed such a programme to its electorate, which is perhaps why governments are generally at pains to disguise these effects of IMF programmes.

This is not all. Within the emerging nations themselves, the arrival of the IMF is typically used as the excuse needed by governments to raise taxation in order to 'recapitalise' their domestic banking industries. Once again, this involves taxing the general population to bail out bank owners, who are usually mega-rich industrial oligarchs. These transfers within the emerging nations have recently been of truly herculean scale, amounting to 25 per cent of GDP or more.

Many economists would argue that these latter transfers have little to do with the IMF, since they would be necessary anyway in order to rescue the banking systems in countries like Mexico or Thailand. But there is a genuine issue here. Why have these bank losses recently become so extraordinarily large? When bank failures were common in the industrial countries during the last century, the losses rarely amounted to more than a few per cent of GDP. Even the widespread bank failures in the US in the 1930s cost no more than 4 per cent of GDP. So what has suddenly happened to produce a position in which bank losses have increased almost tenfold?

It is hard to avoid the conclusion that the massive growth in international bank lending from the OECD economies to the emerging world has been central to this process. After all, in the Asian crisis economies, foreign bank debt had grown to 25 to 45 per cent of GDP just before the storm broke. And it is hard also to escape the suspicion that Western banks were willing to take on such huge exposures partly because they expected IMF help to be available in case of problems. The 1995 Mexican bailout certainly encouraged this belief.

If Western governments subsidise risk-taking activities, they can hardly be surprised when levels of risk rise to intolerable levels. This is a problem that needs to be addressed as soon as the present crisis subsides.

Q12. D. From August 1993 to the start of the euro in 1999, the band was fixed at a ±15 per cent divergence from any other ERM currency (the exception being the German mark and the Dutch guilder, where the band was ±2¹/₄ per cent). Previous to that the band was ±2¹/₄ per cent for all currencies other that those of Spain and Portugal (and the UK before it left the system in 1992), where the band was ±6 per cent.

Q13. D. Interest rates could not be raised because this would put further upward pressure on the exchange rate.

Q14. D. Speculators did not generally doubt the commitment of Italy and the UK to maintaining their exchange rates within their ERM bands: it was their ability to do so that was in doubt. (Note in the case of (iii) that low US interest rates led to speculative flows of finance to Germany, thus further strengthening the mark and weakening the relative position of the lira and the pound.)

Q15. *True.* There was divergence not only between economic indicators such as growth and government finances, but also between the different economic objectives of the member states.

Q16. *True.*

Q17. Yes: (c), (d), (f), (g), (h) and (j).
No: (a), (b), (e) and (i).
Note that when the euro has fully replaced the previous currencies (by 1 July 2002) there will be no 'exchange rates' between member countries – any more than there is between England and Wales. Note also that, although types of tax must be harmonised and rates of indirect taxes should be similar, direct taxes could differ: they would be like different local taxes within a country.

Q18. Advantages include: elimination of the costs of converting currencies; elimination of uncertainties associated with possible exchange rate realignments and fluctuations within the permitted band; a lower average rate of inflation (provided that the European Central Bank is truly independent from short-term political considerations); greater macroeconomic stability which will promote higher levels of investment.

Q19. Disadvantages include: problems of domestic adjustment if the economy is not in harmony with other members (e.g. if it has higher cost-push inflationary pressures), with the country maybe becoming a depressed 'region' of the union; adjustment to asym-

metric shocks (shocks that have different effects on the various member countries); loss of political sovereignty (some see this as an advantage).

Q20. E. The benefits (or costs) of a single currency are not confined to one indicator (such as inflation or trade or economic growth). An optimal currency area is one which maximises the *overall* benefit to the members. If the current area is the optimal size, then altering the size (either increasing it or decreasing it) will lead to a decrease in the overall benefit from having the currency area.

Q21. *True* (50 per cent of 20 per cent).

Q22. *False.* 10 per cent per week compounded over a year is equivalent to over 14 000 per cent per annum.

Q23. *Yes* (a) and (d). With a free-floating exchange rate, there is no need for exchange rate intervention at all. With a common currency, you give up monetary policy, but there can be no speculation as there is no possibility of a currency depreciating against itself! With anything other than these extremes, as soon as the pegged or fixed rate ceases to be the perceived equilibrium rate, speculation is likely to force an exchange rate adjustment.

Q24. They may discourage international investment; they may discourage international trade; they are disliked as 'anti-market'.

Q25. *True.* Such a tax would help to discourage speculation by making it more expensive.

Q26. Because speculation, if dampened, is likely to be stabilising and may help force countries to move towards an equilibrium exchange rate, rather than maintaining one which does not reflect underlying economic fundamentals, such as purchasing power parities.

Q27. (a) *True*; (b) *False* (bands would be wide: e.g. ±10%); (c) *True*; (d) *False* (the central parity may have to be adjusted very frequently, if the country's rate of inflation diverges from the weighted average of its trading partners; (e) *True* (the closer the rate approached these buffers, the greater would be the scale of exchange market intervention).

Q28. It removes pressure on high-inflation countries to bring their inflation under control; monetary policy may have to be geared to keeping the exchange rate within the bands, rather than being used for domestic purposes (though this problem is not as great as it would be with a more rigid exchange rate system).

CHAPTER TWENTY-SIX

26 Economic Problems of Developing Countries

A REVIEW

In this last chapter we look at some of the economic problems of the poorer countries of the world, problems beside which those of the affluent North pale into insignificance. We start by examining the nature and extent of poverty in developing countries. This poverty cannot be examined in isolation from these countries' relationships with the rest of the world and thus we turn to this topic next. We continue by looking at some specific internal problems such the neglect of agriculture and the huge scale of unemployment. Finally we examine the massive international debts that many poor countries have incurred and the difficulties in overcoming them.

26.1 The problem of underdevelopment

(Pages 733–4) One way of defining the level of development is the extent to which a country provides the basic needs of life.

Q1. Which of the following would you include as basic needs?

(a) Adequate food.   *Yes/No*
(b) Free education for all children up to 12.   *Yes/No*
(c) Sufficient time free from work to be able to rest and
     enjoy social interaction.   *Yes/No*
(d) Adequate clothing, warmth and shelter.   *Yes/No*
(e) Freedom to choose where to work and live.   *Yes/No*
(f) Adequate health care.   *Yes/No*
(g) Adequate care for the elderly and those without work.
                                                                              Yes/No
(h) Fulfilment at work.   *Yes/No*
(i) Proper sanitation.   *Yes/No*
(j) Self-esteem.   *Yes/No*

Q2. Give three problems in defining development in terms of basic needs.

1. ....

2. ....

3. ....

(Pages 744–7) The single most commonly used measure of economic development is GNY per head, measured in some international currency such as the US dollar.

Q3. Which of the following are advantages of using GNY as an indicator of the level of a country's economic development?

(a) GNY statistics are available for all countries.   *Yes/No*
(b) A sustained rise in GNY is generally considered to be a
     necessary condition for a sustained increase in eco-
     nomic welfare.   *Yes/No*
(c) A sustained rise in GNY is generally considered as a
     sufficient condition for a sustained increase in eco-
     nomic welfare.   *Yes/No*
(d) Exchange rates accurately reflect domestic purchasing
     power.   *Yes/No*

 Multiple Choice   Written answer   Delete wrong word   Diagram/table manipulation   Calculation   Matching/ordering

(a) When the IMF was set up at the end of World War Two, what was its principal role?

(b) How was the IMF's role to change, following the demise of the Bretton Woods system in the early 1970s?

(c) What concerns does Davies have about the IMF's approach to financial bail-outs, such as those of south-east Asian countries in 1997/98?

 E ANSWERS

Q1. *an expansion of output in other countries.* This will occur via the following process. A rise in US national income will lead to a rise in US expenditure on imports. These increased US imports represent an increase in exports for other countries, and hence an injection into their economies. These increased injections lead to an expansion in output of these other countries.

Q2. E.

Q3. *(a)* *False.* The higher interest rate will attract an *inflow* of finance.

(b) *True.* The inflow of finance will drive up the exchange rate.

(c) *True.* The higher exchange rate will cause exports to be less competitive.

(d) *True.* The higher interest rate will cause lower investment. This, combined with lower exports, will cause national income to be lower than it would otherwise have been.

(e) *Uncertain.* A higher exchange rate will make imports relatively cheaper and hence increase them, but a lower national income will tend to reduce expenditure on imports.

(f) *True.* Lower US exports (and possibly higher imports) will mean lower imports (and possibly higher exports) for the USA's trading partners.

(g) *False.* A rise in US interest rates will tend to drive up interest rates in the rest of the world (albeit by probably not so much as in the USA).

(h) *Uncertain* (although probably *False*). Higher interest rates in other countries will cause their investment to fall and lead to a fall in confidence. It is possible, however, that higher exports to the USA (injections) combined with lower imports from the USA (withdrawals) could lead to *higher* national income, and, via the accelerator, to *higher* investment. It is likely, however, that the first effect would be the dominant one.

(i) *Uncertain* (although probably *False*). There are two effects here: (i) the fall in their imports (and possible rise in their exports) will cause their national income to rise; (ii) the rise in their interest rates and probable fall in investment will cause their national income to fall. Probably the interest rate effect will be the dominant one, leading to a net fall in national income.

Q4. *similar.*

Q5. *international financial flows.*

Q6. *more.*

Q7. C. In the case of (i), an expansionary fiscal policy in the USA will lead, via the international trade multiplier, to higher national incomes in other countries. This effect will be amplified by lower interest rates, transmitted to them from the USA via international financial flows. In the case of (iv), the contractionary international trade multiplier effects of a contractionary fiscal policy will be amplified by higher interest rates, again transmitted via international financial flows.

Q8. (a) and (e) will help to stimulate other countries too, via the international trade multiplier. They thus *benefit* other countries.

(b), (c) and (d) reduce other countries' exports and/or increase their imports and thus *hinder* their recovery.

Q9. *Yes.* All of them. In the case of (c), with monetary policy determined by central banks, it make it impossible for G7 politicians to use changes in interest rates as a means of achieving harmonisation. In the case of (d), with different rates of productivity growth, different underlying inflation rates, different propensities to import, and different sizes of budget deficits and national debts as a proportion of GDP, achieving similar growth rates may involve considerable interest rate differences and currency instability.

Q10. *(a)* With different underlying rates of inflation (e.g. different cost-push pressures), to achieve similar rates of inflation between countries may require quite different rates of interest.

(b) Budget deficits differ substantially from one country to another as does the balance between saving and investment. To achieve similar budget deficits will entail considerable fiscal policy changes between countries and different rates of economic growth.

(c) To achieve similar rates of inflation between countries will involve changing interest rates for this purpose. These changes in interest rates can cause considerable exchange rate volatility.

Q11. E. Each one would cause a different rate of growth of imports and exports (the last one because it would affect the rate of inflation) and thus a change in the equilibrium rate of exchange over time.

Q12. D. From August 1993 to the start of the euro in 1999, the band was fixed at a ±15 per cent divergence from any other ERM currency (the exception being the German mark and the Dutch guilder, where the band was ±2¼ per cent). Previous to that the band was ±2¼ per cent for all currencies other that those of Spain and Portugal (and the UK before it left the system in 1992), where the band was ±6 per cent.

Q13. D. Interest rates could not be raised because this would put further upward pressure on the exchange rate.

Q14. D. Speculators did not generally doubt the commitment of Italy and the UK to maintaining their exchange rates within their ERM bands: it was their ability to do so that was in doubt. (Note in the case of (iii) that low US interest rates led to speculative flows of finance to Germany, thus further strengthening the mark and weakening the relative position of the lira and the pound.)

Q15. *True.* There was divergence not only between economic indicators such as growth and government finances, but also between the different economic objectives of the member states.

Q16. *True.*

Q17. Yes: (c), (d), (f), (g), (h) and (j).
No: (a), (b), (e) and (i).
Note that when the euro has fully replaced the previous currencies (by 1 July 2002) there will be no 'exchange rates' between member countries – any more than there is between England and Wales. Note also that, although types of tax must be harmonised and rates of indirect taxes should be similar, direct taxes could differ: they would be like different local taxes within a country.

Q18. Advantages include: elimination of the costs of converting currencies; elimination of uncertainties associated with possible exchange rate realignments and fluctuations within the permitted band; a lower average rate of inflation (provided that the European Central Bank is truly independent from short-term political considerations); greater macroeconomic stability which will promote higher levels of investment.

Q19. Disadvantages include: problems of domestic adjustment if the economy is not in harmony with other members (e.g. if it has higher cost-push inflationary pressures), with the country maybe becoming a depressed 'region' of the union; adjustment to asymmetric shocks (shocks that have different effects on the various member countries); loss of political sovereignty (some see this as an advantage).

Q20. E. The benefits (or costs) of a single currency are not confined to one indicator (such as inflation or trade or economic growth). An optimal currency area is one which maximises the *overall* benefit to the members. If the current area is the optimal size, then altering the size (either increasing it or decreasing it) will lead to a decrease in the overall benefit from having the currency area.

Q21. *True* (50 per cent of 20 per cent).

Q22. *False.* 10 per cent per week compounded over a year is equivalent to over 14 000 per cent per annum.

Q23. *Yes* (a) and (d). With a free-floating exchange rate, there is no need for exchange rate intervention at all. With a common currency, you give up monetary policy, but there can be no speculation as there is no possibility of a currency depreciating against itself! With anything other than these extremes, as soon as the pegged or fixed rate ceases to be the perceived equilibrium rate, speculation is likely to force an exchange rate adjustment.

Q24. They may discourage international investment; they may discourage international trade; they are disliked as 'anti-market'.

Q25. *True.* Such a tax would help to discourage speculation by making it more expensive.

Q26. Because speculation, if dampened, is likely to be stabilising and may help force countries to move towards an equilibrium exchange rate, rather than maintaining one which does not reflect underlying economic fundamentals, such as purchasing power parities.

Q27. (a) *True*; (b) *False* (bands would be wide: e.g. ±10%); (c) *True*; (d) *False* (the central parity may have to be adjusted very frequently, if the country's rate of inflation diverges from the weighted average of its trading partners); (e) *True* (the closer the rate approached these buffers, the greater would be the scale of exchange market intervention).

Q28. It removes pressure on high-inflation countries to bring their inflation under control; monetary policy may have to be geared to keeping the exchange rate within the bands, rather than being used for domestic purposes (though this problem is not as great as it would be with a more rigid exchange rate system).

26 Economic Problems of Developing Countries

A REVIEW

In this last chapter we look at some of the economic problems of the poorer countries of the world, problems beside which those of the affluent North pale into insignificance. We start by examining the nature and extent of poverty in developing countries. This poverty cannot be examined in isolation from these countries' relationships with the rest of the world and thus we turn to this topic next. We continue by looking at some specific internal problems such the neglect of agriculture and the huge scale of unemployment. Finally we examine the massive international debts that many poor countries have incurred and the difficulties in overcoming them.

26.1 The problem of underdevelopment

(Pages 733–4) One way of defining the level of development is the extent to which a country provides the basic needs of life.

Q1. Which of the following would you include as basic needs?

(a) Adequate food.   *Yes/No*

(b) Free education for all children up to 12.   *Yes/No*

(c) Sufficient time free from work to be able to rest and enjoy social interaction.   *Yes/No*

(d) Adequate clothing, warmth and shelter.   *Yes/No*

(e) Freedom to choose where to work and live.   *Yes/No*

(f) Adequate health care.   *Yes/No*

(g) Adequate care for the elderly and those without work.
                                                       Yes/No

(h) Fulfilment at work.   *Yes/No*

(i) Proper sanitation.   *Yes/No*

(j) Self-esteem.   *Yes/No*

Q2. Give three problems in defining development in terms of basic needs.

1. ....

2. ....

3. ....

(Pages 744–7) The single most commonly used measure of economic development is GNY per head, measured in some international currency such as the US dollar.

Q3. Which of the following are advantages of using GNY as an indicator of the level of a country's economic development?

(a) GNY statistics are available for all countries.   *Yes/No*

(b) A sustained rise in GNY is generally considered to be a necessary condition for a sustained increase in economic welfare.   *Yes/No*

(c) A sustained rise in GNY is generally considered as a sufficient condition for a sustained increase in economic welfare.   *Yes/No*

(d) Exchange rates accurately reflect domestic purchasing power.   *Yes/No*

(e) Virtually all goods and services that are produced are included in GNY. *Yes/No*

(f) Prices, although not exactly equal to marginal costs, do roughly reflect the opportunity costs of production. *Yes/No*

(g) The rules for measurement of GNY are generally agreed. *Yes/No*

(h) GNY takes externalities into account. *Yes/No*

(i) There is a fairly close correlation between the ranking of countries by GNY per head and by other indicators of development (taken as a whole). *Yes/No*

As a country's economy grows, it is likely that there will be movement from subsistence agriculture to cash crops and industrial production. This structure of production means that GNY statistics for developing countries will tend to **Q4.** *overstate/understate* the level of production and **Q5.** *overstate/understate* the rate of growth of production.

Q6. GNY is based on market prices, but market prices are often distorted. Which of the following are typical market distortions in developing countries?

(a) Rates of interest in the towns are below the opportunity cost of capital. *Yes/No*

(b) Producers of manufactured goods often have considerable market power. *Yes/No*

(c) Wage rates in the modern sector are typically below the market-clearing level. *Yes/No*

(d) Exchange rates are typically overvalued. *Yes/No*

(e) Protection (in the form of tariffs or quotas) is given unevenly to different industries. *Yes/No*

(f) Rates of interest in the countryside are often much higher than those in the towns. *Yes/No*

(g) Prices of foodstuffs are kept artificially high. *Yes/No*

(h) Mine and plantation owners often have considerable monopsony power to drive down wages. *Yes/No*

26.2 International trade and development

(Pages 747–51) Trade is of vital importance for most developing countries, and yet most suffer from chronic balance of trade deficits. It is therefore of vital importance for countries to adopt the most appropriate trade policies.

Traditionally, developing countries have been **Q7.** *primary/secondary* exporters and **Q8.** *primary/secondary* importers.

Q9. There are various arguments why developing countries should export food and raw materials. These include:

(i) the vent for surplus theory;

(ii) the Heckscher–Ohlin theory;

(iii) the engine for growth argument;

(iv) differences in technology and labour skills.

Match each of the following arguments to the above.

(a) As industrial expansion takes place in advanced countries, so their demand for developing countries' primary products will increase.

....

(b) Advanced countries can produce industrial goods with comparatively fewer resources than primary products when compared with developing countries.

....

(c) Developing countries have a relative abundance of labour and a relative scarcity of capital when compared with advanced countries.

....

(d) Trade allows developing countries to exploit resources that would not otherwise be used.

....

Q10. According to the Heckscher–Ohlin theory, international trade will lead to an increase in income inequalities. *True/False*

Q11. Which of the following are problems that might arise from a policy of specialising in the production of primaries for export?

(a) Technological progress is less rapid in the production of primaries than in manufactures. *Yes/No*

(b) The benefits from the trade may only accrue in small part to the nationals of the country. *Yes/No*

(c) Primary products have a high income elasticity of demand. *Yes/No*

(d) The price elasticity of demand for primary products from an *individual* country is very low. *Yes/No*

(e) Relying on primary exports may lead to long-term balance of payments deficits. *Yes/No*

(f) Relying on primary exports may lead to long-term increases in the terms of trade. *Yes/No*

(g) The income elasticity of demand for manufactured imports is high. *Yes/No*

(h) The price elasticity of demand for manufactured imports is high. *Yes/No*

(i) The world price of primaries is subject to sharper price fluctuations than the world price of manufactures. *Yes/No*

(j) Exporting primary products may involve substantial external costs. *Yes/No*

(Pages 751–3) A second approach to trade is that of *import-substituting industrialisation* (ISI).

(?) Q12. Define *import-substituting industrialisation*.

....

....

ISI has typically involved a process of *tariff escalation*.

Q13. Tariff escalation is where the government imposes larger and larger tariffs on products:

A. the closer they are to the finished stage.

B. over time.

C. the greater the monopolistic power of the foreign importers.

D. the more established the domestic producer becomes.

E. the higher the rate of domestic inflation.

◑ *Q14.* Import substitution through protectionism is likely to encourage multinational investment in a country.

True/False

Despite its popularity with developing country governments, ISI has involved some serious disadvantages.

◑ *Q15.* Which of the following have tended to result from ISI?

(a) It has encouraged the establishment of monopolies and oligopolies. *Yes/No*

(b) It has involved artificially high real interest rates. *Yes/No*

(c) It has led to an overvaluation of the exchange rate. *Yes/No*

(d) It has led to urban wages being kept down relative to rural wages. *Yes/No*

(e) It has led to a bias against the agricultural sector. *Yes/No*

(f) Effective protective rates have differed widely from one product to another. *Yes/No*

(g) Effective protective rates have generally been below nominal protective rates. *Yes/No*

⑦ *Q16.* Give three other problems with import-substituting industrialisation.

1. ....

2. ....

3. ....

(Pages 753–6) A third approach, and one that many countries have turned to after their experiences with the limitations of ISI, is export-orientated manufacturing.

⑦ *Q17.* The developing countries which have experienced the most rapid rates of economic growth have tended to be export-orientated manufacturing countries. *True/False*

⑦ *Q18.* What does the Heckscher–Ohlin theory suggest about the type of manufactured goods in which developing countries should specialise?

....

▤ *Q19.* Which of the following will help promote the development of export-orientated industries?

(i) Devaluation.

(ii) Removal of tariff barriers.

(iii) Reduction in taxes on employing labour.

A. (i).

B. (ii).

C. (i) and (ii).

D. (i) and (iii).

E. (i), (ii) and (iii).

The gains from an export-orientated manufacturing policy will tend to be greatest for *Q20. small/large* countries and when there are *Q21. minimal/substantial* internal economies of scale in the potential export industries.

⑦ *Q22.* Give three possible drawbacks of pursuing a policy of export-orientated manufacturing.

1. ....

2. ....

3. ....

26.3 Structural problems within developing countries

(Pages 756–7) The neglect of agriculture

Policies of import-substituting industrialisation have tended to involve an urban bias.

◑ *Q23.* Examples of urban bias include:

(a) *High/Low* food prices.

(b) *High/Low* rural rates of interest.

(c) *Overvalued/Undervalued* exchange rates.

(d) *High/Low* manufactured prices.

(e) *High/Low* tariffs on imported manufactures.

(f) *High/Low* tariffs on imported foodstuffs.

⑦ *Q24.* Give three examples of policies that can help to develop the agricultural sector.

1. ....

2. ....

3. ....

(Pages 757–9) Inappropriate technology

In the urban sector of developing countries, the wage/interest rate ratio has typically been *Q25. above/below* the market-clearing level. The effect has been to create a *Q26. capital/labour* intensity bias in the choice of techniques. This *Q27. is in accordance with/contradicts* the implications of the Heckscher–Ohlin theory.

Nevertheless, capital-intensive techniques may bring some advantages.

Q28. Which of the following are possible advantages for developing countries of capital-intensive techniques?
 (i) They are in accordance with the law of comparative advantage.
 (ii) They typically yield a higher rate of profit, which can be used for reinvestment.
(iii) They may have a lower capital/output ratio despite having a higher capital/labour ratio.

A. (i).
B. (ii).
C. (iii).
D. (i) and (ii).
E. (ii) and (iii).

Q29. Give three possible disadvantages of capital-intensive technologies.

1. ....

2. ....

3. ....

(Pages 759–61) Unemployment
In addition to high rates of open unemployment, developing countries may suffer from considerable disguised unemployment and underemployment.

Q30. Which of the following two definitions is of disguised unemployment and which of underemployment?
(a) Where people are unable to find sufficient work to occupy them full time.
disguised unemployment/underemployment
(b) Where the same work could be done by fewer people.
disguised unemployment/underemployment

Q31. A cause of disguised unemployment in the countryside is the level of overcrowding on the land and the resulting low marginal productivity of labour.
True/False

Q32. How may the creation of jobs in towns also create more open unemployment in the towns?

....

....

Q33. Rural–urban migration will be greater:
(a) The greater the income differential between the towns and the countryside. *True/False*
(b) The higher the level of unemployment in the towns. *True/False*
(c) The greater the level of disguised unemployment in the countryside. *True/False*

(d) The higher the cost of living in the towns. *True/False*
(e) The lower the costs of migration. *True/False*
(f) The more risk averse a potential migrant is. *True/False*
(g) The more attractive the potential migrant believes city life to be. *True/False*

Q34. Of the following, which will help to reduce urban unemployment?
 (i) Concentrating investment in the towns.
 (ii) The adoption of more capital-intensive techniques.
(iii) Increasing food prices.
(iv) Labour-intensive rural infrastructure projects.

A. (i) and (iv).
B. (ii) and (iii).
C. (iii) and (iv).
D. (i), (iii) and (iv)
E. (i), (ii), (iii) and (iv).

(Pages 761–2) Inflation
Inflation rates are generally higher in developing countries than in advanced countries.

Q35. Structuralists blame inflation on:
A. excessive growth in the money supply.
B. the adoption of labour-intensive technology.
C. adaptive expectations.
D. rational expectations.
E. supply bottlenecks.

Q36. High rates of inflation in developing countries are generally accompanied by rapid rates of increase in the money supply. *True/False*

Q37. What problems arise from attempting to control inflation by reducing the rate of growth of the money supply?

....

....

26.4 The problem of debt
(Pages 763–4) After the 1973 oil crisis, many developing countries borrowed heavily in order to finance their balance of trade deficits and maintain a programme of investment. After the 1979 oil price rises, however, the problem became much more serious.

Q38. In the world economy after 1979, when compared with the period after 1973:
(a) real interest rates were *higher/lower*.
(b) nominal interest rates were *higher/lower*.
(c) monetary policy was generally *tighter/more relaxed*.

(d) the resulting recession was *deeper/shallower*.

(e) the resulting recession was *shorter/longer lasting*.

(f) a greater proportion of debt was at *variable/fixed* interest rates.

(g) a greater proportion of debt was in the form of *official government/commercial bank* loans.

(h) the effect on developing countries was *more/less* severe.

(Pages 764–8) To cope with the debt crisis and the difficulties of servicing these debts, many countries' debts have been *rescheduled*.

(?) Q39. Give three ways in which debts could be rescheduled.

1. ....

2. ....

3. ....

Official loans are renegotiated through the **Q40.** *London/Paris/Houston/Toronto* Club, whereas commercial bank loans are often rescheduled by collective action of banks which form a Bank Advisory Committee. Such arrangements are referred to as the **Q41.** *London/Paris/Houston/Toronto* Club.

Q42. One of the difficulties in solving the debt problem has been the phenomenon of 'capital flight'. This is defined as:

A. loans made to developing countries that are then merely put on deposit back in rich countries.

B. investors in developing countries pulling out of their investments and reinvesting their money in rich countries.

C. a reduction in new investment in developing countries by investors in rich countries.

D. profits made by multinationals from their activities in developing countries being used for investment in rich countries.

E. illegal repatriating of profits from developing countries to rich countries in order to evade taxes.

Q43. The following are various types of swap arrangement for reducing countries' debt burden:

(i) Debt-for-cash swaps.

(ii) Debt-for-equity swaps.

(iii) Debt-for-development swaps.

(iv) Debt-for-bonds swaps.

(v) Debt-for-nature swaps.

(vi) Debt-for-export swaps.

(vii) Debt-to-local-debt swaps.

Match each of the above to the following definitions:

(a) Where banks help developing countries sell their products in rich countries on the condition that the revenues gained are used to pay off the debt.

(b) Where banks allow developing countries to buy back their own debt (i.e. repay it) at a discount.

(c) Where banks agree to convert debt into low-interest-rate securities.

(d) Where debt is sold to companies exporting to or investing in the debtor country. These companies then sell the debt to the central bank for local currency at a discount. This provides these companies with a cheap source of local currency.

(e) Where banks sell debt. The purchasers can then exchange this debt with the central bank of the debtor country for local currency to use for purchasing shares in companies in the debtor country.

(f) Where debts are sold to an international environmental agency. This agency then swaps this debt with the central bank of the debtor country for a local bond which pays interest. The interest is then used to finance environmental projects.

(g) As (f) except that the interest is used to finance a range of projects in such fields as education, health, transport infrastructure and agriculture.

(Pages 768–70) A long-term solution to the debt problem will involve a restructuring of the economies of developing countries and their relationships with the advanced countries.

Q44. Which of the following policies for highly indebted developing countries are recommended by the IMF?

(a) Tight monetary policies. *Yes/No*

(b) Tight fiscal policies. *Yes/No*

(c) Greater economic planning to direct resources into investment. *Yes/No*

(d) Import controls in order to reduce balance of payments deficits. *Yes/No*

(e) Policies to promote greater national economic self-sufficiency. *Yes/No*

(f) Privatisation. *Yes/No*

(g) Devaluation. *Yes/No*

(h) Market-orientated supply-side policies. *Yes/No*

(i) A more open trade policy. *Yes/No*

(j) The abolition of price controls. *Yes/No*

(?) Q45. Give three disadvantages of the policies recommended by the IMF.

1. ....

2. ....

3. ....

Another requirement for a long-term solution to the debt problem is the cancellation of some of the debts of the most heavily indebted poor countries. Under the HIPC initiative of 1996, and revised in 1999, some of these countries would have a proportion of their debts cancelled.

(?) **Q46.** Give three criticisms of the HIPC arrangements:

1. ....

2. ....

3. ....

 PROBLEMS, EXERCISES AND PROJECTS

No questions in this section.

 DISCUSSION TOPICS AND ESSAYS

Q47. Is GNY a suitable measure of the level of a country's development?

Q48. Why do developing countries tend to suffer from chronic balance of payments problems?

Q49. Developing countries generally have a comparative advantage in primary products. Why should this be so? Does this imply that investment should be focused in the primary sector?

Q50. What are the problems of using protectionism as a means of encouraging industrialisation?

Q51. Does import-substituting industrialisation inevitably involve a bias against agriculture?

Q52. Should labour-abundant countries always adopt labour-intensive techniques?

Q53. Do all farmers gain equally from the Green Revolution? In what ways could the government help to ensure that the poorest farmers benefit from new agricultural technologies?

Q54. To what extent has unemployment in developing countries been caused by an 'urban bias' in development policy?

Q55. If high inflation in developing countries is generally accompanied by rapid increases in the money supply, does this mean that such countries should adopt monetarist policies?

Q56. To what extent is developing countries' debt problem the direct result of mistaken development policies of the 1960s and 1970s?

Q57. How would you advise a developing country seeking a long-term solution to its massive international debts?

Q58. Would it be desirable to cancel *all* the debts of developing countries? Why might there be a problem of 'moral hazard' if this occurred?

Q59. Debate
The problems of the developing countries have generally been exacerbated by trade and other economic relationships with the developed world.

 ARTICLES

The issue of agricultural policy is not just a debate between the USA and EU as the media may lead you to believe. In fact, the struggle between these two regional giants is having an enormous effect on agricultural markets in the developing world. The article below, taken from the *Oxfam Web Site* on 23 June 1998, discusses the implications of the US/EU agricultural war and the role the WTO should be adopting to support farmers in the developing world.

Farmers, food and the WTO

Governments in Europe and the US may profess faith in free-trade principles, but when it comes to agriculture there is a wide gulf between principle and practice. For decades the US and European Union (EU) have been restricting agricultural imports, subsidising their agricultural producers and dumping highly subsidised surpluses on world markets at prices which undermine other producers – all in defiance of the principle of a 'level playing field'.

The US and EU each spend tens of billions of dollars per year on large and costly systems of protection and subsidy for their farmers – including guaranteed minimum prices, subsidised farm inputs, export subsidies and in the case of the US direct 'deficiency payments' to producers. In 1995 the OECD (Organisation for Economic Co-operation and Development) countries together spent about $182 billion ($112 billion) subsidising their agricultural production, equivalent to about 40 per cent of the total value of farm output (and about four times what they spend on overseas aid). For the EU agricultural support remains the largest single item in its budget, accounting for nearly half of total spending in 1996. The cost to governments of the support schemes has soared in recent years.

While the US and EU may wish to reduce these costs, the intense competition between them means they are not willing to do so at the expense of losing markets to the other. Also, of course, they are under pressure from their domestic farm lobbies to retain them.

These schemes provide support for virtually unlimited production by US and EU farmers, and the result has been that output has far outstripped domestic demand and large surpluses created. To get rid of these surpluses, the US and EU have resorted to selling them at subsidised rates on export markets. In 1992 for example, the EU was selling wheat on the world market for around $80 per ton, for which it was paying producers around $180 a ton.

Inevitably, developing countries are seen as a useful place to dispose of farm surpluses, and concerted efforts are being made to open up these markets.

For countries which export agricultural products, this dumping of subsidised exports onto world markets means depressed prices and the loss of markets to unfair competition. This in turn translates into lower household incomes for producers. For those who produce for the domestic food market, it has a similar effect of reducing prices and incentives to agricultural production. According to one study of the maize market in Kenya, competition from subsidised imports resulted in losses to maize farmers of around $439 million in 1994–95.

It is true that these cheap imports means cheaper food for some – for those who have to buy it, which means mainly urban dwellers. But for those who grow it or sell it, it means serious loss of income. In developing countries, farmers are being exposed not to a mythical 'level playing field', but to unfair competition from these surpluses. It is competition which, left unregulated, will destroy livelihoods on a vast scale and leave countries increasingly dependent on food imports.

The inequity in this is immense. Currently each farmer in the US receives over $14 000 in subsidies per year – equivalent to around 30 times the average income in the Philippines for example. This unequal competition between the treasuries of the industrial countries and peasant farmers has led to a fall in rural incomes in developing countries, reduced rural employment, falling investment in agriculture, and migration from the land to the cities.

In theory, countries receiving cheap food imports are supposed to turn from food production to higher-value cash crops or other exports which they then sell on international markets to earn hopefully enough to buy the food they need, plus more. However, for many poor countries this is a very risky and problematic strategy.

For a start, not all developing countries have particularly marketable exports for sale. For example, for the Sub-Saharan African countries which are dependant on primary commodity exports, generating foreign exchange can sometimes be a real problem. Many are heavily indebted and foreign creditors usually have first call on export earnings. Also foreign exchange spent on buying food is then not available for more productive investments needed for long-term economic development. In some circumstances, buying 'cheap' food can be an expensive option.

Unfortunately this is the way things are going. Food imports into Sub-Saharan Africa for example, which were insignificant in the 1960s, now account for almost 20 per cent of the region's total foreign exchange earnings. In West Africa, cereal and livestock imports now account for around half of the region's current account deficit. The group of countries classified as 'low-income food deficit' are now spending about half their foreign exchange earnings on food imports, which is double the proportion they spent 30 years ago.

Another problem is that the farmers who are pushed out of domestic food production are not the ones who will take up the more lucrative cash cropping. If it was as simple as that, they would have all changed years ago. The fact is that it takes capital to get into cash crops like tropical fruit or out-of-season vegetables for export, and peasant farmers just don't have such capital. Their poverty prevents them from changing. It is those with capital who will make the money while the peasant becomes destitute or, if he or she is lucky, a seasonal labourer on a plantation.

The other option for people forced off the land is to move into 'more productive' industrial jobs in factories; but in most cases these jobs are not being created fast enough to soak up the vast numbers who are or will be seeking them. In Mexico for example, now starting to feel the effects of unrestricted cheap agricultural exports from the US, the number estimated to leave the land over the next 15 years ranges from a few hundred thousand to two million. However, the rate of creation of new industrial jobs has levelled off.

A third problem is that this approach leaves developing countries vulnerable. They become dependent for the most basic of all needs, the food to stay alive, on economic factors beyond their control – the depressed and unpredictable market for their commodity exports, or the volatile markets for their manufactured exports, the ups and downs of world food prices – not to mention the vagaries of varying exchange rates. In addition when the level of food self-sufficiency is very low, countries can become politically vulnerable to pressure from those on whom they rely for food.

For decades the US has utilised quotas, subsidies and other distortions of free trade at variance with the rules of the GATT (General Agreement on Tariffs and Trade), under waivers and exemptions of granted to it by GATT in the 1950s. Likewise the EU took advantage of this and refused to subordinate its agricultural support schemes (the 'Common Agricultural Policy') to GATT principles, using quotas, export subsidies and other devices in violation of the GATT.

The recent round of international trade negotiations under GATT, the Uruguay Round, was supposed to be the beginning of the end for this. The agreement on trade in agriculture reached during that Round included a commitment by developed countries to cut spending on agricultural export subsidies by 36 per cent and to reduce the volume of subsidised exports by 21 per cent over a six-year period. Subsidies to producers which are defined as 'trade distorting' also have to be reduced by 20 per cent. Also, all import restrictions have to be converted into tariffs which must then be reduced on average by 36 per cent over six years.

Developing countries also have to reduce such restrictions and supports, but to a lesser extent, and various concessions and exemptions were made for 'least developed' countries. Nevertheless this imposed a constraint on the ability of developing countries to promote increased food security through the use of import restrictions and guaranteed price supports for farmers.

The net result is that the Uruguay Round agreement will have little if any effect on the level of US and EU subsidisation, nor on the dumping of agricultural products in developing countries. So with food exports continuing to be dumped and developing countries' ability to protect themselves against this, or to support increased domestic production being restricted, the threat to food security is very real.

Another outcome of the Uruguay Round was the decision to establish the World Trade Organisation (WTO) to take over from the GATT and administer its agreements. The first ever Ministerial Conference of the WTO is about to take place in Singapore in early December. There will be no negotiations at Singapore on the further liberalisation of trade in agricultural goods. This is not scheduled to happen until 1999. Even so, the opportunity should be taken to highlight the inequities of

the current situation and its negative effects and to suggest what should happen when negotiations on agriculture are reopened. Oxfam believes this should include the following:

1. WTO rules should be amended to include a food security clause which allows developing countries to protect their food production systems for social, environmental or poverty protection and be exempt from some liberalisation measures.

2. The WTO's anti-dumping rules should be extended to include agriculture. Agricultural trade remains the only area of world trade in which dumping is not only accepted but actively sanctioned by multilateral rules. The export of any agricultural commodity at prices which do not reflect the real cost of production and marketing should be outlawed under anti-dumping provisions, just as it is for television sets or cars.

3. Any further liberalisation of agriculture by developing countries or opening of their markets should be conditional on the 'agricultural superpowers' doing likewise; that is liberalising their markets and reducing their levels of subsidisation.

(a) What do you understand by the term 'dumping'?

(b) What impact is the dumping of US/EU food surpluses on world markets having on farmers in developing countries?

(c) Why is the author sceptical that agricultural agreements made under the Uruguay Round will have any

effect on improving the plight of farmers in developing countries?

(d) What policy initiatives do Oxfam argue are necessary, if the WTO is to help farmers in developing countries?

FT

Reliance on the export of commodities can make a country very vulnerable to fluctuations in world commodity prices. In the following article, taken from the *Financial Times* of 2 October 1998, Andrea Mandel-Campbell examines the case of Chile, a country whose development has been largely based on primary exports, particularly copper. With the Asian crisis of 1997/8, the demand for copper fell and the price plummeted. The article examines the country's predicament and its policy options. So what is the future for Chile?

Chile: Tiger of the south takes a tumble

Its economy has been held up as a model for the region. But, as Chile faces its harshest test in recent years, cracks in the once-praised mould are beginning

to show. After averaging 7.7 per cent annual growth for seven consecutive years, the so-called 'tiger of South America' has watched GDP nosedive in

the last quarter of 1998 to an estimated 2 per cent as it suffers from the double effects of low commodity prices and high exposure to Asia.

And, as high interest rates choke liquidity and copper prices continue to slump, private economists are forecasting 1999 GDP growth as low as 2.5 per cent, noticeably lower then the usually conservative government estimates of 3.8 per cent.

'Chile is going to have to wake up to reality,' says Walter Molano, chief economist for SBC Warburg in New York. 'The country got convinced by all the propaganda that it was the model for Latin America when really the big boom of the past few years can be mainly attributed to a high period of copper prices, not expert macroeconomic management.'

What was once a boon to the economy has now turned into its Achilles heel. Copper prices have fallen 30 per cent from the same time last year to hover between 73 and 76 cents a pound. Demand has dropped off as Japan, the world's second largest consumer of copper, fights off recession.

The metal represents 40 per cent of Chile's $17bn in exports while income tax and profit remittances from state-owned copper company Codelco add up to an estimated 4–6 per cent of government revenues, says Ronald Ratcliffe, chief Latin American economist with S G Cowen Securities.

He says that for every 1 cent drop in the price of copper government revenues fall $30m, exports drop by $80m and the current account loses $48m.

But Chile's reliance on commodities does not end with copper. Fishmeal, forestry and agricultural goods, representing another 37 per cent of exports, have been hit by El Niño and a slowdown in demand from Asia, which buys one-third of Chile's exports.

The result is an estimated trade deficit of $3bn, up from $1,3bn in 1997. The current account, registering an already high deficit of 5 per cent of GDP in 1997, is expected to reach between 6.5 and 7 per cent this year and next, largely owing to the trade imbalance.

The last time the current account reached worrying levels in 1982, GDP dropped 15 per cent and the jobless rate rose to 30 per cent, notes Ricardo French-Davis, regional economic adviser for the Economic Commission for Latin America and the Caribbean. 'The Chilean authorities should never have let the deficit go so high,' he adds.

Continued strong foreign direct investment of $3bn in 1998 is expected to cover much of the deficit. The gap is further cushioned by a successful private pension fund system which has accumulated more than $30bn, contributing to a national savings rate equivalent to 25 per cent of GDP.

And, unlike other commodity-dependent countries such as oil-rich Venezuela, Chile has been saving up for a rainy day, depositing excess copper income into a stabilisation fund which has reached close to $2bn.

But, despite Chile's long-standing reputation and enduring economic success, many are sceptical whether government officials have taken the proper steps to gird against the market onslaught.

Announced spending cuts in the order of $200m should have been at least double that, says Brad Solfest, head of research for Chilean investment bank Celfin.

A one-year capital reserve requirement, while reduced from 30 to 10 per cent, continues to act as a barrier to 95 per cent of foreign investors and should be removed altogether, he says.

'Given the way the markets are performing, Chile's central bank needs to make an about-face, otherwise it is difficult to get excited about Chile right now,' he says. 'With such a huge current account deficit, what is going to attract investors to Chile at this point?'

Monetary policy has come under even heavier scrutiny. Faced with a steadily dropping peso, in May the central bank narrowed the band within which the peso is allowed to fluctuate from 12 to 5.5 per cent in an attempt at a controlled devaluation.

To defend the peso, which has depreciated 8 per cent since December 1997, the central bank has paid out $2.7bn in reserves and raised the interbank lending rate from 6.5 to 8.5 per cent.

'Macro-economic success does strange things to countries. It makes them think they are invulnerable and they refuse to face the truth,' says Mr Molano.

What Chile needs to do is further devalue and make the transition from commodities to value-added exports, say analysts.

While copper represented as much as 70 per cent of exports in the late 1980s, exports were more diversified than now and the government's fiscal surplus was higher, says Mr Molano.

Government spending now surpasses GDP, he says, noting the central bank ran a $1.18bn deficit in 1997 representing 1.4 per cent of GDP.

With presidential elections due in December 1999, it is questionable whether the government will be able to keep spending under wraps.

Political concerns have also led government authorities to put a higher priority on reducing inflation, always a touchy subject in Latin America, over making the economy more competitive.

(a) What are the advantages and disadvantages to a country of being a primary commodity exporter?

(b) How has the collapse of commodity prices, especially copper, impacted upon the Chilean economy?

(c) What short-term and long-term policies should Chile adopt to deal with its problems?

Is the giving of aid a good thing? Most would argue that it clearly is, so long as it is not wasted. A book published by the World Bank, however, suggests that a lot of aid is indeed wasted and calls for aid to be targeted on those countries which are pursuing the right economic policies and which can therefore use aid effectively. The article below, taken from *The Economist* of 14 November 1998, looks at the findings of this World Bank study.

Making aid work

This week the World Bank published a new book which will henceforth be *the* book on foreign aid: *Assessing Aid: What Works, What Doesn't, and Why*. The authors, David Dollar and Lant Pritchett, are to be congratulated: by any standards, but especially by Bank standards, they have produced a forthright and lucid piece of work. Too forthright and too lucid for some, one imagines.

Joseph Stiglitz, the Bank's chief economist and overall supervisor of research, deserves credit for letting the report see the light of day; his tepid and convoluted foreword suggests he had his doubts. Mr Stiglitz draws readers' attention to two 'key themes': 'effective aid requires the right timing and . . . the right mix of money and ideas.' Platitudes such as this may be what Mr Stiglitz had hoped to find in the report; or maybe his comments were intended for some other book, and were printed at the front of this one in error. In any event, the true key themes of *Assessing Aid* come through loud and clear: (a) aid works only if it is spent on the right countries and (b) rich-country governments and multilateral agencies (including the Bank) spend a lot of it on the wrong countries.

Reviewing earlier research and drawing on new work for this book, Messrs Dollar and Pritchett establish, first, that the raw correlation between aid and growth is near zero: more aid does not mean more growth. Perhaps other factors mask an underlying link, they concede; perhaps aid is deliberately given to countries growing very slowly (creating a misleading negative correlation between aid and growth, and biasing the numbers). On closer study of such complications, however, the result holds. No correlation: aid does not promote growth.

What transforms the picture is dividing countries according to the quality of their economic policies. Do this and you find that in countries with good economic policies (low inflation, small budget deficits, openness to trade, strong rule of law, competent bureaucracy), aid does indeed spur growth. Aid equivalent to 1 per cent of the recipient's GDP leads, on average, to a sustained increase of 0.5 percentage points in the country's annual rate of growth. In countries with bad policies, on the other hand, the data say that aid actually retards growth – although in this case the estimated multiplier (1 per cent of GDP in aid slows growth by 0.3 percentage points a year) is statistically less robust.

The next question is whether growth reduces poverty – since rich-country governments all say that reducing poverty is what their aid is for. The answer is yes. Recent evidence shows 'conclusively' that growth reduces poverty; its benefits are not undone, as used to be feared, by growing inequality. The converse is also true: in countries with slow or no growth, poverty declines slowly if at all, and in the worst cases it increases. To sum up, in good-policy countries, aid reduces poverty; in bad-policy countries, it doesn't.

A new map

The authors then ask how aid should be spent if the only consideration were (as governments say) to reduce poverty. If that were so, the money would go to countries that combine two things: good policies and lots of poor people. Plenty of countries, many of them recent reformers, meet both tests. Out of the authors' sample of 113 countries, 32 lie in this 'high-impact quadrant', with poverty rates of more than 50 per cent and better-than-average policies. Some of the poorest countries in the world (such as India, Ethiopia and Uganda) are among them.

Now suppose, the authors say, that donors increased the global aid budget by $10 billion. If this were spent across the board, in proportion to existing allocations, an extra 7m people a year would be lifted out of poverty. If it were concentrated instead on the good-policy, lots-of-poverty countries, the corresponding reduction would be 25m people.

This is an indirect way of saying that present allocations are hugely wasteful. The paper on which that calculation is based shows that if the present aid budget were switched entirely to an efficient poverty-reducing allocation, 80m people a year would be lifted out of poverty at a cost of $450 per person, compared with the present 30m a year at a cost of $1,200 per person. (Most of the 80m would in fact be Indians. Their country has vast numbers in poverty and since the early 1990s has had reasonably good policies. Its capacity to absorb aid and use it well is therefore enormous.)

The waste revealed by these figures is the result of a pattern of aid that is almost exactly the opposite of what effective reduction of poverty requires. Countries with good policies should get more aid than countries with bad policies. Actually they get less. This would be justified if aid encouraged countries to improve their policies, but on the whole it does not. For every case where aid has promoted reform there is a case where it has retarded it. Aid can keep bad governments in business; and promises to improve policy, made when the aid is first offered, are often forgotten once it has been delivered. The effort to encourage policy reform – if that is what today's pattern of aid describes – has been made at an enormous cost in terms of unrelieved poverty.

Should countries with bad policies simply be left to their fate? By no means, the authors argue: donors can still help by spreading knowledge of a technological or institutional sort. This is one rationale for (small-scale) project aid. But what donors should not be spreading in these cases is large quantities of cash. That policy not only wastes money; it also undermines political support for every kind of aid, including those that work. While it remains true – as this study makes crystal clear – that the key to development is good economic policy, and that this is something which only the governments concerned can put into effect, aid can play a useful role. It is up to donor governments to see that it does.

(a) What is the aim of giving foreign aid?

(b) What recommendations does the World Bank report make for improving the effectiveness of aid giving?

(c) Should aid go only to countries with good economic policies? Should countries be made to change their economic policies as a condition for receiving aid?

Of all the regions of the world, Africa is the poorest and in need of the greatest help. In the article below, taken from the *Guardian* of 1 June 1998, Larry Elliot considers the plight of Africa and why it is in desperate need of help with its crippling debt burden.

Why the poor are picking up the tab

It is just before dawn in Kinshasa on October 30, 1974. In a boxing ring in the middle of a football stadium lies the prostrate body of George Foreman, knocked out by Muhammad Ali in one of the biggest sporting upsets of the century. As the lightning crackles overhead, 60 000 Zairians cheer Ali, world champion again after seven years.

It took 10 seconds for the referee to count Foreman out and end the Rumble in the Jungle. It has taken 24 years for the West to face up to the enormity of the debt crisis in the developing world.

After years of foot-dragging, the need to relieve the poorest nations of their unpayable debts has moved to the top of the agenda for the meeting of the Group of 8 leaders in Birmingham this weekend. Backed by a coalition of churches and charities, Tony Blair will be urging the West to make deep cuts in the debt burden an urgent priority for the summit.

Chancellor Gordon Brown said at the end of the G8 foreign and finance ministers meeting on Saturday that he was confident that the scene was set for a major debt breakthrough.

Officials will spend the week piecing together a deal to provide speedier relief for seven African countries grappling with mountainous debts in the aftermath of military conflicts – Rwanda, Burundi, Liberia, the two Congos, Sierra Leone and Somalia.

And Britain is attempting to bring all eligible countries under the umbrella of the joint World Bank–International Monetary Fund Highly Indebted Poor Countries (HIPC) initiative by the millennium.

'The millennium objective is . . . now part of the G8 process,' Mr Brown said.

The Prime Minister was still at Oxford when Ali and Foreman left the ring to collect their purses, more than $5 million (£3 million) each for 24 minutes work, provided by Zaire's tyrannical president, Mobutu Sese Seko, to spread his name and the name of his country across the globe. The fight did that all right. But at what a cost – $10 million was money Zaire could ill afford 24

years ago, and the torrential tropical thunderstorm that flooded the Stade du 20 Mai within minutes of the fight's end was symbolic of the economic torrent that was to engulf Africa from the mid-1970s onwards. When the bills started to come in for the continent's collective Rumble in the Jungle, they could not be paid. One poster for the fight, 'From the Slave ship to the championship', had to be withdrawn after it offended Zairians. It has a hollow, ironic ring to it now, because for many African nations the crushing burden of debt has indeed returned them to a new form of slavery.

How so? A few, simple statistics illustrate the horrific cost of the crisis affecting the poorest nations.

According to the United Nations Human Development Report, about a quarter of the world's population – some 1.3 billion people – are living on incomes of less than 50p a day. Nearly a billion are illiterate, some 840 million go hungry or are living from hand to mouth. And whereas those lucky enough to live in the developed West can expect to live until they are almost 80, nearly one third of the people in the least developed countries are not expected to survive to 40.

The epicentre of the problem is Sub-Saharan Africa, which accounts for 33 of the 42 low-income countries which the World Bank rates as highly indebted. In 1962, Sub-Saharan Africa owed $3 billion. By the early 1980s their debts had mounted to $142 billion. Today the debt mountain stands at about $225 billion, which is $379 for every man, woman and child in the continent. It is getting bigger all the time, because countries are falling behind with repayments.

What's more, the gulf between rich and poor is getting wider. The share of the poorest 20 per cent of the world's people in global income stands at a paltry 1.1 per cent, down from 1.4 per cent in 1991 and 2.3 per cent in 1960. The income of the top 20 per cent was 30 times higher than the poorest 20 per cent in 1960. By 1991 it was 61 times higher. The UN says the latest figures put it at 78 times as high.

But it is not just in per capita income that the disparities show up. The UN's annual Human Development Index is effectively a league table for standards of life across the world, looking at a whole range of social indicators including illiteracy, child mortality, numbers without access to health services, and life expectancy.

For the richest 20 countries, the index reveals few, if any serious social problems. In Britain, ranked 15th, nobody lacks access to health care or water, there is no adult illiteracy, 10 000 children die before the age of one, and every child is in primary school.

Now take Ethiopia, 170th out of 175 in the table. There, 54 per cent are without access to health services and 75 per cent lack access to safe water. The adult illiteracy rate is 64.5 per cent, 625 000 children died in 1995 before the age of one. There are no figures for children not in school.

Aid agencies say that a concerted attack on poverty must start with a grassroots expansion of basic social services, particularly health and education. The problem, however, is that the poorest developing nations have precious little to spare on schools and hospitals once they have serviced their enormous debts.

In Britain there would be an outcry if the Government were to introduce charges for education, leave children without desks and roofs on their classrooms, or let hospitals and clinics run out of basic drugs. In the developing world, it happens every day of every year, as money is siphoned off to pay debts.

According to Oxfam, more than 100 000 Ethiopian children die each year from easily preventable diseases, but debt payments are four times more than health spending.

In Africa as a whole, one out of every two children does not go to school, but governments spend four times more in debt payments to northern creditors than they spend on health and education.

Why did this happen? One school of thought says the West is to blame for encouraging developing nations to borrow recklessly recycled petro-dollars from oil-rich Opec nations for inappropriate projects.

Another school of thought says the blame lies squarely with corrupt post-colonial elites, who either squandered the money from loans on grandiose projects or else salted it away in numbered Swiss bank accounts.

There is an element of truth in both arguments, but the real explanation goes deeper. As David Landes puts it in his book, the *Wealth and Poverty of Nations*: 'The continent's problems go much deeper than bad policies, and bad policies are not an accident. Good government is not to be had for the asking. It took Europe centuries to get it, so why should Africa do so in mere decades, especially after the distortions of colonialism?' Many of the nations that gained independence in the 1950s and 1960s were artificial constructs of the colonial era, built around commodities and with borders often cutting

across racial and tribal lines. On top of this was overlaid a centralised state, with power concentrated in a party, a ruling elite and ultimately an all-powerful leader. This quasi-Soviet system of government was a disaster, particularly when the economic climate turned nasty in the mid-1970s.

In the 1950s and 1960s rising commodity prices fed through into higher per capita incomes and more money for health, education and infrastructure, and still left something to be creamed off into Swiss bank accounts. But in the 1970s and 1980s commodity prices fell sharply, so that they are now lower in real terms than during the Great Depression almost 70 years ago.

The problem of falling commodity prices was intensified by higher oil prices, and the debts run up to pay for the imported machinery designed to enhance the prospects of industrialisation. Africa was caught in the jaws of a vice; to make matters worse most of the

borrowed money went on projects utterly inappropriate for the needs of developing countries.

To crown it all, the West then imposed economic policies on the indebted countries that made matters a lot worse. The idea behind structural adjustment was that countries would export their way out of trouble, but since they were often one- or two-commodity economies, attempting to increase exports involved increasing supply, which drove down prices.

Aid agencies argue that action to help the poorest countries is long overdue. Addressing Chase Manhattan shareholders on the eve of the Ali–Foreman showdown, Nelson Rockefeller said: 'I hope you enjoy the fight, because you're paying for it.' Rockefeller was wrong. The banks were bailed out by the IMF, who lent money to poor nations so they could pay off their commercial creditors. Zaire has not been so lucky. The people there are still picking up the tab.

(a) How did Africa's debt originate? How far were the development strategies adopted by the countries themselves to blame?

(b) What facts does the article identify to illustrate the poor economic and social position of the African countries?

(c) What are the most appropriate policies for African countries to adopt in order to tackle the problem of extreme poverty? What should the rich countries' role in this process be?

 E ANSWERS

Q1. Deciding on what constitutes a *basic need* is to some extent a normative judgement. Clearly, adequate food, shelter, clothing, warmth, health care, sanitation, care for the elderly and those without work, etc. can be regarded as basic needs, but there is still the problem of deciding what constitutes 'adequate'. The other items in the list could *all* be regarded as basic needs: it depends on people's value judgements. This is clearly a problem for defining development.

Q2. Problems are: what items to include, how to measure them, how to weight them (given that they are expressed in different units), how to take distribution into account.

Q3. Yes: (a), (b), (f), (g) and (i).
No: (c), (d), (e) and (h).

Q4. *understate*. Many subsistence items will not be included.

Q5. *overstate*. As people now begin to purchase items (which thus get included in GNY statistics) that they would previously have produced themselves (and which would not have been included in GNY statistics), so it appears that production is growing faster than it really is.

Q6. *(a)* Yes. Real rates of interest are often kept deliberately low by governments in order to encourage investment. This has the effect, however, of worsening the shortage of saving.

(b) Yes. The market is often too small to allow effective competition.

(c) No. Although wage rates are very low, they are typically *above* the market-clearing level (perhaps because of minimum wage legislation). There is often high unemployment as a result.

(d) Yes. This is often the result of import restrictions, which thus improve the balance of trade.

Foodstuffs and raw materials thus come cheaply into the country, while exporters find it difficult to export profitably.

(e) *Yes*. There is often huge variation in protection rates.

(f) *Yes*. The only source of loans is often the local moneylender, who may charge exorbitant interest rates.

(g) *No*. Typically they are kept artificially low by price controls. This makes farming less profitable.

(h) *Yes*.

Q7. *primary* (food and minerals).

Q8. *secondary* (manufactures).

Q9. (a) (iii), (b) (iv), (c) (ii), (d) (i).

Q10. *False*. By countries specialising in goods which are intensive in the abundant (and hence relatively low-priced) factors of production, this will result in an increase in the demand for these factors, an increase in their relative price, and hence an erosion of inequalities.

Q11. *(a)* *Yes*: the rate of growth in GNY may thus be correspondingly less for primary producers.

(b) *Yes*: especially if mines and plantations are foreign *owned* and if they have monopsony power in employing local labour.

(c) *No*: they have a low income elasticity of demand. The demand for primaries therefore grows only slowly as the world economy grows.

(d) *No*: developing countries tend to be price takers (facing a virtually infinitely elastic demand curve).

(e) *Yes*: the demand for developing countries' primary exports is likely to grow less rapidly than the demand by developing countries for manufactured imports.

(f) *No*: the terms of trade are likely to decline: the price of manufactured imports is likely to grow more rapidly than the price of primary exports.

(g) *Yes*: and hence their demand grows rapidly over time.

(h) *No*: there are few if any domestic substitutes.

(i) *Yes*: their world demand and supply is less price elastic and the supply curve is subject to shifts.

(j) *Yes*: mining can lead to the despoiling of the countryside, damage to the health of miners and the breaking up of communities. Plantations can also lead to undesirable ecological, social and cultural effects.

Q12. A strategy of building up domestic manufacturing industries by protecting them from competing imports.

Q13. A. Thus a finished product would have higher tariff protection than component parts. This therefore allows a firm setting up in assembly to import the components at a lower tariff than that protecting it from imports of the finished good.

Q14. *True*. By setting up plants in the developing country, the multinationals will receive the protection themselves. If however, they were to attempt to export to the country from plants abroad, they would be faced by the trade barriers.

Q15. *(a)* *Yes*: firms are protected from foreign competition.

(b) *No*: often governments have kept interest rates low in order to encourage investment. Also with less pressure on the current account of the balance of payments, there is less need for a surplus on short-term financial account.

(c) *Yes*: the improvement in the balance of payments from the protectionism pushes up the exchange rate.

(d) *No*: it has led to relatively higher urban wages compared with rural wages.

(e) *Yes*: the overvalued exchange rate has made it less profitable to export primaries. The higher prices of manufactured goods, combined with low food prices, have worsened the rural–urban terms of trade (a unit of agricultural produce buys fewer manufactured products than before).

(f) *Yes*: enormous differences in effective rates occur from one product to another, thus causing huge market distortions.

(g) *No*: given tariff escalation, effective protective rates have generally been above nominal rates.

Q16. Other problems include: social/cultural problems of urban living, often in appalling conditions; environmental costs of industrialisation; increased inequality (between the urban and rural sectors, between the employed and unemployed, between relatively high-paid jobs in some industries and pittance wages in others); increased dependence on specific imports (raw materials, capital equipment and component parts) often from monopoly suppliers; inefficiency due to lack of competition.

Q17. *True*. Export-orientated countries such as South Korea and Singapore have had exceptionally high growth rates (except during the Asian crisis of 1997–8).

Q18. They should be labour-intensive goods (or at least be produced using relatively labour-intensive techniques).

Q19. E. Devaluation increases the profits from exports; removal of tariff barriers helps to reduce the exchange rate and also reverse the bias towards the home market; reductions in employment taxes reduce the costs of producing (labour-intensive) exports.

Q20. *small*: such countries are likely to have a much more limited home market.

Q21. *substantial*: the domestic market under such circumstances is likely to be too small for production at minimum costs.

Q22. Drawbacks include: possible continuing neglect of agricultural sector; trade barriers to developing countries' manufactured exports erected by advanced countries; difficulties in competing against other developing country exporters already established in various markets; risks of shifts in world trading conditions and a rise in protectionism.

Q23. (a) *Low*, (b) *High*, (c) *Overvalued*, (d) *High*, (e) *High*, (f) *Low*.

Q24. Examples include: increasing food prices; provision of rural infrastructure (roads, irrigation schemes, distribution agencies, etc.); provision of low-interest finance to the rural sector; education and training in new techniques; land reform; the encouragement of rural co-operatives.

Q25. *above*.

Q26. *capital*.

Q27. *contradicts*. The Heckscher–Ohlin theory suggests that a labour-abundant country ought to choose labour-intensive techniques.

Q28. E. (i) is incorrect (see answer to Q33). In the case of (iii), if the techniques are more sophisticated they may economise not only on labour, but also (to a lesser extent) on capital costs and thus have a lower capital/output ratio as well as a lower labour/capital and labour/output ratio.

Q29. Possible disadvantages include: capital-intensive techniques may require more maintenance; they may require more imported raw materials, equipment and components; they may involve more pollution; they may provide only very limited employment.

Q30. *(a) underemployment.*
(b) disguised unemployment.

Q31. *True*. This 'surplus' labour is supported because they are either the owners of the land themselves or are part of a family which owns the land and is therefore prepared to support its relatives.

Q32. Because the extra jobs encourage people to migrate from the countryside to the towns, but more than one person migrates for each extra job created.

Q33. *True*: (a), (c), (e) and (g).
False: (b), (d) and (f).

Q34. C. Higher food prices will discourage migration, as will rural infrastructure projects. Investment in the towns may create more urban jobs, but it is likely to encourage more migration and thereby increase urban unemployment.

Q35. E. The economy has various structural rigidities that prevent aggregate supply expanding to meet increases in aggregate demand despite large-scale unemployed resources.

Q36. *True*.

Q37. Just because inflation is accompanied by increases in the money supply, this does not necessarily mean that the cure for inflation is a simple one of controlling the money supply. Money supply may be endogenously determined, and even if governments could control the money supply, they may choose not to, finding it to their advantage to finance government expenditure through the 'printing presses' rather than through higher taxes. Even when governments do attempt to reduce the growth of the money supply (perhaps because of pressure from the IMF) this may involve large-scale cuts in government expenditure or tax increases, and huge problems of hardship for the poor.

Q38. (a) *higher*, (b) *lower* (inflation was generally lower), (c) *tighter*, (d) *deeper*, (e) *longer lasting*, (f) *variable*, (g) *commercial bank*, (h) *more*.

Q39. The length of loan could be extended; a temporary delay could be granted in repaying loans due to mature; countries could be allowed to pay interest only (rather than capital as well) for a period of time; countries could acquire new loans on more favourable terms and use them to pay off the old debts.

Q40. *Paris*. (Note that the Toronto and Houston terms were new Paris Club agreements negotiated at these two places. These new terms allowed greater concessions to be made to low-income debtor countries and lower-middle-income debtor countries respectively.)

Q41. *London*.

Q42. A. Loans are granted to developing countries to help finance their debt, but instead of it being used to pay previous debts or to restructure the economy, it is simply put on deposit by private individuals or firms in foreign banks, or used for the purchase of foreign property or stocks and shares.

Q43. (a) (vi), (b) (i), (c) (iv), (d) (vii), (e) (ii), (f) (v), (g) (iii).

Q44. The IMF generally favours market-based solutions combined with tight demand-side policies. These include (a), (b), (f), (g), (h), (i) and (j).

Q45. Disadvantages include: economic recession while inflation is being squeezed out of the economy – this may take a long time; higher initial inflation as price controls are removed; greater inequality; increased structural unemployment; more vulnerability of the economy to world economic fluctuations.

Q46. The debt thresholds have been set too high, with the resulting reduction in debt being too low; countries have to have adhered to two three-year IMF structural adjustment programmes (reduced to one three-year programme in 1999) before they can receive debt reduction – but debt relief is needed more quickly than that; countries have to pay any arrears to multilateral agencies, such as the IMF or World Bank, before they can receive debt reduction; the IMF structural adjustment programmes are very harsh and can cause great hardship for the very poor.